I0058479

California Cannabis Laws and Regulations

©2019 Omar Figueroa, All rights reserved.

ISBN 978-0-9984215-3-7

Disclaimer

This publication has been created to provide you with accurate and authoritative information concerning California cannabis laws and regulations. It is sold with the understanding that the publisher is not engaged in rendering legal or other professional services. This publication is not a substitute for legal advice of an attorney. If you require legal or other expert advice, you should seek the services of a competent attorney or other professional.

The law is ever changing and sometimes errors happen even with careful attention to detail. Although this publication is designed to aid in the research and practice of cannabis law, it is recommended that you cross check the California Legislature website for any change in the law. The URL for the Legislature's website is:

http://leginfo.legislature.ca.gov/faces/codes.xhtml

Because California's cannabis regulations are also evolving, please check for the latest regulatory updates at the California Cannabis Portal:

http://cannabis.ca.gov

Also, please keep yourself informed by purchasing the most up-to-date edition of this publication as it comes available.

Colophon

Author: Omar Figueroa, Esq.

Legal and Research Assistant: Tina S. Smith, J.D.

Text Design: Jocelyn Bergen

Cover Design: Ophelia Chong

Cover Image: Vivian Shih

Published by Lux Law Publishing

Preface

California cannabis law has greatly expanded in the past few years. After California voters "legalized" cannabis for adults ages 21 and older with the passage of Proposition 64 in 2016, the Legislature merged adult use and medical cannabis laws to create the Medicinal and Adult-Use Cannabis Regulation and Safety Act (MAUCRSA) in 2017. The MAUCRSA regulatory framework created three regulatory agencies for different parts of the cannabis supply chain, and these agencies promulgated emergency regulations as an initial step in the regulatory rulemaking process. The regulatory rulemaking process included public hearings, public comment, and review by the Office of Administrative Law, and it is now complete in 2019, meaning the final permanent regulations are in effect.

This book fulfills an unmet need for a comprehensive reference volume containing California's cannabis laws and regulations, updated for 2019. All of the relevant code sections pertaining to cannabis law in California have been arranged into this comprehensive reference work. Notably, the relevant code sections can be easily found with the annotated table of contents, with detailed section descriptors summarizing the contents of each code section. Of course, the final permanent regulations are included. Finally, a handy Index makes it easy to pinpoint the relevant law or regulation.

Why is such a book necessary in this day of free online access to California's codes and regulations? Because MAUCRSA did not create a legal tabula rasa by repealing all former cannabis laws and establishing a new legal order. Instead, MAUCRSA changed and augmented existing laws, making California cannabis laws even more byzantine than before.

It was not always this way. Cannabis was legal in California until 1913, when the Poison Act was amended to outlaw "narcotic preparations of hemp or loco-weed." (At that point, it was legal under federal law.) In the 1950's, possession was escalated to a felony with mandatory jail. The madness continued until 1976, when the Legislature decriminalized possession of small quantities of marijuana with the Moscone Act. Nevertheless, the cultivation of a single plant, and the sale or possession for sale of any amount, remained non-reducible felonies under California law for decades.

On November 5, 1996, California voters approved Proposition 215, the Compassionate Use Act (CUA), making California the first state in the United States to legalize the possession and cultivation of medical cannabis by patients and primary caregivers. For the first time in nearly a century, patients were allowed to use medical cannabis for the treatment of "cancer, anorexia, AIDS, chronic pain, spasticity, glaucoma, arthritis, migraine, or any other illness for which marijuana provides relief."

Senate Bill 420 was passed in 2003, and became effective on January 1, 2004, establishing a voluntary program for the issuance of official identification cards to qualified medical cannabis patients and caregivers. SB 420 also purported to establish default limits of no more than eight ounces of dried processed flowers per qualified patient and no more than six mature or 12 immature marijuana plants per qualified patient; these "limits" were subsequently struck down by the California Supreme Court as unconstitutional legislative amendments to Proposition 215, to the extent that they burden an accused's defense. SB 420 also established a medical defense for qualified patients and caregivers who associate "in order collectively or cooperatively to cultivate cannabis for medical purposes." The era of collectives and cooperatives was born and lasted until January 9, 2019, when Health and Safety Code Section 11362.775 was repealed.

In 2010, Governor Schwarzenegger signed Senate Bill 1449, which reclassified possession of up to 28.5 grams of marijuana from a no jail misdemeanor punishable by a $100 maximum fine, to an infraction with the same lenient penalties, but without the right to a jury trial afforded to misdemeanor defendants by the California Constitution.

The Medical Marijuana Regulation and Safety Act (with the unfortunate acronym MMRSA) was passed on September 11, 2015, and went into effect on January 1, 2016. It first consisted of three bills: SB 643, AB 266, and AB 243. They established a new regulatory agency, the Bureau of Medical Marijuana Regulation (BMMR, pronounced "bummer"), created a regulatory framework with a dual licensing system requiring local permits and state licenses, and added a sunset clause to the collective and cooperative defense. Within the next year, more legislation was added, which resulted in numerous changes including a renamed Medical Cannabis Regulation and Safety Act (MCRSA) and Bureau of Medical Cannabis Regulation (BMCR).

On November 8, 2016, the California voters approved the Adult Use of Marijuana Act (AUMA), which officially went into effect the next day. AUMA partially legalized marijuana under state law by adults 21 and older, allowing adults to legally grow, possess, and use small quantities of marijuana for non-medical purposes. It also reduced the severity of, and penalties for, many cannabis-related offenses, and established a regulatory framework for non-medical adult-use cannabis similar to the MCRSA framework.

Finally, the laws governing medical and recreational cannabis were merged together by the legislature to create the Medicinal and Adult-Use Cannabis Regulation and Safety act (MAUCRSA). MAUCRSA set forth a comprehensive regulatory framework with different license types overseen by different regulatory agencies. First, cultivation activities are licensed and regulated by Cal Cannabis Cultivation Licensing within the California Department of Food and Agriculture. Second, manufacturing is licensed and regulated by the Manufactured Cannabis Safety Branch within the Department of Public Health. Finally, distribution, laboratory testing, retail (both storefront and delivery-only), microbusinesses, and cannabis events are overseen by the Bureau of Cannabis Control within the Department of Consumer Affairs. These agencies promulgated emergency regulations which became effective on January 1, 2018, and evolved over time, until the final permanent regulations were approved by the Office of Administrative Law on January 16, 2019.

The goal of this publication is to combine all relevant cannabis laws and regulations into a user-friendly guide that can be used by cannabis professionals, scholars, and entrepreneurs. We hope you find California Cannabis Laws and Regulations to be an indispensable tool in your library.

Because California law is rapidly evolving, we suggest that readers check for the latest changes, amendments, and updates at the California Legislature's web site:
http://leginfo.legislature.ca.gov/faces/codes.xhtml

Because California's cannabis regulations are also evolving, please also check for the latest regulatory updates at the California Cannabis Portal:
http://cannabis.ca.gov

A Word About Legal Taxonomy

In order to get the most out of this resource, it's helpful to know the legal classification of California's laws. The California Codes are 29 legal codes enacted by the California State Legislature, which together form the general statutory law of California. The California Codes are organized by subject matter, such as the Business and Professions Code, the Health and Safety Code, and the Vehicle Code. Codes are divided into "Titles," which are numbered and cover a broad area of law within that subject matter. Titles are further broken down into numbered "Divisions" which cover a narrow area of law within that Title. Divisions are broken down into "Parts," followed by "Chapters," then "Articles," and finally into individual "Sections." A law is most typically referred to in the California Courts by its Code name and Section number (for example, Health and Safety Code Section 11362.5).

Contents at a Glance

PART 1: LAWS

I. Business and Professions Code Sections   53

II. Civil Code Sections   139

III. Evidence Code Sections   141

IV. Fish and Game Code Sections   141

V. Food and Agricultural Code Sections   146

VI. Government Code Sections   161

VII. Health and Safety Code Sections   169

VIII. Labor Code Sections   223

IX. Penal Code Sections   225

X. Revenue and Taxation Code Sections   243

XI. Vehicle Code Sections   257

XII. Water Code Sections   260

PART 2: REGULATIONS

I. Title 3. Food and Agriculture
    Division 8. Cannabis Cultivation
       Chapter 1. Cannabis Cultivation Program   279

II. Title 16. Professional and Vocational Regulations
    Division 42. Bureau of Cannabis Control   339

III. Title 17. Public Health
    Division 1. State Department of Health Services
       Chapter 13. Manufactured Cannabis Safety   461

California Cannabis Laws and Regulations: 2019 Edition - Omar Figueroa

Table of Contents
Part 1: Laws

I. Business and Professions Code Sections

§ 27   [The Bureau of Medical Cannabis Regulation Shall Disclose on the Internet Information on its Licensees]   53

§ 101   [The Department of Consumer Affairs is Comprised of, Among Others, the Bureau of Medical Cannabis Regulation]   54

§ 144   [The Bureau of Medical Cannabis Regulation Shall Conduct Criminal History Record Checks]   56

§ 205.1   [Establishing the Medical Cannabis Regulation and Safety Act Fund, a Special Fund Within the Professions and Vocations Fund]   57

§ 2220.05   [Medical Board of California to Prioritize Investigative and Prosecutorial Resources]   57

§ 2241.5   [Treatment of Pain by Doctors; Requirements for Recommending Medical Cannabis]   58

§ 2242.1   [Prohibition on Prescribing, etc. on the Internet Without Appropriate Prior Examination and Medical Indication]   59

§ 2525   [Misdemeanor for Doctor Who Recommends Medical Cannabis to Accept, etc. Any Form of Remuneration From State Licensed Medical Cannabis Facility if Doctor or Immediate Family Have Financial Interest in Facility]   59

§ 2525.1   [The Medical Board Shall Consult with the Center for Medicinal Cannabis Research on Developing Guidelines for the Administration and Use of Medical Cannabis]   59

§ 2525.2   [Doctor or Osteopath Must Be Attending Physician to Recommend Medical Cannabis]   60

§ 2525.3   [Recommending Medical Cannabis Without Appropriate Prior Examination and Medical Indication Constitutes Unprofessional Conduct]   60

§ 2525.4   [Unprofessional Conduct for Physician Recommending Medical Cannabis to Be Employed By Entity Dispensing Medical Cannabis]   60

§ 2525.5   [Advertising for Physician Recommendations for Medical Cannabis; Mandatory Notice to Consumers]   60

§ 2529   [Who May Engage in Psychoanalysis]   61

§ 2529.1   [Conduct Deemed Unprofessional of Registrant, Including Use of Controlled Substance]   61

§ 2529.5   [Registration Fee]   61

§ 2529.6   [Registration Revoked if Registrant Has Been Required to Register as a Sex Offender; Exceptions]   62

§ 4883   [Reasons to Deny, Revoke, or Suspend Veterinary License]   62

§ 4884   [Veterinary License; Cannabis Administration and Recommendation]   63

DIVISION 6. BUSINESS RIGHTS

Chapter 3. Trade Names and Designations

ARTICLE 3. FARM NAMES

§ 14460   ["Farm" Includes Ranch, Estate, and Villa]   64

§ 14461   [Farm Names May be Registered with the Secretary of State; Certificate]   64

§ 14462   [The Name of a Registered Farm May be Used as a Trade-mark on the Products Grown on the Farm]   64

§ 14463   [Registration Under this Article has the Same Effect as A California Trade-mark Registration]   64

§ 14464   [After a Farm Name has been Registered, No Other Farm in California May Register that Name Unless Designating Words are Prefixed or Added]   64

§ 14465   [Misdemeanor to Knowingly Register or Make Use of a Farm Name Already in Use]   65

DIVISION 9. ALCOHOLIC BEVERAGES

§ 25621.5   [A Premises with an Alcohol License is Prohibited from Selling, Offering, or Providing Cannabis or Cannabis Products, Including Alcoholic Beverages that Contain Cannabis]   65

MEDICINAL AND ADULT-USE CANNABIS REGULATION AND SAFETY ACT

DIVISION 10. CANNABIS

Chapter 1. General Provisions and Definitions

§ 26000   [Purpose and Intent of Division 10; Expands Power and Duties of State Agencies to   65
            Control and Regulate the Medicinal and Adult-Use Cannabis Industry; By Majority Vote
            the Legislature May Enact Laws to Implement Division 10]

§ 26001   [Definitions]   66

§ 26001.1   [Definition of Microbusiness]   69

§ 26002   [Cannabidiol Products Not Applicable to this Division]   69

Chapter 2. Administration

§ 26010   [The Bureau of Cannabis Control]   69

§ 26010.5   [Powers, Duties, Purposes, Responsibilities, and Jurisdiction of the Bureau to Regulate   69
            Medicinal and Adult Use Commercial Cannabis Activity]

§ 26011   [Clean Government Restrictions Upon the Chief of the Bureau and Members of the   70
            Cannabis Control Appeals Panel]

§ 26011.5   [Protection of the Public Paramount]   70

§ 26012   [Designation of Licensing Authorities: the Department of Consumer Affairs, the   71
            Department of Food and Agriculture, and the Department of Public Health; Licensing
            Authorities May Collect Fees and Create Additional Licenses; Licensing Authorities Shall
            Begin Issuing Licenses by January 1, 2018]

§26013   [Licensing Authorities to Issue Reasonable Rules and Regulations, Including Emergency   71
            Regulations; Limitations on Regulations]

§26013.5   [Notice of action by Licensing Authority]   72

§ 26014   [Establishment of Advisory Committee to Advise Bureau of Cannabis Control and   72
            Licensing Authorities; Annual Public Report by Advisory Committee]

§ 26015   [Licensing Authority to Conduct Investigations]   72

§ 26016   [Licensing Authority May Delegate Power to Hear and Decide to Administrative Law   72
            Judge]

§ 26017   [Licensing Authority May Pay Expenses of Witness Subpoenaed to Hearing Before   73
            Licensing Authority]

§ 26018   [Licensing Authority May Review Penalty Assessment; Review Limited to Penalty   73
            Reduction]

Chapter 3. Enforcement

§ 26030   [Grounds for Disciplinary Action]   73

§ 26031   [Licensing Authority May Suspend or Revoke Licenses; Procedures for Disciplinary Proceedings]   74

§ 26032   [Disciplinary Action for Violation Committed by Licensee's Agent or Employee Acting on Behalf of Licensee]   74

§ 26033   [Exemption of Licensing Requirement for Personal Medical Use]   74

§ 26034   [Time Limits for Accusations Against Licensees]   75

§ 26035   [Director of the Department of Consumer Affairs Shall Designate Employees for Administration and Enforcement of Division 10; Sufficient Number of Enforcement Employees Must be Qualified Peace Officers]   75

§ 26036   [Division 10 Shall Not Be Interpreted to Supersede or Limit State Agencies From Exercising Existing Enforcement Authority]   75

§ 26037   [No Arrest, Prosecution, Etc. for Actions by Licensee, Employees, and Agents Permitted Pursuant to State License and in Accordance with Requirements and Regulations; Protection for Property Owners]   75

§ 26038   [Penalties for Unlicensed and Licensed Commercial Cannabis Activity; Designation of Where to Deposit Penalty Collected; Clarification of Continued Criminal Penalties]   76

Chapter 4. Appeals

§ 26040   [Establishment of Cannabis Control Appeals Panel; Appointment of Panel Members; Annual Salary; Removal Process]   76

§ 26041   [Cannabis Control Appeals Panel Personnel and Logistics]   77

§ 26042   [Procedures for Appeals]   77

§ 26043   [Review by the Cannabis Control Appeals Panel; Questions to be Considered on Appeal]   77

§ 26044   [Remanding for Reconsideration by the Bureau or Licensing Authority; Affirming or Reversing the Decision of the Bureau or Licensing Authority]   77

§ 26045   [Orders of the Cannabis Control Appeals Panel Subject to Judicial Review]   78

§ 26046   [Basis of Review by the Court]   78

§ 26047   [Findings and Conclusions]   79

Chapter 5. Licensing

§ 26050   [License Classifications; Designation as Commercial Marijuana (Nonmedical); License Valid 12 Months; Each Licensing Authority to Establish Procedures for the Issuance and Renewal of Licenses]   79

§ 26050.2   [Conditions for Provisional License]   80

§ 26051   [Factors for Licensing Authority to Consider on Issuance, Denial, or Renewal of License; Definition of Excessive Concentration of Licensees]   80

§ 26051.5   [Applicant Requirements]   81

§ 26052   [Restrictions of Licensee, Employee, Agent, or Contractor in Regard to Fair Trade and Competition; Personal Liability for Violation; Regulation by Licensing Authority; Any Person or Trade Association May Bring Legal Action]   83

§ 26053   [Testing Laboratories Prohibited from Licensure for Any Other Activity; Multiple Licenses]   84

§ 26054   [Licensee Shall Not Be Licensed as Retailer of Alcoholic Beverages or Tobacco Products; Radius from School, Day Care Center, or Youth Center; Research and Development by Business Engaged in the Manufacture of Cannabis Accessories]   84

§ 26054.2   [Priority Licensing; Identification by Local Jurisdiction of Potential Applicants for Licensure; Sunset Clause]   84

§ 26055   [Licensing Authorities May Issue State License Only to Qualified Applicants; Separate Licenses for Each Premises; Restriction on Changes or Alterations to the Premises After Issuance or Transfer of License; Licensing Authorities Must Deny Application if Approval of State License Will Violate Local Ordinance or Regulation]   85

§ 26056   [Requirements of Health and Safety Code Sections 13143.9, 13145, and 13146 Apply to Licensees]   86

§ 26057   [Grounds for Denial of State License]   87

§ 26058   [Written Notification of Denial of Application]   88

§ 26059   [Denial Shall Not Be Based Solely on Misconduct Where Applicant Has Obtained Certificate of Rehabilitation or Dismissal of Conviction]   88

Chapter 6. Licensed Cultivation Sites

§ 26060   [Regulations by Department of Food and Agriculture and Department of Pesticide Regulation]   88

§ 26060.1   [Conditions Requested by State Water Resources Control Board and Department of Fish and Wildlife]   89

§ 26061   [State Cultivator License Types; Restrictions on Type 5, Type 5A, and Type 5B Licenses]   91

§ 26062   [Certified Organic Designation and Organic Certification Program]   92

§ 26062 .5   [Restriction on Organic Designation and Certification]   92

§ 26063   [Recognition of Appellation of Origin; Misidentification of County of Origin Prohibited]   93

§ 26065   [Employee Engaged in Cultivation Subject to Wage Order No. 4-2001 of the Industrial Welfare Commission]   93

§ 26066   [Licensed Cultivation Shall be Conducted to Ensure Compliance with State and Local Laws; State Agencies Shall Address Environmental Impacts and Coordinate Enforcement Efforts]   93

Chapter 6.5. Unique Identifiers and Track and Trace

§ 26067   [Department to Establish a Track and Trace Program; Information to be Captured Throughout the Distribution Chain; Creation of Electronic Database]   93

§ 26068   [Track and Trace of Cultivation Tax Due; Electronic Seed to Sale Software Tracking System; Third Party Applications, Programs, and Information Technology Systems]   94

§ 26069   [Establishment of Cannabis Cultivation Program; Implementation of Unique Identifier Program]   95

§ 26069.1   [Cooperative Agreement Between State and Local Agencies]   96

§ 26069.9   ["Department" means Department of Food and Agriculture; "Secretary" means Secretary of Food and Agriculture]   96

Chapter 7. Retailers and Distributors

§ 26070   [Retailer, Distributor, and Microbusiness Licenses to be Issued by the Department of Consumer Affairs; Security and Transportation Safety Requirements]   96

§ 26070.1   [Opaque Package Requirement]   98

§ 26070.2   [Licensees are Prohibited from Selling Products Containing Alcohol]   98

§ 26070.5   [Feasibility Determination for Nonprofit Licenses; Temporary Local Licenses to Nonprofit Entities]   99

Chapter 8. Distribution and Transport

§ 26080   [Restriction on Transportation or Distribution Outside California Unless Authorized by Federal Law; Transportation on Public Roads by Licensee and Limits of Local Control]   100

Chapter 9. Delivery

§ 26090   [Deliveries by Licensed Retailer, Microbusiness, or Nonprofit; Customer to Maintain Copy of   100
Delivery Request; Local Jurisdiction Cannot Prevent Delivery on Public Roads by Licensee
Acting in Compliance with Local Law]

Chapter 10. Testing Laboratories

§ 26100   [Cannabis or Cannabis Product Testing Requirements; Chemical Profile; Contaminants;   100
Residual Levels of Volatile Organic Compounds; Testing Methods; Chain of Custody Protocol]

§ 26102   [Testing License Requirements]   102

§ 26104   [Licensed Testing Service to Comply With Applicable Law and Regulations; Procedures to   102
be Established by the Bureau to Ensure Testing Prior to Consumption; Frequency and Cost
of Testing; Destruction of Noncompliant Harvested Batches; Testing Restricted to Cannabis
and Cannabis Products from Licensed Businesses, and Qualified Patients or Their Primary
Caregivers]

§ 26105   [Manufacturing Level 2; Limitation of Risk to Public Safety Created by Volatile Solvents;   103
Department of Public Health to Establish Minimum Standards]

§ 26106   [Standards Developed by the Department of Public Health for the Production and Labeling of   103
Marijuana Products Apply to Licensed Manufacturers, Microbusinesses, and Nonprofits]

Chapter 11. Quality Assurance, Inspection, and Testing

§ 26110   [Quality Assurance, Inspection, and Testing Prior to Sale; Distributor Responsibilities; Quality   103
Assurance Compliance Monitor]

Chapter 12. Packaging and Labeling

§ 26120   [Packaging and Labeling Requirements]   104

§ 26121   [Misbranded Cannabis Products]   105

Chapter 13. Manufacturers and Cannabis Products

§ 26130   [The State Department of Public Health Shall Regulate Manufacturing Licenses; Manufacturing   106
License Categories; Volatile Solvents; Edible Cannabis Products Requirements and Restrictions;
Cannabis Not Considered an Adulterant]

§ 26131   [Factors Making a Cannabis Product Adulterated; Unlawful Actions Associated with Adulterated   106
Cannabis Products]

§ 26132   [Notice to Manufacturer of Adulterated or Misbranded Products; Criteria for Immediate Cease   107
           of Distribution or Recall; Opportunity for Informal Proceeding; State Department of Public
           Health Authority to Order Mandatory Recall]

§ 26133   [Cannabis Product Embargoed for Being Adulterated or Misbranded; Possible Corrections;   108
           Destruction of Adulterated or Misbranded Products]

§ 26134   [The State Department of Pubic Health Citations]   109

§ 26135   [Circumstances for Seizure of Cannabis or Cannabis Products]   109

Chapter 14. Protection of Minors

§ 26140   [Licensees to Shun Persons Under 21 Years of Age; Use of Persons Under 21 Years of Age   110
           Allowed as Decoys for Enforcement; Exceptions for Medicinal Licensee]

Chapter 15. Advertising and Marketing Restrictions

§ 26150   [Definitions]   111

§ 26151   [Requirement of Identification of Licensee in Advertisement or Marketing; Restrictions   111
           on Minor Audience; Age Verification; Advertising Must Be Truthful and Appropriately
           Substantiated]

§ 26152   [Restrictions on Advertising and Marketing by Licensees]   112

§ 26153   [Prohibition on Giving Away Cannabis, Cannabis Products, or Cannabis Accessories for Business   112
           Promotion]

§ 26154   [Restrictions on Health Related Statements in Advertising or Marketing]   112

§ 26155   [Exceptions to Restrictions on Advertising]   113

§ 26156   [The Requirements of Section 5272 Apply to tis Division]   113

Chapter 16. Records

§ 26160   [Record Keeping and Maintenance by Licensees of Commercial Cannabis Activity; Examination   113
           of Records and Inspections of Premises; Citation and Fine for Violation]

§ 26161   [Specific Records Required for Each Sale or Transport Between Licensees; Sales Invoice   113
           Information]

§ 26161.5   [Restrictions on Licensee Disclosure of Consumer Information]   114

§ 26162   [Confidentiality of Medical Information and Records of Medicinal Cannabis Patients]   114

§ 26162.5   [Confidential Medical Information Includes the Patients Name, Address, Social Security   115
            Number, Medical Condition, and Primary Caregiver]

Chapter 18. License Fees

§ 26180   [Licensure and Renewals Fees to be Established by Each Licensing Authority; Fees Set on Scaled   116
            Basis Dependent on Size of the Business; Fees Deposited in Each Licensing Authority's Account
            in the Cannabis Control Fund]

§ 26180.5   [Deadline for Safe and Viable Way to Collect Cash Payments for Taxes and Fees]   116

§ 26181   [Authorization for State Agencies to Establish Fees to Cover Costs of Cannabis Regulatory   116
            Programs]

Chapter 19. Annual Reports; Performance Audit

§ 26190   [Requirement of Annual Report to the Legislature by Each Licensing Authority; Posting on   116
            Authority's Website; Information Included in Report]

§ 26190.5   [Study to Identify the Impact of Cannabis on Motor Skills to be Developed]   118

§ 26191   [Annual Performance Audit by the Bureau of State Audits; Information Included in Report of   118
            Performance Audit]

Chapter 20. Local Control

§ 26200   [Deference to Jurisdiction to Adopt and Enforce Local Ordinances to Regulate Licensed   118
            Businesses or to Completely Prohibit the Establishment or Operation of One or More Types
            of Licensed Businesses; Local Jurisdiction to Notify Bureau Upon Revocation of Local License,
            Permit, or Authorization; State Temporary Event Licenses May be Issued in Local Jurisdictions
            that Authorize Such Events; Local Jurisdiction May Allow Smoking, Vaporizing, and Ingesting of
            Cannabis or Cannabis Products on Premises of Retailer or Microbusiness; Restrictions]

§ 26201   [State to Establish Minimum Standards, Requirements, and Regulations; Local Jurisdiction May   120
            Establish Additional Standards, Requirements, and Regulations]

§ 26202   [Delegation of Enforcement Authority to Local Jurisdiction; Memorandum of Understanding   120
            Between Bureau or Licensing Authority and the Local Jurisdiction]

Chapter 21. Funding

§ 26210   [Change of Fund Name to "Cannabis Control Fund;" General Fund Repayment; Renaming of   120
            Medical Cannabis Fines and Penalties Account to Cannabis Fines and Penalties Account]

§ 26210.5   [Deadline to Establish Offices to Safely Collect Cash Fees and Taxes in Humboldt, Mendocino,   121
            and Trinity County]

§ 26211   [Advances from the General Fund; Annual Funding by the Legislature; Public Information   121
               Program by the Department of Health Care Services]

Chapter 22. Cannabis Cooperative Associations

ARTICLE 1. DEFINITIONS

§ 26220   [Unless the Context Otherwise Requires, Definitions in this Article Govern the Construction of   122
               this Chapter]

§ 26220.1   ["Association" Definition]   122

§ 26220.2   ["Member" Definition]   122

§ 26220.3   ["Cannabis Product" Definition]   122

ARTICLE 2. GENERAL PROVISIONS

§ 26222   [Purpose of this Chapter]   122

§ 26222.1   [Exemption for Possession of Cannabis Product by Cultivator Members]   123

§ 26222.2   [Compliance with This Chapter Required for Use of "Cannabis Cooperative" in Name or   123
               Marketing]

§ 26222.3   [Restriction on Monopolistic Practices]   123

§ 26222.4   [Agreements Shall Not Result in Restraint of Trade or Violation of State Law]   123

§ 26222.5   [Application of the Corporations Code]   123

§ 26222.6   [Proprietary Interest Requirements]   123

ARTICLE 3. PURPOSES

§ 26223   [Cannabis Cooperative Activities; Disclosure of Members Requirement; Limitation on   124
               Cultivation License Type of Members; Four Acre Size Limitation Collectively; Restriction on
               Members Holding Licenses in Any Other State or Country]

ARTICLE 4. ARTICLES OF INCORPORATION

§ 26224   [Required Statements on the Articles of Incorporation for Cannabis Cooperative Associations]   125

§ 26224.1   [General Domestic Corporation Filing Requirements Apply]   125

§ 26224.2   [Articles of Incorporation May be Amended Under General Corporation Law]   125

ARTICLE 5. BYLAWS

§ 26225   [Adoption of Bylaws]   126

§ 26225.1   [Meeting Bylaws]   126

§ 26225.2   [Quorum Bylaws]   126

§ 26225.3   [Voting Bylaws]   126

§ 26225.4   [Director and Officer Bylaws]   126

§ 26225.5   [Penalty Bylaws]   127

§ 26225.6   [Entrance, Organization, and Membership Fee Bylaws]   127

§ 26225.7   [Member or Stockholder Fee Bylaws]   127

§ 26225.8   [Dividend Bylaws]   127

§ 26225.9   [Member and Stockholder Bylaws]   127

§ 26225.95   [Death, Withdrawal, Disqualification, and Expulsion Bylaws]   128

ARTICLE 6. DIRECTORS AND MANAGEMENT

§ 26226   [Election of Board of Directors]   128

§ 26226.1   [District Bylaws]   128

§ 26226.2   [Primary Election Bylaws]   128

§ 26226.3   [District Election Bylaws]   129

§ 26226.4   [Director Bylaws]   129

§ 26226.5   [Executive Committee Bylaws]   129

§ 26226.6   [Fair Remuneration May be Provided]   129

§ 26226.7   [Filling a Vacancy on the Board of Directors]   129

§ 26226.8   [Election of Officers; Option to Use Bank or Depository as Treasurer]   130

§ 26226.9   [Removal of an Officer or Director]   130

ARTICLE 7. POWERS

§ 26227   [General Powers]   130

§ 26227.1   [Power to Borrow; Power to Make Advances to Members]   130

§ 26227.2   [Power to Act as an Agent or Representative]   131

§ 26227.3   [Power to Purchase or Otherwise Acquire, hold, Own, and Exercise All Rights of Ownership]   131

§ 26227.4   [Power to Establish Reserves and Invest the Reserves]   131

§ 26227.5   [Power to Exercise Privileges of Ownership Over Real or Personal Property]   131

§ 26227.6   [Power to Levy Assessments]   131

§ 26227.7   [Power to Use Necessary and Proper Means to Accomplish Purpose and to Benefit the   131
             Corporation; Power to Contract Accordingly; Power to Exercise Any Other Rights, Powers, and
             Privileges Granted to Ordinary Corporations]

§ 26227.75   [Power to Use Facilities for Other Purposes; Restrictions]   132

§ 26227.8   [Power to Hold Interest In or Merge with Other Cannabis Associations]   132

§ 26227.9   [Power to Make Agreements and Contracts with Other Cannabis Associations]   132

ARTICLE 8. FINANCIAL PROVISIONS

§ 26228   [Associations Not Subject to Division 1 of Title 4 of the Corporations Code]   132

§ 26228.1   [Issuance of Nonpar Value Stock]   133

§ 26228.2   [Options for Preferred Shares of Stock]   133

§ 26228.3   [Requirement of Annual Financial Reports]   133

ARTICLE 9. MEMBERS

§ 26229   [Conditions to Admit as a Member or Issue Common Stock]   133

§ 26229.1   [Written Authorization Requirement to Represent a Member of a Nonstock Association that is   133
             Not a Person]

§ 26229.2   [Any Association May Become a Member or Stockholder of Any Other Association]   134

§ 26229.3   [Certificate of Membership]   134

§ 26229.4   [Issuance of Stock Only if Fully Paid; Promissory Notes May Give Right to Vote]   134

§ 26229.5   [Limitation on Common Stock]   134

§ 26229.6   [Restrictions on Membership and Transfer of Common Stock to be in Bylaws and Printed on   134
             Certificate of Stock and Membership]

§ 26229.7   [Association's Purchase of its Common Stock]   134

§ 26229.8   [Liability of Member or Stockholder]   134

ARTICLE 10. MARKETING CONTRACTS

§ 26230   [Execution of Marketing Contracts; Restrictions]   135

§ 26230.1   [Enforceable Contracts]   135

§ 26230.2   [Liquidated Damages Clause]   135

§ 26230.3   [Breach Remedies]   135

ARTICLE 11. REORGANIZATION OF CORPORATIONS ORGANIZED PURSUANT TO OTHER LAWS

§ 26231   [Amendment of the Articles of Incorporation]   136

§ 26231.1   [Requirements To Conform Amended Articles of Incorporation]   136

§ 26231.2   [Conflicting, Inapplicable, or Inconsistent Provisions of the Amended Articles of Incorporation]   136

Chapter 23. The California Cannabis Equity Act

§ 26240   [Definitions]   136

§ 26242   [Technical Assistance to Local Jurisdictions]   137

§ 26244   [Grant to Assist Local Equity Programs]   137

§ 26246   [Bureau Assistance to Local Equity Program]   138

§ 26248   [Progress Report of Local Equity Programs]   139

§ 26250   [Provisions of the Chapter are Severable]   139

II. Civil Code Sections

§ 56.06   [Requirement to Keep Medical Records Confidential]   139

§ 1550.5   [Brief History of California Cannabis Legislation, including Proposition 215, MCRSA, AUMA,   140
                and MAUCRSA; Enforceability of Contracts for Commercial Cannabis Activity Conducted
                in Compliance with California Law and Applicable Local Standards, Requirements, and
                Regulations]

III. Evidence Code Sections

§ 956   [Crime/Fraud Exception to the Lawyer-Client Privilege; Privilege Applies to Legal Services Rendered in Compliance with State and Local Laws on Medicinal or Adult-Use Cannabis Provided Lawyer Advises Client on Conflict with Federal Law]   141

IV. Fish and Game Code Sections

§ 1602   [Notification Requirements for the Diversion or Obstruction of Natural Bodies of Water]   141

§ 1617   [Department General Agreement Related to Cannabis Cultivation Specifics]   143

§ 2080   [Restriction on Import and Export of Endangered or Threatened Species In or Out of California]   143

§ 3513   [Migratory Nongame Bird Law]   144

§ 5650   [List of Materials Unlawful to Deposit In, Permit to Pass Into, or Place Where It Can Pass Into Waters; Exceptions; Defenses]   144

§ 5652   [List of Unlawful Items to Be Deposited, Permitted to Pass Into, Placed Where It Can Pass Into, Abandoned, Disposed of, or Thrown Away Within 150 Feet of the High Water Mark of the Waters of the State; Specifics on Motor Vehicle Violations; Exceptions]   145

§ 12025.2   [Complaint in Accordance with Water Code Section 1055]   145

§ 12029   [Findings of the Legislature on the Environmental Impact of Cannabis Cultivation; Establishment of Watershed Enforcement Program; Establishment of Multiagency Task Force to Address Environmental Impacts; Department May Adopt Regulations to Enhance Fees]   145

V. Food and Agricultural Code Sections

§ 37104   [Medical Cannabis Milk Product Exception]   146

§ 52452   [Cannabis Seed Labeling Requirements; Exceptions to the Labeling Requirement; Definition of "neighbor"]   146

§ 54036   [Restrictions on the Use of the Word "Cooperative" in a Corporate Name or Other Business Name or Title]   147

§ 55403   [Definition of Farm Product]   147

§ 55407   [Definition of Processor]   147

§ 55408   [Definition of Producer]   148

DIVISION 20. PROCESSORS, STORES, DEALERS, AND DISTRIBUTORS OF AGRICULTURAL PRODUCTS

Chapter 6. Processors of Farm Products

ARTICLE 9. PRODUCER'S LIEN

§ 55631   [Right to Producer's Lien for Labor, Care, and Expense in Growing and Harvesting Farm Product; Seed]   148

§ 55631.5   [Nonprofit Cooperative Association May Assert Producer Lien Rights]   148

§ 55632   [Lien Attaches to Delivered Product]   149

§ 55633   [Preferred Lien Prior in Dignity to All Other Liens, Claims, or Encumbrances; Exceptions]   149

§ 55634   [Products Subject to the Lien]   149

§ 55635   [Lien Attaches at Date of Delivery]   149

§ 55636   [Ways to Release Lien Once Suit Commences]   149

§ 55637   [Security Options to Release Lien]   150

§ 55638   [Unlawful to Remove, From this State or Beyond Ownership or Control, Any Farm Product Once Lien is Attached]   150

§ 55638.5   [Required Investigation if Product Reported Removed]   150

§ 55639   [Ways for Processor to Secure a Release of Lien]   150

§ 55640   [Product Released from the Lien May be Sold, Transported, or Otherwise Disposed of]   151

§ 55641   [Bond, Cash Deposit, or Security Given May Allow Processor to Sell, Transport, or Otherwise Dispose of the Product]   151

§ 55642   [Ability of Director to Use Security]   151

§ 55643   [If Bond Given as Security is Unpaid, Legal Action Available]   151

§ 55644   [If Warehouse Receipts for Security are Unpaid, Director May Sell Security]   152

§ 55645   [Claims Shall Have Equal Standing]   152

§ 55646   [Right of Director to Release Liens]   152

§ 55647   [Right of Claimant in Possession of a Lien to Maintain Personal Action to Recover Debt]   152

§ 55648   [Judgment in Personal Action Does Not Impair or Merge Lien Rights]   152

§ 55649   [Processor May File Surety Bond to Release Product]   153

§ 55650   [Court May Order the Release of Product With Evidence of Sufficient Security To Protect the Lien]   153

§ 55651   [Plaintiff May Secure Injunction]   153

§ 55652   [Insufficient Security at Time of Foreclosure Rights]   153

§ 55653   [Consolidation of Actions]   153

DIVISION 24. INDUSTRIAL HEMP

§ 81000   [Definitions Related to Hemp Division]   154

§ 81001   [Industrial Hemp Advisory Board]   154

§ 81002   [Hemp Seed Provisions; Approved Seed Cultivars]   155

§ 81003   [Industrial Hemp Cultivation Registration]   156

§ 81004   [Industrial Hemp Seed Breeder Registration]   157

§ 81005   [Registration and Renewal Fee for Industrial Hemp Cultivation or Seed Breeding]   158

§ 81006   [Industrial Hemp Growth Limitations; Prohibitions; Imports; Laboratory Testing]   158

§ 81007   [Industrial Hemp Agricultural Pilot Program]   160

§ 81008   [Required Attorney General Reports on Industrial Hemp]   160

§ 81009   [Required Economic Impact Report]   160

§ 81010   [Operation of Division]   161

§ 81011   [Requirement to Provide Coordinates of Hemp Research Site]   161

VI. Government Code Sections

§ 9147.7   [Definition of "Eligible Agency"; Creation of Joint Sunset Review Committee; Agency Report Requirements; Procedure for Repeal of Agency]   161

§ 11553   [Annual Salary for the Chairperson of the Cannabis Control Appeals Panel]   162

§ 11553.5   [Annual Salary for a Member of the Cannabis Control Appeals Panel]   163

§ 68152   [Destruction of Court Records]   163

VII. Health and Safety Code Sections

§ 7151.36   [Medical Marijuana Provisions for Organ Transplants]   169

§ 11006.5   [Definition of "Concentrated Cannabis"]   169

§ 11007   [Definition of "Controlled Substance"]   169

§ 11014.5   Definition of "Drug Paraphernalia"]   170

§ 11018   [Definition of "Cannabis"]   171

§ 11018.1   [Definition of "Cannabis Products"]   171

§ 11018.2   [Definition of "Cannabis Accessories"]   171

§ 11018.5   [Definition of "Industrial Hemp"; Industrial Shall be Regulated by the Department of Food and Agriculture]   172

§ 11032   [References Made to the Term "Narcotics" or "Restricted Dangerous Drugs" Explanation; Reference Made to the Term "Marijuana" Means Cannabis]   172

§ 11054   [Schedule 1 Classification]   172

§ 11107.2   [Restrictions on the Sale of Nonodorized Butane]   176

§ 11357   [Possession of Cannabis; Possession of Concentrated Cannabis]   177

§ 11357.5   [Synthetic Cannabinoid Compound or Synthetic Cannabinoid Derivative]   178

§ 11358   [Cultivation of Cannabis]   182

§ 11359   [Possession of Cannabis for Sale]   183

§ 11360   [Unlawful Transportation, Importation, Sale, or Gift of Cannabis]   184

§ 11361   [Restrictions Related to Cannabis and Minors]   184

§ 11361.1   [Drug Education and Counseling Provisions for Cannabis]   185

§ 11361.5   [Destruction of Arrest and Conviction Records; Procedure; Exceptions]   185

§ 11361.7   [Restrictions on Use/Reliability of Records Subject to Destruction Under Section 11361.5]   187

§ 11361.8   [Petition for Reduction or Dismissal of Charges Due to Changes in the Law Under the Control, Regulate, and Tax Adult Use of Marijuana Act; Procedure]   187

§ 11361.9   [Review of Past Convictions for Recall or Dismissal of Sentence, Dismissal and Sealing, or Redesignation]   189

§ 11362   [Meaning of "Felony Offense" and Offense "Punishable as a Felony" Within This Article]   189

§ 11362.1   [Lawful Cannabis Under State and Local Law; Not Subject to Seizure and Shall Not Constitute the Basis For Detention, Search, or Arrest]   190

§ 11362.2   [Restrictions on Personal Cultivation of Cannabis]   190

§ 11362.3   [Restrictions on Lawful Cannabis and Cannabis Products Possession, Use, and Manufacturing]   191

§ 11362.4   [Punishment for Violations of Section 11362.2 and 11362.3; Drug Education, Counseling, and Community Service Provisions]   192

§ 11362.45   [List of Laws and Provisions that 11362.1 Shall Not Amend, Repeal, Affect, Restrict, or Preempt]   192

§ 11362.5   [Compassionate Use Act of 1996 (Proposition 215)]   193

§ 11362.7   [Definitions Related to Medical Cannabis]   194

§ 11362.71   [State Medical Cannabis ID Card Program; Procedures; Protections Against Arrest]   195

§ 11362.712   [Physician's Recommendation and State ID Card Compliance with Article 25 of Chapter 5 of Division 2 of the Business and Professions Code as of January 1, 2018]   196

§ 11362.713   [Confidentiality Requirement of Personal Information of Medical Cannabis Patients and Primary Caregivers]   197

§ 11362.715   [Required Fee and Information in Order to Obtain State Medical Cannabis ID Card; Who May Provide the Application Information]   197

§ 11362.72   [Procedure for County Regarding ID Card Application Approval and Issuance]   198

§ 11362.735   [Information Contained on ID Card; Separate ID Card to be Issued to Designated Primary Caregiver]   199

§ 11362.74   [Reasons for Denial of ID Card; Options if Denied]   199

§ 11362.745   [ID Card Valid for 1 year; Annual Renewal Requires Verification of New or Changed Information]   199

§ 11362.755   [Fee for ID Card; Waiver of Fee; County Repayment Provision to Cover Administration Costs]   200

§ 11362.76   [Information that Card Holder is Required to Update as Changes Occur and Annually]   200

§ 11362.765   [Exceptions for Criminal Liability and Who Specifically Qualifies for the Exceptions Under this Article]   201

§ 11362.768   [Restrictions on Location of Medical Cannabis Cooperative, Collective, Dispensary, Operator, Establishment, or Provider in Relation to a School]   201

§ 11362.769   [State Agencies Shall Coordinate with Cities and Counties and Their Law Enforcement Agencies to Address Environmental Impacts of Cannabis Cultivation]   202

§ 11362.77   [Quantity of Cannabis and Number of Plants Purportedly Allowed for Each Qualified Patient]   202

§ 11362.78   [Law Enforcement's Required Consideration of Medical Cannabis ID Card]   202

§ 11362.785 [No Requirement of Accommodation of Medical Cannabis Use at Place of Employment, During the Hours of Employment, or at a Penal Institution; No Prohibition on Applying for a Medical Cannabis ID Card if Person is in Penal Institution; Use of Medical Cannabis by Prisoner; No Requirement for Health Insurance Provider to be Liable for Claim of Reimbursement for the Medical Use of Cannabis] 202

§ 11362.79 [Restrictions on Where Patients May Smoke Medical Cannabis] 203

§ 11362.795 [Required Court Confirmation to Allow Medical Cannabis Use While a Criminal Defendant is on Probation, Released on Bail, or on Parole; Request for Modification of Terms of Probation or Parole; Appeal] 203

§ 11362.8 [Professional License Protection for Primary Caregivers of Qualified Medical Cannabis Patients or Those Who Possess a Lawful Medical Cannabis ID Card] 204

§ 11362.81 [Offenses Related to Obtaining, Using, Counterfeiting, Etc. of a Medical Cannabis ID Card; Penalties] 204

§ 11362.82 [Part of this Article May Be Removed Without Affecting the Validity of the Remaining Portion] 205

§ 11362.83 [Local Control Over Collectives and Cooperatives] 205

§ 11362.84 [Custodial and Parental Rights to Minor Children Protection for Qualified Medical Cannabis Patients] 205

§ 11362.85 [Amendment or Repeal of Health and Safety Code Sections If Cannabis is Reclassified or Declassified] 205

§ 11362.9 [California Marijuana Research Program] 205

§ 11364.5 [Restrictions on Drug Paraphernalia at a Retail Business; Definition and Description of "Drug Paraphernalia"; Court Considerations in Determining if an Item is Drug Paraphernalia; Exceptions to Application of This Section; Penalties] 209

§ 11366 [Maintaining a Place for the Purpose of Selling, Giving Away, or Using Any Controlled Substance] 211

§ 11366.5 [Knowingly Renting, Leasing, or Making Available for Use a Building, Room, Space, or Enclosure for the Purpose of Unlawfully Manufacturing, Storing, or Distributing Any Controlled Substance for Sale or Distribution; Knowingly Allowing a Building to be Fortified to Suppress Law Enforcement Entry to Further the Sale of Cocaine, Heroin, Etc.] 211

§ 11379.6 [Manufacturing of a Controlled Substance] 212

§ 11470 [Items Subject to Forfeiture for Violations of the Controlled Substances Act] 212

§ 11470.1 [Expenses Recoverable From Defendant] 213

§ 11472 [Items That May Be Seized Pursuant to this Division] 215

§ 11473 [Seized Items Not to be Destroyed; Destruction of Seized Items; Request to be Used for Educational Purposes] 215

§ 11473.5 [Destruction of Seized Items; Request to be Used for Educational Purposes] 215

§ 11474 [Departments Who May Carry Out Destruction of Seized Property] 215

§ 11476 [Plant Species Which May be Seized and Summarily Forfeited to the State] 216

§ 11477 [Failure to Produce Registration Constitutes Authority for the Seizure and Forfeiture of the Plants] 216

§ 11478 [Cannabis Provided by Attorney General for Research Purposes] 216

§ 11479 [Destruction of a Suspected Controlled Substance by Law Enforcement; Restrictions; Guidelines] 216

§ 11479.2 [Destruction of Suspected Controlled Substance] 217

§ 11480 [Research Advisory Panel - Cannabis and Hallucinogenic Drugs] 218

§ 11485 [Notice Requirement for Items Seized Pursuant to a Search Warrant Issued for a Violation of Section 11358; Procedure for Seized Property] 219

§ 11532 [Unlawful to Loiter in a Public Place for Listed Purposes] 219

§ 11553 [Use or Suspected Use of Cannabis is Not Sufficient Grounds to Invoke Section 11551 or 11552] 220

§ 11570 [Nuisance Related to the Use of a Building or Place for the Purpose of Unlawfully Selling, Serving, Storing, Keeping, Manufacturing, or Giving Away Any Controlled Substance] 220

§ 11590 [Registration of Controlled Substance Offenders] 220

§ 25189.5 [Unlawful Disposal, Transportation, Treatment, or Storage of Hazardous Waste] 221

§ 25189.6 [Knowingly or Recklessly Treating, Handling, Transporting, Disposing, or Storing Hazardous Waste In a Manner Which Causes Unreasonable Risk of Fire, Explosion, Serious Injury, or Death] 222

§ 25189.7 [Burning or Incineration of Hazardous Waste] 222

§ 109925 ["Drug" Meaning] 223

VIII. Labor Code Sections

§ 147.5 [Division of Occupational Safety and Health Shall Convene an Advisory Committee Regarding Industry Specific Regulations for Medical Cannabis] 223

§ 147.6 [Division of Occupational Safety and Health Shall Convene an Advisory Committee Regarding Industry Specific Regulations for Nonmedical Marijuana Businesses] 223

§ 432.8 [Marijuana Convictions Subject to the Limitations on Employers and the Penalties Provided for in Section 432.7] 224

§ 1140   [This Part Shall be Known as the Alatorre-Zenovich-Dunlap-Berman Agricultural Labor   224
                Relations Act of 1975]

§ 1140.2   [Rights of Agricultural Employees]   224

§ 1140.4   [Definitions Related to Agricultural Employees]   224

IX. Penal Code Sections

§ 182   [Conspiracy to Commit a Crime]   225

§ 290   [Sex Offender Registration Act]   226

§ 374.8   [Knowingly Causing A Hazardous Substance Spill]   230

§ 667   [Enhancement for Repeat Felony Convictions]   231

§ 830.11   [Persons with the Power of Arrest and Power to Serve Warrants Other than Peace Officers,   234
                Including Employees of the Department of Food and Agriculture Enforcing the Food and
                Agriculture Code or Division 5 or Division 10 of the Business and Professions Code]

§ 1000   [Drug Treatment Program Eligibility and Procedure]   235

§ 1170   [Sentencing Guidelines]   236

§ 12022   [Enhancement for Being Armed with a Firearm in the Commission of a Felony or Attempted   242
                Felony]

X. Revenue and Taxation Code Sections

§ 6479.3   [Electronic Funds Transfer Requirement; Exception for Qualified Licensed Cannabis Businesses   243
                until January 1, 2022]

§ 34010   [Definitions]   244

§ 34011   [Cannabis Excise Tax Specifics]   245

§ 34012   [Cannabis Cultivation Tax Specifics]   246

§ 34012.5   [Cannabis Cultivation Tax Collected by Distributor or Manufacturer]   247

§ 34013   [Cannabis Tax Administration]   248

§ 34014   [Requirement for Separate Permit from Board; Board May Require Security to Cover Liability for   248
                Taxes]

§ 34015   [Tax Due Dates; Tax Report Filing Requirement]   249

§ 34016   [Allowable Inspections by Board Employee or Peace Officer; Punishment for Refusal of Inspection; Punishment for Failure to Tax Cannabis; Punishment for False or Fraudulent Report]   249

§ 34017   [Report Shall be Submitted by The Legislative Analyst's Office for Recommendations for Adjustments to the Tax Rate by January 1, 2020]   250

§ 34018   [Creation of the California Cannabis Tax Fund]   250

§ 34019   [Department of Finance Shall Estimate Revenues From Sections 34011 and 34012 Each Year; Allocation of Disbursement of Funds]   251

§ 34020   [Controller May Periodically Audit the Tax Fund]   256

§ 34021   [Taxes Imposed by this Part are in Addition to Other Tax Imposed by a City, County, or City and County]   256

§ 34021.5   [Local Cannabis Tax Specifics]   256

§ 55044   [Circumstances Beyond Person's Control Allowing Relief of Penalty for Failure to Make a Timely Return or Payment; Statement Requesting Relief Shall Be Filed Under Penalty of Perjury; CDTFA to Establish Criteria for Efficient Resolution of Requests for Penalty Relief]   256

XI. Vehicle Code Sections

§ 2429.7   [Commissioner Shall Appoint Impaired Driving Task Force; Requirements]   257

§ 23152   [Parameters for Unlawful Use of Vehicle Due to Influence of Alcohol or Drugs]   258

§ 23220   [Restriction on Drinking Any Alcoholic Beverage or Smoking or Ingesting Any Marijuana or Marijuana Product While Driving or Riding as a Passenger in a Motor Vehicle on Any Lands; Definition of Lands; Violation Punished as an Infraction]   259

§ 23221   [Restriction on Drinking Any Alcoholic Beverage or Smoking or Ingesting Any Marijuana or Marijuana Product While Driving or Riding as a Passenger in a Motor Vehicle on a Highway; Definition of Highway; Violation Punished as an Infraction]   259

§ 23222   [Unlawful to Possess Open Alcoholic Beverages or Cannabis While Driving a Motor Vehicle; Exceptions/Limitations]   259

§ 40000.15   [List of Vehicle Code Provisions which Constitute a Misdemeanor, and Not an Infraction]   260

XII. Water Code Sections

§ 25   ["Board" = State Water Resources Control Board]   260

§ 1052   [Trespass Water Diversion Injunctive Relief and Civil Liability]   261

§ 1525 [Persons Subject to Fees to Appropriate Water; Board Requirements for Fee Setting] 261

§ 1535 [Fee Payments Shall be Paid to the Board; Board Options for Nonpayment of Fees] 263

§ 1831 [Violations Qualified for a Cease and Desist Order; Board Requirements] 263

§ 1840 [Water Diversion Monitoring, Recording, and Reporting Requirements] 264

§ 1845 [Actions for Failure to Comply with Cease and Desist Order] 265

§ 1846 [Liability for Term, Condition, Regulation, or Order Violation] 265

§ 1847 [Liability for Violations of Water Code § 13149, Business and Professions Code § 26060.1, and Diversion or Use of Water for Cannabis Cultivation Without a Required License] 266

§ 5100 [Definition of "Best Available Technologies", "Best Professional Practices", "Diversion", and "Person"] 266

§ 5101 [Circumstances where a Statement of Diversion and Use is Not Required] 267

§ 5102 [Who May File the Statement of Diversion; Separate Statement for Each Point of Diversion] 267

§ 5103 [Required Information for the Statement of Diversion] 267

§ 13149 [Principle and Guidelines Shall be Adopted for Diversion and Use of Water for Cannabis Cultivation; Board Shall Allow Public Comment and Hearing Before Adoption; Requirement for Interim Principles and Guidelines] 268

§ 13260 [Persons Required to File Report of Discharge; Calculation of Fees Associated with Discharge of Waste; Allocation of Fees Collected; Emergency Regulations; Additional Report Required by Person Discharging Mining Waste] 269

§ 13264 [Requirements Before Discharge of Waste; Actions for Violation; Allocation of Funds for Violations] 272

§ 13272 [Oil or Petroleum Product Discharge Notification Requirement; Punishment for Failure to Notify] 273

§ 13276 [Permanent Multi-agency Task Force Established to Ensure the Reduction of Adverse Impacts of Cannabis Cultivation on Water Quality, and on Fish and Wildlife; List of Conditions to Address] 274

§ 13387 [Persons Subject to Criminal Penalties; Allocation of Funds Collected for Violations] 274

§ 13575 [Definitions for Water Recycling Act of 1991] 276

Table of Contents
Part 2: Regulations

TITLE 3. FOOD AND AGRICULTURE

DIVISION 8. CANNABIS CULTIVATION

Chapter 1.Cannabis Cultivation Program

ARTICLE 1. DEFINITIONS

§ 8000.	Definitions.	279

ARTICLE 2. APPLICATIONS

§ 8100.	Temporary Licenses.	281
§ 8101.	Annual License Application Fees.	282
§ 8102.	Annual License Application Requirements.	282
§ 8103.	Owner and Financial Interest Holders.	287
§ 8104.	Legal Right to Occupy.	288
§ 8105.	Property Diagram.	288
§ 8106.	Cultivation Plan Requirements.	289
§ 8107.	Supplemental Water Source Information.	291
§ 8108.	Cannabis Waste Management Plan.	292
§ 8109.	Applicant Track-and-Trace Training Requirement.	293

§ 8110.   Proof of Local License, Permit, or Other Authorization.   293

§ 8111.   Priority Application Review.   293

§ 8112.   Annual License Application Review for Completeness.   294

§ 8113.   Substantially Related Offenses Review.   294

§ 8114.   Withdrawal of Application.   295

§ 8115.   Notification and Grounds for Denial of License; Petition for Reconsideration.   296

ARTICLE 3. CULTIVATION LICENSE FEES AND REQUIREMENTS

§ 8200.   Annual License Fees.   296

§ 8201.   Cultivation License Types.   297

§ 8202.   General License Requirements.   298

§ 8203.   Renewal of License.   298

§ 8204.   Notification of License Information Change.   300

§ 8205.   Physical Modification of Premises.   300

§ 8206.   Death or Incapacity of an Owner.   301

§ 8207.   Disaster Relief.   302

§ 8208.   Surrender, Revocation, or Suspension of License.   303

§ 8209.   Medium Cultivation License Limits.   303

§ 8210.   Sample Collection by the Bureau.   303

§ 8211.   Prohibition of Product Returns.   303

§ 8212.   Packaging and Labeling of Cannabis and Nonmanufactured Cannabis Products.   304

§ 8213.   Requirements for Weighing Devices and Weighmasters.   304

§ 8214.   Commercial Cannabis Activity Between Licensees.   305

§ 8215.   Personnel Prohibited from Holding Licenses.   305

§ 8216.   License Issuance in an Impacted Watershed.   305

ARTICLE 4. CULTIVATION SITE REQUIREMENTS

§ 8300.   Cultivation Requirements for Specialty Cottage, Specialty, Small, and Medium Licenses.   306

§ 8301.   Seed Production Requirements for Nursery Licensees.   306

§ 8302.   Research and Development Requirements for Nursery Licensees.   306

§ 8303.   Cultivation Requirements for Processor Licensees.   306

§ 8304.   General Environmental Protection Measures.   307

§ 8305.   Renewable Energy Requirements.   307

§ 8306.   Generator Requirements.   308

§ 8307.   Pesticide Use Requirements.   309

§ 8308.   Cannabis Waste Management.   309

ARTICLE 5. RECORDS AND REPORTING

§ 8400.   Record Retention.   311

§ 8401.   Sales Invoice or Receipt Requirements.   312

§ 8402.   Track-and-Trace System.   313

§ 8403.   Track-and-Trace System Unique Identifiers (UID).   313

§ 8404.   Track-and-Trace System User Requirements.   315

§ 8405.   Track-and-Trace System Reporting Requirements.   315

§ 8406.   Track-and-Trace System Inventory Requirements.   317

§ 8407.   Track-and-Trace System Requirements for Cannabis and Nonmanufactured Cannabis Products in Temporary Licensee Possession at the Time of Annual License Issuance.   317

§ 8408.   Inventory Audits.   318

§ 8409.   Notification of Diversion, Theft, Loss, or Criminal Activity.   318

ARTICLE 6. INSPECTIONS, INVESTIGATIONS, AND AUDITS

§ 8500.   Inspections, Investigations, and Audits Applicability.   318

§ 8501.   Inspections, Investigations, Examinations, and Audits.   318

ARTICLE 7. ENFORCEMENT

§ 8600.   Enforcement Applicability.   319

§ 8601.   Administrative Actions - Operations.   319

§ 8602.   Administrative Actions - Record keeping.   332

§ 8603.   Notice of Violation.   335

§ 8604.   Emergency Decisions.   335

§ 8605.   Informal Administrative Hearings.   337

§ 8606.   Informal Hearing Schedule and Notification.   337

§ 8607.   Conduct of Informal Hearings.   338

§ 8608.   Licensing Actions.   338

§ 8609.   Formal Administrative Hearings.   338

TITLE 16. PROFESSIONAL AND VOCATIONAL REGULATIONS

DIVISION 42. BUREAU OF CANNABIS CONTROL

Chapter 1. All Bureau Licensees

ARTICLE 1. DIVISION DEFINITIONS

§ 5000.   Definitions.   339

ARTICLE 2. APPLICATIONS

§ 5001.   Temporary Licenses.   341

§ 5002.   Annual License Application Requirements.   341

§ 5003.   Designation of Owner.   345

§ 5004.   Financial Interest in a Commercial Cannabis Business.   346

§ 5005.   Personnel Prohibited from Holding Licenses.   347

§ 5006.   Premises Diagram.   347

§ 5007.   Landowner Approval.   348

§ 5007.1.   Electronic Signature.   348

§ 5007.2.   Use of Legal Business Name.   348

§ 5008.   Bond.   349

§ 5009.   Limited Waiver of Sovereign Immunity.   349

§ 5010.   Compliance with the California Environmental Quality Act (CEQA).   350

§ 5010.1.   Review of Previously Prepared Environmental Documents Pursuant to CEQA. 351

§ 5010.2.   CEQA Exempt Projects.   351

§ 5010.3.   Preparation of CEQA Environmental Documents for Applicant.   352

§ 5011.   Additional Information.   352

§ 5012.   Incomplete Applications.   352

§ 5013.   Withdrawal of Application.   353

ARTICLE 3. LICENSING

§ 5014.   Fees.   353

§ 5015.   Payment of Fees.   356

§ 5016.   Priority Licensing.   357

§ 5017.   Substantially Related Offenses and Criteria for Rehabilitation.   357

§ 5018.   Additional Grounds for Denial of a License.   358

§ 5019.   Excessive Concentration.   359

§ 5020.   Renewal of License.   360

§ 5021.   Denial of License.   360

§ 5022.   Cancellation of License.   361

§ 5023.   Business Modifications.   361

§ 5024.   Death, Incapacity, or Insolvency of a Licensee.   363

§ 5024.1.   Cannabis Goods After Termination of License.   363

§ 5025.   Premises.   364

§ 5026.   Premises Location.   365

§ 5027.   Physical Modification of Premises.   366

§ 5028.   Subletting of Premises.   366

§ 5029.   Transition to Regulated Commercial Cannabis Market. [Repealed]   366

§ 5030.   Licensee's Responsibility for Acts of Employees and Agents.   366

§ 5031.   Age Restriction.   367

§ 5032.   Commercial Cannabis Activity.   367

§ 5033.   Storage of Inventory.   367

§ 5034.   Significant Discrepancy in Inventory.   368

§ 5035.   Notification of Criminal Acts, Civil Judgments, Violations of Labor Standards, and Revocation of   368
            a Local License, Permit, or Other Authorization After Licensure.

§ 5036.   Notification of Theft, Loss, and Criminal Activity.   369

§ 5037.   Record Retention.   369

§ 5038.   Disaster Relief.   370

ARTICLE 4. POSTING AND ADVERTISING

§ 5039.   License Posting Requirement.   371

§ 5040.   Advertising Placement.   371

§ 5040.1.   Marketing Cannabis Goods as Alcoholic Products.   372

§ 5041.   Age Confirmation in Advertising.   372

§ 5041.1.   Branded Merchandise Approval.   373

ARTICLE 5. SECURITY MEASURES.

§ 5042.   Limited-Access Areas.   373

§ 5043.   Licensee Employee Badge Requirement.   373

§ 5044.   Video Surveillance System.   374

§ 5045.   Security Personnel.   375

§ 5046.   Locks.   375

§ 5047.   Alarm System.   375

ARTICLE 6. TRACK AND TRACE REQUIREMENTS

§ 5048.   Track and Trace System.   376

§ 5049.   Track and Trace Reporting.   377

§ 5050.   Loss of Connectivity.   378

§ 5051.   Track and Trace System Reconciliation.   379

§ 5052.   Temporary Licenses; Licensees in Operation at Time of Licensure.   379

ARTICLE 7. RETURNS AND DESTRUCTION

§ 5052.1.   Acceptance of Shipments.   379

§ 5053.   Returns Between Licensees.   380

§ 5054.   Destruction of Cannabis Goods Prior to Disposal.   380

§ 5055.   Cannabis Waste Management. [Repealed]   381

Chapter 2. Distributors

§ 5300.   Distribution Activities.   381

§ 5301.   Storage Services.   381

§ 5302.   Storage of Batches for Testing.   381

§ 5303.   Packaging, Labeling, and Rolling.   382

§ 5303.1.   Net Weight of Dried Flower.   382

§ 5304.   Testing Arrangements.   383

§ 5305.   Testing Sample.   383

§ 5305.1.   Re-Sampling.   383

§ 5306.   Laboratory Testing Results.   383

§ 5307.   Quality Assurance Review.   384

§ 5307.1.   Quality-Assurance Review for Labeling Cannabinoids and Terpenoids.   385

§ 5307.2.   Licensed Distributor to Licensed Distributor Transfers.   385

§ 5308.   Insurance Requirements.   385

§ 5309.   Inventory Accounting.   386

§ 5310.   Records.   386

§ 5311.   Requirements for the Transportation of Cannabis Goods.   387

§ 5312.   Required Transport Vehicle Information.   388

§ 5313.   Transport Personnel Requirements.   388

§ 5314.   Shipping Manifest.   389

§ 5315.   Distributor Transport Only License.   389

Chapter 3. Retailers

§ 5400.   Access to Retailer Premises.   390

§ 5401.   Limited-Access Areas. [Repealed]   390

§ 5402.   Customer Access to the Retail Area.   390

§ 5403.   Hours of Operation.   391

§ 5403.1. Requirements While Not Open for Business.   391

§ 5404.   Retail Customers.   391

§ 5405.   Cannabis Goods Display.   392

§ 5406.   Cannabis Goods for Sale.   392

§ 5407.   Sale of Non-Cannabis Goods.   392

§ 5408.   Sale of Live Plants and Seeds.   393

§ 5409.   Daily Limits.   393

§ 5410.   Customer Return of Cannabis Goods.   394

§ 5411.   Free Cannabis Goods.   394

§ 5412.   Prohibition on Packaging and Labeling by a Retailer.   395

§ 5413.   Cannabis Goods Packaging and Exit Packaging.   395

§ 5414.   Non-Storefront Retailer.   395

§ 5415.   Delivery Employees.   396

§ 5415.1.   Deliveries Facilitated by Technology Platforms.   396

§ 5416.   Delivery to a Physical Address.   397

§ 5417.   Delivery Vehicle Requirements.   397

§ 5418.   Cannabis Goods Carried During Delivery.   398

§ 5419.   Cannabis Consumption During Delivery.   399

§ 5420.   Delivery Request Receipt.   399

§ 5421.   Delivery Route.   400

§ 5422.   Receiving Shipments of Inventory.   400

§ 5423.   Inventory Documentation.   401

§ 5424.   Inventory Reconciliation.   401

§ 5425.   Record of Sales.   401

§ 5426.   Records.   401

§ 5427.   Retailer Premises to Retailer Premises Transfer.   402

Chapter 4. Microbusiness

§ 5500.   Microbusiness.   402

§ 5501.   Microbusiness Applications Including Cultivation Activities.   403

§ 5502.   Cultivation Plan Requirements.   404

§ 5503.   Supplemental Water Source Information.   405

§ 5504.   License Issuance in an Impacted Watershed.   407

§ 5505.   Cultivation Records for Licensees Engaging in Cultivation Activities. 407

§ 5506.   Microbusiness Applications Including Manufacturing Activities.   407

§ 5506.1.   Microbusiness Failed Manufactured Cannabis Product Batches.   408

§ 5507.   Microbusiness Records for Licensees Engaging in Manufacturing Activities. 409

Chapter 5. Cannabis Events

§ 5600.   Cannabis Event Organizer License.   409

§ 5601.   Temporary Cannabis Event License.   412

§ 5602.   Temporary Cannabis Event Sales.   414

§ 5603.   Temporary Cannabis Event Consumption.   416

§ 5604.   Informational or Educational Cannabis Events.   416

Chapter 6. Testing Laboratories

ARTICLE 1. CHAPTER DEFINITIONS

§ 5700.   Definitions.   416

ARTICLE 2. LABORATORY LICENSE

§ 5701.   General Laboratory License Requirements.   421

§ 5702.   Laboratory License Application.   421

§ 5703.   Interim Testing Laboratory License.   422

ARTICLE 3. SAMPLING CANNABIS AND CANNABIS PRODUCTS

§ 5704.   Sampling Standard Operating Procedures.   423

§ 5705.   General Sampling Requirements.   424

§ 5706.   Chain of Custody (COC).   425

§ 5707.   Harvest Batch Sampling.   425

§ 5708.   Cannabis Product Batch and Pre-Roll Sampling.   426

§ 5709.   Laboratory Transportation of Cannabis Goods Samples.   427

§ 5710.   Laboratory Receipt of Samples Obtained from a Distributor or Microbusiness.   428

ARTICLE 4. STANDARD OPERATING PROCEDURES

§ 5711.   Laboratory Analyses Standard Operating Procedures.   428

§ 5712.   Test Methods.   429

§ 5713.   Validation of Test Methods.   429

ARTICLE 5. LABORATORY TESTING AND REPORTING

§ 5714.   Required Testing.   431

§ 5715.   Phase-in of Required Laboratory Testing.   431

§ 5716.   Homogeneity Testing of Edible Cannabis Products. [Repealed]   432

§ 5717.   Moisture Content and Water Activity Testing.   432

§ 5718.   Residual Solvents and Processing Chemicals Testing.   433

§ 5719.   Residual Pesticides Testing.   434

§ 5720.   Microbial Impurities Testing.   436

§ 5721.   Mycotoxin Testing.   437

§ 5722.   Foreign Material Testing.   437

§ 5723.   Heavy Metals Testing.   438

§ 5724.   Cannabinoid Testing.   438

§ 5725.   Terpenoid Testing.   440

§ 5726.   Certificate of Analysis (COA).   440

ARTICLE 6. POST TESTING PROCEDURES

§ 5727.   Remediation and Retesting.   441

§ 5728.   Post Testing Sample Retention.   442

ARTICLE 7. LABORATORY QUALITY ASSURANCE AND QUALITY CONTROL

§ 5729.   Laboratory Quality Assurance (Lqa) Program.   442

§ 5730.   Laboratory Quality Control (Lqc) Samples.   443

§ 5731.   Limits of Detection (Lod) and Limits of Quantitation (Loq) for Quantitative Analyses.   444

§ 5732.   Data Package.   445

§ 5733.   Required Proficiency Testing.   445

§ 5734.   Satisfactory and Unsatisfactory Proficiency Test Performance.   446

§ 5735.   Laboratory Audits.   446

ARTICLE 8. LABORATORY EMPLOYEE QUALIFICATIONS

§ 5736.   General Laboratory Employee Qualifications.   447

§ 5737.   Supervisor or Management Responsibilities and Qualifications.   447

§ 5738.   Analyst and Sampler Qualifications.   447

ARTICLE 9. RECORD RETENTION

§ 5739.   Records.   448

Chapter 7. Enforcement

§ 5800.   Right of Access.   448

§ 5801.   Notice to Comply.   449

§ 5802.   Citations; Orders of Abatement; Administrative Fines.   449

§ 5803.   Contesting Citations.   450

§ 5804.   Citation Compliance.   450

§ 5805.   Minor Decoys.   451

§ 5806.   Attire and Conduct.   451

§ 5807.   Entertainers and Conduct.   452

§ 5808.   Additional Grounds for Discipline.   452

§ 5809.   Disciplinary Actions.   453

§ 5810.   Interim Suspension.   454

§ 5811.   Posting of Notice of Suspension.   454

§ 5812.   Posting of Notice of Revocation.   455

§ 5813.   Enforcement Costs.   455

§ 5814.   Disciplinary Guidelines.   456

§ 5815.   Emergency Decision and Order.   456

Chapter 8. Other Provisions

ARTICLE 1. RESEARCH FUNDING

§ 5900.	Eligibility.	458
§ 5901.	Request for Proposals.	458
§ 5902.	Selection Process and Criteria.	459
§ 5903.	Release of Funds.	459
§ 5904.	Reports to the Bureau.	460
§ 5905.	Research Records.	460

Title 17. Public Health

DIVISION 1. STATE DEPARTMENT OF HEALTH SERVICES

Chapter 13. Manufactured Cannabis Safety

SUBCHAPTER 1. GENERAL PROVISIONS AND DEFINITIONS

ARTICLE 1. DEFINITIONS

§ 40100.	Definitions.	461
§ 40101.	Applicability.	464
§ 40102.	Owners and Financial Interest Holders.	465
§ 40105.	Premises Diagram.	465

ARTICLE 2. GENERAL PROVISIONS

§ 40115.	License Required.	466
§ 40116.	Personnel Prohibited from Holding Licenses.	466
§ 40118.	Manufacturing License Types.	467
§ 40120.	Additional Activities.	468

SUBCHAPTER 2. MANUFACTURING LICENSES

ARTICLE 1. APPLICATIONS FOR LICENSURE

§ 40126.   Temporary Licenses.   468

§ 40127.   Temporary Shared-Use Facility Registration; Temporary Licenses: Type S.   468

§ 40128.   Annual License Application Requirements.   469

§ 40129.   Annual License Application Requirements - Business Information.   470

§ 40130.   Annual License Application Requirements - Owners.   471

§ 40131.   Annual License Application Requirements - Manufacturing Premises and Operations Information.   472

§ 40132.   Annual License Application Requirements - Compliance with CEQA.   473

§ 40133.   Limited Waiver of Sovereign Immunity.   474

§ 40135.   Incomplete and Abandoned Applications.   475

§ 40137.   Application Withdrawal.   475

ARTICLE 3. FEES

§ 40150.   Application and License Fees.   475

§ 40152.   Gross Annual Revenue Calculation.   476

ARTICLE 4. APPROVAL OR DENIAL OF APPLICATION FOR LICENSURE

§ 40155.   New License Approval.   476

§ 40156.   Priority License Issuance.   477

§ 40159.   Denial of License.   477

§ 40162.   Substantially Related Acts.   478

§ 40165.   Criteria for Evidence of Rehabilitation.   478

§ 40167.   Appeal of License Denial.   479

§ 40169.   Notification of Criminal Acts, Civil Judgments, and Revocation of a Local License, Permit, or Other Authorization After Licensure. [Repealed]   479

ARTICLE 5. LICENSING

§ 40175.	License Constraints.	479
§ 40177.	Change in Licensed Operations.	480
§ 40178.	Add or Remove Owner(s) and Financial Interest Holders.	480
§ 40179.	Death, Incapacity, or Insolvency of a Licensee.	481
§ 40180.	License Renewal.	481
§ 40182.	Disaster Relief.	482
§ 40184.	Notification of Criminal Acts, Civil Judgments, and Revocation of a Local License, Permit, or Other Authorization After Licensure.	483

ARTICLE 6. SHARED-USE FACILITIES

§ 40190.	Definitions.	484
§ 40191.	Type S License.	484
§ 40192.	Registration to Operate a Shared-Use Facility.	485
§ 40194.	Shared-Use Facility Conditions for Operation.	485
§ 40196.	Shared-Use Facility Compliance Requirements.	486

Subchapter 3. Requirements of Operation

ARTICLE 1. SAFETY AND SECURITY

§ 40200.	Security Plan.	486
§ 40205.	Video Surveillance.	487
§ 40207.	Notification of Theft, Loss, or Diversion.	488

ARTICLE 2. EXTRACTIONS

§ 40220.	Permissible Extractions.	488
§ 40222.	Volatile Solvent Extractions.	489
§ 40223.	Ethanol Extractions.	489
§ 40225.	Closed-Loop Extraction System Requirements.	489

ARTICLE 3. GOOD MANUFACTURING PRACTICES

§ 40230.   Manufacturing Practices Definitions.   490

§ 40232.   Requirements for Personnel. [Repealed]   492

§ 40234.   Grounds. [Repealed]   492

§ 40235.   Quality Control Program.   492

§ 40236.   Premises Construction and Design. [Repealed]   493

§ 40238.   Sanitary Operations. [Repealed]   493

§ 40240.   Grounds, Building, and Manufacturing Premises.   493

§ 40242.   Equipment and Utensils. [Repealed]   494

§ 40243.   Equipment and Utensils.   494

§ 40246.   Personnel.   495

§ 40248.   Cannabis Product Components.   496

§ 40250.   Manufacturing Processes and Procedures.   496

§ 40252.   Quality of Raw Materials and Ingredients. [Repealed]   497

§ 40253.   Product Quality Plan.   497

§ 40254.   Manufacturing Operations. [Repealed]   498

§ 40255.   Master Manufacturing Protocol.   498

§ 40256.   Hazard Analysis. [Repealed]   499

§ 40258.   Batch Production Record.   499

§ 40260.   Equipment and Machinery Qualification. [Repealed]   501

§ 40262.   Master Manufacturing Protocol. [Renumbered]   501

§ 40264.   Batch Production Record. [Renumbered]   501

§ 40266.   Product Complaints. [Repealed]   501

§ 40268.   Recalls. [Repealed]   501

ARTICLE 5. SPECIAL PROCESSING REQUIREMENTS

§ 40270.   Juice Processing.   501

§ 40272.   Dried Meat Processing.   501

ARTICLE 6. OTHER RESPONSIBILITIES

§ 40275.   Standard Operating Procedures.   501

§ 40277.   Weights and Measures.   502

§ 40280.   Training Program.   502

§ 40282.   Inventory Control - Cannabis and Cannabis Products.   504

§ 40290.   Waste Management.   504

§ 40292.   Consent to Sample Collection.   505

§ 40295.   Product Complaints.   505

§ 40297.   Recalls.   506

SUBCHAPTER 4. PRODUCTS

ARTICLE 1. CANNABIS PRODUCT STANDARDS

§ 40299.   Applicability. [Repealed]   507

§ 40300.   Prohibited Products.   507

§ 40305.   Requirements for Edible Cannabis Products.   508

§ 40306.   Requirements for Topical Cannabis Products, Concentrates, and Other Cannabis Products.   508

§ 40308.   Orally-Consumed Products Containing Alcohol.   508

§ 40310.   Failed Product Batches. [Repealed]   509

ARTICLE 2. CANNABINOID CONCENTRATION LIMITS

§ 40315.   Thc Concentration Limits.   509

ARTICLE 3. FAILED PRODUCT BATCHES

§ 40330.   Failed Product Batches.   509

SUBCHAPTER 5. LABELING AND PACKAGING REQUIREMENTS

ARTICLE 1. GENERAL PROVISIONS

§ 40400.   Applicability.   510

§ 40401.   Release to Distributor as Finished Product.   511

ARTICLE 2. LABELING REQUIREMENTS

§ 40403.   General Provisions.   511

§ 40404.   Labeling Requirements: Pre-Rolls and Packaged Flower.   511

§ 40405.   Primary Panel Labeling Requirements: Manufactured Products.   512

§ 40406.   Additional Primary Panel Labeling Requirements: Edible Products.   512

§ 40408.   Informational Panel Labeling Requirements.   513

§ 40409.   Cannabinoid Content Labeling.   514

§ 40410.   Labeling Restrictions.   515

§ 40411.   Statement of Characteristic Anticipated Effects.   515

§ 40412.   Universal Symbol.   516

ARTICLE 3. PACKAGING

§ 40415.   Packaging.   516

§ 40417.   Child-Resistant Packaging Requirements.   517

Subchapter 6. Compliance

ARTICLE 1. RECORDS

§ 40500.   Record Keeping Requirements.   517

§ 40505.   Sales Invoices and Receipts.   518

ARTICLE 2. TRACK-AND-TRACE SYSTEM

§ 40510.   Track-and-Trace System General Requirements.   519

§ 40512.   Track-and-Trace System Reporting Requirements.   520

§ 40513.   Track-and-Trace System - Loss of Access.   520

§ 40515.   Track-and-Trace System - Temporary Licenses.   521

§ 40517.   Track-and-Trace System - UID Tag Order.   521

ARTICLE 3. ADVERTISING AND MARKETING

§ 40525.   Advertising and Marketing.   522

ARTICLE 4. INSPECTIONS

§ 40550.   Inspections.   522

§ 40551.   Notice to Comply.   523

ARTICLE 5. SUSPENSIONS AND REVOCATIONS OF A LICENSE

§ 40570.   Emergency Decision and Order.   523

SUBCHAPTER 7. TRANSITIONAL PERIOD [REPEALED]

§ 40600.   License Designations. [Repealed]   525

§ 40601.   Packaging and Labeling. [Repealed]   525

Part 1: Laws

I. Business and Professions Code Sections

Business and Professions Code § 27

(Amended by Stats. 2018, Ch. 703, Sec. 1.3. (SB 1491) Effective January 1, 2019.)

(a) Each entity specified in subdivisions (c), (d), and (e) shall provide on the Internet information regarding the status of every license issued by that entity in accordance with the California Public Records Act (Chapter 3.5 (commencing with Section 6250) of Division 7 of Title 1 of the Government Code) and the Information Practices Act of 1977 (Chapter 1 (commencing with Section 1798) of Title 1.8 of Part 4 of Division 3 of the Civil Code). The public information to be provided on the Internet shall include information on suspensions and revocations of licenses issued by the entity and other related enforcement action, including accusations filed pursuant to the Administrative Procedure Act (Chapter 3.5 (commencing with Section 11340) of Part 1 of Division 3 of Title 2 of the Government Code) taken by the entity relative to persons, businesses, or facilities subject to licensure or regulation by the entity. The information may not include personal information, including home telephone number, date of birth, or social security number. Each entity shall disclose a licensee's address of record. However, each entity shall allow a licensee to provide a post office box number or other alternate address, instead of his or her home address, as the address of record. This section shall not preclude an entity from also requiring a licensee, who has provided a post office box number or other alternative mailing address as his or her address of record, to provide a physical business address or residence address only for the entity's internal administrative use and not for disclosure as the licensee's address of record or disclosure on the Internet.

(b) In providing information on the Internet, each entity specified in subdivisions (c) and (d) shall comply with the Department of Consumer Affairs' guidelines for access to public records.

(c) Each of the following entities within the Department of Consumer Affairs shall comply with the requirements of this section:

(1) The Board for Professional Engineers, Land Surveyors, and Geologists shall disclose information on its registrants and licensees.

(2) The Bureau of Automotive Repair shall disclose information on its licensees, including auto repair dealers, smog stations, lamp and brake stations, smog check technicians, and smog inspection certification stations.

(3) The Bureau of Household Goods and Services shall disclose information on its licensees and registrants, including major appliance repair dealers, combination dealers (electronic and appliance), electronic repair dealers, service contract sellers, and service contract administrators.

(4) The Cemetery and Funeral Bureau shall disclose information on its licensees, including cemetery brokers, cemetery salespersons, cemetery managers, crematory managers, cemetery authorities, crematories, cremated remains disposers, embalmers, funeral establishments, and funeral directors.

(5) The Professional Fiduciaries Bureau shall disclose information on its licensees.

(6) The Contractors' State License Board shall disclose information on its licensees and registrants in accordance with Chapter 9 (commencing with Section 7000) of Division 3. In addition to information related to licenses as specified in subdivision (a), the board shall also disclose information provided to the board by the Labor Commissioner pursuant to Section 98.9 of the Labor Code.

(7) The Bureau for Private Postsecondary Education shall disclose information on private postsecondary institutions under its jurisdiction, including disclosure of notices to comply issued pursuant to Section 94935

of the Education Code.

(8) The California Board of Accountancy shall disclose information on its licensees and registrants.

(9) The California Architects Board shall disclose information on its licensees, including architects and landscape architects.

(10) The State Athletic Commission shall disclose information on its licensees and registrants.

(11) The State Board of Barbering and Cosmetology shall disclose information on its licensees.

(12) The State Board of Guide Dogs for the Blind shall disclose information on its licensees and registrants.

(13) The Acupuncture Board shall disclose information on its licensees.

(14) The Board of Behavioral Sciences shall disclose information on its licensees and registrants.

(15) The Dental Board of California shall disclose information on its licensees.

(16) The State Board of Optometry shall disclose information on its licensees and registrants.

(17) The Board of Psychology shall disclose information on its licensees, including psychologists, psychological assistants, and registered psychologists.

(18) The Veterinary Medical Board shall disclose information on its licensees, registrants, and permitholders.

(d) The State Board of Chiropractic Examiners shall disclose information on its licensees.

(e) The Structural Pest Control Board shall disclose information on its licensees, including applicators, field representatives, and operators in the areas of fumigation, general pest and wood destroying pests and organisms, and wood roof cleaning and treatment.

(f) The Bureau of Cannabis Control shall disclose information on its licensees.

(g) "Internet" for the purposes of this section has the meaning set forth in paragraph (6) of subdivision (f) of Section 17538.

Business and Professions Code § 101

(Amended (as added by Stats. 2017, Ch. 828, Sec. 4) by Stats. 2018, Ch. 858, Sec. 1.5. (SB 1482) Effective January 1, 2019.)

The department is comprised of the following:

(a) The Dental Board of California.

(b) The Medical Board of California.

(c) The State Board of Optometry.

(d) The California State Board of Pharmacy.

(e) The Veterinary Medical Board.

(f) The California Board of Accountancy.

(g) The California Architects Board.

(h) The State Board of Barbering and Cosmetology.

(i) The Board for Professional Engineers, Land Surveyors, and Geologists.

(j) The Contractors' State License Board.

(k) The Bureau for Private Postsecondary Education.

(l) The Bureau of Household Goods and Services.

(m) The Board of Registered Nursing.

(n) The Board of Behavioral Sciences.

(o) The State Athletic Commission.

(p) The Cemetery and Funeral Bureau.

(q) The Bureau of Security and Investigative Services.

(r) The Court Reporters Board of California.

(s) The Board of Vocational Nursing and Psychiatric Technicians.

(t) The Landscape Architects Technical Committee.

(u) The Division of Investigation.

(v) The Bureau of Automotive Repair.

(w) The Respiratory Care Board of California.

(x) The Acupuncture Board.

(y) The Board of Psychology.

(z) The California Board of Podiatric Medicine.

(aa) The Physical Therapy Board of California.

(ab) The Arbitration Review Program.

(ac) The Physician Assistant Board.

(ad) The Speech-Language Pathology and Audiology and Hearing Aid Dispensers Board.

(ae) The California Board of Occupational Therapy.

(af) The Osteopathic Medical Board of California.

(ag) The Naturopathic Medicine Committee.

(ah) The Dental Hygiene Board of California.

(ai) The Professional Fiduciaries Bureau.

(aj) The State Board of Chiropractic Examiners.

(ak) The Bureau of Real Estate Appraisers.

(al) The Structural Pest Control Board.

(am) The Bureau of Cannabis Control.

(an) Any other boards, offices, or officers subject to its jurisdiction by law.

(ao) This section shall become operative on July 1, 2018.

Business and Professions Code § 144

(Amended by Stats. 2018, Ch. 6, Sec. 1. (AB 106) Effective March 13, 2018.)

(a) Notwithstanding any other law, an agency designated in subdivision (b) shall require an applicant to furnish to the agency a full set of fingerprints for purposes of conducting criminal history record checks. Any agency designated in subdivision (b) may obtain and receive, at its discretion, criminal history information from the Department of Justice and the United States Federal Bureau of Investigation.

(b) Subdivision (a) applies to the following:

(1) California Board of Accountancy.

(2) State Athletic Commission.

(3) Board of Behavioral Sciences.

(4) Court Reporters Board of California.

(5) State Board of Guide Dogs for the Blind.

(6) California State Board of Pharmacy.

(7) Board of Registered Nursing.

(8) Veterinary Medical Board.

(9) Board of Vocational Nursing and Psychiatric Technicians.

(10) Respiratory Care Board of California.

(11) Physical Therapy Board of California.

(12) Physician Assistant Committee of the Medical Board of California.

(13) Speech-Language Pathology and Audiology and Hearing Aid Dispensers Board.

(14) Medical Board of California.

(15) State Board of Optometry.

(16) Acupuncture Board.

(17) Cemetery and Funeral Bureau.

(18) Bureau of Security and Investigative Services.

(19) Division of Investigation.

(20) Board of Psychology.

(21) California Board of Occupational Therapy.

(22) Structural Pest Control Board.

(23) Contractors' State License Board.

(24) Naturopathic Medicine Committee.

(25) Professional Fiduciaries Bureau.

(26) Board for Professional Engineers, Land Surveyors, and Geologists.

(27) Bureau of Cannabis Control.

(28) California Board of Podiatric Medicine.

(29) Osteopathic Medical Board of California.

(c) For purposes of paragraph (26) of subdivision (b), the term "applicant" shall be limited to an initial applicant who has never been registered or licensed by the board or to an applicant for a new licensure or registration category.

Business and Professions Code § 205.1

(MCRSA- SB 837, Effective June 27, 2016.)

Notwithstanding subdivision (a) of Section 205, the Medical Cannabis Regulation and Safety Act Fund is a special fund within the Professions and Vocations Fund, and is subject to subdivision (b) of Section 205.

Business and Professions Code § 2220.05

(Amended by Stats. 2017, Ch. 775, Sec. 72. (SB 798) Effective January 1, 2018.)

(a) In order to ensure that its resources are maximized for the protection of the public, the Medical Board of California and the California Board of Podiatric Medicine shall prioritize their investigative and prosecutorial resources to ensure that physicians and surgeons and doctors of podiatric medicine representing the greatest threat of harm are identified and disciplined expeditiously. Cases involving any of the following allegations shall be handled on a priority basis, as follows, with the highest priority being given to cases in the first paragraph:

(1) Gross negligence, incompetence, or repeated negligent acts that involve death or serious bodily injury to one or more patients, such that the physician and surgeon or the doctor of podiatric medicine represents a danger to the public.

(2) Drug or alcohol abuse by a physician and surgeon or a doctor of podiatric medicine involving death or serious bodily injury to a patient.

(3) Repeated acts of clearly excessive prescribing, furnishing, or administering of controlled substances, or repeated acts of prescribing, dispensing, or furnishing of controlled substances without a good faith prior examination of the patient and medical reason therefor. However, in no event shall a physician and surgeon prescribing, furnishing, or administering controlled substances for intractable pain consistent with lawful prescribing, including, but not limited to, Sections 725, 2241.5, and 2241.6 of this code and Sections 11159.2 and 124961 of the Health and Safety Code, be prosecuted for excessive prescribing and prompt review of the applicability of these provisions shall be made in any complaint that may implicate these provisions.

(4) Repeated acts of clearly excessive recommending of cannabis to patients for medical purposes, or repeated acts of recommending cannabis to patients for medical purposes without a good faith prior examination of the patient and a medical reason for the recommendation.

(5) Sexual misconduct with one or more patients during a course of treatment or an examination.

(6) Practicing medicine while under the influence of drugs or alcohol.

(7) Repeated acts of clearly excessive prescribing, furnishing, or administering psychotropic medications to a minor without a good faith prior examination of the patient and medical reason therefor.

(b) The board may by regulation prioritize cases involving an allegation of conduct that is not described in subdivision (a). Those cases prioritized by regulation shall not be assigned a priority equal to or higher than the priorities established in subdivision (a).

(c) The Medical Board of California shall indicate in its annual report mandated by Section 2312 the number of temporary restraining orders, interim suspension orders, and disciplinary actions that are taken in each priority category specified in subdivisions (a) and (b).

Business and Professions Code § 2241.5

(MCRSA- SB 643, Effective January 1, 2016.)

(a) A physician and surgeon may prescribe for, or dispense or administer to, a person under his or her treatment for a medical condition dangerous drugs or prescription controlled substances for the treatment of pain or a condition causing pain, including, but not limited to, intractable pain.

(b) No physician and surgeon shall be subject to disciplinary action for prescribing, dispensing, or administering dangerous drugs or prescription controlled substances in accordance with this section.

(c) This section shall not affect the power of the board to take any action described in Section 2227 against a physician and surgeon who does any of the following:

(1) Violates subdivision (b), (c), or (d) of Section 2234 regarding gross negligence, repeated negligent acts, or incompetence.

(2) Violates Section 2241 regarding treatment of an addict.

(3) Violates Section 2242 or 2525.3 regarding performing an appropriate prior examination and the existence of a medical indication for prescribing, dispensing, or furnishing dangerous drugs or recommending medical cannabis.

(4) Violates Section 2242.1 regarding prescribing on the Internet.

(5) Fails to keep complete and accurate records of purchases and disposals of substances listed in the California Uniform Controlled Substances Act (Division 10 (commencing with Section 11000) of the Health and Safety Code) or controlled substances scheduled in the federal Comprehensive Drug Abuse Prevention and Control Act of 1970 (21 U.S.C. Sec. 801 et seq.), or pursuant to the federal Comprehensive Drug Abuse Prevention and Control Act of 1970. A physician and surgeon shall keep records of his or her purchases and disposals of these controlled substances or dangerous drugs, including the date of purchase, the date and records of the sale or disposal of the drugs by the physician and surgeon, the name and address of the person receiving the drugs, and the reason for the disposal or the dispensing of the drugs to the person, and shall otherwise comply with all state recordkeeping requirements for controlled substances.

(6) Writes false or fictitious prescriptions for controlled substances listed in the California Uniform Controlled Substances Act or scheduled in the federal Comprehensive Drug Abuse Prevention and Control Act of 1970.

(7) Prescribes, administers, or dispenses in violation of this chapter, or in violation of Chapter 4 (commencing with Section 11150) or Chapter 5 (commencing with Section 11210) of Division 10 of the Health and Safety Code.

(d) A physician and surgeon shall exercise reasonable care in determining whether a particular patient or condition, or the complexity of a patient's treatment, including, but not limited to, a current or recent pattern of drug abuse, requires consultation with, or referral to, a more qualified specialist.

(e) Nothing in this section shall prohibit the governing body of a hospital from taking disciplinary actions against a physician and surgeon pursuant to Sections 809.05, 809.4, and 809.5.

Business and Professions Code § 2242.1

(MCRSA- SB 643, Effective January 1, 2016.)

(a) No person or entity may prescribe, dispense, or furnish, or cause to be prescribed, dispensed, or furnished, dangerous drugs or dangerous devices, as defined in Section 4022, on the Internet for delivery to any person in this state, without an appropriate prior examination and medical indication, except as authorized by Section 2242.

(b) Notwithstanding any other provision of law, a violation of this section may subject the person or entity that has committed the violation to either a fine of up to twenty-five thousand dollars ($25,000) per occurrence pursuant to a citation issued by the board or a civil penalty of twenty-five thousand dollars ($25,000) per occurrence.

(c) The Attorney General may bring an action to enforce this section and to collect the fines or civil penalties authorized by subdivision (b).

(d) For notifications made on and after January 1, 2002, the Franchise Tax Board, upon notification by the Attorney General or the board of a final judgment in an action brought under this section, shall subtract the amount of the fine or awarded civil penalties from any tax refunds or lottery winnings due to the person who is a defendant in the action using the offset authority under Section 12419.5 of the Government Code, as delegated by the Controller, and the processes as established by the Franchise Tax Board for this purpose. That amount shall be forwarded to the board for deposit in the Contingent Fund of the Medical Board of California.

(e) If the person or entity that is the subject of an action brought pursuant to this section is not a resident of this state, a violation of this section shall, if applicable, be reported to the person's or entity's appropriate professional licensing authority.

(f) Nothing in this section shall prohibit the board from commencing a disciplinary action against a physician and surgeon pursuant to Section 2242 or 2525.3.

Business and Professions Code § 2525

(Amended by Stats. 2018, Ch. 599, Sec. 3. (AB 3261) Effective January 1, 2019.)

(a) It is unlawful for a physician and surgeon who recommends cannabis to a patient for a medical purpose to accept, solicit, or offer any form of remuneration from or to a facility issued a state license pursuant to Division 10 (commencing with Section 26000), if the physician and surgeon or his or her immediate family have a financial interest in that facility.

(b) For the purposes of this section, "financial interest" shall have the same meaning as in Section 650.01.

(c) A violation of this section shall be a misdemeanor punishable by up to one year in county jail and a fine of up to five thousand dollars ($5,000) or by civil penalties of up to five thousand dollars ($5,000) and shall constitute unprofessional conduct.

Business and Professions Code § 2525.1

(MCRSA- SB 643, Effective January 1, 2016.)

The Medical Board of California shall consult with the California Marijuana Research Program, known as the Center for Medicinal Cannabis Research, authorized pursuant to Section 11362.9 of the Health and Safety Code, on developing and adopting medical guidelines for the appropriate administration and use of medical cannabis.

Business and Professions Code § 2525.2

(Amended by Stats. 2017, Ch. 775, Sec. 96. (SB 798) Effective January 1, 2018.)

An individual who possesses a license in good standing to practice medicine or osteopathy issued by the Medical Board of California, the California Board of Podiatric Medicine, or the Osteopathic Medical Board of California shall not recommend medical cannabis to a patient, unless that person is the patient's attending physician, as defined by subdivision (a) of Section 11362.7 of the Health and Safety Code.

Business and Professions Code § 2525.3

(MCRSA- SB 643, Effective January 1, 2016.)

Recommending medical cannabis to a patient for a medical purpose without an appropriate prior examination and a medical indication constitutes unprofessional conduct.

Business and Professions Code § 2525.4

(MCRSA- SB 643, Effective January 1, 2016.)

It is unprofessional conduct for any attending physician recommending medical cannabis to be employed by, or enter into any other agreement with, any person or entity dispensing medical cannabis.

Business and Professions Code § 2525.5

(MCRSA- SB 643, Effective January 1, 2016.)

(a) A person shall not distribute any form of advertising for physician recommendations for medical cannabis in California unless the advertisement bears the following notice to consumers:

NOTICE TO CONSUMERS: The Compassionate Use Act of 1996 ensures that seriously ill Californians have the right to obtain and use cannabis for medical purposes where medical use is deemed appropriate and has been recommended by a physician who has determined that the person's health would benefit from the use of medical cannabis. Recommendations must come from an attending physician as defined in Section 11362.7 of the Health and Safety Code. Cannabis is a Schedule I drug according to the federal Controlled Substances Act. Activity related to cannabis use is subject to federal prosecution, regardless of the protections provided by state law.

(b) Advertising for attending physician recommendations for medical cannabis shall meet all of the requirements in Section 651. Price advertising shall not be fraudulent, deceitful, or misleading, including statements or advertisements of bait, discounts, premiums, gifts, or statements of a similar nature.

Business and Professions Code § 2529

(Amended by Stats. 2017, Ch. 775, Sec. 98. (SB 798) Effective January 1, 2018.)

(a) Graduates of the Southern California Psychoanalytic Institute, the Los Angeles Psychoanalytic Society and Institute, the San Francisco Psychoanalytic Institute, the San Diego Psychoanalytic Center, or institutes deemed equivalent by the Medical Board of California who have completed clinical training in psychoanalysis may engage in psychoanalysis as an adjunct to teaching, training, or research and hold themselves out to the public as psychoanalysts, and students in those institutes may engage in psychoanalysis under supervision, if the students and graduates do not hold themselves out to the public by any title or description of services incorporating the words "psychological," "psychologist," "psychology," "psychometrists," "psychometrics," or "psychometry," or that they do not state or imply that they are licensed to practice psychology.

(b) Those students and graduates seeking to engage in psychoanalysis under this chapter shall register with the Medical Board of California, presenting evidence of their student or graduate status. The board may suspend or revoke the exemption of those persons for unprofessional conduct as defined in Sections 726, 2234, 2235, and 2529.1

Business and Professions Code § 2529.1

(Amended by Stats. 2018, Ch. 571, Sec. 9. (SB 1480) Effective January 1, 2019.)

(a) The use of any controlled substance or the use of any of the dangerous drugs specified in Section 4022, or of alcoholic beverages, to the extent, or in such a manner as to be dangerous or injurious to the registrant, or to any other person or to the public, or to the extent that this use impairs the ability of the registrant to practice safely or more than one misdemeanor or any felony conviction involving the use, consumption, or self-administration of any of the substances referred to in this section, or any combination thereof, constitutes unprofessional conduct. The record of the conviction is conclusive evidence of this unprofessional conduct.

(b) A plea or verdict of guilty or a conviction following a plea of nolo contendere is deemed to be a conviction within the meaning of this section. The board may order discipline of the registrant in accordance with Section 2227 or may order the denial of the registration when the time for appeal has elapsed or the judgment of conviction has been affirmed on appeal or when an order granting probation is made suspending imposition of sentence, irrespective of a subsequent order under the provisions of Section 1203.4 of the Penal Code allowing this person to withdraw his or her plea of guilty and to enter a plea of not guilty, or setting aside the verdict of guilty, or dismissing the accusation, complaint, information, or indictment.

Business and Professions Code § 2529.5

(Amended by Stats. 2018, Ch. 571, Sec. 10. (SB 1480) Effective January 1, 2019.)

(a) Each person to whom registration is granted under the provisions of this chapter shall pay into the Contingent Fund of the Medical Board of California a fee to be fixed by the Medical Board of California at a sum not in excess of one hundred dollars ($100).

(b) The registration shall expire after two years. The registration may be renewed biennially at a fee to be fixed by the board at a sum not in excess of fifty dollars ($50). Students seeking to renew their registration shall present to the board evidence of their continuing student status.

(c) The money in the Contingent Fund of the Medical Board of California shall be used for the administration of this chapter.

Business and Professions Code § 2529.6

(Amended by Stats. 2018, Ch. 571, Sec. 11. (SB 1480) Effective January 1, 2019.)

(a) Except as provided in subdivisions (b) and (c), the board shall revoke the registration of any person who has been required to register as a sex offender pursuant to Section 290 of the Penal Code for conduct that occurred on or after January 1, 2017.

(b) This section shall not apply to a person who is required to register as a sex offender pursuant to Section 290 of the Penal Code solely because of a misdemeanor conviction under Section 314 of the Penal Code.

(c) This section shall not apply to a person who has been relieved under Section 290.5 of the Penal Code of his or her duty to register as a sex offender, or whose duty to register has otherwise been formally terminated under California law.

(d) A proceeding to revoke a registration pursuant to this section shall be conducted in accordance with Chapter 5 (commencing with Section 11500) of Part 1 of Division 3 of Title 2 of the Government Code.

Business and Professions Code § 4883

(Amended by Stats. 2018, Ch. 819, Sec. 1. (AB 2215) Effective January 1, 2019.)

The board may deny, revoke, or suspend a license or registration or assess a fine as provided in Section 4875 for any of the following:

(a) Conviction of a crime substantially related to the qualifications, functions, or duties of veterinary medicine, surgery, or dentistry, in which case the record of the conviction shall be conclusive evidence.

(b) For having professional connection with, or lending the licensee's or registrant's name to, any illegal practitioner of veterinary medicine and the various branches thereof.

(c) Violation or attempting to violate, directly or indirectly, any of the provisions of this chapter.

(d) Fraud or dishonesty in applying, treating, or reporting on tuberculin or other biological tests.

(e) Employment of anyone but a veterinarian licensed in the state to demonstrate the use of biologics in the treatment of animals.

(f) False or misleading advertising.

(g) Unprofessional conduct, that includes, but is not limited to, the following:

(1) Conviction of a charge of violating any federal statutes or rules or any statute or rule of this state regulating dangerous drugs or controlled substances. The record of the conviction is conclusive evidence thereof. A plea or verdict of guilty or a conviction following a plea of nolo contendere is deemed to be a conviction within the meaning of this section. The board may order the license or registration to be suspended or revoked, or assess a fine, or decline to issue a license or registration, when the time for appeal has elapsed, or the judgment of conviction has been affirmed on appeal or when an order granting probation is made suspending the imposition of sentence, irrespective of a subsequent order under Section 1203.4, 1210.1, or 3063.1 of the Penal Code allowing the person to withdraw his or her plea of guilty and to enter a plea of not guilty, or setting aside the verdict of guilty, or dismissing the accusation, information, or indictment.

(2) (A) The use of or prescribing for or administering to himself or herself, any controlled substance.

(B) The use of any of the dangerous drugs specified in Section 4022, or of alcoholic beverages to the extent, or in any manner as to be dangerous or injurious to a person licensed or registered under this chapter, or to any other person or to the public, or to the extent that the use impairs the ability of the person so licensed or registered to conduct with safety the practice authorized by the license or registration.

(C) The conviction of more than one misdemeanor or any felony involving the use, consumption, or self-administration of any of the substances referred to in this section or any combination thereof, and the record of the conviction is conclusive evidence.

A plea or verdict of guilty or a conviction following a plea of nolo contendere is deemed to be a conviction within the meaning of this section. The board may order the license or registration to be suspended or revoked or assess a fine, or may decline to issue a license or registration, when the time for appeal has elapsed or the judgment of conviction has been affirmed on appeal or when an order granting probation is made suspending imposition of sentence, irrespective of a subsequent order under Section 1203.4, 1210.1, or 3063.1 of the Penal Code allowing the person to withdraw his or her plea of guilty and to enter a plea of not guilty, or setting aside the verdict of guilty, or dismissing the accusation, information, or indictment.

(3) A violation of any federal statute, rule, or regulation or any of the statutes, rules, or regulations of this state regulating dangerous drugs or controlled substances.

(h) Failure to keep the licensee's or registrant's premises and all equipment therein in a clean and sanitary condition.

(i) Fraud, deception, negligence, or incompetence in the practice of veterinary medicine.

(j) Aiding or abetting in any acts that are in violation of any of the provisions of this chapter.

(k) The employment of fraud, misrepresentation, or deception in obtaining the license or registration.

(l) The revocation, suspension, or other discipline by another state or territory of a license, certificate, or registration to practice veterinary medicine or as a veterinary technician in that state or territory.

(m) Cruelty to animals, conviction on a charge of cruelty to animals, or both.

(n) Disciplinary action taken by any public agency in any state or territory for any act substantially related to the practice of veterinary medicine or the practice of a veterinary technician.

(o) Violation, or the assisting or abetting violation, of any regulations adopted by the board pursuant to this chapter.

(p) Accepting, soliciting, or offering any form of remuneration from or to a cannabis licensee if the veterinarian or his or her immediate family have a financial interest with the cannabis licensee. For purposes of this subdivision, the following definitions shall apply:

(1) "Cannabis licensee" shall have the same meaning as "licensee" in Section 26001.

(2) "Financial interest" shall have the same meaning as in Section 650.01.

(q) Discussing medicinal cannabis with a client while the veterinarian is employed by, or has an agreement with, a cannabis licensee. For purposes of this subdivision, "cannabis licensee" shall have the same meaning as "licensee" in Section 26001.

(r) Distributing any form of advertising for cannabis in California.

Business and Professions Code § 4884

(Added by Stats. 2018, Ch. 819, Sec. 2. (AB 2215) Effective January 1, 2019.)

(a) A licensee shall not dispense or administer cannabis or cannabis products to an animal patient.

(b) Notwithstanding any other law and absent negligence or incompetence, a veterinarian licensed under this chapter shall not be disciplined by the board or have his or her license denied, revoked, or suspended solely for discussing the use of cannabis on an animal for medicinal purposes.

(c) On or before January 1, 2020, the board shall adopt guidelines for veterinarians to follow when discussing cannabis within the veterinarian-client-patient relationship. These guidelines shall be posted on the board's Internet Web site.

DIVISION 6. BUSINESS RIGHTS

Chapter 3. Trade Names and Designations

ARTICLE 3. FARM NAMES

Business and Professions Code § 14460

(Added by Stats. 1941, Ch. 59.)

"Farm," as used in this article, includes ranch, estate and villa.

Business and Professions Code 14461

(Amended by Stats. 1999, Ch. 1000, Sec. 6. Effective January 1, 2000.)

Any farm owner or lessee in this state may register the name of his or her farm with the Secretary of State, and the Secretary of State shall issue a certificate setting forth the name and location of the farm and the name of the owner upon payment of the fee as set forth in subdivision (g) of Section 12193 of the Government Code.

Business and Professions Code § 14462

(Added by Stats. 1941, Ch. 59.)

Any person selling or marketing the products grown on a farm may use the name of the farm as a trade-mark on the products of the farm, in the same manner as provided for other trade-marks, and subject to the same rights and duties, as provided in this code.

Business and Professions Code § 14463

(Added by Stats. 1941, Ch. 59.)

Registration under this article shall have the same effect as the registration of a trade-mark.

Business and Professions Code § 14464

(Added by Stats. 1941, Ch. 59.)

When any name has been registered as the name of any farm, that name shall not be registered as the name of any other farm in this State, unless designating words have been prefixed or added thereto. The Secretary of State shall register such name only for the person entitled thereto.

Business and Professions Code § 14465

(Added by Stats. 1941, Ch. 59.)

Any person who registers as his own, any name already in use in this State, knowing that the name is already adopted as the name of a farm, or makes use of the name when regularly registered and in use by any other person entitled thereto under this article is guilty of a misdemeanor.

DIVISION 9. ALCOHOLIC BEVERAGES

Business and Professions Code § 25621.5

(Added by Stats. 2018, Ch. 827, Sec. 2. (AB 2914) Effective January 1, 2019.)

(a) A licensee shall not, at its licensed premises, sell, offer, or provide cannabis or cannabis products, as defined in Section 26001, including an alcoholic beverage that contains cannabis or a cannabis product, and no alcoholic beverage shall be manufactured, sold, or offered for sale if it contains tetrahydrocannabinol or cannabinoids, regardless of source.

(b) The department shall take disciplinary action against a licensee that violates this section, including, but not limited to, suspension or revocation of the license.

DIVISION 10. CANNABIS

Chapter 1. General Provisions and Definitions

Business and Professions Code § 26000

(MAUCRSA, Effective June 27, 2017.)

(a) This division shall be known, and may be cited, as the Medicinal and Adult-Use Cannabis Regulation and Safety Act.

(b) The purpose and intent of this division is to establish a comprehensive system to control and regulate the cultivation, distribution, transport, storage, manufacturing, processing, and sale of both of the following:

(1) Medicinal cannabis and medicinal cannabis products for patients with valid physician's recommendations.

(2) Adult-use cannabis and adult-use cannabis products for adults 21 years of age and over.

(c) In the furtherance of subdivision (b), this division sets forth the power and duties of the state agencies responsible for controlling and regulating the commercial medicinal and adult-use cannabis industry.

(d) The Legislature may, by majority vote, enact laws to implement this division, provided those laws are consistent with the purposes and intent of the Control, Regulate and Tax Adult Use of Marijuana Act.

Business and Professions Code § 26001

(Amended by Stats. 2018, Ch. 92, Sec. 19. (SB 1289) Effective January 1, 2019. Note: This section was added on Nov. 8, 2016, by initiative Prop. 64.)

For purposes of this division, the following definitions apply:

(a) "A-license" means a state license issued under this division for cannabis or cannabis products that are intended for adults who are 21 years of age and older and who do not possess a physician's recommendation.

(b) "A-licensee" means any person holding a license under this division for cannabis or cannabis products that are intended for adults who are 21 years of age and older and who do not possess a physician's recommendation.

(c) "Applicant" means an owner applying for a state license pursuant to this division.

(d) "Batch" means a specific quantity of homogeneous cannabis or cannabis product that is one of the following types:

> (1) Harvest batch. "Harvest batch" means a specifically identified quantity of dried flower or trim, leaves, and other cannabis plant matter that is uniform in strain, harvested at the same time, and, if applicable, cultivated using the same pesticides and other agricultural chemicals, and harvested at the same time.

> (2) Manufactured cannabis batch. "Manufactured cannabis batch" means either of the following:

>> (A) An amount of cannabis concentrate or extract that is produced in one production cycle using the same extraction methods and standard operating procedures.

>> (B) An amount of a type of manufactured cannabis produced in one production cycle using the same formulation and standard operating procedures.

(e) "Bureau" means the Bureau of Cannabis Control within the Department of Consumer Affairs, formerly named the Bureau of Marijuana Control, the Bureau of Medical Cannabis Regulation, and the Bureau of Medical Marijuana Regulation.

(f) "Cannabis" means all parts of the plant Cannabis sativa Linnaeus, Cannabis indica, or Cannabis ruderalis, whether growing or not; the seeds thereof; the resin, whether crude or purified, extracted from any part of the plant; and every compound, manufacture, salt, derivative, mixture, or preparation of the plant, its seeds, or resin. "Cannabis" also means the separated resin, whether crude or purified, obtained from cannabis. "Cannabis" does not include the mature stalks of the plant, fiber produced from the stalks, oil or cake made from the seeds of the plant, any other compound, manufacture, salt, derivative, mixture, or preparation of the mature stalks (except the resin extracted therefrom), fiber, oil, or cake, or the sterilized seed of the plant which is incapable of germination. For the purpose of this division, "cannabis" does not mean "industrial hemp" as defined by Section 11018.5 of the Health and Safety Code.

(g) "Cannabis accessories" has the same meaning as in Section 11018.2 of the Health and Safety Code.

(h) "Cannabis concentrate" means cannabis that has undergone a process to concentrate one or more active cannabinoids, thereby increasing the product's potency. Resin from granular trichomes from a cannabis plant is a concentrate for purposes of this division. A cannabis concentrate is not considered food, as defined by Section 109935 of the Health and Safety Code, or a drug, as defined by Section 109925 of the Health and Safety Code.

(i) "Cannabis products" has the same meaning as in Section 11018.1 of the Health and Safety Code.

(j) "Child resistant" means designed or constructed to be significantly difficult for children under five years of age to open, and not difficult for normal adults to use properly.

(k) "Commercial cannabis activity" includes the cultivation, possession, manufacture, distribution, processing, storing, laboratory testing, packaging, labeling, transportation, delivery, or sale of cannabis and cannabis products as provided for in this division.

(l) "Cultivation" means any activity involving the planting, growing, harvesting, drying, curing, grading, or trimming of cannabis.

(m) "Cultivation site" means a location where cannabis is planted, grown, harvested, dried, cured, graded, or trimmed, or a location where any combination of those activities occurs.

(n) "Customer" means a natural person 21 years of age or older or a natural person 18 years of age or older who possesses a physician's recommendation, or a primary caregiver.

(o) "Day care center" has the same meaning as in Section 1596.76 of the Health and Safety Code.

(p) "Delivery" means the commercial transfer of cannabis or cannabis products to a customer. "Delivery" also includes the use by a retailer of any technology platform.

(q) "Director" means the Director of Consumer Affairs.

(r) "Distribution" means the procurement, sale, and transport of cannabis and cannabis products between licensees.

(s) "Dried flower" means all dead cannabis that has been harvested, dried, cured, or otherwise processed, excluding leaves and stems.

(t) "Edible cannabis product" means cannabis product that is intended to be used, in whole or in part, for human consumption, including, but not limited to, chewing gum, but excluding products set forth in Division 15 (commencing with Section 32501) of the Food and Agricultural Code. An edible cannabis product is not considered food, as defined by Section 109935 of the Health and Safety Code, or a drug, as defined by Section 109925 of the Health and Safety Code.

(u) "Fund" means the Cannabis Control Fund established pursuant to Section 26210.

(v) "Kind" means applicable type or designation regarding a particular cannabis variant or cannabis product type, including, but not limited to, strain name or other grower trademark, or growing area designation.

(w) "Labeling" means any label or other written, printed, or graphic matter upon a cannabis product, upon its container or wrapper, or that accompanies any cannabis product.

(x) "Labor peace agreement" means an agreement between a licensee and any bona fide labor organization that, at a minimum, protects the state's proprietary interests by prohibiting labor organizations and members from engaging in picketing, work stoppages, boycotts, and any other economic interference with the applicant's business. This agreement means that the applicant has agreed not to disrupt efforts by the bona fide labor organization to communicate with, and attempt to organize and represent, the applicant's employees. The agreement shall provide a bona fide labor organization access at reasonable times to areas in which the applicant's employees work, for the purpose of meeting with employees to discuss their right to representation, employment rights under state law, and terms and conditions of employment. This type of agreement shall not mandate a particular method of election or certification of the bona fide labor organization.

(y) "License" means a state license issued under this division, and includes both an A-license and an M-license, as well as a testing laboratory license.

(z) "Licensee" means any person holding a license under this division, regardless of whether the license held is an A-license or an M-license, and includes the holder of a testing laboratory license.

(aa) "Licensing authority" means the state agency responsible for the issuance, renewal, or reinstatement of the license, or the state agency authorized to take disciplinary action against the licensee.

(ab) "Live plants" means living cannabis flowers and plants, including seeds, immature plants, and vegetative stage plants.

(ac) "Local jurisdiction" means a city, county, or city and county.

(ad) "Lot" means a batch or a specifically identified portion of a batch.

(ae) "M-license" means a state license issued under this division for commercial cannabis activity involving medicinal cannabis.

(af) "M-licensee" means any person holding a license under this division for commercial cannabis activity involving medicinal cannabis.

(ag) "Manufacture" means to compound, blend, extract, infuse, or otherwise make or prepare a cannabis product.

(ah) "Manufacturer" means a licensee that conducts the production, preparation, propagation, or compounding of cannabis or cannabis products either directly or indirectly or by extraction methods, or independently by means of chemical synthesis, or by a combination of extraction and chemical synthesis at a fixed location that packages or repackages cannabis or cannabis products or labels or relabels its container.

(ai) "Medicinal cannabis" or "medicinal cannabis product" means cannabis or a cannabis product, respectively, intended to be sold for use pursuant to the Compassionate Use Act of 1996 (Proposition 215), found at Section 11362.5 of the Health and Safety Code, by a medicinal cannabis patient in California who possesses a physician's recommendation.

(aj) "Nursery" means a licensee that produces only clones, immature plants, seeds, and other agricultural products used specifically for the propagation and cultivation of cannabis.

(ak) "Operation" means any act for which licensure is required under the provisions of this division, or any commercial transfer of cannabis or cannabis products.

(al) "Owner" means any of the following:

> (1) A person with an aggregate ownership interest of 20 percent or more in the person applying for a license or a licensee, unless the interest is solely a security, lien, or encumbrance.

> (2) The chief executive officer of a nonprofit or other entity.

> (3) A member of the board of directors of a nonprofit.

> (4) An individual who will be participating in the direction, control, or management of the person applying for a license.

(am) "Package" means any container or receptacle used for holding cannabis or cannabis products.

(an) "Person" includes any individual, firm, partnership, joint venture, association, corporation, limited liability company, estate, trust, business trust, receiver, syndicate, or any other group or combination acting as a unit, and the plural as well as the singular.

(ao) "Physician's recommendation" means a recommendation by a physician and surgeon that a patient use cannabis provided in accordance with the Compassionate Use Act of 1996 (Proposition 215), found at Section 11362.5 of the Health and Safety Code.

(ap) "Premises" means the designated structure or structures and land specified in the application that is owned, leased, or otherwise held under the control of the applicant or licensee where the commercial cannabis activity will be or is conducted. The premises shall be a contiguous area and shall only be occupied by one licensee.

(aq) "Primary caregiver" has the same meaning as in Section 11362.7 of the Health and Safety Code.

(ar) "Purchaser" means the customer who is engaged in a transaction with a licensee for purposes of obtaining cannabis or cannabis products.

(as) "Sell," "sale," and "to sell" include any transaction whereby, for any consideration, title to cannabis or cannabis products is transferred from one person to another, and includes the delivery of cannabis or cannabis products pursuant to an order placed for the purchase of the same and soliciting or receiving an order for the same, but does not include the return of cannabis or cannabis products by a licensee to the licensee from whom the cannabis or cannabis product was purchased.

(at) "Testing laboratory" means a laboratory, facility, or entity in the state that offers or performs tests of cannabis or cannabis products and that is both of the following:

(1) Accredited by an accrediting body that is independent from all other persons involved in commercial cannabis activity in the state.

(2) Licensed by the bureau.

(au) "Unique identifier" means an alphanumeric code or designation used for reference to a specific plant on a licensed premises and any cannabis or cannabis product derived or manufactured from that plant.

(av) "Youth center" has the same meaning as in Section 11353.1 of the Health and Safety Code.

Business and Professions Code § 26001.1

(Added by Stats. 2018, Ch. 599, Sec. 4. (AB 3261) Effective January 1, 2019.)

In addition to the definitions listed in Section 26001, for purposes of this division, "microbusiness" means a person holding a license issued under paragraph (3) of subdivision (a) of Section 26070.

Business and Professions Code § 26002

(Added by Stats. 2018, Ch. 62, Sec. 2. (AB 710) Effective July 9, 2018.)

This division shall not apply to any product containing cannabidiol that has been approved by the federal Food and Drug Administration that has either been placed on a schedule of the federal Controlled Substances Act other than Schedule I or has been exempted from one or more provisions of that act, and that is intended for prescribed use for the treatment of a medical condition.

Chapter 2. Administration

Business and Professions Code § 26010

(MAUCRSA, Effective June 27, 2017.)

There is in the Department of Consumer Affairs the Bureau of Cannabis Control, under the supervision and control of the director. The director shall administer and enforce the provisions of this division related to the bureau.

Business and Professions Code § 26010.5

(MAUCRSA, Effective June 27, 2017.)

(a) The Governor shall appoint a chief of the bureau, subject to confirmation by the Senate, at a salary to be fixed and determined by the Director of Consumer Affairs with the approval of the Director of Finance. The chief shall serve under the direction and supervision of the Director of Consumer Affairs and at the pleasure of the Governor.

(b) Every power granted to or duty imposed upon the Director of Consumer Affairs under this division may be exercised or performed in the name of the director by a deputy or assistant director or by the chief, subject to conditions and limitations that the director may prescribe. In addition to every power granted or duty imposed under this division, the director shall have all other powers and duties generally applicable in relation to bureaus that are part of the Department of Consumer Affairs.

(c) The Director of Consumer Affairs may employ and appoint all employees necessary to properly administer the work of the bureau, in accordance with civil service laws and regulations. The Governor may also appoint a deputy chief and an assistant chief counsel to the bureau. These positions shall hold office at the pleasure of the Governor.

(d) The bureau has the power, duty, purpose, responsibility, and jurisdiction to regulate commercial cannabis activity as provided in this division.

(e) The bureau and the director shall succeed to and are vested with all the duties, powers, purposes, responsibilities, and jurisdiction formerly vested in the Bureau of Marijuana Control, also formerly known as the Bureau of Medical Cannabis Regulation and the Bureau of Medical Marijuana Regulation, under the former Medical Cannabis Regulation and Safety Act (former Chapter 3.5 (commencing with Section 19300) of Division 8).

(f) Upon the effective date of this section, whenever "Bureau of Marijuana Control," "Bureau of Medical Cannabis Regulation," or "Bureau of Medical Marijuana Regulation" appears in any statute, regulation, or contract, or in any other code, it shall be construed to refer to the bureau.

(g) Upon the effective date of this section, whenever any reference to the "Medical Cannabis Regulation and Safety Act," "Medical Marijuana Regulation and Safety Act," or former Chapter 3.5 (commencing with Section 19300) of Division 8 appears in any statute, regulation, contract, or in any other code, it shall be construed to refer to this division as it relates to medicinal cannabis and medicinal cannabis products.

Business and Professions Code § 26011

(MAUCRSA, Effective June 27, 2017.)

Neither the chief of the bureau nor any member of the Cannabis Control Appeals Panel established under Section 26040 shall do any of the following:

(a) Receive any commission or profit whatsoever, directly or indirectly, from any person applying for or receiving any license or permit under this division.

(b) Engage or have any interest in the sale or any insurance covering a licensee's business or premises.

(c) Engage or have any interest in the sale of equipment for use upon the premises of a licensee engaged in commercial cannabis activity.

(d) Knowingly solicit any licensee for the purchase of tickets for benefits or contributions for benefits.

(e) Knowingly request any licensee to donate or receive money, or any other thing of value, for the benefit of any person whatsoever.

Business and Professions Code § 26011.5

(MAUCRSA, Effective June 27, 2017.)

The protection of the public shall be the highest priority for all licensing authorities in exercising licensing, regulatory, and disciplinary functions under this division. Whenever the protection of the public is inconsistent with other interests sought to be promoted, the protection of the public shall be paramount.

Business and Professions Code § 26012

(MAUCRSA, Effective June 27, 2017.)

(a) It being a matter of statewide concern, except as otherwise authorized in this division:

(1) The bureau shall have the sole authority to create, issue, deny, renew, discipline, suspend, or revoke licenses for microbusinesses, transportation, storage unrelated to manufacturing activities, distribution, testing, and sale of cannabis and cannabis products within the state.

(2) The Department of Food and Agriculture shall administer the provisions of this division related to and associated with the cultivation of cannabis. The Department of Food and Agriculture shall have the authority to create, issue, deny, and suspend or revoke cultivation licenses for violations of this division.

(3) The State Department of Public Health shall administer the provisions of this division related to and associated with the manufacturing of cannabis products. The State Department of Public Health shall have the authority to create, issue, deny, and suspend or revoke manufacturing licenses for violations of this division.

(b) The licensing authorities shall have the authority to collect fees in connection with activities they regulate concerning cannabis. The licensing authorities may create licenses in addition to those identified in this division that the licensing authorities deem necessary to effectuate their duties under this division.

(c) For the performance of its duties, each licensing authority has the power conferred by Sections 11180 to 11191, inclusive, of the Government Code.

(d) Licensing authorities shall begin issuing licenses under this division by January 1, 2018.

Business and Professions Code § 26013

(Amended by Stats. 2018, Ch. 92, Sec. 20. (SB 1289) Effective January 1, 2019. Note: This section was added on Nov. 8, 2016, by initiative Prop. 64.)

(a) Licensing authorities shall make and prescribe reasonable rules and regulations as may be necessary to implement, administer, and enforce their respective duties under this division in accordance with Chapter 3.5 (commencing with Section 11340) of Part 1 of Division 3 of Title 2 of the Government Code. Those rules and regulations shall be consistent with the purposes and intent of the Control, Regulate and Tax Adult Use of Marijuana Act.

(b) (1) Each licensing authority may adopt emergency regulations to implement this division.

(2) Each licensing authority may readopt any emergency regulation authorized by this section that is the same as, or substantially equivalent to, an emergency regulation previously adopted as authorized by this section. Any such readoption shall be limited to one time for each regulation.

(3) Notwithstanding any other law, the initial adoption of emergency regulations and the readoption of emergency regulations authorized by this section shall be deemed an emergency and necessary for the immediate preservation of the public peace, health, safety, or general welfare. The initial emergency regulations and the readopted emergency regulations authorized by this section shall be each submitted to the Office of Administrative Law for filing with the Secretary of State and shall remain in effect for no more than 180 days, by which time final regulations may be adopted.

(c) Regulations issued under this division shall be necessary to achieve the purposes of this division, based on best available evidence, and shall mandate only commercially feasible procedures, technology, or other requirements, and shall not unreasonably restrain or inhibit the development of alternative procedures or technology to achieve the same substantive requirements, nor shall the regulations make compliance so onerous that the operation under a cannabis license is not worthy of being carried out in practice by a reasonably prudent businessperson.

Business and Professions Code § 26013 .5

(MAUCRSA, Effective June 27, 2017.)

Notice of any action of a licensing authority required by this division to be given may be signed and given by the director of the licensing authority or an authorized employee of the licensing authority and may be made personally or in the manner prescribed by Section 1013 of the Code of Civil Procedure, or in the manner prescribed by Section

124 of this code.

Business and Professions Code § 26014

(MAUCRSA, Effective June 27, 2017.)

(a) The bureau shall convene an advisory committee to advise the licensing authorities on the development of standards and regulations pursuant to this division, including best practices and guidelines that protect public health and safety while ensuring a regulated environment for commercial cannabis activity that does not impose such barriers so as to perpetuate, rather than reduce and eliminate, the illicit market for cannabis.

(b) The advisory committee members shall include, but not be limited to, representatives of the cannabis industry, including medicinal cannabis, representatives of labor organizations, appropriate state and local agencies, persons who work directly with racially, ethnically, and economically diverse populations, public health experts, and other subject matter experts, including representatives from the Department of Alcoholic Beverage Control, with expertise in regulating commercial activity for adult-use intoxicating substances. The advisory committee members shall be determined by the director.

(c) Commencing on January 1, 2019, the advisory committee shall publish an annual public report describing its activities including, but not limited to, the recommendations the advisory committee made to the licensing authorities during the immediately preceding calendar year and whether those recommendations were implemented by the licensing authorities.

Business and Professions Code § 26015

(AUMA, Effective November 9, 2016.)

A licensing authority may make or cause to be made such investigation as it deems necessary to carry out its duties under this division.

Business and Professions Code § 26016

(AUMA, Effective November 9, 2016.)

For any hearing held pursuant to this division, except a hearing held under Chapter 4, a licensing authority may delegate the power to hear and decide to an administrative law judge. Any hearing before an administrative law judge shall be pursuant to the procedures, rules, and limitations prescribed in Chapter 5 (commencing with Section 11500) of Part 1 of Division 3 of Title 2 of the Government Code.

Business and Professions Code § 26017

(AUMA, Effective November 9, 2016.)

In any hearing before a licensing authority pursuant to this division, the licensing authority may pay any person appearing as a witness at the hearing at the request of the licensing authority pursuant to a subpoena, his or her actual, necessary, and reasonable travel, food, and lodging expenses, not to exceed the amount authorized for state employees.

Business and Professions Code § 26018

(AUMA, Effective November 9, 2016.)

A licensing authority may on its own motion at any time before a penalty assessment is placed into effect, and without any further proceedings, review the penalty, but such review shall be limited to its reduction.

Chapter 3. Enforcement

Business and Professions Code § 26030

(MAUCRSA, Effective June 27, 2017.)

Grounds for disciplinary action include, but are not limited to, all of the following:

(a) Failure to comply with the provisions of this division or any rule or regulation adopted pursuant to this division.

(b) Conduct that constitutes grounds for denial of licensure pursuant to Chapter 2 (commencing with Section 480) of Division 1.5 or discipline of a license pursuant to Chapter 3 (commencing with Section 490) of Division 1.5.

(c) Any other grounds contained in regulations adopted by a licensing authority pursuant to this division.

(d) Failure to comply with any state law including, but not limited to, the payment of taxes as required under the Revenue and Taxation Code, except as provided for in this division or other California law.

(e) Knowing violations of any state or local law, ordinance, or regulation conferring worker protections or legal rights on the employees of a licensee.

(f) Failure to comply with the requirement of a local ordinance regulating commercial cannabis activity.

(g) The intentional and knowing sale of cannabis or cannabis products by an A-licensee to a person under 21 years of age.

(h) The intentional and knowing sale of medicinal cannabis or medicinal cannabis products by an M-licensee to a person without a physician's recommendation.

(i) Failure to maintain safe conditions for inspection by a licensing authority.

(j) Failure to comply with any operating procedure submitted to the licensing authority pursuant to subdivision (b) of Section 26051.5.

(k) Failure to comply with license conditions established pursuant to subdivision (b) of Section 26060.1.

Business and Professions Code § 26031

(MAUCRSA, Effective June 27, 2017.)

(a) Each licensing authority may suspend, revoke, place on probation with terms and conditions, or otherwise discipline licenses issued by that licensing authority and fine a licensee, after proper notice and hearing to the licensee, if the licensee is found to have committed any of the acts or omissions constituting grounds for disciplinary action. The disciplinary proceedings under this chapter shall be conducted in accordance with Chapter 5 (commencing with Section 11500) of Part 1 of Division 3 of Title 2 of the Government Code, and the director of each licensing authority shall have all the powers granted therein.

(b) A licensing authority may suspend or revoke a license when a local agency has notified the licensing authority that a licensee within its jurisdiction is in violation of state rules and regulations relating to commercial cannabis activities, and the licensing authority, through an investigation, has determined that the violation is grounds for suspension or revocation of the license.

(c) Each licensing authority may take disciplinary action against a licensee for any violation of this division when the violation was committed by the licensee's officers, directors, owners, agents, or employees while acting on behalf of the licensee or engaged in commercial cannabis activity.

(d) A licensing authority may recover the costs of investigation and enforcement of a disciplinary proceeding pursuant to Section 125.3 of this code.

(e) Upon suspension or revocation of a license, the licensing authority shall inform the bureau. The bureau shall then inform all other licensing authorities. Upon any other enforcement action against a licensee, the licensing authority shall notify all other licensing authorities.

Business and Professions Code § 26032

(MAUCRSA, Effective June 27, 2017.)

(a) The actions of a licensee, its employees, and its agents are not unlawful under state law and shall not be an offense subject to arrest, prosecution, or other sanction under state law, or be subject to a civil fine or be a basis for seizure or forfeiture of assets under state law if they are all of the following:

(1) Permitted pursuant to a state license.

(2) Permitted pursuant to a local authorization, license, or permit issued by the local jurisdiction, if any.

(3) Conducted in accordance with the requirements of this division and regulations adopted pursuant to this division.

(b) The actions of a person who, in good faith, allows his or her property to be used by a licensee, its employees, and its agents, as permitted pursuant to a state license and, if required by the applicable local ordinances, a local license or permit, are not unlawful under state law and shall not be an offense subject to arrest, prosecution, or other sanction under state law, or be subject to a civil fine or be a basis for seizure or forfeiture of assets under state law.

Business and Professions Code § 26033

(MAUCRSA, Effective June 27, 2017.)

(a) A qualified patient, as defined in Section 11362.7 of the Health and Safety Code, who cultivates, possesses, stores, manufactures, or transports cannabis exclusively for his or her personal medical use but who does not provide, donate, sell, or distribute cannabis to any other person is not thereby engaged in commercial cannabis activity and is therefore exempt from the licensure requirements of this division.

(b) A primary caregiver who cultivates, possesses, stores, manufactures, transports, donates, or provides cannabis exclusively for the personal medical purposes of no more than five specified qualified patients for whom he or she is the primary caregiver within the meaning of Section 11362.7 of the Health and Safety Code, but who does not receive remuneration for these activities except for compensation in full compliance with subdivision (c) of Section 11362.765 of the Health and Safety Code, is exempt from the licensure requirements of this division.

Business and Professions Code § 26034

(MAUCRSA, Effective June 27, 2017.)

All accusations against licensees shall be filed by the licensing authority within five years after the performance of the act or omission alleged as the ground for disciplinary action; provided, however, that the foregoing provision shall not constitute a defense to an accusation alleging fraud or misrepresentation as a ground for disciplinary action. The cause for disciplinary action in that case shall not be deemed to have accrued until discovery, by the licensing authority, of the facts constituting the fraud or misrepresentation, and, in that case, the accusation shall be filed within five years after that discovery.

Business and Professions Code § 26035

(AUMA, Effective November 9, 2016.)

The director shall designate the persons employed by the Department of Consumer Affairs for purposes of the administration and enforcement of this division. The director shall ensure that a sufficient number of employees are qualified peace officers for purposes of enforcing this division.

Business and Professions Code § 26036

(AUMA, Effective November 9, 2016.)

Nothing in this division shall be interpreted to supersede or limit state agencies from exercising their existing enforcement authority, including, but not limited to, under the Fish and Game Code, the Food and Agricultural Code, the Government Code, the Health and Safety Code, the Public Resources Code, the Water Code, or the application of those laws.

Business and Professions Code § 26037

(AUMA, Effective November 9, 2016.)

(a) The actions of a licensee, its employees, and its agents that are:

   (1) permitted under a license issued under this division and any applicable local ordinances; and

   (2) conducted in accordance with the requirements of this division and regulations adopted pursuant to this division, are not unlawful under state law and shall not be an offense subject to arrest, prosecution, or other sanction under state law, or be subject to a civil fine or be a basis for seizure or forfeiture of assets under state

law.

(b) The actions of a person who, in good faith, allows his or her property to be used by a licensee, its employees, and its agents, as permitted pursuant to a state license and any applicable local ordinances, are not unlawful under state law and shall not be an offense subject to arrest, prosecution, or other sanction under state law, or be subject to a civil fine or be a basis for seizure or forfeiture of assets under state law.

Business and Professions Code § 26038

(MAUCRSA, Effective June 27, 2017.)

(a) A person engaging in commercial cannabis activity without a license required by this division shall be subject to civil penalties of up to three times the amount of the license fee for each violation, and the court may order the destruction of cannabis associated with that violation in accordance with Section 11479 of the Health and Safety Code. Each day of operation shall constitute a separate violation of this section. All civil penalties imposed and collected pursuant to this section by a licensing authority shall be deposited into the General Fund except as provided in subdivision (b). A violator shall be responsible for the cost of the destruction of cannabis associated with his or her violation.

(b) If an action for civil penalties is brought against a person pursuant to this division by the Attorney General on behalf of the people, the penalty collected shall be deposited into the General Fund. If the action is brought by a district attorney or county counsel, the penalty shall first be used to reimburse the district attorney or county counsel for the costs of bringing the action for civil penalties, with the remainder, if any, to be deposited into the General Fund. If the action is brought by a city attorney or city prosecutor, the penalty collected shall first be used to reimburse the city attorney or city prosecutor for the costs of bringing the action for civil penalties, with the remainder, if any, to be deposited into the General Fund.

(c) Notwithstanding subdivision (a), criminal penalties shall continue to apply to an unlicensed person engaging in commercial cannabis activity in violation of this division.

Chapter 4. Appeals

Business and Professions Code § 26040

(Amended by Stats. 2018, Ch. 95, Sec. 1. (AB 1527) Effective July 16, 2018. Note: This section was added on Nov. 8, 2016, by initiative Prop. 64.)

(a) (1) There is established in state government a Cannabis Control Appeals Panel which shall consist of the following members:

    (A) One member appointed by the Senate Committee on Rules.

    (B) One member appointed by the Speaker of the Assembly.

    (C) Three members appointed by the Governor and subject to confirmation by a majority vote of all of the members elected to the Senate.

  (2) Each member, at the time of his or her initial appointment, shall be a resident of a different county from the one in which either of the other members resides. Members of the panel shall receive an annual salary as provided for by Chapter 6 (commencing with Section 11550) of Part 1 of Division 3 of Title 2 of the Government Code.

(b) The members of the panel may be removed from office by their appointing authority.

Business and Professions Code § 26041

(AUMA, Effective November 9, 2016.)

All personnel of the panel shall be appointed, employed, directed, and controlled by the panel consistent with state civil service requirements. The director shall furnish the equipment, supplies, and housing necessary for the authorized activities of the panel and shall perform such other mechanics of administration as the panel and the director may agree upon.

Business and Professions Code § 26042

(AUMA, Effective November 9, 2016.)

The panel shall adopt procedures for appeals similar to the procedures used in Articles 3 and 4 in Chapter 1.5 in Division 9 of the Business and Professions Code. Such procedures shall be adopted in accordance with the Administrative Procedure Act (Government Code, Title 2, Division 3, section 11340 et seq.).

Business and Professions Code § 26043

(MAUCRSA, Effective June 27, 2017.)

(a) After proceedings pursuant to Section 26031 or 26058 or Chapter 2 (commencing with Section 480) or Chapter 3 (commencing with Section 490) of Division 1.5, any person aggrieved by the decision of a licensing authority denying the person's application for any license, denying the person's renewal of any license, placing any license on probation, imposing any condition on any license, imposing any fine on any license, assessing any penalty on any license, or canceling, suspending, revoking, or otherwise disciplining any license as provided for under this division, may appeal the licensing authority's written decision to the panel.

(b) The panel shall review the decision subject to such limitations as may be imposed by the Legislature. In such cases, the panel shall not receive evidence in addition to that considered by the licensing authority.

(c) Review by the panel of a decision of a licensing authority shall be limited to the following questions:

   (1) Whether the licensing authority has proceeded without or in excess of its jurisdiction.

   (2) Whether the licensing authority has proceeded in the manner required by law.

   (3) Whether the decision is supported by the findings.

   (4) Whether the findings are supported by substantial evidence in the light of the whole record.

Business and Professions Code § 26044

(MAUCRSA, Effective June 27, 2017.)

(a) In appeals where the panel finds that there is relevant evidence which, in the exercise of reasonable diligence, could not have been produced or which was improperly excluded at the hearing before the licensing authority, it may enter an order remanding the matter to the licensing authority for reconsideration in the light of that evidence.

(b) Except as provided in subdivision (a), in all appeals, the panel shall enter an order either affirming or reversing the decision of the licensing authority. When the order reverses the decision of the licensing authority, the panel may direct the reconsideration of the matter in the light of its order and may direct the licensing authority to take such further action as is specially enjoined upon it by law, but the order shall not limit or control in any way the discretion vested by law in the licensing authority.

Business and Professions Code § 26045

(MAUCRSA, Effective June 27, 2017.)

(a) No court of this state, except the Supreme Court and the courts of appeal to the extent specified in this chapter, shall have jurisdiction to review, affirm, reverse, correct, or annul any order, rule, or decision of a licensing authority or to suspend, stay, or delay the operation or execution thereof, or to restrain, enjoin, or interfere with a licensing authority in the performance of its duties, but a writ of mandate shall lie from the Supreme Court or the courts of appeal in any proper case.

(b) Any person affected by a final order of the panel, including a licensing authority, may apply to the Supreme Court or to the court of appeal for the appellate district in which the proceeding arose, for a writ of review of that final order.

(c) The application for writ of review shall be made within 30 days after filing of the final order.

(d) The provisions of the Code of Civil Procedure relating to writs of review shall, insofar as applicable, apply to proceedings in the courts as provided by this chapter. A copy of every pleading filed pursuant to this chapter shall be served on the panel, the licensing authority, and on each party who entered an appearance before the panel.

(e) No decision of a licensing authority that has been appealed to the panel and no final order of the panel shall become effective during the period in which application may be made for a writ of review, as provided by subdivision (c).

(f) The filing of a petition for, or the pendency of, a writ of review shall not of itself stay or suspend the operation of any order, rule, or decision of a licensing authority, but the court before which the petition is filed may stay or suspend, in whole or in part, the operation of the order, rule, or decision of the licensing authority subject to review, upon the terms and conditions which it by order directs.

Business and Professions Code § 26046

(MAUCRSA, Effective June 27, 2017.)

(a) The review by the court shall not extend further than to determine, based on the whole record of the licensing authority as certified by the panel, whether:

(1) The licensing authority has proceeded without or in excess of its jurisdiction.

(2) The licensing authority has proceeded in the manner required by law.

(3) The decision of the licensing authority is supported by the findings.

(4) The findings in the licensing authority's decision are supported by substantial evidence in the light of the whole record.

(5) There is relevant evidence which, in the exercise of reasonable diligence, could not have been produced or which was improperly excluded at the hearing before the licensing authority.

(b) Nothing in this chapter shall permit the court to hold a trial de novo, to take evidence, or to exercise its independent judgment on the evidence.

Business and Professions Code § 26047

(MAUCRSA, Effective June 27, 2017.)

The findings and conclusions of the licensing authority on questions of fact are conclusive and final and are not subject to review. Those questions of fact shall include ultimate facts and the findings and conclusions of the licensing authority. The panel, the licensing authority, and each party to the action or proceeding before the panel shall have the right to appear in the review proceeding. Following the hearing, the court shall enter judgment either affirming or reversing the decision of the licensing authority, or the court may remand the case for further proceedings before or reconsideration by the licensing authority.

Chapter 5. Licensing

Business and Professions Code § 26050

(MAUCRSA, Effective June 27, 2017.)

(a) The license classification pursuant to this division shall, at a minimum, be as follows:

(1) Type 1—Cultivation; Specialty outdoor; Small.

(2) Type 1A—Cultivation; Specialty indoor; Small.

(3) Type 1B—Cultivation; Specialty mixed-light; Small.

(4) Type 1C—Cultivation; Specialty cottage; Small.

(5) Type 2—Cultivation; Outdoor; Small.

(6) Type 2A—Cultivation; Indoor; Small.

(7) Type 2B—Cultivation; Mixed-light; Small.

(8) Type 3—Cultivation; Outdoor; Medium.

(9) Type 3A—Cultivation; Indoor; Medium.

(10) Type 3B—Cultivation; Mixed-light; Medium.

(11) Type 4—Cultivation; Nursery.

(12) Type 5—Cultivation; Outdoor; Large.

(13) Type 5A—Cultivation; Indoor; Large.

(14) Type 5B—Cultivation; Mixed-light; Large.

(15) Type 6—Manufacturer 1.

(16) Type 7—Manufacturer 2.

(17) Type 8—Testing laboratory.

(18) Type 10—Retailer.

(19) Type 11—Distributor.

(20) Type 12—Microbusiness.

(b) With the exception of testing laboratory licenses, which may be used to test cannabis and cannabis products regardless of whether they are intended for use by individuals who possesses a physician's recommendation, all licenses issued under this division shall bear a clear designation indicating whether the license is for commercial adult-use cannabis activity as distinct from commercial medicinal cannabis activity by prominently affixing an "A" or "M," respectively. Examples of such a designation include, but are not limited to, "A-Type 1" or "M-Type 1." Except as specifically specified in this division, the requirements for A-licenses and M-licenses shall be the same. For testing laboratories, the bureau shall create a license that indicates a testing laboratory may test both adult-use and medicinal cannabis.

(c) A license issued pursuant to this division shall be valid for 12 months from the date of issuance. The license may be renewed annually.

(d) Each licensing authority shall establish procedures for the issuance and renewal of licenses.

Business and Professions Code § 26050.2

(Added by Stats. 2018, Ch. 857, Sec. 1. (SB 1459) Effective September 27, 2018. Repealed as of January 1, 2020, by its own provisions.)

(a) A licensing authority may, in its sole discretion, issue a provisional license to an applicant if the following conditions are met:

(1) The applicant holds or held a temporary license for the same premises and the same commercial cannabis activity for which the license may be issued pursuant to this section.

(2) The applicant has submitted a completed license application to the licensing authority, including evidence that compliance with the California Environmental Quality Act (Division 13 (commencing with Section 21000) of the Public Resources Code) is underway.

(b) A provisional license issued pursuant to this section shall be valid for 12 months from the date issued and shall not be renewed. Except as specified in this section, the provisions of this division shall apply to a provisional license in the same manner as to an annual license.

(c) Without limiting any other statutory exemption or categorical exemption, Division 13 (commencing with Section 21000) of the Public Resources Code does not apply to the issuance of a license pursuant to this section by the licensing authority.

(d) Refusal by the licensing authority to issue a license pursuant to this section or revocation or suspension by the licensing authority of a license issued pursuant to this section shall not entitle the applicant or licensee to a hearing or an appeal of the decision. Chapter 2 (commencing with Section 480) of Division 1.5 and Chapter 4 (commencing with Section 26040) of this division shall not apply to licenses issued pursuant to this section.

(e) This section shall remain in effect only until January 1, 2020, and as of that date is repealed.

Business and Professions Code § 26051

(Amended by Stats. 2018, Ch. 92, Sec. 21. (SB 1289) Effective January 1, 2019.)

(a) The Cartwright Act, the Unfair Practices Act, the Unfair Competition Law, and the other provisions of Part 2 (commencing with Section 16600) of Division 7 apply to all licensees regulated under this division.

(b) It shall be unlawful for any person to monopolize, attempt to monopolize, or combine or conspire with any person or persons to monopolize, any part of the trade or commerce related to cannabis. The Attorney General shall have the sole authority to enforce the provisions of this subdivision.

(c) In determining whether to grant, deny, or renew a retail license, microbusiness license, or a license issued under Section 26070.5, the bureau shall consider if an excessive concentration exists in the area where the licensee will operate. For purposes of this section "excessive concentration" applies when either of the following conditions exist:

(1) The ratio of licensees to population in the census tract or census division in which the applicant premises is located exceeds the ratio of licensees to population in the county in which the applicant premises is located, unless denial of the application would unduly limit the development of the legal market so as to perpetuate the illegal market for cannabis or cannabis products.

(2) The ratio of retail licenses, microbusiness licenses, or licenses under Section 26070.5 to the population in the census tract, census division, or jurisdiction exceeds that allowable by local ordinance adopted under Section 26200.

Business and Professions Code § 26051.5

(Amended by Stats. 2018, Ch. 971, Sec. 1.2. (AB 2799) Effective January 1, 2019.)

(a) An applicant for any type of state license issued pursuant to this division shall do all of the following:

(1) Require that each owner electronically submit to the Department of Justice fingerprint images and related information required by the Department of Justice of all applicants for any type of state license issued pursuant to this division, for the purpose of obtaining information as to the existence and content of a record of state or federal convictions and state and federal arrests, and also information as to the existence and content of a record of state or federal convictions and arrests for which the Department of Justice establishes that the person is free on bail or on his or her recognizance pending trial or appeal.

(A) Notwithstanding any other law, the Bureau of Cannabis Control, the Department of Food and Agriculture, and the State Department of Public Health may obtain and receive, at their discretion, criminal history information from the Department of Justice and the Federal Bureau of Investigation for an applicant for any state license under this division, including any license established by a licensing authority by regulation pursuant to subdivision (b) of Section 26012.

(B) When received, the Department of Justice shall transmit fingerprint images and related information received pursuant to this section to the Federal Bureau of Investigation for the purpose of obtaining a federal criminal history records check. The Department of Justice shall review the information returned from the Federal Bureau of Investigation and compile and disseminate a response to the licensing authority.

(C) The Department of Justice shall provide a response to the licensing authority pursuant to paragraph (1) of subdivision (p) of Section 11105 of the Penal Code.

(D) The licensing authority shall request from the Department of Justice subsequent notification service, as provided pursuant to Section 11105.2 of the Penal Code, for applicants.

(E) The Department of Justice shall charge the applicant a fee sufficient to cover the reasonable cost of processing the requests described in this paragraph.

(2) Provide evidence of the legal right to occupy and use the proposed location and provide a statement from the landowner of real property or that landowner's agent where the commercial cannabis activity will occur, as proof to demonstrate the landowner has acknowledged and consented to permit commercial cannabis activities to be conducted on the property by the tenant applicant.

(3) Provide evidence that the proposed location is in compliance with subdivision (b) of Section 26054.

(4) Provide a statement, signed by the applicant under penalty of perjury, that the information provided is complete, true, and accurate.

(5) (A) For an applicant with 20 or more employees, provide a statement that the applicant will enter into, or demonstrate that it has already entered into, and abide by the terms of a labor peace agreement.

(B) For the purposes of this paragraph, "employee" does not include a supervisor.

(C) For the purposes of this paragraph, "supervisor" means an individual having authority, in the interest of the applicant, to hire, transfer, suspend, lay off, recall, promote, discharge, assign, reward, or discipline other employees, or responsibility to direct them or to adjust their grievances, or effectively to recommend such action, if, in connection with the foregoing, the exercise of that authority is not of a merely routine or clerical nature, but requires the use of independent judgment.

(6) Provide the applicant's valid seller's permit number issued pursuant to Part 1 (commencing with Section 6001) of Division 2 of the Revenue and Taxation Code or indicate that the applicant is currently applying for a seller's permit.

(7) Provide any other information required by the licensing authority.

(8) For an applicant seeking a cultivation license, provide a statement declaring the applicant is an "agricultural employer," as defined in the Alatorre-Zenovich-Dunlap-Berman Agricultural Labor Relations Act of 1975 (Part 3.5 (commencing with Section 1140) of Division 2 of the Labor Code), to the extent not prohibited by law.

(9) Pay all applicable fees required for licensure by the licensing authority.

(10) Provide proof of a bond to cover the costs of destruction of cannabis or cannabis products if necessitated by a violation of licensing requirements.

(11) (A) Provide a statement, upon initial application and application for renewal, that the applicant employs, or will employ within one year of receiving or renewing a license, one supervisor and one employee who have successfully completed a Cal-OSHA 30-hour general industry outreach course offered by a training provider that is authorized by an OSHA Training Institute Education Center to provide the course. This paragraph shall not be construed to alter or amend existing requirements for employers to provide occupational safety and health training to employees.

(B) An applicant with only one employee shall not be subject to subparagraph (A).

(C) For purposes of this paragraph "employee" has the same meaning as provided in subparagraph (B) of paragraph (5) and "supervisor" has the same meaning as provided in subparagraph (C) of paragraph (5).

(b) An applicant shall also include in the application a detailed description of the applicant's operating procedures for all of the following, as required by the licensing authority:

(1) Cultivation.

(2) Extraction and infusion methods.

(3) The transportation process.

(4) Inventory procedures.

(5) Quality control procedures.

(6) Security protocols.

(7) For applicants seeking licensure to cultivate, the source or sources of water the applicant will use for

cultivation, as provided in subdivisions (a) to (c), inclusive, of Section 26060.1. For purposes of this paragraph, "cultivation" as used in Section 26060.1 shall have the same meaning as defined in Section 26001. The Department of Food and Agriculture shall consult with the State Water Resources Control Board and the Department of Fish and Wildlife in the implementation of this paragraph.

(c) The applicant shall also provide a complete detailed diagram of the proposed premises wherein the license privileges will be exercised, with sufficient particularity to enable ready determination of the bounds of the premises, showing all boundaries, dimensions, entrances and exits, interior partitions, walls, rooms, and common or shared entryways, and include a brief statement or description of the principal activity to be conducted therein, and, for licenses permitting cultivation, measurements of the planned canopy, including aggregate square footage and individual square footage of separate cultivation areas, if any, roads, water crossings, points of diversion, water storage, and all other facilities and infrastructure related to the cultivation.

(d) Provide a complete list of every person with a financial interest in the person applying for the license as required by the licensing authority. For purposes of this subdivision, "persons with a financial interest" does not include persons whose only interest in a licensee is an interest in a diversified mutual fund, blind trust, or similar instrument.

Business and Professions Code § 26052

(MAUCRSA, Effective June 27, 2017.)

(a) A licensee shall not perform any of the following acts, or permit any of the following acts to be performed by any employee, agent, or contractor of the licensee:

(1) Make any contract in restraint of trade in violation of Section 16600.

(2) Form a trust or other prohibited organization in restraint of trade in violation of Section 16720.

(3) Make a sale or contract for the sale of cannabis or cannabis products, or to fix a price charged therefor, or discount from, or rebate upon, that price, on the condition, agreement, or understanding that the consumer or purchaser thereof shall not use or deal in the goods, merchandise, machinery, supplies, commodities, or services of a competitor or competitors of the seller, where the effect of that sale, contract, condition, agreement, or understanding may be to substantially lessen competition or tend to create a monopoly in any line of trade or commerce.

(4) Sell any cannabis or cannabis products at less than cost for the purpose of injuring competitors, destroying competition, or misleading or deceiving purchasers or prospective purchasers.

(5) Discriminate between different sections, communities, or cities or portions thereof, or between different locations in those sections, communities, or cities or portions thereof in this state, by selling or furnishing cannabis or cannabis products at a lower price in one section, community, or city or any portion thereof, or in one location in that section, community, or city or any portion thereof, than in another, for the purpose of injuring competitors or destroying competition.

(6) Sell any cannabis or cannabis products at less than the cost thereof to such vendor, or to give away any article or product for the purpose of injuring competitors or destroying competition.

(b) Any person who, either as director, officer, or agent of any firm or corporation, or as agent of any person, violates the provisions of this chapter, or assists or aids, directly or indirectly, in that violation is responsible therefor equally with the person, firm, or corporation for which that person acts.

(c) Any person or trade association may bring an action to enjoin and restrain any violation of this section for the recovery of damages.

Business and Professions Code § 26053

(Amended by AB 133, Effective September 16, 2017.)

(a) All commercial cannabis activity shall be conducted between licensees, except as otherwise provided in this division.

(b) A person that holds a state testing laboratory license under this division is prohibited from licensure for any other activity, except testing, as authorized under this division. A person that holds a state testing laboratory license shall not employ an individual who is also employed by any other licensee that does not hold a state testing laboratory license.

(c) Except as provided in subdivision (b), a person may apply for and be issued more than one license under this division.

(d) Each applicant or licensee shall apply for, and if approved, shall obtain, a separate license for each location where it engages in commercial cannabis activity.

Business and Professions Code § 26054

(MAUCRSA, Effective June 27, 2017.)

(a) A licensee shall not sell alcoholic beverages or tobacco products on or at any premises licensed under this division.

(b) A premises licensed under this division shall not be located within a 600-foot radius of a school providing instruction in kindergarten or any grades 1 through 12, day care center, or youth center that is in existence at the time the license is issued, unless a licensing authority or a local jurisdiction specifies a different radius. The distance specified in this section shall be measured in the same manner as provided in subdivision (c) of Section 11362.768 of the Health and Safety Code unless otherwise provided by law.

(c) It shall not be a violation of state or local law for a business engaged in the manufacture of cannabis accessories to possess, transport, purchase, or otherwise obtain small amounts of cannabis or cannabis products as necessary to conduct research and development related to the cannabis accessories, provided the cannabis and cannabis products are obtained from a person licensed under this division permitted to provide or deliver the cannabis or cannabis products.

(d) It shall not be a violation of state or local law for an agent of a licensing authority to possess, transport, or obtain cannabis or cannabis products as necessary to conduct activities reasonably related to the duties of the licensing authority.

Business and Professions Code § 26054.2

(MAUCRSA, Effective June 27, 2017; Inoperative December 31, 2019, by its Own Provisions.)

(a) A licensing authority shall give priority in issuing licenses under this division to applicants that can demonstrate to the authority's satisfaction that the applicant operated in compliance with the Compassionate Use Act of 1996 (Section 11362.5 of the Health and Safety Code) and its implementing laws before September 1, 2016.

(b) The licensing authorities shall request that local jurisdictions identify for the licensing authorities potential applicants for licensure based on the applicants' prior operation in the local jurisdiction in compliance with state law, including the Compassionate Use Act of 1996 (Section 11362.5 of the Health and Safety Code) and its implementing laws, and any applicable local laws.

(c) In addition to or in lieu of the information described in subdivision (b), an applicant may furnish other evidence as deemed appropriate by the licensing authority to demonstrate operation in compliance with the Compassionate Use Act of 1996 (Section 11362.5 of the Health and Safety Code). The licensing authorities may accept such evidence to demonstrate eligibility for the priority provided for in subdivision (a).

(d) This section shall cease to be operative on December 31, 2019, unless otherwise provided by law.

Business and Professions Code § 26055

(Amended by Stats. 2018, Ch. 92, Sec. 22. (SB 1289) Effective January 1, 2019. Note: This section was added on Nov. 8, 2016, by initiative Prop. 64.)

(a) Licensing authorities may issue state licenses only to qualified applicants.

(b) Revocation of a state license issued under this division shall terminate the ability of the licensee to operate pursuant to that license within California until a new license is obtained.

(c) A licensee shall not change or alter the premises in a manner which materially or substantially alters the premises, the usage of the premises, or the mode or character of business operation conducted from the premises, from the plan contained in the diagram on file with the application, unless and until written approval by the licensing authority has been obtained. For purposes of this section, material or substantial physical changes of the premises, or in the usage of the premises, shall include, but not be limited to, a substantial increase or decrease in the total area of the licensed premises previously diagrammed, or any other physical modification resulting in substantial change in the mode or character of business operation.

(d) Licensing authorities shall not approve an application for a state license under this division if approval of the state license will violate the provisions of any local ordinance or regulation adopted in accordance with Section 26200.

(e) An applicant may voluntarily provide proof of a license, permit, or other authorization from the local jurisdiction verifying that the applicant is in compliance with the local jurisdiction. An applicant that voluntarily submits a valid, unexpired license, permit, or other authorization from the local jurisdiction shall be presumed to be in compliance with all local ordinances unless the licensing authority is notified otherwise by the local jurisdiction. The licensing authority shall notify the contact person for the local jurisdiction of any applicant that voluntarily submits a valid, unexpired license, permit, or other authorization from the local jurisdiction.

(f) (1) A local jurisdiction shall provide to the bureau a copy of any ordinance or regulation related to commercial cannabis activity and the name and contact information for the person who will serve as the contact for state licensing authorities regarding commercial cannabis activity within the jurisdiction. If a local jurisdiction does not provide a contact person, the bureau shall assume that the clerk of the legislative body of the local jurisdiction is the contact person.

(2) Whenever there is a change in a local ordinance or regulation adopted pursuant to Section 26200 or a change in the contact person for the jurisdiction, the local jurisdiction shall provide that information to the bureau.

(3) The bureau shall share the information required by this subdivision with the other licensing authorities.

(g) (1) The licensing authority shall deny an application for a license under this division for a commercial cannabis activity that the local jurisdiction has notified the bureau is prohibited in accordance with subdivision (f). The licensing authority shall notify the contact person for the local jurisdiction of each application denied due to the local jurisdiction's indication that the commercial cannabis activity for which a license is sought is prohibited by a local ordinance or regulation.

(2) Prior to issuing a state license under this division for any commercial cannabis activity, if an applicant has

not provided adequate proof of compliance with local laws pursuant to subdivision (e):

(A) The licensing authority shall notify the contact person for the local jurisdiction of the receipt of an application for commercial cannabis activity within their jurisdiction.

(B) A local jurisdiction may notify the licensing authority that the applicant is not in compliance with a local ordinance or regulation. In this instance, the licensing authority shall deny the application.

(C) A local jurisdiction may notify the licensing authority that the applicant is in compliance with all applicable local ordinances and regulations. In this instance, the licensing authority may proceed with the licensing process.

(D) If the local jurisdiction does not provide notification of compliance or noncompliance with applicable local ordinances or regulations, or otherwise does not provide notification indicating that the completion of the local permitting process is still pending, within 60 business days of receiving the inquiry from a licensing authority submitted pursuant to subparagraph (A), the licensing authority shall make a rebuttable presumption that the applicant is in compliance with all local ordinances and regulations adopted in accordance with Section 26200, except as provided in subparagraphs (E) and (F).

(E) At any time after expiration of the 60-business-day period set forth in subparagraph (D), the local jurisdiction may provide written notification to the licensing authority that the applicant or licensee is not in compliance with a local ordinance or regulation adopted in accordance with Section 26200. Upon receiving this notification, the licensing authority shall not presume that the applicant or licensee has complied with all local ordinances and regulations adopted in accordance with Section 26200, and may commence disciplinary action in accordance with Chapter 3 (commencing with Section 26030). If the licensing authority does not take action against the licensee before the time of the renewal of the license, the license shall not be renewed until and unless the local jurisdiction notifies the licensing authority that the licensee is once again in compliance with local ordinances.

(F) A presumption by a licensing authority pursuant to this paragraph that an applicant has complied with all local ordinances and regulations adopted in accordance with Section 26200 shall not prevent, impair, or preempt the local government from enforcing all applicable local ordinances or regulations against the applicant, nor shall the presumption confer any right, vested or otherwise, upon the applicant to commence or continue operating in any local jurisdiction except in accordance with all local ordinances or regulations.

(3) For purposes of this section, "notification" includes written notification or access by a licensing authority to a local jurisdiction's registry, database, or other platform designated by a local jurisdiction, containing information specified by the licensing authority, on applicants to determine local compliance.

(h) Without limiting any other statutory exemption or categorical exemption, Division 13 (commencing with Section 21000) of the Public Resources Code does not apply to the adoption of an ordinance, rule, or regulation by a local jurisdiction that requires discretionary review and approval of permits, licenses, or other authorizations to engage in commercial cannabis activity. To qualify for this exemption, the discretionary review in any such law, ordinance, rule, or regulation shall include any applicable environmental review pursuant to Division 13 (commencing with Section 21000) of the Public Resources Code. This subdivision shall become inoperative on July 1, 2019.

(i) A local or state public agency may charge and collect a fee from a person proposing a project pursuant to subdivision (a) of Section 21089 of the Public Resources Code.

Business and Professions Code § 26056

(MAUCRSA, Effective June 27, 2017.)

The requirements of Sections 13143.9, 13145, and 13146 of the Health and Safety Code shall apply to all licensees.

Business and Professions Code § 26057

(Amended by Stats. 2018, Ch. 92, Sec. 23. (SB 1289) Effective January 1, 2019. Note: This section was added on Nov. 8, 2016, by initiative Prop. 64.)

(a) The licensing authority shall deny an application if either the applicant, or the premises for which a state license is applied, do not qualify for licensure under this division.

(b) The licensing authority may deny the application for licensure or renewal of a state license if any of the following conditions apply:

(1) Failure or inability to comply with the provisions of this division, any rule or regulation adopted pursuant to this division, or any requirement imposed to protect natural resources, including, but not limited to, protections for instream flow, water quality, and fish and wildlife.

(2) Conduct that constitutes grounds for denial of licensure under Chapter 2 (commencing with Section 480) of Division 1.5, except as otherwise specified in this section and Section 26059.

(3) Failure to provide information required by the licensing authority.

(4) The applicant, owner, or licensee has been convicted of an offense that is substantially related to the qualifications, functions, or duties of the business or profession for which the application is made, except that if the licensing authority determines that the applicant, owner, or licensee is otherwise suitable to be issued a license, and granting the license would not compromise public safety, the licensing authority shall conduct a thorough review of the nature of the crime, conviction, circumstances, and evidence of rehabilitation of the applicant or owner, and shall evaluate the suitability of the applicant, owner, or licensee to be issued a license based on the evidence found through the review. In determining which offenses are substantially related to the qualifications, functions, or duties of the business or profession for which the application is made, the licensing authority shall include, but not be limited to, the following:

(A) A violent felony conviction, as specified in subdivision (c) of Section 667.5 of the Penal Code.

(B) A serious felony conviction, as specified in subdivision (c) of Section 1192.7 of the Penal Code.

(C) A felony conviction involving fraud, deceit, or embezzlement.

(D) A felony conviction for hiring, employing, or using a minor in transporting, carrying, selling, giving away, preparing for sale, or peddling, any controlled substance to a minor; or selling, offering to sell, furnishing, offering to furnish, administering, or giving any controlled substance to a minor.

(E) A felony conviction for drug trafficking with enhancements pursuant to Section 11370.4 or 11379.8 of the Health and Safety Code.

(5) Except as provided in subparagraphs (D) and (E) of paragraph (4) and notwithstanding Chapter 2 (commencing with Section 480) of Division 1.5, a prior conviction, where the sentence, including any term of probation, incarceration, or supervised release, is completed, for possession, possession for sale, sale, manufacture, transportation, or cultivation of a controlled substance is not considered substantially related, and shall not be the sole ground for denial of a license. Conviction for any controlled substance felony subsequent to licensure shall be grounds for revocation of a license or denial of the renewal of a license.

(6) The applicant, or any of its officers, directors, or owners, has been subject to fines, penalties, or otherwise been sanctioned for cultivation or production of a controlled substance on public or private lands pursuant to Section 12025 or 12025.1 of the Fish and Game Code.

(7) The applicant, or any of its officers, directors, or owners, has been sanctioned by a licensing authority or a city, county, or city and county for unauthorized commercial cannabis activities, has had a license suspended or revoked under this division in the three years immediately preceding the date the application is filed with the licensing authority.

(8) Failure to obtain and maintain a valid seller's permit required pursuant to Part 1 (commencing with Section 6001) of Division 2 of the Revenue and Taxation Code.

(9) Any other condition specified in law.

Business and Professions Code § 26058

(MAUCRSA, Effective June 27, 2017.)

Upon the denial of any application for a license, the licensing authority shall notify the applicant in writing. Within 30 days of service of the notice, the applicant may file a written petition for a license with the licensing authority. Upon receipt of a timely filed petition, the licensing authority shall set the petition for hearing. The hearing shall be conducted in accordance with Chapter 5 (commencing with Section 11500) of Part 1 of Division 3 of Title 2 of the Government Code, and the director of each licensing authority shall have all the powers granted therein. Any appeal from a final decision of the licensing authority shall be conducted in accordance with Chapter 4 (commencing with Section 26040).

Business and Professions Code § 26059

(AUMA, Effective November 9, 2016.)

An applicant shall not be denied a state license if the denial is based solely on any of the following:

(a) A conviction or act that is substantially related to the qualifications, functions, or duties of the business or profession for which the application is made for which the applicant or licensee has obtained a certificate of rehabilitation pursuant to Chapter 3.5 (commencing with Section 4852.01) of Title 6 of Part 3 of the Penal Code.

(b) A conviction that was subsequently dismissed pursuant to Sections 1203.4, 1203.4a, or 1203.41 of the Penal Code or any other provision allowing for dismissal of a conviction.

Chapter 6. Licensed Cultivation Sites

Business and Professions Code § 26060

(Amended by Stats. 2018, Ch. 92, Sec. 24. (SB 1289) Effective January 1, 2019. Note: This section was added on Nov. 8, 2016, by initiative Prop. 64.)

(a) Regulations issued by the Department of Food and Agriculture governing the licensing of indoor, outdoor, nursery, special cottage, and mixed-light cultivation sites shall apply to licensed cultivators under this division. The Department of Food and Agriculture shall have the authority necessary for the implementation of the regulations it adopts pursuant to this division, including regulations governing the licensing of indoor, outdoor, mixed-light cultivation site, nursery, and special cottage cultivation.

(b) The regulations shall do all of the following:

(1) Provide that weighing or measuring devices used in connection with the sale or distribution of cannabis are

required to meet standards equivalent to Division 5 (commencing with Section 12001).

(2) Require that cannabis cultivation by licensees is conducted in accordance with state and local laws.

(3) Establish procedures for the issuance and revocation of unique identifiers for activities associated with a cannabis cultivation license, pursuant to Chapter 6.5 (commencing with Section 26067). All cannabis shall be labeled with the unique identifier issued by the Department of Food and Agriculture.

(4) Prescribe standards, in consultation with the bureau, for the reporting of information as necessary related to unique identifiers pursuant to Chapter 6.5 (commencing with Section 26067).

(c) The Department of Food and Agriculture shall serve as the lead agency for purposes of the California Environmental Quality Act (Division 13 (commencing with Section 21000) of the Public Resources Code) related to the licensing of cannabis cultivation.

(d) The Department of Pesticide Regulation shall develop guidelines for the use of pesticides in the cultivation of cannabis and residue in harvested cannabis.

(e) A cannabis cultivator shall not use any pesticide that has been banned for use in the state.

(f) The regulations promulgated by the Department of Food and Agriculture under this division shall implement the requirements of subdivision (b) of Section 26060.1.

(g) The Department of Pesticide Regulation shall require that the application of pesticides or other pest control in connection with the indoor, outdoor, nursery, specialty cottage, or mixed-light cultivation of cannabis complies with Division 6 (commencing with Section 11401) of the Food and Agricultural Code and its implementing regulations.

Business and Professions Code § 26060.1

(Amended by Stats. 2018, Ch. 92, Sec. 25. (SB 1289) Effective January 1, 2019.)

(a) An application for a license for cultivation issued by the Department of Food and Agriculture shall identify the source of water supply as follows:

(1) (A) If water will be supplied by a retail water supplier, as defined in Section 13575 of the Water Code, the application shall identify the retail water supplier.

(B) Paragraphs (2) and (3) do not apply to any water subject to subparagraph (A) unless the retail water supplier has 10 or fewer customers, the applicant receives 10 percent or more of the water supplied by the retail water supplier, 25 percent or more of the water delivered by the retail water supplier is used for cannabis cultivation, or the applicant and the retail water supplier are affiliates, as defined in Section 2814.20 of Title 23 of the California Code of Regulations.

(2) If the water supply includes a diversion within the meaning of Section 5100 of the Water Code, the application shall identify the point of diversion and the maximum amount to be diverted as follows:

(A) For an application submitted before January 1, 2019, the application shall include a copy of one of the following:

(i) A small irrigation use registration certificate, permit, or license issued pursuant to Part 2 (commencing with Section 1200) of Division 2 of the Water Code that covers the diversion.

(ii) A statement of water diversion and use filed with the State Water Resources Control Board on or before October 31, 2017, that covers the diversion and specifies the amount of water used for cannabis cultivation.

(iii) A pending application for a permit to appropriate water, filed with the State Water Resources Control Board on or before October 31, 2017.

(iv) Documentation submitted to the State Water Resources Control Board on or before January 1, 2019, demonstrating that the diversion is subject to subdivision (a), (c), (d), or (e) of Section 5101 of the Water Code.

(v) Documentation submitted to the State Water Resources Control Board on or before October 31, 2017, demonstrating that the diversion is authorized under a riparian right and that no diversion occurred after January 1, 2010, and before January 1, 2017. The documentation shall be submitted on or accompany a form provided by the State Water Resources Control Board and shall include all of the information outlined in subdivisions (a) to (d), inclusive, and (e) of Section 5103 of the Water Code. The documentation shall also include a general description of the area in which the water will be used in accordance with subdivision (g) of Section 5103 of the Water Code and the year in which the diversion is planned to commence.

(B) For an application submitted after December 31, 2018, the application shall include a copy of one of the following:

(i) A small irrigation use registration certificate, permit, or license issued pursuant to Part 2 (commencing with Section 1200) of Division 2 of the Water Code that covers the diversion.

(ii) A statement of water diversion and use filed with the State Water Resources Control Board that covers the diversion and specifies the amount of water used for cannabis cultivation.

(iii) Documentation submitted to the State Water Resources Control Board demonstrating that the diversion is subject to subdivision (a), (c), (d), or (e) of Section 5101 of the Water Code.

(iv) Documentation submitted to the State Water Resources Control Board demonstrating that the diversion is authorized under a riparian right and that no diversion occurred after January 1, 2010, and in the calendar year in which the application is submitted. The documentation shall be submitted on or accompany a form provided by the State Water Resources Control Board and shall include all of the information outlined in subdivisions (a) to (d), inclusive, and (e) of Section 5103 of the Water Code. The documentation shall also include a general description of the area in which the water will be used in accordance with subdivision (g) of Section 5103 of the Water Code and the year in which the diversion is planned to commence.

(3) If water will be supplied from a groundwater extraction not subject to paragraph (2), the application shall identify the location of the extraction and the maximum amount to be diverted for cannabis cultivation in any year.

(b) The Department of Food and Agriculture shall include in any license for cultivation all of the following:

(1) Conditions requested by the Department of Fish and Wildlife and the State Water Resources Control Board to: (A) ensure that individual and cumulative effects of water diversion and discharge associated with cultivation do not affect the instream flows needed for fish spawning, migration, and rearing, and the flows needed to maintain natural flow variability; (B) ensure that cultivation does not negatively impact springs, riparian habitat, wetlands, or aquatic habitat; and (C) otherwise protect fish, wildlife, fish and wildlife habitat, and water quality. The conditions shall include, but not be limited to, the principles, guidelines, and requirements established pursuant to Section 13149 of the Water Code.

(2) Any relevant mitigation requirements the Department of Food and Agriculture identifies as part of its approval of the final environmental documentation for the cannabis cultivation licensing program as requirements that should be included in a license for cultivation. Chapter 3.5 (commencing with Section 11340) of Part 1 of Division 3 of Title 2 of the Government Code does not apply to the identification of these mitigation measures. This paragraph does not reduce any requirements established pursuant to Division 13

(commencing with Section 21000) of the Public Resources Code.

(3) A condition that the license shall not be effective until the licensee has demonstrated compliance with Section 1602 of the Fish and Game Code or receives written verification from the Department of Fish and Wildlife that a streambed alteration agreement is not required.

(c) The Department of Food and Agriculture shall consult with the State Water Resources Control Board and the Department of Fish and Wildlife in the implementation of this section.

(d) Notwithstanding paragraph (1) of subdivision (b), the Department of Food and Agriculture is not responsible for verifying compliance with the conditions requested or imposed by the Department of Fish and Wildlife or the State Water Resources Control Board. The Department of Fish and Wildlife or the State Water Resources Control Board, upon finding and making the final determination of a violation of a condition included pursuant to paragraph (1) of subdivision (b), shall notify the Department of Food and Agriculture, which may take appropriate action with respect to the licensee in accordance with Chapter 3 (commencing with Section 26030).

Business and Professions Code § 26061

(MAUCRSA, Effective June 27, 2017.)

(a) The state cultivator license types to be issued by the Department of Food and Agriculture under this division shall include all of the following:

(1) Type 1, or "specialty outdoor," for outdoor cultivation using no artificial lighting of less than or equal to 5,000 square feet of total canopy size on one premises, or up to 50 mature plants on noncontiguous plots.

(2) Type 1A, or "specialty indoor," for indoor cultivation using exclusively artificial lighting of between 501 and 5,000 square feet of total canopy size on one premises.

(3) Type 1B, or "specialty mixed-light," for cultivation using a combination of natural and supplemental artificial lighting at a maximum threshold to be determined by the licensing authority, of between 2,501 and 5,000 square feet of total canopy size on one premises.

(4) Type 1C, or "specialty cottage," for cultivation using a combination of natural and supplemental artificial lighting at a maximum threshold to be determined by the licensing authority, of 2,500 square feet or less of total canopy size for mixed-light cultivation, up to 25 mature plants for outdoor cultivation, or 500 square feet or less of total canopy size for indoor cultivation, on one premises.

(5) Type 2, or "small outdoor," for outdoor cultivation using no artificial lighting between 5,001 and 10,000 square feet, inclusive, of total canopy size on one premises.

(6) Type 2A, or "small indoor," for indoor cultivation using exclusively artificial lighting between 5,001 and 10,000 square feet, inclusive, of total canopy size on one premises.

(7) Type 2B, or "small mixed-light," for cultivation using a combination of natural and supplemental artificial lighting at a maximum threshold to be determined by the licensing authority, between 5,001 and 10,000 square feet, inclusive, of total canopy size on one premises.

(8) Type 3, or "outdoor," for outdoor cultivation using no artificial lighting from 10,001 square feet to one acre, inclusive, of total canopy size on one premises. The Department of Food and Agriculture shall limit the number of licenses allowed of this type.

(9) Type 3A, or "indoor," for indoor cultivation using exclusively artificial lighting between 10,001 and 22,000 square feet, inclusive, of total canopy size on one premises. The Department of Food and Agriculture shall limit the number of licenses allowed of this type.

(10) Type 3B, or "mixed-light," for cultivation using a combination of natural and supplemental artificial lighting at a maximum threshold to be determined by the licensing authority, between 10,001 and 22,000 square feet, inclusive, of total canopy size on one premises. The Department of Food and Agriculture shall limit the number of licenses allowed of this type.

(11) Type 4, or "nursery" for cultivation of cannabis solely as a nursery.

(b) Except as otherwise provided by law:

(1) Type 5, or "outdoor," means for outdoor cultivation using no artificial lighting greater than one acre, inclusive, of total canopy size on one premises.

(2) Type 5A, or "indoor," means for indoor cultivation using exclusively artificial lighting greater than 22,000 square feet, inclusive, of total canopy size on one premises.

(3) Type 5B, or "mixed-light," means for cultivation using a combination of natural and supplemental artificial lighting at a maximum threshold to be determined by the licensing authority, greater than 22,000 square feet, inclusive, of total canopy size on one premises.

(c) No Type 5, Type 5A, or Type 5B cultivation licenses may be issued before January 1, 2023.

(d) Commencing on January 1, 2023, a Type 5, Type 5A, or Type 5B licensee may apply for and hold a Type 6 or Type 7 license and apply for and hold a Type 10 license. A Type 5, Type 5A, or Type 5B licensee shall not be eligible to apply for or hold a Type 8, Type 11, or Type 12 license.

Business and Professions Code § 26062

(MAUCRSA, Effective June 27, 2017.)

(a) No later than January 1, 2021, the Department of Food and Agriculture shall establish a program for cannabis that is comparable to the National Organic Program (Section 6517 of the federal Organic Foods Production Act of 1990 (7 U.S.C. Sec. 6501 et seq.)), and the California Organic Food and Farming Act (Chapter 10 (commencing with Section 46000) of Division 17 of the Food and Agricultural Code) and Article 7 (commencing with Section 110810) of Chapter 5 of Part 5 of Division 104 of the Health and Safety Code. The Department of Food and Agriculture shall be the sole determiner of designation and certification.

(b) If at any time preceding or following the establishment of a program by the Department of Food and Agriculture pursuant to subdivision (a), the National Organic Program (Section 6517 of the federal Organic Foods Production Act of 1990 (7 U.S.C. Sec. 6501 et seq.)) authorizes organic designation and certification for cannabis, this section shall become inoperative and, as of January 1, of the following year, is repealed.

Business and Professions Code § 26062.5

(MAUCRSA, Effective June 27, 2017.)

A person shall not represent, sell, or offer for sale any cannabis or cannabis product as organic except in accordance with the National Organic Program (Section 6517 of the federal Organic Foods Production Act of 1990 (7 U.S.C. Sec. 6501 et seq.)), if applicable. A person shall not represent, sell, or offer for sale any cannabis or cannabis product with the designation or certification established by the Department of Food and Agriculture pursuant to subdivision (a) of Section 26062 except in accordance with that subdivision.

Business and Professions Code § 26063

(MAUCRSA, Effective June 27, 2017.)

(a) No later than January 1, 2018, the Department of Food and Agriculture shall establish standards by which a licensed cultivator may designate a county of origin for cannabis. To be eligible for the designation, 100 percent of the cannabis shall be produced within the designated county, as defined by finite political boundaries.

(1) Cannabis shall not be advertised, marketed, labeled, or sold as grown in a California county when the cannabis was not grown in that county.

(2) The name of a California county, including any similar name that is likely to mislead consumers as to the origin of the product, shall not be used in the advertising, labeling, marketing, or packaging of cannabis products unless the cannabis contained in the product was grown in that county.

(b) No later than January 1, 2021, the Department of Food and Agriculture shall establish a process by which licensed cultivators may establish appellations of standards, practices, and varietals applicable to cannabis grown in a certain geographical area in California, not otherwise specified in subdivision (a).

Business and Professions Code § 26065

(MAUCRSA, Effective June 27, 2017.)

An employee engaged in the cultivation of cannabis under this division shall be subject to Wage Order No. 4-2001 of the Industrial Welfare Commission.

Business and Professions Code § 26066

(MAUCRSA, Effective June 27, 2017.)

Indoor and outdoor cannabis cultivation by persons and entities licensed under this division shall be conducted in accordance with state and local laws related to land conversion, current building and fire standards, grading, electricity usage, water usage, water quality, woodland and riparian habitat protection, agricultural discharges, and similar matters. State agencies, including, but not limited to, the State Board of Forestry and Fire Protection, the Department of Fish and Wildlife, the State Water Resources Control Board, the California regional water quality control boards, and traditional state law enforcement agencies, shall address environmental impacts of cannabis cultivation and shall coordinate when appropriate with cities and counties and their law enforcement agencies in enforcement efforts.

Chapter 6.5. Unique Identifiers and Track and Trace

Business and Professions Code § 26067

(Amended by Stats. 2018, Ch. 599, Sec. 6. (AB 3261) Effective January 1, 2019.)

(a) The department, in consultation with the bureau, shall establish a track and trace program for reporting the movement of cannabis and cannabis products throughout the distribution chain that utilizes a unique identifier pursuant to Section 26069, secure packaging, and is capable of providing information that captures, at a minimum, all of the following:

(1) The licensee receiving the product.

(2) The transaction date.

(3) The cultivator from which the product originates, including the associated unique identifier pursuant to Section 26069.

(b) (1) The department, in consultation with the California Department of Tax and Fee Administration, shall create an electronic database containing the electronic shipping manifests to facilitate the administration of the track and trace program, which shall include, but not be limited to, the following information:

(A) The variety and quantity or weight of products shipped.

(B) The estimated times of departure and arrival.

(C) The variety and quantity or weight of products received.

(D) The actual time of departure and arrival.

(E) A categorization of the product.

(F) The license number and the unique identifier pursuant to Section 26069 issued by the licensing authority for all licensees involved in the shipping process, including, but not limited to, cultivators, manufacturers, distributors, and dispensaries.

(2) (A) The database shall be designed to flag irregularities for all licensing authorities in this division to investigate. All licensing authorities pursuant to this division may access the database and share information related to licensees under this chapter, including social security and individual taxpayer identifications notwithstanding Section 30.

(B) The department shall immediately inform the bureau upon the finding of an irregularity or suspicious finding related to a licensee, applicant, or commercial cannabis activity for investigatory purposes.

(3) Licensing authorities and state and local agencies may, at any time, inspect shipments and request documentation for current inventory.

(4) The bureau shall have 24-hour access to the electronic database administered by the department. The California Department of Tax and Fee Administration shall have read access to the electronic database for the purpose of taxation and regulation of cannabis and cannabis products.

(5) The department shall be authorized to enter into memoranda of understandings with licensing authorities for data sharing purposes, as deemed necessary by the department.

(6) Information received and contained in records kept by the department or licensing authorities for the purposes of administering this chapter are confidential and shall not be disclosed pursuant to the California Public Records Act (Chapter 3.5 (commencing with Section 6250) of Division 7 of Title 1 of the Government Code), except as necessary for authorized employees of the State of California or any city, county, or city and county to perform official duties pursuant to this division or a local ordinance.

(7) Upon the request of a state or local law enforcement agency, licensing authorities shall allow access to or provide information contained within the database to assist law enforcement in their duties and responsibilities pursuant to this division.

Business and Professions Code § 26068

(Amended by Stats. 2018, Ch. 599, Sec. 7. (AB 3261) Effective January 1, 2019.)

(a) The department, in consultation with the bureau and the California Department of Tax and Fee Administration, shall ensure that the track and trace program can also track and trace the amount of the cultivation tax due pursuant to Part 14.5 (commencing with Section 34010) of Division 2 of the Revenue and Taxation Code. The track and trace program shall include an electronic seed to sale software tracking system with data points for the different stages of commercial activity, including, but not limited to, cultivation, harvest, processing, distribution, inventory, and sale.

(b) The department, in consultation with the bureau, shall ensure that licensees under this division are allowed to use third-party applications, programs, and information technology systems to comply with the requirements of the expanded track and trace program described in subdivision (a) to report the movement of cannabis and cannabis products throughout the distribution chain and communicate the information to licensing agencies as required by law.

(c) Any software, database, or other information technology system utilized by the department to implement the expanded track and trace program shall support interoperability with third-party cannabis business software applications and allow all licensee-facing system activities to be performed through a secure application programming interface (API) or comparable technology that is well documented, bi-directional, and accessible to any third-party application that has been validated and has appropriate credentials. The API or comparable technology shall have version control and provide adequate notice of updates to third-party applications. The system should provide a test environment for third-party applications to access that mirrors the production environment.

Business and Professions Code § 26069

(Amended by AB 133, Effective September 16, 2017.)

(a) The department shall establish a Cannabis Cultivation Program to be administered by the secretary. The secretary shall administer this section as it pertains to the cultivation of cannabis. For purposes of this division, cannabis is an agricultural product.

(b) A person or entity shall not cultivate cannabis without first obtaining a state license issued by the department pursuant to this division.

(c) (1) The department, in consultation with, but not limited to, the bureau, shall implement a unique identification program for cannabis. In implementing the program, the department shall consider issues including, but not limited to, water use and environmental impacts. If the State Water Resources Control Board or the Department of Fish and Wildlife finds, based on substantial evidence, that cannabis cultivation is causing significant adverse impacts on the environment in a watershed or other geographic area, the department shall not issue new licenses or increase the total number of plant identifiers within that watershed or area.

  (2) (A) The department shall establish a program for the identification of permitted cannabis plants at a cultivation site during the cultivation period. A unique identifier shall be issued for each cannabis plant. The department shall ensure that unique identifiers are issued as quickly as possible to ensure the implementation of this division. The unique identifier shall be attached at the base of each plant or as otherwise required by law or regulation.

    (B) Unique identifiers shall only be issued to those persons appropriately licensed by this section.

    (C) Information associated with the assigned unique identifier and licensee shall be included in the trace and track program specified in Section 26067.

    (D) The department may charge a fee to cover the reasonable costs of issuing the unique identifier and monitoring, tracking, and inspecting each cannabis plant.

    (E) The department may promulgate regulations to implement this section.

  (3) The department shall take adequate steps to establish protections against fraudulent unique identifiers and limit illegal diversion of unique identifiers to unlicensed persons.

(d) A city, county, or city and county may administer unique identifiers and associated identifying information but a city, county, or city and county's identifiers shall not supplant the department's track and trace program.

(e) (1) This section does not apply to the cultivation of cannabis in accordance with Section 11362.1 of the Health and Safety Code or the Compassionate Use Act.

(2) Subdivision (b) does not apply to persons or entities licensed under subdivision (b) of Section 26070.5.

Business and Professions Code § 26069.1

(MAUCRSA, Effective June 27, 2017.)

The secretary may enter into a cooperative agreement with a county agricultural commissioner or other state or local agency to assist the department in implementing the provisions of this division related to administration, investigation, inspection, fee collection, document management, education and outreach, distribution of individual licenses approved by the secretary, and technical assistance pertaining to the cultivation of cannabis. The department shall pay compensation under a cooperative agreement from fees collected and deposited pursuant to this division and shall provide reimbursement to a county agricultural commissioner, state, or local agency for associated costs. The secretary shall not delegate through a cooperative agreement, or otherwise, its authority to issue cultivation licenses to a county agricultural commissioner, local agency, or another state agency. The secretary shall provide notice of any cooperative agreement entered into pursuant to this section to other relevant state agencies involved in the regulation of cannabis cultivation. No cooperative agreement under this section shall relieve the department of its obligations under paragraph (2) of subdivision (a) of Section 26012 to administer the provisions of this division related to, and associated with, the cultivation of cannabis.

Business and Professions Code § 26069.9

(MAUCRSA, Effective June 27, 2017.)

For purposes of this chapter:

(a) "Department" means the Department of Food and Agriculture.

(b) "Secretary" means the Secretary of Food and Agriculture.

Chapter 7. Retailers and Distributors

Business and Professions Code § 26070

(Amended by Stats. 2018, Ch. 599, Sec. 9. (AB 3261) Effective January 1, 2019. Note: This section was added on Nov. 8, 2016, by initiative Prop. 64.)

Retailers, Distributors, and Microbusinesses.

(a) State licenses to be issued by the bureau related to the sale and distribution of cannabis and cannabis products are as follows:

(1) "Retailer," for the retail sale and delivery of cannabis or cannabis products to customers. A retailer shall have a licensed premises which is a physical location from which commercial cannabis activities are conducted. A retailer's premises may be closed to the public. A retailer may conduct sales exclusively by delivery.

(2) "Distributor," for the distribution of cannabis and cannabis products. A distributor licensee shall be bonded

and insured at a minimum level established by the licensing authority.

(3) (A) "Microbusiness," for the cultivation of cannabis on an area less than 10,000 square feet and to act as a licensed distributor, Level 1 manufacturer, and retailer under this division, provided such licensee can demonstrate compliance with all requirements imposed by this division on licensed cultivators, distributors, Level 1 manufacturers, and retailers to the extent the licensee engages in such activities. Microbusiness licenses that authorize cultivation of cannabis shall include the license conditions described in subdivision (b) of Section 26060.1.

(B) In coordination with each other, the licensing authorities shall establish a process by which an applicant for a microbusiness license can demonstrate compliance with all the requirements under this division for the activities that will be conducted under the license.

(C) The bureau may enter into interagency agreements with licensing authorities to implement and enforce the provisions of this division related to microbusinesses. The costs of activities carried out by the licensing authorities as requested by the bureau pursuant to the interagency agreement shall be calculated into the application and licensing fees collected pursuant to this division, and shall provide for reimbursement to state agencies for associated costs as provided for in the interagency agreement.

(b) The bureau shall establish minimum security and transportation safety requirements for the commercial distribution and delivery of cannabis and cannabis products. Except as provided in subdivision (d) of Section 26110, the transportation of cannabis and cannabis products shall only be conducted by persons holding a distributor license under this division or employees of those persons. Transportation safety standards established by the bureau shall include, but not be limited to, minimum standards governing the types of vehicles in which cannabis and cannabis products may be distributed and delivered and minimum qualifications for persons eligible to operate such vehicles.

(c) The driver of a vehicle transporting or transferring cannabis or cannabis products shall be directly employed by a licensee authorized to transport or transfer cannabis or cannabis products.

(d) Notwithstanding any other law, all vehicles transporting cannabis and cannabis products for hire shall be required to have a valid motor carrier permit pursuant to Chapter 2 (commencing with Section 34620) of Division 14.85 of the Vehicle Code. The Department of the California Highway Patrol shall have authority over the safe operation of these vehicles, including, but not limited to, requiring licensees engaged in the transportation of cannabis or cannabis products to participate in the Basic Inspection of Terminals (BIT) program pursuant to Section 34501.12 of the Vehicle Code.

(e) Prior to transporting cannabis or cannabis products, a licensed distributor shall do both of the following:

(1) Complete an electronic shipping manifest as prescribed by the licensing authority. The shipping manifest shall include the unique identifier, pursuant to Section 26069, issued by the Department of Food and Agriculture for the original cannabis product.

(2) Securely transmit the manifest to the bureau and the licensee that will receive the cannabis product. The bureau shall inform the Department of Food and Agriculture of information pertaining to commercial cannabis activity for the purpose of the track and trace program identified in Section 26067.

(f) During transportation, the licensed distributor shall maintain a physical copy of the shipping manifest and make it available upon request to agents of the Department of Consumer Affairs and law enforcement officers.

(g) The licensee receiving the shipment shall maintain each electronic shipping manifest and shall make it available upon request to the Department of Consumer Affairs and any law enforcement officers.

(h) Upon receipt of the transported shipment, the licensee receiving the shipment shall submit to the licensing authority a record verifying receipt of the shipment and the details of the shipment.

(i) Transporting, or arranging for or facilitating the transport of, cannabis or cannabis products in violation of this chapter is grounds for disciplinary action against the license.

(j) Licensed retailers and microbusinesses, and licensed nonprofits under Section 26070.5, shall implement security measures reasonably designed to prevent unauthorized entrance into areas containing cannabis or cannabis products and theft of cannabis or cannabis products from the premises. These security measures shall include, but not be limited to, all of the following:

(1) Prohibiting individuals from remaining on the licensee's premises if they are not engaging in activity expressly related to the operations of the retailer.

(2) Establishing limited access areas accessible only to authorized personnel.

(3) Other than limited amounts of cannabis used for display purposes, samples, or immediate sale, storing all finished cannabis and cannabis products in a secured and locked room, safe, or vault, and in a manner reasonably designed to prevent diversion, theft, and loss.

(k) A retailer shall notify the licensing authority and the appropriate law enforcement authorities within 24 hours after discovering any of the following:

(1) Significant discrepancies identified during inventory. The level of significance shall be determined by the bureau.

(2) Diversion, theft, loss, or any criminal activity pertaining to the operation of the retailer.

(3) Diversion, theft, loss, or any criminal activity by any agent or employee of the retailer pertaining to the operation of the retailer.

(4) The loss or unauthorized alteration of records related to cannabis or cannabis products, registered qualifying patients, primary caregivers, or retailer employees or agents.

(5) Any other breach of security.

(l) Beginning January 1, 2018, a licensee may sell cannabis or cannabis products that have not been tested for a limited and finite time as determined by the bureau. The cannabis or cannabis products must have a label affixed to each package containing the cannabis or cannabis products that clearly states "This product has not been tested as required by the Medicinal and Adult-Use Cannabis Regulation and Safety Act" and must comply with any other requirement as determined by the bureau.

Business and Professions Code § 26070.1

(MAUCRSA, Effective June 27, 2017.)

Cannabis or cannabis products purchased by a customer shall not leave a licensed retail premises unless they are placed in an opaque package.

Business and Professions Code § 26070.2

(Added by Stats. 2018, Ch. 827, Sec. 2. (AB 2914) Effective January 1, 2019.)

A licensee shall not sell, offer, or provide a cannabis product that is an alcoholic beverage, including, but not limited to, an infusion of cannabis or cannabinoids derived from industrial hemp into an alcoholic beverage.

Business and Professions Code § 26070.5

(Amended by Stats. 2018, Ch. 92, Sec. 28. (SB 1289) Effective January 1, 2019. Note: This section was added on Nov. 8, 2016, by initiative Prop. 64.)

(a) The bureau shall, by January 1, 2020, investigate the feasibility of creating one or more classifications of nonprofit licenses under this section. The feasibility determination shall be made in consultation with the relevant licensing agencies and representatives of local jurisdictions which issue temporary licenses pursuant to subdivision (b). The bureau shall consider factors including, but not limited to, the following:

(1) Should nonprofit licensees be exempted from any or all state taxes, licensing fees, and regulatory provisions applicable to other licenses in this division?

(2) Should funding incentives be created to encourage others licensed under this division to provide professional services at reduced or no cost to nonprofit licensees?

(3) Should nonprofit licenses be limited to, or prioritize those, entities previously operating on a not-for-profit basis primarily providing whole-plant cannabis and cannabis products and a diversity of cannabis strains and seed stock to low-income persons?

(b) Any local jurisdiction may issue temporary local licenses to nonprofit entities primarily providing whole-plant cannabis and cannabis products and a diversity of cannabis strains and seed stock to low-income persons so long as the local jurisdiction does all of the following:

(1) Confirms the license applicant's status as a nonprofit entity registered with the California Attorney General's Registry of Charitable Trusts and that the applicant is in good standing with all state requirements governing nonprofit entities.

(2) Licenses and regulates any such entity to protect public health and safety, and so as to require compliance with all environmental requirements in this division.

(3) Provides notice to the bureau of any such local licenses issued, including the name and location of any such licensed entity and all local regulations governing the licensed entity's operation.

(4) Certifies to the bureau that any such licensed entity will not generate annual gross revenues in excess of two million dollars ($2,000,000).

(c) Temporary local licenses authorized under subdivision (b) shall expire after 12 months unless renewed by the local jurisdiction.

(d) The bureau may impose reasonable additional requirements on the local licenses authorized under subdivision (b).

(e) (1) New temporary local licenses shall not be issued pursuant to this section after the date the bureau determines that creation of nonprofit licenses under this division is not feasible, or if the bureau determines that creation of nonprofit licenses under this division is feasible, after the date a licensing agency commences issuing state nonprofit licenses.

(2) If the bureau determines that creation of nonprofit licenses under this division is feasible, no temporary license issued under subdivision (b) shall be renewed or extended after the date on which a licensing agency commences issuing state nonprofit licenses.

(3) If the bureau determines that creation of nonprofit licenses under this division is not feasible, the bureau shall provide notice of this determination to all local jurisdictions that have issued temporary licenses under subdivision (b). The bureau may, in its discretion, permit any such local jurisdiction to renew or extend on an annual basis any temporary license previously issued under subdivision (b).

Chapter 8. Distribution and Transport

Business and Professions Code § 26080

(MAUCRSA, Effective June 27, 2017.)

(a) This division shall not be construed to authorize or permit a licensee to transport or distribute, or cause to be transported or distributed, cannabis or cannabis products outside the state, unless authorized by federal law.

(b) A local jurisdiction shall not prevent transportation of cannabis or cannabis products on public roads by a licensee transporting cannabis or cannabis products in compliance with this division.

Chapter 9. Delivery

Business and Professions Code § 26090

(Amended by AB 133, Effective September 16, 2017.)

(a) Deliveries, as defined in this division, may only be made by a licensed retailer or microbusiness, or a licensed nonprofit under Section 26070.5.

(b) All employees of a retailer, microbusiness, or nonprofit delivering cannabis or cannabis products shall carry a copy of the licensee's current license and a government-issued identification with a photo of the employee, such as a driver's license. The employee shall present that license and identification upon request to state and local law enforcement, employees of regulatory authorities, and other state and local agencies enforcing this division.

(c) During delivery, the licensee shall maintain a copy of the delivery request and shall make it available upon request of the licensing authority and law enforcement officers. The delivery request documentation shall comply with state and federal law regarding the protection of confidential medical information.

(d) A customer requesting delivery shall maintain a physical or electronic copy of the delivery request and shall make it available upon request by the licensing authority and law enforcement officers.

(e) A local jurisdiction shall not prevent delivery of cannabis or cannabis products on public roads by a licensee acting in compliance with this division and local law as adopted under Section 26200.

Chapter 10. Testing Laboratories

Business and Professions Code § 26100

(MAUCRSA, Effective June 27, 2017.)

(a) Except as otherwise provided by law, cannabis or cannabis products shall not be sold pursuant to a license provided for under this division unless a representative sample of the cannabis or cannabis products has been tested by a licensed testing laboratory.

(b) The bureau shall develop criteria to determine which batches shall be tested. All testing of the samples shall be performed on the final form in which the cannabis or cannabis product will be consumed or used.

(c) Testing of batches to meet the requirements of this division shall only be conducted by a licensed testing laboratory.

(d) For each batch tested, the testing laboratory shall issue a certificate of analysis for selected lots at a frequency determined by the bureau with supporting data, to report both of the following:

(1) Whether the chemical profile of the sample conforms to the labeled content of compounds, including, but not limited to, all of the following, unless limited through regulation by the bureau:

(A) Tetrahydrocannabinol (THC).

(B) Tetrahydrocannabinolic Acid (THCA).

(C) Cannabidiol (CBD).

(D) Cannabidiolic Acid (CBDA).

(E) The terpenes required by the bureau in regulation.

(F) Cannabigerol (CBG).

(G) Cannabinol (CBN).

(H) Any other compounds or contaminants required by the bureau.

(2) That the presence of contaminants does not exceed the levels established by the bureau. In establishing the levels, the bureau shall consider the American Herbal Pharmacopoeia monograph, guidelines set by the Department of Pesticide Regulation pursuant to subdivision (d) of Section 26060, and any other relevant sources. For purposes of this paragraph, "contaminants" includes, but is not limited to, all of the following:

(A) Residual solvent or processing chemicals.

(B) Foreign material, including, but not limited to, hair, insects, or similar or related adulterant.

(C) Microbiological impurities as identified by the bureau in regulation.

(e) Standards for residual levels of volatile organic compounds shall be established by the bureau.

(f) The testing laboratory shall conduct all testing required by this section in a manner consistent with general requirements for the competence of testing and calibrations activities, including sampling and using verified methods.

(g) All testing laboratories performing tests pursuant to this section shall obtain and maintain ISO/IEC 17025 accreditation as required by the bureau in regulation.

(h) If a test result falls outside the specifications authorized by law or regulation, the testing laboratory shall follow a standard operating procedure to confirm or refute the original result.

(i) A testing laboratory shall destroy the remains of the sample of medical cannabis or medical cannabis product upon completion of the analysis, as determined by the bureau through regulations.

(j) Any presale inspection, testing transfer, or transportation of cannabis products pursuant to this section shall conform to a specified chain of custody protocol and any other requirements imposed under this division.

(k) This division does not prohibit a licensee from performing testing on the licensee's premises for the purposes of quality assurance of the product in conjunction with reasonable business operations. This division also does not prohibit a licensee from performing testing on the licensee's premises of cannabis or cannabis products obtained from another licensee. Onsite testing by the licensee shall not be certified by the bureau and does not exempt the licensee from the requirements of quality assurance testing at a testing laboratory pursuant to this section.

Business and Professions Code § 26102

(MAUCRSA, Effective June 27, 2017.)

A testing laboratory shall not be licensed by the bureau unless the laboratory meets all of the following:

(a) Complies with any other requirements specified by the bureau.

(b) Notifies the bureau within one business day after the receipt of notice of any kind that its accreditation has been denied, suspended, or revoked.

(c) Has established standard operating procedures that provide for adequate chain of custody controls for samples transferred to the testing laboratory for testing.

Business and Professions Code § 26104

(Amended by Stats. 2018, Ch. 546, Sec. 1. (AB 2721) Effective January 1, 2019. Note: This section was added on Nov. 8, 2016, by initiative Prop. 64.)

(a) A licensed testing laboratory shall, in performing activities concerning cannabis and cannabis products, comply with the requirements and restrictions set forth in applicable law and regulations.

(b) The bureau shall develop procedures to do all of the following:

> (1) Ensure that testing of cannabis and cannabis products occurs prior to distribution to retailers, microbusinesses, or nonprofits licensed under Section 26070.5.

> (2) Specify how often licensees shall test cannabis and cannabis products, and that the cost of testing cannabis shall be borne by the licensed cultivators and the cost of testing cannabis products shall be borne by the licensed manufacturer, and that the costs of testing cannabis and cannabis products shall be borne by a nonprofit licensed under Section 26070.5.

> (3) Require destruction of harvested batches whose testing samples indicate noncompliance with health and safety standards required by the bureau, unless remedial measures can bring the cannabis or cannabis products into compliance with quality assurance standards as specified by law and implemented by the bureau.

> (4) Ensure that a testing laboratory employee takes the sample of cannabis or cannabis products from the distributor's premises for testing required by this division and that the testing laboratory employee transports the sample to the testing laboratory.

(c) Except as provided in this division, a testing laboratory shall not acquire or receive cannabis or cannabis products except from a licensee in accordance with this division, and shall not distribute, sell, or dispense cannabis or cannabis products, from the licensed premises from which the cannabis or cannabis products were acquired or received. All transfer or transportation shall be performed pursuant to a specified chain of custody protocol.

(d) A testing laboratory may receive and test samples of cannabis or cannabis products from a qualified patient or primary caregiver with a valid physician's recommendation for cannabis for medicinal purposes. A testing laboratory shall not certify samples from a qualified patient or primary caregiver for resale or transfer to another person or licensee. All tests performed by a testing laboratory for a qualified patient or primary caregiver shall be recorded with the name of the qualified patient or primary caregiver and the amount of cannabis or cannabis product received.

(e) A testing laboratory may receive and test samples of cannabis or cannabis products from a person over 21 years of age when the cannabis has been grown by that person and will be used solely for his or her personal use, as authorized pursuant to Section 11362.1 of the Health and Safety Code. A testing laboratory shall not certify samples from the person over 21 years of age for resale or transfer to another person or licensee. All tests recorded pursuant to this subdivision shall be recorded with the name of the person submitting the sample and the amount of cannabis or cannabis product received.

Business and Professions Code § 26105

(AUMA, Effective November 9, 2016.)

Manufacturing Level 2 licensees shall enact sufficient methods or procedures to capture or otherwise limit risk of explosion, combustion, or any other unreasonably dangerous risk to public safety created by volatile solvents. The Department of Public Health shall establish minimum standards concerning such methods and procedures for Level 2 licensees.

Business and Professions Code § 26106

(MAUCRSA, Effective June 27, 2017.)

Standards for the production, packaging, and labeling of all cannabis products developed by the State Department of Public Health apply to all licensed manufacturers and microbusinesses, and nonprofits licensed under Section 26070.5, unless otherwise specified by the State Department of Public Health.

Chapter 11. Quality Assurance, Inspection, and Testing

Business and Professions Code § 26110

(Amended by Stats. 2018, Ch. 556, Sec. 1. (SB 311) Effective September 19, 2018.)

(a) Cannabis batches are subject to quality assurance and testing prior to sale at a retailer, microbusiness, or nonprofit licensed under Section 26070.5, except for immature cannabis plants and seeds, as provided for in this division.

(b) A licensee that holds a valid distributor license may act as the distributor for the licensee's cannabis and cannabis products.

(c) The distributor shall store, as determined by the bureau, the cannabis batches on the premises of the distributor before testing and continuously until either of the following occurs:

(1) The cannabis batch passes the testing requirements pursuant to this division and is transported to a licensed retailer or to another licensed distributor.

(2) The cannabis batch fails the testing requirements pursuant to this division and is destroyed or transported to a manufacturer for remediation as allowed by the bureau or the State Department of Public Health.

(d) The distributor shall arrange for a testing laboratory to obtain a representative sample of each cannabis batch at the distributor's licensed premises. After obtaining the sample, the testing laboratory representative shall maintain custody of the sample and transport it to the testing laboratory.

(e) Upon issuance of a certificate of analysis by the testing laboratory that the cannabis batch has passed the testing requirements pursuant to this division, the distributor shall conduct a quality assurance review before distribution to ensure the labeling and packaging of the cannabis and cannabis products conform to the requirements of this division.

(f) (1) There shall be a quality assurance compliance monitor who is an employee or contractor of the bureau and who shall not hold a license in any category or own or have an ownership interest in a licensee or the premises of a licensee.

(2) The quality assurance compliance monitor shall conduct random quality assurance reviews at a distributor's licensed premises before distribution to ensure the labeling and packaging of the cannabis and cannabis products conform to the requirements of this division.

(3) The quality assurance compliance monitor shall have access to all records and test results required of a licensee by law in order to conduct quality assurance analysis and to confirm test results. All records of inspection and verification by the quality assurance compliance monitor shall be provided to the bureau. Failure to comply shall be noted by the quality assurance compliance monitor for further investigation. Violations shall be reported to the bureau. The quality assurance compliance monitor shall also verify the tax payments collected and paid under Sections 34011 and 34012 of the Revenue and Taxation Code are accurate. The monitor shall also have access to the inputs and assumptions in the track and trace system and shall be able to verify their accuracy and that they are commensurate with the tax payments.

(g) After testing, all cannabis and cannabis products fit for sale may be transported only from the distributor's premises to the premises of another licensed distributor for further distribution, or to a licensed retailer, microbusiness, or nonprofit for retail sale.

(h) A licensee is not required to sell cannabis or cannabis products to a distributor and may directly contract for sale with a licensee authorized to sell cannabis and cannabis products to purchasers.

(i) A distributor performing services pursuant to this section may collect a fee from the licensee for the services provided. The fee may include, but is not limited to, the costs incurred for laboratory testing. A distributor may also collect applicable state or local taxes and fees.

(j) This section does not prohibit a licensee from performing testing on the licensee's premises for the purposes of quality assurance of the product in conjunction with reasonable business operations. The testing conducted on the licensee's premises by the licensee does not meet the testing requirements pursuant to this division.

Chapter 12. Packaging and Labeling

Business and Professions Code § 26120

(MAUCRSA, Effective June 27, 2017.)

(a) Prior to delivery or sale at a retailer, cannabis and cannabis products shall be labeled and placed in a resealable, tamper-evident, child-resistant package and shall include a unique identifier for the purposes of identifying and tracking cannabis and cannabis products.

(b) Packages and labels shall not be made to be attractive to children.

(c) All cannabis and cannabis product labels and inserts shall include the following information prominently displayed in a clear and legible fashion in accordance with the requirements, including font size, prescribed by the bureau or the State Department of Public Health:

(1) The following statements, in bold print:

(A) For cannabis: "GOVERNMENT WARNING: THIS PACKAGE CONTAINS CANNABIS, A SCHEDULE I CONTROLLED SUBSTANCE. KEEP OUT OF REACH OF CHILDREN AND ANIMALS. CANNABIS MAY ONLY BE POSSESSED OR CONSUMED BY PERSONS 21 YEARS OF AGE OR OLDER UNLESS THE PERSON IS A QUALIFIED PATIENT. CANNABIS USE WHILE PREGNANT OR BREASTFEEDING MAY BE HARMFUL.

CONSUMPTION OF CANNABIS IMPAIRS YOUR ABILITY TO DRIVE AND OPERATE MACHINERY. PLEASE USE EXTREME CAUTION."

(B) For cannabis products: "GOVERNMENT WARNING: THIS PRODUCT CONTAINS CANNABIS, A SCHEDULE I CONTROLLED SUBSTANCE. KEEP OUT OF REACH OF CHILDREN AND ANIMALS. CANNABIS PRODUCTS MAY ONLY BE POSSESSED OR CONSUMED BY PERSONS 21 YEARS OF AGE OR OLDER UNLESS THE PERSON IS A QUALIFIED PATIENT. THE INTOXICATING EFFECTS OF CANNABIS PRODUCTS MAY BE DELAYED UP TO TWO HOURS. CANNABIS USE WHILE PREGNANT OR BREASTFEEDING MAY BE HARMFUL. CONSUMPTION OF CANNABIS PRODUCTS IMPAIRS YOUR ABILITY TO DRIVE AND OPERATE MACHINERY. PLEASE USE EXTREME CAUTION."

(2) For packages containing only dried flower, the net weight of cannabis in the package.

(3) Identification of the source and date of cultivation, the type of cannabis or cannabis product and the date of manufacturing and packaging.

(4) The appellation of origin, if any.

(5) List of pharmacologically active ingredients, including, but not limited to, tetrahydrocannabinol (THC), cannabidiol (CBD), and other cannabinoid content, the THC and other cannabinoid amount in milligrams per serving, servings per package, and the THC and other cannabinoid amount in milligrams for the package total.

(6) A warning if nuts or other known allergens are used.

(7) Information associated with the unique identifier issued by the Department of Food and Agriculture.

(8) For a medicinal cannabis product sold at a retailer, the statement "FOR MEDICAL USE ONLY."

(9) Any other requirement set by the bureau or the State Department of Public Health.

(d) Only generic food names may be used to describe the ingredients in edible cannabis products.

(e) In the event the Attorney General determines that cannabis is no longer a Schedule I controlled substance under federal law, the label prescribed in subdivision (c) shall no longer require a statement that cannabis is a Schedule I controlled substance.

Business and Professions Code § 26121

(MAUCRSA, Effective June 27, 2017.)

(a) A cannabis product is misbranded if it is any of the following:

(1) Manufactured, packed, or held in this state in a manufacturing premises not duly licensed as provided in this division.

(2) Its labeling is false or misleading in any particular.

(3) Its labeling or packaging does not conform to the requirements of Section 26120 or any other labeling or packaging requirement established pursuant to this division.

(b) It is unlawful for any person to manufacture, sell, deliver, hold, or offer for sale a cannabis product that is misbranded.

(c) It is unlawful for any person to misbrand a cannabis product.

(d) It is unlawful for any person to receive in commerce a cannabis product that is misbranded or to deliver or offer for delivery any such cannabis product.

Chapter 13. Manufacturers and Cannabis Products

Business and Professions Code § 26130

(Amended by AB 133, Effective September 16, 2017.)

(a) The State Department of Public Health shall promulgate regulations governing the licensing of cannabis manufacturers and standards for the manufacturing, packaging, and labeling of all manufactured cannabis products. Licenses to be issued are as follows:

(1) "Manufacturing Level 1," for sites that manufacture cannabis products using nonvolatile solvents, or no solvents.

(2) "Manufacturing Level 2," for sites that manufacture cannabis products using volatile solvents.

(b) For purposes of this section, "volatile solvents" shall have the same meaning as in paragraph (3) of subdivision (b) of Section 11362.3 of the Health and Safety Code, unless otherwise provided by law or regulation.

(c) Edible cannabis products shall be:

(1) Not designed to be appealing to children or easily confused with commercially sold candy or foods that do not contain cannabis.

(2) Produced and sold with a standardized concentration of cannabinoids not to exceed 10 milligrams tetrahydrocannabinol (THC) per serving.

(3) Delineated or scored into standardized serving sizes if the cannabis product contains more than one serving and is an edible cannabis product in solid form.

(4) Homogenized to ensure uniform disbursement of cannabinoids throughout the product.

(5) Manufactured and sold under sanitation standards established by the State Department of Public Health, in consultation with the bureau, that are similar to the standards for preparation, storage, handling, and sale of food products.

(6) Provided to customers with sufficient information to enable the informed consumption of the product, including the potential effects of the cannabis product and directions as to how to consume the cannabis product, as necessary.

(7) Marked with a universal symbol, as determined by the State Department of Public Health through regulation.

(d) Cannabis, including concentrated cannabis, included in a cannabis product manufactured in compliance with law is not considered an adulterant under state law.

Business and Professions Code § 26131

(MAUCRSA, Effective June 27, 2017.)

(a) A cannabis product is adulterated if it is any of the following:

(1) It has been produced, prepared, packed, or held under unsanitary conditions in which it may have become contaminated with filth or in which it may have been rendered injurious.

(2) It consists in whole or in part of any filthy, putrid, or decomposed substance.

(3) It bears or contains any poisonous or deleterious substance that may render it injurious to users under the conditions of use suggested in the labeling or under conditions as are customary or usual.

(4) It bears or contains a substance that is restricted or limited under this division or regulations promulgated pursuant to this division and the level of substance in the product exceeds the limits specified pursuant to this division or in regulation.

(5) Its concentrations differ from, or its purity or quality is below, that which it is represented to possess.

(6) The methods, facilities, or controls used for its manufacture, packing, or holding do not conform to, or are not operated or administered in conformity with, practices established by regulations adopted under this division to ensure that the cannabis product meets the requirements of this division as to safety and has the concentrations it purports to have and meets the quality and purity characteristics that it purports or is represented to possess.

(7) Its container is composed, in whole or in part, of any poisonous or deleterious substance that may render the contents injurious to health.

(8) It is an edible cannabis product and a substance has been mixed or packed with it after testing by a testing laboratory so as to reduce its quality or concentration or if any substance has been substituted, wholly or in part, for the edible cannabis product.

(b) It is unlawful for a person to manufacture, sell, deliver, hold, or offer for sale a cannabis product that is adulterated.

(c) It is unlawful for a person to adulterate a cannabis product.

(d) It is unlawful for a person to receive in commerce a cannabis product that is adulterated or to deliver or proffer for delivery any such cannabis product.

Business and Professions Code § 26132

(MAUCRSA, Effective June 27, 2017.)

(a) When the State Department of Public Health has evidence that a cannabis product is adulterated or misbranded, the department shall notify the manufacturer.

(b) The State Department of Public Health may order a manufacturer to immediately cease distribution of a cannabis product and recall the product if the department determines both of the following:

(1) The manufacture, distribution, or sale of the cannabis product creates or poses an immediate and serious threat to human life or health.

(2) Other procedures available to the State Department of Public Health to remedy or prevent the occurrence of the situation would result in an unreasonable delay.

(c) The State Department of Public Health shall provide the manufacturer an opportunity for an informal proceeding on the matter, as determined by the department, within five days, on the actions required by the order and on why the product should not be recalled. Following the proceeding, the order shall be affirmed, modified, or set aside as determined appropriate by the State Department of Public Health.

(d) The State Department of Public Health's powers set forth in this section expressly include the power to order movement, segregation, isolation, or destruction of cannabis products, as well as the power to hold those products in place.

(e) If the State Department of Public Health determines it is necessary, it may issue the mandatory recall order and may use all appropriate measures to obtain reimbursement from the manufacturer for any and all costs associated with these orders. All funds obtained by the State Department of Public Health from these efforts shall be deposited into a fee account specific to the State Department of Public Health, to be established in the Cannabis Control Fund, and will be available for use by the department upon appropriation by the Legislature.

(f) It is unlawful for any person to move or allow to be moved a cannabis product subject to an order issued pursuant to this section unless that person has first obtained written authorization from the State Department of Public Health.

Business and Professions Code § 26133

(MAUCRSA, Effective June 27, 2017.)

(a) If the State Department of Public Health finds or has probable cause to believe that a cannabis product is adulterated or misbranded within the meaning of this division or the sale of the cannabis product would be in violation of this division, the department shall affix to the cannabis product, or component thereof, a tag or other appropriate marking. The State Department of Public Health shall give notice that the cannabis product is, or is suspected of being, adulterated or misbranded, or the sale of the cannabis would be in violation of this division and has been embargoed and that no person shall remove or dispose of the cannabis product by sale or otherwise until permission for removal or disposal is given by the State Department of Public Health or a court.

(b) It is unlawful for a person to remove, sell, or dispose of a detained or embargoed cannabis product without written permission of the State Department of Public Health or a court. A violation of this subdivision is punishable by a fine of not more than ten thousand dollars ($10,000).

(c) If the adulteration or misbranding can be corrected by proper labeling or additional processing of the cannabis product and all of the provisions of this division can be complied with, the licensee or owner may request the State Department of Public Health to remove the tag or other marking. If, under the supervision of the State Department of Public Health, the adulteration or misbranding has been corrected, the department may remove the tag or other marking.

(d) If the State Department of Public Health finds that a cannabis product that is embargoed is not adulterated or misbranded, or that its sale is not otherwise in violation of this division, the State Department of Public Health may remove the tag or other marking.

(e) The cannabis product may be destroyed by the owner pursuant to a corrective action plan approved by the State Department of Public Health and under the supervision of the department. The cannabis product shall be destroyed at the expense of the licensee or owner.

(f) A proceeding for condemnation of a cannabis product under this section shall be subject to appropriate notice to, and the opportunity for a hearing with regard to, the person affected in accordance with Section 26016.

(g) Upon a finding by the administrative law judge that the cannabis product is adulterated or misbranded, or that its sale is otherwise in violation of this division, the administrative law judge may direct the cannabis product to be destroyed at the expense of the licensee or owner. The administrative law judge may also direct a licensee or owner of the affected cannabis product to pay fees and reasonable costs, including the costs of storage and testing, incurred by the bureau or the State Department of Public Health in investigating and prosecuting the action taken pursuant to this section.

(h) When, under the supervision of the State Department of Public Health, the adulteration or misbranding has been corrected by proper labeling or additional processing of the cannabis and cannabis product and when all provisions of this division have been complied with, and after costs, fees, and expenses have been paid, the State Department of Public Health may release the embargo and remove the tag or other marking.

(i) The State Department of Public Health may condemn a cannabis product under provisions of this division. The cannabis product shall be destroyed at the expense of the licensee or owner.

Business and Professions Code § 26134

(MAUCRSA, Effective June 27, 2017.)

(a) The State Department of Public Health may issue a citation, which may contain an order of abatement and an order to pay an administrative fine assessed by the department if the licensee is in violation of this division or any regulation adopted pursuant to it.

(1) Citations shall be in writing and shall describe with particularity the nature of the violation, including specific reference to the law determined to have been violated.

(2) If appropriate, the citation shall contain an order of abatement fixing a reasonable time for abatement of the violation.

(3) The administrative fine assessed by the State Department of Public Health shall not exceed five thousand dollars ($5,000) for each violation, unless a different fine amount is expressly provided by this division. In assessing a fine, the department shall give due consideration to the appropriateness of the amount of the fine with respect to factors such as the gravity of the violation, the good faith of the licensee, and the history of previous violations.

(4) A citation issued or a fine assessed pursuant to this section shall notify the licensee that if the licensee desires a hearing to contest the finding of a violation, that hearing shall be requested by written notice to the State Department of Public Health within 30 days of the date of issuance of the citation or fine. If a hearing is not requested pursuant to this section, payment of any fine shall not constitute an admission of the violation charged. Hearings shall be held pursuant to Chapter 5 (commencing with Section 11500) of Part 1 of Division 3 of Title 2 of the Government Code.

(5) Failure of a licensee to pay a fine within 30 days of the date of assessment of the fine, unless assessment of the fine or the citation is being appealed, may result in further legal action being taken by the State Department of Public Health. If a licensee does not contest a citation or pay the fine, the full amount of the fine shall be added to the fee for renewal of the license. A license shall not be renewed without payment of the renewal fee, including the amount of the fine.

(6) A citation may be issued without the assessment of an administrative fine.

(7) The State Department of Public Health may limit the assessment of administrative fines to only particular violations of this division and establish any other requirement for implementation of the citation system by regulation.

(b) Notwithstanding any other law, if a fine is paid to satisfy an assessment based on the finding of a violation, payment of the fine shall be represented as satisfactory resolution of the matter for purposes of public disclosure.

Business and Professions Code § 26135

(MAUCRSA, Effective June 27, 2017.)

A peace officer, including a peace officer within the State Department of Public Health or the bureau, may seize cannabis and cannabis products in any of the following circumstances:

(a) The cannabis or cannabis product is subject to recall or embargo by any licensing authority.

(b) The cannabis or cannabis product is subject to destruction pursuant to this division.

(c) The cannabis or cannabis product is seized related to an investigation or disciplinary action for violation of this division.

Chapter 14. Protection of Minors

Business and Professions Code § 26140

(Amended by AB 133, Effective September 16, 2017.)

(a) An A-licensee shall not:

(1) Sell cannabis or cannabis products to persons under 21 years of age.

(2) Allow any person under 21 years of age on its premises, unless the A-licensee holds an M-license and the licensed premises for the A-license and M-license are the same.

(3) Employ or retain persons under 21 years of age.

(4) Sell or transfer cannabis or cannabis products unless the person to whom the cannabis or cannabis product is to be sold first presents documentation which reasonably appears to be a valid government-issued identification card showing that the person is 21 years of age or older.

(b) Persons under 21 years of age may be used by peace officers in the enforcement of this division and to apprehend licensees, or employees or agents of licensees, or other persons who sell or furnish cannabis to minors. Notwithstanding any provision of law, any person under 21 years of age who purchases or attempts to purchase any cannabis while under the direction of a peace officer is immune from prosecution for that purchase or attempt to purchase cannabis. Guidelines with respect to the use of persons under 21 years of age as decoys shall be adopted and published by the bureau in accordance with the rulemaking portion of the Administrative Procedure Act (Chapter 3.5 (commencing with Section 11340) of Part 1 of Division 3 of Title 2 of the Government Code).

(c) Notwithstanding subdivision (a), an M-licensee may:

(1) Allow on the premises any person 18 years of age or older who possesses a valid government-issued identification card, and either a valid county-issued identification card under Section 11362.712 of the Health and Safety Code or a valid physician's recommendation for himself or herself or for a person for whom he or she is a primary caregiver.

(2) Allow any person 21 years of age or older on its premises if the M-licensee holds an A-license and the licensed premises for the M-license and A-license are the same.

(3) Sell cannabis, cannabis products, and cannabis accessories to a person 18 years of age or older who possesses a valid government-issued identification card and either a valid county-issued identification card under Section 11362.712 of the Health and Safety Code or a valid physician's recommendation for himself or herself or for a person for whom he or she is a primary caregiver.

(4) The bureau may establish requirements for the purchase of cannabis, cannabis products, or cannabis accessories by a primary caregiver for a patient to ensure that the status of a person as a primary caregiver is verified.

Chapter 15. Advertising and Marketing Restrictions

Business and Professions Code § 26150

(MAUCRSA, Effective June 27, 2017.)

For purposes of this chapter:

(a) "Advertise" means the publication or dissemination of an advertisement.

(b) "Advertisement" includes any written or verbal statement, illustration, or depiction which is calculated to induce sales of cannabis or cannabis products, including any written, printed, graphic, or other material, billboard, sign, or other outdoor display, public transit card, other periodical literature, publication, or in a radio or television broadcast, or in any other media; except that such term shall not include:

> (1) Any label affixed to any cannabis or cannabis products, or any individual covering, carton, or other wrapper of that container that constitutes a part of the labeling under provisions of this division.

> (2) Any editorial or other reading material, such as a news release, in any periodical or publication or newspaper for the publication of which no money or valuable consideration is paid or promised, directly or indirectly, by any licensee, and which is not written by or at the direction of the licensee.

(c) "Advertising sign" is any sign, poster, display, billboard, or any other stationary or permanently affixed advertisement promoting the sale of cannabis or cannabis products which are not cultivated, manufactured, distributed, or sold on the same lot.

(d) "Health-related statement" means any statement related to health, and includes statements of a curative or therapeutic nature that, expressly or by implication, suggest a relationship between the consumption of cannabis or cannabis products and health benefits, or effects on health.

(e) "Market" or "Marketing" means any act or process of promoting or selling cannabis or cannabis products, including, but not limited to, sponsorship of sporting events, point-of-sale advertising, and development of products specifically designed to appeal to certain demographics.

Business and Professions Code § 26151

(MAUCRSA, Effective June 27, 2017.)

(a) (1) All advertisements and marketing shall accurately and legibly identify the licensee responsible for its content, by adding, at a minimum, the licensee's license number.

> (2) A technology platform shall not display an advertisement by a licensee on an Internet Web page unless the advertisement displays the license number of the licensee.

> (3) An outdoor advertising company subject to the Outdoor Advertising Act (Chapter 2 (commencing with Section 5200) of Division 3) shall not display an advertisement by a licensee unless the advertisement displays the license number of the licensee.

(b) Any advertising or marketing placed in broadcast, cable, radio, print, and digital communications shall only be displayed where at least 71.6 percent of the audience is reasonably expected to be 21 years of age or older, as determined by reliable, up-to-date audience composition data.

(c) Any advertising or marketing involving direct, individualized communication or dialogue controlled by the licensee shall utilize a method of age affirmation to verify that the recipient is 21 years of age or older before engaging in that communication or dialogue controlled by the licensee. For purposes of this section, that method of age affirmation may include user confirmation, birth date disclosure, or other similar registration method.

(d) All advertising shall be truthful and appropriately substantiated.

Business and Professions Code § 26152

(Amended by Stats. 2018, Ch. 923, Sec. 1. (AB 2899) Effective January 1, 2019. Note: This section was added on Nov. 8, 2016, by initiative Prop. 64.)

A licensee shall not do any of the following:

(a) Advertise or market in a manner that is false or untrue in any material particular, or that, irrespective of falsity, directly, or by ambiguity, omission, or inference, or by the addition of irrelevant, scientific, or technical matter, tends to create a misleading impression.

(b) Publish or disseminate advertising or marketing containing any statement concerning a brand or product that is inconsistent with any statement on the labeling thereof.

(c) Publish or disseminate advertising or marketing containing any statement, design, device, or representation which tends to create the impression that the cannabis originated in a particular place or region, unless the label of the advertised product bears an appellation of origin, and such appellation of origin appears in the advertisement.

(d) Advertise or market on a billboard or similar advertising device located on an Interstate Highway or on a State Highway which crosses the California border.

(e) Advertise or market cannabis or cannabis products in a manner intended to encourage persons under 21 years of age to consume cannabis or cannabis products.

(f) Publish or disseminate advertising or marketing that is attractive to children.

(g) Advertise or market cannabis or cannabis products on an advertising sign within 1,000 feet of a day care center, school providing instruction in kindergarten or any grades 1 to 12, inclusive, playground, or youth center.

(h) Publish or disseminate advertising or marketing while the licensee's license is suspended.

Business and Professions Code § 26153

(MAUCRSA, Effective June 27, 2017.)

A licensee shall not give away any amount of cannabis or cannabis products, or any cannabis accessories, as part of a business promotion or other commercial activity.

Business and Professions Code § 26154

(MAUCRSA, Effective June 27, 2017.)

A licensee shall not include on the label of any cannabis or cannabis product or publish or disseminate advertising or marketing containing any health-related statement that is untrue in any particular manner or tends to create a misleading impression as to the effects on health of cannabis consumption.

Business and Professions Code § 26155

(MAUCRSA, Effective June 27, 2017.)

(a) The provisions of subdivision (g) of Section 26152 shall not apply to the placement of advertising signs inside a licensed premises and which are not visible by normal unaided vision from a public place, provided that such advertising signs do not advertise cannabis or cannabis products in a manner intended to encourage persons under 21 years of age to consume cannabis or cannabis products.

(b) This chapter does not apply to any noncommercial speech.

Business and Professions Code § 26156

(MAUCRSA, Effective June 27, 2017.)

The requirements of Section 5272 apply to this division.

Chapter 16. Records

Business and Professions Code § 26160

(MAUCRSA, Effective June 27, 2017.)

(a) A licensee shall keep accurate records of commercial cannabis activity.

(b) All records related to commercial cannabis activity as defined by the licensing authorities shall be maintained for a minimum of seven years.

(c) Licensing authorities may examine the records of a licensee and inspect the premises of a licensee as the licensing authority, or a state or local agency, deems necessary to perform its duties under this division. All inspections and examinations of records shall be conducted during standard business hours of the licensed facility or at any other reasonable time. Licensees shall provide and deliver records to the licensing authority upon request.

(d) Licensees shall keep records identified by the licensing authorities on the premises of the location licensed. The licensing authorities may make any examination of the records of any licensee. Licensees shall also provide and deliver copies of documents to the licensing authority upon request.

(e) A licensee, or its agent or employee, that refuses, impedes, obstructs, or interferes with an inspection of the premises or records of the licensee pursuant to this section, has engaged in a violation of this division.

(f) If a licensee, or an agent or employee of a licensee, fails to maintain or provide the records required pursuant to this section, the licensee shall be subject to a citation and fine of up to thirty thousand dollars ($30,000) per individual violation.

Business and Professions Code § 26161

(Amended by Stats. 2018, Ch. 599, Sec. 10. (AB 3261) Effective January 1, 2019. Note: This section was added on Nov. 8, 2016, by initiative Prop. 64.)

(a) Every sale or transport of cannabis or cannabis products from one licensee to another licensee must be recorded on a sales invoice or receipt. Sales invoices and receipts may be maintained electronically and must be filed in such manner as to be readily accessible for examination by employees of the licensing authorities or California Department of Tax and Fee Administration and shall not be commingled with invoices covering other commodities.

(b) Each sales invoice required by subdivision (a) shall include the name and address of the seller and shall include the following information:

(1) Name and address of the purchaser.

(2) Date of sale and invoice number.

(3) Kind, quantity, size, and capacity of packages of cannabis or cannabis products sold.

(4) The cost to the purchaser, together with any discount applied to the price as shown on the invoice.

(5) The place from which transport of the cannabis or cannabis product was made unless transport was made from the premises of the licensee.

(6) Any other information specified by the licensing authority.

Business and Professions Code § 26161.5

(Added by Stats. 2018, Ch. 583, Sec. 1. (AB 2402) Effective January 1, 2019.)

(a) A licensee shall not disclose a consumer's personal information to a third party, except to the extent necessary to allow responsibility for payment to be determined and payment to be made or if the consumer has consented to the licensee's disclosure of the personal information. This section does not prohibit the disclosure of nonpublic personal information to the State of California or a city, county, or city and county to perform official duties pursuant to this division or a local ordinance.

(b) A licensee shall not discriminate against a consumer, or deny a consumer a product or service, because the consumer has not provided consent, pursuant to subdivision (a), to authorize the licensee to disclose the consumer's nonpublic personal information to a third party not directly related to the transaction.

(c) For purposes of this section, "personal information" has the same meaning as defined in subdivision (d) of Section 1798.81.5 of the Civil Code.

(d) For the purposes of this section, "third party" does not include a contractor providing software services to a licensee for the purpose of conducting a transaction or verifying eligibility, provided that the contractor does not use or retain a consumer's personal information for any other purpose or share a consumer's personal information with any party other than the contracting licensee.

(e) This section provides greater protection to personal information than that provided by Section 1798.81.5 of the Civil Code, which does not apply to licensees under this division pursuant to paragraph (5) of subdivision (e) of Section 1798.81.5 of the Civil Code.

Business and Professions Code § 26162

(MAUCRSA, Effective June 27, 2017.)

(a) Information identifying the names of patients, their medical conditions, or the names of their primary caregivers received and contained in records kept by the office or licensing authorities for the purposes of administering this chapter are confidential and shall not be disclosed pursuant to the California Public Records Act (Chapter 3.5 (commencing with Section 6250) of Division 7 of Title 1 of the Government Code), except as necessary for authorized employees of the State of California or any city, county, or city and county to perform official duties pursuant to this chapter, or a local ordinance.

(b) Information identifying the names of patients, their medical conditions, or the names of their primary caregivers received and contained in records kept by the bureau for the purposes of administering this chapter shall be maintained in accordance with Chapter 1 (commencing with Section 123100) of Part 1 of Division 106 of the Health and Safety Code, Part 2.6 (commencing with Section 56) of Division 1 of the Civil Code, and other state and federal laws relating to confidential patient information.

(c) Nothing in this section precludes the following:

(1) Employees of the bureau or any licensing authorities notifying state or local agencies about information submitted to the agency that the employee suspects is falsified or fraudulent.

(2) Notifications from the bureau or any licensing authorities to state or local agencies about apparent violations of this chapter or applicable local ordinance.

(3) Verification of requests by state or local agencies to confirm licenses and certificates issued by the regulatory authorities or other state agency.

(4) Provision of information requested pursuant to a court order or subpoena issued by a court or an administrative agency or local governing body authorized by law to issue subpoenas.

(d) Information shall not be disclosed by any state or local agency beyond what is necessary to achieve the goals of a specific investigation, notification, or the parameters of a specific court order or subpoena.

Business and Professions Code § 26162.5

(Amended by Stats. 2018, Ch. 583, Sec. 2. (AB 2402) Effective January 1, 2019.)

(a) Identification cards issued pursuant to Section 11362.71 of the Health and Safety Code are hereby deemed "medical information" within the meaning of the Confidentiality of Medical Information Act (Part 2.6 (commencing with Section 56) of Division 1 of the Civil Code) and shall not be disclosed by a licensee except as (1) necessary for the State of California or any city, county, or city and county to perform official duties pursuant to this chapter, or a local ordinance, or (2) to a contractor providing software services to a licensee for the purpose of conducting a transaction or verifying eligibility, provided that the contractor does not use or retain medical information for any other purpose or share information with any party other than the contracting licensee.

(b) Information contained in a physician's recommendation issued in accordance with Article 25 (commencing with Section 2525) of Chapter 5 of Division 2 and received by a licensee, including, but not limited to, the name, address, or social security number of the patient, the patient's medical condition, or the name of the patient's primary caregiver is hereby deemed "medical information" within the meaning of the Confidentiality of Medical Information Act (Part 2.6 (commencing with Section 56) of Division 1 of the Civil Code) and shall not be disclosed by a licensee except as (1) necessary for the State of California or any city, county, or city and county to perform official duties pursuant to this chapter, or a local ordinance, or (2) to a contractor providing software services to a licensee for the purpose of conducting a transaction or verifying eligibility, provided that the contractor does not use or retain medical information for any other purpose or share information with any party other than the contracting licensee.

Chapter 18. License Fees

Business and Professions Code § 26180

(MAUCRSA, Effective June 27, 2017.)

Each licensing authority shall establish a scale of application, licensing, and renewal fees, based upon the cost of enforcing this division, as follows:

(a) Each licensing authority shall charge each licensee a licensure and renewal fee, as applicable. The licensure and renewal fee shall be calculated to cover the costs of administering this division. The licensure fee may vary depending upon the varying costs associated with administering the various regulatory requirements of this division as they relate to the nature and scope of the different licensure activities, including, but not limited to, the track and trace program required pursuant to Section 26067, but shall not exceed the reasonable regulatory costs to the licensing authority.

(b) The total fees assessed pursuant to this division shall be set at an amount that will fairly and proportionately generate sufficient total revenue to fully cover the total costs of administering this division.

(c) All license fees shall be set on a scaled basis by the licensing authority, dependent on the size of the business.

(d) The licensing authority shall deposit all fees collected in a fee account specific to that licensing authority, to be established in the Cannabis Control Fund. Moneys in the licensing authority fee accounts shall be used, upon appropriation by the Legislature, by the designated licensing authority for the administration of this division.

Business and Professions Code § 26180.5

(MAUCRSA, Effective June 27, 2017.)

No later than January 1, 2018, the Secretary of Business, Consumer Services, and Housing or his or her designee shall initiate work with the Legislature, the Department of Consumer Affairs, the Department of Food and Agriculture, the State Department of Public Health, and any other related departments to ensure that there is a safe and viable way to collect cash payments for taxes and fees related to the regulation of cannabis activity throughout the state.

Business and Professions Code § 26181

(MAUCRSA, Effective June 27, 2017.)

The State Water Resources Control Board, the Department of Fish and Wildlife, and other agencies may establish fees to cover the costs of their cannabis programs.

Chapter 19. Annual Reports; Performance Audit

Business and Professions Code § 26190

(MAUCRSA, Effective June 27, 2017.)

Beginning on March 1, 2023, and on or before March 1 of each year thereafter, each licensing authority shall prepare and submit to the Legislature an annual report on the authority's activities, in compliance with Section 9795 of the Government Code, and post the report on the authority's Internet Web site. The report shall include, but not be limited to, the following information for the previous fiscal year:

(a) The amount of funds allocated and spent by the licensing authority for cannabis licensing, enforcement, and administration.

(b) The number of state licenses issued, renewed, denied, suspended, and revoked, by state license category.

(c) The average time for processing state license applications, by state license category.

(d) The number of appeals from the denial of state licenses or other disciplinary actions taken by the licensing authority and the average time spent on these appeals.

(e) The number of complaints submitted by citizens or representatives of cities or counties regarding licensees, provided as both a comprehensive statewide number and by geographical region.

(f) The number and type of enforcement activities conducted by the licensing authorities and by local law enforcement agencies in conjunction with the licensing authorities.

(g) The number, type, and amount of penalties, fines, and other disciplinary actions taken by the licensing authorities.

(h) A detailed list of the petitions for regulatory relief or rulemaking changes received by the licensing authorities from licensees requesting modifications of the enforcement of rules under this division.

(i) (1) For the first publication of the reports, the licensing authorities shall provide a joint report to the Legislature regarding the state of the cannabis market in California. This report shall identify any statutory or regulatory changes necessary to ensure that the implementation of this division does not do any of the following:

> (A) Allow unreasonable restraints on competition by creation or maintenance of unlawful monopoly power.

> (B) Perpetuate the presence of an illegal market for cannabis or cannabis products in the state or out of the state.

> (C) Encourage underage use or adult abuse of cannabis or cannabis products, or illegal diversion of cannabis or cannabis products out of the state.

> (D) Result in an excessive concentration of licensees in a given city, county, or both.

> (E) Present an unreasonable risk of minors being exposed to cannabis or cannabis products.

> (F) Result in violations of any environmental protection laws.

(2) For purposes of this subdivision, "excessive concentration" means when the premises for a retail license, microbusiness license, or a license issued under Section 26070.5 is located in an area where either of the following conditions exist:

> (A) The ratio of licensees to population in a census tract or census division exceeds the ratio of licensees to population in the county in which the census tract or census division is located, unless reduction of that ratio would unduly limit the development of the legal market so as to perpetuate the illegal market for cannabis or cannabis products.

> (B) The ratio of retail licenses, microbusiness licenses, or licenses under Section 26070.5 to population in the census tract, division, or jurisdiction exceeds that allowable by local ordinance adopted under Section 26200.

Business and Professions Code § 26190.5

(MAUCRSA, Effective June 27, 2017.)

The bureau shall contract with the California Cannabis Research Program, known as the Center for Medicinal Cannabis Research, and formerly known as the California Marijuana Research Program, authorized pursuant to Section 11362.9 of the Health and Safety Code, to develop a study that identifies the impact that cannabis has on motor skills.

Business and Professions Code § 26191

(MAUCRSA, Effective June 27, 2017.)

(a) Commencing January 1, 2019, and by January 1 triennially thereafter, the Office of State Audits and Evaluations within the Department of Finance shall conduct a performance audit of the bureau's activities under this division, and shall report its findings to the bureau and the Legislature by July 1 of that same year. The report shall include, but not be limited to, the following:

> (1) The actual costs of the program.

> (2) The overall effectiveness of enforcement programs.

> (3) Any report submitted pursuant to this section shall be submitted in compliance with Section 9795 of the Government Code.

(b) The Legislature shall provide sufficient funds to the Department of Finance to conduct the triennial audit required by this section.

Chapter 20. Local Control

Business and Professions Code § 26200

(Amended by Stats. 2018, Ch. 749, Sec. 1. (AB 2020) Effective January 1, 2019. Note: This section was added on Nov. 8, 2016, by initiative Prop. 64.)

(a) (1) This division shall not be interpreted to supersede or limit the authority of a local jurisdiction to adopt and enforce local ordinances to regulate businesses licensed under this division, including, but not limited to, local zoning and land use requirements, business license requirements, and requirements related to reducing exposure to secondhand smoke, or to completely prohibit the establishment or operation of one or more types of businesses licensed under this division within the local jurisdiction.

> (2) This division shall not be interpreted to supersede or limit existing local authority for law enforcement activity, enforcement of local zoning requirements or local ordinances, or enforcement of local license, permit, or other authorization requirements.

(b) This division shall not be interpreted to require a licensing authority to undertake local law enforcement responsibilities, enforce local zoning requirements, or enforce local licensing, permitting, or other authorization requirements.

(c) A local jurisdiction shall notify the bureau upon revocation of any local license, permit, or authorization for a licensee to engage in commercial cannabis activity within the local jurisdiction. Within 10 days of notification, the bureau shall inform the relevant licensing authorities. Within 60 days of being so informed by the bureau, the relevant licensing authorities shall begin the process to determine whether a license issued to the licensee should be suspended or revoked pursuant to Chapter 3 (commencing with Section 26030).

(d) For facilities issued a state license that are located within the incorporated area of a city, the city shall have full power and authority to enforce this division and the regulations promulgated by the bureau or any licensing authority, if delegated by the state. Notwithstanding Sections 101375, 101400, and 101405 of the Health and Safety Code or any contract entered into pursuant thereto, or any other law, the city shall assume complete responsibility for any regulatory function pursuant to this division within the city limits that would otherwise be performed by the county or any county officer or employee, including a county health officer, without liability, cost, or expense to the county.

(e) (1) This division does not prohibit the issuance of a state temporary event license to a licensee authorizing onsite cannabis sales to, and consumption by, persons 21 years of age or older at a county fair event, district agricultural association event, or at another venue expressly approved by a local jurisdiction for the purpose of holding temporary events of this nature, provided that the activities, at a minimum, comply with all the following:

(A) The requirements of paragraphs (1) to (3), inclusive, of subdivision (g).

(B) All participants who are engaged in the onsite retail sale of cannabis or cannabis products at the event are licensed under this division to engage in that activity.

(C) The activities are otherwise consistent with regulations promulgated and adopted by the bureau governing state temporary event licenses.

(D) A state temporary event license shall only be issued in local jurisdictions that authorize such events.

(E) A licensee who submits an application for a state temporary event license shall, 60 days before the event, provide to the bureau a list of all licensees that will be providing onsite sales of cannabis or cannabis products at the event. If any changes occur in that list, the licensee shall provide the bureau with a final updated list to reflect those changes. A person shall not engage in the onsite retail sale of cannabis or cannabis products, or in any way participate in the event, who is not included in the list, including any updates, provided to the bureau.

(2) The bureau may impose a civil penalty on any person who violates this subdivision, or any regulations adopted by the bureau governing state temporary event licenses, in an amount up to three times the amount of the license fee for each violation, consistent with Sections 26018 and 26038.

(3) The bureau may require the event and all participants to cease operations without delay if in the opinion of the bureau or local law enforcement it is necessary to protect the immediate public health and safety of the people of the state. The bureau may also require the event organizer to immediately expel from the event any participant selling cannabis or cannabis products without a license from the bureau that authorizes the participant to sell cannabis or cannabis products. If the unlicensed participant does not leave the event, the bureau may require the event and all participants to cease operations immediately.

(4) The order by the bureau for the event to cease operations pursuant to paragraph (3) does not entitle the event organizer or any participant in the event to a hearing or an appeal of the decision. Chapter 3 (commencing with Section 490) of Division 1.5 and Chapter 4 (commencing with Section 26040) of this division shall not apply to the order by the bureau for the event to cease operations pursuant to paragraph (3).

(5) The smoking of cannabis or cannabis products at temporary events authorized pursuant to this subdivision is prohibited in locations where smoking is prohibited. For purposes of this section, "smoking" has the same meaning as defined in subdivision (c) of Section 22950.5.

(f) This division, or any regulations promulgated thereunder, shall not be deemed to limit the authority or remedies of a city, county, or city and county under any provision of law, including, but not limited to, Section 7 of Article XI of the California Constitution.

(g) Notwithstanding paragraph (1) of subdivision (a) of Section 11362.3 of the Health and Safety Code, a local jurisdiction may allow for the smoking, vaporizing, and ingesting of cannabis or cannabis products on the premises of a retailer or microbusiness licensed under this division if all of the following are met:

(1) Access to the area where cannabis consumption is allowed is restricted to persons 21 years of age or older.

(2) Cannabis consumption is not visible from any public place or nonage-restricted area.

(3) Sale or consumption of alcohol or tobacco is not allowed on the premises.

(h) This division shall not be interpreted to supersede Section 6404.5 of the Labor Code.

Business and Professions Code § 26201

(AUMA, Effective November 9, 2016.)

Any standards, requirements, and regulations regarding health and safety, environmental protection, testing, security, food safety, and worker protections established by the state shall be the minimum standards for all licensees under this division statewide. A local jurisdiction may establish additional standards, requirements, and regulations.

Business and Professions Code § 26202

(MAUCRSA, Effective June 27, 2017.)

(a) A local jurisdiction may enforce this division and the regulations promulgated by any licensing authority if delegated the power to do so by the licensing authority.

(b) A licensing authority shall implement the delegation of enforcement authority in subdivision (a) through an agreement between the licensing authority and the local jurisdiction to which enforcement authority is to be delegated.

Chapter 21. Funding

Business and Professions Code § 26210

(MAUCRSA, Effective June 27, 2017.)

(a) The Marijuana Control Fund, formerly known as the Medical Cannabis Regulation and Safety Act Fund and the Medical Marijuana Regulation and Safety Act Fund, is hereby renamed the Cannabis Control Fund. Notwithstanding Section 16305.7 of the Government Code, the fund shall include any interest and dividends earned on moneys in the fund.

(b) Upon the effective date of this section, whenever "Marijuana Control Fund," "Medical Cannabis Regulation and Safety Act Fund," or "Medical Marijuana Regulation and Safety Act Fund" appears in any statute, regulation, or contract, or in any other code, it shall be construed to refer to the Cannabis Control Fund.

(c) Any General Fund or special fund loan that was used to establish and support the regulatory activities of the state licensing entities pursuant to former Section 19351 shall be repaid by the initial proceeds from fees collected pursuant to this division or any rule or regulation adopted pursuant to this division, by January 1, 2022. Should the initial proceeds from fees not be sufficient to repay the loan, moneys from the Cannabis Fines and Penalties Account shall be made available to the bureau, by appropriation of the Legislature, to repay the loan.

(d) The Medical Cannabis Fines and Penalties Account established in former Section 19351 is hereby renamed the Cannabis Fines and Penalties Account.

Business and Professions Code § 26210.5

(MAUCRSA, Effective June 27, 2017.)

By July 1, 2018, the bureau, in coordination with the Department of General Services, shall establish an office to collect fees and taxes in the County of Humboldt, County of Trinity, or County of Mendocino in order to ensure the safe payment and collection of cash in those counties.

Business and Professions Code § 26211

(Amended by Stats. 2018, Ch. 599, Sec. 11. (AB 3261) Effective January 1, 2019. Note: This section was added on Nov. 8, 2016, by initiative Prop. 64.)

(a) Funds for the initial establishment and support of the regulatory activities under this division, including the public information program described in subdivision (c), and for the activities of the State Board of Equalization under Part 14.5 (commencing with Section 34010) of Division 2 of the Revenue and Taxation Code until July 1, 2017, or until the 2017 Budget Act is enacted, whichever occurs later, shall be advanced from the General Fund and shall be repaid by the initial proceeds from fees collected pursuant to this division, any rule or regulation adopted pursuant to this division, or revenues collected from the tax imposed by Sections 34011 and 34012 of the Revenue and Taxation Code, by January 1, 2025.

(1) Funds advanced pursuant to this subdivision shall be appropriated to the bureau, which shall distribute the moneys to the appropriate licensing authorities, as necessary to implement the provisions of this division, and to the State Board of Equalization, as necessary, to implement the provisions of Part 14.5 (commencing with Section 34010) of Division 2 of the Revenue and Taxation Code.

(2) Within 45 days of November 9, 2016, the date this section became operative:

(A) The Director of Finance shall determine an amount of the initial advance from the General Fund to the Cannabis Control Fund that does not exceed thirty million dollars ($30,000,000); and

(B) There shall be advanced a sum of five million dollars ($5,000,000) from the General Fund to the State Department of Health Care Services to provide for the public information program described in subdivision (c).

(b) Notwithstanding subdivision (a), the Legislature shall provide sufficient funds to the Cannabis Control Fund to support the activities of the bureau, state licensing authorities under this division, and the California Department of Tax and Fee Administration to support its activities under Part 14.5 (commencing with Section 34010) of Division 2 of the Revenue and Taxation Code. It is anticipated that this funding will be provided annually beginning on July 1, 2017.

(c) The State Department of Health Care Services shall establish and implement a public information program no later than September 1, 2017. This public information program shall, at a minimum, describe the provisions of the Control, Regulate and Tax Adult Use of Marijuana Act of 2016, the scientific basis for restricting access of cannabis and cannabis products to persons under the age of 21 years, describe the penalties for providing access to cannabis and cannabis products to persons under the age of 21 years, provide information regarding the dangers of driving a motor vehicle, boat, vessel, aircraft, or other vehicle used for transportation while impaired from cannabis use, the potential harms of using cannabis while pregnant or breastfeeding, and the potential harms of overusing cannabis or cannabis products.

Chapter 22. Cannabis Cooperative Associations

ARTICLE 1. DEFINITIONS

Business and Professions Code § 26220

(MAUCRSA, Effective June 27, 2017.)

Unless the context otherwise requires, the definitions in this article govern the construction of this chapter.

Business and Professions Code § 26220.1

(MAUCRSA, Effective June 27, 2017.)

"Association" means any cannabis cooperative that is organized pursuant to this chapter. An association shall be deemed incorporated pursuant to this chapter, or organized pursuant to this chapter and shall be deemed a cultivator of a cannabis product within the meaning of this chapter, if it is functioning under, or is subject to, the provisions of this chapter, irrespective of whether it was originally incorporated pursuant to those provisions or was incorporated under other provisions.

Business and Professions Code § 26220.2

(MAUCRSA, Effective June 27, 2017.)

"Member" includes members of associations without capital stock and holders of common stock in associations that are organized with shares of stock.

Business and Professions Code § 26220.3

(MAUCRSA, Effective June 27, 2017.)

"Cannabis product" includes any cannabis associated with a licensed cultivator.

ARTICLE 2. GENERAL PROVISIONS

Business and Professions Code § 26222

(MAUCRSA, Effective June 27, 2017.)

The purpose of this chapter is to do all of the following:

(a) Promote, foster, and encourage the intelligent and orderly marketing of cannabis product through cooperation.

(b) Eliminate speculation and waste.

(c) Make the distribution of cannabis product as direct as can be efficiently done.

(d) Stabilize the marketing of cannabis product.

(e) Satisfy the conditions of Section 26052.

Business and Professions Code § 26222.1

(MAUCRSA, Effective June 27, 2017.)

An exemption under law that applies to a cannabis product in the possession, or under the control, of the individual cultivator, shall apply similarly and completely to the cannabis product that is delivered by its cultivator members that are in the possession, or under the control, of the association.

Business and Professions Code § 26222.2

(MAUCRSA, Effective June 27, 2017.)

A person, firm, corporation, or association, that is hereafter organized or doing business in this state, may not use the word "cannabis cooperative" as part of its corporate name or other business name or title for producers' cooperative marketing activities, unless it has complied with this chapter.

Business and Professions Code § 26222.3

(MAUCRSA, Effective June 27, 2017.)

An association that is organized pursuant to this chapter shall not conspire in restraint of trade, or serve as an illegal monopoly, attempt to lessen competition, or to fix prices in violation of law of this state.

Business and Professions Code § 26222.4

(MAUCRSA, Effective June 27, 2017.)

The marketing contracts and agreements between an association that is organized pursuant to this chapter and its members and any agreements authorized in this chapter shall not result in restraint of trade, or violation of law of this state.

Business and Professions Code § 26222.5

(MAUCRSA, Effective June 27, 2017.)

The General Corporation Law (Division 1 (commencing with Section 100) of Title 1 of the Corporations Code) applies to each association that is organized pursuant to this chapter, except where those provisions are in conflict with or inconsistent with the express provisions of this chapter. For the purpose of associations organized without shares of stock, the members shall be deemed to be "shareholders" as the term is used in the General Corporation Law.

Business and Professions Code § 26222.6

(MAUCRSA, Effective June 27, 2017.)

(a) Except as provided in subdivision (c), Chapter 7 (commencing with Section 1500) of Title 10 of Part 3 of the Code of Civil Procedure does not apply to a proprietary interest in an association organized in accordance with this chapter. A proprietary interest that would otherwise escheat to the state pursuant to Chapter 7 (commencing with Section 1500) of Title 10 of Part 3 of the Code of Civil Procedure shall instead become the property of the association.

(b) Notwithstanding subdivision (a), no proprietary interest shall become the property of the association under this section unless all of the following requirements are satisfied:

(1) At least 60 days' prior notice of the proposed transfer of the proprietary interest to the association is given to the affected member by first-class or certified mail to the last address of the member shown on the association's records, and by publication in a newspaper of general circulation in the county in which the member last resided as shown on the association's records. Notice given pursuant to this paragraph constitutes actual notice.

(2) No written notice objecting to the transfer is received by the association from the affected member or, if the member is deceased, from the member's heirs or the executor or executrix of the estate, prior to the date of the proposed transfer.

(c) "Proprietary interest" means and includes any membership, membership certificate, membership share, share certificate, or equity or dividend certificate of any class representing a proprietary interest in, and issued by, the association together with all accrued and unpaid earnings, dividends, and patronage distributions relating thereto.

ARTICLE 3. PURPOSES

Business and Professions Code § 26223

(MAUCRSA, Effective June 27, 2017.)

(a) Three or more natural persons, who are engaged in the cultivation of any cannabis product, may form an association pursuant to this chapter for the purpose of engaging in any activity in connection with any of the following:

(1) The cultivation, marketing, or selling of the cannabis products of its members.

(2) The growing, harvesting, curing, drying, trimming, packing, grading, storing, or handling of any product of its members.

(3) The manufacturing, selling, or supplying to its members of machinery, equipment, or supplies.

(4) The financing of the activities that are specified by this section.

(b) Members of a cannabis cooperative shall be disclosed to the licensing authority before the application is processed.

(c) Members of a cannabis cooperative formed pursuant to this chapter shall be limited to cultivators who only hold a single Type 1 or Type 2 license.

(d) Collectively, members of a cannabis cooperative shall not grow more than four acres of total canopy size of cultivation throughout the state during the period that the respective licensees are valid.

(e) No member of a cooperative formed pursuant to this section shall be licensed to operate a cannabis business in another state or country.

ARTICLE 4. ARTICLES OF INCORPORATION

Business and Professions Code § 26224

(MAUCRSA, Effective June 27, 2017.)

The articles of incorporation of an association shall show that the signers of the articles of incorporation are engaged in the cultivation of cannabis products, and that they propose to incorporate an association pursuant to this chapter, and shall state all of the following:

(a) The name of the association.

(b) The purposes for which it is formed.

(c) The city, county, or city and county where the principal office for the transaction of business of the association is to be located.

(d) The number of directors of the association, which shall not be less than three, and the names and addresses of the persons who are to serve as first directors. If it is desired that the first directors shall serve for terms of different lengths, the term for which each person so named to serve shall also be stated.

(e) If organized without shares of stock, whether the voting power and the property rights and interest of each member are equal or unequal. If voting power and property rights and interest of each member are unequal, the general rule or rules that are applicable to all members by which the voting power and the property rights and interests, respectively, of each member may be and are determined and fixed shall also be stated.

(f) (1) If organized with shares of stock, the number of shares that may be issued and if the shares are to have a par value, the par value of each share, and the aggregate par value of all shares. If the shares are to be without par value, it shall be so stated.

> (2) If the shares of stock are to be classified, a description of the classes of shares and a statement of the number of shares of each kind or class and the nature and extent of the preferences, rights, privileges, and restrictions that are granted to or imposed upon the holders of the respective classes of stock. Except as to the matters and things so stated, no distinction shall exist between the classes of stock or the holders of them. One class of stock shall always be known as common stock, and voting power may be restricted to holders of common stock.

Business and Professions Code § 26224.1

(MAUCRSA, Effective June 27, 2017.)

Articles of incorporation shall be signed, acknowledged, and filed in the manner that is prescribed by the general laws of this state for domestic corporations.

Business and Professions Code § 26224.2

(MAUCRSA, Effective June 27, 2017.)

The articles of incorporation of any association may be amended in the manner and for the purposes which are authorized by the General Corporation Law, Division 1 (commencing with Section 100) of Title 1 of the Corporations Code.

ARTICLE 5. BYLAWS

Business and Professions Code § 26225

(MAUCRSA, Effective June 27, 2017.)

Each association shall, within 30 days after its incorporation, adopt for its government and management, a code of bylaws, consistent with this chapter. The vote or written assent of shareholders or members that hold at least a majority of the voting power is necessary to adopt the bylaws and is effectual to repeal or amend a bylaw, or to adopt an additional bylaw. The power to repeal and amend the bylaws, and adopt new bylaws, may, by a similar vote, or similar written assent, be delegated to the board of directors, which authority may, by a similar vote, or similar written assent, be revoked.

Business and Professions Code § 26225.1

(MAUCRSA, Effective June 27, 2017.)

The bylaws may prescribe the time, place, and manner of calling and conducting its meetings. Meetings of members or stockholders shall be held at the place as provided in the bylaws, or, if no provision is made, in the city, county, or city and county where the principal place of business is located at a place designated by the board of directors. Meetings of the board of directors may be held at any place within or without the state that is fixed by a quorum of the board of directors unless otherwise provided in the articles of incorporation or bylaws.

Business and Professions Code § 26225.2

(MAUCRSA, Effective June 27, 2017.)

The bylaws may prescribe the number of stockholders, directors, or members that constitutes a quorum.

Business and Professions Code § 26225.3

(MAUCRSA, Effective June 27, 2017.)

The bylaws may prescribe the following:

(a) The right of members or stockholders to vote by proxy or by mail or both, and the conditions, manner, form, and effects of those votes.

(b) The right of members or stockholders to cumulate their votes and the prohibition, if any, of cumulative voting.

Business and Professions Code § 26225.4

(MAUCRSA, Effective June 27, 2017.)

(a) The bylaws may prescribe the qualifications, compensation, duties, and term of office of directors and officers and the time of their election.

(b) The number of directors set forth in the articles of incorporation shall be either a fixed number or a variable number. If a fixed number, it shall not be less than three, and if a variable number, the stated minimum shall not be less than three and the stated maximum shall not be greater than two times the stated minimum minus one.

(c) The number of directors may also be set forth in the bylaws either as a fixed number or as a variable number subject to the same limitations as in subdivision (b). After shares have been issued or members have been admitted, any adoption or amendment of the bylaw provision shall be approved by the outstanding shares as provided in Section 152 of the Corporations Code.

(d) In the event of an inconsistency between an article provision referred to in subdivision (b) and a bylaw provision referred to in subdivision (c), the provision more recently adopted or amended shall prevail.

(e) If a variable number of directors is set forth in the articles of incorporation or the bylaws, the exact number of directors shall be fixed, within the limits specified, by approval of the board of directors or the shareholders as provided in Section 153 of the Corporations Code in the manner designated in the bylaws.

Business and Professions Code § 26225.5

(MAUCRSA, Effective June 27, 2017.)

The bylaws may prescribe penalties for violations of the bylaws.

Business and Professions Code § 26225.6

(MAUCRSA, Effective June 27, 2017.)

The bylaws may prescribe the amount of entrance, organization, and membership fees, if any, the manner and method of collection of the fees, and the purposes for which they may be used.

Business and Professions Code § 26225.7

(MAUCRSA, Effective June 27, 2017.)

The bylaws may prescribe the amount that each member or stockholder shall be required to pay annually, or from time to time, if at all, to carry on the business of the association, the charge, if any, to be paid by each member or stockholder for services that are rendered by the association to him, the time of payment and the manner of collection, and the marketing contract between the association and its members or stockholders that every member or stockholder may be required to sign.

Business and Professions Code § 26225.8

(MAUCRSA, Effective June 27, 2017.)

The bylaws may prescribe the amount of dividends, if any, that may be declared on the stock or membership capital. To the extent that dividends are payable out of the excess of association income over association expenses attributable to business transacted with or for members, dividends shall not exceed 8 percent per annum.

Business and Professions Code § 26225.9

(MAUCRSA, Effective June 27, 2017.)

The bylaws may prescribe any of the following:

(a) The number and qualification of members or stockholders of the association and the conditions precedent to membership or ownership of common stock.

(b) The method, time, and manner of permitting members to withdraw or the holders of common stock to transfer their stock.

(c) The manner of assignment and transfer of the interest of members, and of the shares of common stock.

(d) The conditions under which, and time when, membership of a member shall cease.

(e) The automatic suspension of the rights of a member when he or she ceases to be eligible to membership in the association.

(f) The mode, manner, and effect of the expulsion of a member.

Business and Professions Code § 26225.95

(MAUCRSA, Effective June 27, 2017.)

(a) The bylaws may prescribe any of the following:

(1) The manner of determining the value of a member's interest and provision for its purchase by the association upon the death or withdrawal of a member or upon the expulsion of a member or forfeiture of his or her membership, or at the option of the association, the purchase at a price fixed by conclusive appraisal by the board of directors.

(2) The conditions and terms for the repurchase by the association from its stockholders of their stock upon their disqualification as stockholders.

(b) If a member is expelled and the bylaws do not provide any procedure or penalty for expulsion, the board of directors shall equitably and conclusively appraise his or her property interest in the association and shall fix the amount of his or her property interest in money, which shall be paid to him or her within one year after such expulsion.

ARTICLE 6. DIRECTORS AND MANAGEMENT

Business and Professions Code § 26226

(MAUCRSA, Effective June 27, 2017.)

The affairs of the association shall be managed by a board of not less than three directors who are elected by the members or stockholders.

Business and Professions Code § 26226.1

(MAUCRSA, Effective June 27, 2017.)

The bylaws may provide that the territory in which the association has members shall be divided into districts and that directors shall be elected from the several districts. If the bylaws divides the territory into districts for the election of directors, the bylaws shall specify the number of directors to be elected by each district and the manner and method of reapportioning the directors and of redistricting the territory covered by the association.

Business and Professions Code § 26226.2

(MAUCRSA, Effective June 27, 2017.)

The bylaws may provide that primary elections shall be held to nominate directors. If the bylaws provide that the territory in which the association has members shall be divided into districts, the bylaws may also provide that the results of the primary elections in the various districts shall be final and shall be ratified at the annual meeting of the association.

Business and Professions Code § 26226.3

(MAUCRSA, Effective June 27, 2017.)

The bylaws may provide that the territory in which the association has members shall be divided into districts, and that the directors shall be elected by representatives or advisers, who themselves have been elected by the members or stockholders from the several territorial districts. If the bylaws divide the territory into districts for the election of representatives or advisers who elect the directors, the bylaws shall specify the number of representatives or advisers to be elected by each district and the manner and method of reapportioning the representatives or advisers and of redistricting the territory that is covered by the association.

Business and Professions Code § 26226.4

(MAUCRSA, Effective June 27, 2017.)

The bylaws may provide that one or more directors may be chosen by a public official or commission or by the other directors selected by the members. The director shall represent primarily the interest of the general public in the association. The director shall have the same powers and rights as other directors. These directors shall not number more than one-fifth of the entire number of directors.

Business and Professions Code § 26226.5

(MAUCRSA, Effective June 27, 2017.)

The bylaws may provide for an executive committee and may allot to the committee all the functions and powers of the board of directors, subject to the general direction and control of the board.

Business and Professions Code § 26226.6

(MAUCRSA, Effective June 27, 2017.)

An association may provide a fair remuneration for the time that is actually spent by its officers and directors in its service and for the service of the members of its executive committee.

Business and Professions Code § 26226.7

(MAUCRSA, Effective June 27, 2017.)

If a vacancy on the board of directors occurs, except by expiration of term, the remaining members of the board, by a majority vote, shall fill the vacancy, unless the bylaws provide for an election of directors by districts. If the bylaws provide for an election of directors by districts, the vacancy shall be filled either by the election of a director from the district in which the vacancy occurs or by the board of directors calling a special meeting of the members or stockholders in that district to fill the vacancy.

Business and Professions Code § 26226.8

(MAUCRSA, Effective June 27, 2017.)

(a) The directors shall elect a president, one or more vice presidents, a secretary, a treasurer, and such other officers as may be prescribed by the bylaws. Any two or more offices, except those of president and secretary, may be held by the same person.

(b) The treasurer may be a bank or a depository and, as such, shall not be considered as an officer, but as a function of the board of directors. In such case, the secretary shall perform the usual accounting duties of the treasurer, except that the funds shall be deposited only as and where authorized by the board of directors.

Business and Professions Code § 26226.9

(MAUCRSA, Effective June 27, 2017.)

(a) A member may bring charges against an officer or director by filing them in writing with the secretary of the association, together with a petition that is signed by 5 percent of the members, which requests the removal of the officer or director in question. The removal shall be voted upon at the next regular or special meeting of the association and, by a vote of a majority of the members, the association may remove the officer or director and fill the vacancy. The director or officer, against whom the charges have been brought, shall be informed in writing of the charges previous to the meeting and shall have an opportunity at the meeting to be heard in person or by counsel and to present witnesses. The person bringing the charges against him or her shall have the same opportunity.

(b) If the bylaws provide for election of directors by districts with primary elections in each district, the petition for removal of a director shall be signed by 20 percent of the members that reside in the district from which the director was elected. The board of directors shall call a special meeting of the members who reside in that district to consider the removal of the director. By a vote of the majority of the members of that district at the special meeting, the director in question shall be removed from office.

ARTICLE 7. POWERS

Business and Professions Code § 26227

(MAUCRSA, Effective June 27, 2017.)

An association may engage in any activity in connection with the growing, harvesting, curing, drying, trimming, packing, grading, storing, or handling of any cannabis product that is produced or delivered to it by its members; or any activity in connection with the purchase, hiring, or use by its members of supplies, machinery, or equipment, or in the financing of any such activities; or in any one or more of the activities that are specified in this section with a valid license.

Business and Professions Code § 26227.1

(MAUCRSA, Effective June 27, 2017.)

An association may borrow without limitation as to the amount of corporate indebtedness or liability and may make advances to members.

Business and Professions Code § 26227.2

(MAUCRSA, Effective June 27, 2017.)

An association may act as the agent or representative of any member or members in any of the activities specified in Section 26226.2 or 26226.3.

Business and Professions Code § 26227.3

(MAUCRSA, Effective June 27, 2017.)

An association may purchase or otherwise acquire, hold, own, and exercise all rights of ownership in, sell, transfer, pledge, or guarantee the payment of dividends or interest on, or the retirement or redemption of, shares of the capital stock or bonds of an association that is engaged in any related activity or in the growing, harvesting, curing, drying, trimming, packing, grading, storing, or handling of a cannabis product that is handled by the association.

Business and Professions Code § 26227.4

(MAUCRSA, Effective June 27, 2017.)

An association may establish reserves and invest the funds of the reserves in bonds or in other property as may be provided in the bylaws.

Business and Professions Code § 26227.5

(MAUCRSA, Effective June 27, 2017.)

An association may buy, hold, and exercise all privileges of ownership over such real or personal property as may be necessary or convenient for the conduct and operation of, or incidental to, the business of the association.

Business and Professions Code § 26227.6

(MAUCRSA, Effective June 27, 2017.)

An association may levy assessments in the manner and in the amount as may be provided in its bylaws.

Business and Professions Code § 26227.7

(MAUCRSA, Effective June 27, 2017.)

An association may do any of the following anywhere:

(a) That which is what is necessary, suitable, or proper for the accomplishment of a purpose, or the attainment of an object, that is enumerated in this article.

(b) That which is conducive to, or expedient for, the interest or benefit of the association.

(c) Contract accordingly.

(d) Exercise and possess all powers, rights, and privileges that are necessary or incidental to the purposes for which the association is organized or to the activities in which it is engaged.

(e) Exercise any other rights, powers, and privileges that are granted by the laws of this state to ordinary corporations, except such as are inconsistent with the express provisions of this chapter.

Business and Professions Code § 26227.75

(MAUCRSA, Effective June 27, 2017.)

An association may use or employ any of its facilities for any purpose, provided the proceeds that arise from such use and employment shall go to reduce the cost of operation for its members. The cannabis products that are handled for, or the services, machinery, equipment, or supplies or facilities that are furnished to, nonmembers shall not, however, exceed in value the cannabis products that are handled for, or the services, merchandise, or facilities that are supplied to, members during the same period.

Business and Professions Code § 26227.8

(MAUCRSA, Effective June 27, 2017.)

(a) An association may organize, form, operate, own, control, have an interest in, own stock of, or be a member of any other association, with or without capital stock, that is engaged in growing, harvesting, curing, drying, trimming, packing, grading, storing, or handling of any cannabis product that is handled by the association, or the byproducts of the cannabis product.

(b) Any two or more associations that are organized pursuant to this section may be merged into one constituent association or consolidated into a new association. The merger or consolidation shall be made in the manner that is prescribed by the general laws of the state that cover domestic corporations.

Business and Professions Code § 26227.9

(Amended by AB 133, Effective September 16, 2017.)

(a) Any association may, upon resolution adopted by its board of directors, enter into all necessary and proper contracts and agreements and make all necessary and proper stipulations and arrangements with another cannabis cooperative or association that is formed in this state for the cannabis cooperative and more economical carrying on of its business or any part of its business.

(b) Any two or more associations may, by agreement between them, unite in employing and using, or may separately employ and use, the same personnel, methods, means, and agencies for carrying on and conducting their respective business.

ARTICLE 8. FINANCIAL PROVISIONS

Business and Professions Code § 26228

(MAUCRSA, Effective June 27, 2017.)

An association is not subject in any manner to the terms of the Corporate Securities Law (Division 1 (commencing with Section 25000) of Title 4 of the Corporations Code), and any association may issue its membership certificates or stock or other securities as provided in this chapter without the necessity of any qualification under that law.

Business and Professions Code § 26228.1

(MAUCRSA, Effective June 27, 2017.)

If an association issues nonpar value stock, the issuance of the stock shall be governed by the terms of all general laws that cover the issuance of nonpar value stock in domestic corporations.

Business and Professions Code § 26228.2

(MAUCRSA, Effective June 27, 2017.)

If an association with preferred shares of stock purchases the stock or any property, or any interest in any property of any person, it may discharge the obligations that are so incurred, wholly or in part, by exchanging for the acquired interest, shares of its preferred stock to an amount that at par value would equal the fair market value of the stock or interest so purchased, as determined by the board of directors. In that case, the transfer to the association of the stock or interest that is purchased is equivalent to payment in cash for the shares of stock that are issued.

Business and Professions Code § 26228.3

(MAUCRSA, Effective June 27, 2017.)

The board of directors of every association shall cause to be sent to the members of the association not later than 120 days after the close of the fiscal or calendar year an annual report of the operations of the association, unless the report is expressly dispensed with in the bylaws. If required by the bylaws, interim reports of the operations of the association for the three-month, six-month, or nine-month periods of the current fiscal year of the association shall be furnished to the members of the association. Such annual report and any such interim reports shall include a balance sheet as of such closing date. Such financial statement shall be prepared from, and be in accordance with, the books. It shall be prepared in a form that is sanctioned by sound accounting practice for the association or approved by a duly certified public accountant or a public accountant.

ARTICLE 9. MEMBERS

Business and Professions Code § 26229

(MAUCRSA, Effective June 27, 2017.)

Under the terms and conditions that are prescribed in the bylaws adopted by it, an association may admit as members or issue common stock only to persons engaged in the cultivation of a cannabis product that is to be handled by or through the association.

Business and Professions Code § 26229.1

(MAUCRSA, Effective June 27, 2017.)

If a member of a nonstock association is other than a natural person, the member may be represented by any individual, associate, officer, or manager or member of it, who is duly authorized in writing.

Business and Professions Code § 26229.2

(MAUCRSA, Effective June 27, 2017.)

Any association may become a member or stockholder of any other association.

Business and Professions Code § 26229.3

(MAUCRSA, Effective June 27, 2017.)

If a member of an association that is established without shares of stock has paid his membership fee in full, he or she shall receive a certificate of membership.

Business and Professions Code § 26229.4

(MAUCRSA, Effective June 27, 2017.)

An association shall not issue a certificate for stock to a member until it has been fully paid for. The promissory notes of the members may be accepted by the association as full or partial payment. The association shall hold the stock as security for the payment of the note, but the retention as security does not affect the member's right to vote.

Business and Professions Code § 26229.5

(MAUCRSA, Effective June 27, 2017.)

An association, in its bylaws, may limit the amount of common stock that any member may own.

Business and Professions Code § 26229.6

(MAUCRSA, Effective June 27, 2017.)

The bylaws shall prohibit the transfer of the common stock or membership certificates of the associations to a person that is not qualified to be a shareholder or member as specified in this chapter. These restrictions shall be printed upon every certificate of stock or membership that is subject to them.

Business and Professions Code § 26229.7

(MAUCRSA, Effective June 27, 2017.)

The association may, at any time, as specified in the bylaws, except when the debts of the association exceed 50 percent of its assets, buy in or purchase its common stock at the book value of the common stock, as conclusively determined by the board of directors, and pay for it in cash within one year thereafter.

Business and Professions Code § 26229.8

(MAUCRSA, Effective June 27, 2017.)

A member or stockholder is not liable for the debts of the association to an amount that exceeds the sum that remains unpaid on his membership fee or his subscription to the capital stock, including any unpaid balance on any promissory note that is given in payment of the membership fee or the subscription to the capital stock.

ARTICLE 10. MARKETING CONTRACTS

Business and Professions Code § 26230

(MAUCRSA, Effective June 27, 2017.)

The association and its members may make and execute marketing contracts that require the members to sell, for any period of time, but not over 15 years, all or a specified part of a cannabis product exclusively to or through the association, or a facility that is created by the association. If the members contract a sale to the association, title to the cannabis product passes absolutely and unreservedly, except for recorded liens, to the association upon delivery or at another specified time that is expressly and definitely agreed in the contract.

Business and Professions Code § 26230.1

(MAUCRSA, Effective June 27, 2017.)

Notwithstanding any provisions of the Civil Code, a contract that is entered into by a member or stockholder of an association that provides for the delivery to the association of a cannabis product that is produced or acquired by the member or stockholder may be specifically enforced by the association to secure the delivery to it of the cannabis product.

Business and Professions Code § 26230.2

(MAUCRSA, Effective June 27, 2017.)

The bylaws or a marketing contract may fix, as liquidated damages, specific sums to be paid by the member or stockholder to the association upon the breach by him or her of any provision of the marketing contract regarding the sale or delivery or withholding of a cannabis product and may provide that the member will pay all costs, premiums for bonds, expenses, and fees, if any action is brought upon the contract by the association. These provisions are valid and enforceable in the courts of this state. The clauses that provide for liquidated damages are enforceable as such and shall not be regarded as penalties.

Business and Professions Code § 26230.3

(MAUCRSA, Effective June 27, 2017.)

If there is a breach or threatened breach of a marketing contract by a member, the association shall be entitled to an injunction to prevent the further breach of the contract and to a decree of specific performance of the contract. Pending the adjudication of the action and upon filing a verified complaint that shows the breach or threatened breach, and upon filing a sufficient bond, the association shall be entitled to a temporary restraining order and preliminary injunction against the member.

ARTICLE 11. REORGANIZATION OF CORPORATIONS ORGANIZED PURSUANT TO OTHER LAWS

Business and Professions Code § 26231

(Amended by Stats. 2018, Ch. 92, Sec. 32. (SB 1289) Effective January 1, 2019.)

A corporation that is organized or existing pursuant to any law except Part 12 (commencing with Section 14550) of Division 3 of Title 1 of the Corporations Code may be brought under the provisions of this chapter by amending its articles of incorporation, in the manner that is prescribed by the general corporation laws, to conform to this chapter. If a corporation amends its articles of incorporation to conform to this chapter, it shall be deemed to be organized and existing pursuant to, and entitled to the benefit of, and subject to this chapter for all purposes and as fully as though it had been originally organized pursuant to this chapter.

Business and Professions Code § 26231.1

(MAUCRSA, Effective June 27, 2017.)

Articles of incorporation shall be deemed to conform to this chapter within the meaning of Section 26231 if it clearly appears from the articles of incorporation that the corporation desires to be subject to, and to be organized, exist, and function pursuant to this chapter.

Business and Professions Code § 26231.2

(MAUCRSA, Effective June 27, 2017.)

If the amended articles conform, as provided in Section 26231.1, provisions in the articles of incorporation that appeared in the original articles or some previous amended articles, are ineffective if, and to the extent that, they are inapplicable to, or inconsistent with, this chapter.

Chapter 23. The California Cannabis Equity Act

Business and Professions Code § 26240

(Added by Stats. 2018, Ch. 794, Sec. 3. (SB 1294) Effective January 1, 2019.)

For purposes of this chapter, the following definitions apply:

(a) "Eligible local jurisdiction" means a local jurisdiction that has adopted or operates a local equity program.

(b) "Local equity applicant" means an applicant who has submitted, or will submit, an application to a local jurisdiction to engage in commercial cannabis activity within the jurisdictional boundaries of that jurisdiction and who meets the requirements of that jurisdiction's local equity program.

(c) "Local equity licensee" means a person who has obtained a license from a local jurisdiction to engage in commercial cannabis activity within the jurisdictional boundaries of that jurisdiction and who meets the requirements of that jurisdiction's local equity program.

(d) "Local equity program" means a program adopted or operated by a local jurisdiction that focuses on inclusion and support of individuals and communities in California's cannabis industry who are linked to populations or neighborhoods that were negatively or disproportionately impacted by cannabis criminalization. Local equity programs may include, but are not limited to, the following types of services:

    (1) Small business support services offering technical assistance to those persons from economically

disadvantaged communities that experience high rates of poverty or communities most harmed by cannabis prohibition, determined by historically high rates of arrests or convictions for cannabis law violations.

(2) Tiered fees or fee waivers for cannabis-related permits and licenses.

(3) Assistance in paying state regulatory and licensing fees.

(4) Assistance securing business locations prior to or during the application process.

(5) Assistance securing capital investments.

(6) Assistance with regulatory compliance.

(7) Assistance in recruitment, training, and retention of a qualified and diverse workforce, including transitional workers.

(e) "Transitional worker" means a person who, at the time of starting employment at the business premises, resides in a ZIP Code or census track area with higher than average unemployment, crime, or child death rates, and faces at least one of the following barriers to employment: (1) is homeless;   (2) is a custodial single parent; (3) is receiving public assistance; (4) lacks a GED or high school diploma; (5) has a criminal record or other involvement with the criminal justice system; (6) suffers from chronic unemployment; (7) is emancipated from the foster care system; (8) is a veteran; or (9) is over 65 years of age and is financially compromised.

Business and Professions Code § 26242

(Added by Stats. 2018, Ch. 794, Sec. 3. (SB 1294) Effective January 1, 2019.)

(a) The bureau may, upon request by a local jurisdiction, provide technical assistance to a local equity program that helps local equity applicants or local equity licensees. When determining whether to provide technical assistance, the bureau shall make individual determinations based on the reasonableness of the request and available resources.

(b) "Technical assistance" includes providing training and educational sessions regarding state cannabis licensing processes and requirements to equity applicants or equity licensees that are coordinated with the local equity program.

Business and Professions Code § 26244

(Added by Stats. 2018, Ch. 794, Sec. 3. (SB 1294) Effective January 1, 2019.)

(a) (1) Upon appropriation of funds by the Legislature, an eligible local jurisdiction may, in the form and manner prescribed by the bureau, submit an application to the bureau for a grant to assist local equity applicants and local equity licensees through that local jurisdiction's equity program.

(2) The bureau shall review an application based on the following factors:

(A) Whether the local jurisdiction is an eligible local jurisdiction.

(B) Whether the local jurisdiction has adopted or operates a local equity program.

(C) Whether the local jurisdiction has identified a local equity applicant or a local equity licensee that the local jurisdiction could assist, as defined in subdivision (b), through use of the grant funding.

(D) Whether the local jurisdiction has demonstrated the ability to provide, or created a plan to provide, the services identified in subdivision (b).

(E) The number of existing and potential local equity applicants and local equity licensees in the local jurisdiction.

(F) Any additional relevant and reasonable criteria the bureau deems necessary.

(3) The bureau shall grant funding to an eligible local jurisdiction based on its review of the factors in paragraph (2). If applications for funding are greater than the amount appropriated for this grant program, the bureau shall prorate the funding as necessary.

(b) An eligible local jurisdiction that receives a grant pursuant to subdivision (a) shall use grant funds to assist local equity applicants and local equity licensees in that local jurisdiction to gain entry to, and to successfully operate in, the state's regulated cannabis marketplace. For purposes of this subdivision, "assist" includes, but is not limited to, any of the following methods:

(1) To provide a loan or a grant to a local equity applicant or local equity licensee to assist the applicant or licensee with startup and ongoing costs. For purposes of this paragraph, "startup and ongoing costs" include, but are not limited to, rent, leases, local and state application and licensing fees, regulatory adherence, testing of cannabis, equipment, capital improvements, and training and retention of a qualified and diverse workforce.

(2) To support local equity program efforts to provide sources of capital to local equity applicants and local equity licensees.

(3) To provide direct technical assistance to local equity applicants and local equity licensees.

(4) To assist in the administration of local equity programs.

(c) An eligible local jurisdiction that receives a grant pursuant to subdivision (a) shall, on or before January 1 of the year following receipt of the grant and annually thereafter for each year that grant funds are expended, submit an annual report to the bureau that includes all of the following information:

(1) How the local jurisdiction disbursed grant funds.

(2) How the local jurisdiction identified local equity applicants or local equity licensees, including how the local jurisdiction determines who qualifies as a local equity applicant or local equity licensee.

(3) The number of local equity applicants and local equity licensees that were served by the grant funds.

(4) Demographic data on equity applicants, equity licensees, and other applicants and licensees in the jurisdiction, including, but not limited to, race, ethnicity, gender, sexual orientation, income level, prior convictions, and veteran status. This information will be consolidated and reported without the individual's identifying information.

(d) An eligible local jurisdiction that receives a grant pursuant to this section shall use no more than 10 percent of the state grant for administration, including employing staff or hiring consultants to administer grants and the program.

Business and Professions Code § 26246

(Added by Stats. 2018, Ch. 794, Sec. 3. (SB 1294) Effective January 1, 2019.)

To facilitate greater equity in business ownership and employment in the cannabis market, the bureau shall do all of the following:

(a) Serve as a point of contact for local equity programs.

(b) On or before July 1, 2019, publish approved local equity ordinances and model local equity ordinances created by advocacy groups and experts to the bureau's Internet Web site. Advocacy groups and experts may include, but are not limited to, minority business owners and entrepreneurs, organizations with expertise in addressing barriers to employment and licensure for low-income communities or persons with prior arrests or convictions, and unions representing cannabis workers.

(c) To the extent feasible, coordinate with the relevant local jurisdictions to carry out the responsibilities described in this section.

Business and Professions Code § 26248

(Added by Stats. 2018, Ch. 794, Sec. 3. (SB 1294) Effective January 1, 2019.)

(a) On or before July 1, 2020, the bureau shall submit a report to the Legislature regarding the progress of local equity programs that have received funding pursuant to Section 26244.

(b) The report shall include, but is not limited to, the following information:

(1) The cities, counties, and cities and counties that have enacted local equity programs.

(2) The number of local equity applicants and general applicants applying for and receiving licenses in the jurisdictions that received grants.

(3) Information collected pursuant to subdivision (c) of Section 26244.

(c) The bureau shall post the report required by this section on its Internet Web site.

(d) The report required by this section shall be submitted in compliance with Section 9795 of the Government Code, and shall apply notwithstanding Section 10231.5 of the Government Code.

Business and Professions Code § 26250

(Added by Stats. 2018, Ch. 794, Sec. 3. (SB 1294) Effective January 1, 2019.)

The provisions of this chapter are severable. If any provision of this chapter or its application is held invalid, that invalidity shall not affect other provisions or applications that can be given effect without the invalid provision or application.

II. Civil Code Sections

Civil Code § 56.06

(Amended by Stats. 2018, Ch. 583, Sec. 3. (AB 2402) Effective January 1, 2019.)

(a) Any business organized for the purpose of maintaining medical information, as defined in subdivision (j) of Section 56.05, in order to make the information available to an individual or to a provider of health care at the request of the individual or a provider of health care, for purposes of allowing the individual to manage his or her information, or for the diagnosis and treatment of the individual, shall be deemed to be a provider of health care subject to the requirements of this part. However, this section shall not be construed to make a business specified in this subdivision a provider of health care for purposes of any law other than this part, including laws that specifically incorporate by reference the definitions of this part.

(b) Any business that offers software or hardware to consumers, including a mobile application or other related device that is designed to maintain medical information, as defined in subdivision (j) of Section 56.05, in order to make the information available to an individual or a provider of health care at the request of the individual or a provider of health care, for purposes of allowing the individual to manage his or her information, or for the diagnosis, treatment, or management of a medical condition of the individual, shall be deemed to be a provider of health care subject to the requirements of this part. However, this section shall not be construed to make a business specified in this subdivision a provider of health care for purposes of any law other than this part, including laws that specifically incorporate by reference the definitions of this part.

(c) Any business that is licensed pursuant to Division 10 (commencing with Section 26000) of the Business and Professions Code that is authorized to receive or receives identification cards issued pursuant to Section 11362.71 of the Health and Safety Code or information contained in a physician's recommendation issued in accordance with Article 25 (commencing with Section 2525) of Chapter 5 of Division 2 of the Business and Professions Code shall be deemed to be a provider of health care subject to the requirements of this part. However, this section shall not be construed to make a business specified in this subdivision a provider of health care for purposes of any law other than this part, including laws that specifically incorporate by reference the definitions of this part.

(d) Any business described in this section shall maintain the same standards of confidentiality required of a provider of health care with respect to medical information disclosed to the business.

(e) Any business described in this section is subject to the penalties for improper use and disclosure of medical information prescribed in this part.

Civil Code § 1550.5

(Amended by Stats. 2018, Ch. 92, Sec. 35. (SB 1289) Effective January 1, 2019.)

(a) The Legislature finds and declares all of the following:

(1) The Compassionate Use Act of 1996, an initiative measure enacted by the approval of Proposition 215 at the November 5, 1996, statewide general election, authorized the use of marijuana for medical purposes in this state.

(2) The Legislature passed the Medical Cannabis Regulation and Safety Act, formerly Chapter 3.5 (commencing with Section 19300) of Division 8 of the Business and Professions Code, to regulate and license medical cannabis in the state.

(3) The Control, Regulate and Tax Adult Use of Marijuana Act (AUMA), an initiative measure enacted by the approval of Proposition 64 at the November 8, 2016, statewide general election, authorized the consumption of nonmedical marijuana by persons over 21 years of age and provided for the licensure and regulation of certain commercial nonmedical marijuana activities in this state.

(4) The Legislature passed the Medicinal and Adult-Use Cannabis Regulation and Safety Act (Division 10 (commencing with Section 26000) of the Business and Professions Code) to consolidate the licensure and regulation of certain commercial activities with respect to medicinal cannabis and nonmedical marijuana, now known as adult-use cannabis.

(b) Notwithstanding any law, including, but not limited to, Sections 1550, 1667, and 1668 and federal law, commercial activity relating to medicinal cannabis or adult-use cannabis conducted in compliance with California law and any applicable local standards, requirements, and regulations shall be deemed to be all of the following:

(1) A lawful object of a contract.

(2) Not contrary to, an express provision of law, any policy of express law, or good morals.

(3) Not against public policy.

III. Evidence Code Sections

Evidence Code § 956

(Amended by AB 1159, Effective January 1, 2018.)

(a) There is no privilege under this article if the services of the lawyer were sought or obtained to enable or aid anyone to commit or plan to commit a crime or a fraud.

(b) This exception to the privilege granted by this article shall not apply to legal services rendered in compliance with state and local laws on medicinal cannabis or adult-use cannabis, and confidential communications provided for the purpose of rendering those services are confidential communications between client and lawyer, as defined in Section 952, provided the lawyer also advises the client on conflicts with respect to federal law.

IV. Fish and Game Code Sections

Fish and Game Code § 1602

(MAUCRSA, Effective June 27, 2017.)

(a) An entity shall not substantially divert or obstruct the natural flow of, or substantially change or use any material from the bed, channel, or bank of, any river, stream, or lake, or deposit or dispose of debris, waste, or other material containing crumbled, flaked, or ground pavement where it may pass into any river, stream, or lake, unless all of the following occur:

(1) The department receives written notification regarding the activity in the manner prescribed by the department. The notification shall include, but is not limited to, all of the following:

(A) A detailed description of the project's location and a map.

(B) The name, if any, of the river, stream, or lake affected.

(C) A detailed project description, including, but not limited to, construction plans and drawings, if applicable.

(D) A copy of any document prepared pursuant to Division 13 (commencing with Section 21000) of the Public Resources Code.

(E) A copy of any other applicable local, state, or federal permit or agreement already issued.

(F) Any other information required by the department.

(2) The department determines the notification is complete in accordance with Chapter 4.5 (commencing with Section 65920) of Division 1 of Title 7 of the Government Code, irrespective of whether the activity constitutes a development project for the purposes of that chapter.

(3) The entity pays the applicable fees, pursuant to Section 1609.

(4) One of the following occurs:

(A) (i) The department informs the entity, in writing, that the activity will not substantially adversely affect an existing fish or wildlife resource, and that the entity may commence the activity without an agreement, if the entity conducts the activity as described in the notification, including any measures in the notification that are intended to protect fish and wildlife resources.

(ii) Each region of the department shall log the notifications of activities where no agreement is required. The log shall list the date the notification was received by the department, a brief description of the proposed activity, and the location of the activity. Each item shall remain on the log for one year. Upon written request by any person, a regional office shall send the log to that person monthly for one year. A request made pursuant to this clause may be renewed annually.

(B) The department determines that the activity may substantially adversely affect an existing fish or wildlife resource and issues a final agreement to the entity that includes reasonable measures necessary to protect the resource, and the entity conducts the activity in accordance with the agreement.

(C) A panel of arbitrators issues a final agreement to the entity in accordance with subdivision (b) of Section 1603, and the entity conducts the activity in accordance with the agreement.

(D) The department does not issue a draft agreement to the entity within 60 days from the date notification is complete, and the entity conducts the activity as described in the notification, including any measures in the notification that are intended to protect fish and wildlife resources.

(b) (1) If an activity involves the routine maintenance and operation of water supply, drainage, flood control, or waste treatment and disposal facilities, notice to and agreement with the department shall not be required after the initial notification and agreement, unless the department determines either of the following:

(A) The work described in the agreement has substantially changed.

(B) Conditions affecting fish and wildlife resources have substantially changed, and those resources are adversely affected by the activity conducted under the agreement.

(2) This subdivision applies only if notice to, and agreement with, the department was attained prior to January 1, 1977, and the department has been provided a copy of the agreement or other proof of the existence of the agreement that satisfies the department, if requested.

(c) Notwithstanding subdivision (a), the department is not required to determine whether the notification is complete or otherwise process the notification until the department has received the applicable fees.

(d) (1) Notwithstanding subdivision (a), an entity shall not be required to obtain an agreement with the department pursuant to this chapter for activities authorized by a license or renewed license for cannabis cultivation issued by the Department of Food and Agriculture for the term of the license or renewed license if all of the following occur:

(A) The entity submits all of the following to the department:

(i) The written notification described in paragraph (1) of subdivision (a).

(ii) A copy of the license or renewed license for cannabis cultivation issued by the Department of Food and Agriculture that includes the requirements specified in subdivisions (d), (e), and (f) of Section 19332.2 of the Business and Professions Code.

(iii) The fee specified in paragraph (3) of subdivision (a).

(B) The department determines in its sole discretion that compliance with the requirements specified in Section 26060.1of the Business and Professions Code that are included in the license will adequately protect existing fish and wildlife resources that may be substantially adversely affected by the cultivation without the need for additional measures that the department would include in a draft streambed alteration agreement in accordance with Section 1603.

(C) The department notifies the entity in writing that the exemption applies to the cultivation authorized by the license or renewed license.

(2) The department shall notify the entity in writing whether the exemption in paragraph (1) applies to the cultivation authorized by the license or renewed license within 60 days from the date that the notification is complete and the fee has been paid.

(3) If an entity receives an exemption pursuant to this subdivision and fails to comply with any of the requirements described in Section 26060.1 of the Business and Professions Code that are included in the license, the failure shall constitute a violation under this section, and the department shall notify the Department of Food and Agriculture of any enforcement action taken.

(e) It is unlawful for any entity to violate this chapter.

Fish and Game Code § 1617

(MAUCRSA, Effective June 27, 2017.)

(a) The department may adopt general agreements for the cultivation of cannabis.

(b) Any general agreement adopted by the department subsequent to adoption of regulations under this section shall be in lieu of an individual agreement described in subparagraph (B) of paragraph (4) of subdivision (a) of Section 1602.

(c) Subparagraph (D) of paragraph (4) of subdivision (a) of Section 1602 and all other time periods to process agreements specified in this chapter do not apply to the issuance of a general agreement adopted by the department pursuant to this section.

(d) Any general agreement issued by the department pursuant to this section is a final agreement and is not subject to Section 1603 or 1604.

(e) The department shall charge a fee for a general agreement adopted by the department under this section in accordance with Section 1609.

(f) If the department adopts or amends a general agreement under this section, it shall do so as an emergency regulation. An emergency regulation adopted pursuant to this section, and any amendments to it, shall be adopted by the department in accordance with Chapter 3.5 (commencing with Section 11340) of Part 1 of Division 3 of Title 2 of the Government Code. The adoption of these regulations is an emergency and shall be considered by the Office of Administrative Law as necessary for the immediate preservation of the public peace, health and safety, and general welfare. Notwithstanding Chapter 3.5 (commencing with Section 11340) of Part 1 of Division 3 of Title 2 of the Government Code, an emergency regulation adopted by the department, or any amendments to it made by the department pursuant to this section, shall stay in effect until revised by the department.

(g) Regulations adopted pursuant to this section, and any amendment thereto, shall not be subject to Division 13 (commencing with Section 21000) of the Public Resources Code.

Fish and Game Code § 2080

(Amended by Statute, Effective January 1, 1995.)

No person shall import into this state, export out of this state, or take, possess, purchase, or sell within this state, any species, or any part or product thereof, that the commission determines to be an endangered species or a threatened species, or attempt any of those acts, except as otherwise provided in this chapter, the Native Plant Protection Act (Chapter 10 (commencing with Section 1900) of this code), or the California Desert Native Plants Act (Division 23 (commencing with Section 80001) of the Food and Agricultural Code).

Fish and Game Code § 3513

(Amended by Statute, Effective 1977.)

It is unlawful to take or possess any migratory nongame bird as designated in the Migratory Bird Treaty Act or any part of such migratory nongame bird except as provided by rules and regulations adopted by the Secretary of the Interior under provisions of the Migratory Treaty Act.

Fish and Game Code § 5650

(Amended by Statute, Effective January 1, 2008.)

(a) Except as provided in subdivision (b), it is unlawful to deposit in, permit to pass into, or place where it can pass into the waters of this state any of the following:

(1) Any petroleum, acid, coal or oil tar, lampblack, aniline, asphalt, bitumen, or residuary product of petroleum, or carbonaceous material or substance.

(2) Any refuse, liquid or solid, from any refinery, gas house, tannery, distillery, chemical works, mill, or factory of any kind.

(3) Any sawdust, shavings, slabs, or edgings.

(4) Any factory refuse, lime, or slag.

(5) Any cocculus indicus.

(6) Any substance or material deleterious to fish, plant life, mammals, or bird life.

(b) This section does not apply to a discharge or a release that is expressly authorized pursuant to, and in compliance with, the terms and conditions of a waste discharge requirement pursuant to Section 13263 of the Water Code or a waiver issued pursuant to subdivision (a) of Section 13269 of the Water Code issued by the State Water Resources Control Board or a regional water quality control board after a public hearing, or that is expressly authorized pursuant to, and in compliance with, the terms and conditions of a federal permit for which the State Water Resources Control Board or a regional water quality control board has, after a public hearing, issued a water quality certification pursuant to Section 13160 of the Water Code. This section does not confer additional authority on the State Water Resources Control Board, a regional water quality control board, or any other entity.

(c) It shall be an affirmative defense to a violation of this section if the defendant proves, by a preponderance of the evidence, all of the following:

(1) The defendant complied with all applicable state and federal laws and regulations requiring that the discharge or release be reported to a government agency.

(2) The substance or material did not enter the waters of the state or a storm drain that discharges into the waters of the state.

(3) The defendant took reasonable and appropriate measures to effectively mitigate the discharge or release in a timely manner.

(d) The affirmative defense in subdivision (c) does not apply and may not be raised in an action for civil penalties or injunctive relief pursuant to Section 5650.1.

(e) The affirmative defense in subdivision (c) does not apply and may not be raised by any defendant who has on two prior occasions in the preceding five years, in any combination within the same county in which the case is prosecuted, either pleaded nolo contendere, been convicted of a violation of this section, or suffered a judgment for a violation of this section or Section 5650.1. This subdivision shall apply only to cases filed on or after January 1, 1997.

(f) The affirmative defense in subdivision (c) does not apply and may not be raised by the defendant in any case in which a district attorney, city attorney, or Attorney General alleges, and the court finds, that the defendant acted willfully.

Fish and Game Code § 5652

(Amended by Statute, Effective January 1, 2008.)

(a) It is unlawful to deposit, permit to pass into, or place where it can pass into the waters of the state, or to abandon, dispose of, or throw away, within 150 feet of the high water mark of the waters of the state, any cans, bottles, garbage, motor vehicle or parts thereof, rubbish, litter, refuse, waste, debris, or the viscera or carcass of any dead mammal, or the carcass of any dead bird.

(b) The abandonment of any motor vehicle in any manner that violates this section shall constitute a rebuttable presumption affecting the burden of producing evidence that the last registered owner of record, not having complied with Section 5900 of the Vehicle Code, is responsible for that abandonment and is thereby liable for the cost of removal and disposition of the vehicle. This section prohibits the placement of a vehicle body on privately owned property along a streambank by the property owner or tenant for the purpose of preventing erosion of the streambank.

(c) This section does not apply to a refuse disposal site that is authorized by the appropriate local agency having jurisdiction or to the depositing of those materials in a container from which the materials are routinely removed to a legal point of disposal.

(d) This section shall be enforced by all law enforcement officers of this state.

Fish and Game Code § 12025.2

(MCRSA- SB-837, Effective June 27, 2016.)

The director or his or her designee may issue a complaint to any person or entity in accordance with Section 1055 of the Water Code alleging a violation for which liability may be imposed under Section 1052 or 1847 of the Water Code that harms fish and wildlife resources. The complaint is subject to the substantive and procedural requirements set forth in Section 1055 of the Water Code, and the department shall be designated a party to any proceeding before the State Water Resources Control Board regarding a complaint filed pursuant to this section.

Fish and Game Code § 12029

(MCRSA- SB 837, Effective June 27, 2016.)

(a) The Legislature finds and declares all of the following:

(1) The environmental impacts associated with cannabis cultivation have increased, and unlawful water diversions for cannabis irrigation have a detrimental effect on fish and wildlife and their habitat, which are held

in trust by the state for the benefit of the people of the state.

(2) The remediation of existing cannabis cultivation sites is often complex and the permitting of these sites requires greater department staff time and personnel expenditures. The potential for cannabis cultivation sites to significantly impact the state's fish and wildlife resources requires immediate action on the part of the department's lake and streambed alteration permitting staff.

(b) In order to address unlawful water diversions and other violations of the Fish and Game Code associated with cannabis cultivation, the department shall establish the watershed enforcement program to facilitate the investigation, enforcement, and prosecution of these offenses.

(c) The department, in coordination with the State Water Resources Control Board and the Department of Food and Agriculture, shall establish a permanent multiagency task force to address the environmental impacts of cannabis cultivation. The multiagency task force, to the extent feasible and subject to available resources, shall expand its enforcement efforts on a statewide level to ensure the reduction of adverse impacts of cannabis cultivation on fish and wildlife and their habitats throughout the state.

(d) In order to facilitate the remediation and permitting of cannabis cultivation sites, the department may adopt regulations to enhance the fees on any entity subject to Section 1602 for cannabis cultivation sites that require remediation. The fee schedule established pursuant to this subdivision shall not exceed the fee limits in Section 1609.

V. Food and Agricultural Code Sections

Food and Agricultural Code § 37104

(MAUCRSA, Effective June 27, 2017.)

Notwithstanding Section 26001 of the Business and Professions Code, butter purchased from a licensed milk products plant or retail location that is subsequently infused or mixed with medicinal or adult-use cannabis at the premises or location that is not subject to licensing as a milk product plant is exempt from the provisions of this division.

Food and Agricultural Code § 52452

(MCRSA- SB 837, Effective June 27, 2016.)

(a) Except as otherwise provided in Section 52454, each container of agricultural seed that is for sale or sold within this state for sowing purposes shall bear upon it or have attached to it in a conspicuous place a plainly written or printed label or tag in the English language that includes all of the following information:

(1) The commonly accepted name of the kind, kind and variety, or kind and type of each agricultural seed component in excess of 5 percent of the whole, and the percentage by weight of each. If the aggregate of agricultural seed components, each present in an amount not exceeding 5 percent of the whole, exceeds 10 percent of the whole, each component in excess of 1 percent of the whole shall be named together with the percentage by weight of each. If more than one component is required to be named, the names of all components shall be shown in letters of the same type and size.

(2) The lot number or other lot identification.

(3) The percentage by weight of all weed seeds.

(4) The name and approximate number of each kind of restricted noxious weed seed per pound.

(5) The percentage by weight of any agricultural seed except that which is required to be named on the label.

(6) The percentage by weight of inert matter. If a percentage by weight is required to be shown by any provision of this section, that percentage shall be exclusive of any substance that is added to the seed as a coating and shown on the label as such.

(7) For each agricultural seed in excess of 5 percent of the whole, stated in accordance with paragraph (1), the percentage of germination exclusive of hard seed, the percentage of hard seed, if present, and the calendar month and year the test was completed to determine the percentages. Following the statement of those percentages, the additional statement "total germination and hard seed" may be stated.

(8) The name and address of the person who labeled the seed or of the person who sells the seed within this state.

(b) Subdivision (a) does not apply in the following instances:

(1) The sale is an occasional sale of seed grain by the producer of the seed grain to his or her neighbor for use by the purchaser within the county of production.

(2) Any cannabis seed, as defined in subdivision (f) of Section 19300.5 of the Business and Professions Code, sold or offered for sale in the state.

(c) All determinations of noxious weed seeds are subject to tolerances and methods of determination prescribed in the regulations that are adopted pursuant to this chapter.

(d) For purposes of this section, "neighbor" means a person who lives in close proximity, not to exceed three miles, to another.

Food and Agricultural Code § 54036

(MAUCRSA, Effective June 27, 2017.)

A person, firm, corporation, or association, that is hereafter organized or doing business in this state, may not use the word "cooperative" as part of its corporate name or other business name or title for producers' cooperative marketing activities, unless it has complied with this chapter or is otherwise authorized by Chapter 22 (commencing with Section 26220) of Division 10 of the Business and Professions Code.

Food and Agricultural Code § 55403

(Amended by Stats. 1997, Ch. 696, Sec. 2. Effective January 1, 1998.)

"Farm product" includes every agricultural, horticultural, viticultural, or vegetable product of the soil, honey and beeswax, oilseeds, poultry, poultry product, livestock product, and livestock for immediate slaughter. It does not include timber or any timber product, milk or any milk product, any aquacultural product, or cattle sold to any person who is bonded under the federal Packers and Stockyards Act, 1921 (7 U.S.C. Sec. 181, et seq.).

Food and Agricultural Code § 55407

(Amended by Stats. 1967, Ch. 807.)

"Processor" means any person that is engaged in the business of processing or manufacturing any farm product, that solicits, buys, contracts to buy, or otherwise takes title to, or possession or control of, any farm product from the producer of the farm product for the purpose of processing or manufacturing it and selling, reselling, or redelivering it in any dried, canned, extracted, fermented, distilled, frozen, eviscerated, or other preserved or processed form. It does not, however, include any retail merchant that has a fixed or established place of business in this state and does not sell at wholesale any farm product which is processed or manufactured by him.

Food and Agricultural Code § 55408

(Enacted by Stats. 1967, Ch. 15.)

"Producer" means any person that is engaged in the business of growing or producing any farm product.

DIVISION 20. PROCESSORS, STORES, DEALERS, AND DISTRIBUTORS OF AGRICULTURAL PRODUCTS

Chapter 6. Processors of Farm Products

ARTICLE 9. PRODUCER'S LIEN

Food and Agricultural Code § 55631

(Amended by Stats. 2016, Ch. 86, Sec. 144. (SB 1171) Effective January 1, 2017.)

(a) Every producer of any farm product that sells any product that is grown by him or her to any processor under contract, express or implied, in addition to all other rights and remedies that are provided for by law, has a lien upon that product and upon all processed or manufactured forms of that farm product for his or her labor, care, and expense in growing and harvesting that product. The lien shall be to the extent of the agreed price, if any, for that product so sold. If there is no agreed price or a method for determining the price that is agreed upon, the extent of the lien is the value of the farm product as of the date of the delivery. Any portion of that product or the processed or manufactured forms of that product, in excess of the amount necessary to satisfy the total amount owed to producers under contract, shall be free and clear of that lien.

(b) Every producer of a flower, agricultural, or vegetable seed that sells seed that is grown by him or her, when the seed was purchased or supplied by the grower and not supplied by the dealer or an independent third party who paid for the seed, to any seed dealer under contract, express or implied, in addition to all other rights and remedies that are provided for by law, has a lien upon that product and upon all processed or manufactured forms of that product for his or her labor, care, and expense in growing and harvesting that product. The lien shall be to the extent of the agreed price, if any, for that product so sold. If there is no agreed price or a method for determining the price that is agreed upon, the extent of the lien is the value of that product as of the date of the delivery. Any portion of that product or the processed or manufactured forms of that product, in excess of the amount necessary to satisfy the total amount owed to producers under contract, shall be free and clear of that lien.

Food and Agricultural Code § 55631.5

(Added by Stats. 1986, Ch. 1109, Sec. 2.)

Notwithstanding Section 55461, a nonprofit cooperative association acting as a producer bargaining association may assert producer's lien rights for, or on behalf of, its members.

Food and Agricultural Code § 55632

(Enacted by Stats. 1967, Ch. 15.)

This producer's lien attaches on all of such delivered product from the date of delivery of such farm product or any portion of it by a producer to any processor.

Food and Agricultural Code § 55633

(Amended by Stats. 1979, Ch. 969.)

The producer's lien is a preferred lien prior in dignity to all other liens, claims, or encumbrances except the following:

(a) Labor claims for wages and salaries for personal services which are rendered by any person to any processor in connection with such processing business after the delivery of any such product for processing.

(b) The lien of a warehouseman as provided by Division 7 (commencing with Section 7101) of the Uniform Commercial Code.

Food and Agricultural Code § 55634

(Amended by Stats. 1986, Ch. 1109, Sec. 3.)

Every lien which is provided for in this article is on every farm product and any processed form of the farm product which is in the possession of the processor without segregation of the product. For purposes of this chapter, any and all farm products or processed form of farm products deposited by a processor with a warehouse, whether or not warehouse receipts are given as security to a lender, shall be considered as being in the possession of the processor and subject to the lien.

Food and Agricultural Code § 55635

(Amended by Stats. 1986, Ch. 1109, Sec. 4.)

The lien of a producer, unless sooner released by payment or by security which is given for the payment as provided in this article, attaches from the date of delivery of the product, or if there is a series of deliveries, it attaches from the date of the last delivery.

Food and Agricultural Code § 55636

(Amended by Stats. 1979, Ch. 969.)

If suit is commenced by any such producer to enforce any lien, such lien shall remain in effect until one of the following occurs:

(a) The payment of the agreed price or the value of such product.

(b) Deposit of the amount of the lien or claims with the clerk of the court in which any such action is pending.

(c) The final determination of such court proceeding.

Food and Agricultural Code § 55637

(Enacted by Stats. 1967, Ch. 15.)

Any lien on any product or processed product may, however, be released, to the extent the value of the claim upon such product is secured, by a surety bond or a cash deposit or other security given as provided in this article. Any producer may also release any lien which is possessed by him upon payment being made to him for the agreed or reasonable value of the product which is so sold and delivered, or upon arrangements being made for such payment which are satisfactory to the producer.

Food and Agricultural Code § 55638

(Amended by Stats. 1979, Ch. 969.)

It is unlawful for any processor to remove, from this state or beyond his ownership or control, any farm product which is delivered to him, or any processed form of the farm product, to which any of the liens provided for in this chapter has attached, except for any of such product or processed product as may be in excess of a quantity on hand which is of a value that is sufficient to satisfy all existing liens. Furthermore, this section shall not prohibit the sale of any farm product or processed form of the product to which such a lien has attached, so long as the total proceeds of the sale are used to satisfy obligations to producers which are secured by a lien established pursuant to this chapter.

Food and Agricultural Code § 55638.5

(Added by Stats. 1986, Ch. 1109, Sec. 5.)

The director, within 15 days of the filing of a verified complaint by a producer, shall investigate any charge that a purchaser of a farm product to which a lien has attached has removed any farm product, or any processed form of a farm product, in violation of Section 55638.

Food and Agricultural Code § 55639

(Enacted by Stats. 1967, Ch. 15.)

Any processor that desires to secure a release of any or all of such liens on any product or processed product may do so in any of the following ways:

(a) By paying the agreed or actual value of any farm product which is purchased by such processor within 20 days from the date of delivery of the farm product unless the date of payment is otherwise agreed upon in writing or such payment is secured other than by lien.

(b) By depositing with the director a surety bond which is executed by such processor as principal and by a surety company which is qualified and authorized to do business in this state as surety in an amount which equals the current market value of the product or processed product which is intended by such processor to be sold or otherwise disposed of, as such value may appear by the sworn statement of such processor in accordance with quotations from the federal-state market news service or other evidence which is satisfactory to the director. The bond shall be conditioned that if the processor fails to pay up to the amount of such bond the lawful claims of all producers whose liens have been released by the bond, within 35 days after date of the bond, the surety shall be liable to and shall pay to the state on behalf of such claimants all such lawful claims as may be covered by the amount of the bond, together with costs of suit if an action is filed on the bond.

(c) By depositing with the director a cash sum in lawful money of the United States which is expressly set apart by an instrument in writing that is signed by the processor for the purpose of guaranteeing to the extent of such sum, payment of all existing claims of producers whose liens are released by the deposit, within 35 days from the date of such deposit. The director shall be named in such instrument as trustee to carry out the purpose and intent of the instrument.

(d) By designating, setting apart, and depositing in a public warehouse a quantity of any processed farm products and indorsing over to the director and delivering to him the warehouse receipt for such products for the purpose of guaranteeing to the extent of the value of such deposit, payment within 35 days from the date of such deposit, all existing claims of producers and labor claimants whose liens are released by it.

(e) By securing a release from the director after payment in full for such farm product.

Food and Agricultural Code § 55640

(Enacted by Stats. 1967, Ch. 15.)

If all lawful claims of the producers have been paid in accordance with this article by any processor, any product which is released by such action may be sold, transported, or otherwise disposed of.

Food and Agricultural Code § 55641

(Enacted by Stats. 1967, Ch. 15.)

If a bond, cash deposit, or security is given to the director by any processor as provided in this article, such processor may sell, transport, or otherwise dispose of the product or processed product to the value which is represented by such security as such value may appear by the sworn statement of such processor in accordance with quotations from the federal-state market news service or other evidence satisfactory to the director.

Food and Agricultural Code § 55642

(Enacted by Stats. 1967, Ch. 15.)

The director may accept such bond, if approved by him, and such other security. If the claims or any of them are not paid in accordance with the condition of such security, the director may, on proof being made to his satisfaction of the amounts which are due such claimants, pay all such unpaid claims insofar as possible out of the deposit money, or proceeds from any sale made by him of any securities or processed products which are given as security.

Food and Agricultural Code § 55643

(Enacted by Stats. 1967, Ch. 15.)

If a bond has been given as security, the director shall notify the principal and surety of any default on the part of the principal under the bond, and make demand for payment on behalf of such unpaid claimants. If payment is not made, the director may take any legal action he may deem necessary to enforce payment under such bond.

Food and Agricultural Code § 55644

(Enacted by Stats. 1967, Ch. 15.)

If the director has received warehouse receipts for any processed product as security, and the processor giving them has failed to pay the claims in accordance with the terms of such security, the director may sell such security with or without notice, and in such manner as he shall determine.

Food and Agricultural Code § 55645

(Enacted by Stats. 1967, Ch. 15.)

All claims in relation to payment shall have equal standing and payment shall be prorated if necessary among the claimants.

Food and Agricultural Code § 55646

(Enacted by Stats. 1967, Ch. 15.)

This article does not prevent the director if in his opinion the rights of all of the claimants are fully protected, as provided for in this article, from issuing a certificate in the name of the department and signed by him which releases any specific lot or quantity of any product or processed product from all liens of the claimants. No security which is held by the director shall, however, be released by him to any processor unless and until it is made to appear to his satisfaction that all claims have been fully paid, or that the rights of all of the claimants are fully protected.

A fee of five dollars ($5) shall be paid to the director for issuing any certificate or release which is provided for in this section.

Food and Agricultural Code § 55647

(Enacted by Stats. 1967, Ch. 15.)

This article does not impair or affect the right of any claimant that possesses a lien to maintain a personal action to recover such debt against a processor, either in an action to foreclose his lien or in a separate action. He is not required to state in his affidavit to procure an attachment that his demand is not secured by a lien.

Food and Agricultural Code § 55648

(Enacted by Stats. 1967, Ch. 15.)

The judgment, if any, which is obtained by the plaintiff in such personal action, or personal judgment which is obtained in such lien action, does not impair or merge any lien right or claim which is held by such plaintiff. Any money, however, which is collected on the judgment shall be credited on the amount of such lien or claims in any action which is brought to enforce the lien or in any action which is filed pursuant to this article by the director.

Food and Agricultural Code § 55649

(Amended by Stats. 1982, Ch. 517, Sec. 234.)

In an action that is filed by any such lien claimant, the defendant processor may file with the court in which the action is pending a surety bond in an amount that is sufficient to cover the demand of plaintiff's complaint, including the costs, whereupon the court may order the release of a portion or the whole of any product or processed product upon which the lien of plaintiff has attached.

Food and Agricultural Code § 55650

(Enacted by Stats. 1967, Ch. 15.)

Such processor may also, on motion duly noticed, introduce evidence to the court before whom any such action is pending to the effect that he has sufficient security or money on deposit with the director to protect the lien or other rights of plaintiff. If he does so, the court may order the release of a portion or the whole of such product upon which the lien of plaintiff is attached, and deny to plaintiff any recovery in such action. Such action by the court does not, however, prejudice any other rights or remedies which are possessed by the plaintiff.

Food and Agricultural Code § 55651

(Enacted by Stats. 1967, Ch. 15.)

The plaintiff in an action which is brought to foreclose any of the liens which are provided for in this article may, in a proper case, and upon proper allegations, secure an injunction against the processor in accordance with the provisions of Chapter 3 (commencing with Section 525), Title 7, Part 2 of the Code of Civil Procedure to restrain the doing of any acts on the part of such processor which are designed to or which would, in effect, remove any processed product in his possession or under his control and upon which valid liens exist, beyond the process of the court, to plaintiff's injury.

Food and Agricultural Code § 55652

(Enacted by Stats. 1967, Ch. 15.)

If in a court proceeding to foreclose such lien, it is found and determined by the court that there is no cash, bond, or other deposit placed with the director as security for the payment of any of the lien claims as set out in the complaint, the judgment of foreclosure shall be against a sufficient quantity in value of such farm product or processed product in the possession or under the control of the defendant processor, as may be necessary to satisfy such claim or render judgment and declare forfeited any bond which is deposited in the court by such processor to secure the lawful claims of the plaintiff as determined by the court.

Food and Agricultural Code § 55653

(Enacted by Stats. 1967, Ch. 15.)

All actions filed by the director or producers against any processor for the foreclosure of the liens or other security which are provided for in this article may be consolidated by the court and all persons that are necessary to a determination of such action may be made parties to such actions. Any judgment which is rendered shall determine the lawfulness of the amount of each claim as represented by the pleadings.

DIVISION 24. INDUSTRIAL HEMP

Food and Agricultural Code § 81000

(AUMA, Operative January 1, 2017, pursuant to Section 81010.)

For purposes of this division, the following terms have the following meanings:

(a) "Board" means the Industrial Hemp Advisory Board.

(b) "Commissioner" means the county agricultural commissioner.

(c) "Established agricultural research institution" means any institution that is either:

> (1) a public or private institution or organization that maintains land or facilities for agricultural research, including colleges, universities, agricultural research centers, and conservation research centers; or

> (2) an institution of higher education (as defined in Section 1001 of the Higher Education Act of 1965 (20 USC. 1001)) that grows, cultivates or manufactures industrial hemp for purposes of research conducted under an agricultural pilot program or other agricultural or academic research.

(d) "Industrial hemp" has the same meaning as the term is defined in Section 11018.5 of the Health and Safety Code.

(e) "Secretary" means the Secretary of Food and Agriculture.

(f) "Seed breeder" means an individual or public or private institution or organization that is registered with the commissioner to develop seed cultivars intended for sale or research.

(g) "Seed cultivar" means a variety of industrial hemp.

(h) "Seed development plan" means a strategy devised by a seed breeder, or applicant seed breeder, detailing his or her plam1ed approach to growing and developing a new seed cultivar for industrial hemp.

Food and Agriculture Code § 81001

(Added by Stats. 2013, Ch. 398, Sec. 4. (SB 566) Effective January 1, 2014. Section operative January 1, 2017, pursuant to Section 81010.)

(a) There is in the department an Industrial Hemp Advisory Board. The board shall consist of 11 members, appointed by the secretary as follows:

> (1) Three of the board members shall be growers of industrial hemp that are registered pursuant to the provisions of this division. In the case of forming the initial board, and if the registration program established pursuant to this division has not yet been implemented, these board members shall be those who intend to register as growers of industrial hemp. A member of the board who is a grower of industrial hemp, or who intends to register as a grower of industrial hemp, shall be a representative of at least one of the following functions:

>> (A) Seed production.

>> (B) Seed condition.

>> (C) Marketing.

>> (D) Seed utilization.

(2) Two of the board members shall be members of an established agricultural research institution.

(3) One member of the board shall be a representative as provided by the California State Sheriffs' Association and approved by the secretary.

(4) One member of the board shall be a county agricultural commissioner.

(5) One member of the board shall be a representative of the Hemp Industries Association or its successor industry association.

(6) One member of the board shall be a representative of industrial hemp product processors or manufacturers.

(7) One member of the board shall be a representative of businesses that sell industrial hemp products.

(8) One member of the board shall be a member of the public.

(b) It is hereby declared, as a matter of legislative determination, that growers and representatives of industrial hemp product manufacturers and businesses appointed to the board pursuant to this division are intended to represent and further the interest of a particular agricultural industry, and that the representation and furtherance is intended to serve the public interest. Accordingly, the Legislature finds that persons who are appointed to the board shall be subject to the conflict-of-interest provisions described in Section 87103 of the Government Code.

(c) The term of office for a member of the board is three years. If a vacancy exists, the secretary shall, consistent with the membership requirements described in subdivision (a), appoint a replacement member to the board for the duration of the term.

(d) A member of the board shall not receive a salary but may be reimbursed by the department for attendance at meetings and other board activities authorized by the board and approved by the secretary.

(e) The board shall advise the secretary and may make recommendations on all matters pertaining to this division, including, but not limited to, industrial hemp seed law and regulations, enforcement, annual budgets required to accomplish the purposes of this division, and the setting of an appropriate assessment rate necessary for the administration of this division.

(f) The board shall annually elect a chair from its membership and, from time to time, other officers as it deems necessary.

(g) The board shall meet at the call of its chair or the secretary, or at the request of any four members of the board. The board shall meet at least once a year to review budget proposals and fiscal matters related to the proposals.

Food and Agriculture Code § 81002

(Amended by Stats. 2018, Ch. 986, Sec. 1. (SB 1409) Effective January 1, 2019.)

(a) Except when grown by an established agricultural research institution or by a seed breeder developing a new California seed cultivar, industrial hemp shall only be grown if it is on the list of approved seed cultivars, or produced by clonal propagation of industrial hemp that is on the list of approved seed cultivars and therefore genetically identical to, and capable of exhibiting the same range of characteristics as, the parent cultivar.

(b) The list of approved seed cultivars shall include all of the following:

(1) Industrial hemp seed cultivars that have been certified by member organizations of the Association of Official Seed Certifying Agencies, including, but not limited to, the Canadian Seed Growers' Association.

(2) Industrial hemp seed cultivars that have been certified by the Organization of Economic Cooperation and Development.

(3) California varieties of industrial hemp seed cultivars that have been certified by a seed-certifying agency pursuant to Article 6.5 (commencing with Section 52401) of Chapter 2 of Division 18.

(c) (1) Upon recommendation by the board or the department, the secretary may update the list of approved seed cultivars by adding, amending, or removing seed cultivars.

(2) The adoption, amendment, or repeal of the list of approved seed cultivars, and the adoption of a methodology and procedure to add, amend, or remove a seed cultivar from the list of approved seed cultivars, pursuant to this section shall not be subject to the requirements of the Administrative Procedure Act (Chapter 3.5 (commencing with Section 11340) of Part 1 of Division 3 of Title 2 of the Government Code).

(3) The department, in consultation with the board, shall hold at least one public hearing with public comment to determine the methodology and procedure by which a seed cultivar is added, amended, or removed from the list of approved seed cultivars.

(4) The department shall finalize the methodology and procedure to add, amend, or remove a seed cultivar from the list of approved seed cultivars and send the methodology and procedure to the Office of Administrative Law. The Office of Administrative Law shall file the methodology and procedure promptly with the Secretary of State without further review pursuant to Article 6 (commencing with Section 11349) of Chapter 3.5 of Part 1 of Division 3 of Title 2 of the Government Code. The methodology and procedure shall do all of the following:

(A) Indicate that the methodology and procedure are adopted pursuant to this division.

(B) State that the methodology and procedure are being transmitted for filing.

(C) Request that the Office of Administrative Law publish a notice of the filing of the methodology and procedure and print an appropriate reference in Title 3 of the California Code of Regulations.

(d) The department, in consultation with the board, may determine the manner in which the public is given notice of the list of approved seed cultivars, and any addition, amendment, or removal from that list.

Food and Agriculture Code § 81003

(Amended by Stats. 2018, Ch. 986, Sec. 2. (SB 1409) Effective January 1, 2019.)

(a) (1) Except for an established agricultural research institution, and before cultivation, a grower of industrial hemp for commercial purposes shall register with the commissioner of the county in which the grower intends to engage in industrial hemp cultivation.

(2) The application shall include all of the following:

(A) The name, physical address, and mailing address of the applicant.

(B) The legal description, Global Positioning System coordinates, and map of the land area on which the applicant plans to engage in industrial hemp cultivation, storage, or both.

(C) The approved seed cultivar to be grown, including the state or county of origin.

(3) (A) The application shall be accompanied by a registration fee, as determined pursuant to Section 81005.

(B) A registration issued pursuant to this section shall be valid for one year, after which the registrant shall renew his or her registration and pay an accompanying renewal fee, as determined pursuant to Section 81005.

(b) If the commissioner determines that the requirements for registration pursuant to this division are met, the commissioner shall issue a registration to the applicant.

(c) A registrant that wishes to alter the land area on which the registrant conducts industrial hemp cultivation, storage, or both, shall, before altering the area, submit to the commissioner an updated legal description, Global Positioning System coordinates, and map specifying the proposed alteration. Once the commissioner has received the change to the registration, the commissioner shall notify the registrant that it may cultivate industrial hemp on the altered land area.

(d) A registrant that wishes to change the seed cultivar grown shall submit to the commissioner the name of the new, approved seed cultivar to be grown. Once the commissioner has received the change to the registration, the commissioner shall notify the registrant that it may cultivate the new seed cultivar.

(e) The commissioner shall transmit information collected under this section to the department.

Food and Agriculture Code § 81004

(Amended by Stats. 2018, Ch. 986, Sec. 3. (SB 1409) Effective January 1, 2019.)

(a) (1) Except when grown by an established agricultural research institution, and before cultivation, a seed breeder shall register with the commissioner of the county in which the seed breeder intends to engage in industrial hemp cultivation.

(2) The application shall include all of the following:

(A) The name, physical address, and mailing address of the applicant.

(B) The legal description, Global Positioning System coordinates, and map of the land area on which the applicant plans to engage in industrial hemp cultivation, storage, or both.

(C) The approved seed cultivar to be grown for seed production, including the state or county of origin.

(D) If an applicant intends to develop a new California seed cultivar to be certified by a seed-certifying agency, the applicant shall include all of the following:

(i) The name of the seed-certifying agency that will be conducting the certification.

(ii) The industrial hemp varieties that will be used in the development of the new California seed cultivar.

(iii) A seed development plan specifying how the listed industrial hemp varieties will be used in the development of the new seed cultivar, measures that will be taken to prevent the unlawful use of industrial hemp or seed cultivars under this division, and a procedure for the maintenance of records documenting the development of the new seed cultivar.

(3) (A) The application shall be accompanied by a registration fee, as determined pursuant to Section 81005.

(B) A registration issued pursuant to this section shall be valid for one year, after which the registrant shall renew its registration and pay an accompanying renewal fee, as determined pursuant to Section 81005.

(b) If the commissioner determines that the requirements for registration pursuant to this division are met, the commissioner shall issue a seed breeder registration to the applicant.

(c) A registrant that wishes to alter the land area on which the registrant conducts industrial hemp cultivation, storage, or both, shall, before altering the area, submit to the commissioner an updated legal description, Global Positioning System coordinates, and map specifying the proposed alteration. Once the commissioner has received the change to the registration, the commissioner shall notify the registrant that it may cultivate industrial hemp on the altered land area.

(d) A registrant that wishes to change the seed cultivar grown shall submit to the commissioner the name of the new, approved seed cultivar to be grown. Once the commissioner has received the change to the registration, the commissioner shall notify the registrant that it may cultivate the new seed cultivar.

(e) A registrant developing a new California seed cultivar who wishes to change any provision of the seed development plan shall submit to the commissioner the revised seed development plan. Once the commissioner has received the change to the registration, the commissioner shall notify the registrant that he or she may cultivate under the revised seed development plan.

(f) All records pertaining to the seed development plan shall be kept and maintained by the seed breeder and be available upon request by the commissioner, a law enforcement agency, or a seed certifying agency.

(g) The commissioner shall transmit information collected under this section to the department.

Food and Agriculture Code § 81005

(Amended by Stats. 2018, Ch. 986, Sec. 4. (SB 1409) Effective January 1, 2019.)

(a) The department shall establish a registration fee and appropriate renewal fee to be paid by growers of industrial hemp for commercial purposes and seed breeders, not including an established agricultural research institution, to cover the actual costs of implementing, administering, and enforcing the provisions of this division.

(b) Fees established pursuant to subdivision (a) that are collected by the commissioners upon registration or renewal pursuant to Section 81003 or 81004, except for amounts retained pursuant to this subdivision, shall be forwarded, according to procedures set by the department, to the department for deposit into the Department of Food and Agriculture Fund to be used for the administration and enforcement of this division. A commissioner or the county, as appropriate, may retain the amount of a fee necessary to reimburse direct costs incurred by the commissioner in the collection of the fee.

(c) The board of supervisors of a county may establish a reasonable fee, in an amount necessary to cover the actual costs of the commissioner and the county of implementing, administering, and enforcing the provisions of this division, except for costs that are otherwise reimbursed pursuant to subdivision (b), to be charged and collected by the commissioner upon registrations or renewals required pursuant to Section 81003 or 81004 and retained by the commissioner or the county, as appropriate.

Food and Agriculture Code § 81006

(Amended by Stats. 2018, Ch. 986, Sec. 5. (SB 1409) Effective January 1, 2019. Note: This section was added on Nov. 8, 2016, by initiative Prop. 64.)

Industrial Hemp Growth Limitations; Prohibitions; Imports; Laboratory Testing.

(a) (1) Except when grown by an established agricultural research institution or a seed breeder, industrial hemp shall be grown in acreages of not less than one-tenth of an acre at the same time.

(2) Seed breeders, for purposes of seed production, shall only grow industrial hemp in acreages of not less than one-tenth of an acre at the same time.

(3) Seed breeders, for purposes of developing a new California seed cultivar, shall grow industrial hemp in dedicated acreage of not less than one-tenth of an acre and in accordance with the seed development plan. The entire area of the dedicated acreage is not required to be used for the cultivation of the particular seed cultivar.

(b) Clandestine cultivation of industrial hemp is prohibited. All plots shall have adequate signage indicating they are industrial hemp.

(c) Industrial hemp shall include products imported under the Harmonized Tariff Schedule of the United States (2013) of the United States International Trade Commission, including, but not limited to, hemp seed, per subheading 1207.99.03, hemp oil, per subheading 1515.90.80, oilcake, per subheading 2306.90.01, true hemp, per heading 5302, true hemp yarn, per subheading 5308.20.00, and woven fabrics of true hemp fibers, per subheading 5311.00.40.

(d) (1) Except when industrial hemp is grown by an established agricultural research institution, a registrant that grows industrial hemp under this section shall, before the harvest of each crop and as provided below, obtain a laboratory test report indicating the THC levels of a random sampling of the dried flowering tops of the industrial hemp grown.

(2) Sampling shall occur no more than 30 days before harvest.

(3) The sample collected for THC testing shall be taken with the grower or seed breeder present. The department shall establish, by regulation, the sampling procedures, including all of the following:

(A) The number of plants to be sampled per field, and any composting of samples.

(B) The portions of the plant to be sampled.

(C) The plant parts to be included in a sample.

(D) Additional procedures as necessary to ensure accuracy and the sanitation of samples and fields.

(4) The sample collected for THC testing shall be accompanied by the following documentation:

(A) The registrant's proof of registration.

(B) Seed certification documentation for the seed cultivar used.

(C) The THC testing report for each certified seed cultivar used.

(5) The laboratory test report shall be issued by a laboratory approved by the department, using a department-approved testing method, and indicate the percentage content of THC on a dry-weight basis, indicate the date and location of samples taken, and state the Global Positioning System coordinates and total acreage of the crop. If the laboratory test report indicates a percentage content of THC that is equal to or less than three-tenths of 1 percent, the words "PASSED AS CALIFORNIA INDUSTRIAL HEMP" shall appear at or near the top of the laboratory test report. If the laboratory test report indicates a percentage content of THC that is greater than three-tenths of 1 percent, the words "FAILED AS CALIFORNIA INDUSTRIAL HEMP" shall appear at or near the top of the laboratory test report.

(6) If the laboratory test report indicates a percentage content of THC that is equal to or less than three-tenths of 1 percent, the laboratory shall provide the person who requested the testing not less than 10 original copies signed by an employee authorized by the laboratory and shall retain one or more original copies of the laboratory test report for a minimum of two years from its date of sampling.

(7) If the laboratory test report indicates a percentage content of THC that is greater than three-tenths of 1 percent and does not exceed 1 percent, the registrant that grows industrial hemp shall submit additional samples for testing of the industrial hemp grown.

(8) A registrant that grows industrial hemp shall destroy the industrial hemp grown upon receipt of a first laboratory test report indicating a percentage content of THC that exceeds 1 percent or a second laboratory test report pursuant to paragraph (7) indicating a percentage content of THC that exceeds three-tenths of 1 percent but is less than 1 percent. If the percentage content of THC exceeds 1 percent, the destruction shall begin within 48 hours, and be completed within 7 days, after receipt of the laboratory test report. If the percentage content of THC in the second laboratory test report exceeds three-tenths of 1 percent but is less than 1 percent, the destruction shall take place as soon as practicable, but no later than 45 days after receipt of the second test report.

(9) A registrant that intends to grow industrial hemp and who complies with this section shall not be prosecuted for the cultivation or possession of marijuana as a result of a laboratory test report that indicates a percentage content of THC that is greater than three-tenths of 1 percent but does not exceed 1 percent.

(10) Established agricultural research institutions shall be permitted to cultivate or possess industrial hemp with a laboratory test report that indicates a percentage content of THC that is greater than three-tenths of 1 percent if that cultivation or possession contributes to the development of types of industrial hemp that will comply with the three-tenths of 1 percent THC limit established in this division.

(11) Except for an established agricultural research institution, a registrant that grows industrial hemp shall retain an original signed copy of the laboratory test report for two years from its date of sampling, make an original signed copy of the laboratory test report available to the department, the commissioner, or law enforcement officials or their designees upon request, and shall provide an original copy of the laboratory test report to each person purchasing, transporting, or otherwise obtaining from the registrant that grows industrial hemp the fiber, oil, cake, or seed, or any component of the seed, of the plant.

(e) If, in the Attorney General's opinion issued pursuant to Section 8 of the act that added this division, it is determined that the provisions of this section are not sufficient to comply with federal law, the department, in consultation with the board, shall establish procedures for this section that meet the requirements of federal law.

Food and Agriculture Code § 81007

(Added by Stats. 2018, Ch. 986, Sec. 6. (SB 1409) Effective January 1, 2019.)

As part of the registration program established pursuant to this division, the department may establish and carry out, by regulation, an agricultural pilot program pursuant to Section 7606 of the federal Agricultural Act of 2014 (7 U.S.C. Sec. 5940) in accordance with the purposes of that section.

Food and Agricultural Code § 81008

(AUMA, operative January 1, 2017, pursuant to Section 81010. Repealed on January 1, 2023, or later as prescribed by its own provisions.)

(a) Not later than January 1, 2019, the Attorney General shall report to the Assembly and Senate Committees on Agriculture and the Assembly and Senate Committees on Public Safety the reported incidents, if any, of the following:

(1) A field of industrial hemp being used to disguise marijuana cultivation.

(2) Claims in a court hearing by persons other than those exempted in subdivision (f) of Section 81006 that marijuana is industrial hemp.

(b) A report submitted pursuant to subdivision (a) shall be submitted in compliance with Section 9795 of the Government Code.

(c) Pursuant to Section 10231.5 of the Government Code, this section is repealed on January 1, 2023, or four years after the date that the report is due, whichever is later.

Food and Agricultural Code § 81009

(Added by Stats. 2013, Ch. 398, Sec. 4. (SB 566) Effective January 1, 2014. Section operative January 1, 2017, pursuant to Section 81010.)

Not later than January 1, 2019, or five years after the provisions of this division are authorized under federal law, whichever is later, the board, in consultation with the Hemp Industries Association, or its successor industry association, shall report the following to the Assembly and Senate Committees on Agriculture and the Assembly and Senate Committees on Public Safety:

(a) The economic impacts of industrial hemp cultivation, processing, and product manufacturing in California.

(b) The economic impacts of industrial hemp cultivation, processing, and product manufacturing in other states that may have permitted industrial hemp cultivation.

Food and Agricultural Code § 81010

(MAUCRSA, Effective June 27, 2017.)

This division, and Section 221 shall become operative on January 1, 2017.

Food and Agriculture Code § 81011

(Added by Stats. 2018, Ch. 986, Sec. 7. (SB 1409) Effective January 1, 2019.)

Before cultivating industrial hemp, an established agricultural research institution shall provide the Global Positioning System coordinates of the planned cultivation site to the commissioner of the county in which the site is located.

VI. Government Code Sections

Government Code § 9147.7

(Amended by Stats. 2018, Ch. 92, Sec. 92. (SB 1289) Effective January 1, 2019.)

(a) For the purpose of this section, "eligible agency" means any agency, authority, board, bureau, commission, conservancy, council, department, division, or office of state government, however denominated, excluding an agency that is constitutionally created or an agency related to postsecondary education, for which a date for repeal has been established by statute on or after January 1, 2011.

(b) The Joint Sunset Review Committee is hereby created to identify and eliminate waste, duplication, and inefficiency in government agencies. The purpose of the committee is to conduct a comprehensive analysis over 15 years, and on a periodic basis thereafter, of every eligible agency to determine if the agency is still necessary and cost effective.

(c) Each eligible agency scheduled for repeal shall submit to the committee, on or before December 1 before the year it is set to be repealed, a complete agency report covering the entire period since last reviewed, including, but not limited to, the following:

(1) The purpose and necessity of the agency.

(2) A description of the agency budget, priorities, and job descriptions of employees of the agency.

(3) Programs and projects under the direction of the agency.

(4) Measures of the success or failures of the agency and justifications for the metrics used to evaluate

successes and failures.

(5) Recommendations of the agency for changes or reorganization in order to better fulfill its purpose.

(d) The committee shall take public testimony and evaluate the eligible agency before the date the agency is scheduled to be repealed. An eligible agency shall be eliminated unless the Legislature enacts a law to extend, consolidate, or reorganize the eligible agency. An eligible agency shall not be extended in perpetuity unless specifically exempted from the provisions of this section. The committee may recommend that the Legislature extend the statutory sunset date for no more than one year to allow the committee more time to evaluate the eligible agency.

(e) The committee shall be comprised of 10 members of the Legislature. The Senate Committee on Rules shall appoint five members of the Senate to the committee, not more than three of whom shall be members of the same political party. The Speaker of the Assembly shall appoint five members of the Assembly to the committee, not more than three of whom shall be members of the same political party. Members shall be appointed within 15 days after the commencement of the regular session. Each member of the committee who is appointed by the Senate Committee on Rules or the Speaker of the Assembly shall serve during that committee member's term of office or until that committee member no longer is a Member of the Senate or the Assembly, whichever is applicable. A vacancy on the committee shall be filled in the same manner as the original appointment. Three Assembly Members and three Senators who are members of the committee shall constitute a quorum for the conduct of committee business. Members of the committee shall receive no compensation for their work with the committee.

(f) The committee shall meet not later than 30 days after the first day of the regular session to choose a chairperson and to establish the schedule for eligible agency review provided for in the statutes governing the eligible agencies. The chairperson of the committee shall alternate every two years between a Member of the Senate and a Member of the Assembly, and the vice chairperson of the committee shall be a member of the opposite house as the chairperson.

(g) This section shall not be construed to change the existing jurisdiction of the budget or policy committees of the Legislature.

(h) This section does not apply to the Bureau of Cannabis Control.

Government Code § 11553

(Amended by AB 133, Effective September 16, 2017.)

(a) Effective January 1, 1988, an annual salary of eighty-one thousand six hundred thirty-five dollars ($81,635) shall be paid to each of the following:

(1) Chairperson of the Unemployment Insurance Appeals Board.

(2) Chairperson of the Agricultural Labor Relations Board.

(3) President of the Public Utilities Commission.

(4) Chairperson of the Fair Political Practices Commission.

(5) Chairperson of the Energy Resources Conservation and Development Commission.

(6) Chairperson of the Public Employment Relations Board.

(7) Chairperson of the Workers' Compensation Appeals Board.

(8) Administrative Director of the Division of Industrial Accidents.

(9) Chairperson of the State Water Resources Control Board.

(10) Chairperson of the Cannabis Control Appeals Panel.

(b) The annual compensation provided by this section shall be increased in any fiscal year in which a general salary increase is provided for state employees. The amount of the increase provided by this section shall be comparable to, but shall not exceed, the percentage of the general salary increases provided for state employees during that fiscal year.

(c) Notwithstanding subdivision (b), any salary increase is subject to Section 11565.5.

Government Code § 11553.5

(Amended by AB 133, Effective September 16, 2017.)

(a) Effective January 1, 1988, an annual salary of seventy-nine thousand one hundred twenty-two dollars ($79,122) shall be paid to the following:

 (1) Member of the Agricultural Labor Relations Board.

 (2) Member of the State Energy Resources Conservation and Development Commission.

 (3) Member of the Public Utilities Commission.

 (4) Member of the Public Employment Relations Board.

 (5) Member of the Unemployment Insurance Appeals Board.

 (6) Member of the Workers' Compensation Appeals Board.

 (7) Member of the State Water Resources Control Board.

 (8) Member of the Cannabis Control Appeals Panel.

(b) The annual compensation provided by this section shall be increased in any fiscal year in which a general salary increase is provided for state employees. The amount of the increase provided by this section shall be comparable to, but shall not exceed, the percentage of the general cost-of-living salary increases provided for state employees during that fiscal year.

(c) Notwithstanding subdivision (b), any salary increase is subject to Section 11565.5.

Government Code § 68152

(Amended by Stats. 2018, Ch. 423, Sec. 31. (SB 1494) Effective January 1, 2019.)

The trial court clerk may destroy court records under Section 68153 after notice of destruction, and if there is no request and order for transfer of the records, except the comprehensive historical and sample superior court records preserved for research under the California Rules of Court, when the following times have expired after the date of final disposition of the case in the categories listed:

(a) Civil actions and proceedings, as follows:

 (1) Except as otherwise specified: retain 10 years.

 (2) Civil unlimited cases, limited cases, and small claims cases, including after trial de novo, if any, except as otherwise specified: retain for 10 years.

 (3) Civil judgments for unlimited civil cases: retain permanently.

 (4) Civil judgments for limited and small claims cases: retain for 10 years, unless judgment is renewed. If

judgment is renewed, retain judgment for length of renewal pursuant to Article 2 (commencing with Section 683.110) of Chapter 3 of Division 1 of Title 9 of Part 2 of the Code of Civil Procedure.

(5) If a party in a civil case appears by a guardian ad litem: retain for 10 years after termination of the court's jurisdiction.

(6) Civil harassment, domestic violence, elder and dependent adult abuse, private postsecondary school violence, gun violence, and workplace violence cases: retain for the same period of time as the duration of the restraining or other orders and any renewals thereof, then retain the restraining or other orders permanently as a judgment; 60 days after expiration of the temporary restraining or other temporary orders; retain judgments establishing paternity under Section 6323 of the Family Code permanently.

(7) Family law, except as otherwise specified: retain for 30 years.

(8) Adoption: retain permanently.

(9) Parentage: retain permanently.

(10) Change of name, gender, or name and gender: retain permanently.

(11) Probate:

(A) Decedent estates: retain permanently all orders, judgments, and decrees of the court, all inventories and appraisals, and all wills and codicils of the decedent filed in the case, including those not admitted to probate. All other records: retain for five years after final disposition of the estate proceeding.

(B) Wills and codicils transferred or delivered to the court pursuant to Section 732, 734, or 8203 of the Probate Code: retain permanently. For wills and codicils delivered to the clerk of the court under Section 8200 of the Probate Code, retain the original documents as provided in Section 26810.

(C) Substitutes for decedent estate administration:

(i) Affidavit procedures for real property of small value under Chapter 3 (commencing with Section 13100) of Part 1 of Division 8 of the Probate Code: retain permanently.

(ii) Proceedings for determining succession to property under Chapter 4 (commencing with Section 13150) of Part 1 of Division 8 of the Probate Code: retain permanently all inventories and appraisals and court orders. Other records: retain for five years after final disposition of the proceeding.

(iii) Proceedings for determination of property passing or belonging to surviving spouse under Chapter 5 (commencing with Section 13650) of Part 2 of Division 8 of the Probate Code: retain permanently all inventories and appraisals and court orders. Other records: retain for five years after final disposition of the proceeding.

(D) Conservatorships: retain permanently all court orders. Documents of trusts established under substituted judgment pursuant to Section 2580 of the Probate Code: retain as provided in clause (iii) of subparagraph (G). Other records: retain for five years after the later of either (i) the final disposition of the conservatorship proceeding, or (ii) the date of the conservatee's death, if that date is disclosed in the court's file.

(E) Guardianships: retain permanently orders terminating the guardianship, if any, and court orders settling final account and ordering distribution of the estate. Other records: retain for five years after the later of (i) the final disposition of the guardianship proceeding, or (ii) the earlier of the date of the ward's death, if that date is disclosed in the court's file, or the date the ward reaches 23 years of age.

(F) Compromise of minor's or disabled person's claim or action, and disposition of judgment for minors and disabled persons under Section 372 of the Code of Civil Procedure and Chapter 4 (commencing with Section 3600) of Part 8 of Division 4 of the Probate Code:

(i) Retain permanently judgments in favor of minors or disabled persons, orders approving compromises of claims and actions and disposition of the proceeds of judgments, orders directing payment of expenses, costs, and fees, orders directing deposits into blocked accounts and receipts and acknowledgments of those orders, and orders for the withdrawal of funds from blocked accounts.

(ii) Retain other records for the same retention period as for records in the underlying case. If there is no underlying case, retain for five years after the later of either (I) the date the order for payment or delivery of the final balance of the money or property is entered, or (II) the earlier of the date of the minor's death, if that date is disclosed in the court's file, or the date the minor reaches 23 years of age.

(G) Trusts:

(i) Proceedings under Part 5 (commencing with Section 17000) of Division 9 of the Probate Code: retain permanently.

(ii) Trusts created by substituted judgment under Section 2580 of the Probate Code: retain permanently all trust instruments and court orders. Other records: retain as long as the underlying conservatorship file is retained.

(iii) Special needs trusts: retain permanently all trust instruments and court orders. Other records: retain until the later of either (I) the retention date of "other records" in the beneficiary's conservatorship or guardianship file under subparagraph (D) or (E), if any, or (II) five years after the date of the beneficiary's death, if that date is disclosed in the court's file.

(H) All other proceedings under the Probate Code: retain as provided for civil cases.

(12) Mental health:

(A) Lanterman Developmental Disabilities Services Act: retain for 10 years.

(B) Lanterman-Petris-Short Act: retain for 20 years.

(C) Riese (capacity) hearings under Sections 5333 and 5334 of the Welfare and Institutions Code: retain for the later of either (i) 20 years after the date of the capacity determination order, or (ii) the court records retention date of the underlying involuntary treatment or commitment proceeding, if any.

(D) Petitions under Chapter 3 (commencing with Section 8100) of Division 8 of the Welfare and Institutions Code for the return of firearms to petitioners who relinquished them to law enforcement while detained in a mental health facility: retain for 10 years.

(13) Eminent domain: retain permanently.

(14) Real property other than unlawful detainer: retain permanently if the action affects title or an interest in real property.

(15) Unlawful detainer: retain for one year if judgment is only for possession of the premises; retain for 10 years if judgment is for money, or money and possession.

(b) Notwithstanding subdivision (a), any civil or small claims case in the trial court:

(1) Involuntarily dismissed by the court for delay in prosecution or failure to comply with state or local rules: retain for one year.

(2) Voluntarily dismissed by a party without entry of judgment: retain for one year.

(c) Criminal actions and proceedings, as follows:

(1) Capital felony in which the defendant is sentenced to death, and any felony resulting in a sentence of life or life without the possibility of parole: retain permanently, including records of the cases of any codefendants and any related cases, regardless of the disposition. For the purpose of this paragraph, "capital felony" means murder with special circumstances when the prosecution seeks the death penalty. Records of the cases of codefendants and related cases required to be retained under this paragraph shall be limited to those cases that are factually linked or related to the charged offense, that are identified in the courtroom, and that are placed on the record. If a capital felony is disposed of by a sentence less than death, or imprisonment for life or life without the possibility of parole, the judgment shall be retained permanently, and the record shall be retained for 50 years or for 10 years after the official written notification of the death of the defendant. If a capital felony is disposed of by an acquittal, the record shall be retained for 10 years.

(2) Felony, except as otherwise specified, and in any felony or misdemeanor case resulting in a requirement that the defendant register as a sex offender under Section 290 of the Penal Code: retain judgment permanently. For all other documents: retain for 50 years or the maximum term of the sentence, whichever is longer. However, any record other than the judgment may be destroyed 10 years after the death of the defendant. Felony case files that do not include final sentencing or other final disposition because the case was bound over from a former municipal court to the superior court and not already consolidated with the superior court felony case file: retain for 10 years from the disposition of the superior court case.

(3) Felony reduced to a misdemeanor: retain in accordance with the retention period for the relevant misdemeanor.

(4) Felony, if the charge is dismissed, except as provided in paragraph (6): retain for three years.

(5) Misdemeanor, if the charge is dismissed, except as provided in paragraph (6): retain for one year.

(6) Dismissal under Section 1203.4 or 1203.4a of the Penal Code: retain for the same retention period as for records of the underlying case. If the records in the underlying case have been destroyed, retain for five years after dismissal.

(7) Misdemeanor, except as otherwise specified: retain for five years. For misdemeanors alleging a violation of Section 23103, 23152, or 23153 of the Vehicle Code: retain for 10 years.

(8) Misdemeanor alleging a marijuana violation under subdivision (b) or (c) of Section 11357 of the Health and Safety Code, or subdivision (b) of Section 11360 of the Health and Safety Code: records shall be destroyed, or redacted in accordance with subdivision (c) of Section 11361.5 of the Health and Safety Code, two years from the date of conviction, or from the date of arrest if no conviction, if the case is no longer subject to review on appeal, all applicable fines and fees have been paid, and the defendant has complied with all terms and conditions of the sentence or grant of probation. As provided in subdivision (a) of Section 11361.5 of the Health and Safety Code and paragraph (5) of subdivision (e) of this section, records of an infraction alleging a marijuana violation under subdivision (d) of Section 11357 of the Health and Safety Code shall be retained until the offender attains 18 years of age, at which time the records shall be destroyed as provided in subdivision (c) of Section 11361.5 of the Health and Safety Code.

(9) Misdemeanor reduced to an infraction: retain in accordance with the retention period for the relevant infraction.

(10) Infraction, except as otherwise specified: retain for one year. Vehicle Code infraction: retain for three years. Infraction alleging a marijuana violation under subdivision (a) of Section 11357 of the Health and Safety Code: if records are retained past the one-year minimum retention period, the records shall be destroyed or redacted in accordance with subdivision (c) of Section 11361.5 of the Health and Safety Code two years from the date of conviction, or from the date of arrest if no conviction, if the case is no longer subject to review

on appeal, all applicable fines and fees have been paid, and the defendant has complied with all terms and conditions of the sentence or grant of probation.

(11) Criminal protective order: retain until the order expires or is terminated.

(12) Arrest warrant: retain for the same retention period as for records in the underlying case. If there is no underlying case, retain for one year from the date of issue.

(13) Search warrant:

(A) If there is no underlying case, retain for five years from the date of issue.

(B) If there is any underlying case, retain for 10 years from the date of issue or, if the retention period for records in the underlying case is less than 10 years or if the underlying case is a capital felony described in paragraph (1) of subdivision (c), retain for the same retention period as for records in the underlying case.

(14) Probable cause declarations: retain for the same retention period as for records in the underlying case. If there is no underlying case, retain for one year from the date of declaration.

(15) Proceedings for revocation of postrelease community supervision or postrelease parole supervision: retain for five years after the period of supervision expires or is terminated.

(d) Habeas corpus:

(1) Habeas corpus in criminal and family law matters: retain for the same retention period as for records in the underlying case, whether granted or denied.

(2) Habeas corpus in mental health matters: retain all records for the same retention period as for records in the underlying case, whether granted or denied. If there is no underlying case, retain records for 20 years.

(e) Juveniles:

(1) Dependent pursuant to Section 300 of the Welfare and Institutions Code: upon reaching 28 years of age, or on written request, shall be released to the juvenile five years after jurisdiction over the person has terminated under subdivision (a) of Section 826 of the Welfare and Institutions Code. Sealed records shall be destroyed upon court order five years after the records have been sealed pursuant to subdivision (c) of Section 389 of the Welfare and Institutions Code.

(2) Ward pursuant to Section 601 of the Welfare and Institutions Code: upon reaching 21 years of age, or on written request, shall be released to the juvenile five years after jurisdiction over the person has terminated under subdivision (a) of Section 826 of the Welfare and Institutions Code. Sealed records shall be destroyed upon court order five years after the records have been sealed under subdivision (d) of Section 781 of the Welfare and Institutions Code.

(3) Ward pursuant to Section 602 of the Welfare and Institutions Code: upon reaching 38 years of age under subdivision (a) of Section 826 of the Welfare and Institutions Code. Sealed records shall be destroyed upon court order when the subject of the record reaches 38 years of age under subdivision (d) of Section 781 of the Welfare and Institutions Code.

(4) Traffic and some nontraffic misdemeanors and infractions pursuant to Section 601 of the Welfare and Institutions Code: upon reaching 21 years of age, or five years after jurisdiction over the person has terminated under subdivision (c) of Section 826 of the Welfare and Institutions Code. Records may be microfilmed or photocopied.

(5) Marijuana infraction under subdivision (d) of Section 11357 of the Health and Safety Code in accordance with procedures specified in subdivision (a) of Section 11361.5 of the Health and Safety Code: upon reaching 18

years of age, the records shall be destroyed.

(f) Court records of the appellate division of the superior court: retain for five years.

(g) Other records:

(1) Bench warrant: retain for the same retention period as for records in the underlying case. For a bench warrant issued for a misdemeanor, retain records for the same retention period as for records in the underlying misdemeanor following issuance. If there is no return on the warrant, the court may dismiss on its own motion and immediately destroy the records.

(2) Body attachment: retain for same retention period as for records in the underlying case.

(3) Bond: retain for three years after exoneration and release.

(4) Court reporter notes:

(A) Criminal and juvenile proceedings: retain notes for 10 years, except as otherwise specified. Notes reporting proceedings in capital felony cases (murder with special circumstances when the prosecution seeks the death penalty and the sentence is death), including notes reporting the preliminary hearing, shall be retained permanently, unless the Supreme Court on request of the court clerk authorizes the destruction.

(B) Civil and all other proceedings: retain notes for five years.

(5) Electronic recordings made as the official record of the oral proceedings under the California Rules of Court may be destroyed or deleted as follows:

(A) Any time after final disposition of the case in infraction and misdemeanor proceedings.

(B) After 10 years in all other criminal proceedings.

(C) After five years in all other proceedings.

(6) Electronic recordings not made as the official record of the oral proceedings under the California Rules of Court may be destroyed at any time at the discretion of the court.

(7) Fee waiver applications: retain for the same retention period as for records in the underlying case.

(8) Judgments within the jurisdiction of the superior court other than in a limited civil case, misdemeanor case, or infraction case: retain permanently.

(9) Judgments in misdemeanor cases, infraction cases, and limited civil cases: retain for the same retention period as for records in the underlying case.

(10) Juror proceedings, including sanctions: retain for one year.

(11) Minutes: retain for the same retention period as for records in the underlying case.

(12) Orders not associated with an underlying case, such as orders for the destruction of court records for telephone taps, orders to destroy drugs, and other miscellaneous court orders: retain for one year.

(13) Naturalization index: retain permanently.

(14) Index for cases alleging traffic violations: retain for the same retention period as for records in the underlying case.

(15) Index, except as otherwise specified: retain permanently.

(16) Register of actions or docket: retain for the same retention period as for records in the underlying case, but

in no event less than 10 years for civil and small claims cases.

(h) Retention of the court records under this section shall be extended by order of the court on its own motion, or on application of a party or an interested member of the public for good cause shown and on those terms as are just. A fee shall not be charged for making the application.

(i) The record retention periods provided in this section, as amended effective January 1, 2014, apply to all court records in existence prior to that date as well as to records created on or after that date.

VII. Health and Safety Code Sections

Health and Safety Code § 7151.36

(AB 258, Effective January 1, 2016.)

(a) A hospital, physician and surgeon, procurement organization, or other person shall not determine the ultimate recipient of an anatomical gift based solely upon a potential recipient's status as a qualified patient, as defined in Section 11362.7, or based solely upon a positive test for the use of medical marijuana by a potential recipient who is a qualified patient, as defined in Section 11362.7, except to the extent that the qualified patient's use of medical marijuana has been found by a physician and surgeon, following a case-by-case evaluation of the potential recipient, to be medically significant to the provision of the anatomical gift.

(b) Subdivision (a) shall apply to each part of the organ transplant process. The organ transplant process includes, but is not limited to, all of the following:

(1) The referral from a primary care provider to a specialist.

(2) The referral from a specialist to a transplant center.

(3) The evaluation of the patient for the transplant by the transplant center.

(4) The consideration of the patient for placement on the official waiting list.

(c) The court shall accord priority on its calendar and handle expeditiously any action brought to seek any remedy authorized by law for purposes of enforcing compliance with this section.

(d) This section shall not be deemed to require referrals or recommendations for, or the performance of, medically inappropriate organ transplants.

Health and Safety Code § 11006.5

(MAUCRSA, Effective June 27, 2017.)

"Concentrated cannabis" means the separated resin, whether crude or purified, obtained from cannabis.

Health and Safety Code § 11007

(Added by Statute, Effective September 26, 1987.)

"Controlled substance," unless otherwise specified, means a drug, substance, or immediate precursor which is listed in any schedule in Section 11054, 11055, 11056, 11057, or 11058.

Health and Safety Code § 11014.5

(MAUCRSA, Effective June 27, 2017.)

(a) "Drug paraphernalia" means all equipment, products and materials of any kind which are designed for use or marketed for use, in planting, propagating, cultivating, growing, harvesting, manufacturing, compounding, converting, producing, processing, preparing, testing, analyzing, packaging, repackaging, storing, containing, concealing, injecting, ingesting, inhaling, or otherwise introducing into the human body a controlled substance in violation of this division. It includes, but is not limited to:

(1) Kits designed for use or marketed for use in planting, propagating, cultivating, growing, or harvesting of any species of plant which is a controlled substance or from which a controlled substance can be derived.

(2) Kits designed for use or marketed for use in manufacturing, compounding, converting, producing, processing, or preparing controlled substances.

(3) Isomerization devices designed for use or marketed for use in increasing the potency of any species of plant which is a controlled substance.

(4) Testing equipment designed for use or marketed for use in identifying, or in analyzing the strength, effectiveness, or purity of controlled substances.

(5) Scales and balances designed for use or marketed for use in weighing or measuring controlled substances.

(6) Containers and other objects designed for use or marketed for use in storing or concealing controlled substances.

(7) Hypodermic syringes, needles, and other objects designed for use or marketed for use in parenterally injecting controlled substances into the human body.

(8) Objects designed for use or marketed for use in ingesting, inhaling, or otherwise introducing marijuana, cocaine, hashish, or hashish oil into the human body, such as:

(A) Carburetion tubes and devices.

(B) Smoking and carburetion masks.

(C) Roach clips, meaning objects used to hold burning material, such as a cannabis cigarette, that has become too small or too short to be held in the hand.

(D) Miniature cocaine spoons, and cocaine vials.

(E) Chamber pipes.

(F) Carburetor pipes.

(G) Electric pipes.

(H) Air-driven pipes.

(I) Chillums.

(J) Bongs.

(K) Ice pipes or chillers.

(b) For the purposes of this section, the phrase "marketed for use" means advertising, distributing, offering for sale, displaying for sale, or selling in a manner which promotes the use of equipment, products, or materials with controlled substances.

(c) In determining whether an object is drug paraphernalia, a court or other authority may consider, in addition to all other logically relevant factors, the following:

(1) Statements by an owner or by anyone in control of the object concerning its use.

(2) Instructions, oral or written, provided with the object concerning its use for ingesting, inhaling, or otherwise introducing a controlled substance into the human body.

(3) Descriptive materials accompanying the object which explain or depict its use.

(4) National and local advertising concerning its use.

(5) The manner in which the object is displayed for sale.

(6) Whether the owner, or anyone in control of the object, is a legitimate supplier of like or related items to the community, such as a licensed distributor or dealer of tobacco products.

(7) Expert testimony concerning its use.

(d) If any provision of this section or the application thereof to any person or circumstance is held invalid, it is the intent of the Legislature that the invalidity shall not affect other provisions or applications of the section which can be given effect without the invalid provision or application and to this end the provisions of this section are severable.

Health and Safety Code § 11018

(MAUCRSA, Effective June 27, 2017.)

"Cannabis" means all parts of the plant Cannabis sativa L., whether growing or not; the seeds thereof; the resin extracted from any part of the plant; and every compound, manufacture, salt, derivative, mixture, or preparation of the plant, its seeds or resin. It does not include either of the following:

(a) Industrial hemp, as defined in Section 11018.5; or

(b) The weight of any other ingredient combined with cannabis to prepare topical or oral administrations, food, drink, or other product.

Health and Safety Code § 11018.1

(MAUCRSA, Effective June 27, 2017.)

"Cannabis products" means cannabis that has undergone a process whereby the plant material has been transformed into a concentrate, including, but not limited to, concentrated cannabis, or an edible or topical product containing cannabis or concentrated cannabis and other ingredients.

Health and Safety Code § 11018.2

(MAUCRSA, Effective June 27, 2017.)

"Cannabis accessories" means any equipment, products or materials of any kind which are used, intended for use, or designed for use in planting, propagating, cultivating, growing, harvesting, manufacturing, compounding, converting, producing, processing, preparing, testing, analyzing, packaging, repackaging, storing, smoking, vaporizing, or containing cannabis, or for ingesting, inhaling, or otherwise introducing cannabis or cannabis products into the human body.

Health & Safety Code § 11018.5

(Amended by Stats. 2018, Ch. 986, Sec. 8. (SB 1409) Effective January 1, 2019. Note: This section was amended on Nov. 8, 2016, by initiative Prop. 64.)

(a) "Industrial hemp" means a crop that is limited to types of the plant Cannabis sativa L. having no more than three-tenths of 1 percent tetrahydrocannabinol (THC) contained in the dried flowering tops, whether growing or not; the seeds of the plant; the resin extracted from any part of the plant; and every compound, manufacture, salt, derivative, mixture, or preparation of the plant, its seeds or resin produced therefrom.

(b) Industrial hemp shall not be subject to the provisions of this division or of Division 10 (commencing with Section 26000) of the Business and Professions Code, but instead shall be regulated by the Department of Food and Agriculture in accordance with the provisions of Division 24 (commencing with Section 81000) of the Food and Agricultural Code, inclusive.

Health and Safety Code § 11032

(MAUCRSA, Effective June 27, 2017.)

If reference is made to the term "narcotics" in any law not in this division, unless otherwise expressly provided, it means those controlled substances classified in Schedules I and II, as defined in this division. If reference is made to "restricted dangerous drugs" not in this division, unless otherwise expressly provided, it means those controlled substances classified in Schedules III and IV. If reference is made to the term "marijuana" in any law not in this division, unless otherwise expressly provided, it means cannabis as defined in this division.

Health and Safety Code § 11054

(MAUCRSA, Effective June 27, 2017.)

(a) The controlled substances listed in this section are included in Schedule I.

(b) Opiates. Unless specifically excepted or unless listed in another schedule, any of the following opiates, including their isomers, esters, ethers, salts, and salts of isomers, esters, and ethers whenever the existence of those isomers, esters, ethers, and salts is possible within the specific chemical designation:

    (1) Acetylmethadol.

    (2) Allylprodine.

    (3) Alphacetylmethadol (except levoalphacetylmethadol, also known as levo-alpha- acetylmethadol, levomethadyl acetate, or LAAM).

    (4) Alphameprodine.

    (5) Alphamethadol.

    (6) Benzethidine.

    (7) Betacetylmethadol.

(8) Betameprodine.

(9) Betamethadol.

(10) Betaprodine.

(11) Clonitazene.

(12) Dextromoramide.

(13) Diampromide.

(14) Diethylthiambutene.

(15) Difenoxin.

(16) Dimenoxadol.

(17) Dimepheptanol.

(18) Dimethylthiambutene.

(19) Dioxaphetyl butyrate.

(20) Dipipanone.

(21) Ethylmethylthiambutene.

(22) Etonitazene.

(23) Etoxeridine.

(24) Furethidine.

(25) Hydroxypethidine.

(26) Ketobemidone.

(27) Levomoramide.

(28) Levophenacylmorphan.

(29) Morpheridine.

(30) Noracymethadol.

(31) Norlevorphanol.

(32) Normethadone.

(33) Norpipanone.

(34) Phenadoxone.

(35) Phenampromide.

(36) Phenomorphan.

(37) Phenoperidine.

(38) Piritramide.

(39) Proheptazine.

(40) Properidine.

(41) Propiram.

(42) Racemoramide.

(43) Tilidine.

(44) Trimeperidine.

(45) Any substance which contains any quantity of acetylfentanyl (N-[1-phenethyl-4-piperidinyl] acetanilide) or a derivative thereof.

(46) Any substance which contains any quantity of the thiophene analog of acetylfentanyl (N-[1-[2-(2-thienyl) ethyl]-4-piperidinyl] acetanilide) or a derivative thereof.

(47) 1-Methyl-4-Phenyl-4-Propionoxypiperidine (MPPP).

(48) 1-(2-Phenethyl)-4-Phenyl-4-Acetyloxypiperidine (PEPAP).

(c) Opium derivatives. Unless specifically excepted or unless listed in another schedule, any of the following opium derivatives, its salts, isomers, and salts of isomers whenever the existence of those salts, isomers, and salts of isomers is possible within the specific chemical designation:

(1) Acetorphine.

(2) Acetyldihydrocodeine.

(3) Benzylmorphine.

(4) Codeine methylbromide.

(5) Codeine-N-Oxide.

(6) Cyprenorphine.

(7) Desomorphine.

(8) Dihydromorphine.

(9) Drotebanol.

(10) Etorphine (except hydrochloride salt).

(11) Heroin.

(12) Hydromorphinol.

(13) Methyldesorphine.

(14) Methyldihydromorphine.

(15) Morphine methylbromide.

(16) Morphine methylsulfonate.

(17) Morphine-N-Oxide.

(18) Myrophine.

(19) Nicocodeine.

(20) Nicomorphine.

(21) Normorphine.

(22) Pholcodine.

(23) Thebacon.

(d) Hallucinogenic substances. Unless specifically excepted or unless listed in another schedule, any material, compound, mixture, or preparation, which contains any quantity of the following hallucinogenic substances, or which contains any of its salts, isomers, and salts of isomers whenever the existence of those salts, isomers, and salts of isomers is possible within the specific chemical designation (for purposes of this subdivision only, the term "isomer" includes the optical, position, and geometric isomers):

(1) 4-bromo-2,5-dimethoxy-amphetamine—Some trade or other names: 4-bromo-2,5-dimethoxy-alphamethylphenethylamine; 4-bromo-2,5-DMA.

(2) 2,5-dimethoxyamphetamine—Some trade or other names: 2,5-dimethoxy-alpha-methylphenethylamine; 2,5-DMA.

(3) 4-methoxyamphetamine—Some trade or other names: 4-methoxy-alpha-methylphenethylamine, paramethoxyamphetamine, PMA.

(4) 5-methoxy-3,4-methylenedioxy-amphetamine.

(5) 4-methyl-2,5-dimethoxy-amphetamine—Some trade or other names: 4-methyl-2,5-dimethoxy-alphamethylphenethylamine; "DOM"; and "STP."

(6) 3,4-methylenedioxy amphetamine.

(7) 3,4,5-trimethoxy amphetamine.

(8) Bufotenine—Some trade or other names: 3-(beta-dimethylaminoethyl)-5-hydroxyindole; 3-(2-dimethylaminoethyl)-5 indolol; N,N-dimethylserolonin, 5-hydroxy-N,N-dimethyltryptamine; mappine.

(9) Diethyltryptamine—Some trade or other names: N,N-Diethyltryptamine; DET.

(10) Dimethyltryptamine—Some trade or other names: DMT.

(11) Ibogaine—Some trade or other names: 7-Ethyl-6,6beta, 7,8,9,10,12,13-octahydro-2-methoxy-6,9-methano-5H-pyrido [1',2':1,2] azepino [5,4-b] indole; Tabernantheiboga.

(12) Lysergic acid diethylamide.

(13) Cannabis.

(14) Mescaline.

(15) Peyote—Meaning all parts of the plant presently classified botanically as Lophophora williamsii Lemaire, whether growing or not, the seeds thereof, any extract from any part of the plant, and every compound, manufacture, salts, derivative, mixture, or preparation of the plant, its seeds or extracts (interprets 21 U.S.C. Sec. 812(c), Schedule 1(c)(12)).

(16) N-ethyl-3-piperidyl benzilate.

(17) N-methyl-3-piperidyl benzilate.

(18) Psilocybin.

(19) Psilocyn.

(20) Tetrahydrocannabinols. Synthetic equivalents of the substances contained in the plant, or in the resinous extractives of Cannabis, sp. and/or synthetic substances, derivatives, and their isomers with similar chemical structure and pharmacological activity such as the following: delta 1 cis or trans tetrahydrocannabinol, and their optical isomers; delta 6 cis or trans tetrahydrocannabinol, and their optical isomers; delta 3,4 cis or trans tetrahydrocannabinol, and its optical isomers.

Because nomenclature of these substances is not internationally standardized, compounds of these structures, regardless of numerical designation of atomic positions covered.

(21) Ethylamine analog of phencyclidine—Some trade or other names: N-ethyl-1-phenylcyclohexylamine, (1-phenylcyclohexyl) ethylamine, N-(1-phenylcyclohexyl) ethylamine, cyclohexamine, PCE.

(22) Pyrrolidine analog of phencyclidine—Some trade or other names: 1-(1-phenylcyclohexyl)-pyrrolidine, PCP, PHP.

(23) Thiophene analog of phencyclidine—Some trade or other names: 1-[1-(2 thienyl)-cyclohexyl]-piperidine, 2-thienyl analog of phencyclidine, TPCP, TCP.

(e) Depressants. Unless specifically excepted or unless listed in another schedule, any material, compound, mixture, or preparation which contains any quantity of the following substances having a depressant effect on the central nervous system, including its salts, isomers, and salts of isomers whenever the existence of those salts, isomers, and salts of isomers is possible within the specific chemical designation:

(1) Mecloqualone.

(2) Methaqualone.

(3) Gamma hydroxybutyric acid (also known by other names such as GHB; gamma hydroxy butyrate; 4-hydroxybutyrate; 4-hydroxybutanoic acid; sodium oxybate; sodium oxybutyrate), including its immediate precursors, isomers, esters, ethers, salts, and salts of isomers, esters, and ethers, including, but not limited to, gammabutyrolactone, for which an application has not been approved under Section 505 of the Federal Food, Drug, and Cosmetic Act (21 U.S.C. Sec. 355).

(f) Unless specifically excepted or unless listed in another schedule, any material, compound, mixture, or preparation which contains any quantity of the following substances having a stimulant effect on the central nervous system, including its isomers:

(1) Cocaine base.

(2) Fenethylline, including its salts.

(3) N-Ethylamphetamine, including its salts.

Health and Safety Code § 11107.2

(Added by Stats. 2018, Ch. 595, Sec. 1. (AB 3112) Effective January 1, 2019. Section operative July 1, 2019, by its own provisions.)

(a) Except as otherwise provided in subdivision (b), it is unlawful for a manufacturer, wholesaler, reseller, retailer, or other person or entity to sell to any customer any quantity of nonodorized butane.

(b) The limitations in subdivisions (a) shall not apply to any of the following transactions:

(1) Butane sold to manufacturers, wholesalers, resellers, or retailers solely for the purpose of resale.

(2) Butane sold to a person for use in a lawful commercial enterprise, including, but not limited to, a volatile solvent extraction activity licensed under Division 10 (commencing with Section 26000) of the Business and Professions Code or a medical cannabis collective or cooperative described in subdivision (b) of Section 11362.775 of this code, operating in compliance with all applicable state licensing requirements and local regulations governing that type of business.

(3) The sale of pocket lighters, utility lighters, grill lighters, torch lighters, butane gas appliances, refill canisters, gas cartridges, or other products that contain or use nonodorized butane and contain less than 150 milliliters of butane.

(4) The sale of any product in which butane is used as an aerosol propellant.

(c) (1) Any person or business that violates subdivision (a) is subject to a civil penalty of two thousand five hundred dollars ($2,500).

(2) The Attorney General, a city attorney, a county counsel, or a district attorney may bring a civil action to enforce this section.

(3) The civil penalty shall be deposited into the General Fund if the action is brought by the Attorney General. If the action is brought by a city attorney, the civil penalty shall be paid to the treasurer of the city in which the judgment is entered. If the action is brought by a county counsel or district attorney, the civil penalty shall be paid to the treasurer of the county in which the judgment is entered.

(d) As used in this section, the following definitions shall apply:

(1) "Customer" means any person or entity other than those described in paragraphs (1) and (2) of subdivision (b) that purchases or acquires nonodorized butane from a seller during a transaction.

(2) "Nonodorized butane" means iso-butane, n-butane, butane, or a mixture of butane and propane of any power that may also use the words "refined," "pure," "purified," "premium," or "filtered," to describe the butane or butane mixture, which does not contain ethyl mercaptan or a similar odorant.

(3) "Sell" or "sale" means to furnish, give away, exchange, transfer, deliver, surrender, distribute, or supply, in exchange for money or any other consideration.

(4) "Seller" means any person, business entity, or employee thereof that sells nonodorized butane to any customer within this state.

(e) This section shall become operative on July 1, 2019.

Health and Safety Code § 11357

(Amended by AB 133, Effective September 16, 2017.)

(a) Except as authorized by law, possession of not more than 28.5 grams of cannabis, or not more than eight grams of concentrated cannabis, or both, shall be punished or adjudicated as follows:

(1) Persons under 18 years of age are guilty of an infraction and shall be required to:

(A) Upon a finding that a first offense has been committed, complete four hours of drug education or counseling and up to 10 hours of community service over a period not to exceed 60 days.

(B) Upon a finding that a second offense or subsequent offense has been committed, complete six hours of drug education or counseling and up to 20 hours of community service over a period not to exceed 90 days.

(2) Persons at least 18 years of age but less than 21 years of age are guilty of an infraction and punishable by a fine of not more than one hundred dollars ($100).

(b) Except as authorized by law, possession of more than 28.5 grams of cannabis, or more than eight grams of concentrated cannabis, shall be punished as follows:

(1) Persons under 18 years of age who possess more than 28.5 grams of cannabis or more than eight grams of concentrated cannabis, or both, are guilty of an infraction and shall be required to:

(A) Upon a finding that a first offense has been committed, complete eight hours of drug education or counseling and up to 40 hours of community service over a period not to exceed 90 days.

(B) Upon a finding that a second or subsequent offense has been committed, complete 10 hours of drug education or counseling and up to 60 hours of community service over a period not to exceed 120 days.

(2) Persons 18 years of age or older who possess more than 28.5 grams of cannabis, or more than eight grams of concentrated cannabis, or both, shall be punished by imprisonment in a county jail for a period of not more than six months or by a fine of not more than five hundred dollars ($500), or by both that fine and imprisonment.

(c) Except as authorized by law, a person 18 years of age or older who possesses not more than 28.5 grams of cannabis, or not more than eight grams of concentrated cannabis, upon the grounds of, or within, any school providing instruction in kindergarten or any of grades 1 to 12, inclusive, during hours the school is open for classes or school-related programs is guilty of a misdemeanor and shall be punished as follows:

(1) A fine of not more than two hundred fifty dollars ($250), upon a finding that a first offense has been committed.

(2) A fine of not more than five hundred dollars ($500), or by imprisonment in a county jail for a period of not more than 10 days, or both, upon a finding that a second or subsequent offense has been committed.

(d) Except as authorized by law, a person under 18 years of age who possesses not more than 28.5 grams of cannabis, or not more than eight grams of concentrated cannabis, upon the grounds of, or within, any school providing instruction in kindergarten or any of grades 1 to 12, inclusive, during hours the school is open for classes or school-related programs is guilty of an infraction and shall be punished in the same manner provided in paragraph (1) of subdivision (b).

Health and Safety Code § 11357.5

(Amended by Statute, Effective September 25, 2016.)

(a) Every person who sells, dispenses, distributes, furnishes, administers, or gives, or offers to sell, dispense, distribute, furnish, administer, or give, or possesses for sale any synthetic cannabinoid compound, or any synthetic cannabinoid derivative, to any person, is guilty of a misdemeanor, punishable by imprisonment in a county jail not to exceed six months, or by a fine not to exceed one thousand dollars ($1,000), or by both that fine and imprisonment.

(b) Every person who uses or possesses any synthetic cannabinoid compound, or any synthetic cannabinoid derivative, is guilty of a public offense, punishable as follows:

(1) A first offense is an infraction punishable by a fine not exceeding two hundred fifty dollars ($250).

(2) A second offense is an infraction punishable by a fine not exceeding two hundred fifty dollars ($250) or a misdemeanor punishable by imprisonment in a county jail not exceeding six months, a fine not exceeding five hundred dollars ($500), or by both that fine and imprisonment.

(3) A third or subsequent offense is a misdemeanor punishable by imprisonment in a county jail not exceeding

six months, or by a fine not exceeding one thousand dollars ($1,000), or by both that fine and imprisonment.

(c) As used in this section, the term "synthetic cannabinoid compound" refers to any of the following substances or an analog of any of the following substances:

(1) Adamantoylindoles or adamantoylindazoles, which includes adamantyl carboxamide indoles and adamantyl carboxamide indazoles, or any compound structurally derived from 3-(1-adamantoyl)indole, 3-(1-adamantoyl) indazole, 3-(2-adamantoyl)indole, N-(1-adamantyl)-1H-indole-3-carboxamide, or N-(1-adamantyl)-1H-indazole-3-carboxamide by substitution at the nitrogen atom of the indole or indazole ring with alkyl, haloalkyl, alkenyl, cyanoalkyl, hydroxyalkyl, cycloalkylmethyl, cycloalkylethyl, 1-(N-methyl-2-piperidinyl) methyl, 2-(4-morpholinyl)ethyl, or 1-(N-methyl-2-pyrrolidinyl)methyl, 1-(N-methyl-3-morpholinyl)methyl, or (tetrahydropyran-4-yl)methyl group, whether or not further substituted in the indole or indazole ring to any extent and whether or not substituted in the adamantyl ring to any extent, including, but not limited to, 2NE1, 5F-AKB-48, AB-001, AKB-48, AM-1248, JWH-018 adamantyl carboxamide, STS-135.

(2) Benzoylindoles, which includes any compound structurally derived from a 3-(benzoyl)indole structure with substitution at the nitrogen atom of the indole ring with alkyl, haloalkyl, cyanoalkyl, hydroxyalkyl, alkenyl, cycloalkylmethyl, cycloalkylethyl, 1-(N-methyl-2-piperidinyl)methyl, 2-(4-morpholinyl)ethyl, or 1-(N-methyl-2-pyrrolidinyl)methyl, 1-(N-methyl-3-morpholinyl)methyl, or (tetrahydropyran-4-yl)methyl group, whether or not further substituted in the indole ring to any extent and whether or not substituted in the phenyl ring to any extent, including, but not limited to, AM-630, AM-661, AM-679, AM-694, AM-1241, AM-2233, RCS-4, WIN 48,098 (Pravadoline).

(3) Cyclohexylphenols, which includes any compound structurally derived from 2-(3-hydroxycyclohexyl)phenol by substitution at the 5-position of the phenolic ring by alkyl, haloalkyl, cyanoalkyl, hydroxyalkyl, alkenyl, cycloalkylmethyl, cycloalkylethyl, 1-(N-methyl-2-piperidinyl)methyl, 2-(4-morpholinyl)ethyl, or 1-(N-methyl-2-pyrrolidinyl)methyl, 1-(N-methyl-3-morpholinyl)methyl, or tetrahydropyran-4-yl)methyl group, whether or not further substituted in the cyclohexyl ring to any extent, including, but not limited to, CP 47,497, CP 55,490, CP 55,940, CP 56,667, cannabicyclohexanol.

(4) Cyclopropanoylindoles, which includes any compound structurally derived from 3-(cyclopropylmethanoyl) indole, 3-(cyclopropylmethanone)indole, 3-(cyclobutylmethanone)indole or 3-(cyclopentylmethanone)indole by substitution at the nitrogen atom of the indole ring, whether or not further substituted in the indole ring to any extent, whether or not substituted on the cyclopropyl, cyclobutyl, or cyclopentyl rings to any extent.

(5) Naphthoylindoles, which includes any compound structurally derived from 3-(1-naphthoyl)indole or 1H-indol-3-yl-(1-naphthyl)methane by substitution at the nitrogen atom of the indole ring by alkyl, haloalkyl, cyanoalkyl, hydroxyalkyl, alkenyl, cycloalkylmethyl, cycloalkylethyl, 1-(N-methyl-2-piperidinyl)methyl, 2-(4-morpholinyl)ethyl group, 1-(N-methyl-2-pyrrolidinyl)methyl, 1-(N-methyl-3-morpholinyl)methyl, or (tetrahydropyran-4-yl)methyl group, whether or not further substituted in the naphthyl ring to any extent, including, but not limited to, AM-678, AM-1220, AM-1221, AM-1235, AM-2201, AM-2232, EAM-2201, JWH-004, JWH-007, JWH-009, JWH-011, JWH-015, JWH-016, JWH-018, JWH-019, JWH-020, JWH-022, JWH-046, JWH-047, JWH-048, JWH-049, JWH-050, JWH-070, JWH-071, JWH-072, JWH-073, JWH-076, JWH-079, JWH-080, JWH-081, JWH-082, JWH-094, JWH-096, JWH-098, JWH-116, JWH-120, JWH-122, JWH-148, JWH-149, JWH-164, JWH-166, JWH-180, JWH-181, JWH-182, JWH-189, JWH-193, JWH-198, JWH-200, JWH-210, JWH-211, JWH-212, JWH-213, JWH-234, JWH-235, JWH-236, JWH-239, JWH-240, JWH-241, JWH-242, JWH-258, JWH-262, JWH-386, JWH-387, JWH-394, JWH-395, JWH-397, JWH-398, JWH-399, JWH-400, JWH-412, JWH-413, JWH-414, JWH-415, JWH-424, MAM-2201, WIN 55,212.

(6) Naphthoylnaphthalenes, which includes any compound structurally derived from naphthalene-1-yl-(naphthalene-1-yl) methanone with substitutions on either of the naphthalene rings to any extent, including, but not limited to, CB-13.

(7) Naphthoylpyrroles, which includes any compound structurally derived from 3-(1-naphthoyl)pyrrole by substitution at the nitrogen atom of the pyrrole ring by alkyl, haloalkyl, cyanoalkyl, hydroxyalkyl, alkenyl,

cycloalkylmethyl, cycloalkylethyl, 1-(N-methyl-2-piperidinyl)methyl, 2-(4-morpholinyl)ethyl, or 1-N-methyl-2-pyrrolidinyl)methyl, 1-(N-methyl-3-morpholinyl)methyl, or (tetrahydropyran-4-yl)methyl group, whether or not further substituted in the pyrrole ring to any extent and whether or not substituted in the naphthyl ring to any extent, including, but not limited to, JWH-030, JWH-031, JWH-145, JWH-146, JWH-147, JWH-150, JWH-156, JWH-243, JWH-244, JWH-245, JWH-246, JWH-292, JWH-293, JWH-307, JWH-308, JWH-309, JWH-346, JWH-348, JWH-363, JWH-364, JWH-365, JWH-367, JWH-368, JWH-369, JWH-370, JWH-371, JWH-373, JWH-392.

(8) Naphthylmethylindenes, which includes any compound containing a naphthylideneindene structure or which is structurally derived from 1-(1-naphthylmethyl)indene with substitution at the 3-position of the indene ring by alkyl, haloalkyl, cyanoalkyl, hydroxyalkyl, alkenyl, cycloalkylmethyl, cycloalkylethyl, 1-(N-methyl-2-piperidinyl)methyl, 2-(4-morpholinyl)ethyl, or 1-(N-methyl-2-pyrrolidinyl)methyl, 1-(N-methyl-3-morpholinyl)methyl, or (tetrahydropyran-4-yl)methyl group, whether or not further substituted in the indene ring to any extent and whether or not substituted in the naphthyl ring to any extent, including, but not limited to, JWH-171, JWH-176, JWH-220.

(9) Naphthylmethylindoles, which includes any compound structurally derived from an H-indol-3-yl-(1-naphthyl) methane by substitution at the nitrogen atom of the indole ring by alkyl, haloalkyl, cyanoalkyl, hydroxyalkyl, alkenyl, cycloalkylmethyl, cycloalkylethyl, 1-(N-methyl-2-piperidinyl)methyl, 2-(4-morpholinyl) ethyl, or 1-(N-methyl-2-pyrrolidinyl)methyl, 1-(N-methyl-3-morpholinyl)methyl, or (tetrahydropyran-4-yl)methyl group, whether or not further substituted in the indole ring to any extent and whether or not substituted in the naphthyl ring to any extent, including, but not limited to, JWH-175, JWH-184, JWH-185, JWH-192, JWH-194, JWH-195, JWH-196, JWH-197, JWH-199.

(10) Phenylacetylindoles, which includes any compound structurally derived from 3-phenylacetylindole by substitution at the nitrogen atom of the indole ring with alkyl, haloalkyl, cyanoalkyl, hydroxyalkyl, alkenyl, cycloalkylmethyl, cycloalkylethyl, 1-(N-methyl-2-piperidinyl)methyl, 2-(4-morpholinyl)ethyl, or 1-N-methyl-2-pyrrolidinyl)methyl, 1-(N-methyl-3-morpholinyl)methyl, or (tetrahydropyran-4-yl)methyl group, whether or not further substituted in the indole ring to any extent and whether or not substituted in the phenyl ring to any extent, including, but not limited to, cannabipiperidiethanone, JWH-167, JWH-201, JWH-202, JWH-203, JWH-204, JWH-205, JWH-206, JWH-207, JWH-208, JWH-209, JWH-237, JWH-248, JWH-249, JWH-250, JWH-251, JWH-253, JWH-302, JWH-303, JWH-304, JWH-305, JWH-306, JWH-311, JWH-312, JWH-313, JWH-314, JWH-315, JWH-316, RCS-8.

(11) Quinolinylindolecarboxylates, which includes any compound structurally derived from quinolin-8-yl-1H-indole-3-carboxylate by substitution at the nitrogen atom of the indole ring with alkyl, haloalkyl, benzyl, halobenzyl, alkenyl, haloalkenyl, alkoxy, cyanoalkyl, hydroxyalkyl, cycloalkylmethyl, cycloalkylethyl, (N-methylpiperidin-2-yl)alkyl, (4-tetrahydropyran)alkyl, or 2-(4-morpholinyl)alkyl, whether or not further substituted in the indole ring to any extent, whether or not substituted in the quinoline ring to any extent, including, but not limited to, BB-22, 5-Fluoro-PB-22, PB-22.

(12) Tetramethylcyclopropanoylindoles, which includes any compound structurally derived from 3-tetramethylcyclopropanoylindole, 3-(1- tetramethylcyclopropyl)indole, 3-(2,2,3,3-tetramethylcyclopropyl) indole or 3-(2,2,3,3-tetramethylcyclopropylcarbonyl)indole with substitution at the nitrogen atom of the indole ring by an alkyl, haloalkyl, cyanoalkyl, hydroxyalkyl, alkenyl, cycloalkylmethyl, cycloalkylethyl, 1-(N-methyl-2-piperidinyl)methyl, 2-(4-morpholinyl)ethyl, 1-(N-methyl-2-pyrrolidinyl)methyl, 1-(N-methyl-3-morpholinyl)methyl, or (tetrahydropyran-4-yl)methyl group whether or not further substituted in the indole ring to any extent and whether or not substituted in the tetramethylcyclopropanoyl ring to any extent, including, but not limited to, 5-bromo-UR-144, 5-chloro-UR-144, 5-fluoro-UR-144, A-796,260, A-834,735, AB-034, UR-144, XLR11.

(13) Tetramethylcyclopropane-thiazole carboxamides, which includes any compound structurally derived from 2,2,3,3-tetramethyl-N-(thiazol-2-ylidene)cyclopropanecarboxamide by substitution at the nitrogen atom of the thiazole ring by alkyl, haloalkyl, benzyl, halobenzyl, alkenyl, haloalkenyl, alkoxy, cyanoalkyl, hydroxyalkyl, cycloalkylmethyl, cycloalkylethyl, (N-methylpiperidin-2-yl)alkyl, (4-tetrahydropyran)alkyl, or

2-(4-morpholinyl)alkyl, whether or not further substituted in the thiazole ring to any extent, whether or not substituted in the tetramethylcyclopropyl ring to any extent, including, but not limited to, A-836,339.

(14) Unclassified synthetic cannabinoids, which includes all of the following:

(A) AM-087, (6aR,10aR)-3-(2-methyl-6-bromohex-2-yl)-6,6,9-t rimethyl-6a,7,10,10a-tetrahydrobenzo[c] chromen-1-ol.

(B) AM-356, methanandamide, including (5Z,8Z,11Z,14Z)--[(1R)-2-hydroxy-1-methylethyl]icosa-5,8,11,14-tetraenamide and arachidonyl-1'-hydroxy-2'-propylamide.

(C) AM-411, (6aR,10aR)-3-(1-adamantyl)-6,6,9-trimethyl-6 a,7,10,10a-tetrahydrobenzo[c]chromen-1-ol.

(D) AM-855, (4aR,12bR)-8-hexyl-2,5,5-trimethyl-1 ,4,4a,8,9,10,11,12b-octahydronaphtho[3,2-c] isochromen-12-ol.

(E) AM-905, (6aR,9R,10aR)-3-[(E)-hept-1-enyl]-9-(hydroxymethyl)-6,6-dimethyl-6a,7,8,9,10,10a-hexahydrobenzo[c]chromen-1-ol.

(F) AM-906, (6aR,9R,10aR)-3-[(Z)-hept-1-enyl]-9-(hydroxymethyl)-6,6-dimethyl-6a,7,8,9,10,10a-hexahydrobenzo[c]chromen-1-ol.

(G) AM-2389, (6aR,9R,10aR)-3-(1-hexyl-cyclobut-1-yl)-6 a,7,8,9,10,10a-hexahydro-6,6-dimethyl-6H-dibenzo[b,d]pyran-1 ,9 diol.

(H) BAY 38-7271, (-)-(R)-3-(2-Hydroxymethylindanyl-4-o xy)phenyl-4,4,4-trifluorobutyl-1-sulfonate.

(I) CP 50,556-1, Levonantradol, including 9-hydroxy-6-methyl-3 -[5-phenylpentan-2-yl]oxy-5,6,6a,7,8,9,10,10a-octahydrophenant hridin-1-yl]acetate; [(6S,6aR,9R, 10aR)-9-hydroxy-6-methyl-3-[(2R)-5-phenylpentan-2-yl]oxy-5,6,6a,7,8,9,10,10a-octahydrophenanthridin-1-yl]acetate; and [9-hydroxy-6-methyl-3-[5-phenylpentan-2-yl]oxy-5,6,6a,7,8,9,10,10a-octahydrophenanthridin-1-yl] acetate.

(J) HU-210, including (6aR,10aR)-9-(hydroxymethyl)-6,6-d imethyl-3-(2-methyloctan-2-yl)-6a,7,10,10a-tetrahydrobenzo[c] chromen-1-ol; [(6aR,10aR)-9-(hydroxymethyl)-6,6-dimethyl-3-(2-methyl octan-2-yl)-6a,7,10,10a-tetrahydrobenzo[c]chromen-1-o l and 1,1-Dimethylheptyl-11-hydroxytetrahydrocannabinol.

(K) HU-211, Dexanabinol, including (6aS, 10aS)-9-(hydroxy methyl)-6,6-dimethyl-3-(2-methyloctan-2-yl)-6a,7,10,10a-tetrahydrobenzo[c]chromen-1-ol and (6aS, 10aS)-9-(hydroxy methyl)-6,6-dimethyl-3-(2-methyloctan-2-yl)-6a,7,10,10a-tetrahydrobenzo[c]chromen-1-ol.

(L) HU-243, 3-dimethylheptyl-11-hydroxyhexahydrocannabinol.

(M) HU-308, [(91R,2R,5R)-2-[2,6-dimethoxy-4-(2-methyloctan-2 - yl)phenyl]-7,7-dimethyl-4-bicyclo[3.1.1]hept-3-enyl]methanol.

(N) HU-331, 3-hydroxy-2-[(1R,6R)-3-methyl-6-(1-m ethylethenyl)-2-cyclohexen-1-yl]-5-pentyl-2,5-cyclohexadiene-1 ,4-dione.

(O) HU-336, (6aR,10aR)-6,6,9-trimethyl-3-pentyl-6a,7,10,10a-tetrahydro-1H-benzo[c]chromene-1,4(6H)-dione.

(P) JTE-907, N-(benzol[1,3]dioxol-5-ylmethyl)-7-methoxy-2-o xo-8-pentyloxy-1,2-dihydroquinoline-3-carboxamide.

(Q) JWH-051, ((6aR,10aR)-6,6-dimethyl-3-(2-methyloctan-2-y l)-6a,7,10,10a-tetrahydrobenzo[c] chromen-9-yl)methanol.

(R) JWH-057 (6aR,10aR)-3-(1,1-dimethylheptyl)-6a,7,10,10a-t etrahydro-6,6,9-trimethyl-6H-Dibenzo[b,d]pyran.

(S) JWH-133 (6aR,10aR)-3-(1,1-Dimethylbutyl)-6a,7,10,10a-t etrahydro -6,6,9-trimethyl-6H-dibenzo[b,d] pyran.

(T) JWH-359, (6aR,10aR)- 1-methoxy- 6,6,9-trimethyl- 3-[(2R)-1 ,1,2-trimethylbutyl]- 6a,7,10,10a-tetrahydrobenzo[c]chromene.

(U) URB-597 [3-(3-carbamoylphenyl)phenyl]-N-cyclohexylcarb amate.

(V) URB-602 [1,1'-Biphenyl]-3-yl-carbamic acid, cyclohexyl ester; OR cyclohexyl [1,1'-biphenyl]-3-ylcarbamate.

(W) URB-754 6-methyl-2-[(4-methylphenyl)amino]-4H-3,1-b enzoxazin-4-one.

(X) URB-937 3'-carbamoyl-6-hydroxy-[1,1'-biphenyl]-3-yl cyclohexylcarbamate.

(Y) WIN 55,212-2, including (R)-(+)-[2,3-dihydro-5-methyl-3 -(4-morpholinylmethyl)pyrrolo[1,2,3-de]-1,4-benzoxazin-6-yl]-1 -napthalenylmethanone and [2,3-Dihydro-5-methyl-3-(4-morpholinylmethyl) pyrrolo[(1,2,3-de)-1,4-benzoxazin-6-yl]-1-napthalenylmethanone.

(d) The substances or analogs of substances identified in subdivision (c) may be lawfully obtained and used for bona fide research, instruction, or analysis if that possession and use does not violate federal law.

(e) As used in this section, "synthetic cannabinoid compound" does not include either of the following:

(1) Any substance for which there is an approved new drug application, as defined in Section 505 of the federal Food, Drug, and Cosmetic Act (21 U.S.C. Sec. 355) or which is generally recognized as safe and effective for use pursuant to Section 501, 502, and 503 of the federal Food, Drug, and Cosmetic Act and Title 21 of the Code of Federal Regulations.

(2) With respect to a particular person, any substance for which an exemption is in effect for investigational use for that person pursuant to Section 505 of the federal Food, Drug, and Cosmetic Act (21 U.S.C. Sec. 355), to the extent that the conduct with respect to that substance is pursuant to the exemption.

Health and Safety Code § 11358

(MAUCRSA, Effective June 27, 2017.)

Every person who plants, cultivates, harvests, dries, or processes cannabis plants, or any part thereof, except as otherwise provided by law, shall be punished as follows:

(a) Every person under the age of 18 who plants, cultivates, harvests, dries, or processes any cannabis plants shall be punished in the same manner provided in paragraph (1) of subdivision (b) of section 11357.

(b) Every person at least 18 years of age but less than 21 years of age who plants, cultivates, harvests, dries, or processes not more than six living cannabis plants shall be guilty of an infraction and a fine of not more than one hundred dollars ($100).

(c) Every person 18 years of age or over who plants, cultivates, harvests, dries, or processes more than six living cannabis plants shall be punished by imprisonment in a county jail for a period of not more than six months or by a fine of not more than five hundred dollars ($500), or by both such fine and imprisonment.

(d) Notwithstanding subdivision (c), a person 18 years of age or over who plants, cultivates, harvests, dries, or processes more than six living cannabis plants, or any part thereof, except as otherwise provided by law, may be punished by imprisonment pursuant to subdivision (h) of Section 1170 of the Penal Code if any of the following conditions exist:

(1) the person has one or more prior convictions for an offense specified in clause (iv) of subparagraph (C) of paragraph (2) of subdivision (e) of Section 667 of the Penal Code or for an offense requiring registration pursuant to subdivision (c) of Section 290 of the Penal Code.

(2) the person has two or more prior convictions under subdivision (c).

(3) the offense resulted in any of the following:

(A) Violation of Section 1052 of the Water Code relating to illegal diversion of water.

(B) Violation of Section 13260, 13264, 13272, or 13387 of the Water Code relating to discharge of water.

(C) Violation of Section 5650 or Section 5652 of the Fish and Game Code relating to waters of the state.

(D) Violation of Section 1602 of the Fish and Game Code relating to rivers, streams and lakes.

(E) Violation of Section 374.8 of the Penal Code relating to hazardous substances or Sections 25189.5, 25189.6, or 25189.7 of the Health and Safety Code relating to hazardous waste.

(F) Violation of Section 2080 of the Fish and Game Code relating to endangered and threatened species or Section 3513 of the Fish and Game Code relating to the Migratory Bird Treaty Act, or Section 2000 of the Fish and Game Code relating to the unlawful taking of fish and wildlife.

(G) Intentionally or with gross negligence causing substantial environmental harm to public lands or other public resources.

Health and Safety Code § 11359

(MAUCRSA, Effective June 27, 2017.)

Every person who possesses for sale any cannabis, except as otherwise provided by law, shall be punished as follows:

(a) Every person under the age of 18 who possesses cannabis for sale shall be punished in the same manner provided in paragraph (1) of subdivision (b) of Section 11357.

(b) Every person 18 years of age or over who possesses cannabis for sale shall be punished by imprisonment in a county jail for a period of not more than six months or by a fine of not more than five hundred dollars ($500), or by both such fine and imprisonment.

(c) Notwithstanding subdivision (b), a person 18 years of age or over who possesses cannabis for sale may be punished by imprisonment pursuant to subdivision (h) of Section 1170 of the Penal Code if:

(1) the person has one or more prior convictions for an offense specified in clause (iv) of subparagraph (C) of paragraph (2) of subdivision (e) of Section 667 of the Penal Code or for an offense requiring registration pursuant to subdivision (c) of Section 290 of the Penal Code;

(2) the person has two or more prior convictions under subdivision (b); or

(3) the offense occurred in connection with the knowing sale or attempted sale of cannabis to a person under the age of 18 years.

(d) Notwithstanding subdivision (b), a person 21 years of age or over who possesses cannabis for sale may be punished by imprisonment pursuant to subdivision (h) of Section 1170 of the Penal Code if the offense involves knowingly hiring, employing, or using a person 20 years of age or younger in unlawfully cultivating, transporting, carrying, selling, offering to sell, giving away, preparing for sale, or peddling any cannabis.

Health and Safety Code § 11360

(MAUCRSA, Effective June 27, 2017.)

(a) Except as otherwise provided by this section or as authorized by law, every person who transports, imports into this state, sells, furnishes, administers, or gives away, or offers to transport, import into this state, sell, furnish, administer, or give away, or attempts to import into this state or transport any cannabis shall be punished as follows:

> (1) Persons under the age of 18 years shall be punished in the same manner as provided in paragraph (1) of subdivision (b) of section 11357.

> (2) Persons 18 years of age or over shall be punished by imprisonment in a county jail for a period of not more than six months or by a fine of not more than five hundred dollars ($500), or by both such fine and imprisonment.

> (3) Notwithstanding paragraph (2), a person 18 years of age or over may be punished by imprisonment pursuant to subdivision (h) of Section 1170 of the Penal Code for a period two, three, or four years if:

>> (A) The person has one or more prior convictions for an offense specified in clause (iv) of subparagraph (C) of paragraph (2) of subdivision (e) of Section 667 of the Penal Code or for an offense requiring registration pursuant to subdivision (c) of Section 290 of the Penal Code;

>> (B) The person has two or more prior convictions under paragraph (2);

>> (C) The offense involved the knowing sale, attempted sale, or the knowing offer to sell, furnish, administer or give away cannabis to a person under the age of 18 years; or

>> (D) The offense involved the import, offer to import; or attempted import into this state, or the transport for sale, offer to transport for sale, or attempted transport for sale out of this state, of more than 28.5 grams of cannabis or more than four grams of concentrated cannabis.

(b) Except as authorized by law, every person who gives away, offers to give away, transports, offers to transport, or attempts to transport not more than 28.5 grams of cannabis, other than concentrated cannabis, is guilty of an infraction and shall be punished by a fine of not more than one hundred dollars ($100). In any case in which a person is arrested for a violation of this subdivision and does not demand to be taken before a magistrate, such person shall be released by the arresting officer upon presentation of satisfactory evidence of identity and giving his or her written promise to appear in court, as provided in Section 853.6 of the Penal Code, and shall not be subjected to booking.

(c) For purposes of this section, "transport" means to transport for sale.

(d) This section does not preclude or limit prosecution for any aiding and abetting or conspiracy offenses.

Health & Safety Code § 11361

(MAUCRSA, Effective June 27, 2017.)

(a) A person 18 years of age or over who hires, employs, or uses a minor in unlawfully transporting, carrying, selling, giving away, preparing for sale, or peddling any cannabis, who unlawfully sells, or offers to sell, any cannabis to a minor, or who furnishes, administers, or gives, or offers to furnish, administer, or give any cannabis to a minor under 14 years of age, or who induces a minor to use cannabis in violation of law shall be punished by imprisonment in the state prison for a period of three, five, or seven years.

(b) A person 18 years of age or over who furnishes, administers, or gives, or offers to furnish, administer, or give, any cannabis to a minor 14 years of age or older in violation of law shall be punished by imprisonment in the state prison for a period of three, four, or five years.

Health and Safety Code § 11361.1

(MAUCRSA, Effective June 27, 2017.)

(a) The drug education and counseling requirements under sections 11357, 11358, 11359, and 11360 shall be:

(1) Mandatory, unless the court finds that such drug education or counseling is unnecessary for the person, or that a drug education or counseling program is unavailable;

(2) Free to participants, and shall consist of at least four hours of group discussion or instruction based on science and evidence-based principles and practices specific to the use and abuse of cannabis and other controlled substances.

(b) For good cause, the court may grant an extension of time not to exceed 30 days for a person to complete the drug education and counseling required under sections 11357, 11358, 11359, and 11360.

Health and Safety Code § 11361.5

(Amended by Stats. 2018, Ch. 92, Sec. 140. (SB 1289) Effective January 1, 2019. Note: This section was amended on Nov. 8, 2016, by initiative Prop. 64.)

(a) Records of any court of this state, any public or private agency that provides services upon referral under Section 1000.2 of the Penal Code, or of any state agency pertaining to the arrest or conviction of any person for a violation of Section 11357 or subdivision (b) of Section 11360, or pertaining to the arrest or conviction of any person under the age of 18 for a violation of any provision of this article except Section 11357.5, shall not be kept beyond two years from the date of the conviction, or from the date of the arrest if there was no conviction, except with respect to a violation of subdivision (d) of Section 11357, or any other violation by a person under the age of 18 occurring upon the grounds of, or within, any school providing instruction in kindergarten or any of grades 1 to 12, inclusive, during hours the school is open for classes or school-related programs, the records shall be retained until the offender attains the age of 18 years at which time the records shall be destroyed as provided in this section. A court or agency having custody of the records, including the statewide criminal databases, shall provide for the timely destruction of the records in accordance with subdivision (c), and those records shall also be purged from the statewide criminal databases. As used in this subdivision, "records pertaining to the arrest or conviction" shall include records of arrests resulting in the criminal proceeding and records relating to other offenses charged in the accusatory pleading, whether the defendant was acquitted or charges were dismissed. The two-year period beyond which records shall not be kept pursuant to this subdivision does not apply to any person who is, at the time at which this subdivision would otherwise require record destruction, incarcerated for an offense subject to this subdivision. For such persons, the two-year period shall commence from the date the person is released from custody. The requirements of this subdivision do not apply to records of any conviction occurring before January 1, 1976, or records of any arrest not followed by a conviction occurring before that date, or records of any arrest for an offense specified in subdivision (c) of Section 1192.7, or subdivision (c) of Section 667.5, of the Penal Code.

(b) This subdivision applies only to records of convictions and arrests not followed by conviction occurring before January 1, 1976, for any of the following offenses:

(1) A violation of Section 11357 or a statutory predecessor thereof.

(2) Unlawful possession of a device, contrivance, instrument, or paraphernalia used for unlawfully smoking cannabis, in violation of Section 11364, as it existed before January 1, 1976, or a statutory predecessor thereof.

(3) Unlawful visitation or presence in a room or place in which cannabis is being unlawfully smoked or used, in violation of Section 11365, as it existed before January 1, 1976, or a statutory predecessor thereof.

(4) Unlawfully using or being under the influence of cannabis, in violation of Section 11550, as it existed before January 1, 1976, or a statutory predecessor thereof.

(A) A person subject to an arrest or conviction for those offenses may apply to the Department of Justice for destruction of records pertaining to the arrest or conviction if two or more years have elapsed since the date of the conviction, or since the date of the arrest if not followed by a conviction. The application shall be submitted upon a form supplied by the Department of Justice and shall be accompanied by a fee, which shall be established by the department in an amount which will defray the cost of administering this subdivision and costs incurred by the state under subdivision (c), but which shall not exceed thirty-seven dollars and fifty cents ($37.50). The application form may be made available at every local police or sheriff's department and from the Department of Justice and may require that information which the department determines is necessary for purposes of identification.

(B) The department may request, but not require, the applicant to include a self-administered fingerprint upon the application. If the department is unable to sufficiently identify the applicant for purposes of this subdivision without the fingerprint or without additional fingerprints, it shall so notify the applicant and shall request the applicant to submit any fingerprints which may be required to effect identification, including a complete set if necessary, or, alternatively, to abandon the application and request a refund of all or a portion of the fee submitted with the application, as provided in this section. If the applicant fails or refuses to submit fingerprints in accordance with the department's request within a reasonable time which shall be established by the department, or if the applicant requests a refund of the fee, the department shall promptly mail a refund to the applicant at the address specified in the application or at any other address which may be specified by the applicant. However, if the department has notified the applicant that election to abandon the application will result in forfeiture of a specified amount which is a portion of the fee, the department may retain a portion of the fee which the department determines will defray the actual costs of processing the application, provided the amount of the portion retained shall not exceed ten dollars ($10).

(C) Upon receipt of a sufficient application, the Department of Justice shall destroy records of the department, if any, pertaining to the arrest or conviction in the manner prescribed by subdivision (c) and shall notify the Federal Bureau of Investigation, the law enforcement agency which arrested the applicant, and, if the applicant was convicted, the probation department which investigated the applicant and the Department of Motor Vehicles, of the application.

(c) Destruction of records of arrest or conviction pursuant to subdivision (a) or (b) shall be accomplished by permanent obliteration of all entries or notations upon the records pertaining to the arrest or conviction, and the record shall be prepared again so that it appears that the arrest or conviction never occurred. However, where (1) the only entries upon the record pertain to the arrest or conviction and (2) the record can be destroyed without necessarily effecting the destruction of other records, then the document constituting the record shall be physically destroyed.

(d) Notwithstanding subdivision (a) or (b), written transcriptions of oral testimony in court proceedings and published judicial appellate reports are not subject to this section. Additionally, no records shall be destroyed pursuant to subdivision (a) if the defendant or a codefendant has filed a civil action against the peace officers or law enforcement jurisdiction which made the arrest or instituted the prosecution and if the agency which is the custodian of those records has received a certified copy of the complaint in the civil action, until the civil action has finally been resolved. Immediately following the final resolution of the civil action, records subject to subdivision (a) shall be destroyed pursuant to subdivision (c) if more than two years have elapsed from the date of the conviction or arrest without conviction.

Health and Safety Code § 11361.7

(Added by Statute, Effective 1976.)

(a) Any record subject to destruction or permanent obliteration pursuant to Section 11361.5, or more than two years of age, or a record of a conviction for an offense specified in subdivision (a) or (b) of Section 11361.5 which became final more than two years previously, shall not be considered to be accurate, relevant, timely, or complete for any purposes by any agency or person. The provisions of this subdivision shall be applicable for purposes of the Privacy Act of 1974 (5 U.S.C. Section 552a) to the fullest extent permissible by law, whenever any information or record subject to destruction or permanent obliteration under Section 11361.5 was obtained by any state agency, local public agency, or any public or private agency that provides services upon referral under Section 1000.2 of the Penal Code, and is thereafter shared with or disseminated to any agency of the federal government.

(b) No public agency shall alter, amend, assess, condition, deny, limit, postpone, qualify, revoke, surcharge, or suspend any certificate, franchise, incident, interest, license, opportunity, permit, privilege, right, or title of any person because of an arrest or conviction for an offense specified in subdivision (a) or (b) of Section 11361.5, or because of the facts or events leading to such an arrest or conviction, on or after the date the records of such arrest or conviction are required to be destroyed by subdivision (a) of Section 11361.5, or two years from the date of such conviction or arrest without conviction with respect to arrests and convictions occurring prior to January 1, 1976. As used in this subdivision, "public agency" includes, but is not limited to, any state, county, city and county, city, public or constitutional corporation or entity, district, local or regional political subdivision, or any department, division, bureau, office, board, commission or other agency thereof.

(c) Any person arrested or convicted for an offense specified in subdivision (a) or (b) of Section 11361.5 may, two years from the date of such a conviction, or from the date of the arrest if there was no conviction, indicate in response to any question concerning his prior criminal record that he was not arrested or convicted for such offense.

(d) The provisions of this section shall be applicable without regard to whether destruction or obliteration of records has actually been implemented pursuant to Section 11361.5.

Health and Safety Code § 11361.8

(AUMA, Effective November 9, 2016.)

(a) A person currently serving a sentence for a conviction, whether by trial or by open or negotiated plea, who would not have been guilty of an offense or who would have been guilty of a lesser offense under the Control, Regulate and Tax Adult Use of Marijuana Act had that Act been in effect at the time of the offense may petition for a recall or dismissal of sentence before the trial court that entered the judgment of conviction in his or her case to request resentencing or dismissal in accordance with Sections 11357, 11358, 11359, 11360, 11362.1, 11362.2, 11362.3, and 11362. 4 as those sections have been amended or added by this Act.

(b) Upon receiving a petition under subdivision (a), the court shall presume the petitioner satisfies the criteria in subdivision (a) unless the party opposing the petition proves by clear and convincing evidence that the petitioner does not satisfy the criteria. If the petitioner satisfies the criteria in subdivision (a), the court shall grant the petition to recall the sentence or dismiss the sentence because it is legally invalid unless the court determines that granting the petition would pose an unreasonable risk of danger to public safety.

> (1) In exercising its discretion, the court may consider, but shall not be limited to evidence provided for in subdivision (b) of Section 1170.18 of the Penal Code.

> (2) As used in this section, "unreasonable risk of danger to public safety" has the same meaning as provided in subdivision (c) of Section 1170.18 of the Penal Code.

(c) A person who is serving a sentence and resentenced pursuant to subdivision (b) shall be given credit for any time already served and shall be subject to supervision for one year following completion of his or her time in custody or shall be subject to whatever supervision time he or she would have otherwise been subject to after release, whichever is shorter, unless the court, in its discretion, as part of its resentencing order, releases the person from supervision. Such person is subject to parole supervision under Penal Code Section 3000.08 or post-release community supervision under subdivision (a) of Section 3451 of the Penal Code by the designated agency and the jurisdiction of the court in the county in which the offender is released or resides, or in which an alleged violation of supervision has occurred, for the purpose of hearing petitions to revoke supervision and impose a term of custody.

(d) Under no circumstances may resentencing under this section result in the imposition of a term longer than the original sentence, or the reinstatement of charges dismissed pursuant to a negotiated plea agreement.

(e) A person who has completed his or her sentence for a conviction under Sections 11357, 11358, 11359, and 11360, whether by trial or open or negotiated plea, who would not have been guilty of an offense or who would have been guilty of a lesser offense under the Control, Regulate and Tax Adult Use of Marijuana Act had that Act been in effect at the time of the offense, may file an application before the trial court that entered the judgment of conviction in his or her case to have the conviction dismissed and sealed because the prior conviction is now legally invalid or redesignated as a misdemeanor or infraction in accordance with Sections 11357, 11358, 11359, 11360, 11362.1, 11362.2, 11362.3, and 11362.4 as those sections have been amended or added by this Act.

(f) The court shall presume the petitioner satisfies the criteria in subdivision (e) unless the party opposing the application proves by clear and convincing evidence that the petitioner does not satisfy the criteria in subdivision (e). Once the applicant satisfies the criteria in subdivision (e), the court shall redesignate the conviction as a misdemeanor or infraction or dismiss and seal the conviction as legally invalid as now established under the Control, Regulate and Tax Adult Use of Marijuana Act.

(g) Unless requested by the applicant, no hearing is necessary to grant or deny an application filed under subdivision (e).

(h) Any felony conviction that is recalled and resentenced under subdivision (b) or designated as a misdemeanor or infraction under subdivision (f) shall be considered a misdemeanor or infraction for all purposes. Any misdemeanor conviction that is recalled and resentenced under subdivision (b) or designated as an infraction under subdivision (f) shall be considered an infraction for all purposes.

(i) If the court that originally sentenced the petitioner is not available, the presiding judge shall designate another judge to rule on the petition or application.

(j) Nothing in this section is intended to diminish or abrogate any rights or remedies otherwise available to the petitioner or applicant.

(k) Nothing in this and related sections is intended to diminish or abrogate the finality of judgments in any case not falling within the purview of the Control, Regulate and Tax Adult Use of Marijuana Act.

(l) A resentencing hearing ordered under this act shall constitute a "post-conviction release proceeding" under paragraph (7) of subdivision (b) of Section 28 of Article I of the California Constitution (Marsy's Law).

(m) The provisions of this section shall apply equally to juvenile delinquency adjudications and dispositions under Section 602 of the Welfare and Institutions Code if the juvenile would not have been guilty of an offense or would have been guilty of a lesser offense under the Control, Regulate and Tax Adult Use of Marijuana Act.

(n) The Judicial Council shall promulgate and make available all necessary forms to enable the filing of the petitions and applications provided in this section.

Health & Safety Code § 11361.9

(Added by Stats. 2018, Ch. 993, Sec. 1. (AB 1793) Effective January 1, 2019.)

(a) On or before July 1, 2019, the Department of Justice shall review the records in the state summary criminal history information database and shall identify past convictions that are potentially eligible for recall or dismissal of sentence, dismissal and sealing, or redesignation pursuant to Section 11361.8. The department shall notify the prosecution of all cases in their jurisdiction that are eligible for recall or dismissal of sentence, dismissal and sealing, or redesignation.

(b) The prosecution shall have until July 1, 2020, to review all cases and determine whether to challenge the recall or dismissal of sentence, dismissal and sealing, or redesignation.

(c) (1) The prosecution may challenge the resentencing of a person pursuant to this section when the person does not meet the criteria established in Section 11361.8 or presents an unreasonable risk to public safety.

(2) The prosecution may challenge the dismissal and sealing or redesignation of a person pursuant to this section who has completed his or her sentence for a conviction when the person does not meet the criteria established in Section 11361.8.

(3) On or before July 1, 2020, the prosecution shall inform the court and the public defender's office in their county when they are challenging a particular recall or dismissal of sentence, dismissal and sealing, or redesignation. The prosecution shall inform the court when they are not challenging a particular recall or dismissal of sentence, dismissal and sealing, or redesignation.

(4) The public defender's office, upon receiving notice from the prosecution pursuant to paragraph (3), shall make a reasonable effort to notify the person whose resentencing or dismissal is being challenged.

(d) If the prosecution does not challenge the recall or dismissal of sentence, dismissal and sealing, or redesignation by July 1, 2020, the court shall reduce or dismiss the conviction pursuant to Section 11361.8.

(e) The court shall notify the department of the recall or dismissal of sentence, dismissal and sealing, or redesignation and the department shall modify the state summary criminal history information database accordingly.

(f) The department shall post general information on its Internet Web site about the recall or dismissal of sentences, dismissal and sealing, or redesignation authorized in this section.

(g) It is the intent of the Legislature that persons who are currently serving a sentence or who proactively petition for a recall or dismissal of sentence, dismissal and sealing, or redesignation pursuant to Section 11361.8 be prioritized for review.

Health and Safety Code § 11362

(Amended by Statute, Effective April 4, 2011, and Operative October 1, 2011.)

As used in this article "felony offense," and offense "punishable as a felony" refer to an offense prior to July 1, 2011, for which the law prescribes imprisonment in the state prison, or for an offense on or after July 1, 2011, imprisonment in either the state prison or pursuant to subdivision (h) of Section 1170 of the Penal Code, as either an alternative or the sole penalty, regardless of the sentence the particular defendant received.

Health and Safety Code § 11362.1

(MAUCRSA, Effective June 27, 2017.)

(a) Subject to Sections 11362.2, 11362.3, 11362.4, and 11362.45, but notwithstanding any other provision of law, it shall be lawful under state and local law, and shall not be a violation of state or local law, for persons 21 years of age or older to:

(1) Possess, process, transport, purchase, obtain, or give away to persons 21 years of age or older without any compensation whatsoever, not more than 28.5 grams of cannabis not in the form of concentrated cannabis;

(2) Possess, process, transport, purchase, obtain, or give away to persons 21 years of age or older without any compensation whatsoever, not more than eight grams of cannabis in the form of concentrated cannabis, including as contained in cannabis products;

(3) Possess, plant, cultivate, harvest, dry, or process not more than six living cannabis plants and possess the cannabis produced by the plants;

(4) Smoke or ingest cannabis or cannabis products; and

(5) Possess, transport, purchase, obtain, use, manufacture, or give away cannabis accessories to persons 21 years of age or older without any compensation whatsoever.

(b) Paragraph (5) of subdivision (a) is intended to meet the requirements of subdivision (f) of Section 863 a/Title 21 of the United States Code (21 US.C. § 863(f)) by authorizing, under state law, any person in compliance with this section to manufacture, possess, or distribute cannabis accessories.

(c) Cannabis and cannabis products involved in any way with conduct deemed lawful by this section are not contraband nor subject to seizure, and no conduct deemed lawful by this section shall constitute the basis for detention, search, or arrest.

Health and Safety Code § 11362.2

(MAUCRSA, Effective June 27, 2017.)

(a) Personal cultivation of cannabis under paragraph (3) of subdivision (a) of Section 11362.1 is subject to the following restrictions:

(1) A person shall plant, cultivate, harvest, dry, or process plants in accordance with local ordinances, if any, adopted in accordance with subdivision (b).

(2) The living plants and any cannabis produced by the plants in excess of 28.5 grams are kept within the person's private residence, or upon the grounds of that private residence (e.g., in an outdoor garden area), are in a locked space, and are not visible by normal unaided vision from a public place.

(3) Not more than six living plants may be planted, cultivated, harvested, dried, or processed within a single private residence, or upon the grounds of that private residence, at one time.

(b)(1) A city, county, or city and county may enact and enforce reasonable regulations to regulate the actions and conduct in paragraph (3) of subdivision (a) of Section 11362.1.

(2) Notwithstanding paragraph (1), a city, county, or city and county shall not completely prohibit persons engaging in the actions and conduct under paragraph (3) of subdivision (a) of Section 11362.1 inside a private residence, or inside an accessory structure to a private residence located upon the grounds of a private residence that is fully enclosed and secure.

(3) Notwithstanding paragraph (3) of subdivision (a) of Section 11362.1, a city, county, or city and county may completely prohibit persons from engaging in actions and conduct under paragraph (3) of subdivision (a) of Section 11362.1 outdoors upon the grounds of a private residence.

(4) Paragraph (3) shall become inoperable upon a determination by the California Attorney General that adult use of cannabis is lawful in the State of California under federal law, and an act taken by a city, county, or city and county under paragraph (3) is unenforceable upon the date of that determination by the Attorney General.

(5) For purposes of this section, "private residence" means a house, an apartment unit, a mobile home, or other similar dwelling.

Health and Safety Code § 11362.3

(MAUCRSA, Effective June 27, 2017.)

(a) Section 11362.1 does not permit any person to:

(1) Smoke or ingest cannabis or cannabis products in a public place, except in accordance with Section 26200 of the Business and Professions Code.

(2) Smoke cannabis or cannabis products in a location where smoking tobacco is prohibited.

(3) Smoke cannabis or cannabis products within 1,000 feet of a school, day care center, or youth center while children are present at the school, day care center, or youth center, except in or upon the grounds of a private residence or in accordance with Section 26200 of the Business and Professions Code and only if such smoking is not detectable by others on the grounds of the school, day care center, or youth center while children are present.

(4) Possess an open container or open package of cannabis or cannabis products while driving, operating, or riding in the passenger seat or compartment of a motor vehicle, boat, vessel, aircraft, or other vehicle used for transportation.

(5) Possess, smoke or ingest cannabis or cannabis products in or upon the grounds of a school, day care center, or youth center while children are present.

(6) Manufacture concentrated cannabis using a volatile solvent, unless done in accordance with a license under Division 10 (commencing with section 26000) of the Business and Professions Code.

(7) Smoke or ingest cannabis or cannabis products while driving, operating a motor vehicle, boat, vessel, aircraft, or other vehicle used for transportation.

(8) Smoke or ingest cannabis or cannabis products while riding in the passenger seat or compartment of a motor vehicle, boat, vessel, aircraft, or other vehicle used for transportation except as permitted on a motor vehicle, boat, vessel, aircraft, or other vehicle used for transportation that is operated in accordance with Section 26200 of the Business and Professions Code and while no persons under the age of 21 years are present.

(b) For purposes of this section, the following definitions apply:

(1) "Day care center" has the same meaning as in Section 1596.76.

(2) "Smoke" means to inhale, exhale, burn, or carry any lighted or heated device or pipe, or any other lighted or heated cannabis or cannabis product intended for inhalation, whether natural or synthetic, in any manner or in any form. "Smoke" includes the use of an electronic smoking device that creates an aerosol or vapor, in any manner or in any form, or the use of any oral smoking device for the purpose of circumventing the prohibition of smoking in a place.

(3) "Volatile solvent" means a solvent that is or produces a flammable gas or vapor that, when present in the air in sufficient quantities, will create explosive or ignitable mixtures.

(4) "Youth center" has the same meaning as in Section 11353.1.

(c) Nothing in this section shall be construed or interpreted to amend, repeal, affect, restrict, or preempt laws pertaining to the Compassionate Use Act of 1996.

Health and Safety Code § 11362.4

(Amended by Stats. 2018, Ch. 92, Sec. 141. (SB 1289) Effective January 1, 2019. Note: This section was added on Nov. 8, 2016, by initiative Prop. 64.)

(a) A person who engages in the conduct described in paragraph (1) of subdivision (a) of Section 11362.3 is guilty of an infraction punishable by no more than a one-hundred-dollar ($100) fine; provided, however, that persons under 18 years of age shall instead be required to complete four hours of a drug education program or counseling, and up to 10 hours of community service, over a period not to exceed 60 days once the drug education program or counseling and community service opportunity are made available to the person.

(b) A person who engages in the conduct described in paragraph (2), (3), or (4) of subdivision (a) of Section 11362.3 is guilty of an infraction punishable by no more than a two-hundred-fifty-dollar ($250) fine, unless that activity is otherwise permitted by state and local law; provided, however, that a person under 18 years of age shall instead be required to complete four hours of drug education or counseling, and up to 20 hours of community service, over a period not to exceed 90 days once the drug education program or counseling and community service opportunity are made available to the person.

(c) A person who engages in the conduct described in paragraph (5) of subdivision (a) of Section 11362.3 is subject to the same punishment as provided under subdivision (c) or (d) of Section 11357.

(d) A person who engages in the conduct described in paragraph (6) of subdivision (a) of Section 11362.3 is subject to punishment under Section 11379.6.

(e) A person who violates the restrictions in subdivision (a) of Section 11362.2 is guilty of an infraction punishable by no more than a two-hundred-fifty-dollar ($250) fine.

(f) Notwithstanding subdivision (e), a person under 18 years of age who violates the restrictions in subdivision (a) of Section 11362.2 shall be punished under paragraph (1) of subdivision (b) of Section 11357.

(g) (1) The drug education program or counseling hours required by this section shall be mandatory unless the court makes a finding that the program or counseling is unnecessary for the person or that a drug education program or counseling is unavailable.

(2) The drug education program required by this section for persons under 18 years of age shall be free to participants and provide at least four hours of group discussion or instruction based on science and evidence-based principles and practices specific to the use and abuse of cannabis and other controlled substances.

(h) Upon a finding of good cause, the court may extend the time for a person to complete the drug education or counseling, and community service required under this section.

Health and Safety Code § 11362.45

(MAUCRSA, Effective June 27, 2017.)

Section 11362.1 does not amend, repeal, affect, restrict, or preempt:

(a) Laws making it unlawful to drive or operate a vehicle, boat, vessel, or aircraft, while smoking, ingesting, or impaired by, cannabis or cannabis products, including, but not limited to, subdivision (e) of Section 23152 of the Vehicle Code, or the penalties prescribed for violating those laws.

(b) Laws prohibiting the sale, administering, furnishing, or giving away of cannabis, cannabis products, or cannabis accessories, or the offering to sell, administer, furnish, or give away cannabis, cannabis products, or cannabis accessories to a person younger than 21 years of age.

(c) Laws prohibiting a person younger than 21 years of age from engaging in any of the actions or conduct otherwise permitted under Section 11362.1.

(d) Laws pertaining to smoking or ingesting cannabis or cannabis products on the grounds of, or within, any facility or institution under the jurisdiction of the Department of Corrections and Rehabilitation or the Division of Juvenile Justice, or on the grounds of, or within, any other facility or institution referenced in Section 4573 of the Penal Code.

(e) Laws providing that it would constitute negligence or professional malpractice to undertake any task while impaired from smoking or ingesting cannabis or cannabis products.

(f) The rights and obligations of public and private employers to maintain a drug and alcohol free workplace or require an employer to permit or accommodate the use, consumption, possession, transfer, display, transportation, sale, or growth of cannabis in the workplace, or affect the ability of employers to have policies prohibiting the use of cannabis by employees and prospective employees, or prevent employers from complying with state or federal law.

(g) The ability of a state or local government agency to prohibit or restrict any of the actions or conduct otherwise permitted under Section 11362.1 within a building owned, leased, or occupied by the state or local government agency.

(h) The ability of an individual or private entity to prohibit or restrict any of the actions or conduct otherwise permitted under Section 11362.1 on the individual's or entity's privately owned property.

(i) Laws pertaining to the Compassionate Use Act of 1996.

Health And Safety Code § 11362.5

(Proposition 215, Effective November 5, 1996.)

SEC. 1.

(a) This section shall be known and may be cited as the Compassionate Use Act of 1996.

(b)(1) The people of the State of California hereby find and declare that the purposes of the Compassionate Use Act of 1996 are as follows:

> (A) To ensure that seriously ill Californians have the right to obtain and use marijuana for medical purposes where that medical use is deemed appropriate and has been recommended by a physician who has determined that the person's health would benefit from the use of marijuana in the treatment of cancer, anorexia, AIDS, chronic pain, spasticity, glaucoma, arthritis, migraine, or any other illness for which marijuana provides relief.

> (B) To ensure that patients and their primary caregivers who obtain and use marijuana for medical purposes upon the recommendation of a physician are not subject to criminal prosecution or sanction.

> (C) To encourage the federal and state governments to implement a plan to provide for the safe and affordable distribution of marijuana to all patients in medical need of marijuana.

(b)(2) Nothing in this section shall be construed to supersede legislation prohibiting persons from engaging in conduct that endangers others, nor to condone the diversion of marijuana for nonmedical purposes.

(c) Notwithstanding any other provision of law, no physician in this state shall be punished, or denied any right or privilege, for having recommended marijuana to a patient for medical purposes.

(d) Section 11357, relating to the possession of marijuana, and Section 11358, relating to the cultivation of marijuana, shall not apply to a patient, or to a patient's primary caregiver, who possesses or cultivates marijuana for the personal medical purposes of the patient upon the written or oral recommendation or approval of a physician.

(e) For the purposes of this section, "primary caregiver" means the individual designated by the person exempted under this section who has consistently assumed responsibility for the housing, health, or safety of that person.

SEC. 2.

If any provision of this measure or the application thereof to any person or circumstance is held invalid, that invalidity shall not affect other provisions or applications of the measure that can be given effect without the invalid provision or application, and to this end the provisions of this measure are severable.

Heath and Safety Code § 11362.7

(Amended by Stats. 2017, Ch. 775, Sec. 112. (SB 798) Effective January 1, 2018.)

For purposes of this article, the following definitions shall apply:

(a) "Attending physician" means an individual who possesses a license in good standing to practice medicine, podiatry, or osteopathy issued by the Medical Board of California, the California Board of Podiatric Medicine, or the Osteopathic Medical Board of California and who has taken responsibility for an aspect of the medical care, treatment, diagnosis, counseling, or referral of a patient and who has conducted a medical examination of that patient before recording in the patient's medical record the physician's assessment of whether the patient has a serious medical condition and whether the medical use of cannabis is appropriate.

(b) "Department" means the State Department of Public Health.

(c) "Person with an identification card" means an individual who is a qualified patient who has applied for and received a valid identification card pursuant to this article.

(d) "Primary caregiver" means the individual, designated by a qualified patient, who has consistently assumed responsibility for the housing, health, or safety of that patient, and may include any of the following:

> (1) In a case in which a qualified patient or person with an identification card receives medical care or supportive services, or both, from a clinic licensed pursuant to Chapter 1 (commencing with Section 1200) of Division 2, a health care facility licensed pursuant to Chapter 2 (commencing with Section 1250) of Division 2, a residential care facility for persons with chronic life-threatening illness licensed pursuant to Chapter 3.01 (commencing with Section 1568.01) of Division 2, a residential care facility for the elderly licensed pursuant to Chapter 3.2 (commencing with Section 1569) of Division 2, a hospice, or a home health agency licensed pursuant to Chapter 8 (commencing with Section 1725) of Division 2, the owner or operator, or no more than three employees who are designated by the owner or operator, of the clinic, facility, hospice, or home health agency, if designated as a primary caregiver by that qualified patient or person with an identification card.

> (2) An individual who has been designated as a primary caregiver by more than one qualified patient or person with an identification card, if every qualified patient or person with an identification card who has designated that individual as a primary caregiver resides in the same city or county as the primary caregiver.

> (3) An individual who has been designated as a primary caregiver by a qualified patient or person with an identification card who resides in a city or county other than that of the primary caregiver, if the individual has

not been designated as a primary caregiver by any other qualified patient or person with an identification card.

(e) A primary caregiver shall be at least 18 years of age, unless the primary caregiver is the parent of a minor child who is a qualified patient or a person with an identification card or the primary caregiver is a person otherwise entitled to make medical decisions under state law pursuant to Section 6922, 7002, 7050, or 7120 of the Family Code.

(f) "Qualified patient" means a person who is entitled to the protections of Section 11362.5, but who does not have an identification card issued pursuant to this article.

(g) "Identification card" means a document issued by the department that identifies a person authorized to engage in the medical use of cannabis and the person's designated primary caregiver, if any.

(h) "Serious medical condition" means all of the following medical conditions:

(1) Acquired immune deficiency syndrome (AIDS).

(2) Anorexia.

(3) Arthritis.

(4) Cachexia.

(5) Cancer.

(6) Chronic pain.

(7) Glaucoma.

(8) Migraine.

(9) Persistent muscle spasms, including, but not limited to, spasms associated with multiple sclerosis.

(10) Seizures, including, but not limited to, seizures associated with epilepsy.

(11) Severe nausea.

(12) Any other chronic or persistent medical symptom that either:

(A) Substantially limits the ability of the person to conduct one or more major life activities as defined in the federal Americans with Disabilities Act of 1990 (Public Law 101-336).

(B) If not alleviated, may cause serious harm to the patient's safety or physical or mental health.

(i) "Written documentation" means accurate reproductions of those portions of a patient's medical records that have been created by the attending physician, that contain the information required by paragraph (2) of subdivision (a) of Section 11362.715, and that the patient may submit as part of an application for an identification card.

Health and Safety Code § 11362.71

(MAUCRSA, Effective June 27, 2017.)

(a) (1) The department shall establish and maintain a voluntary program for the issuance of identification cards to qualified patients who satisfy the requirements of this article and voluntarily apply to the identification card program.

(2) The department shall establish and maintain a 24-hour, toll-free telephone number that will enable state and local law enforcement officers to have immediate access to information necessary to verify the validity

of an identification card issued by the department, until a cost-effective Internet Web-based system can be developed for this purpose.

(b) Every county health department, or the county's designee, shall do all of the following:

(1) Provide applications upon request to individuals seeking to join the identification card program.

(2) Receive and process completed applications in accordance with Section 11362.72.

(3) Maintain records of identification card programs.

(4) Utilize protocols developed by the department pursuant to paragraph (1) of subdivision (d).

(5) Issue identification cards developed by the department to approved applicants and designated primary caregivers.

(c) The county board of supervisors may designate another health-related governmental or nongovernmental entity or organization to perform the functions described in subdivision (b), except for an entity or organization that cultivates or distributes cannabis.

(d) The department shall develop all of the following:

(1) Protocols that shall be used by a county health department or the county's designee to implement the responsibilities described in subdivision (b), including, but not limited to, protocols to confirm the accuracy of information contained in an application and to protect the confidentiality of program records.

(2) Application forms that shall be issued to requesting applicants.

(3) An identification card that identifies a person authorized to engage in the medical use of cannabis and an identification card that identifies the person's designated primary caregiver, if any. The two identification cards developed pursuant to this paragraph shall be easily distinguishable from each other.

(e) No person or designated primary caregiver in possession of a valid identification card shall be subject to arrest for possession, transportation, delivery, or cultivation of medicinal cannabis in an amount established pursuant to this article, unless there is probable cause to believe that the information contained in the card is false or falsified, the card has been obtained by means of fraud, or the person is otherwise in violation of the provisions of this article.

(f) It shall not be necessary for a person to obtain an identification card in order to claim the protections of Section 11362.5.

Health and Safety Code § 11362.712

(AUMA, Effective November 9, 2016.)

(a) Commencing on January 1, 2018, a qualified patient must possess a physician's recommendation that complies with Article 25 (commencing with Section 2525) of Chapter 5 of Division 2 of the Business and Professions Code. Failure to comply with this requirement shall not, however, affect any of the protections provided to patients or their primary caregivers by Section 11362.5.

(b) A county health department or the county's designee shall develop protocols to ensure that, commencing upon January 1, 2018, all identification cards issued pursuant to Section 11362.71 are supported by a physician's recommendation that complies with Article 25 (commencing with Section 2525) of Chapter 5 of Division 2 of the Business and Professions Code.

Health and Safety Code § 11362.713

(AUMA, Effective November 9, 2016.)

(a) Information identifying the names, addresses, or social security numbers of patients, their medical conditions, or the names of their primary caregivers, received and contained in the records of the Department of Public Health and by any county public health department are hereby deemed "medical information" within the meaning of the Confidentiality of Medical Information Act (Civil Code§ 56, et seq.) and shall not be disclosed by the Department or by any county public health department except in accordance with the restrictions on disclosure of individually identifiable information under the Confidentiality of Medical Information Act.

(b) Within 24 hours of receiving any request to disclose the name, address, or social security number of a patient, their medical condition, or the name of their primary caregiver, the Department of Public Health or any county public health agency shall contact the patient and inform the patient of the request and if the request was made in writing, a copy of the request.

(c) Notwithstanding Section 56.10 of the Civil Code, neither the Department of Public Health, nor any county public health agency, shall disclose, nor shall they be ordered by agency or court to disclose, the names, addresses, or social security numbers of patients, their medical conditions, or the names of their primary caregivers, sooner than the 10th day after which the patient whose records are sought to be disclosed has been contacted.

(d) No identification card application system or database used or maintained by the Department of Public Health or by any county department of public health or the county's designee as provided in Section 11362.71 shall contain any personal information of any qualified patient, including but not limited to, the patient's name, address, social security number, medical conditions, or the names of their primary caregivers. Such an application system or database may only contain a unique user identification number, and when that number is entered, the only information that may be provided is whether the card is valid or invalid.

Health and Safety Code § 11362.715

(MAUCRSA, Effective June 27, 2017.)

(a) A person who seeks an identification card shall pay the fee, as provided in Section 11362.755, and provide all of the following to the county health department or the county's designee on a form developed and provided by the department:

   (1) The name of the person and proof of his or her residency within the county.

   (2) Written documentation by the attending physician in the person's medical records stating that the person has been diagnosed with a serious medical condition and that the medicinal use of cannabis is appropriate.

   (3) The name, office address, office telephone number, and California medical license number of the person's attending physician.

   (4) The name and the duties of the primary caregiver.

   (5) A government-issued photo identification card of the person and of the designated primary caregiver, if any. If the applicant is a person under 18 years of age, a certified copy of a birth certificate shall be deemed sufficient proof of identity.

(b) If the person applying for an identification card lacks the capacity to make medical decisions, the application may be made by the person's legal representative, including, but not limited to, any of the following:

   (1) A conservator with authority to make medical decisions.

(2) An attorney-in-fact under a durable power of attorney for health care or surrogate decisionmaker authorized under another advanced health care directive.

(3) Any other individual authorized by statutory or decisional law to make medical decisions for the person.

(c) The legal representative described in subdivision (b) may also designate in the application an individual, including himself or herself, to serve as a primary caregiver for the person, provided that the individual meets the definition of a primary caregiver.

(d) The person or legal representative submitting the written information and documentation described in subdivision (a) shall retain a copy thereof.

Health and Safety Code § 11362.72

(SB 420, Effective January 1, 2004.)

(a) Within 30 days of receipt of an application for an identification card, a county health department or the county's designee shall do all of the following:

(1) For purposes of processing the application, verify that the information contained in the application is accurate. If the person is less than 18 years of age, the county health department or its designee shall also contact the parent with legal authority to make medical decisions, legal guardian, or other person or entity with legal authority to make medical decisions, to verify the information.

(2) Verify with the Medical Board of California or the Osteopathic Medical Board of California that the attending physician has a license in good standing to practice medicine or osteopathy in the state.

(3) Contact the attending physician by facsimile, telephone, or mail to confirm that the medical records submitted by the patient are a true and correct copy of those contained in the physician's office records. When contacted by a county health department or the county' s designee, the attending physician shall confirm or deny that the contents of the medical records are accurate.

(4) Take a photograph or otherwise obtain an electronically transmissible image of the applicant and of the designated primary caregiver, if any.

(5) Approve or deny the application. If an applicant who meets the requirements of Section 11362.715 can establish that an identification card is needed on an emergency basis, the county or its designee shall issue a temporary identification card that shall be valid for 30 days from the date of issuance. The county, or its designee, may extend the temporary identification card for no more than 30 days at a time, so long as the applicant continues to meet the requirements of this paragraph.

(b) If the county health department or the county's designee approves the application, it shall, within 24 hours, or by the end of the next working day of approving the application, electronically transmit the following information to the department:

(1) A unique user identification number of the applicant.

(2) The date of expiration of the identification card.

(3) The name and telephone number of the county health department or the county's designee that has approved the application.

(c) The county health department or the county's designee shall issue an identification card to the applicant and to his or her designated primary caregiver, if any, within five working days of approving the application.

(d) In any case involving an incomplete application, the applicant shall assume responsibility for rectifying the deficiency. The county shall have 14 days from the receipt of information from the applicant pursuant to this subdivision to approve or deny the application.

Health and Safety Code § 11362.735

(SB 420, Effective January 1, 2004.)

(a) An identification card issued by the county health department shall be serially numbered and shall contain all of the following:

(1) A unique user identification number of the cardholder.

(2) The date of expiration of the identification card.

(3) The name and telephone number of the county health department or the county's designee that has approved the application.

(4) A 24-hour, toll-free telephone number, to be maintained by the department, that will enable state and local law enforcement officers to have immediate access to information necessary to verify the validity of the card.

(5) Photo identification of the cardholder.

(b) A separate identification card shall be issued to the person's designated primary caregiver, if any, and shall include a photo identification of the caregiver.

Health and Safety Code § 11362.74

(SB 420, Effective January 1, 2004.)

(a) The county health department or the county's designee may deny an application only for any of the following reasons:

(1) The applicant did not provide the information required by Section 11362.715, and upon notice of the deficiency pursuant to subdivision (d) of Section 11362.72, did not provide the information within 30 days.

(2) The county health department or the county's designee determines that the information provided was false.

(3) The applicant does not meet the criteria set forth in this article.

(b) Any person whose application has been denied pursuant to subdivision (a) may not reapply for six months from the date of denial unless otherwise authorized by the county health department or the county's designee or by a court of competent jurisdiction.

(c) Any person whose application has been denied pursuant to subdivision (a) may appeal that decision to the department. The county health department or the county's designee shall make available a telephone number or address to which the denied applicant can direct an appeal.

Health and Safety Code § 11362.745

(SB 420, Effective January 1, 2004.)

(a) An identification card shall be valid for a period of one year.

(b) Upon annual renewal of an identification card, the county health department or its designee shall verify all new information and may verify any other information that has not changed.

(c) The county health department or the county's designee shall transmit its determination of approval or denial of a renewal to the department.

Health and Safety Code § 11362.755

(AUMA, Effective November 9, 2016.)

(a) Each county health department or the county's designee may charge a fee for all costs incurred by the county or the county's designee for administering the program pursuant to this article.

(b) In no event shall the amount of the fee charged by a county health department exceed $100 per application or renewal.

(c) Upon satisfactory proof of participation and eligibility in the Medi-Cal program, a Medi-Cal beneficiary shall receive a 50 percent reduction in the fees established pursuant to this section.

(d) Upon satisfactory proof that a qualified patient, or the legal guardian of a qualified patient under the age of 18, is a medically indigent adult who is eligible for and participates in the County Medical Services Program, the fee established pursuant to this section shall be waived.

(e) In the event the fees charged and collected by a county health department are not sufficient to pay for the administrative costs incurred in discharging the county health department's duties with respect to the mandatory identification card system, the Legislature, upon request by the county health department, shall reimburse the county health department for those reasonable administrative costs in excess of the fees charged and collected by the county health department.

Health and Safety Code § 11362.76

(SB 420, Effective January 1, 2004.)

(a) A person who possesses an identification card shall:

(1) Within seven days, notify the county health department or the county's designee of any change in the person's attending physician or designated primary caregiver, if any.

(2) Annually submit to the county health department or the county' s designee the following:

(A) Updated written documentation of the person's serious medical condition.

(B) The name and duties of the person's designated primary caregiver, if any, for the forthcoming year.

(b) If a person who possesses an identification card fails to comply with this section, the card shall be deemed expired. If an identification card expires, the identification card of any designated primary caregiver of the person shall also expire.

(c) If the designated primary caregiver has been changed, the previous primary caregiver shall return his or her identification card to the department or to the county health department or the county's designee.

(d) If the owner or operator or an employee of the owner or operator of a provider has been designated as a primary caregiver pursuant to paragraph (1) of subdivision (d) of Section 11362.7, of the qualified patient or person with an identification card, the owner or operator shall notify the county health department or the county's designee, pursuant to Section 11362.715, if a change in the designated primary caregiver has occurred.

Health and Safety Code § 11362.765

(MAUCRSA, Effective June 27, 2017.)

(a) Subject to the requirements of this article, the individuals specified in subdivision (b) shall not be subject, on that sole basis, to criminal liability under Section 11357, 11358, 11359, 11360, 11366, 11366.5, or 11570. This section does not authorize the individual to smoke or otherwise consume cannabis unless otherwise authorized by this article, nor shall anything in this section authorize any individual or group to cultivate or distribute cannabis for profit.

(b) Subdivision (a) shall apply to all of the following:

(1) A qualified patient or a person with an identification card who transports or processes cannabis for his or her own personal medical use.

(2) A designated primary caregiver who transports, processes, administers, delivers, or gives away cannabis for medical purposes, in amounts not exceeding those established in subdivision (a) of Section 11362.77, only to the qualified patient of the primary caregiver, or to the person with an identification card who has designated the individual as a primary caregiver.

(3) An individual who provides assistance to a qualified patient or a person with an identification card, or his or her designated primary caregiver, in administering medicinal cannabis to the qualified patient or person or acquiring the skills necessary to cultivate or administer cannabis for medical purposes to the qualified patient or person.

(c) A primary caregiver who receives compensation for actual expenses, including reasonable compensation incurred for services provided to an eligible qualified patient or person with an identification card to enable that person to use cannabis under this article, or for payment for out-of-pocket expenses incurred in providing those services, or both, shall not, on the sole basis of that fact, be subject to prosecution or punishment under Section 11359 or 11360.

Health and Safety Code § 11362.768

(MAUCRSA, Effective June 27, 2017.)

(a) This section shall apply to individuals specified in subdivision (b) of Section 11362.765.

(b) No medicinal cannabis cooperative, collective, dispensary, operator, establishment, or provider who possesses, cultivates, or distributes medicinal cannabis pursuant to this article shall be located within a 600-foot radius of a school.

(c) The distance specified in this section shall be the horizontal distance measured in a straight line from the property line of the school to the closest property line of the lot on which the medicinal cannabis cooperative, collective, dispensary, operator, establishment, or provider is to be located without regard to intervening structures.

(d) This section shall not apply to a medicinal cannabis cooperative, collective, dispensary, operator, establishment, or provider that is also a licensed residential medical or elder care facility.

(e) This section shall apply only to a medicinal cannabis cooperative, collective, dispensary, operator, establishment, or provider that is authorized by law to possess, cultivate, or distribute medicinal cannabis and that has a storefront or mobile retail outlet which ordinarily requires a local business license.

(f) Nothing in this section shall prohibit a city, county, or city and county from adopting ordinances or policies that further restrict the location or establishment of a medicinal cannabis cooperative, collective, dispensary, operator, establishment, or provider.

(g) This section does not preempt local ordinances, adopted prior to January 1, 2011, that regulate the location or establishment of a medicinal cannabis cooperative, collective, dispensary, operator, establishment, or provider.

(h) For the purposes of this section, "school" means any public or private school providing instruction in kindergarten or any of grades 1 to 12, inclusive, but does not include any private school in which education is primarily conducted in private homes.

Health and Safety Code § 11362.769

(MCRSA- SB 837, Effective June 27, 2016.)

Indoor and outdoor medical cannabis cultivation shall be conducted in accordance with state and local laws. State agencies, including, but not limited to, the Department of Food and Agriculture, the State Board of Forestry and Fire Protection, the Department of Fish and Wildlife, the State Water Resources Control Board, the California regional water quality control boards, and traditional state law enforcement agencies shall address environmental impacts of medical cannabis cultivation and shall coordinate, when appropriate, with cities and counties and their law enforcement agencies in enforcement efforts.

Health and Safety Code § 11362.77

(MAUCRSA, Effective June 27, 2017.)

(a) A qualified patient or primary caregiver may possess no more than eight ounces of dried cannabis per qualified patient. In addition, a qualified patient or primary caregiver may also maintain no more than six mature or 12 immature cannabis plants per qualified patient.

(b) If a qualified patient or primary caregiver has a physician's recommendation that this quantity does not meet the qualified patient's medical needs, the qualified patient or primary caregiver may possess an amount of cannabis consistent with the patient's needs.

(c) Counties and cities may retain or enact medicinal cannabis guidelines allowing qualified patients or primary caregivers to exceed the state limits set forth in subdivision (a).

(d) Only the dried mature processed flowers of female cannabis plant or the plant conversion shall be considered when determining allowable quantities of cannabis under this section.

(e) A qualified patient or a person holding a valid identification card, or the designated primary caregiver of that qualified patient or person, may possess amounts of cannabis consistent with this article.

Health and Safety Code § 11362.78

(MAUCRSA, Effective June 27, 2017.)

A state or local law enforcement agency or officer shall not refuse to accept an identification card issued pursuant to this article unless the state or local law enforcement agency or officer has probable cause to believe that the information contained in the card is false or fraudulent, or the card is being used fraudulently.

Health and Safety Code § 11362.785

(MAUCRSA, Effective June 27, 2017.)

(a) Nothing in this article shall require any accommodation of medicinal use of cannabis on the property or premises of a place of employment or during the hours of employment or on the property or premises of a jail, correctional facility, or other type of penal institution in which prisoners reside or persons under arrest are detained.

(b) Notwithstanding subdivision (a), a person shall not be prohibited or prevented from obtaining and submitting the written information and documentation necessary to apply for an identification card on the basis that the person is incarcerated in a jail, correctional facility, or other penal institution in which prisoners reside or persons under arrest are detained.

(c) This article does not prohibit a jail, correctional facility, or other penal institution in which prisoners reside or persons under arrest are detained, from permitting a prisoner or a person under arrest who has an identification card, to use cannabis for medicinal purposes under circumstances that will not endanger the health or safety of other prisoners or the security of the facility.

(d) This article does not require a governmental, private, or any other health insurance provider or health care service plan to be liable for a claim for reimbursement for the medicinal use of cannabis.

Health and Safety Code § 11362.79

(MAUCRSA, Effective June 27, 2017.)

This article does not authorize a qualified patient or person with an identification card to engage in the smoking of medicinal cannabis under any of the following circumstances:

(a) In a place where smoking is prohibited by law.

(b) In or within 1,000 feet of the grounds of a school, recreation center, or youth center, unless the medicinal use occurs within a residence.

(c) On a schoolbus.

(d) While in a motor vehicle that is being operated.

(e) While operating a boat.

Health and Safety Code § 11362.795

(MAUCRSA, Effective June 27, 2017.)

(a) (1) Any criminal defendant who is eligible to use cannabis pursuant to Section 11362.5 may request that the court confirm that he or she is allowed to use medicinal cannabis while he or she is on probation or released on bail.

(2) The court's decision and the reasons for the decision shall be stated on the record and an entry stating those reasons shall be made in the minutes of the court.

(3) During the period of probation or release on bail, if a physician recommends that the probationer or defendant use medicinal cannabis, the probationer or defendant may request a modification of the conditions of probation or bail to authorize the use of medicinal cannabis.

(4) The court's consideration of the modification request authorized by this subdivision shall comply with the requirements of this section.

(b) (1) Any person who is to be released on parole from a jail, state prison, school, road camp, or other state or local institution of confinement and who is eligible to use medicinal cannabis pursuant to Section 11362.5 may request that he or she be allowed to use medicinal cannabis during the period he or she is released on parole. A parolee's written conditions of parole shall reflect whether or not a request for a modification of the conditions of his or her parole to use medicinal cannabis was made, and whether the request was granted or denied.

(2) During the period of the parole, where a physician recommends that the parolee use medicinal cannabis, the parolee may request a modification of the conditions of the parole to authorize the use of medicinal cannabis.

(3) Any parolee whose request to use medicinal cannabis while on parole was denied may pursue an administrative appeal of the decision. Any decision on the appeal shall be in writing and shall reflect the reasons for the decision.

(4) The administrative consideration of the modification request authorized by this subdivision shall comply with the requirements of this section.

Health and Safety Code § 11362.8

(MAUCRSA, Effective June 27, 2017.)

A professional licensing board shall not impose a civil penalty or take other disciplinary action against a licensee based solely on the fact that the licensee has performed acts that are necessary or appropriate to carry out the licensee's role as a designated primary caregiver to a person who is a qualified patient or who possesses a lawful identification card issued pursuant to Section 11362.72. However, this section shall not apply to acts performed by a physician relating to the discussion or recommendation of the medical use of cannabis to a patient. These discussions or recommendations, or both, shall be governed by Section 11362.5.

Health and Safey Code § 11362.81

(MAUCRSA, Effective June 27, 2017.)

(a) A person specified in subdivision (b) shall be subject to the following penalties:

(1) For the first offense, imprisonment in the county jail for no more than six months or a fine not to exceed one thousand dollars ($1,000), or both.

(2) For a second or subsequent offense, imprisonment in the county jail for no more than one year, or a fine not to exceed one thousand dollars ($1,000), or both.

(b) Subdivision (a) applies to any of the following:

(1) A person who fraudulently represents a medical condition or fraudulently provides any material misinformation to a physician, county health department or the county's designee, or state or local law enforcement agency or officer, for the purpose of falsely obtaining an identification card.

(2) A person who steals or fraudulently uses any person's identification card in order to acquire, possess, cultivate, transport, use, produce, or distribute cannabis.

(3) A person who counterfeits, tampers with, or fraudulently produces an identification card.

(4) A person who breaches the confidentiality requirements of this article to information provided to, or contained in the records of, the department or of a county health department or the county's designee pertaining to an identification card program.

(c) In addition to the penalties prescribed in subdivision (a), a person described in subdivision (b) may be precluded from attempting to obtain, or obtaining or using, an identification card for a period of up to six months at the discretion of the court.

(d) In addition to the requirements of this article, the Attorney General shall develop and adopt appropriate guidelines to ensure the security and nondiversion of cannabis grown for medicinal use by patients qualified under the Compassionate Use Act of 1996.

Health and Safety Code § 11362.82

(SB 420, Effective January 1, 2004.)

If any section, subdivision, sentence, clause, phrase, or portion of this article is for any reason held invalid or unconstitutional by any court of competent jurisdiction, that portion shall be deemed a separate, distinct, and independent provision, and that holding shall not affect the validity of the remaining portion thereof.

Health and Safety Code § 11362.83

(MAUCRSA, Effective June 27, 2017.)

Nothing in this article shall prevent a city or other local governing body from adopting and enforcing any of the following:

(a) Adopting local ordinances that regulate the location, operation, or establishment of a medicinal cannabis cooperative or collective.

(b) The civil and criminal enforcement of local ordinances described in subdivision (a).

(c) Enacting other laws consistent with this article.

Health and Safety Code § 11362.84

(AUMA, Effective November 9, 2016.)

The status and conduct of a qualified patient who acts in accordance with the Compassionate Use Act shall not, by itself, be used to restrict or abridge custodial or parental rights to minor children in any action or proceeding under the jurisdiction of family or juvenile court.

Health and Safety Code § 11362.85

(MAUCRSA, Effective June 27, 2017.)

Upon a determination by the California Attorney General that the federal schedule of controlled substances has been amended to reclassify or declassify cannabis, the Legislature may amend or repeal the provisions of this code, as necessary, to conform state law to such changes in federal law.

Health and Safety Code § 11362.9

(MAUCRSA, Effective June 27, 2017.)

(a) (1) It is the intent of the Legislature that the state commission objective scientific research by the premier research institute of the world, the University of California, regarding the efficacy and safety of administering cannabis as part of medical treatment. If the Regents of the University of California, by appropriate resolution, accept this responsibility, the University of California shall create a program, to be known as the California Cannabis Research Program. Whenever "California Marijuana Research Program" appears in any statute, regulation, or contract, or in any other code, it shall be construed to refer to the California Cannabis Research Program.

(2) The program shall develop and conduct studies intended to ascertain the general medical safety and efficacy of cannabis and, if found valuable, shall develop medical guidelines for the appropriate administration and use of cannabis. The studies may include studies to ascertain the effect of cannabis on motor skills.

(b) The program may immediately solicit proposals for research projects to be included in the cannabis studies. Program requirements to be used when evaluating responses to its solicitation for proposals, shall include, but not be limited to, all of the following:

(1) Proposals shall demonstrate the use of key personnel, including clinicians or scientists and support personnel, who are prepared to develop a program of research regarding cannabis' general medical efficacy and safety.

(2) Proposals shall contain procedures for outreach to patients with various medical conditions who may be suitable participants in research on cannabis.

(3) Proposals shall contain provisions for a patient registry.

(4) Proposals shall contain provisions for an information system that is designed to record information about possible study participants, investigators, and clinicians, and deposit and analyze data that accrues as part of clinical trials.

(5) Proposals shall contain protocols suitable for research on cannabis, addressing patients diagnosed with acquired immunodeficiency syndrome (AIDS) or human immunodeficiency virus (HIV), cancer, glaucoma, or seizures or muscle spasms associated with a chronic, debilitating condition. The proposal may also include research on other serious illnesses, provided that resources are available and medical information justifies the research.

(6) Proposals shall demonstrate the use of a specimen laboratory capable of housing plasma, urine, and other specimens necessary to study the concentration of cannabinoids in various tissues, as well as housing specimens for studies of toxic effects of cannabis.

(7) Proposals shall demonstrate the use of a laboratory capable of analyzing cannabis, provided to the program under this section, for purity and cannabinoid content and the capacity to detect contaminants.

(c) In order to ensure objectivity in evaluating proposals, the program shall use a peer review process that is modeled on the process used by the National Institutes of Health, and that guards against funding research that is biased in favor of or against particular outcomes. Peer reviewers shall be selected for their expertise in the scientific substance and methods of the proposed research, and their lack of bias or conflict of interest regarding the applicants or the topic of an approach taken in the proposed research. Peer reviewers shall judge research proposals on several criteria, foremost among which shall be both of the following:

(1) The scientific merit of the research plan, including whether the research design and experimental procedures are potentially biased for or against a particular outcome.

(2) Researchers' expertise in the scientific substance and methods of the proposed research, and their lack of bias or conflict of interest regarding the topic of, and the approach taken in, the proposed research.

(d) If the program is administered by the Regents of the University of California, any grant research proposals approved by the program shall also require review and approval by the research advisory panel.

(e) It is the intent of the Legislature that the program be established as follows:

(1) The program shall be located at one or more University of California campuses that have a core of faculty experienced in organizing multidisciplinary scientific endeavors and, in particular, strong experience in clinical trials involving psychopharmacologic agents. The campuses at which research under the auspices of the

program is to take place shall accommodate the administrative offices, including the director of the program, as well as a data management unit, and facilities for storage of specimens.

(2) When awarding grants under this section, the program shall utilize principles and parameters of the other well-tested statewide research programs administered by the University of California, modeled after programs administered by the National Institutes of Health, including peer review evaluation of the scientific merit of applications.

(3) The scientific and clinical operations of the program shall occur, partly at University of California campuses, and partly at other postsecondary institutions, that have clinicians or scientists with expertise to conduct the required studies. Criteria for selection of research locations shall include the elements listed in subdivision (b) and, additionally, shall give particular weight to the organizational plan, leadership qualities of the program director, and plans to involve investigators and patient populations from multiple sites.

(4) The funds received by the program shall be allocated to various research studies in accordance with a scientific plan developed by the Scientific Advisory Council. As the first wave of studies is completed, it is anticipated that the program will receive requests for funding of additional studies. These requests shall be reviewed by the Scientific Advisory Council.

(5) The size, scope, and number of studies funded shall be commensurate with the amount of appropriated and available program funding.

(f) All personnel involved in implementing approved proposals shall be authorized as required by Section 11604.

(g) Studies conducted pursuant to this section shall include the greatest amount of new scientific research possible on the medical uses of, and medical hazards associated with, cannabis. The program shall consult with the Research Advisory Panel analogous agencies in other states, and appropriate federal agencies in an attempt to avoid duplicative research and the wasting of research dollars.

(h) The program shall make every effort to recruit qualified patients and qualified physicians from throughout the state.

(i) The cannabis studies shall employ state-of-the-art research methodologies.

(j) The program shall ensure that all cannabis used in the studies is of the appropriate medical quality and shall be obtained from the National Institute on Drug Abuse or any other federal agency designated to supply cannabis for authorized research. If these federal agencies fail to provide a supply of adequate quality and quantity within six months of the effective date of this section, the Attorney General shall provide an adequate supply pursuant to Section 11478.

(k) The program may review, approve, or incorporate studies and research by independent groups presenting scientifically valid protocols for medical research, regardless of whether the areas of study are being researched by the committee.

(l) (1) To enhance understanding of the efficacy and adverse effects of cannabis as a pharmacological agent, the program shall conduct focused controlled clinical trials on the usefulness of cannabis in patients diagnosed with AIDS or HIV, cancer, glaucoma, or seizures or muscle spasms associated with a chronic, debilitating condition. The program may add research on other serious illnesses, provided that resources are available and medical information justifies the research. The studies shall focus on comparisons of both the efficacy and safety of methods of administering the drug to patients, including inhalational, tinctural, and oral, evaluate possible uses of cannabis as a primary or adjunctive treatment, and develop further information on optimal dosage, timing, mode of administration, and variations in the effects of different cannabinoids and varieties of cannabis.

(2) The program shall examine the safety of cannabis in patients with various medical disorders, including cannabis's interaction with other drugs, relative safety of inhalation versus oral forms, and the effects on

mental function in medically ill persons.

(3) The program shall be limited to providing for objective scientific research to ascertain the efficacy and safety of cannabis as part of medical treatment, and should not be construed as encouraging or sanctioning the social or recreational use of cannabis.

(m) (1) Subject to paragraph (2), the program shall, prior to any approving proposals, seek to obtain research protocol guidelines from the National Institutes of Health and shall, if the National Institutes of Health issues research protocol guidelines, comply with those guidelines.

(2) If, after a reasonable period of time of not less than six months and not more than a year has elapsed from the date the program seeks to obtain guidelines pursuant to paragraph (1), no guidelines have been approved, the program may proceed using the research protocol guidelines it develops.

(n) In order to maximize the scope and size of the cannabis studies, the program may do any of the following:

(1) Solicit, apply for, and accept funds from foundations, private individuals, and all other funding sources that can be used to expand the scope or timeframe of the cannabis studies that are authorized under this section. The program shall not expend more than 5 percent of its General Fund allocation in efforts to obtain money from outside sources.

(2) Include within the scope of the cannabis studies other cannabis research projects that are independently funded and that meet the requirements set forth in subdivisions (a) to (c), inclusive. In no case shall the program accept any funds that are offered with any conditions other than that the funds be used to study the efficacy and safety of cannabis as part of medical treatment. Any donor shall be advised that funds given for purposes of this section will be used to study both the possible benefits and detriments of cannabis and that he or she will have no control over the use of these funds.

(o) (1) Within six months of the effective date of this section, the program shall report to the Legislature, the Governor, and the Attorney General on the progress of the cannabis studies.

(2) Thereafter, the program shall issue a report to the Legislature every six months detailing the progress of the studies. The interim reports required under this paragraph shall include, but not be limited to, data on all of the following:

(A) The names and number of diseases or conditions under study.

(B) The number of patients enrolled in each study by disease.

(C) Any scientifically valid preliminary findings.

(p) If the Regents of the University of California implement this section, the President of the University of California shall appoint a multidisciplinary Scientific Advisory Council, not to exceed 15 members, to provide policy guidance in the creation and implementation of the program. Members shall be chosen on the basis of scientific expertise. Members of the council shall serve on a voluntary basis, with reimbursement for expenses incurred in the course of their participation. The members shall be reimbursed for travel and other necessary expenses incurred in their performance of the duties of the council.

(q) No more than 10 percent of the total funds appropriated may be used for all aspects of the administration of this section.

(r) This section shall be implemented only to the extent that funding for its purposes is appropriated by the Legislature in the annual Budget Act.

Health & Safety Code § 11364.5

(MAUCRSA, Effective June 27, 2017.)

(a) Except as authorized by law, no person shall maintain or operate any place of business in which drug paraphernalia is kept, displayed or offered in any manner, sold, furnished, transferred or given away unless such drug paraphernalia is completely and wholly kept, displayed or offered within a separate room or enclosure to which persons under the age of 18 years not accompanied by a parent or legal guardian are excluded. Each entrance to such a room or enclosure shall be signposted in reasonably visible and legible words to the effect that drug paraphernalia is kept, displayed or offered in such room or enclosure and that minors, unless accompanied by a parent or legal guardian, are excluded.

(b) Except as authorized by law, no owner, manager, proprietor or other person in charge of any room or enclosure, within any place of business, in which drug paraphernalia is kept, displayed or offered in any manner, sold, furnished, transferred or given away shall permit or allow any person under the age of 18 years to enter, be in, remain in or visit such room or enclosure unless that minor person is accompanied by one of his or her parents or by his or her legal guardian.

(c) Unless authorized by law, no person under the age of 18 years shall enter, be in, remain in, or visit any room or enclosure in any place of business in which drug paraphernalia is kept, displayed or offered in any manner, sold, furnished, transferred, or given away unless accompanied by one of his or her parents or by his or her legal guardian.

(d) As used in this section, "drug paraphernalia" means all equipment, products, and materials of any kind which are intended for use or designed for use, in planting, propagating, cultivating, growing, harvesting, manufacturing, compounding, converting, producing, processing, preparing, testing, analyzing, packaging, repackaging, storing, containing, concealing, injecting, ingesting, inhaling, or otherwise introducing into the human body a controlled substance. "Drug paraphernalia" includes, but is not limited to, all of the following:

(1) Kits intended for use or designed for use in planting, propagating, cultivating, growing, or harvesting of any species of plant which is a controlled substance or from which a controlled substance can be derived.

(2) Kits intended for use or designed for use in manufacturing, compounding, converting, producing, processing, or preparing controlled substances.

(3) Isomerization devices intended for use or designed for use in increasing the potency of any species of plant which is a controlled substance.

(4) Testing equipment intended for use or designed for use in identifying, or in analyzing the strength, effectiveness, or purity of controlled substances.

(5) Scales and balances intended for use or designed for use in weighing or measuring controlled substances.

(6) Diluents and adulterants, such as quinine hydrochloride, mannitol, mannite, dextrose, and lactose, intended for use or designed for use in cutting controlled substances.

(7) Separation gins and sifters intended for use or designed for use in removing twigs and seeds from, or in otherwise cleaning or refining, cannabis.

(8) Blenders, bowls, containers, spoons, and mixing devices intended for use or designed for use in compounding controlled substances.

(9) Capsules, balloons, envelopes, and other containers intended for use or designed for use in packaging small quantities of controlled substances.

(10) Containers and other objects intended for use or designed for use in storing or concealing controlled substances.

(11) Hypodermic syringes, needles, and other objects intended for use or designed for use in parenterally injecting controlled substances into the human body.

(12) Objects intended for use or designed for use in ingesting, inhaling, or otherwise introducing cannabis, cocaine, hashish, or hashish oil into the human body, such as the following:

    (A) Metal, wooden, acrylic, glass, stone, plastic, or ceramic pipes with or without screens, permanent screens, hashish heads, or punctured metal bowls.

    (B) Water pipes.

    (C) Carburetion tubes and devices.

    (D) Smoking and carburetion masks.

    (E) Roach clips, meaning objects used to hold burning material, such as a cannabis cigarette that has become too small or too short to be held in the hand.

    (F) Miniature cocaine spoons, and cocaine vials.

    (G) Chamber pipes.

    (H) Carburetor pipes.

    (I) Electric pipes.

    (J) Air-driven pipes.

    (K) Chillums.

    (L) Bongs.

    (M) Ice pipes or chillers.

(e) In determining whether an object is drug paraphernalia, a court or other authority may consider, in addition to all other logically relevant factors, the following:

(1) Statements by an owner or by anyone in control of the object concerning its use.

(2) Prior convictions, if any, of an owner, or of anyone in control of the object, under any state or federal law relating to any controlled substance.

(3) Direct or circumstantial evidence of the intent of an owner, or of anyone in control of the object, to deliver it to persons whom he or she knows, or should reasonably know, intend to use the object to facilitate a violation of this section. The innocence of an owner, or of anyone in control of the object, as to a direct violation of this section shall not prevent a finding that the object is intended for use, or designed for use, as drug paraphernalia.

(4) Instructions, oral or written, provided with the object concerning its use.

(5) Descriptive materials, accompanying the object which explain or depict its use.

(6) National and local advertising concerning its use.

(7) The manner in which the object is displayed for sale.

(8) Whether the owner, or anyone in control of the object, is a legitimate supplier of like or related items to the community, such as a licensed distributor or dealer of tobacco products.

(9) The existence and scope of legitimate uses for the object in the community.

(10) Expert testimony concerning its use.

(f) This section shall not apply to any of the following:

(1) Any pharmacist or other authorized person who sells or furnishes drug paraphernalia described in paragraph (11) of subdivision (d) upon the prescription of a physician, dentist, podiatrist, or veterinarian.

(2) Any physician, dentist, podiatrist, or veterinarian who furnishes or prescribes drug paraphernalia described in paragraph (11) of subdivision (d) to his or her patients.

(3) Any manufacturer, wholesaler, or retailer licensed by the California State Board of Pharmacy to sell or transfer drug paraphernalia described in paragraph (11) of subdivision (d).

(g) Notwithstanding any other provision of law, including Section 11374, violation of this section shall not constitute a criminal offense, but operation of a business in violation of the provisions of this section shall be grounds for revocation or nonrenewal of any license, permit, or other entitlement previously issued by a city, county, or city and county for the privilege of engaging in such business and shall be grounds for denial of any future license, permit, or other entitlement authorizing the conduct of such business or any other business, if the business includes the sale of drug paraphernalia.

Health & Safety Code § 11366

(Amended by Statute, Effective 1991.)

Every person who opens or maintains any place for the purpose of unlawfully selling, giving away, or using any controlled substance which is

(1) specified in subdivision (b), (c), or (e), or paragraph (1) of subdivision (f) of Section 11054, specified in paragraph (13), (14), (15), or (20) of subdivision (d) of Section 11054, or specified in subdivision (b), (c), paragraph (1) or (2) of subdivision (d), or paragraph (3) of subdivision (e) of Section 11055, or

(2) which is a narcotic drug classified in Schedule III, IV, or V, shall be punished by imprisonment in the county jail for a period of not more than one year or the state prison.

Health & Safety Code § 11366.5

(Amended by Statute, Effective April 4, 2011, and Operative October 1, 2011.)

(a) Any person who has under his or her management or control any building, room, space, or enclosure, either as an owner, lessee, agent, employee, or mortgagee, who knowingly rents, leases, or makes available for use, with or without compensation, the building, room, space, or enclosure for the purpose of unlawfully manufacturing, storing, or distributing any controlled substance for sale or distribution shall be punished by imprisonment in the county jail for not more than one year, or pursuant to subdivision (h) of Section 1170 of the Penal Code.

(b) Any person who has under his or her management or control any building, room, space, or enclosure, either as an owner, lessee, agent, employee, or mortgagee, who knowingly allows the building, room, space, or enclosure to be fortified to suppress law enforcement entry in order to further the sale of any amount of cocaine base as specified in paragraph (1) of subdivision (f) of Section 11054, cocaine as specified in paragraph (6) of subdivision (b) of Section 11055, heroin, phencyclidine, amphetamine, methamphetamine, or lysergic acid diethylamide and who obtains excessive profits from the use of the building, room, space, or enclosure shall be punished by imprisonment pursuant to subdivision (h) of Section 1170 of the Penal Code for two, three, or four years.

(c) Any person who violates subdivision (a) after previously being convicted of a violation of subdivision (a) shall be punished by imprisonment pursuant to subdivision (h) of Section 1170 of the Penal Code for two, three, or four years.

(d) For the purposes of this section, excessive profits means the receipt of consideration of a value substantially higher than fair market value.

Health & Safety Code § 11379.6

(Amended by Statute, Effective January 1, 2016.)

(a) Except as otherwise provided by law, every person who manufactures, compounds, converts, produces, derives, processes, or prepares, either directly or indirectly by chemical extraction or independently by means of chemical synthesis, any controlled substance specified in Section 11054, 11055, 11056, 11057, or 11058 shall be punished by imprisonment pursuant to subdivision (h) of Section 1170 of the Penal Code for three, five, or seven years and by a fine not exceeding fifty thousand dollars ($50,000).

(b) Except when an enhancement pursuant to Section 11379.7 is pled and proved, the fact that a person under 16 years of age resided in a structure in which a violation of this section involving methamphetamine occurred shall be considered a factor in aggravation by the sentencing court.

(c) Except when an enhancement pursuant to Section 11379.7 is pled and proved, the fact that a violation of this section involving methamphetamine occurred within 200 feet of an occupied residence or any structure where another person was present at the time the offense was committed may be considered a factor in aggravation by the sentencing court.

(d) The fact that a violation of this section involving the use of a volatile solvent to chemically extract concentrated cannabis occurred within 300 feet of an occupied residence or any structure where another person was present at the time the offense was committed may be considered a factor in aggravation by the sentencing court.

(e) Except as otherwise provided by law, every person who offers to perform an act which is punishable under subdivision (a) shall be punished by imprisonment pursuant to subdivision (h) of Section 1170 of the Penal Code for three, four, or five years.

(f) All fines collected pursuant to subdivision (a) shall be transferred to the State Treasury for deposit in the Clandestine Drug Lab Clean-up Account, as established by Section 5 of Chapter 1295 of the Statutes of 1987. The transmission to the State Treasury shall be carried out in the same manner as fines collected for the state by the county.

Health and Safety Code § 11470

(MAUCRSA, Effective June 27, 2017.)

The following are subject to forfeiture:

(a) All controlled substances which have been manufactured, distributed, dispensed, or acquired in violation of this division.

(b) All raw materials, products, and equipment of any kind which are used, or intended for use, in manufacturing, compounding, processing, delivering, importing, or exporting any controlled substance in violation of this division.

(c) All property except real property or a boat, airplane, or any vehicle which is used, or intended for use, as a container for property described in subdivision (a) or (b).

(d) All books, records, and research products and materials, including formulas, microfilm, tapes, and data which are used, or intended for use, in violation of this division.

(e) The interest of any registered owner of a boat, airplane, or any vehicle other than an implement of husbandry, as defined in Section 36000 of the Vehicle Code, which has been used as an instrument to facilitate the manufacture of, or possession for sale or sale of 14.25 grams or more of heroin, or a substance containing 14.25 grams or more of heroin, or 14.25 grams or more of a substance containing heroin, or 28.5 grams or more of Schedule I controlled substances except cannabis, peyote, or psilocybin; 10 pounds dry weight or more of cannabis, peyote, or psilocybin; or 28.5 grams or more of cocaine, as specified in paragraph (6) of subdivision (b) of Section 11055, cocaine base as specified in paragraph (1) of subdivision (f) of Section 11054, or methamphetamine; or a substance containing 28.5 grams or more of cocaine, as specified in paragraph (6) of subdivision (b) of Section 11055, cocaine base as specified in paragraph (1) of subdivision (f) of Section 11054, or methamphetamine; or 57 grams or more of a substance containing cocaine, as specified in paragraph (6) of subdivision (b) of Section 11055, cocaine base as specified in paragraph (1) of subdivision (f) of Section 11054, or methamphetamine; or 28.5 grams or more of Schedule II controlled substances. An interest in a vehicle which may be lawfully driven on the highway with a class C, class M1, or class M2 license, as prescribed in Section 12804.9 of the Vehicle Code, shall not be forfeited under this subdivision if there is a community property interest in the vehicle by a person other than the defendant and the vehicle is the sole class C, class M1, or class M2 vehicle available to the defendant's immediate family.

(f) All moneys, negotiable instruments, securities, or other things of value furnished or intended to be furnished by any person in exchange for a controlled substance, all proceeds traceable to such an exchange, and all moneys, negotiable instruments, or securities used or intended to be used to facilitate any violation of Section 11351, 11351.5, 11352, 11355, 11359, 11360, 11378, 11378.5, 11379, 11379.5, 11379.6, 11380, 11382, or 11383 of this code, or Section 182 of the Penal Code, or a felony violation of Section 11366.8 of this code, insofar as the offense involves manufacture, sale, possession for sale, offer for sale, or offer to manufacture, or conspiracy to commit at least one of those offenses, if the exchange, violation, or other conduct which is the basis for the forfeiture occurred within five years of the seizure of the property, or the filing of a petition under this chapter, or the issuance of an order of forfeiture of the property, whichever comes first.

(g) The real property of any property owner who is convicted of violating Section 11366, 11366.5, or 11366.6 with respect to that property. However, property which is used as a family residence or for other lawful purposes, or which is owned by two or more persons, one of whom had no knowledge of its unlawful use, shall not be subject to forfeiture.

(h) (1) Subject to the requirements of Section 11488.5 and except as further limited by this subdivision to protect innocent parties who claim a property interest acquired from a defendant, all right, title, and interest in any personal property described in this section shall vest in the state upon commission of the act giving rise to forfeiture under this chapter, if the state or local governmental entity proves a violation of Section 11351, 11351.5, 11352, 11355, 11359, 11360, 11378, 11378.5, 11379, 11379.5, 11379.6, 11380, 11382, or 11383 of this code, or Section 182 of the Penal Code, or a felony violation of Section 11366.8 of this code, insofar as the offense involves the manufacture, sale, possession for sale, offer for sale, offer to manufacture, or conspiracy to commit at least one of those offenses, in accordance with the burden of proof set forth in paragraph (1) of subdivision (i) of Section 11488.4 or, in the case of cash or negotiable instruments in excess of twenty-five thousand dollars ($25,000), paragraph (4) of subdivision (i) of Section 11488.4.

(2) The operation of the special vesting rule established by this subdivision shall be limited to circumstances where its application will not defeat the claim of any person, including a bona fide purchaser or encumbrancer who, pursuant to Section 11488.5, 11488.6, or 11489, claims an interest in the property seized, notwithstanding that the interest in the property being claimed was acquired from a defendant whose property interest would otherwise have been subject to divestment pursuant to this subdivision.

Health and Safety Code § 11470.1

(Amended by Stats. 2016, Ch. 831, Sec. 1. (SB 443) Effective January 1, 2017.)

(a) The expenses of seizing, eradicating, destroying, or taking remedial action with respect to, any controlled substance or its precursors shall be recoverable from:

(1) Any person who manufactures or cultivates a controlled substance or its precursors in violation of this division.

(2) Any person who aids and abets or who knowingly profits in any manner from the manufacture or cultivation of a controlled substance or its precursors on property owned, leased, or possessed by the defendant, in violation of this division.

(b) The expenses of taking remedial action with respect to any controlled substance or its precursors shall also be recoverable from any person liable for the costs of that remedial action under Chapter 6.8 (commencing with Section 25300) of Division 20 of the Health and Safety Code.

(c) It shall be necessary to seek or obtain a criminal conviction for the unlawful manufacture or cultivation of any controlled substance or its precursors prior to the entry of judgment for the recovery of expenses. If criminal charges are pending against the defendant for the unlawful manufacture or cultivation of any controlled substance or its precursors, an action brought pursuant to this section shall, upon a defendant's request, be continued while the criminal charges are pending.

(d) The action may be brought by the district attorney, county counsel, city attorney, the State Department of Health Care Services, or Attorney General. All expenses recovered pursuant to this section shall be remitted to the law enforcement agency which incurred them.

(e) (1) The burden of proof as to liability shall be on the plaintiff and shall be by a preponderance of the evidence in an action alleging that the defendant is liable for expenses pursuant to paragraph (1) of subdivision (a). The burden of proof as to liability shall be on the plaintiff and shall be by clear and convincing evidence in an action alleging that the defendant is liable for expenses pursuant to paragraph (2) of subdivision (a). The burden of proof as to the amount of expenses recoverable shall be on the plaintiff and shall be by a preponderance of the evidence in any action brought pursuant to subdivision (a).

(2) Notwithstanding paragraph (1), for any person convicted of a criminal charge of the manufacture or cultivation of a controlled substance or its precursors there shall be a presumption affecting the burden of proof that the person is liable.

(f) Only expenses which meet the following requirements shall be recoverable under this section:

(1) The expenses were incurred in seizing, eradicating, or destroying the controlled substance or its precursors or in taking remedial action with respect to a hazardous substance. These expenses may not include any costs incurred in use of the herbicide paraquat.

(2) The expenses were incurred as a proximate result of the defendant's manufacture or cultivation of a controlled substance in violation of this division.

(3) The expenses were reasonably incurred.

(g) For purposes of this section, "remedial action" shall have the meaning set forth in Section 25322.

(h) For the purpose of discharge in bankruptcy, a judgment for recovery of expenses under this section shall be deemed to be a debt for willful and malicious injury by the defendant to another entity or to the property of another entity.

(i) Notwithstanding Section 526 of the Code of Civil Procedure, the plaintiff may be granted a temporary restraining order or a preliminary injunction, pending or during trial, to restrain the defendant from transferring, encumbering, hypothecating, or otherwise disposing of any assets specified by the court, if it appears by the complaint that the plaintiff is entitled to the relief demanded and it appears that the defendant may dispose of those assets to thwart enforcement of the judgment.

(j) The Legislature finds and declares that civil penalties for the recovery of expenses incurred in enforcing the provisions of this division shall not supplant criminal prosecution for violation of those provisions, but shall be a supplemental remedy to criminal enforcement.

(k) Any testimony, admission, or any other statement made by the defendant in any proceeding brought pursuant to this section, or any evidence derived from the testimony, admission, or other statement, shall not be admitted or otherwise used in any criminal proceeding arising out of the same conduct.

(l) No action shall be brought or maintained pursuant to this section against a person who has been acquitted of criminal charges for conduct that is the basis for an action under this section.

Health & Safety Code § 11472

(Added by renumbering Section 11473 by Stats. 1980, Ch. 1019.)

Controlled substances and any device, contrivance, instrument, or paraphernalia used for unlawfully using or administering a controlled substance, which are possessed in violation of this division, may be seized by any peace officer and in the aid of such seizure a search warrant may be issued as prescribed by law.

Health and Safety Code § 11473

(Amended by Stats. 1994, Ch. 979, Sec. 2. Effective January 1, 1995.)

(a) All seizures under provisions of this chapter, except seizures of vehicles, boats, or airplanes, as specified in subdivision (e) of Section 11470, or seizures of moneys, negotiable instruments, securities, or other things of value as specified in subdivision (f) of Section 11470, shall, upon conviction of the owner or defendant, be ordered destroyed by the court in which conviction was had.

(b) Law enforcement may request of the court that certain uncontaminated science equipment be relinquished to a school or school district for science classroom education in lieu of destruction.

Health and Safety Code § 11473.5

(Amended by Stats. 1994, Ch. 979, Sec. 3. Effective January 1, 1995.)

(a) All seizures of controlled substances, instruments, or paraphernalia used for unlawfully using or administering a controlled substance which are in possession of any city, county, or state official as found property, or as the result of a case in which no trial was had or which has been disposed of by way of dismissal or otherwise than by way of conviction, shall be destroyed by order of the court, unless the court finds that the controlled substances, instruments, or paraphernalia were lawfully possessed by the defendant.

(b) If the court finds that the property was not lawfully possessed by the defendant, law enforcement may request of the court that certain uncontaminated instruments or paraphernalia be relinquished to a school or school district for science classroom education in lieu of destruction.

Health and Safety Code § 11474

(Amended by Stats. 1999, Ch. 787, Sec. 7. Effective January 1, 2000.)

A court order for the destruction of controlled substances, instruments, or paraphernalia pursuant to the provisions of Section 11473 or 11473.5 may be carried out by a police or sheriff's department, the Department of Justice, the Department of the California Highway Patrol, or the Department of Alcoholic Beverage Control. The court order shall specify the agency responsible for the destruction. Controlled substances, instruments, or paraphernalia not in the possession of the designated agency at the time the order of the court is issued shall be delivered to the designated agency for destruction in compliance with the order.

Health and Safety Code § 11476

(Added by Stats. 1972, Ch. 1407.)

Species of plants from which controlled substances in Schedules I and II may be derived which have been planted or cultivated in violation of this division, or of which the owners or cultivators are unknown, or which are wild growths, may be seized and summarily forfeited to the state.

Health and Safety Code § 11477

(Amended by Stats. 1980, Ch. 1019.)

The failure, upon demand by a peace officer of the person in occupancy or in control of land or premises upon which the species of plants are growing or being stored, to produce an appropriate registration, or proof that he is the holder thereof, constitutes authority for the seizure and forfeiture of the plants.

Health & Safety Code § 11478

(MAUCRSA, Effective June 27, 2017.)

Cannabis may be provided by the Attorney General to the heads of research projects which have been registered by the Attorney General, and which have been approved by the research advisory panel pursuant to Section 11480.

The head of the approved research project shall personally receipt for such quantities of cannabis and shall make a record of their disposition. The receipt and record shall be retained by the Attorney General. The head of the approved research project shall also, at intervals and in the manner required by the research advisory panel, report the progress or conclusions of the research project.

Health & Safety Code § 11479

(MAUCRSA, Effective June 27, 2017.)

Notwithstanding Sections 11473 and 11473.5, at any time after seizure by a law enforcement agency of a suspected controlled substance, except in the case of growing or harvested cannabis, that amount in excess of 10 pounds in gross weight may be destroyed without a court order by the chief of the law enforcement agency or a designated subordinate. In the case of growing or harvested cannabis, that amount in excess of two pounds, or the amount of cannabis a medicinal cannabis patient or designated caregiver is authorized to possess by ordinance in the city or county where the cannabis was seized, whichever is greater, may be destroyed without a court order by the chief of the law enforcement agency or a designated subordinate. Destruction shall not take place pursuant to this section until all of the following requirements are satisfied:

(a) At least five random and representative samples have been taken, for evidentiary purposes, from the total amount of suspected controlled substances to be destroyed. These samples shall be in addition to the 10 pounds required above. When the suspected controlled substance consists of growing or harvested cannabis plants, at least one 2-pound sample or a sample in the amount of medicinal cannabis a medicinal cannabis patient or designated caregiver is authorized to possess by ordinance in the city or county where the cannabis was seized, whichever is greater, shall be retained. This sample may include stalks, branches, or leaves. In addition, five representative samples of leaves or buds shall be retained for evidentiary purposes from the total amount of suspected controlled substances to be destroyed.

(b) Photographs and videos have been taken that reasonably and accurately demonstrate the total amount of the suspected controlled substance to be destroyed.

(c) The gross weight of the suspected controlled substance has been determined, either by actually weighing the suspected controlled substance or by estimating that weight after dimensional measurement of the total suspected controlled substance.

(d) The chief of the law enforcement agency has determined that it is not reasonably possible to preserve the suspected controlled substance in place, or to remove the suspected controlled substance to another location. In making this determination, the difficulty of transporting and storing the suspected controlled substance to another site and the storage facilities may be taken into consideration.

Subsequent to any destruction of a suspected controlled substance pursuant to this section, an affidavit shall be filed within 30 days in the court that has jurisdiction over any pending criminal proceedings pertaining to that suspected controlled substance, reciting the applicable information required by subdivisions (a), (b), (c), and (d) together with information establishing the location of the suspected controlled substance, and specifying the date and time of the destruction. In the event that there are no criminal proceedings pending that pertain to that suspected controlled substance, the affidavit may be filed in any court within the county that would have jurisdiction over a person against whom those criminal charges might be filed.

Health & Safety Code § 11479.2

(MAUCRSA, Effective June 27, 2017.)

Notwithstanding the provisions of Sections 11473, 11473.5, 11474, 11479, and 11479.1, at any time after seizure by a law enforcement agency of a suspected controlled substance, except cannabis, any amount, as determined by the court, in excess of 57 grams may, by court order, be destroyed by the chief of a law enforcement agency or a designated subordinate. Destruction shall not take place pursuant to this section until all of the following requirements are satisfied:

(a) At least five random and representative samples have been taken, for evidentiary purposes, from the total amount of suspected controlled substances to be destroyed. Those samples shall be in addition to the 57 grams required above and each sample shall weigh not less than one gram at the time the sample is collected.

(b) Photographs have been taken which reasonably demonstrate the total amount of the suspected controlled substance to be destroyed.

(c) The gross weight of the suspected controlled substance has been determined, either by actually weighing the suspected controlled substance or by estimating such weight after dimensional measurement of the total suspected controlled substance.

(d) In cases involving controlled substances suspected of containing cocaine or methamphetamine, an analysis has determined the qualitative and quantitative nature of the suspected controlled substance.

(e) The law enforcement agency with custody of the controlled substance sought to be destroyed has filed a written motion for the order of destruction in the court which has jurisdiction over any pending criminal proceeding in which a defendant is charged by accusatory pleading with a crime specifically involving the suspected controlled substance sought to be destroyed. The motion shall, by affidavit of the chief of the law enforcement agency or designated subordinate, recite the applicable information required by subdivisions (a), (b), (c), and (d), together with information establishing the location of the suspected controlled substance and the title of any pending criminal proceeding as defined in this subdivision. The motion shall bear proof of service upon all parties to any pending criminal proceeding. No motion shall be made when a defendant is without counsel until the defendant has entered his or her plea to the charges.

(f) The order for destruction shall issue pursuant to this section upon the motion and affidavit in support of the order, unless within 20 days after application for the order, a defendant has requested, in writing, a hearing on the motion. Within 10 days after the filing of that request, or a longer period of time upon good cause shown by either party, the court shall conduct a hearing on the motion in which each party to the motion for destruction shall be permitted to call and examine witnesses. The hearing shall be recorded. Upon conclusion of the hearing, if the court finds that the defendant would not be prejudiced by the destruction, it shall grant the motion and make an order for destruction. In making the order, the court shall ensure that the representative samples to be retained are of sufficient quantities to allow for qualitative analyses by both the prosecution and the defense. Any order for destruction pursuant to this section shall include the applicable information required by subdivisions (a), (b), (c), (d), and (e) and the name of the agency responsible for the destruction. Unless waived, the order shall provide for a 10-day delay prior to destruction in order to allow expert analysis of the controlled substance by the defense.

Subsequent to any destruction of a suspected controlled substance pursuant to this section, an affidavit shall be filed within 30 days in the court which ordered destruction stating the location of the retained, suspected controlled substance and specifying the date and time of destruction.

This section does not apply to seizures involving hazardous chemicals or controlled substances in mixture or combination with hazardous chemicals.

Health and Safety Code § 11480

(MAUCRSA, Effective June 27, 2017.)

(a) The Legislature finds that there is a need to encourage further research into the nature and effects of cannabis and hallucinogenic drugs and to coordinate research efforts on such subjects.

(b) There is a Research Advisory Panel that consists of a representative of the State Department of Health Services, a representative of the California State Board of Pharmacy, the State Public Health Officer, a representative of the Attorney General, a representative of the University of California who shall be a pharmacologist, a physician, or a person holding a doctorate degree in the health sciences, a representative of a private university in this state who shall be a pharmacologist, a physician, or a person holding a doctorate degree in the health sciences, a representative of a statewide professional medical society in this state who shall be engaged in the private practice of medicine and shall be experienced in treating controlled substance dependency, a representative appointed by and serving at the pleasure of the Governor who shall have experience in drug abuse, cancer, or controlled substance research and who is either a registered nurse, licensed pursuant to Chapter 6 (commencing with Section 2700) of Division 2 of the Business and Professions Code, or other health professional. The Governor shall annually designate the private university and the professional medical society represented on the panel. Members of the panel shall be appointed by the heads of the entities to be represented, and they shall serve at the pleasure of the appointing power.

(c) The Research Advisory Panel shall appoint two special members to the Research Advisory Panel, who shall serve at the pleasure of the Research Advisory Panel only during the period Article 6 (commencing with Section 11260) of Chapter 5 remains effective. The additional members shall be physicians and surgeons, and who are board certified in oncology, ophthalmology, or psychiatry.

(d) The panel shall annually select a chairperson from among its members.

(e) The panel may hold hearings on, and in other ways study, research projects concerning cannabis or hallucinogenic drugs in this state. Members of the panel shall serve without compensation, but shall be reimbursed for any actual and necessary expenses incurred in connection with the performance of their duties.

(f) The panel may approve research projects, which have been registered by the Attorney General, into the nature and effects of cannabis or hallucinogenic drugs, and shall inform the Attorney General of the head of the approved research projects that are entitled to receive quantities of cannabis pursuant to Section 11478.

(g) The panel may withdraw approval of a research project at any time, and when approval is withdrawn shall notify the head of the research project to return any quantities of cannabis to the Attorney General.

(h) The panel shall report annually to the Legislature and the Governor those research projects approved by the panel, the nature of each research project, and, where available, the conclusions of the research project.

Health and Safety Code § 11485

(MAUCRSA, Effective June 27, 2017.)

Any peace officer of this state who, incident to a search under a search warrant issued for a violation of Section 11358 with respect to which no prosecution of a defendant results, seizes personal property suspected of being used in the planting, cultivation, harvesting, drying, processing, or transporting of cannabis, shall, if the seized personal property is not being held for evidence or destroyed as contraband, and if the owner of the property is unknown or has not claimed the property, provide notice regarding the seizure and manner of reclamation of the property to any owner or tenant of real property on which the property was seized. In addition, this notice shall be posted at the location of seizure and shall be published at least once in a newspaper of general circulation in the county in which the property was seized. If, after 90 days following the first publication of the notice, no owner appears and proves his or her ownership, the seized personal property shall be deemed to be abandoned and may be disposed of by sale to the public at public auction as set forth in Article 1 (commencing with Section 2080) of Chapter 4 of Title 6 of Part 4 of Division 3 of the Civil Code, or may be disposed of by transfer to a government agency or community service organization. Any profit from the sale or transfer of the property shall be expended for investigative services with respect to crimes involving cannabis.

Health and Safety Code § 11532

(MAUCRSA, Effective June 27, 2017.)

(a) It is unlawful for any person to loiter in any public place in a manner and under circumstances manifesting the purpose and with the intent to commit an offense specified in Chapter 6 (commencing with Section 11350) and Chapter 6.5 (commencing with Section 11400).

(b) Among circumstances that may be considered in determining whether a person has the requisite intent to engage in drug-related activity are that the person:

(1) Acts as a "look-out."

(2) Transfers small objects or packages for currency in a furtive fashion.

(3) Tries to conceal himself or herself or any object that reasonably could be involved in an unlawful drug-related activity.

(4) Uses signals or language indicative of summoning purchasers of illegal drugs.

(5) Repeatedly beckons to, stops, attempts to stop, or engages in conversations with passersby, whether on foot or in a motor vehicle, indicative of summoning purchasers of illegal drugs.

(6) Repeatedly passes to or receives from passersby, whether on foot or in a motor vehicle, money or small objects.

(7) Is under the influence of a controlled substance or possesses narcotic or drug paraphernalia. For the

purposes of this paragraph, "narcotic or drug paraphernalia" means any device, contrivance, instrument, or apparatus designed or marketed for the use of smoking, injecting, ingesting, or consuming cannabis, hashish, PCP, or any controlled substance, including, but not limited to, roach clips, cigarette papers, and rollers designed or marketed for use in smoking a controlled substance.

(8) Has been convicted in any court within this state, within five years prior to the arrest under this chapter, of any violation involving the use, possession, or sale of any of the substances referred to in Chapter 6 (commencing with Section 11350) or Chapter 6.5 (commencing with Section 11400), or has been convicted of any violation of those provisions or substantially similar laws of any political subdivision of this state or of any other state.

(9) Is currently subject to any order prohibiting his or her presence in any high drug activity geographic area.

(10) Has engaged, within six months prior to the date of arrest under this section, in any behavior described in this subdivision, with the exception of paragraph (8), or in any other behavior indicative of illegal drug-related activity.

(c) The list of circumstances set forth in subdivision (b) is not exclusive. The circumstances set forth in subdivision (b) should be considered particularly salient if they occur in an area that is known for unlawful drug use and trafficking, or if they occur on or in premises that have been reported to law enforcement as a place suspected of unlawful drug activity. Any other relevant circumstances may be considered in determining whether a person has the requisite intent. Moreover, no one circumstance or combination of circumstances is in itself determinative of intent. Intent must be determined based on an evaluation of the particular circumstances of each case.

Health and Safety Code § 11553

(MAUCRSA, Effective June 27, 2017.)

The fact that a person is or has been, or is suspected of being, a user of cannabis is not alone sufficient grounds upon which to invoke Section 11551 or 11552.

This section shall not be construed to limit the discretion of a judge to invoke Section 11551 or 11552 if the court has reason to believe a person is or has been a user of narcotics or drugs other than cannabis.

Health & Safety Code § 11570

(Amended by Statute, Effective 1986.)

Every building or place used for the purpose of unlawfully selling, serving, storing, keeping, manufacturing, or giving away any controlled substance, precursor, or analog specified in this division, and every building or place wherein or upon which those acts take place, is a nuisance which shall be enjoined, abated, and prevented, and for which damages may be recovered, whether it is a public or private nuisance.

Health & Safety Code § 11590

(Amended by statute, Effective January 1, 1996.)

(a) Except as provided in subdivisions (c) and (d), any person who is convicted in the State of California of any offense defined in Section 11350, 11351, 11351.5, 11352, 11353, 11353.5, 11353.7, 11354, 11355, 11357, 11358, 11359, 11360, 11361, 11363, 11366, 11366.5, 11366.6, 11368, 11370.1, 11378, 11378.5, 11379, 11379.5, 11379.6, 11380, 11380.5, 11383, or 11550, or subdivision (a) of Section 11377, or any person who is discharged or paroled from a penal institution where he or she was confined because of the commission of any such offense, or any person who is convicted in any other state of any offense which, if committed or attempted in this state, would have been punishable as one or more of the above-mentioned offenses, shall within 30 days of his or her coming into any county or city, or city and county in which he or she resides or is temporarily domiciled for that length of time, register with the chief of police of the city in which he or she resides or the sheriff of the county if he or she resides in an unincorporated area.

For persons convicted of an offense defined in Section 11377, 11378, 11379, or 11380, this subdivision shall apply only to offenses involving controlled substances specified in paragraph (12) of subdivision (d) of Section 11054 and paragraph (2) of subdivision (d) of Section 11055, and to analogs of these substances, as defined in Section 11401. For persons convicted of an offense defined in Section 11379 or 11379.5, this subdivision shall not apply if the conviction was for transporting, offering to transport, or attempting to transport a controlled substance.

(b) Any person who is convicted in any federal court of any offense which, if committed or attempted in this state would have been punishable as one or more of the offenses enumerated in subdivision (a) shall, within 30 days of his or her coming into any county or city, or city and county, in which he or she resides or is temporarily domiciled for that length of time, register with the chief of police of the city in which he or she resides or the sheriff of the county if he or she resides in an unincorporated area.

(c) This section does not apply to a conviction of a misdemeanor under Section 11357, 11360, or 11377.

(d) The registration requirements imposed by this section for the conviction of offenses defined in Section 11353.7, 11366.5, 11366.6, 11370.1, 11377, 11378, 11378.5, 11379, 11379.5, 11379.6, 11380, 11380.5, or 11383, shall apply to any person who commits any of those offenses on and after January 1, 1990.

Health & Safety Code § 25189.5

(Amended by Statute, Effective April 4, 2011, and Operative October 1, 2011. Subd. (e) Amended on Nov. 4, 1986, by Prop. 65.)

(a) The disposal of any hazardous waste, or the causing thereof, is prohibited when the disposal is at a facility which does not have a permit from the department issued pursuant to this chapter, or at any point which is not authorized according to this chapter.

(b) Any person who is convicted of knowingly disposing or causing the disposal of any hazardous waste, or who reasonably should have known that he or she was disposing or causing the disposal of any hazardous waste, at a facility which does not have a permit from the department issued pursuant to this chapter, or at any point which is not authorized according to this chapter shall, upon conviction, be punished by imprisonment in a county jail for not more than one year or by imprisonment pursuant to subdivision (h) of Section 1170 of the Penal Code.

(c) Any person who knowingly transports or causes the transportation of hazardous waste, or who reasonably should have known that he or she was causing the transportation of any hazardous waste, to a facility which does not have a permit from the department issued pursuant to this chapter, or at any point which is not authorized according to this chapter, shall, upon conviction, be punished by imprisonment in a county jail for not more than one year or by imprisonment pursuant to subdivision (h) of Section 1170 of the Penal Code.

(d) Any person who knowingly treats or stores any hazardous waste at a facility which does not have a permit from the department issued pursuant to this chapter, or at any point which is not authorized according to this chapter, shall, upon conviction, be punished by imprisonment in a county jail for not more than one year or by imprisonment pursuant to subdivision (h) of Section 1170 of the Penal Code.

(e) The court also shall impose upon a person convicted of violating subdivision (b), (c), or (d), a fine of not less than five thousand dollars ($5,000) nor more than one hundred thousand dollars ($100,000) for each day of violation, except as further provided in this subdivision. If the act which violated subdivision (b), (c), or (d) caused great bodily injury, or caused a substantial probability that death could result, the person convicted of violating subdivision (b), (c), or (d) may be punished by imprisonment pursuant to subdivision (h) of Section 1170 of the Penal Code for one, two, or three years, in addition and consecutive to the term specified in subdivision (b), (c), or (d), and may be fined up to two hundred fifty thousand dollars ($250,000) for each day of violation.

(f) For purposes of this section, except as otherwise provided in this subdivision, "each day of violation" means each day on which a violation continues. In any case where a person has disposed or caused the disposal of any hazardous waste in violation of this section, each day that the waste remains disposed of in violation of this section and the person has knowledge thereof is a separate additional violation, unless the person has filed a report of the disposal with the department and is complying with any order concerning the disposal issued by the department, a hearing officer, or court of competent jurisdiction.

Health & Safety Code § 25189.6

(Amended by Statute, Effective April 4, 2011, and Operative October 1, 2011.)

(a) Any person who knowingly, or with reckless disregard for the risk, treats, handles, transports, disposes, or stores any hazardous waste in a manner which causes any unreasonable risk of fire, explosion, serious injury, or death is guilty of a public offense and shall, upon conviction, be punished by a fine of not less than five thousand dollars ($5,000) nor more than two hundred fifty thousand dollars ($250,000) for each day of violation, or by imprisonment in a county jail for not more than one year, or by imprisonment pursuant to subdivision (h) of Section 1170 of the Penal Code, or by both that fine and imprisonment.

(b) Any person who knowingly, at the time the person takes the actions specified in subdivision (a), places another person in imminent danger of death or serious bodily injury, is guilty of a public offense and shall, upon conviction, be punished by a fine of not less than five thousand dollars ($5,000) nor more than two hundred fifty thousand dollars ($250,000) for each day of violation, and by imprisonment pursuant to subdivision (h) of Section 1170 of the Penal Code for three, six, or nine years.

Health & Safety Code § 25189.7

(Amended by Statute, Effective April 4, 2011, and Operative October 1, 2011.)

(a) The burning or incineration of any hazardous waste, or the causing thereof, is prohibited when the burning or incineration is at a facility which does not have a permit from the department issued pursuant to this chapter, or at any point which is not authorized according to this chapter.

(b) Any person who is convicted of knowingly burning or incinerating, or causing the burning or incineration of, any hazardous waste, or who reasonably should have known that he or she was burning or incinerating, or causing the burning or incineration of, any hazardous waste, at a facility which does not have a permit from the department issued pursuant to this chapter, or at any point which is not authorized according to this chapter, shall, upon conviction, be punished by imprisonment in a county jail for not more than one year or by imprisonment pursuant to subdivision (h) of Section 1170 of the Penal Code.

(c) The court also shall impose upon a person convicted of violating subdivision (b) a fine of not less than five thousand dollars ($5,000) nor more than one hundred thousand dollars ($100,000) for each day of violation, except as otherwise provided in this subdivision. If the act which violated subdivision (b) caused great bodily injury or caused a substantial probability that death could result, the person convicted of violating subdivision (b) may be punished by imprisonment pursuant to subdivision (h) of Section 1170 of the Penal Code for one, two, or three years, in addition and consecutive to the term specified in subdivision (b), and may be fined up to two hundred fifty thousand dollars ($250,000) for each day of violation.

Health and Safety Code § 109925

(MAUCRSA, Effective June 27, 2017.)

(a) "Drug" means any of the following:

(1) An article recognized in an official compendium.

(2) An article used or intended for use in the diagnosis, cure, mitigation, treatment, or prevention of disease in human beings or any other animal.

(3) An article other than food, that is used or intended to affect the structure or any function of the body of human beings or any other animal.

(4) An article used or intended for use as a component of an article designated in paragraphs (1) to (3), inclusive.

(b) The term "drug" does not include any device.

(c) Any food for which a claim (as described in Sections 403(r)(1)(B) (21 U.S.C. Sec. 343(r)(1)(B)) and 403(r)(3) (21 U.S.C. Sec. 343(r)(3)) or Sections 403(r)(1)(B) (21 U.S.C. Sec. 343(r)(1)(B)) and 403(r)(5)(D) (21 U.S.C. Sec. 343(r)(5)(D)) of the federal act), is made in accordance with the requirements set forth in Section 403(r) (21 U.S.C. Sec. 343(r)) of the federal act, is not a drug under subdivision (b) solely because the label or labeling contains such a claim.

(d) Cannabis product, including any cannabis product intended for external use, is not a drug.

VIII. Labor Code Sections

Labor Code § 147.5

(MCRSA- AB 266, Effective January 1, 2016)

(a) By January 1, 2017, the Division of Occupational Safety and Health shall convene an advisory committee to evaluate whether there is a need to develop industry-specific regulations related to the activities of facilities issued a license pursuant to Chapter 3.5 (commencing with Section 19300) of Division 8 of the Business and Professions Code.

(b) By July 1, 2017, the advisory committee shall present to the board its findings and recommendations for consideration by the board. By July 1, 2017, the board shall render a decision regarding the adoption of industry-specific regulations pursuant to this section.

Labor Code § 147.6

(AUMA, Effective November 9, 2016.)

(a) By March 1, 2018, the Division of Occupational Safety and Health shall convene an advisory committee to evaluate whether there is a need to develop industry-specific regulations related to the activities of licensees under Division 10 of the Business and Professions Code, including but not limited to, whether specific requirements are needed to address exposure to second-hand marijuana smoke by employees at facilities where on-site consumption of marijuana is permitted under subdivision (d) of Section 26200 of the Business and Professions Code, and whether specific requirements are needed to address the potential risks of combustion, inhalation, armed robberies or repetitive strain injuries.

(b) By October 1, 2018, the advisory committee shall present to the board its findings and recommendations for consideration by the board. By October 1, 2018, the board shall render a decision regarding the adoption of industry-specific regulations pursuant to this section.

Labor Code § 432.8

(Added by Statute, Effective 1976.)

The limitations on employers and the penalties provided for in Section 432.7 shall apply to a conviction for violation of subdivision (b) or (c) of Section 11357 of the Health and Safety Code or a statutory predecessor thereof, or subdivision (c) of Section 11360 of the Health and Safety Code, or Section 11364, 11365, or 11550 of the Health and Safety Code as they related to marijuana prior to January 1, 1976, or a statutory predecessor thereof, two years from the date of such a conviction.

Labor Code § 1140

(Added by Statute, Effective 1975.)

This part shall be known and may be referred to as the Alatorre-Zenovich-Dunlap-Berman Agricultural Labor Relations Act of 1975.

Labor Code § 1140.2

(Added by Statute, Effective 1975.)

It is hereby stated to be the policy of the State of California to encourage and protect the right of agricultural employees to full freedom of association, self-organization, and designation of representatives of their own choosing, to negotiate the terms and conditions of their employment, and to be free from the interference, restraint, or coercion of employers of labor, or their agents, in the designation of such representatives or in self-organization or in other concerted activities for the purpose of collective bargaining or other mutual aid or protection. For this purpose this part is adopted to provide for collective-bargaining rights for agricultural employees.

Labor Code § 1140.4

(Amended by Statute, Effective January 1, 1995.)

As used in this part:

(a) The term "agriculture" includes farming in all its branches, and, among other things, includes the cultivation and tillage of the soil, dairying, the production, cultivation, growing, and harvesting of any agricultural or horticultural commodities (including commodities defined as agricultural commodities in Section 1141j(g) of Title 12 of the United States Code), the raising of livestock, bees, furbearing animals, or poultry, and any practices (including any forestry or lumbering operations) performed by a farmer or on a farm as an incident to or in conjunction with such farming operations, including preparation for market and delivery to storage or to market or to carriers for transportation to market.

(b) The term "agricultural employee" or "employee" shall mean one engaged in agriculture, as such term is defined in subdivision (a). However, nothing in this subdivision shall be construed to include any person other than those employees excluded from the coverage of the National Labor Relations Act, as amended, as agricultural employees, pursuant to Section 2(3) of the Labor Management Relations Act (Section 152(3), Title 29, United States Code), and

Section 3(f) of the Fair Labor Standards Act (Section 203(f), Title 29, United States Code).

Further, nothing in this part shall apply, or be construed to apply, to any employee who performs work to be done at the site of the construction, alteration, painting, or repair of a building, structure, or other work (as these terms have been construed under Section 8(e) of the Labor Management Relations Act, 29 U.S.C. Sec. 158(e)) or logging or timber-clearing operations in initial preparation of land for farming, or who does land leveling or only land surveying for any of the above.

As used in this subdivision, "land leveling" shall include only major land moving operations changing the contour of the land, but shall not include annual or seasonal tillage or preparation of land for cultivation.

(c) The term "agricultural employer" shall be liberally construed to include any person acting directly or indirectly in the interest of an employer in relation to an agricultural employee, any individual grower, corporate grower, cooperative grower, harvesting association, hiring association, land management group, any association of persons or cooperatives engaged in agriculture, and shall include any person who owns or leases or manages land used for agricultural purposes, but shall exclude any person supplying agricultural workers to an employer, any farm labor contractor as defined by Section 1682, and any person functioning in the capacity of a labor contractor. The employer engaging such labor contractor or person shall be deemed the employer for all purposes under this part.

(d) The term "person" shall mean one or more individuals, corporations, partnerships, limited liability companies, associations, legal representatives, trustees in bankruptcy, receivers, or any other legal entity, employer, or labor organization having an interest in the outcome of a proceeding under this part.

(e) The term "representatives" includes any individual or labor organization.

(f) The term "labor organization" means any organization of any kind, or any agency or employee representation committee or plan, in which employees participate and which exists, in whole or in part, for the purpose of dealing with employers concerning grievances, labor disputes, wages, rates of pay, hours of employment, or conditions of work for agricultural employees.

(g) The term "unfair labor practice" means any unfair labor practice specified in Chapter 4 (commencing with Section 1153) of this part.

(h) The term "labor dispute" includes any controversy concerning terms, tenure, or conditions of employment, or concerning the association or representation of persons in negotiating, fixing, maintaining, changing, or seeking to arrange terms or conditions of employment, regardless of whether the disputants stand in the proximate relation of employer and employee.

(i) The term "board" means Agricultural Labor Relations Board.

(j) The term "supervisor" means any individual having the authority, in the interest of the employer, to hire, transfer, suspend, lay off, recall, promote, discharge, assign, reward, or discipline other employees, or the responsibility to direct them, or to adjust their grievances, or effectively to recommend such action, if, in connection with the foregoing, the exercise of such authority is not of a merely routine or clerical nature, but requires the use of independent judgment.

IX. Penal Code Sections

Penal Code § 182

(Amended by Statute, Effective April 4, 2011, and Operative October 1, 2011.)

(a) If two or more persons conspire:

(1) To commit any crime.

(2) Falsely and maliciously to indict another for any crime, or to procure another to be charged or arrested for any crime.

(3) Falsely to move or maintain any suit, action, or proceeding.

(4) To cheat and defraud any person of any property, by any means which are in themselves criminal, or to obtain money or property by false pretenses or by false promises with fraudulent intent not to perform those promises.

(5) To commit any act injurious to the public health, to public morals, or to pervert or obstruct justice, or the due administration of the laws.

(6) To commit any crime against the person of the President or Vice President of the United States, the Governor of any state or territory, any United States justice or judge, or the secretary of any of the executive departments of the United States. They are punishable as follows: When they conspire to commit any crime against the person of any official specified in paragraph (6), they are guilty of a felony and are punishable by imprisonment pursuant to subdivision (h) of Section 1170 for five, seven, or nine years. When they conspire to commit any other felony, they shall be punishable in the same manner and to the same extent as is provided for the punishment of that felony. If the felony is one for which different punishments are prescribed for different degrees, the jury or court which finds the defendant guilty thereof shall determine the degree of the felony the defendant conspired to commit. If the degree is not so determined, the punishment for conspiracy to commit the felony shall be that prescribed for the lesser degree, except in the case of conspiracy to commit murder, in which case the punishment shall be that prescribed for murder in the first degree. If the felony is conspiracy to commit two or more felonies which have different punishments and the commission of those felonies constitute but one offense of conspiracy, the penalty shall be that prescribed for the felony which has the greater maximum term.

When they conspire to do an act described in paragraph (4), they shall be punishable by imprisonment in a county jail for not more than one year, or by imprisonment pursuant to subdivision (h) of Section 1170, or by a fine not exceeding ten thousand dollars ($10,000), or by both that imprisonment and fine. When they conspire to do any of the other acts described in this section, they shall be punishable by imprisonment in a county jail for not more than one year, or pursuant to subdivision (h) of Section 1170, or by a fine not exceeding ten thousand dollars ($10,000), or by both that imprisonment and fine. When they receive a felony conviction for conspiring to commit identity theft, as defined in Section 530.5, the court may impose a fine of up to twenty-five thousand dollars ($25,000). All cases of conspiracy may be prosecuted and tried in the superior court of any county in which any overt act tending to effect the conspiracy shall be done.

(b) Upon a trial for conspiracy, in a case where an overt act is necessary to constitute the offense, the defendant cannot be convicted unless one or more overt acts are expressly alleged in the indictment or information, nor unless one of the acts alleged is proved; but other overt acts not alleged may be given in evidence.

Penal Code § 290

(Amended (as added by Stats. 2017, Ch. 541, Sec. 2.5) by Stats. 2018, Ch. 423, Sec. 52. (SB 1494) Effective January 1, 2019. Section operative January 1, 2021, by its own provisions. Note: This section was amended on November 6, 2012, by initiative Prop. 35.)

(a) Sections 290 to 290.024, inclusive, shall be known, and may be cited, as the Sex Offender Registration Act. All references to "the Act" in those sections are to the Sex Offender Registration Act.

(b) Every person described in subdivision (c), for the period specified in subdivision (d) while residing in California, or while attending school or working in California, as described in Sections 290.002 and 290.01, shall register with the chief of police of the city in which he or she is residing, or the sheriff of the county if he or she is residing in an unincorporated area or city that has no police department, and, additionally, with the chief of police of a campus of the University of California, the California State University, or community college if he or she is residing upon the campus or in any of its facilities, within five working days of coming into, or changing his or her residence within, any city, county, or city and county, or campus in which he or she temporarily resides, and shall register thereafter in accordance with the Act, unless the duty to register is terminated pursuant to Section 290.5 or as otherwise provided by law.

(c) The following persons shall register:

Every person who, since July 1, 1944, has been or is hereafter convicted in any court in this state or in any federal or military court of a violation of Section 187 committed in the perpetration, or an attempt to perpetrate, rape or any act punishable under Section 286, 287, 288, or 289 or former Section 288a, Section 207 or 209 committed with intent to violate Section 261, 286, 287, 288, or 289 or former Section 288a, Section 220, except assault to commit mayhem, subdivision (b) or (c) of Section 236.1, Section 243.4, Section 261, paragraph (1) of subdivision (a) of Section 262 involving the use of force or violence for which the person is sentenced to the state prison, Section 264.1, 266, or 266c, subdivision (b) of Section 266h, subdivision (b) of Section 266i, Section 266j, 267, 269, 285, 286, 287, 288, 288.3, 288.4, 288.5, 288.7, 289, or 311.1, or former Section 288a, subdivision (b), (c), or (d) of Section 311.2, Section 311.3, 311.4, 311.10, 311.11, or 647.6, former Section 647a, subdivision (c) of Section 653f, subdivision 1 or 2 of Section 314, any offense involving lewd or lascivious conduct under Section 272, or any felony violation of Section 288.2; any statutory predecessor that includes all elements of one of the offenses described in this subdivision; or any person who since that date has been or is hereafter convicted of the attempt or conspiracy to commit any of the offenses described in this subdivision.

(d) A person described in subdivision (c), or who is otherwise required to register pursuant to the Act shall register for 10 years, 20 years, or life, following a conviction and release from incarceration, placement, commitment, or release on probation or other supervision, as follows:

(1) (A) A tier one offender is subject to registration for a minimum of 10 years. A person is a tier one offender if the person is required to register for conviction of a misdemeanor described in subdivision (c), or for conviction of a felony described in subdivision (c) that was not a serious or violent felony as described in subdivision (c) of Section 667.5 or subdivision (c) of Section 1192.7.

(B) This paragraph does not apply to a person who is subject to registration pursuant to paragraph (2) or (3).

(2) (A) A tier two offender is subject to registration for a minimum of 20 years. A person is a tier two offender if the person was convicted of an offense described in subdivision (c) that is also described in subdivision (c) of Section 667.5 or subdivision (c) of Section 1192.7, Section 285, subdivision (g) or (h) of Section 286, subdivision (g) or (h) of Section 287 or former Section 288a, subdivision (b) of Section 289, or Section 647.6 if it is a second or subsequent conviction for that offense that was brought and tried separately.

(B) This paragraph does not apply if the person is subject to lifetime registration as required in paragraph (3).

(3) A tier three offender is subject to registration for life. A person is a tier three offender if any one of the following applies:

(A) Following conviction of a registerable offense, the person was subsequently convicted in a separate proceeding of committing an offense described in subdivision (c) and the conviction is for commission of a violent felony described in subdivision (c) of Section 667.5, or the person was subsequently convicted of committing an offense for which the person was ordered to register pursuant to Section 290.006, and the conviction is for the commission of a violent felony described in subdivision (c) of Section 667.5.

(B) The person was committed to a state mental hospital as a sexually violent predator pursuant to Article 4 (commencing with Section 6600) of Chapter 2 of Part 2 of Division 6 of the Welfare and Institutions Code.

(C) The person was convicted of violating any of the following:

(i) Section 187 while attempting to commit or committing an act punishable under Section 261, 286, 287, 288, or 289 or former Section 288a.

(ii) Section 207 or 209 with intent to violate Section 261, 286, 287, 288, or 289 or former Section 288a.

(iii) Section 220.

(iv) Subdivision (b) of Section 266h.

(v) Subdivision (b) of Section 266i.

(vi) Section 266j.

(vii) Section 267.

(viii) Section 269.

(ix) Subdivision (b) or (c) of Section 288.

(x) Section 288.2.

(xi) Section 288.3, unless committed with the intent to commit a violation of subdivision (b) of Section 286, subdivision (b) of Section 287 or former Section 288a, or subdivision (h) or (i) of Section 289.

(xii) Section 288.4.

(xiii) Section 288.5.

(xiv) Section 288.7.

(xv) Subdivision (c) of Section 653f.

(xvi) Any offense for which the person is sentenced to a life term pursuant to Section 667.61.

(D) The person's risk level on the static risk assessment instrument for sex offenders (SARATSO), pursuant to Section 290.04, is well above average risk at the time of release on the index sex offense into the community, as defined in the Coding Rules for that instrument.

(E) The person is a habitual sex offender pursuant to Section 667.71.

(F) The person was convicted of violating subdivision (a) of Section 288 in two proceedings brought and tried separately.

(G) The person was sentenced to 15 to 25 years to life for an offense listed in Section 667.61.

(H) The person is required to register pursuant to Section 290.004.

(I) The person was convicted of a felony offense described in subdivision (b) or (c) of Section 236.1.

(J) The person was convicted of a felony offense described in subdivision (a), (c), or (d) of Section 243.4.

(K) The person was convicted of violating paragraph (2), (3), or (4) of subdivision (a) of Section 261 or was convicted of violating Section 261 and punished pursuant to paragraph (1) or (2) of subdivision (c) of

Section 264.

(L) The person was convicted of violating paragraph (1) of subdivision (a) of Section 262.

(M) The person was convicted of violating Section 264.1.

(N) The person was convicted of any offense involving lewd or lascivious conduct under Section 272.

(O) The person was convicted of violating paragraph (2) of subdivision (c) or subdivision (d), (f), or (i) of Section 286.

(P) The person was convicted of violating paragraph (2) of subdivision (c) or subdivision (d), (f), or (i) of Section 287 or former Section 288a.

(Q) The person was convicted of violating paragraph (1) of subdivision (a) or subdivision (d), (e), or (j) of Section 289.

(R) The person was convicted of a felony violation of Section 311.1 or 311.11 or of violating subdivision (b), (c), or (d) of Section 311.2, Section 311.3, 311.4, or 311.10.

(4) (A) A person who is required to register pursuant to Section 290.005 shall be placed in the appropriate tier if the offense is assessed as equivalent to a California registerable offense described in subdivision (c).

(B) If the person's duty to register pursuant to Section 290.005 is based solely on the requirement of registration in another jurisdiction, and there is no equivalent California registerable offense, the person shall be subject to registration as a tier two offender, except that the person is subject to registration as a tier three offender if one of the following applies:

(i) The person's risk level on the static risk assessment instrument (SARATSO), pursuant to Section 290.06, is well above average risk at the time of release on the index sex offense into the community, as defined in the Coding Rules for that instrument.

(ii) The person was subsequently convicted in a separate proceeding of an offense substantially similar to an offense listed in subdivision (c) which is also substantially similar to an offense described in subdivision (c) of Section 667.5, or is substantially similar to Section 269 or 288.7.

(iii) The person has ever been committed to a state mental hospital or mental health facility in a proceeding substantially similar to civil commitment as a sexually violent predator pursuant to Article 4 (commencing with Section 6600) of Chapter 2 of Part 2 of Division 6 of the Welfare and Institutions Code.

(5) (A) The Department of Justice may place a person described in subdivision (c), or who is otherwise required to register pursuant to the Act, in a tier-to-be-determined category if his or her appropriate tier designation described in this subdivision cannot be immediately ascertained. An individual placed in this tier-to-be-determined category shall continue to register in accordance with the Act. The individual shall be given credit for any period for which he or she registers towards his or her mandated minimum registration period.

(B) The Department of Justice shall ascertain an individual's appropriate tier designation as described in this subdivision within 24 months of his or her placement in the tier-to-be-determined category.

(e) The minimum time period for the completion of the required registration period in tier one or two commences on the date of release from incarceration, placement, or commitment, including any related civil commitment on the registerable offense. The minimum time for the completion of the required registration period for a designated tier is tolled during any period of subsequent incarceration, placement, or commitment, including any subsequent civil commitment, except that arrests not resulting in conviction, adjudication, or revocation of probation or parole shall not toll the required registration period. The minimum time period shall be extended by one year for each misdemeanor conviction of failing to register under this act, and by three years for each felony conviction of failing to register under this act, without regard to the actual time served in custody for the conviction. If a registrant is subsequently convicted of another offense requiring registration pursuant to the Act, a new minimum time period for the completion of the registration requirement for the applicable tier shall commence upon that person's release from incarceration, placement, or commitment, including any related civil commitment. If the subsequent conviction requiring registration pursuant to the Act occurs prior to an order to terminate the registrant from the registry after completion of a tier associated with the first conviction for a registerable offense, the applicable tier shall be the highest tier associated with the convictions.

(f) Nothing in this section shall be construed to require a ward of the juvenile court to register under the Act, except as provided in Section 290.008.

(g) This section shall become operative on January 1, 2021.

Penal Code § 374.8

(Amended by Statute, Effective April 4, 2011, and Operative October 1, 2011.)

(a) In any prosecution under this section, proof of the elements of the offense shall not be dependent upon the requirements of Title 22 of the California Code of Regulations.

(b) Any person who knowingly causes any hazardous substance to be deposited into or upon any road, street, highway, alley, or railroad right-of-way, or upon the land of another, without the permission of the owner, or into the waters of this state is punishable by imprisonment in the county jail for not more than one year or by imprisonment pursuant to subdivision (h) of Section 1170 for a term of 16 months, two years, or three years, or by a fine of not less than fifty dollars ($50) nor more than ten thousand dollars ($10,000), or by both the fine and imprisonment, unless the deposit occurred as a result of an emergency that the person promptly reported to the appropriate regulatory authority.

(c) For purposes of this section, "hazardous substance" means either of the following:

(1) Any material that, because of its quantity, concentration, or physical or chemical characteristics, poses a significant present or potential hazard to human health and safety or to the environment if released into the environment, including, but not limited to, hazardous waste and any material that the administering agency or a handler, as defined in Chapter 6.91 (commencing with Section 25410) of Division 20 of the Health and Safety Code, has a reasonable basis for believing would be injurious to the health and safety of persons or harmful to the environment if released into the environment.

(2) Any substance or chemical product for which one of the following applies:

(A) The manufacturer or producer is required to prepare a MSDS, as defined in Section 6374 of the Labor Code, for the substance or product pursuant to the Hazardous Substances Information Training Act (Chapter 2.5 (commencing with Section 6360) of Part 1 of Division 5 of the Labor Code) or pursuant to any applicable federal law or regulation.

(B) The substance is described as a radioactive material in Chapter 1 of Title 10 of the Code of Federal Regulations maintained and updated by the Nuclear Regulatory Commission.

(C) The substance is designated by the Secretary of Transportation in Chapter 27 (commencing with Section 1801) of the appendix to Title 49 of the United States Code and taxed as a radioactive substance or material.

(D) The materials listed in subdivision (b) of Section 6382 of the Labor Code.

Penal Code § 667

(Amended by Stats. 2018, Ch. 1013, Sec. 1. (SB 1393) Effective January 1, 2019. Note: This section was added on June 8, 1982, by initiative Prop. 8.)

(a) (1) Any person convicted of a serious felony who previously has been convicted of a serious felony in this state or of any offense committed in another jurisdiction which includes all of the elements of any serious felony, shall receive, in addition to the sentence imposed by the court for the present offense, a five-year enhancement for each such prior conviction on charges brought and tried separately. The terms of the present offense and each enhancement shall run consecutively.

> (2) This subdivision shall not be applied when the punishment imposed under other provisions of law would result in a longer term of imprisonment. There is no requirement of prior incarceration or commitment for this subdivision to apply.

> (3) The Legislature may increase the length of the enhancement of sentence provided in this subdivision by a statute passed by majority vote of each house thereof.

> (4) As used in this subdivision, "serious felony" means a serious felony listed in subdivision (c) of Section 1192.7.

> (5) This subdivision shall not apply to a person convicted of selling, furnishing, administering, or giving, or offering to sell, furnish, administer, or give to a minor any methamphetamine-related drug or any precursors of methamphetamine unless the prior conviction was for a serious felony described in subparagraph (24) of subdivision (c) of Section 1192.7.

(b) It is the intent of the Legislature in enacting subdivisions (b) to (i), inclusive, to ensure longer prison sentences and greater punishment for those who commit a felony and have been previously convicted of one or more serious or violent felony offenses.

(c) Notwithstanding any other law, if a defendant has been convicted of a felony and it has been pled and proved that the defendant has one or more prior serious or violent felony convictions as defined in subdivision (d), the court shall adhere to each of the following:

(1) There shall not be an aggregate term limitation for purposes of consecutive sentencing for any subsequent felony conviction.

(2) Probation for the current offense shall not be granted, nor shall execution or imposition of the sentence be suspended for any prior offense.

(3) The length of time between the prior serious or violent felony conviction and the current felony conviction shall not affect the imposition of sentence.

(4) There shall not be a commitment to any other facility other than the state prison. Diversion shall not be granted nor shall the defendant be eligible for commitment to the California Rehabilitation Center as provided in Article 2 (commencing with Section 3050) of Chapter 1 of Division 3 of the Welfare and Institutions Code.

(5) The total amount of credits awarded pursuant to Article 2.5 (commencing with Section 2930) of Chapter 7 of Title 1 of Part 3 shall not exceed one-fifth of the total term of imprisonment imposed and shall not accrue until the defendant is physically placed in the state prison.

(6) If there is a current conviction for more than one felony count not committed on the same occasion, and not arising from the same set of operative facts, the court shall sentence the defendant consecutively on each count pursuant to subdivision (e).

(7) If there is a current conviction for more than one serious or violent felony as described in paragraph (6), the

court shall impose the sentence for each conviction consecutive to the sentence for any other conviction for which the defendant may be consecutively sentenced in the manner prescribed by law.

(8) Any sentence imposed pursuant to subdivision (e) will be imposed consecutive to any other sentence which the defendant is already serving, unless otherwise provided by law.

(d) Notwithstanding any other law and for the purposes of subdivisions (b) to (i), inclusive, a prior conviction of a serious and/or violent felony shall be defined as:

(1) Any offense defined in subdivision (c) of Section 667.5 as a violent felony or any offense defined in subdivision (c) of Section 1192.7 as a serious felony in this state. The determination of whether a prior conviction is a prior felony conviction for purposes of subdivisions (b) to (i), inclusive, shall be made upon the date of that prior conviction and is not affected by the sentence imposed unless the sentence automatically, upon the initial sentencing, converts the felony to a misdemeanor. None of the following dispositions shall affect the determination that a prior conviction is a prior felony for purposes of subdivisions (b) to (i), inclusive:

(A) The suspension of imposition of judgment or sentence.

(B) The stay of execution of sentence.

(C) The commitment to the State Department of Health Services as a mentally disordered sex offender following a conviction of a felony.

(D) The commitment to the California Rehabilitation Center or any other facility whose function is rehabilitative diversion from the state prison.

(2) A prior conviction in another jurisdiction for an offense that, if committed in California, is punishable by imprisonment in the state prison shall constitute a prior conviction of a particular serious and/or violent felony if the prior conviction in the other jurisdiction is for an offense that includes all of the elements of a particular violent felony as defined in subdivision (c) of Section 667.5 or serious felony as defined in subdivision (c) of Section 1192.7.

(3) A prior juvenile adjudication shall constitute a prior serious and/or violent felony conviction for purposes of sentence enhancement if:

(A) The juvenile was 16 years of age or older at the time he or she committed the prior offense.

(B) The prior offense is listed in subdivision (b) of Section 707 of the Welfare and Institutions Code or described in paragraph (1) or (2) as a serious or violent felony.

(C) The juvenile was found to be a fit and proper subject to be dealt with under the juvenile court law.

(D) The juvenile was adjudged a ward of the juvenile court within the meaning of Section 602 of the Welfare and Institutions Code because the person committed an offense listed in subdivision (b) of Section 707 of the Welfare and Institutions Code.

(e) For purposes of subdivisions (b) to (i), inclusive, and in addition to any other enhancement or punishment provisions which may apply, the following shall apply where a defendant has one or more prior serious or violent felony convictions:

(1) If a defendant has one prior serious or violent felony conviction as defined in subdivision (d) that has been pled and proved, the determinate term or minimum term for an indeterminate term shall be twice the term otherwise provided as punishment for the current felony conviction.

(2) (A) Except as provided in subparagraph (C), if a defendant has two or more prior serious or violent felony convictions as defined in subdivision (d) that have been pled and proved, the term for the current felony

conviction shall be an indeterminate term of life imprisonment with a minimum term of the indeterminate sentence calculated as the greatest of:

(i) Three times the term otherwise provided as punishment for each current felony conviction subsequent to the two or more prior serious or violent felony convictions.

(ii) Imprisonment in the state prison for 25 years.

(iii) The term determined by the court pursuant to Section 1170 for the underlying conviction, including any enhancement applicable under Chapter 4.5 (commencing with Section 1170) of Title 7 of Part 2, or any period prescribed by Section 190 or 3046.

(B) The indeterminate term described in subparagraph (A) shall be served consecutive to any other term of imprisonment for which a consecutive term may be imposed by law. Any other term imposed subsequent to any indeterminate term described in subparagraph (A) shall not be merged therein but shall commence at the time the person would otherwise have been released from prison.

(C) If a defendant has two or more prior serious or violent felony convictions as defined in subdivision (c) of Section 667.5 or subdivision (c) of Section 1192.7 that have been pled and proved, and the current offense is not a serious or violent felony as defined in subdivision (d), the defendant shall be sentenced pursuant to paragraph (1) of subdivision (e) unless the prosecution pleads and proves any of the following:

(i) The current offense is a controlled substance charge, in which an allegation under Section 11370.4 or 11379.8 of the Health and Safety Code was admitted or found true.

(ii) The current offense is a felony sex offense, defined in subdivision (d) of Section 261.5 or Section 262, or any felony offense that results in mandatory registration as a sex offender pursuant to subdivision (c) of Section 290 except for violations of Sections 266 and 285, paragraph (1) of subdivision (b) and subdivision (e) of Section 286, paragraph (1) of subdivision (b) and subdivision (e) of Section 288a, Section 311.11, and Section 314.

(iii) During the commission of the current offense, the defendant used a firearm, was armed with a firearm or deadly weapon, or intended to cause great bodily injury to another person.

(iv) The defendant suffered a prior serious or violent felony conviction, as defined in subdivision (d) of this section, for any of the following felonies:

(I) A "sexually violent offense" as defined in subdivision (b) of Section 6600 of the Welfare and Institutions Code.

(II) Oral copulation with a child who is under 14 years of age, and who is more than 10 years younger than he or she as defined by Section 288a, sodomy with another person who is under 14 years of age and more than 10 years younger than he or she as defined by Section 286, or sexual penetration with another person who is under 14 years of age, and who is more than 10 years younger than he or she, as defined by Section 289.

(III) A lewd or lascivious act involving a child under 14 years of age, in violation of Section 288.

(IV) Any homicide offense, including any attempted homicide offense, defined in Sections 187 to 191.5, inclusive.

(V) Solicitation to commit murder as defined in Section 653f.

(VI) Assault with a machine gun on a peace officer or firefighter, as defined in paragraph (3) of subdivision (d) of Section 245.

(VII) Possession of a weapon of mass destruction, as defined in paragraph (1) of subdivision (a) of Section 11418.

(VIII) Any serious or violent felony offense punishable in California by life imprisonment or death.

(f) (1) Notwithstanding any other law, subdivisions (b) to (i), inclusive, shall be applied in every case in which a defendant has one or more prior serious or violent felony convictions as defined in subdivision (d). The prosecuting attorney shall plead and prove each prior serious or violent felony conviction except as provided in paragraph (2).

(2) The prosecuting attorney may move to dismiss or strike a prior serious or violent felony conviction allegation in the furtherance of justice pursuant to Section 1385, or if there is insufficient evidence to prove the prior serious or violent felony conviction. If upon the satisfaction of the court that there is insufficient evidence to prove the prior serious or violent felony conviction, the court may dismiss or strike the allegation. Nothing in this section shall be read to alter a court's authority under Section 1385.

(g) Prior serious or violent felony convictions shall not be used in plea bargaining as defined in subdivision (b) of Section 1192.7. The prosecution shall plead and prove all known prior felony serious or violent convictions and shall not enter into any agreement to strike or seek the dismissal of any prior serious and/or violent felony conviction allegation except as provided in paragraph (2) of subdivision (f).

(h) All references to existing statutes in subdivisions (c) to (g), inclusive, are to statutes as they existed on November 7, 2012.

(i) If any provision of subdivisions (b) to (h), inclusive, or the application thereof to any person or circumstance is held invalid, that invalidity shall not affect other provisions or applications of those subdivisions which can be given effect without the invalid provision or application, and to this end the provisions of those subdivisions are severable.

(j) The provisions of this section shall not be amended by the Legislature except by statute passed in each house by rollcall vote entered in the journal, two-thirds of the membership concurring, or by a statute that becomes effective only when approved by the electors.

Penal Code § 830.11

(Amended by Stats. 2018, Ch. 138, Sec. 1. (AB 873) Effective January 1, 2019.)

(a) The following persons are not peace officers but may exercise the powers of arrest of a peace officer as specified in Section 836 and the power to serve warrants as specified in Sections 1523 and 1530 during the course and within the scope of their employment, if they receive a course in the exercise of those powers pursuant to Section 832. The authority and powers of the persons designated under this section extend to any place in the state:

(1) A person employed by the Department of Business Oversight designated by the Commissioner of Business Oversight, provided that the person's primary duty is the enforcement of, and investigations relating to, the provisions of law administered by the Commissioner of Business Oversight.

(2) A person employed by the Bureau of Real Estate designated by the Real Estate Commissioner, provided that the person's primary duty is the enforcement of the laws set forth in Part 1 (commencing with Section 10000) and Part 2 (commencing with Section 11000) of Division 4 of the Business and Professions Code. The Real Estate Commissioner may designate a person under this section who, at the time of his or her designation, is assigned to the Special Investigations Unit, internally known as the Crisis Response Team.

(3) A person employed by the State Lands Commission designated by the executive officer, provided that the person's primary duty is the enforcement of the law relating to the duties of the State Lands Commission.

(4) A person employed as an investigator of the Investigations Bureau of the Department of Insurance,

who is designated by the Chief of the Investigations Bureau, provided that the person's primary duty is the enforcement of the Insurance Code and other laws relating to persons and businesses, licensed and unlicensed by the Department of Insurance, who are engaged in the business of insurance.

(5) A person employed as an investigator or investigator supervisor by the Public Utilities Commission, who is designated by the commission's executive director and approved by the commission, provided that the person's primary duty is the enforcement of the law as that duty is set forth in Section 308.5 of the Public Utilities Code.

(6) (A) A person employed by the State Board of Equalization, Investigations Division, who is designated by the board's executive director, provided that the person's primary duty is the enforcement of laws administered by the State Board of Equalization.

(B) A person designated pursuant to this paragraph is not entitled to peace officer retirement benefits.

(7) A person employed by the Department of Food and Agriculture and designated by the Secretary of Food and Agriculture as an investigator, investigator supervisor, or investigator manager, provided that the person's primary duty is enforcement of, and investigations relating to, the Food and Agricultural Code or Division 5 (commencing with Section 12001) or Division 10 (commencing with Section 26000) of the Business and Professions Code.

(8) The Inspector General and those employees of the Office of the Inspector General designated by the Inspector General, provided that the person's primary duty is the enforcement of the law relating to the duties of the Office of the Inspector General.

(b) Notwithstanding any other law, a person designated pursuant to this section may not carry a firearm.

(c) A person designated pursuant to this section shall be included as a "peace officer of the state" under paragraph (2) of subdivision (c) of Section 11105 for the purpose of receiving state summary criminal history information and shall be furnished that information on the same basis as other peace officers designated in paragraph (2) of subdivision (c) of Section 11105.

Penal Code § 1000

(Amended by Stats. 2017, Ch. 778, Sec. 1. (AB 208) Effective January 1, 2018.)

(a) This chapter shall apply whenever a case is before any court upon an accusatory pleading for a violation of Section 11350, 11357, 11364, or 11365, paragraph (2) of subdivision (b) of Section 11375, Section 11377, or Section 11550 of the Health and Safety Code, or subdivision (b) of Section 23222 of the Vehicle Code, or Section 11358 of the Health and Safety Code if the marijuana planted, cultivated, harvested, dried, or processed is for personal use, or Section 11368 of the Health and Safety Code if the narcotic drug was secured by a fictitious prescription and is for the personal use of the defendant and was not sold or furnished to another, or subdivision (d) of Section 653f if the solicitation was for acts directed to personal use only, or Section 381 or subdivision (f) of Section 647 of the Penal Code, if for being under the influence of a controlled substance, or Section 4060 of the Business and Professions Code, and it appears to the prosecuting attorney that, except as provided in subdivision (b) of Section 11357 of the Health and Safety Code, all of the following apply to the defendant:

(1) Within five years prior to the alleged commission of the charged offense, the defendant has not suffered a conviction for any offense involving controlled substances other than the offenses listed in this subdivision.

(2) The offense charged did not involve a crime of violence or threatened violence.

(3) There is no evidence of a contemporaneous violation relating to narcotics or restricted dangerous drugs other than a violation of the offenses listed in this subdivision.

(4) The defendant has no prior felony conviction within five years prior to the alleged commission of the

charged offense.

(b) The prosecuting attorney shall review his or her file to determine whether or not paragraphs (1) to (4), inclusive, of subdivision (a) apply to the defendant. If the defendant is found eligible, the prosecuting attorney shall file with the court a declaration in writing or state for the record the grounds upon which the determination is based, and shall make this information available to the defendant and his or her attorney. This procedure is intended to allow the court to set the hearing for pretrial diversion at the arraignment. If the defendant is found ineligible for pretrial diversion, the prosecuting attorney shall file with the court a declaration in writing or state for the record the grounds upon which the determination is based, and shall make this information available to the defendant and his or her attorney. The sole remedy of a defendant who is found ineligible for pretrial diversion is a postconviction appeal.

(c) All referrals for pretrial diversion granted by the court pursuant to this chapter shall be made only to programs that have been certified by the county drug program administrator pursuant to Chapter 1.5 (commencing with Section 1211) of Title 8, or to programs that provide services at no cost to the participant and have been deemed by the court and the county drug program administrator to be credible and effective. The defendant may request to be referred to a program in any county, as long as that program meets the criteria set forth in this subdivision.

(d) Pretrial diversion for an alleged violation of Section 11368 of the Health and Safety Code shall not prohibit any administrative agency from taking disciplinary action against a licensee or from denying a license. This subdivision does not expand or restrict the provisions of Section 1000.4.

(e) Any defendant who is participating in a program authorized in this section may be required to undergo analysis of his or her urine for the purpose of testing for the presence of any drug as part of the program. However, urinalysis results shall not be admissible as a basis for any new criminal prosecution or proceeding.

Penal Code § 1170

(Amended (as amended by Stats. 2018, Ch. 36, Sec. 17) by Stats. 2018, Ch. 1001, Sec. 1. (AB 2942) Effective January 1, 2019. Repealed as of January 1, 2022, by its own provisions. See later operative version, as amended by Sec. 2 of Stats. 2018, Ch. 1001.)

(a) (1) The Legislature finds and declares that the purpose of sentencing is public safety achieved through punishment, rehabilitation, and restorative justice. When a sentence includes incarceration, this purpose is best served by terms that are proportionate to the seriousness of the offense with provision for uniformity in the sentences of offenders committing the same offense under similar circumstances.

(2) The Legislature further finds and declares that programs should be available for inmates, including, but not limited to, educational, rehabilitative, and restorative justice programs that are designed to promote behavior change and to prepare all eligible offenders for successful reentry into the community. The Legislature encourages the development of policies and programs designed to educate and rehabilitate all eligible offenders. In implementing this section, the Department of Corrections and Rehabilitation is encouraged to allow all eligible inmates the opportunity to enroll in programs that promote successful return to the community. The Department of Corrections and Rehabilitation is directed to establish a mission statement consistent with these principles.

(3) In any case in which the sentence prescribed by statute for a person convicted of a public offense is a term of imprisonment in the state prison or a term pursuant to subdivision (h) of any specification of three time periods, the court shall sentence the defendant to one of the terms of imprisonment specified unless the convicted person is given any other disposition provided by law, including a fine, jail, probation, or the suspension of imposition or execution of sentence or is sentenced pursuant to subdivision (b) of Section 1168 because he or she had committed his or her crime prior to July 1, 1977. In sentencing the convicted person, the court shall apply the sentencing rules of the Judicial Council. The court, unless it determines that there are

circumstances in mitigation of the sentence prescribed, shall also impose any other term that it is required by law to impose as an additional term. Nothing in this article shall affect any provision of law that imposes the death penalty, that authorizes or restricts the granting of probation or suspending the execution or imposition of sentence, or expressly provides for imprisonment in the state prison for life, except as provided in paragraph (2) of subdivision (d). In any case in which the amount of preimprisonment credit under Section 2900.5 or any other law is equal to or exceeds any sentence imposed pursuant to this chapter, except for the remaining portion of mandatory supervision pursuant to subparagraph (B) of paragraph (5) of subdivision (h), the entire sentence shall be deemed to have been served, except for the remaining period of mandatory supervision, and the defendant shall not be actually delivered to the custody of the secretary or to the custody of the county correctional administrator. The court shall advise the defendant that he or she shall serve an applicable period of parole, postrelease community supervision, or mandatory supervision, and order the defendant to report to the parole or probation office closest to the defendant's last legal residence, unless the in-custody credits equal the total sentence, including both confinement time and the period of parole, postrelease community supervision, or mandatory supervision. The sentence shall be deemed a separate prior prison term or a sentence of imprisonment in a county jail under subdivision (h) for purposes of Section 667.5, and a copy of the judgment and other necessary documentation shall be forwarded to the secretary.

(b) When a judgment of imprisonment is to be imposed and the statute specifies three possible terms, the choice of the appropriate term shall rest within the sound discretion of the court. At least four days prior to the time set for imposition of judgment, either party or the victim, or the family of the victim if the victim is deceased, may submit a statement in aggravation or mitigation. In determining the appropriate term, the court may consider the record in the case, the probation officer's report, other reports, including reports received pursuant to Section 1203.03, and statements in aggravation or mitigation submitted by the prosecution, the defendant, or the victim, or the family of the victim if the victim is deceased, and any further evidence introduced at the sentencing hearing. The court shall select the term which, in the court's discretion, best serves the interests of justice. The court shall set forth on the record the reasons for imposing the term selected and the court may not impose an upper term by using the fact of any enhancement upon which sentence is imposed under any provision of law. A term of imprisonment shall not be specified if imposition of sentence is suspended.

(c) The court shall state the reasons for its sentence choice on the record at the time of sentencing. The court shall also inform the defendant that as part of the sentence after expiration of the term he or she may be on parole for a period as provided in Section 3000 or 3000.08 or postrelease community supervision for a period as provided in Section 3451.

(d) (1) When a defendant subject to this section or subdivision (b) of Section 1168 has been sentenced to be imprisoned in the state prison or a county jail pursuant to subdivision (h) and has been committed to the custody of the secretary or the county correctional administrator, the court may, within 120 days of the date of commitment on its own motion, or at any time upon the recommendation of the secretary or the Board of Parole Hearings in the case of state prison inmates, the county correctional administrator in the case of county jail inmates, or the district attorney of the county in which the defendant was sentenced, recall the sentence and commitment previously ordered and resentence the defendant in the same manner as if he or she had not previously been sentenced, provided the new sentence, if any, is no greater than the initial sentence. The court resentencing under this subdivision shall apply the sentencing rules of the Judicial Council so as to eliminate disparity of sentences and to promote uniformity of sentencing. The court resentencing under this paragraph may reduce a defendant's term of imprisonment and modify the judgment, including a judgment entered after a plea agreement, if it is in the interest of justice. The court may consider postconviction factors, including, but not limited to, the inmate's disciplinary record and record of rehabilitation while incarcerated, evidence that reflects whether age, time served, and diminished physical condition, if any, have reduced the inmate's risk for future violence, and evidence that reflects that circumstances have changed since the inmate's original sentencing so that the inmate's continued incarceration is no longer in the interest of justice. Credit shall be given for time served.

(2) (A) (i) When a defendant who was under 18 years of age at the time of the commission of the offense for which the defendant was sentenced to imprisonment for life without the possibility of parole has been incarcerated for at least

15 years, the defendant may submit to the sentencing court a petition for recall and resentencing.

(ii) Notwithstanding clause (i), this paragraph shall not apply to defendants sentenced to life without parole for an offense where it was pled and proved that the defendant tortured, as described in Section 206, his or her victim or the victim was a public safety official, including any law enforcement personnel mentioned in Chapter 4.5 (commencing with Section 830) of Title 3, or any firefighter as described in Section 245.1, as well as any other officer in any segment of law enforcement who is employed by the federal government, the state, or any of its political subdivisions.

(B) The defendant shall file the original petition with the sentencing court. A copy of the petition shall be served on the agency that prosecuted the case. The petition shall include the defendant's statement that he or she was under 18 years of age at the time of the crime and was sentenced to life in prison without the possibility of parole, the defendant's statement describing his or her remorse and work towards rehabilitation, and the defendant's statement that one of the following is true:

(i) The defendant was convicted pursuant to felony murder or aiding and abetting murder provisions of law.

(ii) The defendant does not have juvenile felony adjudications for assault or other felony crimes with a significant potential for personal harm to victims prior to the offense for which the sentence is being considered for recall.

(iii) The defendant committed the offense with at least one adult codefendant.

(iv) The defendant has performed acts that tend to indicate rehabilitation or the potential for rehabilitation, including, but not limited to, availing himself or herself of rehabilitative, educational, or vocational programs, if those programs have been available at his or her classification level and facility, using self-study for self-improvement, or showing evidence of remorse.

(C) If any of the information required in subparagraph (B) is missing from the petition, or if proof of service on the prosecuting agency is not provided, the court shall return the petition to the defendant and advise the defendant that the matter cannot be considered without the missing information.

(D) A reply to the petition, if any, shall be filed with the court within 60 days of the date on which the prosecuting agency was served with the petition, unless a continuance is granted for good cause.

(E) If the court finds by a preponderance of the evidence that one or more of the statements specified in clauses (i) to (iv), inclusive, of subparagraph (B) is true, the court shall recall the sentence and commitment previously ordered and hold a hearing to resentence the defendant in the same manner as if the defendant had not previously been sentenced, provided that the new sentence, if any, is not greater than the initial sentence. Victims, or victim family members if the victim is deceased, shall retain the rights to participate in the hearing.

(F) The factors that the court may consider when determining whether to resentence the defendant to a term of imprisonment with the possibility of parole include, but are not limited to, the following:

(i) The defendant was convicted pursuant to felony murder or aiding and abetting murder provisions of law.

(ii) The defendant does not have juvenile felony adjudications for assault or other felony crimes with a significant potential for personal harm to victims prior to the offense for which the defendant was sentenced to life without the possibility of parole.

(iii) The defendant committed the offense with at least one adult codefendant.

(iv) Prior to the offense for which the defendant was sentenced to life without the possibility of parole, the defendant had insufficient adult support or supervision and had suffered from psychological or physical trauma, or significant stress.

(v) The defendant suffers from cognitive limitations due to mental illness, developmental disabilities, or other factors that did not constitute a defense, but influenced the defendant's involvement in the offense.

(vi) The defendant has performed acts that tend to indicate rehabilitation or the potential for rehabilitation, including, but not limited to, availing himself or herself of rehabilitative, educational, or vocational programs, if those programs have been available at his or her classification level and facility, using self-study for self-improvement, or showing evidence of remorse.

(vii) The defendant has maintained family ties or connections with others through letter writing, calls, or visits, or has eliminated contact with individuals outside of prison who are currently involved with crime.

(viii) The defendant has had no disciplinary actions for violent activities in the last five years in which the defendant was determined to be the aggressor.

(G) The court shall have the discretion to resentence the defendant in the same manner as if the defendant had not previously been sentenced, provided that the new sentence, if any, is not greater than the initial sentence. The discretion of the court shall be exercised in consideration of the criteria in subparagraph (F). Victims, or victim family members if the victim is deceased, shall be notified of the resentencing hearing and shall retain their rights to participate in the hearing.

(H) If the sentence is not recalled or the defendant is resentenced to imprisonment for life without the possibility of parole, the defendant may submit another petition for recall and resentencing to the sentencing court when the defendant has been committed to the custody of the department for at least 20 years. If the sentence is not recalled or the defendant is resentenced to imprisonment for life without the possibility of parole under that petition, the defendant may file another petition after having served 24 years. The final petition may be submitted, and the response to that petition shall be determined, during the 25th year of the defendant's sentence.

(I) In addition to the criteria in subparagraph (F), the court may consider any other criteria that the court deems relevant to its decision, so long as the court identifies them on the record, provides a statement of reasons for adopting them, and states why the defendant does or does not satisfy the criteria.

(J) This subdivision shall have retroactive application.

(K) Nothing in this paragraph is intended to diminish or abrogate any rights or remedies otherwise available to the defendant.

(e) (1) Notwithstanding any other law and consistent with paragraph (1) of subdivision (a), if the secretary or the Board of Parole Hearings or both determine that a prisoner satisfies the criteria set forth in paragraph (2), the secretary or the board may recommend to the court that the prisoner's sentence be recalled.

(2) The court shall have the discretion to resentence or recall if the court finds that the facts described in subparagraphs (A) and (B) or subparagraphs (B) and (C) exist:

(A) The prisoner is terminally ill with an incurable condition caused by an illness or disease that would produce death within six months, as determined by a physician employed by the department.

(B) The conditions under which the prisoner would be released or receive treatment do not pose a threat to public safety.

(C) The prisoner is permanently medically incapacitated with a medical condition that renders him or her permanently unable to perform activities of basic daily living, and results in the prisoner requiring 24-hour total care, including, but not limited to, coma, persistent vegetative state, brain death, ventilator-dependency, loss of control of muscular or neurological function, and that incapacitation did not exist at the time of the original sentencing.

The Board of Parole Hearings shall make findings pursuant to this subdivision before making a recommendation for resentence or recall to the court. This subdivision does not apply to a prisoner sentenced to death or a term of life without the possibility of parole.

(3) Within 10 days of receipt of a positive recommendation by the secretary or the board, the court shall hold a hearing to consider whether the prisoner's sentence should be recalled.

(4) Any physician employed by the department who determines that a prisoner has six months or less to live shall notify the chief medical officer of the prognosis. If the chief medical officer concurs with the prognosis, he or she shall notify the warden. Within 48 hours of receiving notification, the warden or the warden's representative shall notify the prisoner of the recall and resentencing procedures, and shall arrange for the prisoner to designate a family member or other outside agent to be notified as to the prisoner's medical condition and prognosis, and as to the recall and resentencing procedures. If the inmate is deemed mentally unfit, the warden or the warden's representative shall contact the inmate's emergency contact and provide the information described in paragraph (2).

(5) The warden or the warden's representative shall provide the prisoner and his or her family member, agent, or emergency contact, as described in paragraph (4), updated information throughout the recall and resentencing process with regard to the prisoner's medical condition and the status of the prisoner's recall and resentencing proceedings.

(6) Notwithstanding any other provisions of this section, the prisoner or his or her family member or designee may independently request consideration for recall and resentencing by contacting the chief medical officer at the prison or the secretary. Upon receipt of the request, the chief medical officer and the warden or the warden's representative shall follow the procedures described in paragraph (4). If the secretary determines that the prisoner satisfies the criteria set forth in paragraph (2), the secretary or board may recommend to the court that the prisoner's sentence be recalled. The secretary shall submit a recommendation for release within 30 days in the case of inmates sentenced to determinate terms and, in the case of inmates sentenced to indeterminate terms, the secretary shall make a recommendation to the Board of Parole Hearings with respect to the inmates who have applied under this section. The board shall consider this information and make an independent judgment pursuant to paragraph (2) and make findings related thereto before rejecting the request or making a recommendation to the court. This action shall be taken at the next lawfully noticed board meeting.

(7) Any recommendation for recall submitted to the court by the secretary or the Board of Parole Hearings shall include one or more medical evaluations, a postrelease plan, and findings pursuant to paragraph (2).

(8) If possible, the matter shall be heard before the same judge of the court who sentenced the prisoner.

(9) If the court grants the recall and resentencing application, the prisoner shall be released by the department within 48 hours of receipt of the court's order, unless a longer time period is agreed to by the inmate. At the time of release, the warden or the warden's representative shall ensure that the prisoner has each of the following in his or her possession: a discharge medical summary, full medical records, state identification, parole or postrelease community supervision medications, and all property belonging to the prisoner. After discharge, any additional records shall be sent to the prisoner's forwarding address.

(10) The secretary shall issue a directive to medical and correctional staff employed by the department that details the guidelines and procedures for initiating a recall and resentencing procedure. The directive shall clearly state that any prisoner who is given a prognosis of six months or less to live is eligible for recall and

resencing consideration, and that recall and resentencing procedures shall be initiated upon that prognosis.

(11) The provisions of this subdivision shall be available to an inmate who is sentenced to a county jail pursuant to subdivision (h). For purposes of those inmates, "secretary" or "warden" shall mean the county correctional administrator and "chief medical officer" shall mean a physician designated by the county correctional administrator for this purpose.

(f) Notwithstanding any other provision of this section, for purposes of paragraph (3) of subdivision (h), any allegation that a defendant is eligible for state prison due to a prior or current conviction, sentence enhancement, or because he or she is required to register as a sex offender shall not be subject to dismissal pursuant to Section 1385.

(g) A sentence to the state prison for a determinate term for which only one term is specified, is a sentence to the state prison under this section.

(h) (1) Except as provided in paragraph (3), a felony punishable pursuant to this subdivision where the term is not specified in the underlying offense shall be punishable by a term of imprisonment in a county jail for 16 months, or two or three years.

(2) Except as provided in paragraph (3), a felony punishable pursuant to this subdivision shall be punishable by imprisonment in a county jail for the term described in the underlying offense.

(3) Notwithstanding paragraphs (1) and (2), where the defendant (A) has a prior or current felony conviction for a serious felony described in subdivision (c) of Section 1192.7 or a prior or current conviction for a violent felony described in subdivision (c) of Section 667.5, (B) has a prior felony conviction in another jurisdiction for an offense that has all the elements of a serious felony described in subdivision (c) of Section 1192.7 or a violent felony described in subdivision (c) of Section 667.5, (C) is required to register as a sex offender pursuant to Chapter 5.5 (commencing with Section 290) of Title 9 of Part 1, or (D) is convicted of a crime and as part of the sentence an enhancement pursuant to Section 186.11 is imposed, an executed sentence for a felony punishable pursuant to this subdivision shall be served in the state prison.

(4) Nothing in this subdivision shall be construed to prevent other dispositions authorized by law, including pretrial diversion, deferred entry of judgment, or an order granting probation pursuant to Section 1203.1.

(5) (A) Unless the court finds that, in the interests of justice, it is not appropriate in a particular case, the court, when imposing a sentence pursuant to paragraph (1) or (2), shall suspend execution of a concluding portion of the term for a period selected at the court's discretion.

(B) The portion of a defendant's sentenced term that is suspended pursuant to this paragraph shall be known as mandatory supervision, and, unless otherwise ordered by the court, shall commence upon release from physical custody or an alternative custody program, whichever is later. During the period of mandatory supervision, the defendant shall be supervised by the county probation officer in accordance with the terms, conditions, and procedures generally applicable to persons placed on probation, for the remaining unserved portion of the sentence imposed by the court. The period of supervision shall be mandatory, and may not be earlier terminated except by court order. Any proceeding to revoke or modify mandatory supervision under this subparagraph shall be conducted pursuant to either subdivisions (a) and (b) of Section 1203.2 or Section 1203.3. During the period when the defendant is under that supervision, unless in actual custody related to the sentence imposed by the court, the defendant shall be entitled to only actual time credit against the term of imprisonment imposed by the court. Any time period which is suspended because a person has absconded shall not be credited toward the period of supervision.

(6) When the court is imposing a judgment pursuant to this subdivision concurrent or consecutive to a judgment or judgments previously imposed pursuant to this subdivision in another county or counties, the court rendering the second or other subsequent judgment shall determine the county or counties of incarceration and supervision of the defendant.

(7) The sentencing changes made by the act that added this subdivision shall be applied prospectively to any person sentenced on or after October 1, 2011.

(8) The sentencing changes made to paragraph (5) by the act that added this paragraph shall become effective and operative on January 1, 2015, and shall be applied prospectively to any person sentenced on or after January 1, 2015.

(i) This section shall remain in effect only until January 1, 2022, and as of that date is repealed, unless a later enacted statute, that is enacted before January 1, 2022, deletes or extends that date.

Penal Code § 12022

(Amended by Statute, Effective January 1, 2014.)

(a) (1) Except as provided in subdivisions (c) and (d), a person who is armed with a firearm in the commission of a felony or attempted felony shall be punished by an additional and consecutive term of imprisonment pursuant to subdivision (h) of Section 1170 for one year, unless the arming is an element of that offense. This additional term shall apply to a person who is a principal in the commission of a felony or attempted felony if one or more of the principals is armed with a firearm, whether or not the person is personally armed with a firearm.

(2) Except as provided in subdivision (c), and notwithstanding subdivision (d), if the firearm is an assault weapon, as defined in Section 30510 or 30515, or a machinegun, as defined in Section 16880, or a .50 BMG rifle, as defined in Section 30530, the additional and consecutive term described in this subdivision shall be three years imprisonment pursuant to subdivision (h) of Section 1170 whether or not the arming is an element of the offense of which the person was convicted. The additional term provided in this paragraph shall apply to any person who is a principal in the commission of a felony or attempted felony if one or more of the principals is armed with an assault weapon, machinegun, or a .50 BMG rifle, whether or not the person is personally armed with an assault weapon, machinegun, or a .50 BMG rifle.

(b) (1) A person who personally uses a deadly or dangerous weapon in the commission of a felony or attempted felony shall be punished by an additional and consecutive term of imprisonment in the state prison for one year, unless use of a deadly or dangerous weapon is an element of that offense.

(2) If the person described in paragraph (1) has been convicted of carjacking or attempted carjacking, the additional term shall be in the state prison for one, two, or three years.

(3) When a person is found to have personally used a deadly or dangerous weapon in the commission of a felony or attempted felony as provided in this subdivision and the weapon is owned by that person, the court shall order that the weapon be deemed a nuisance and disposed of in the manner provided in Sections 18000 and 18005.

(c) Notwithstanding the enhancement set forth in subdivision (a), a person who is personally armed with a firearm in the commission of a violation or attempted violation of Section 11351, 11351.5, 11352, 11366.5, 11366.6, 11378, 11378.5, 11379, 11379.5, or 11379.6 of the Health and Safety Code shall be punished by an additional and consecutive term of imprisonment pursuant to subdivision (h) of Section 1170 for three, four, or five years.

(d) Notwithstanding the enhancement set forth in subdivision (a), a person who is not personally armed with a firearm who, knowing that another principal is personally armed with a firearm, is a principal in the commission of an offense or attempted offense specified in subdivision (c), shall be punished by an additional and consecutive term of imprisonment pursuant to subdivision (h) of Section 1170 for one, two, or three years.

(e) For purposes of imposing an enhancement under Section 1170.1, the enhancements under this section shall count as a single enhancement.

(f) Notwithstanding any other provision of law, the court may strike the additional punishment for the enhancements provided in subdivision (c) or (d) in an unusual case where the interests of justice would best be served, if the court specifies on the record and enters into the minutes the circumstances indicating that the interests of justice would best be served by that disposition.

X. Revenue and Taxation Code Sections

Revenue and Taxation Code § 6479.3

(Amended by Stats. 2018, Ch. 228, Sec. 1. (AB 1741) Effective August 28, 2018.)

(a) Except as provided in subdivision (k), any person whose estimated tax liability under this part averages ten thousand dollars ($10,000) or more per month, as determined by the department pursuant to methods of calculation prescribed by the department, shall remit amounts due by an electronic funds transfer under procedures prescribed by the department. Any person who collects use tax on a voluntary basis is not required to remit amounts due by electronic funds transfer.

(b) Any person whose estimated tax liability under this part averages less than ten thousand dollars ($10,000) per month or any person who voluntarily collects use tax may elect to remit amounts due by electronic funds transfer with the approval of the department.

(c) Any person remitting amounts due pursuant to subdivision (a) or (b) shall perform electronic funds transfer in compliance with the due dates set forth in Article 1 (commencing with Section 6451) and Article 1.1 (commencing with Section 6470). Payment is deemed complete on the date the electronic funds transfer is initiated, if settlement to the state's demand account occurs on or before the banking day following the date the transfer is initiated. If settlement to the state's demand account does not occur on or before the banking day following the date the transfer is initiated, payment is deemed to occur on the date settlement occurs.

(d) Any person remitting taxes by electronic funds transfer shall, on or before the due date of the remittance, file a return for the preceding reporting period in the form and manner prescribed by the department. Any person who fails to timely file the required return shall pay a penalty of 10 percent of the amount of taxes, exclusive of prepayments, with respect to the period for which the return is required.

(e) (1) Except as provided in paragraph (2), any person required to remit taxes pursuant to this article who remits those taxes by means other than appropriate electronic funds transfer shall pay a penalty of 10 percent of the taxes incorrectly remitted.

(2) A person required to remit prepayments pursuant to this article who remits a prepayment by means other than an appropriate electronic funds transfer shall pay a penalty of 6 percent of the prepayment amount incorrectly remitted.

(f) Except as provided in Sections 6476 and 6477, any person who fails to pay any tax to the state or any amount of tax required to be collected and paid to the state, except amounts of determinations made by the department under Article 2 (commencing with Section 6481) or Article 3 (commencing with Section 6511), within the time required shall pay a penalty of 10 percent of the tax or amount of tax, in addition to the tax or amount of tax, plus interest at the modified adjusted rate per month, or fraction thereof, established pursuant to Section 6591.5, from the date on which the tax or the amount of tax required to be collected became due and payable to the state until the date of payment.

(g) In determining whether a person's estimated tax liability averages ten thousand dollars ($10,000) or more per month, the department may consider tax returns filed pursuant to this part and any other information in the department's possession.

(h) Except as provided in subdivision (i), the penalties imposed by subdivisions (d), (e), and (f) shall be limited to a maximum of 10 percent of the taxes due, exclusive of prepayments, for any one return. Any person remitting taxes by electronic funds transfer shall be subject to the penalties under this section and not Section 6591.

(i) The penalties imposed with respect to paragraph (2) of subdivision (e) and Sections 6476 and 6477 shall be limited to a maximum of 6 percent of the prepayment amount.

(j) The department shall promulgate regulations pursuant to Chapter 3.5 (commencing with Section 11340) of Part 1 of Division 3 of Title 2 of the Government Code for purposes of implementing this section.

(k) Until January 1, 2022, a person licensed to engage in commercial cannabis activity under Division 10 (commencing with Section 26000) of the Business and Professions Code, may remit amounts due by a means other than electronic funds transfer, if the department deems it necessary to facilitate collection of amounts due.

Revenue and Taxation Code § 34010

(Amended by Stats. 2018, Ch. 92, Sec. 200. (SB 1289) Effective January 1, 2019. Note: This section was added on Nov. 8, 2016, by initiative Prop. 64.)

For purposes of this part:

(a) "Arm's length transaction" shall mean a sale entered into in good faith and for valuable consideration that reflects the fair market value in the open market between two informed and willing parties, neither under any compulsion to participate in the transaction.

(b) "Average market price" shall mean:

(1) In an arm's length transaction, the average retail price determined by the wholesale cost of the cannabis or cannabis products sold or transferred to a cannabis retailer, plus a mark-up, as determined by the department on a biannual basis in six-month intervals.

(2) In a nonarm's length transaction, the cannabis retailer's gross receipts from the retail sale of the cannabis or cannabis products.

(c) "Department" means the California Department of Tax and Fee Administration or its successor agency.

(d) "Bureau" means the Bureau of Cannabis Control within the Department of Consumer Affairs.

(e) "Tax Fund" means the California Cannabis Tax Fund created by Section 34018.

(f) "Cannabis" has the same meaning as set forth in Section 11018 of the Health and Safety Code and shall also mean medicinal cannabis.

(g) "Cannabis products" has the same meaning as set forth in Section 11018.1 of the Health and Safety Code and shall also mean medicinal concentrates and medicinal cannabis products.

(h) "Cannabis flowers" means the dried flowers of the cannabis plant as defined by the board.

(i) "Cannabis leaves" means all parts of the cannabis plant other than cannabis flowers that are sold or consumed.

(j) "Cannabis retailer" means a person required to be licensed as a retailer, microbusiness, or nonprofit pursuant to Division 10 (commencing with Section 26000) of the Business and Professions Code.

(k) "Cultivator" means all persons required to be licensed to cultivate cannabis pursuant to Division 10 (commencing with Section 26000) of the Business and Professions Code.

(l) "Distributor" means a person required to be licensed as a distributor pursuant to Division 10 (commencing with

Section 26000) of the Business and Professions Code.

(m) "Enters the commercial market" means cannabis or cannabis product, except for immature cannabis plants and seeds, that complete and comply with a quality assurance review and testing, as described in Section 26110 of the Business and Professions Code.

(n) "Gross receipts" has the same meaning as set forth in Section 6012.

(o) "Microbusiness" has the same meaning as set forth in paragraph (3) of subdivision (a) of Section 26070 of the Business and Professions Code.

(p) "Nonprofit" has the same meaning as set forth in Section 26070.5 of the Business and Professions Code.

(q) "Person" has the same meaning as set forth in Section 6005.

(r) "Retail sale" has the same meaning as set forth in Section 6007.

(s) "Sale" and "purchase" mean any change of title or possession, exchange, or barter, conditional or otherwise, in any manner or by any means whatsoever, for consideration.

(t) "Transfer" means to grant, convey, hand over, assign, sell, exchange, or barter, in any manner or by any means, with or without consideration.

(u) "Unprocessed cannabis" includes cannabis flowers, cannabis leaves, or other categories of harvested cannabis, categories for unprocessed or frozen cannabis or immature plants, or cannabis that is shipped directly to manufacturers.

(v) "Manufacturer" means a person required to be licensed as a manufacturer pursuant to Division 10 (commencing with Section 26000) of the Business and Professions Code.

Revenue and Taxation Code § 34011

(Amended by Stats. 2018, Ch. 92, Sec. 201. (SB 1289) Effective January 1, 2019. Note: This section was added on Nov. 8, 2016, by initiative Prop. 64.)

(a) (1) Effective January 1, 2018, a cannabis excise tax shall be imposed upon purchasers of cannabis or cannabis products sold in this state at the rate of 15 percent of the average market price of any retail sale by a cannabis retailer. A purchaser's liability for the cannabis excise tax is not extinguished until the cannabis excise tax has been paid to this state except that an invoice, receipt, or other document from a cannabis retailer given to the purchaser pursuant to this subdivision is sufficient to relieve the purchaser from further liability for the tax to which the invoice, receipt, or other document refers.

(2) Each cannabis retailer shall provide a purchaser with an invoice, receipt, or other document that includes a statement that reads: "The cannabis excise taxes are included in the total amount of this invoice."

(3) The department may prescribe other means to display the cannabis excise tax on an invoice, receipt, or other document from a cannabis retailer given to the purchaser.

(b) (1) A distributor in an arm's length transaction shall collect the cannabis excise tax from the cannabis retailer on or before 90 days after the sale or transfer of cannabis or cannabis product to the cannabis retailer. A distributor in a nonarm's length transaction shall collect the cannabis excise tax from the cannabis retailer on or before 90 days after the sale or transfer of cannabis or cannabis product to the cannabis retailer, or at the time of retail sale by the cannabis retailer, whichever is earlier. A distributor shall report and remit the cannabis excise tax to the department pursuant to Section 34015. A cannabis retailer shall be responsible for collecting the cannabis excise tax from the purchaser and remitting the cannabis excise tax to the distributor in accordance with rules and procedures established under law and any regulations adopted by the department.

(2) A distributor shall provide an invoice, receipt, or other similar document to the cannabis retailer that identifies the licensee receiving the product, the distributor from which the product originates, including the associated unique identifier, the amount of cannabis excise tax, and any other information deemed necessary by the department. The department may authorize other forms of documentation under this paragraph.

(c) The excise tax imposed by this section shall be in addition to the sales and use tax imposed by the state and local governments.

(d) Gross receipts from the sale of cannabis or cannabis products for purposes of assessing the sales and use taxes under Part 1 (commencing with Section 6001) shall include the tax levied pursuant to this section.

(e) Cannabis or cannabis products shall not be sold to a purchaser unless the excise tax required by law has been paid by the purchaser at the time of sale.

(f) The sales and use taxes imposed by Part 1 (commencing with Section 6001) shall not apply to retail sales of medicinal cannabis, medicinal cannabis concentrate, edible medicinal cannabis products, or topical cannabis as those terms are defined in Division 10 (commencing with Section 26000) of the Business and Professions Code when a qualified patient or primary caregiver for a qualified patient provides his or her card issued under Section 11362.71 of the Health and Safety Code and a valid government-issued identification card.

Revenue and Taxation Code § 34012

(Amended by AB 133, Effective September 16, 2017.)

(a) Effective January 1, 2018, there is hereby imposed a cultivation tax on all harvested cannabis that enters the commercial market upon all cultivators. The tax shall be due after the cannabis is harvested and enters the commercial market.

    (1) The tax for cannabis flowers shall be nine dollars and twenty-five cents ($9.25) per dry-weight ounce.

    (2) The tax for cannabis leaves shall be set at two dollars and seventy-five cents ($2.75) per dry-weight ounce.

(b) The department may adjust the tax rate for cannabis leaves annually to reflect fluctuations in the relative price of cannabis flowers to cannabis leaves.

(c) The department may from time to time establish other categories of harvested cannabis, categories for unprocessed or frozen cannabis or immature plants, or cannabis that is shipped directly to manufacturers. These categories shall be taxed at their relative value compared with cannabis flowers.

(d) The department may prescribe by regulation a method and manner for payment of the cultivation tax that utilizes tax stamps or state-issued product bags that indicate that all required tax has been paid on the product to which the tax stamp is affixed or in which the cannabis is packaged.

(e) The tax stamps and product bags shall be of the designs, specifications, and denominations as may be prescribed by the department and may be purchased by any licensee under Division 10 (commencing with Section 26000) of the Business and Professions Code.

(f) Subsequent to the establishment of a tax stamp program, the department may by regulation provide that cannabis shall not be removed from a licensed cultivation facility or transported on a public highway unless in a state-issued product bag bearing a tax stamp in the proper denomination.

(g) The tax stamps and product bags shall be capable of being read by a scanning or similar device and must be traceable utilizing the track and trace system pursuant to Section 26068 of the Business and Professions Code.

(h) Cultivators shall be responsible for payment of the tax pursuant to regulations adopted by the department. A cultivator's liability for the tax is not extinguished until the tax has been paid to this state except that an invoice, receipt, or other document from a distributor or manufacturer given to the cultivator pursuant to paragraph (3) is sufficient to relieve the cultivator from further liability for the tax to which the invoice, receipt, or other document refers. Cannabis shall not be sold unless the tax has been paid as provided in this part.

(1) A distributor shall collect the cultivation tax from a cultivator on all harvested cannabis that enters the commercial market. This paragraph shall not apply where a cultivator is not required to send, and does not send, the harvested cannabis to a distributor.

(2) (A) A manufacturer shall collect the cultivation tax from a cultivator on the first sale or transfer of unprocessed cannabis by a cultivator to a manufacturer. The manufacturer shall remit the cultivation tax collected on the cannabis product sold or transferred to a distributor for quality assurance, inspection, and testing, as described in Section 26110 of the Business and Professions Code. This paragraph shall not apply where a distributor collects the cultivation tax from a cultivator pursuant to paragraph (1).

(B) Notwithstanding subparagraph (A), the department may prescribe a substitute method and manner for collection and remittance of the cultivation tax under this paragraph, including a method and manner for collection of the cultivation tax by a distributor.

(3) A distributor or manufacturer shall provide to the cultivator, and a distributor that collects the cultivation tax from a manufacturer pursuant to paragraph (2) shall provide to the manufacturer, an invoice, receipt, or other similar document that identifies the licensee receiving the product, the cultivator from which the product originates, including the associated unique identifier, the amount of cultivation tax, and any other information deemed necessary by the department. The department may authorize other forms of documentation under this paragraph.

(4) The department may adopt regulations prescribing procedures for the refund of cultivation tax collected on cannabis or cannabis product that fails quality assurance, inspection, and testing as described in Section 26110 of the Business and Professions Code.

(i) All cannabis removed from a cultivator's premises, except for plant waste, shall be presumed to be sold and thereby taxable under this section.

(j) The tax imposed by this section shall be imposed on all cannabis cultivated in the state pursuant to rules and regulations promulgated by the department, but shall not apply to cannabis cultivated for personal use under Section 11362.1 of the Health and Safety Code or cultivated by a qualified patient or primary caregiver in accordance with the Compassionate Use Act of 1996 (Section 11362.5 of the Health and Safety Code).

(k) Beginning January 1, 2020, the rates set forth in subdivisions (a), (b), and (c) shall be adjusted by the department annually thereafter for inflation.

(l) The Department of Food and Agriculture is not responsible for enforcing any provisions of the cultivation tax.

Revenue and Taxation Code § 34012.5

(Amended by AB 133, Effective September 16, 2017.)

(a) The cultivation tax and cannabis excise tax required to be collected by the distributor, or required to be collected by the manufacturer pursuant to paragraph (2) of subdivision (h) of Section 34012, and any amount unreturned to the cultivator or cannabis retailer that is not tax but was collected from the cultivator or cannabis retailer under the representation by the distributor or the manufacturer that it was tax constitute debts owed by the distributor or the manufacturer to this state.

(b) A distributor or manufacturer that has collected any amount of tax in excess of the amount of tax imposed by this part and actually due from a cultivator or cannabis retailer, may refund such amount to the cultivator or cannabis retailer, even though such tax amount has already been paid over to the department and no corresponding credit or refund has yet been secured. The distributor or manufacturer may claim credit for that overpayment against the amount of tax imposed by this part that is due upon any other quarterly return, providing that credit is claimed in a return dated no later than three years from the date of overpayment.

(c) Any tax collected from a cultivator or cannabis retailer that has not been remitted to the department shall be deemed a debt owed to the State of California by the person required to collect and remit the tax.

Revenue and Taxation Code § 34013

(Amended by Stats. 2018, Ch. 228, Sec. 2. (AB 1741) Effective August 28, 2018. Note: This section was amended on Nov. 8, 2016, by initiative Prop. 64.)

(a) The department shall administer and collect the taxes imposed by this part pursuant to the Fee Collection Procedures Law (Part 30 (commencing with Section 55001)). For purposes of this part, the references in the Fee Collection Procedures Law to "fee" shall include the taxes imposed by this part, and references to "feepayer" shall include a person required to pay or collect the taxes imposed by this part.

(b) Until January 1, 2022, subdivision (a) of Section 55050 shall not apply to a person required to pay or collect the taxes imposed by this part on a person licensed to engage in commercial cannabis activity under Division 10 (commencing with Section 26000) of the Business and Professions Code if the department deems it necessary to facilitate the collection of amounts due.

(c) The department may prescribe, adopt, and enforce regulations relating to the administration and enforcement of this part, including, but not limited to, collections, reporting, refunds, and appeals.

(d) The department shall adopt necessary rules and regulations to administer the taxes in this part. Such rules and regulations may include methods or procedures to tag cannabis or cannabis products, or the packages thereof, to designate prior tax payment.

(e) Until January 1, 2019, the department may prescribe, adopt, and enforce any emergency regulations as necessary to implement, administer, and enforce its duties under this division. Any emergency regulation prescribed, adopted, or enforced pursuant to this section shall be adopted in accordance with Chapter 3.5 (commencing with Section 11340) of Part 1 of Division 3 of Title 2 of the Government Code, and, for purposes of that chapter, including Section 11349.6 of the Government Code, the adoption of the regulation is an emergency and shall be considered by the Office of Administrative Law as necessary for the immediate preservation of the public peace, health and safety, and general welfare. Notwithstanding any other law, the emergency regulations adopted by the department may remain in effect for two years from adoption.

(f) Any person required to be licensed pursuant to Division 10 (commencing with Section 26000) of the Business and Professions Code who fails to pay the taxes imposed under this part shall, in addition to owing the taxes not paid, be subject to a penalty of at least one-half the amount of the taxes not paid, and shall be subject to having its license revoked pursuant to Section 26031 of the Business and Professions Code.

(g) The department may bring such legal actions as are necessary to collect any deficiency in the tax required to be paid, and, upon the department's request, the Attorney General shall bring the actions.

Revenue and Taxation Code § 34014

(MAUCRSA, Effective June 27, 2017.)

(a) All distributors must obtain a separate permit from the board pursuant to regulations adopted by the board. No fee shall be charged to any person for issuance of the permit. Any person required to obtain a permit who engages in business as a distributor without a permit or after a permit has been canceled, suspended, or revoked, and each officer of any corporation which so engages in business, is guilty of a misdemeanor.

(b) The board may require every licensed distributor, retailer, cultivator, microbusiness, nonprofit, or other person required to be licensed, to provide security to cover the liability for taxes imposed by state law on cannabis produced or received by the retailer, cultivator, microbusiness, nonprofit, or other person required to be licensed in accordance with procedures to be established by the board. Notwithstanding anything herein to the contrary, the board may waive any security requirement it imposes for good cause, as determined by the board. "Good cause" includes, but is not limited to, the inability of a distributor, retailer, cultivator, microbusiness, nonprofit, or other person required to be licensed to obtain security due to a lack of service providers or the policies of service providers that prohibit service to a cannabis business. A person may not commence or continue any business or operation relating to cannabis cultivation until any surety required by the board with respect to the business or operation has been properly prepared, executed, and submitted under this part.

(c) In fixing the amount of any security required by the board, the board shall give consideration to the financial hardship that may be imposed on licensees as a result of any shortage of available surety providers.

Revenue and Taxation Code § 34015

(MAUCRSA, Effective June 27, 2017.)

(a) Unless otherwise prescribed by the board pursuant to subdivision (c), the excise tax and cultivation tax imposed by this part is due and payable to the board quarterly on or before the last day of the month following each quarterly period of three months. On or before the last day of the month following each quarterly period, a return for the preceding quarterly period shall be filed with the board by each distributor using electronic media. Returns shall be authenticated in a form or pursuant to methods as may be prescribed by the board. If the cultivation tax is paid by stamp pursuant to subdivision (d) of Section 34012 the board may by regulation determine when and how the tax shall be paid.

(b) The board may require every person engaged in the cultivation, distribution, manufacturing, retail sale of cannabis or cannabis products, or any other person required to be licensed pursuant to Division 10 (commencing with Section 26000) of the Business and Professions Code to file, on or before the 25th day of each month, a report using electronic media respecting the person's inventory, purchases, and sales during the preceding month and any other information as the board may require to carry out the purposes of this part. Reports shall be authenticated in a form or pursuant to methods as may be prescribed by the board.

(c) The board may adopt regulations prescribing the due date for returns and remittances of excise tax collected by a distributor in an arm's length transaction pursuant to subdivision (b) of Section 34011.

(d) The board may make examinations of the books and records of any person licensed, or required to be licensed, pursuant to Division 10 (commencing with Section 26000) of the Business and Professions Code, as it may deem necessary in carrying out this part.

Revenue and Taxation Code § 34016

(MAUCRSA, Effective June 27, 2017.)

(a) Any peace officer or board employee granted limited peace officer status pursuant to paragraph (6) of subdivision (a) of Section 830.11 of the Penal Code, upon presenting appropriate credentials, is authorized to enter any place as described in paragraph (3) and to conduct inspections in accordance with the following paragraphs, inclusive.

(1) Inspections shall be performed in a reasonable manner and at times that are reasonable under the circumstances, taking into consideration the normal business hours of the place to be entered.

(2) Inspections may be at any place at which cannabis or cannabis products are sold to purchasers, cultivated, or stored, or at any site where evidence of activities involving evasion of tax may be discovered.

(3) Inspections shall be conducted no more than once in a 24-hour period.

(b) Any person who fails or refuses to allow an inspection shall be guilty of a misdemeanor. Each offense shall be punished by a fine not to exceed five thousand dollars ($5,000), or imprisonment not exceeding one year in a county jail, or both the fine and imprisonment. The court shall order any fines assessed be deposited in the California Cannabis Tax Fund.

(c) Upon discovery by the board or a law enforcement agency that a licensee or any other person possesses, stores, owns, or has made a retail sale of cannabis or cannabis products, without evidence of tax payment or not contained in secure packaging, the board or the law enforcement agency shall be authorized to seize the cannabis or cannabis products. Any cannabis or cannabis products seized by a law enforcement agency or the board shall within seven days be deemed forfeited and the board shall comply with the procedures set forth in Sections 30436 through 30449, inclusive.

(d) Any person who renders a false or fraudulent report is guilty of a misdemeanor and subject to a fine not to exceed one thousand dollars ($1,000) for each offense.

(e) Any violation of any provisions of this part, except as otherwise provided, is a misdemeanor and is punishable as such.

(f) All moneys remitted to the board under this part shall be credited to the California Cannabis Tax Fund.

Revenue and Taxation Code § 34017

(AUMA, Effective November 9, 2016.)

The Legislative Analyst's Office shall submit a report to the Legislature by January 1, 2020, with recommendations to the Legislature for adjustments to the tax rate to achieve the goals of undercutting illicit market prices and discouraging use by persons younger than 21 years of age while ensuring sufficient revenues are generated for the programs identified in Section 34019.

Revenue and Taxation Code § 34018

(Amended by Stats. 2018, Ch. 92, Sec. 202. (SB 1289) Effective January 1, 2019. Note: This section was added on Nov. 8, 2016, by initiative Prop. 64.)

(a) The California Cannabis Tax Fund is hereby created in the State Treasury. The Tax Fund shall consist of all taxes, interest, penalties, and other amounts collected and paid to the board pursuant to this part, less payment of refunds.

(b) Notwithstanding any other law, the California Cannabis Tax Fund is a special trust fund established solely to carry out the purposes of the Control, Regulate and Tax Adult Use of Marijuana Act and all revenues deposited into the Tax Fund, together with interest or dividends earned by the fund, are hereby continuously appropriated for the purposes of the Control, Regulate and Tax Adult Use of Marijuana Act without regard to fiscal year and shall be expended only in accordance with the provisions of this part and its purposes.

(c) Notwithstanding any other law, the taxes imposed by this part and the revenue derived therefrom, including investment interest, shall not be considered to be part of the General Fund, as that term is used in Chapter 1 (commencing with Section 16300) of Part 2 of Division 4 of Title 2 of the Government Code, shall not be considered General Fund revenue for purposes of Section 8 of Article XVI of the California Constitution and its implementing statutes, and shall not be considered "moneys" for purposes of subdivisions (a) and (b) of Section 8 of Article XVI of the California Constitution and its implementing statutes.

Revenue and Taxation Code § 34019

(MAUCRSA, Effective June 27, 2017.)

(a) Beginning with the 2017–18 fiscal year, the Department of Finance shall estimate revenues to be received pursuant to Sections 34011 and 34012 and provide those estimates to the Controller no later than June 15 of each year. The Controller shall use these estimates when disbursing funds pursuant to this section. Before any funds are disbursed pursuant to subdivisions (b), (c), (d), and (e) of this section, the Controller shall disburse from the Tax Fund to the appropriate account, without regard to fiscal year, the following:

(1) Reasonable costs incurred by the board for administering and collecting the taxes imposed by this part; provided, however, such costs shall not exceed 4 percent of tax revenues received.

(2) Reasonable costs incurred by the bureau, the Department of Consumer Affairs, the Department of Food and Agriculture, and the State Department of Public Health for implementing, administering, and enforcing Division 10 (commencing with Section 26000) of the Business and Professions Code to the extent those costs are not reimbursed pursuant to Section 26180 of the Business and Professions Code. This paragraph shall remain operative through the 2022–23 fiscal year.

(3) Reasonable costs incurred by the Department of Fish and Wildlife, the State Water Resources Control Board, and the Department of Pesticide Regulation for carrying out their respective duties under Division 10 (commencing with Section 26000) of the Business and Professions Code to the extent those costs are not otherwise reimbursed.

(4) Reasonable costs incurred by the Controller for performing duties imposed by the Control, Regulate and Tax Adult Use of Marijuana Act, including the audit required by Section 34020.

(5) Reasonable costs incurred by the Department of Finance for conducting the performance audit pursuant to Section 26191 of the Business and Professions Code.

(6) Reasonable costs incurred by the Legislative Analyst's Office for performing duties imposed by Section 34017.

(7) Sufficient funds to reimburse the Division of Labor Standards Enforcement and the Division of Occupational Safety and Health within the Department of Industrial Relations and the Employment Development Department for the costs of applying and enforcing state labor laws to licensees under Division 10 (commencing with Section 26000) of the Business and Professions Code.

(b) The Controller shall next disburse the sum of ten million dollars ($10,000,000) to a public university or universities in California annually beginning with the 2018–19 fiscal year until the 2028–29 fiscal year to research and evaluate the implementation and effect of the Control, Regulate and Tax Adult Use of Marijuana Act, and shall, if appropriate, make recommendations to the Legislature and Governor regarding possible amendments to the Control, Regulate and Tax Adult Use of Marijuana Act. The recipients of these funds shall publish reports on their findings at a minimum of every two years and shall make the reports available to the public. The bureau shall select the universities to be funded. The research funded pursuant to this subdivision shall include but not necessarily be limited to:

(1) Impacts on public health, including health costs associated with cannabis use, as well as whether cannabis use is associated with an increase or decrease in use of alcohol or other drugs.

(2) The impact of treatment for maladaptive cannabis use and the effectiveness of different treatment programs.

(3) Public safety issues related to cannabis use, including studying the effectiveness of the packaging and labeling requirements and advertising and marketing restrictions contained in the act at preventing underage access to and use of cannabis and cannabis products, and studying the health-related effects among users of varying potency levels of cannabis and cannabis products.

(4) Cannabis use rates, maladaptive use rates for adults and youth, and diagnosis rates of cannabis-related substance use disorders.

(5) Cannabis market prices, illicit market prices, tax structures and rates, including an evaluation of how to best tax cannabis based on potency, and the structure and function of licensed cannabis businesses.

(6) Whether additional protections are needed to prevent unlawful monopolies or anti-competitive behavior from occurring in the adult-use cannabis industry and, if so, recommendations as to the most effective measures for preventing such behavior.

(7) The economic impacts in the private and public sectors, including, but not necessarily limited to, job creation, workplace safety, revenues, taxes generated for state and local budgets, and criminal justice impacts, including, but not necessarily limited to, impacts on law enforcement and public resources, short and long term consequences of involvement in the criminal justice system, and state and local government agency administrative costs and revenue.

(8) Whether the regulatory agencies tasked with implementing and enforcing the Control, Regulate and Tax Adult Use of Marijuana Act are doing so consistent with the purposes of the act, and whether different agencies might do so more effectively.

(9) Environmental issues related to cannabis production and the criminal prohibition of cannabis production.

(10) The geographic location, structure, and function of licensed cannabis businesses, and demographic data, including race, ethnicity, and gender, of license holders.

(11) The outcomes achieved by the changes in criminal penalties made under the Control, Regulate and Tax Adult Use of Marijuana Act for cannabis-related offenses, and the outcomes of the juvenile justice system, in particular, probation-based treatments and the frequency of up-charging illegal possession of cannabis or cannabis products to a more serious offense.

(c) The Controller shall next disburse the sum of three million dollars ($3,000,000) annually to the Department of the California Highway Patrol beginning with the 2018–19 fiscal year until the 2022–23 fiscal year to establish and adopt protocols to determine whether a driver is operating a vehicle while impaired, including impairment by the use of cannabis or cannabis products, and to establish and adopt protocols setting forth best practices to assist law enforcement agencies. The department may hire personnel to establish the protocols specified in this subdivision. In addition, the department may make grants to public and private research institutions for the purpose of developing technology for determining when a driver is operating a vehicle while impaired, including impairment by the use of cannabis or cannabis products.

(d) The Controller shall next disburse the sum of ten million dollars ($10,000,000) beginning with the 2018–19 fiscal year and increasing ten million dollars ($10,000,000) each fiscal year thereafter until the 2022–23 fiscal year, at which time the disbursement shall be fifty million dollars ($50,000,000) each year thereafter, to the Governor's Office of Business and Economic Development, in consultation with the Labor and Workforce Development Agency and the State Department of Social Services, to administer a community reinvestments grants program to local health departments and at least 50 percent to qualified community-based nonprofit organizations to support job placement, mental health treatment, substance use disorder treatment, system navigation services, legal services to address barriers to reentry, and linkages to medical care for communities disproportionately affected by past federal and state drug policies. The office shall solicit input from community-based job skills, job placement, and legal service providers with relevant expertise as to the administration of the grants program. In addition, the office shall periodically evaluate the programs it is funding to determine the effectiveness of the programs, shall not spend more than 4 percent for administrative costs related to implementation, evaluation, and oversight of the programs, and shall award grants annually, beginning no later than January 1, 2020.

(e) The Controller shall next disburse the sum of two million dollars ($2,000,000) annually to the University of California San Diego Center for Medicinal Cannabis Research to further the objectives of the center, including the enhanced understanding of the efficacy and adverse effects of cannabis as a pharmacological agent.

(f) By July 15 of each fiscal year beginning in the 2018–19 fiscal year, the Controller shall, after disbursing funds pursuant to subdivisions (a), (b), (c), (d), and (e), disburse funds deposited in the Tax Fund during the prior fiscal year into sub-trust accounts, which are hereby created, as follows:

(1) Sixty percent shall be deposited in the Youth Education, Prevention, Early Intervention and Treatment Account, and disbursed by the Controller to the State Department of Health Care Services for programs for youth that are designed to educate about and to prevent substance use disorders and to prevent harm from substance use. The State Department of Health Care Services shall enter into interagency agreements with the State Department of Public Health and the State Department of Education to implement and administer these programs. The programs shall emphasize accurate education, effective prevention, early intervention, school retention, and timely treatment services for youth, their families and caregivers. The programs may include, but are not limited to, the following components:

(A) Prevention and early intervention services including outreach, risk survey and education to youth, families, caregivers, schools, primary care health providers, behavioral health and substance use disorder service providers, community and faith-based organizations, fostercare providers, juvenile and family courts, and others to recognize and reduce risks related to substance use, and the early signs of problematic use and of substance use disorders.

(B) Grants to schools to develop and support student assistance programs, or other similar programs, designed to prevent and reduce substance use, and improve school retention and performance, by supporting students who are at risk of dropping out of school and promoting alternatives to suspension or expulsion that focus on school retention, remediation, and professional care. Schools with higher than average dropout rates should be prioritized for grants.

(C) Grants to programs for outreach, education, and treatment for homeless youth and out-of-school youth with substance use disorders.

(D) Access and linkage to care provided by county behavioral health programs for youth, and their families and caregivers, who have a substance use disorder or who are at risk for developing a substance use disorder.

(E) Youth-focused substance use disorder treatment programs that are culturally and gender competent, trauma-informed, evidence-based and provide a continuum of care that includes screening and assessment (substance use disorder as well as mental health), early intervention, active treatment, family involvement, case management, overdose prevention, prevention of communicable diseases related to substance use, relapse management for substance use and other cooccurring behavioral health disorders, vocational services, literacy services, parenting classes, family therapy and counseling services, medication-assisted treatments, psychiatric medication and psychotherapy. When indicated, referrals must be made to other providers.

(F) To the extent permitted by law and where indicated, interventions shall utilize a two-generation approach to addressing substance use disorders with the capacity to treat youth and adults together. This would include supporting the development of family-based interventions that address substance use disorders and related problems within the context of families, including parents, foster parents, caregivers and all their children.

(G) Programs to assist individuals, as well as families and friends of drug using young people, to reduce the stigma associated with substance use including being diagnosed with a substance use disorder or seeking substance use disorder services. This includes peer-run outreach and education to reduce stigma, anti-stigma campaigns, and community recovery networks.

(H) Workforce training and wage structures that increase the hiring pool of behavioral health staff with substance use disorder prevention and treatment expertise. Provide ongoing education and coaching that increases substance use treatment providers' core competencies and trains providers on promising and evidenced-based practices.

(I) Construction of community-based youth treatment facilities.

(J) The departments may contract with each county behavioral health program for the provision of services.

(K) Funds shall be allocated to counties based on demonstrated need, including the number of youth in the county, the prevalence of substance use disorders among adults, and confirmed through statistical data, validated assessments, or submitted reports prepared by the applicable county to demonstrate and validate need.

(L) The departments shall periodically evaluate the programs they are funding to determine the effectiveness of the programs.

(M) The departments may use up to 4 percent of the moneys allocated to the Youth Education, Prevention, Early Intervention and Treatment Account for administrative costs related to implementation, evaluation, and oversight of the programs.

(N) If the Department of Finance ever determines that funding pursuant to cannabis taxation exceeds demand for youth prevention and treatment services in the state, the departments shall provide a plan to the Department of Finance to provide treatment services to adults as well as youth using these funds.

(O) The departments shall solicit input from volunteer health organizations, physicians who treat addiction, treatment researchers, family therapy and counseling providers, and professional education associations with relevant expertise as to the administration of any grants made pursuant to this paragraph.

(2) Twenty percent shall be deposited in the Environmental Restoration and Protection Account, and disbursed by the Controller as follows:

(A) To the Department of Fish and Wildlife and the Department of Parks and Recreation for the cleanup, remediation, and restoration of environmental damage in watersheds affected by cannabis cultivation and related activities including, but not limited to, damage that occurred prior to enactment of this part, and to support local partnerships for this purpose. The Department of Fish and Wildlife and the Department of Parks and Recreation may distribute a portion of the funds they receive from the Environmental Restoration and Protection Account through grants for purposes specified in this paragraph.

(B) To the Department of Fish and Wildlife and the Department of Parks and Recreation for the stewardship and operation of state-owned wildlife habitat areas and state park units in a manner that discourages and prevents the illegal cultivation, production, sale, and use of cannabis and cannabis products on public lands, and to facilitate the investigation, enforcement, and prosecution of illegal cultivation, production, sale, and use of cannabis or cannabis products on public lands.

(C) To the Department of Fish and Wildlife to assist in funding the watershed enforcement program and multiagency taskforce established pursuant to subdivisions (b) and (c) of Section 12029 of the Fish and Game Code to facilitate the investigation, enforcement, and prosecution of these offenses and to ensure the reduction of adverse impacts of cannabis cultivation, production, sale, and use on fish and wildlife habitats throughout the state.

(D) For purposes of this paragraph, the Secretary of the Natural Resources Agency shall determine the allocation of revenues between the departments. During the first five years of implementation, first consideration should be given to funding purposes specified in subparagraph (A).

(E) Funds allocated pursuant to this paragraph shall be used to increase and enhance activities described in subparagraphs (A), (B), and (C), and not replace allocation of other funding for these purposes. Accordingly, annual General Fund appropriations to the Department of Fish and Wildlife and the Department of Parks and Recreation shall not be reduced below the levels provided in the Budget Act of 2014 (Chapter 25 of the Statutes of 2014).

(3) Twenty percent shall be deposited into the State and Local Government Law Enforcement Account and disbursed by the Controller as follows:

(A) To the Department of the California Highway Patrol for conducting training programs for detecting, testing and enforcing laws against driving under the influence of alcohol and other drugs, including driving under the influence of cannabis. The department may hire personnel to conduct the training programs specified in this subparagraph.

(B) To the Department of the California Highway Patrol to fund internal California Highway Patrol programs and grants to qualified nonprofit organizations and local governments for education, prevention, and enforcement of laws related to driving under the influence of alcohol and other drugs, including cannabis; programs that help enforce traffic laws, educate the public in traffic safety, provide varied and effective means of reducing fatalities, injuries, and economic losses from collisions; and for the purchase of equipment related to enforcement of laws related to driving under the influence of alcohol and other drugs, including cannabis.

(C) To the Board of State and Community Corrections for making grants to local governments to assist with law enforcement, fire protection, or other local programs addressing public health and safety associated with the implementation of the Control, Regulate and Tax Adult Use of Marijuana Act. The board shall not make any grants to local governments which have banned the cultivation, including personal cultivation under paragraph (3) of subdivision (b) of Section 11362.2 of the Health and Safety Code, or retail sale of cannabis or cannabis products pursuant to Section 26200 of the Business and Professions Code or as otherwise provided by law.

(D) For purposes of this paragraph, the Department of Finance shall determine the allocation of revenues between the agencies; provided, however, beginning in the 2022–23 fiscal year the amount allocated pursuant to subparagraph (A) shall not be less than ten million dollars ($10,000,000) annually and the amount allocated pursuant to subparagraph (B) shall not be less than forty million dollars ($40,000,000) annually. In determining the amount to be allocated before the 2022–23 fiscal year pursuant to this paragraph, the Department of Finance shall give initial priority to subparagraph (A).

(g) Funds allocated pursuant to subdivision (f) shall be used to increase the funding of programs and purposes identified and shall not be used to replace allocation of other funding for these purposes.

(h) Effective July 1, 2028, the Legislature may amend this section by majority vote to further the purposes of the Control, Regulate and Tax Adult Use of Marijuana Act, including allocating funds to programs other than those specified in subdivisions (d) and (f). Any revisions pursuant to this subdivision shall not result in a reduction of funds to accounts established pursuant to subdivisions (d) and (f) in any subsequent year from the amount allocated to each account in the 2027–28 fiscal year. Prior to July 1, 2028, the Legislature may not change the allocations to programs specified in subdivisions (d) and (f).

Revenue and Taxation Code § 34020

(AUMA, Effective November 9, 2016.)

The Controller shall periodically audit the Tax Fund to ensure that those funds are used and accounted for in a manner consistent with this part and as otherwise required by law.

Revenue and Taxation Code § 34021

(AUMA, Effective November 9, 2016.)

(a) The taxes imposed by this Part shall be in addition to any other tax imposed by a city, county, or city and county.

Revenue and Taxation Code § 34021.5

(MAUCRSA, Effective June 27, 2017.)

(a) (1) A county may impose a tax on the privilege of cultivating, manufacturing, producing, processing, preparing, storing, providing, donating, selling, or distributing cannabis or cannabis products by a licensee operating under Division 10 (commencing with Section 26000) of the Business and Professions Code.

   (2) The board of supervisors shall specify in the ordinance proposing the tax the activities subject to the tax, the applicable rate or rates, the method of apportionment, if necessary, and the manner of collection of the tax. The tax may be imposed for general governmental purposes or for purposes specified in the ordinance by the board of supervisors.

   (3) In addition to any other method of collection authorized by law, the board of supervisors may provide for the collection of the tax imposed pursuant to this section in the same manner, and subject to the same penalties and priority of lien, as other charges and taxes fixed and collected by the county. A tax imposed pursuant to this section is a tax and not a fee or special assessment. The board of supervisors shall specify whether the tax applies throughout the entire county or within the unincorporated area of the county.

   (4) The tax authorized by this section may be imposed upon any or all of the activities set forth in paragraph (1), as specified in the ordinance, regardless of whether the activity is undertaken individually, collectively, or cooperatively, and regardless of whether the activity is for compensation or gratuitous, as determined by the board of supervisors.

(b) A tax imposed pursuant to this section shall be subject to applicable voter approval requirements imposed by law.

(c) This section is declaratory of existing law and does not limit or prohibit the levy or collection of any other fee, charge, or tax, or a license or service fee or charge upon, or related to, the activities set forth in subdivision (a) as otherwise provided by law. This section shall not be construed as a limitation upon the taxing authority of a county as provided by law.

(d) This section shall not be construed to authorize a county to impose a sales or use tax in addition to the sales and use taxes imposed under an ordinance conforming to the provisions of Sections 7202 and 7203 of this code.

Revenue and Taxation Code § 55044

(Amended by AB 133, Effective September 16, 2017.)

(a) If the department finds that a person's failure to make a timely return or payment is due to reasonable cause and circumstances beyond the person's control, and occurred notwithstanding the exercise of ordinary care and the absence of willful neglect, the person may be relieved of the penalty provided by Sections 34013, 55042, 55050, and 55086.

(b) Except as provided in subdivision (c), any person seeking to be relieved of the penalty shall file with the department a statement, under penalty of perjury, setting forth the facts upon which he or she bases his or her claim for relief.

(c) The department shall establish criteria that provide for efficient resolution of requests for relief pursuant to this section.

XI. Vehicle Code Sections

Vehicle Code § 2429.7

(MAUCRSA, Effective June 27, 2017.)

(a) The commissioner shall appoint an impaired driving task force to develop recommendations for best practices, protocols, proposed legislation, and other policies that will address the issue of impaired driving, including driving under the influence of cannabis and controlled substances. The task force shall also examine the use of technology, including field testing technologies and validated field sobriety tests, to identify drivers under the influence of prescription drugs, cannabis, and controlled substances. The task force shall include, but is not limited to, the commissioner, who shall serve as chairperson, and at least one member from each of the following:

(1) The Office of Traffic Safety.

(2) The National Highway Traffic Safety Administration.

(3) Local law enforcement.

(4) District attorneys.

(5) Public defenders.

(6) California Association of Crime Laboratory Directors.

(7) California Attorneys for Criminal Justice.

(8) The California Cannabis Research Program, known as the Center for Medicinal Cannabis Research, authorized pursuant to Section 11362.9 of the Health and Safety Code.

(9) An organization that represents medicinal cannabis patients.

(10) Licensed physicians with expertise in substance abuse disorder treatment.

(11) Researchers with expertise in identifying impairment caused by prescription medications and controlled substances.

(12) Nongovernmental organizations committed to social justice issues.

(13) A nongovernmental organization that focuses on improving roadway safety.

(b) The members of the task force shall serve at the pleasure of the commissioner and without compensation.

(c) The task force members shall be free of economic relationships with any company that profits from the sale of technologies or equipment that is intended to identify impairment. Members and their organizations shall not receive pay from, grants from, or any form of financial support from companies or entities that sell such technologies or equipment.

(d) The task force shall make recommendations regarding prevention of impaired driving, means of identifying impaired driving, and responses to impaired driving that reduce reoccurrence, including, but not limited to, evidence-based approaches that do not rely on incarceration.

(e) The task force shall make recommendations regarding how to best capture data to evaluate the impact that cannabis legalization is having on roadway safety.

(f) By January 1, 2021, the task force shall report to the Legislature its policy recommendations and the steps state agencies are taking regarding impaired driving. The report shall be submitted in compliance with Section 9795 of the Government Code.

Vehicle Code § 23152

(Amended by Stats. 2016, Ch. 765, Sec. 1. (AB 2687) Effective January 1, 2017.)

(a) It is unlawful for a person who is under the influence of any alcoholic beverage to drive a vehicle.

(b) It is unlawful for a person who has 0.08 percent or more, by weight, of alcohol in his or her blood to drive a vehicle.

For purposes of this article and Section 34501.16, percent, by weight, of alcohol in a person's blood is based upon grams of alcohol per 100 milliliters of blood or grams of alcohol per 210 liters of breath.

In any prosecution under this subdivision, it is a rebuttable presumption that the person had 0.08 percent or more, by weight, of alcohol in his or her blood at the time of driving the vehicle if the person had 0.08 percent or more, by weight, of alcohol in his or her blood at the time of the performance of a chemical test within three hours after the driving.

(c) It is unlawful for a person who is addicted to the use of any drug to drive a vehicle. This subdivision shall not apply to a person who is participating in a narcotic treatment program approved pursuant to Article 3 (commencing with Section 11875) of Chapter 1 of Part 3 of Division 10.5 of the Health and Safety Code.

(d) It is unlawful for a person who has 0.04 percent or more, by weight, of alcohol in his or her blood to drive a commercial motor vehicle, as defined in Section 15210. In a prosecution under this subdivision, it is a rebuttable presumption that the person had 0.04 percent or more, by weight, of alcohol in his or her blood at the time of driving the vehicle if the person had 0.04 percent or more, by weight, of alcohol in his or her blood at the time of the performance of a chemical test within three hours after the driving.

(e) Commencing July 1, 2018, it shall be unlawful for a person who has 0.04 percent or more, by weight, of alcohol in his or her blood to drive a motor vehicle when a passenger for hire is a passenger in the vehicle at the time of the offense. For purposes of this subdivision, "passenger for hire" means a passenger for whom consideration is contributed or expected as a condition of carriage in the vehicle, whether directly or indirectly flowing to the owner, operator, agent, or any other person having an interest in the vehicle. In a prosecution under this subdivision, it is a rebuttable presumption that the person had 0.04 percent or more, by weight, of alcohol in his or her blood at the time of driving the vehicle if the person had 0.04 percent or more, by weight, of alcohol in his or her blood at the time of the performance of a chemical test within three hours after the driving.

(f) It is unlawful for a person who is under the influence of any drug to drive a vehicle.

(g) It is unlawful for a person who is under the combined influence of any alcoholic beverage and drug to drive a vehicle.

Vehicle Code § 23220

(Amended by SB 65, Effective January 1, 2018.)

(a) A person shall not drink any alcoholic beverage or smoke or ingest marijuana or any marijuana product while driving a motor vehicle on any lands described in subdivision (c).

(b) A person shall not drink any alcoholic beverage or smoke or ingest marijuana or any marijuana product while riding as a passenger in any motor vehicle being driven on any lands described in subdivision (c).

(c) As used in this section, "lands" means those lands to which the Chappie-Z'berg Off-Highway Motor Vehicle Law of 1971 (Division 16.5 (commencing with Section 38000)) applies as to off-highway motor vehicles, as described in Section 38001.

(d) A violation of subdivision (a) or (b) shall be punished as an infraction.

Vehicle Code § 23221

(Amended by SB 65, Effective January 1, 2018.)

(a) A driver shall not drink any alcoholic beverage or smoke or ingest marijuana or any marijuana product while driving a motor vehicle upon a highway.

(b) A passenger shall not drink any alcoholic beverage or smoke or ingest marijuana or any marijuana product while in a motor vehicle being driven upon a highway.

(c) A violation of this section shall be punished as an infraction.

Vehicle Code § 23222

(MAUCRSA, Effective June 27, 2017.)

(a) No person shall have in his or her possession on his or her person, while driving a motor vehicle upon a highway or on lands, as described in subdivision (b) of Section 23220, any bottle, can, or other receptacle, containing any alcoholic beverage which has been opened, or a seal broken, or the contents of which have been partially removed.

(b) (1) Except as authorized by law, every person who has in his or her possession on his or her person, while driving a motor vehicle upon a highway or on lands, as described in subdivision (b) of Section 23220, any receptacle containing any cannabis or cannabis products, as defined by Section 11018.1 of the Health and Safety Code, which has been opened or has a seal broken, or loose cannabis flower not in a container, is guilty of an infraction punishable by a fine of not more than one hundred dollars ($100).

    (2) Paragraph (1) does not apply to a person who has a receptacle containing cannabis or cannabis products that has been opened, has a seal broken, or the contents of which have been partially removed, or to a person who has loose cannabis flower not in a container, if the receptacle or loose cannabis flower not in a container is in the trunk of the vehicle.

(c) Subdivision (b) does not apply to a qualified patient or person with an identification card, as defined in Section 11362.7 of the Health and Safety Code, if both of the following apply:

    (1) The person is carrying a current identification card or a physician's recommendation.

    (2) The cannabis or cannabis product is contained in a container or receptacle that is either sealed, resealed, or closed.

Vehicle Code § 40000.15

(Amended by Statute, Effective January 1, 2007.)

A violation of any of the following provisions shall constitute a misdemeanor, and not an infraction:

Subdivision (g), (j), (k), (l), or (m) of Section 22658, relating to unlawfully towed or stored vehicles.

Sections 23103 and 23104, relating to reckless driving.

Section 23109, relating to speed contests or exhibitions.

Subdivision (a) of Section 23110, relating to throwing at vehicles.

Section 23152, relating to driving under the influence.

Subdivision (b) of Section 23222, relating to possession of marijuana.

Subdivision (a) or (b) of Section 23224, relating to persons under 21 years of age knowingly driving, or being a passenger in, a motor vehicle carrying any alcoholic beverage.

Section 23253, relating to directions on toll highways or vehicular crossings.

Section 23332, relating to trespassing.

Section 24002.5, relating to unlawful operation of a farm vehicle.

Section 24011.3, relating to vehicle bumper strength notices.

Section 27150.1, relating to sale of exhaust systems.

Section 27362, relating to child passenger seat restraints.

Section 28050, relating to true mileage driven.

Section 28050.5, relating to nonfunctional odometers.

Section 28051, relating to resetting odometers.

Section 28051.5, relating to devices to reset odometers.

Subdivision (d) of Section 28150, relating to possessing four or more jamming devices.

XII. Water Code Sections

Water Code § 25

(Added by Statute, Effective 1967.)

"Board," unless otherwise specified, means the State Water Resources Control Board.

Water Code § 1052

(Amended by Statute, Effective March 1, 2014.)

(a) The diversion or use of water subject to this division other than as authorized in this division is a trespass.

(b) The Attorney General, upon request of the board, shall institute in the superior court in and for any county where the diversion or use is threatened, is occurring, or has occurred an action for the issuance of injunctive relief as may be warranted by way of temporary restraining order, preliminary injunction, or permanent injunction.

(c) Any person or entity committing a trespass as defined in this section may be liable in an amount not to exceed the following:

(1) If the unauthorized diversion or use occurs in a critically dry year immediately preceded by two or more consecutive below normal, dry, or critically dry years or during a period for which the Governor has issued a proclamation of a state of emergency under the California Emergency Services Act (Chapter 7 (commencing with Section 8550) of Division 1 of Title 2 of the Government Code) based on drought conditions, the sum of the following:

(A) One thousand dollars ($1,000) for each day in which the trespass occurs.

(B) Two thousand five hundred dollars ($2,500) for each acre-foot of water diverted or used in excess of that diverter's water rights.

(2) If the unauthorized diversion or use is not described by paragraph (1), five hundred dollars ($500) for each day in which the unauthorized diversion or use occurs.

(d) Civil liability for a violation of this section may be imposed by the superior court or the board as follows:

(1) The superior court may impose civil liability in an action brought by the Attorney General, upon request of the board, to impose, assess, and recover any sums pursuant to subdivision (c). In determining the appropriate amount, the court shall take into consideration all relevant circumstances, including, but not limited to, the extent of harm caused by the violation, the nature and persistence of the violation, the length of time over which the violation occurs, and the corrective action, if any, taken by the violator.

(2) The board may impose civil liability in accordance with Section 1055.

(e) All funds recovered pursuant to this section shall be deposited in the Water Rights Fund established pursuant to Section 1550.

(f) The remedies prescribed in this section are cumulative and not alternative.

Water Code § 1525

(SB 837, Effective June 27, 2016.)

(a) Each person or entity who holds a permit or license to appropriate water, and each lessor of water leased under Chapter 1.5 (commencing with Section 1020) of Part 1, shall pay an annual fee according to a fee schedule established by the board.

(b) Each person or entity who files any of the following shall pay a fee according to a fee schedule established by the board:

(1) An application for a permit to appropriate water.

(2) A registration of appropriation for a small domestic use, small irrigation use, or livestock stockpond use.

(3) A petition for an extension of time within which to begin construction, to complete construction, or to apply the water to full beneficial use under a permit.

(4) A petition to change the point of diversion, place of use, or purpose of use, under a permit, license, or registration.

(5) A petition to change the conditions of a permit or license, requested by the permittee or licensee, that is not otherwise subject to paragraph (3) or (4).

(6) A petition to change the point of discharge, place of use, or purpose of use, of treated wastewater, requested pursuant to Section 1211.

(7) An application for approval of a water lease agreement.

(8) A request for release from priority pursuant to Section 10504.

(9) An application for an assignment of a state-filed application pursuant to Section 10504.

(10) A statement of water diversion and use pursuant to Part 5.1 (commencing with Section 5100) that reports that water was used for cannabis cultivation.

(c) The board shall set the fee schedule authorized by this section so that the total amount of fees collected pursuant to this section equals that amount necessary to recover costs incurred in connection with the issuance, administration, review, monitoring, and enforcement of permits, licenses, certificates, and registrations to appropriate water, water leases, statements of water diversion and use for cannabis cultivation, and orders approving changes in point of discharge, place of use, or purpose of use of treated wastewater. The board may include, as recoverable costs, but is not limited to including, the costs incurred in reviewing applications, registrations, statements of water diversion and use for cannabis cultivation, petitions and requests, prescribing terms of permits, licenses, registrations, and change orders, enforcing and evaluating compliance with permits, licenses, certificates, registrations, change orders, and water leases, inspection, monitoring, planning, modeling, reviewing documents prepared for the purpose of regulating the diversion and use of water, applying and enforcing the prohibition set forth in Section 1052 against the unauthorized diversion or use of water subject to this division and the water diversion related provisions of Article 6 (commencing with Section 19331) of Chapter 3.5 of Division 8 of the Business and Professions Code, and the administrative costs incurred in connection with carrying out these actions.

(d) (1) The board shall adopt the schedule of fees authorized under this section as emergency regulations in accordance with Section 1530.

(2) For filings subject to subdivision (b), the schedule may provide for a single filing fee or for an initial filing fee followed by an annual fee, as appropriate to the type of filing involved, and may include supplemental fees for filings that have already been made but have not yet been acted upon by the board at the time the schedule of fees takes effect.

(3) The board shall set the amount of total revenue collected each year through the fees authorized by this section at an amount equal to the amounts appropriated by the Legislature for expenditure for support of water rights program activities from the Water Rights Fund established under Section 1550, taking into account the reserves in the Water Rights Fund. The board shall review and revise the fees each fiscal year as necessary to conform with the amounts appropriated. If the board determines that the revenue collected during the preceding year was greater than, or less than, the amounts appropriated, the board may further adjust the annual fees to compensate for the over or under collection of revenue.

(e) Annual fees imposed pursuant to this section for the 2003–04 fiscal year shall be assessed for the entire 2003–04 fiscal year.

Water Code § 1535

(SB 837, Effective June 27, 2016.)

(a) Any fee subject to this chapter that is required in connection with the filing of an application, registration, request, statement, or proof of claim, other than an annual fee required after the period covered by the initial filing fee, shall be paid to the board.

(b) If a fee established under subdivision (b) of Section 1525, Section 1528, or Section 13160.1 is not paid when due, the board may cancel the application, registration, petition, request, statement, or claim, or may refer the matter to the State Board of Equalization for collection of the unpaid fee.

Water Code § 1831

(MAUCRSA, Effective June 27, 2017.)

(a) When the board determines that any person is violating, or threatening to violate, any requirement described in subdivision (d), the board may issue an order to that person to cease and desist from that violation.

(b) The cease and desist order shall require that person to comply forthwith or in accordance with a time schedule set by the board.

(c) The board may issue a cease and desist order only after notice and an opportunity for hearing pursuant to Section 1834.

(d) The board may issue a cease and desist order in response to a violation or threatened violation of any of the following:

(1) The prohibition set forth in Section 1052 against the unauthorized diversion or use of water subject to this division.

(2) Any term or condition of a permit, license, certification, or registration issued under this division.

(3) Any decision or order of the board issued under this part, Section 275, Chapter 11 (commencing with Section 10735) of Part 2.74 of Division 6, or Article 7 (commencing with Section 13550) of Chapter 7 of Division 7, in which decision or order the person to whom the cease and desist order will be issued, or a predecessor in interest to that person, was named as a party directly affected by the decision or order.

(4) A regulation adopted under Section 1058.5.

(5) Any extraction restriction, limitation, order, or regulation adopted or issued under Chapter 11 (commencing with Section 10735) of Part 2.74 of Division 6.

(6) Any diversion or use of water for cannabis cultivation if any of paragraphs (1) to (5), inclusive, or any of the following applies:

(A) A license is required, but has not been obtained, under Chapter 6 (commencing with Section 26060) or Chapter 7 (commencing with Section 26070) of Division 10 of the Business and Professions Code.

(B) The diversion is not in compliance with an applicable limitation or requirement established by the board or the Department of Fish and Wildlife under Section 13149.

(C) The diversion or use is not in compliance with a requirement imposed under paragraphs (1) and (2) of subdivision (b) of Section 26060.1 of, and paragraph (3) of subdivision (a) of Section 26070 of, the Business and Professions Code.

(e) This article does not alter the regulatory authority of the board under other provisions of law.

Water Code § 1840

(MCRSA- SB 837, Effective June 27, 2016.)

(a) (1) Except as provided in subdivision (b), a person who, on or after January 1, 2016, diverts 10 acre-feet of water per year or more under a permit or license shall install and maintain a device or employ a method capable of measuring the rate of direct diversion, rate of collection to storage, and rate of withdrawal or release from storage. The measurements shall be made using the best available technologies and best professional practices, as defined in Section 5100, using a device or methods satisfactory to the board, as follows:

(A) A device shall be capable of continuous monitoring of the rate and quantity of water diverted and shall be properly maintained. The permittee or licensee shall provide the board with evidence that the device has been installed with the first report submitted after installation of the device. The permittee or licensee shall provide the board with evidence demonstrating that the device is functioning properly as part of the reports submitted at five-year intervals after the report documenting installation of the device, or upon request of the board.

(B) In developing regulations pursuant to Section 1841, the board shall consider devices and methods that provide accurate measurement of the total amount diverted and the rate of diversion. The board shall consider devices and methods that provide accurate measurements within an acceptable range of error, including the following:

(i) Electricity records dedicated to a pump and recent pump test.

(ii) Staff gage calibrated with an acceptable streamflow rating curve.

(iii) Staff gage calibrated for a flume or weir.

(iv) Staff gage calibrated with an acceptable storage capacity curve.

(v) Pressure transducer and acceptable storage capacity curve.

(2) The permittee or licensee shall maintain a record of all diversion monitoring that includes the date, time, and diversion rate at time intervals of one hour or less, and the total amount of water diverted. These records shall be included with reports submitted under the permit or license, as required under subdivision (c), or upon request of the board.

(b) (1) The board may modify the requirements of subdivision (a) upon finding either of the following:

(A) That strict compliance is infeasible, is unreasonably expensive, would unreasonably affect public trust uses, or would result in the waste or unreasonable use of water.

(B) That the need for monitoring and reporting is adequately addressed by other conditions of the permit or license.

(2) The board may increase the 10-acre-foot reporting threshold of subdivision (a) in a watershed or subwatershed, after considering the diversion reporting threshold in relation to quantity of water within the watershed or subwatershed. The board may increase the 10-acre-foot reporting threshold to 25 acre-feet or above if it finds that the benefits of the additional information within the watershed or subwatershed are substantially outweighed by the cost of installing measuring devices or employing methods for measurement for diversions at the 10-acre-foot threshold.

(c) At least annually, a person who diverts water under a registration, permit, or license shall report to the board the following information:

(1) The quantity of water diverted by month.

(2) The maximum rate of diversion by months in the preceding calendar year.

(3) The information required by subdivision (a), if applicable.

(4) The amount of water used, if any, for cannabis cultivation.

(d) Compliance with the applicable requirements of this section is a condition of every registration, permit, or license.

Water Code § 1845

(SB 837, Effective June 27, 2016.)

(a) Upon the failure of any person to comply with a cease and desist order issued by the board pursuant to this chapter, the Attorney General, upon the request of the board, shall petition the superior court for the issuance of prohibitory or mandatory injunctive relief as appropriate, including a temporary restraining order, preliminary injunction, or permanent injunction.

(b) (1) A person or entity who violates a cease and desist order issued pursuant to this chapter may be liable in an amount not to exceed the following:

(A) If the violation occurs in a critically dry year immediately preceded by two or more consecutive below normal, dry, or critically dry years or during a period for which the Governor has issued a proclamation of a state of emergency under the California Emergency Services Act (Chapter 7 (commencing with Section 8550) of Division 1 of Title 2 of the Government Code) based on drought conditions, ten thousand dollars ($10,000) for each day in which the violation occurs.

(B) If the violation is not described by subparagraph (A), one thousand dollars ($1,000) for each day in which the violation occurs.

(2) Civil liability may be imposed by the superior court. The Attorney General, upon the request of the board, shall petition the superior court to impose, assess, and recover those sums.

(3) Civil liability may be imposed administratively by the board pursuant to Section 1055.

Water Code § 1846

(SB 837, Effective June 27, 2016.)

(a) A person or entity may be liable for a violation of any of the following in an amount not to exceed five hundred dollars ($500) for each day in which the violation occurs:

(1) A term or condition of a permit, license, certificate, or registration issued under this division.

(2) A regulation or order adopted by the board.

(b) Civil liability may be imposed by the superior court. The Attorney General, upon the request of the board, shall petition the superior court to impose, assess, and recover those sums.

(c) Civil liability may be imposed administratively by the board pursuant to Section 1055.

Water Code § 1847

(MAUCRSA, Effective June 27, 2017.)

(a) A person or entity may be liable for a violation of any of the requirements of subdivision (b) in an amount not to exceed the sum of the following:

(1) Five hundred dollars ($500), plus two hundred fifty dollars ($250) for each additional day on which the violation continues if the person fails to correct the violation within 30 days after the board has called the violation to the attention of that person.

(2) Two thousand five hundred dollars ($2,500) for each acre-foot of water diverted or used in violation of the applicable requirement.

(b) Liability may be imposed for any of the following violations:

(1) Violation of a principle, guideline, or requirement established by the board or the Department of Fish and Wildlife under Section 13149.

(2) Failure to submit information, or making a material misstatement in information submitted, under Section 26060.1 of the Business and Professions Code.

(3) Violation of any requirement imposed under subdivision (b) of Section 26060.1 of the Business and Professions Code.

(4) Diversion or use of water for cannabis cultivation for which a license is required, but has not been obtained, under Chapter 6 (commencing with Section 26060) or Chapter 7 (commencing with Section 26070) of Division 10 of the Business and Professions Code.

(c) Civil liability may be imposed by the superior court. The Attorney General, upon the request of the board, shall petition the superior court to impose, assess, and recover those sums.

(d) Civil liability may be imposed administratively by the board pursuant to Section 1055.

Water Code § 5100

(Amended by Statute, Effective February 3, 2010.)

As used in this part:

(a) "Best available technologies" means technologies at the highest technically practical level, using flow totaling devices, and if necessary, data loggers and telemetry.

(b) "Best professional practices" means practices attaining and maintaining the accuracy of measurement and reporting devices and methods.

(c) "Diversion" means taking water by gravity or pumping from a surface stream or subterranean stream flowing through a known and definite channel, or other body of surface water, into a canal, pipeline, or other conduit, and includes impoundment of water in a reservoir.

(d) "Person" means all persons whether natural or artificial, including the United States of America, State of California, and all political subdivisions, districts, municipalities, and public agencies.

Water Code § 5101

(Amended by Statute, Effective January 1, 2012.)

Each person who, after December 31, 1965, diverts water shall file with the board, prior to July 1 of the succeeding year, a statement of his or her diversion and use, except that a statement is not required to be filed if the diversion is any of the following:

(a) From a spring that does not flow off the property on which it is located and from which the person's aggregate diversions do not exceed 25 acre-feet in any year.

(b) Covered by a registration for small domestic use, small irrigation use, or livestock stockpond use, or permit or license to appropriate water on file with the board.

(c) Included in a notice filed pursuant to Part 5 (commencing with Section 4999).

(d) Regulated by a watermaster appointed by the department and included in annual reports filed with a court or the board by the watermaster, which reports identify the persons who have diverted water and describe the general purposes and the place, the use, and the quantity of water that has been diverted from each source.

(e) Included in annual reports filed with a court or the board by a watermaster appointed by a court or pursuant to statute to administer a final judgment determining rights to water, which reports identify the persons who have diverted water and give the general place of use and the quantity of water that has been diverted from each source.

(f) For use in compliance with Article 2.5 (commencing with Section 1226) or Article 2.7 (commencing with Section 1228) of Chapter 1 of Part 2.

(g) A diversion that occurs before January 1, 2009, if any of the following applies:

(1) The diversion is from a spring that does not flow off the property on which it is located, and the person's aggregate diversions do not exceed 25 acre-feet in any year.

(2) The diversion is covered by an application to appropriate water on file with the board.

(3) The diversion is reported by the department in its hydrologic data bulletins.

(4) The diversion is included in the consumptive use data for the Delta lowlands published by the department in its hydrologic data bulletins.

Water Code § 5102

(Amended by Statute, Effective 1967.)

The statement may be filed either by the person who is diverting water or, on his behalf, by an agency which he designates and which maintains a record of the water diverted. A separate statement shall be filed for each point of diversion.

Water Code § 5103

(SB 837, Effective June 27, 2016.)

Each statement shall be prepared on a form provided by the board. The statement shall include all of the following information:

(a) The name and address of the person who diverted water and of the person filing the statement.

(b) The name of the stream or other source from which water was diverted, and the name of the next major stream or other body of water to which the source is tributary.

(c) The place of diversion. The location of the diversion works shall be depicted on a specific United States Geological Survey topographic map, or shall be identified using the California Coordinate System, or latitude and longitude measurements. If assigned, the public land description to the nearest 40-acre subdivision and the assessor's parcel number shall also be provided.

(d) The capacity of the diversion works and of the storage reservoir, if any, and the months in which water was used during the preceding calendar year.

(e) (1) (A) At least monthly records of water diversions. The measurements of the diversion shall be made in accordance with Section 1840.

(B) (i) On and after July 1, 2016, the measurement of a diversion of 10 acre-feet or more per year shall comply with regulations adopted by the board pursuant to Article 3 (commencing with Section 1840) of Chapter 12 of Part 2.

(ii) The requirement of clause (i) is extended to January 1, 2017, for any statement filer that enters into a voluntary agreement that is acceptable to the board to reduce the statement filer's diversions during the 2015 irrigation season.

(2) (A) The terms of, and eligibility for, any grant or loan awarded or administered by the department, the board, or the California Bay-Delta Authority on behalf of a person that is subject to paragraph (1) shall be conditioned on compliance with that paragraph.

(B) Notwithstanding subparagraph (A), the board may determine that a person is eligible for a grant or loan even though the person is not complying with paragraph (1), if both of the following apply:

(i) The board determines that the grant or loan will assist the grantee or loan recipient in complying with paragraph (1).

(ii) The person has submitted to the board a one-year schedule for complying with paragraph (1).

(C) It is the intent of the Legislature that the requirements of this subdivision shall complement and not affect the scope of authority granted to the board by provisions of law other than this article.

(f) (1) The purpose of use.

(2) The amount of water used, if any, for cannabis cultivation.

(g) A general description of the area in which the water was used. The location of the place of use shall be depicted on a specific United States Geological Survey topographic map and on any other maps with identifiable landmarks. If assigned, the public land description to the nearest 40-acre subdivision and the assessor's parcel number shall also be provided.

(h) The year in which the diversion was commenced as near as is known.

Water Code § 13149

(MCRSA- SB 837, Effective June 27, 2016.)

(a) (1) (A) The board, in consultation with the Department of Fish and Wildlife, shall adopt principles and guidelines for diversion and use of water for cannabis cultivation in areas where cannabis cultivation may have the potential to substantially affect instream flows. The principles and guidelines adopted under this section may include, but are not limited to, instream flow objectives, limits on diversions, and requirements for screening of diversions and elimination of barriers to fish passage. The principles and guidelines may include requirements that apply to groundwater extractions where the board determines those requirements are reasonably necessary for purposes of this section.

(B) Prior to adopting principles and guidelines under this section, the board shall allow for public comment and hearing, pursuant to Section 13147. The board shall provide an opportunity for the public to review and comment on the proposal for at least 60 days and shall consider the public comments before adopting the principles and guidelines.

(2) The board, in consultation with the Department of Fish and Wildlife, shall adopt principles and guidelines pending the development of long-term principles and guidelines under paragraph (1). The principles and guidelines, including the interim principles and guidelines, shall include measures to protect springs, wetlands, and aquatic habitats from negative impacts of cannabis cultivation. The board may update the interim principles and guidelines as it determines to be reasonably necessary for purposes of this section.

(3) The Department of Fish and Wildlife, in consultation with the board, may establish interim requirements to protect fish and wildlife from the impacts of diversions for cannabis cultivation pending the adoption of long-term principles and guidelines by the board under paragraph (1). The requirements may also include measures to protect springs, wetlands, and aquatic habitats from negative impacts of cannabis cultivation.

(b) (1) Notwithstanding Section 15300.2 of Title 14 of the California Code of Regulations, actions of the board and the Department of Fish and Wildlife under this section shall be deemed to be within Section 15308 of Title 14 of the California Code of regulations, provided that those actions do not involve relaxation of existing streamflow standards.

(2) The board shall adopt principles and guidelines under this section as part of state policy for water quality control adopted pursuant to Article 3 (commencing with Section 13140) of Chapter 3 of Division 7.

(3) If the Department of Fish and Wildlife establishes interim requirements under this section, it shall do so as emergency regulations in accordance with Chapter 3.5 (commencing with Section 11340) of Part 1 of Division 3 of Title 2 of the Government Code. The adoption of those interim requirements is an emergency and shall be considered by the Office of Administrative Law as necessary for the immediate preservation of the public peace, health, safety, and general welfare. Notwithstanding Chapter 3.5 (commencing with Section 11340) of Part 1 of Division 3 of Title 2 of the Government Code, the emergency regulations shall remain in effect until revised by the Department of Fish and Wildlife, provided that the emergency regulations shall not apply after long-term principles and guidelines adopted by the board under this section take effect for the stream or other body of water where the diversion is located.

(4) A diversion for cannabis cultivation is subject to both the interim principles and guidelines and the interim requirements in the period before final principles and guidelines are adopted by the board.

(5) The board shall have primary enforcement responsibility for principles and guidelines adopted under this section, and shall notify the Department of Food and Agriculture of any enforcement action taken.

Water Code § 13260

(Amended by Statute, Effective March 24, 2011.)

(a) Each of the following persons shall file with the appropriate regional board a report of the discharge, containing the information that may be required by the regional board:

(1) A person discharging waste, or proposing to discharge waste, within any region that could affect the quality of the waters of the state, other than into a community sewer system.

(2) A person who is a citizen, domiciliary, or political agency or entity of this state discharging waste, or

proposing to discharge waste, outside the boundaries of the state in a manner that could affect the quality of the waters of the state within any region.

(3) A person operating, or proposing to construct, an injection well.

(b) No report of waste discharge need be filed pursuant to subdivision (a) if the requirement is waived pursuant to Section 13269.

(c) Each person subject to subdivision (a) shall file with the appropriate regional board a report of waste discharge relative to any material change or proposed change in the character, location, or volume of the discharge.

(d) (1) (A) Each person who is subject to subdivision (a) or (c) shall submit an annual fee according to a fee schedule established by the state board.

(B) The total amount of annual fees collected pursuant to this section shall equal that amount necessary to recover costs incurred in connection with the issuance, administration, reviewing, monitoring, and enforcement of waste discharge requirements and waivers of waste discharge requirements.

(C) Recoverable costs may include, but are not limited to, costs incurred in reviewing waste discharge reports, prescribing terms of waste discharge requirements and monitoring requirements, enforcing and evaluating compliance with waste discharge requirements and waiver requirements, conducting surface water and groundwater monitoring and modeling, analyzing laboratory samples, adopting, reviewing, and revising water quality control plans and state policies for water quality control, and reviewing documents prepared for the purpose of regulating the discharge of waste, and administrative costs incurred in connection with carrying out these actions.

(D) In establishing the amount of a fee that may be imposed on a confined animal feeding and holding operation pursuant to this section, including, but not limited to, a dairy farm, the state board shall consider all of the following factors:

(i) The size of the operation.

(ii) Whether the operation has been issued a permit to operate pursuant to Section 1342 of Title 33 of the United States Code.

(iii) Any applicable waste discharge requirement or conditional waiver of a waste discharge requirement.

(iv) The type and amount of discharge from the operation.

(v) The pricing mechanism of the commodity produced.

(vi) Any compliance costs borne by the operation pursuant to state and federal water quality regulations.

(vii) Whether the operation participates in a quality assurance program certified by a regional water quality control board, the state board, or a federal water quality control agency.

(2) (A) Subject to subparagraph (B), the fees collected pursuant to this section shall be deposited in the Waste Discharge Permit Fund, which is hereby created. The money in the fund is available for expenditure by the state board, upon appropriation by the Legislature, solely for the purposes of carrying out this division.

(B) (i) Notwithstanding subparagraph (A), the fees collected pursuant to this section from stormwater dischargers that are subject to a general industrial or construction stormwater permit under the national pollutant discharge elimination system (NPDES) shall be separately accounted for in the Waste Discharge Permit Fund.

(ii) Not less than 50 percent of the money in the Waste Discharge Permit Fund that is separately accounted for pursuant to clause (i) is available, upon appropriation by the Legislature, for expenditure by the regional board with jurisdiction over the permitted industry or construction site that generated the fee to carry out stormwater programs in the region.

(iii) Each regional board that receives money pursuant to clause (ii) shall spend not less than 50 percent of that money solely on stormwater inspection and regulatory compliance issues associated with industrial and construction stormwater programs.

(3) A person who would be required to pay the annual fee prescribed by paragraph (1) for waste discharge requirements applicable to discharges of solid waste, as defined in Section 40191 of the Public Resources Code, at a waste management unit that is also regulated under Division 30 (commencing with Section 40000) of the Public Resources Code, shall be entitled to a waiver of the annual fee for the discharge of solid waste at the waste management unit imposed by paragraph (1) upon verification by the state board of payment of the fee imposed by Section 48000 of the Public Resources Code, and provided that the fee established pursuant to Section 48000 of the Public Resources Code generates revenues sufficient to fund the programs specified in Section 48004 of the Public Resources Code and the amount appropriated by the Legislature for those purposes is not reduced.

(e) Each person that discharges waste in a manner regulated by this section shall pay an annual fee to the state board. The state board shall establish, by regulation, a timetable for the payment of the annual fee. If the state board or a regional board determines that the discharge will not affect, or have the potential to affect, the quality of the waters of the state, all or part of the annual fee shall be refunded.

(f) (1) The state board shall adopt, by emergency regulations, a schedule of fees authorized under subdivision (d). The total revenue collected each year through annual fees shall be set at an amount equal to the revenue levels set forth in the Budget Act for this activity. The state board shall automatically adjust the annual fees each fiscal year to conform with the revenue levels set forth in the Budget Act for this activity. If the state board determines that the revenue collected during the preceding year was greater than, or less than, the revenue levels set forth in the Budget Act, the state board may further adjust the annual fees to compensate for the over and under collection of revenue.

(2) The emergency regulations adopted pursuant to this subdivision, any amendment thereto, or subsequent adjustments to the annual fees, shall be adopted by the state board in accordance with Chapter 3.5 (commencing with Section 11340) of Part 1 of Division 3 of Title 2 of the Government Code. The adoption of these regulations is an emergency and shall be considered by the Office of Administrative Law as necessary for the immediate preservation of the public peace, health, safety, and general welfare. Notwithstanding Chapter 3.5 (commencing with Section 11340) of Part 1 of Division 3 of Title 2 of the Government Code, any emergency regulations adopted by the state board, or adjustments to the annual fees made by the state board pursuant to this section, shall not be subject to review by the Office of Administrative Law and shall remain in effect until revised by the state board.

(g) The state board shall adopt regulations setting forth reasonable time limits within which the regional board shall determine the adequacy of a report of waste discharge submitted under this section.

(h) Each report submitted under this section shall be sworn to, or submitted under penalty of perjury.

(i) The regulations adopted by the state board pursuant to subdivision (f) shall include a provision that annual fees shall not be imposed on those who pay fees under the national pollutant discharge elimination system until the time when those fees are again due, at which time the fees shall become due on an annual basis.

(j) A person operating or proposing to construct an oil, gas, or geothermal injection well subject to paragraph (3) of subdivision (a) shall not be required to pay a fee pursuant to subdivision (d) if the injection well is regulated by the Division of Oil and Gas of the Department of Conservation, in lieu of the appropriate California regional water quality control board, pursuant to the memorandum of understanding, entered into between the state board and the Department of Conservation on May 19, 1988. This subdivision shall remain operative until the memorandum of understanding is revoked by the state board or the Department of Conservation.

(k) In addition to the report required by subdivision (a), before a person discharges mining waste, the person shall first submit both of the following to the regional board:

(1) A report on the physical and chemical characteristics of the waste that could affect its potential to cause pollution or contamination. The report shall include the results of all tests required by regulations adopted by the board, any test adopted by the Department of Toxic Substances Control pursuant to Section 25141 of the Health and Safety Code for extractable, persistent, and bioaccumulative toxic substances in a waste or other material, and any other tests that the state board or regional board may require, including, but not limited to, tests needed to determine the acid-generating potential of the mining waste or the extent to which hazardous substances may persist in the waste after disposal.

(2) A report that evaluates the potential of the discharge of the mining waste to produce, over the long term, acid mine drainage, the discharge or leaching of heavy metals, or the release of other hazardous substances.

(l) Except upon the written request of the regional board, a report of waste discharge need not be filed pursuant to subdivision (a) or (c) by a user of recycled water that is being supplied by a supplier or distributor of recycled water for whom a master recycling permit has been issued pursuant to Section 13523.1.

Water Code § 13264

(Amended by Statute, Effective January 1, 2004.)

(a) No person shall initiate any new discharge of waste or make any material changes in any discharge, or initiate a discharge to, make any material changes in a discharge to, or construct, an injection well, prior to the filing of the report required by Section 13260 and no person shall take any of these actions after filing the report but before whichever of the following occurs first:

(1) The issuance of waste discharge requirements pursuant to Section 13263.

(2) The expiration of 140 days after compliance with Section 13260 if the waste to be discharged does not create or threaten to create a condition of pollution or nuisance and any of the following applies:

(A) The project is not subject to the California Environmental Quality Act (Division 13 (commencing with Section 21000) of the Public Resources Code).

(B) The regional board is the lead agency for purposes of the California Environmental Quality Act, a negative declaration is required, and at least 105 days have expired since the regional board assumed lead agency responsibility.

(C) The regional board is the lead agency for the purposes of the California Environmental Quality Act, and environmental impact report or written documentation prepared to meet the requirements of Section 21080.5 of the Public Resources Code is required, and at least one year has expired since the regional board assumed lead agency responsibility.

(D) The regional board is a responsible agency for purposes of the California Environmental Quality Act, and at least 90 days have expired since certification or approval of environmental documentation by the lead agency.

(3) The issuance of a waiver pursuant to Section 13269.

(b) The Attorney General, at the request of a regional board, shall petition the superior court for the issuance of a temporary restraining order, preliminary injunction, or permanent injunction, or combination thereof, as may be appropriate, prohibiting any person who is violating or threatening to violate this section from doing any of the following, whichever is applicable:

(1) Discharging the waste or fluid.

(2) Making any material change in the discharge.

(3) Constructing the injection well.

(c) (1) Notwithstanding any other provision of law, moneys collected under this division for a violation pursuant to paragraph (2) of subdivision (a) shall be deposited in the Waste Discharge Permit Fund and separately accounted for in that fund.

(2) The funds described in paragraph (1) shall be expended by the state board, upon appropriation by the Legislature, to assist regional boards, and other public agencies with authority to clean up waste or abate the effects of the waste, in cleaning up or abating the effects of the waste on waters of the state or for the purposes authorized in Section 13443.

Water Code § 13272

(Amended by Statute, Effective June 20, 2014.)

(a) Except as provided by subdivision (b), any person who, without regard to intent or negligence, causes or permits any oil or petroleum product to be discharged in or on any waters of the state, or discharged or deposited where it is, or probably will be, discharged in or on any waters of the state, shall, as soon as (1) that person has knowledge of the discharge, (2) notification is possible, and (3) notification can be provided without substantially impeding cleanup or other emergency measures, immediately notify the Office of Emergency Services of the discharge in accordance with the spill reporting provision of the California oil spill contingency plan adopted pursuant to Article 3.5 (commencing with Section 8574.1) of Chapter 7 of Division 1 of Title 2 of the Government Code.

(b) The notification required by this section shall not apply to a discharge in compliance with waste discharge requirements or other provisions of this division.

(c) Any person who fails to provide the notice required by this section is guilty of a misdemeanor and shall be punished by a fine of not less than five hundred dollars ($500) or more than five thousand dollars ($5,000) per day for each day of failure to notify, or imprisonment of not more than one year, or both. Except where a discharge to the waters of this state would have occurred but for cleanup or emergency response by a public agency, this subdivision shall not apply to any discharge to land that does not result in a discharge to the waters of this state. This subdivision shall not apply to any person who is fined by the federal government for a failure to report a discharge of oil.

(d) Notification received pursuant to this section or information obtained by use of that notification shall not be used against any person providing the notification in any criminal case, except in a prosecution for perjury or giving a false statement.

(e) Immediate notification to the appropriate regional board of the discharge, in accordance with reporting requirements set under Section 13267 or 13383, shall constitute compliance with the requirements of subdivision (a).

(f) The reportable quantity for oil or petroleum products shall be one barrel (42 gallons) or more, by direct discharge to the receiving waters, unless a more restrictive reporting standard for a particular body of water is adopted.

Water Code § 13276

(Amended by Stats. 2018, Ch. 92, Sec. 217. (SB 1289) Effective January 1, 2019. Note: This section was amended on Nov. 8, 2016, by initiative Prop. 64.)

(a) The multiagency task force, the Department of Fish and Wildlife and state board pilot project to address the Environmental Impacts of Cannabis Cultivation, assigned to respond to the damages caused by cannabis cultivation on public and private lands in California, shall continue its enforcement efforts on a permanent basis and expand them to a statewide level to ensure the reduction of adverse impacts of cannabis cultivation on water quality and on fish and wildlife throughout the state.

(b) The state board or the appropriate regional board shall address discharges of waste resulting from cannabis cultivation under Division 10 (commencing with Section 26000) of the Business and Professions Code and associated activities, including by adopting a general permit, establishing waste discharge requirements, or taking action pursuant to Section 13269. In addressing these discharges, the state board or the regional board shall include conditions to address items that include, but are not limited to, all of the following:

    (1) Site development and maintenance, erosion control, and drainage features.

    (2) Stream crossing installation and maintenance.

    (3) Riparian and wetland protection and management.

    (4) Soil disposal.

    (5) Water storage and use.

    (6) Irrigation runoff.

    (7) Fertilizers and soil.

    (8) Pesticides and herbicides.

    (9) Petroleum products and other chemicals.

    (10) Cultivation-related waste.

    (11) Refuse and human waste.

    (12) Cleanup, restoration, and mitigation.

Water Code § 13387

(Amended by Statute, Effective April 4, 2011, and Operative October 1, 2011.)

(a) Any person who knowingly or negligently does any of the following is subject to criminal penalties as provided in subdivisions (b), (c), and (d):

    (1) Violates Section 13375 or 13376.

    (2) Violates any waste discharge requirements or dredged or fill material permit issued pursuant to this chapter or any water quality certification issued pursuant to Section 13160.

    (3) Violates any order or prohibition issued pursuant to Section 13243 or 13301, if the activity subject to the order or prohibition is subject to regulation under this chapter.

    (4) Violates any requirement of Section 301, 302, 306, 307, 308, 318, 401, or 405 of the Clean Water Act (33

U.S.C. Sec. 1311, 1312, 1316, 1317, 1318, 1328, 1341, or 1345), as amended.

(5) Introduces into a sewer system or into a publicly owned treatment works any pollutant or hazardous substances that the person knew or reasonably should have known could cause personal injury or property damage.

(6) Introduces any pollutant or hazardous substance into a sewer system or into a publicly owned treatment works, except in accordance with any applicable pretreatment requirements, which causes the treatment works to violate waste discharge requirements.

(b) Any person who negligently commits any of the violations set forth in subdivision (a) shall, upon conviction, be punished by a fine of not less than five thousand dollars ($5,000), nor more than twenty-five thousand dollars ($25,000), for each day in which the violation occurs, by imprisonment for not more than one year in a county jail, or by both that fine and imprisonment. If a conviction of a person is for a violation committed after a first conviction of the person under this subdivision, subdivision (c), or subdivision (d), punishment shall be by a fine of not more than fifty thousand dollars ($50,000) for each day in which the violation occurs, by imprisonment pursuant to subdivision (h) of Section 1170 of the Penal Code for 16, 20, or 24 months, or by both that fine and imprisonment.

(c) Any person who knowingly commits any of the violations set forth in subdivision (a) shall, upon conviction, be punished by a fine of not less than five thousand dollars ($5,000), nor more than fifty thousand dollars ($50,000), for each day in which the violation occurs, by imprisonment pursuant to subdivision (h) of Section 1170 of the Penal Code, or by both that fine and imprisonment. If a conviction of a person is for a violation committed after a first conviction of the person under this subdivision or subdivision (d), punishment shall be by a fine of not more than one hundred thousand dollars ($100,000) for each day in which the violation occurs, by imprisonment pursuant to subdivision (h) of Section 1170 of the Penal Code for two, four, or six years, or by both that fine and imprisonment.

(d) (1) Any person who knowingly commits any of the violations set forth in subdivision (a), and who knows at the time that the person thereby places another person in imminent danger of death or serious bodily injury, shall, upon conviction, be punished by a fine of not more than two hundred fifty thousand dollars ($250,000), imprisonment pursuant to subdivision (h) of Section 1170 of the Penal Code for 5, 10, or 15 years, or by both that fine and imprisonment. A person that is an organization shall, upon conviction under this subdivision, be subject to a fine of not more than one million dollars ($1,000,000). If a conviction of a person is for a violation committed after a first conviction of the person under this subdivision, the punishment shall be by a fine of not more than five hundred thousand dollars ($500,000), by imprisonment pursuant to subdivision (h) of Section 1170 of the Penal Code for 10, 20, or 30 years, or by both that fine and imprisonment. A person that is an organization shall, upon conviction for a violation committed after a first conviction of the person under this subdivision, be subject to a fine of not more than two million dollars ($2,000,000). Any fines imposed pursuant to this subdivision shall be in addition to any fines imposed pursuant to subdivision (c).

(2) In determining whether a defendant who is an individual knew that the defendant's conduct placed another person in imminent danger of death or serious bodily injury, the defendant is responsible only for actual awareness or actual belief that the defendant possessed, and knowledge possessed by a person other than the defendant, but not by the defendant personally, cannot be attributed to the defendant.

(e) Any person who knowingly makes any false statement, representation, or certification in any record, report, plan, notice to comply, or other document filed with a regional board or the state board, or who knowingly falsifies, tampers with, or renders inaccurate any monitoring device or method required under this division shall be punished by a fine of not more than twenty-five thousand dollars ($25,000), by imprisonment pursuant to subdivision (h) of Section 1170 of the Penal Code for 16, 20, or 24 months, or by both that fine and imprisonment. If a conviction of a person is for a violation committed after a first conviction of the person under this subdivision, punishment shall be by a fine of not more than twenty-five thousand dollars ($25,000) per day of violation, by imprisonment pursuant to subdivision (h) of Section 1170 of the Penal Code for two, three, or four years, or by both that fine and imprisonment.

(f) For purposes of this section, a single operational upset which leads to simultaneous violations of more than one pollutant parameter shall be treated as a single violation.

(g) For purposes of this section, "organization," "serious bodily injury," "person," and "hazardous substance" shall have the same meaning as in Section 309(c) of the Clean Water Act (33 U.S.C. Sec. 1319(c)), as amended.

(h) (1) Subject to paragraph (2), funds collected pursuant to this section shall be deposited in the State Water Pollution Cleanup and Abatement Account.

(2) (A) Notwithstanding any other provision of law, fines collected for a violation of a water quality certification in accordance with paragraph (2) of subdivision (a) or for a violation of Section 401 of the Clean Water Act (33 U.S.C. Sec. 1341) in accordance with paragraph (4) of subdivision (a) shall be deposited in the Water Discharge Permit Fund and separately accounted for in that fund.

(B) The funds described in subparagraph (A) shall be expended by the state board, upon appropriation by the Legislature, to assist regional boards, and other public agencies with authority to clean up waste or abate the effects of the waste, in cleaning up or abating the effects of the waste on waters of the state, or for the purposes authorized in Section 13443.

Water Code § 13575

(Amended by Statute, Effective January 1, 1999.)

(a) This chapter shall be known and may be cited as the Water Recycling Act of 1991.

(b) As used in this chapter, the following terms have the following meanings:

(1) "Customer" means a person or entity that purchases water from a retail water supplier.

(2) "Entity responsible for groundwater replenishment" means any person or entity authorized by statute or court order to manage a groundwater basin and acquire water for groundwater replenishment.

(3) "Recycled water" has the same meaning as defined in subdivision (n) of Section 13050.

(4) "Recycled water producer" means any local public entity that produces recycled water.

(5) "Recycled water wholesaler" means any local public entity that distributes recycled water to retail water suppliers and which has constructed, or is constructing, a recycled water distribution system.

(6) "Retail water supplier" means any local entity, including a public agency, city, county, or private water company, that provides retail water service.

(7) "Retailer" means the retail water supplier in whose service area is located the property to which a customer requests the delivery of reycled water service.

Part 2: Regulations

I. Title 3. Food and Agriculture

DIVISION 8. CANNABIS CULTIVATION

Chapter 1. Cannabis Cultivation Program

ARTICLE 1. DEFINITIONS

§ 8000. Definitions.

The following definitions, in addition to those stated in section 26001 of the Business and Professions Code, apply to this chapter.

(a) "Act" means the Medicinal and Adult-Use Cannabis Regulation and Safety Act, division 10, chapter 1 (commencing with section 26000) of the Business and Professions Code.

(b) "Applicant" means an owner of the applicant entity or sole proprietor applying for a state license pursuant to this division.

(c) "Applicant entity" means the entity or sole proprietor applying for a state cannabis cultivation license.

(d) "Batch" or "harvest batch" means a specifically identified quantity of dried flower or trim, leaves, and other cannabis plant matter that is uniform in strain or cultivar, harvested in whole, or in part, at the same time, and, if applicable, cultivated using the same pesticides and other agricultural chemicals.

(e) "Bureau" means the Bureau of Cannabis Control within the Department of Consumer Affairs, formerly named the Bureau of Marijuana Control, the Bureau of Medical Cannabis Regulation, and the Bureau of Medical Marijuana Regulation.

(f) "Canopy" means the designated area(s) at a licensed premises, except nurseries and processors, that will contain mature plants at any point in time, as follows:

> (1) Canopy shall be calculated in square feet and measured using clearly identifiable boundaries of all area(s) that will contain mature plants at any point in time, including all of the space(s) within the boundaries;

> (2) Canopy may be noncontiguous but each unique area included in the total canopy calculation shall be separated by an identifiable boundary that includes, but is not limited to, interior walls, shelves, greenhouse walls, hoop house walls, garden benches, hedgerows, fencing, garden beds, or garden plots; and

(3) If mature plants are being cultivated using a shelving system, the surface area of each level shall be included in the total canopy calculation.

(g) "Commercial cannabis activity" includes the cultivation, possession, manufacture, distribution, processing, storing, laboratory testing, packaging, labeling, transportation, delivery, or sale of cannabis and cannabis products as provided for in this chapter.

(h) "Cultivation" means any activity involving the planting, growing, harvesting, drying, curing, grading, or trimming of cannabis.

(i) "Cultivation site" means a location where commercial cannabis is planted, grown, harvested, dried, cured, graded, or trimmed, or a location where any combinations of those activities occurs.

(j) "Department" means the California Department of Food and Agriculture.

(k) "Dried flower" means all dead cannabis that has been harvested, dried, cured, or otherwise processed, excluding leaves and stems.

(l) "Flowering" means that a cannabis plant has formed a mass of pistils measuring greater than one half inch wide at its widest point.

(m) "Immature plant" or "immature" means a cannabis plant that has a first true leaf measuring greater than one half inch long from base to tip (if started from seed) or a mass of roots measuring greater than one half inch wide at its widest point (if vegetatively propagated), but which is not flowering.

(n) "Indoor cultivation" means the cultivation of cannabis within a permanent structure using exclusively artificial light or within any type of structure using artificial light at a rate above twenty-five watts per square foot.

(o) "Kief" means the resinous trichomes of cannabis that have been separated from the cannabis plant.

(p) "Licensee" means any person holding a license pursuant to this chapter.

(q) "Light deprivation" means the use of any technique to eliminate natural light in order to induce flowering.

(r) "Lot" means a batch, or a specifically identified portion of a batch.

(s) "Mature plant" or "mature" means a cannabis plant that is flowering.

(t) "Mixed-light cultivation" means the cultivation of mature cannabis in a greenhouse, hoop-house, glasshouse, conservatory, hothouse, or other similar structure using a combination of:

  (1) Natural light and light deprivation and one of the artificial lighting models listed below:

    (A) "Mixed-light Tier 1" without the use of artificial light or the use of artificial light at a rate above zero, but no more than six watts per square foot;

    (B) "Mixed-light Tier 2" the use of artificial light at a rate above six and below or equal to twenty-five watts per square foot; or

  (2) Natural light and one of the artificial lighting models listed below:

    (A) "Mixed-light Tier 1" the use of artificial light at a rate above zero, but no more than six watts per square foot;

    (B) "Mixed-light Tier 2" the use of artificial light at a rate above six and below or equal to twenty-five watts per square foot.

(u) "Net weight" means the weight of harvested cannabis and cannabis products, exclusive of all materials, substances, or items not part of the commodity itself, including but not limited to containers, conveyances, bags, wrappers, packaging materials, labels, and individual piece coverings, and that meet the requirements in section 8406(b).

(v) "Nonmanufactured cannabis product" means flower, shake, leaf, pre-rolls, and kief that is obtained from accumulation in containers or sifted from loose, dry cannabis flower or leaf with a mesh screen or sieve.

(w) "Nursery" means all activities associated with producing clones, immature plants, seeds, and other agricultural products used specifically for the propagation and cultivation of cannabis.

(x) "Outdoor cultivation" means the cultivation of mature cannabis without the use of artificial lighting or light deprivation in the canopy area at any point in time. Artificial lighting is permissible only to maintain immature plants outside the canopy area.

(y) "Pest" means any of the following that is, or is liable to become, dangerous or detrimental to the agricultural or nonagricultural environment of the state:

(1) Any insect, predatory animal, rodent, nematode, or weed; and

(2) Any form of terrestrial, aquatic, or aerial plant or animal virus, fungus, bacteria, or other microorganism (except viruses, fungi, bacteria, or other microorganisms on or in living man or other living animals).

(z) "Premises" means the designated structure or structures and land specified in the application that is owned, leased, or otherwise held under the control of the applicant or licensee where the commercial cannabis activity will be or is conducted. The premises shall be a contiguous area and shall only be occupied by one licensee.

(aa) "Pre-roll" means any combination of the following rolled in paper: flower, shake, leaf, or kief that is obtained from accumulation in containers or sifted from loose, dry cannabis flower or leaf with a mesh screen or sieve.

(ab) "Process," "Processing," and "Processes" mean all activities associated with the drying, curing, grading, trimming, rolling, storing, packaging, and labeling of cannabis or nonmanufactured cannabis products.

(ac) "Track-and-trace system" means the state-approved system used to track commercial cannabis activity and movement.

(ad) "Unique identifier" or "UID" means an alphanumeric code or designation used for reference to a specific plant on a licensed premises and any cannabis or cannabis product derived or manufactured from that plant.

(ae) "Watts per square foot" means the sum of the maximum wattage of all lights identified in the designated canopy area(s) in the cultivation plan divided by the sum of the dimensions in square feet of designated canopy area(s) identified in the cultivation plan.

(af) "Wet weight" means the weight of harvested, non-dried cannabis on the licensed premises or being transported between licensees that does not meet the net weight requirements in section 8406(b).

Note: Authority cited: Sections 26012 and 26013, Business and Professions Code. Reference: Sections 26001 and 26013, Business and Professions Code; and Section 12754.5, Food and Agricultural Code.

ARTICLE 2. APPLICATIONS

§ 8100. Temporary Licenses.

(a) A temporary license is a conditional license that authorizes the licensee to engage in commercial cannabis activity as a licensee would be permitted to do under the privileges of an annual license of the same type. A temporary licensee shall follow all applicable statutes and regulations as a licensee would be required to do if the licensee held an annual license of the same type.

(b) A temporary license issued pursuant to this chapter shall be valid for one-hundred twenty (120) calendar days from the effective date. No temporary license shall be effective prior to January 1, 2018.

(c) A temporary license may be extended for additional ninety (90) calendar day periods if a complete application for licensure has been submitted to the department pursuant to section 8102 of this chapter.

(d) A temporary license does not obligate the department to issue an annual license nor does the temporary license create a vested right in the holder to either an extension of the temporary license or to the granting of a subsequent annual license.

(e) The Department shall not issue any temporary licenses or extensions of temporary licenses after December 31, 2018. Any temporary licenses issued or extended with an expiration date after December 31, 2018 will be valid until it expires, but shall not be extended beyond the expiration date.

Note: Authority cited: Sections 26012 and 26013, Business and Professions Code. Reference: Sections 26013, 26050.1 and 26055, Business and Professions Code.

§ 8101. Annual License Application Fees.

The following are nonrefundable application fees for the specified annual license type and shall be paid by the applicant at the time the complete application is submitted to the department:

(a) Specialty Cottage Outdoor	$135
(b) Specialty Cottage Indoor	$205
(c) Specialty Cottage Mixed-Light Tier 1	$340
(d) Specialty Cottage Mixed-Light Tier 2	$580
(e) Specialty Outdoor	$270
(f) Specialty Indoor	$2,170
(g) Specialty Mixed-Light Tier 1	$655
(h) Specialty Mixed-Light Tier 2	$1,125
(i) Small Outdoor	$535
(j) Small Indoor	$3,935
(k) Small Mixed-Light Tier 1	$1,310
(l) Small Mixed-Light Tier 2	$2,250
(m) Medium Outdoor	$1,555
(n) Medium Indoor	$8,655
(o) Medium Mixed-Light Tier 1	$2,885
(p) Medium Mixed-Light Tier 2	$4,945
(q) Nursery	$520
(r) Processor	$1,040

Note: Authority cited: Sections 26012 and 26013, Business and Professions Code. Reference: Sections 26012, 26013, 26050, 26061 and 26180, Business and Professions Code.

§ 8102. Annual License Application Requirements.

Applications for a cultivation license shall be completed and submitted online at calcannabis.cdfa.ca.gov or by mailing a hard copy of the application to the department at P.O. Box 942872, Sacramento, CA 94271-2872. Application fees, pursuant to section 8101 of this chapter, shall accompany the applications submitted online at calcannabis.cdfa.ca.gov or by mail to the department at P.O. Box 942872, Sacramento, CA 94271-2872. Each application shall include the following, if applicable:

(a) The legal business name of the applicant entity and the business entity structure, including but not limited to a corporation, general partnership, joint venture, limited liability company, limited liability partnership, limited partnership, sovereign entity, sole proprietorship, or trust;

(b) The license type, pursuant to section 8201 of this chapter, for which the applicant is applying and whether the application is for an M-license or A-license;

(c) A list of all valid commercial cannabis license types the applicant entity holds and the associated license numbers from the department and other cannabis licensing authorities;

(d) The physical address of the premises;

(e) The mailing address of the applicant entity;

(f) The hours of operation for each day of the week the applicant entity will have staff on the licensed premises. The applicant must provide a minimum of two (2) hours of operation that are between 8:00am and 5:00pm (Pacific Time) on each day, Monday through Friday;

(g) A designated responsible party, who shall also be an owner, with legal authority to bind the applicant entity, and the primary contact for the application. The following information shall be provided for the designated responsible party: full legal name, title, mailing address, primary contact phone number, email address, preferred method of contact (either standard mail or email), and a copy of the owner's government-issued identification. Acceptable forms of identification are a document issued by a federal, state, county, or municipal government, including, but not limited to, a driver's license, that contains the name, date of birth, physical description, and picture of the individual;

(h) An individual or entity serving as agent for service of process for the applicant. The following information shall be provided for the agent for service of process: full legal name, mailing address, primary contact phone number, email address, and preferred method of contact (either standard mail or email);

(i) A complete list of every owner of the applicant entity pursuant to section 8103 of this chapter. Each individual owner named shall submit the following information:

　　(1) Full legal name;

　　(2) Title within the applicant entity;

　　(3) Date of birth;

　　(4) Social security number or individual taxpayer identification number;

　　(5) Home address;

　　(6) Primary phone number;

　　(7) Email address;

　　(8) Preferred method of contact (either standard mail or email);

　　(9) Date ownership interest in the applicant entity was acquired;

　　(10) Percentage of the ownership interest held in the applicant entity by the owner;

　　(11) A list of all the valid licenses, including license type(s) and license number(s), from the department and other cannabis licensing authorities that the owner is listed as either an owner or financial interest holder;

　　(12) A copy of the owner's government-issued identification. Acceptable forms of identification are a document issued by a federal, state, county, or municipal government, including but not limited to, a driver's license, that contains the name, date of birth, physical description, and picture of the individual;

(13) If applicable, a detailed description of any criminal conviction. A conviction within the meaning of this section means a plea or verdict of guilty or a conviction following a plea of nolo contendere. Convictions dismissed under sections 1203.4, 1203.4a and 1203.41 of the Penal Code or equivalent non-California law shall be disclosed. Juvenile adjudications and traffic infractions do not need to be included. For each conviction, all of the following shall be provided:

(A) The date of conviction;

(B) Date(s) of incarceration, if applicable;

(C) Date(s) of probation, if applicable;

(D) Date(s) of parole, if applicable;

(E) A detailed description of the offense for which the owner was convicted; and

(F) A statement of rehabilitation for each conviction. The statement of rehabilitation is to be written by the owner and may contain evidence that the owner would like the department to consider that demonstrates the owner's fitness for licensure. Supporting evidence may be attached to the statement of rehabilitation and may include, but is not limited to, a certificate of rehabilitation under section 4852.01 of the Penal Code, and dated letters of reference from employers, instructors, or professional counselors that contain valid contact information for the individual providing the reference.

(14) A copy of the owner's completed application for electronic fingerprint images submitted to the Department of Justice;

(15) If applicable, a detailed description of any administrative orders or civil judgements for violations of labor standards, any suspension of a commercial cannabis license, revocation of a commercial cannabis license, or sanctions for unlicensed commercial cannabis activity by a licensing authority, local agency, or state agency against the applicant or a business entity in which the applicant was an owner or officer within three years immediately preceding the date of the application.

(j) A complete list of financial interest holders pursuant to section 8103 of this chapter, including the following information for:

(1) Individuals: full legal name, tax identification number (social security number, individual taxpayer identification number, or national identification number), and government identification number and type of government identification; and

(2) Business entities: legal business name and employer identification number.

(k) Copies of all formation documents, which may include, but are not limited to, articles of incorporation, operating agreement, partnership agreement, and fictitious business name statement. The applicant shall also provide all documents filed with the California Secretary of State, which may include but are not limited to, articles of incorporation, certificate of stock, articles of organization, certificate of limited partnership, and statement of partnership authority. If an applicant is a foreign corporation, a certificate of qualification issued by the California Secretary of State;

(l) A valid seller's permit number issued by the California Department of Tax and Fee Administration or confirmation from the California Department of Tax and Fee Administration that a seller's permit is not needed. If the applicant entity has not yet received a seller's permit, the applicant entity shall attest that it is currently applying for a seller's permit;

(m) For applicants that are a cannabis cooperative as defined by division 10, chapter 22 (commencing with section 26220) of the Business and Professions Code, identification of all members. Identifying information shall include each member's license number for commercial cannabis activity, the licensing authority that issued the license, and the name of the licensed business;

(n) Evidence that the applicant entity has the legal right to occupy and use the proposed location pursuant to section 8104 of this chapter;

(o) Evidence of having obtained a surety bond in the amount of not less than $5,000, payable to the department in a form prescribed by the department pursuant to Title 11 of the California Code of Regulations section 26.20. The bond shall be issued by a corporate surety licensed to transact surety business in the State of California;

(p) For all cultivator license types except Processor, evidence of enrollment in an order or waiver of waste discharge requirements with the State Water Resources Control Board or the appropriate Regional Water Quality Control Board. Acceptable documentation for evidence of enrollment can be a Notice of Applicability letter. Acceptable documentation for a Processor that enrollment is not necessary can be a Notice of Non-Applicability;

(q) Evidence that the applicant has conducted a hazardous materials record search of the EnviroStor database for the proposed premises. If hazardous sites were encountered, the applicant shall provide documentation of protocols implemented to protect employee health and safety;

(r) Evidence of exemption from, or compliance with, division 13 (commencing with section 21000) of the Public Resources Code, California Environmental Quality Act (CEQA). The evidence provided shall be one of the following:

(1) A signed copy of a project specific Notice of Determination or Notice of Exemption and a copy of the associated CEQA document, or reference to where it may be located electronically, a project description, and/ or any accompanying permitting documentation from the local jurisdiction used for review in determining site specific environmental compliance;

(2) If an applicant does not have the evidence specified in subsection (1), or if the local jurisdiction did not prepare a CEQA document, the applicant will be responsible for the preparation of an environmental document in compliance with CEQA that can be approved or certified by the department, unless the department specifies otherwise.

(s) For indoor and mixed-light license types, identification of all power sources for cultivation activities, including but not limited to, illumination, heating, cooling, and ventilation;

(t) A property diagram pursuant to section 8105 of this chapter;

(u) A proposed cultivation plan pursuant to section 8106 of this chapter;

(v) Identification of all of the following applicable water sources used for cultivation activities and the applicable supplemental information for each source pursuant to section 8107 of this chapter:

(1) A retail water supplier;

(2) A groundwater well;

(3) A rainwater catchment system;

(4) A diversion from a surface waterbody or an underground stream flowing in a known and definite channel.

(w) A copy of any final lake or streambed alteration agreement issued by the California Department of Fish and Wildlife, pursuant to sections 1602 or 1617 of the Fish and Game Code, or written verification from the California Department of Fish and Wildlife that a lake and streambed alteration agreement is not required;

(x) An attestation that the proposed location is at least a six-hundred (600) foot radius from a school providing instruction in kindergarten or any grades one (1) through twelve (12), or a day care center or youth center as defined in section 26001 of the Business and Professions Code, that is in existence at the time the application is submitted, or that the premises complies with a local ordinance specifying a different radius. The distance shall be measured in the same manner as provided in subsection (c) of section 11362.768 of the Health and Safety Code unless otherwise provided by law;

(y) An attestation that the applicant entity will enter into, or has already entered into, and will abide by the terms of a labor peace agreement if the applicant entity will have twenty (20) or more employees on payroll at any time during the licensed period. The applicant shall submit a copy of the page of the labor peace agreement that contains the signatures of the union representative and the applicant. For applicants who have not yet entered into a labor peace agreement, the applicant shall provide a copy of the page of the labor peace agreement that contains the signatures of the union representative and the licensee as soon as reasonably practicable after licensure;

(z) An attestation that the applicant entity is an "agricultural employer" as defined by the Alatorre-Zenovich-Dunlap-Berman Agricultural Labor Relations Act of 1975; division 2, part 3.5 (commencing with section 1140) of the Labor Code;

(aa) An attestation that the local fire department has been notified of the cultivation site if the application is for an indoor license type;

(bb) For an applicant entity with more than one employee, the applicant entity shall attest that the applicant employs, or will employ within one year of receiving a license, one supervisor and one employee who have successfully completed a Cal-OSHA 30-hour general industry outreach course offered by a training provider that is authorized by an OSHA Training Institute Education Center to provide the course;

(cc) Any applicant that may fall within the scope of sovereign immunity that may be asserted by a federally recognizable tribe or other sovereign entity shall waive any sovereign immunity defense that the applicant may have, may be asserted on its behalf, or may otherwise be asserted in any state or local administrative or judicial enforcement actions against the applicant or licensee, regardless of the form of relief sought, whether monetary or otherwise, under the state laws and regulations governing commercial cannabis activity, and shall provide documentation as may be requested by the department that establishes that the applicant has the lawful authority to enter into the waiver described above and has effectively done so. The limited waiver of sovereign immunity shall meet the requirements of the following:

   (1) The written limited waiver shall include that the applicant or licensee has the lawful authority to enter into the waiver required by this section, the applicant or licensee hereby waives sovereign immunity, and the applicant or licensee agrees to do all of the following:

      (A) Provide documentation to the department that establishes that the applicant or licensee has the lawful authority to enter into the waiver required by this section;

      (B) Conduct all commercial cannabis activity in full compliance with the state laws and regulations governing commercial cannabis activity, including submission to all enforcement provisions thereof;

      (C) Allow access as required by statute or regulation by persons or entities charged with duties under the state laws and regulations governing commercial cannabis activity to any premises or property at which the applicant conducts any commercial cannabis activity, including premises or property where records of commercial cannabis activity are maintained by or for the applicant or licensee;

      (D) Provide any and all records, reports, and other documents as may be required under the state laws and regulations governing commercial cannabis activity;

      (E) Conduct commercial cannabis activity with other state commercial cannabis licensees only, unless otherwise specified by state law;

      (F) Meet all of the requirements for licensure under state laws and regulations governing the conduct of commercial cannabis activity, and provide truthful and accurate documentation and other information of the applicant's qualifications and suitability for licensure as may be requested by the department;

(G) Submit to the personal and subject matter jurisdiction of the California courts to address any matter related to the waiver or commercial cannabis application, license, or activity, and that all such matters and proceedings shall be governed, construed and enforced in accordance with California substantive and procedural law, including but not limited to the Act;

    (2) Any applicant or licensee shall immediately notify the department of any changes that may materially affect the applicant and licensee's compliance with subsection (1).

    (3) Any failure by an applicant or licensee to comply with the requirements of subsections (1) and (2) shall be a basis for denial of an application or renewal or discipline of a licensee.

(dd) If applicable, the applicant shall provide evidence that the proposed premises is not located in whole or in part in a watershed or other geographic area that the State Water Resources Control Board or the Department of Fish and Wildlife has determined to be significantly adversely impacted by cannabis cultivation pursuant to section 8216.

(ee) The department shall not approve an application for a state license if approval of the license would violate the provisions of any local ordinance or regulation adopted in accordance with section 26200 of the Business and Professions Code by a county or, if within a city, a city, within which the licensed premises is to be located.

Note: Authority cited: Sections 26012 and 26013, Business and Professions Code. Reference: Sections 26013, 26051.5, 26054, 26055, 26057, 26060, 26060.1, 26066 and 26069, Business and Professions Code.

§ 8103. Owner and Financial Interest Holders.

(a) "Owner" means any of the following:

    (1) A person with an aggregate ownership interest of twenty (20) percent or more in the person applying for a license or a licensee, unless the interest is solely a security, lien, or encumbrance;

    (2) The chief executive officer of a nonprofit or other entity;

    (3) A member of the board of directors of a nonprofit;

    (4) An individual who will be participating in the direction, control, or management of the person applying for a license.

(b) An owner who is an individual participating in the direction, control, or management of the commercial cannabis business includes any of the following:

    (1) A partner of a commercial cannabis business that is organized as a partnership;

    (2) A managing member of a commercial cannabis business that is organized as a limited liability company;

    (3) An officer or director of a commercial cannabis business that is organized as a corporation.

(c) All individuals and business entities that have a financial interest in a commercial cannabis business but are not owners as defined in subsections (a) or (b) of this section shall be listed on an application for licensure under section 8102(j) of this chapter. "Financial interest" means an investment into a commercial cannabis business, a loan provided to a commercial cannabis business, or any other fully-vested equity interest in a commercial cannabis business.

(d) Notwithstanding subsections (a), (b), or (c), the following are not considered to be owners or financial interest holders:

    (1) A bank or financial institution whose interest constitutes a loan;

    (2) Persons whose only financial interest in the commercial cannabis business is through an interest in a diversified mutual fund, blind trust, or similar instrument;

    (3) Persons whose only financial interest is a security, lien, or encumbrance on property that will be used by the

commercial cannabis business; and

(4) Persons who hold a share of stock that is less than five (5) percent of the total shares in a publicly traded company.

Note: Authority cited: Sections 26012 and 26013, Business and Professions Code. Reference: Sections 26001, 26013 and 26051.5, Business and Professions Code.

§ 8104. Legal Right to Occupy.

(a) If the applicant is the owner of the property on which the premises is located, the applicant shall provide to the department a copy of the title or deed to the property.

(b) If the applicant is not the owner of the property upon which the premises is located, the applicant shall provide the following to the department:

(1) A document from the property owner or property owner's agent where the commercial cannabis activity will occur that states the applicant has the right to occupy the property and acknowledges that the applicant may use the property for commercial cannabis cultivation;

(2) The property owner's mailing address and phone number; and

(3) A copy of the lease or rental agreement, or other contractual documentation.

Note: Authority cited: Sections 26012 and 26013, Business and Professions Code. Reference: Sections 26013 and 26051.5, Business and Professions Code.

§ 8105. Property Diagram.

A property diagram shall be submitted with each application and shall contain the following:

(a) Boundaries of the property and the proposed premises wherein the license privileges will be exercised with sufficient detail to enable ready determination of the bounds of the premises showing all perimeter dimensions, entrances, and exits to both the property and premises;

(b) If the proposed premises consists of only a portion of a property, the diagram shall be labeled indicating which part of the property is the proposed premises and for what purpose the remaining property is used, including any areas shared with other licenses;

(c) All roads and water crossings on the property;

(d) All water sources identified and labeled for beneficial use type, including but not limited to, irrigation, domestic, fire protection, power, fish and wildlife preservation and enhancement, and/or recreation;

(e) If the applicant is proposing to use a diversion from a waterbody or an underground stream flowing in a known and definite channel, groundwater well, or rain catchment system as a water source for cultivation, include the following locations on the property diagram with locations also provided as coordinates in either latitude and longitude or the California Coordinate System:

(1) Sources of water used, including the location of waterbody diversion(s), pump location(s), and distribution system; and

(2) Location, type, and capacity of each storage unit to be used for cultivation.

(f) The assessor's parcel number(s);

(g) The diagram shall be to scale; and

(h) The diagram shall not contain any highlighting.

Note: Authority cited: Sections 26012 and 26013, Business and Professions Code. Reference: Sections 26012, 26013, 26051.5 and 26060.1, Business and Professions Code.

§ 8106. Cultivation Plan Requirements.

(a) The cultivation plan for each Specialty Cottage, Specialty, Small, and Medium licenses shall include all of the following:

(1) A detailed premises diagram showing all boundaries and dimensions in feet of the following proposed areas to scale:

(A) Canopy area(s), including aggregate square footage if the canopy areas are noncontiguous. All unique areas separated by identifiable boundaries pursuant to section 8000(f) shall be clearly described and labeled in the premises diagram;

(B) Area(s) outside of the canopy where only immature plants shall be maintained, if applicable. This area may not be shared among multiple licenses held by one licensee;

(C) Designated pesticide and other agricultural chemical storage area(s);

(D) Designated processing area(s) if the licensee will process on site. This area may not be shared among multiple licenses held by one licensee;

(E) Designated packaging area(s) if the licensee will package products on site. This area may not be shared among multiple licenses held by one licensee;

(F) Designated composting area(s) if the licensee will compost cannabis waste on site;

(G) Designated secured area(s) for cannabis waste if different from subsection (F) above;

(H) Designated area(s) for harvested cannabis storage;

(I) Designated area(s) for physically segregating cannabis or nonmanufactured cannabis products subject to an administrative hold pursuant to section 8604 of this chapter. This area may not be shared among multiple licenses held by one licensee;

(J) Designated area(s) that are shared between licenses held by one licensee. The shared area(s) must be contiguous, be indicated on the property diagram for each application, and be one or more of the following designated area(s) shared between licenses held by one licensee: pesticide and other agricultural chemical storage area(s), composting area(s), and secured area(s) for cannabis waste;

(K) Common use area(s), such as hallways, bathrooms, or break rooms. This area may be shared by multiple licensees.

(2) For indoor and mixed-light license type applications, a lighting diagram with the following information shall be included:

(A) Location of all lights in the canopy area(s); and

(B) Maximum wattage, or wattage equivalent, of each light.

(3) A pest management plan which shall include, but not be limited to, the following:

(A) Product name and active ingredient(s) of all pesticides to be applied to cannabis during any stage of plant growth;

(B) Integrated pest management protocols, including chemical, biological, and cultural methods the applicant anticipates using to control or prevent the introduction of pests on the cultivation site; and

(C) A signed attestation that states the applicant shall contact the appropriate County Agricultural Commissioner regarding requirements for legal use of pesticides on cannabis prior to using any of the active ingredients or products included in the pest management plan and shall comply with all pesticide laws.

(4) A cannabis waste management plan meeting the requirements of section 8108 of this chapter.

(b) The cultivation plan for nursery licenses shall include the following information:

(1) A detailed premises diagram showing all boundaries and dimensions, in feet, of the following proposed areas to scale:

(A) Designated pesticide and other agricultural chemical storage area(s);

(B) Designated composting area(s) if the licensee will compost cannabis waste on site;

(C) Designated secured area(s) for cannabis waste if different from subsection (B) above;

(D) At least one of the following areas:

1. Area(s) which shall contain only immature plants;

2. Designated seed production area(s) that may contain mature plants.

(E) Designated research and development area(s) that may contain mature plants, if the licensee will be conducting research and development activities that require a plant to flower.

(2) A pest management plan that shall include, but not be limited to, the following:

(A) Product name and active ingredient(s) of all pesticides to be applied to cannabis at any time;

(B) Integrated pest management protocols, including chemical, biological, and cultural methods the applicant anticipates using to control or prevent the introduction of pests on the cultivation site; and

(C) A signed attestation that states the applicant shall contact the appropriate County Agricultural Commissioner regarding requirements for legal use of pesticides on cannabis prior to using any of the active ingredients or products included in the pest management plan and shall comply with all pesticide laws.

(3) A cannabis waste management plan pursuant to section 8108 of this chapter.

(c) The cultivation plan for processor licenses shall include a detailed premises diagram showing all boundaries and dimensions, in feet, of the following proposed areas:

(1) Designated processing area(s);

(2) Designated packaging area(s), if the licensee will package and label products on site;

(3) Designated composting area(s) if the licensee will compost cannabis waste on site;

(4) Designated secured area(s) for cannabis waste if different from subsection (3) above;

(5) Designated area(s) for harvested cannabis storage;

(6) A cannabis waste management plan pursuant to section 8108 of this chapter.

Note: Authority cited: Sections 26012 and 26013, Business and Professions Code. Reference: Sections 26012, 26013, 26051.5, 26060 and 26060.1, Business and Professions Code.

§ 8107. Supplemental Water Source Information.

The following information shall be provided for each water source identified by the applicant:

(a) Retail water supply sources:

(1) If the water source is a retail water supplier, as defined in section 13575 of the Water Code, such as a municipal provider, provide the following:

(A) Name of the retail water supplier; and

(B) A copy of the most recent water service bill.

(2) If the water source is a small retail water supplier, such as a delivery service, and is subject to subsection (a)(1)(B) of section 26060.1 of the Business and Professions Code and either:

(A) The retail water supplier contract is for delivery or pickup of water from a surface water body or an underground stream flowing in a known and definite channel, provide all of the following:

1. The name of the retail water supplier under the contract;

2. The water source and geographic location coordinates in either latitude and longitude or the California Coordinate System of any point of diversion used by the retail water supplier to divert water delivered to the applicant under the contract;

3. The authorized place of use of any water right used by the retail water supplier to divert water delivered to the applicant under the contract;

4. The maximum amount of water delivered to the applicant for cannabis cultivation in any year; and

5. A copy of the most recent water service bill; or

(B) The retail water supplier contract is for delivery or pickup of water from a groundwater well, provide all of the following:

1. The name of the retail water supplier under the contract;

2. The geographic location coordinates for any groundwater well used to supply water delivered to the applicant, in either latitude and longitude or the California Coordinate System;

3. The maximum amount of water delivered to the applicant for cannabis cultivation in any year;

4. A copy of the well completion report filed with the Department of Water Resources pursuant to section 13751 of the Water Code for each percolating groundwater well used to divert water delivered to the applicant. If no well completion report is available, the applicant shall provide evidence from the Department of Water Resources indicating that the Department does not have a record of the well completion report. When no well completion report is available, the State Water Resources Control Board may request additional information about the well; and

5. A copy of the most recent water service bill.

(b) If the water source is a groundwater well:

(1) The groundwater well's geographic location coordinates in either latitude and longitude or the California Coordinate System; and

(2) A copy of the well completion report filed with the Department of Water Resources pursuant to section 13751 of the Water Code. If no well completion report is available, the applicant shall provide evidence from the Department of Water Resources indicating that the Department of Water Resources does not have a record of the well completion report. If no well completion report is available, the State Water Resources Control Board may request additional information about the well.

(c) If the water source is a rainwater catchment system:

(1) The total square footage of the catchment footprint area(s);

(2) The total storage capacity, in gallons, of the catchment system(s); and

(3) A detailed description and photographs of the rainwater catchment system infrastructure, including the location, size, and type of all surface areas that collect rainwater. Examples of rainwater collection surface areas include a rooftop and greenhouse.

(d) If the water source is a diversion from a waterbody (such as a river, stream, creek, pond, lake, etc.), provide any applicable water right statement, application, permit, license, or small irrigation use registration identification number(s), and either:

(1) A copy of any applicable statement, registration certificate, permits, licenses, or proof of a pending application issued under part 2 (commencing with section 1200) of division 2 of the California Water Code as evidence of approval of a water diversion by the State Water Resources Control Board;

(2) If the applicant has claimed an exception from the requirement to file a statement of diversion and use pursuant to section 5101 of the Water Code, the applicant shall provide a copy of the documentation submitted to the State Water Resources Control Board before January 1, 2019 demonstrating that the diversion is subject to subsection (a), (c), (d), or (e) of section 5101 of the Water Code.

Note: Authority cited: Sections 26012 and 26013, Business and Professions Code. Reference: Sections 26013 and 26060.1, Business and Professions Code.

§ 8108. Cannabis Waste Management Plan.

For the purposes of this section, "cannabis waste" is organic waste, as defined in section 42649.8(c) of the Public Resources Code. An applicant's cannabis waste management plan shall identify one or more of the following methods for managing cannabis waste generated on its licensed premises:

(a) On-premises composting of cannabis waste;

(b) Collection and processing of cannabis waste by a local agency, a waste hauler franchised or contracted by a local agency, or a private waste hauler permitted by a local agency;

(c) Self-haul cannabis waste to one or more of the following:

(1) A manned, fully permitted solid waste landfill or transformation facility;

(2) A manned, fully permitted composting facility or manned composting operation;

(3) A manned, fully permitted in-vessel digestion operation;

(4) A manned, fully permitted transfer/processing facility or manned transfer/processing operation; or

(5) A manned, fully permitted chip and grind operation or facility.

(6) A recycling center as defined in title 14, section 17402.5(d) of the California Code of Regulations and that meets the following:

(A) The cannabis waste received shall contain at least ninety (90) percent inorganic material;

(B) The inorganic portion of the cannabis waste is recycled into new, reused, or reconstituted products which meet the quality standards necessary to be used in the marketplace; and

(C) The organic portion of the cannabis waste shall be sent to a facility or operation identified in subsection (c)(1) through (5).

(d) Reintroduction of cannabis waste back into agricultural operation through on premises organic waste recycling methods, including but not limited to tilling directly into agricultural land and no-till farming.

Note: Authority cited: Sections 26012 and 26013, Business and Professions Code. Reference: Sections 26013 and 26066, Business and Professions Code.

§ 8109. Applicant Track-and-Trace Training Requirement.

(a) For the purpose of this section, the applicant shall designate an owner to be the licensee's track-and-trace system account manager pursuant to section 8402(c) of this chapter. The designated account manager shall register for track-and-trace system training provided by the department within ten (10) calendar days of receiving notice from the department that its application for licensure has been received and is complete.

(b) Applicants approved for an annual license shall not have access to the track-and-trace system until the designated account manager has completed the track-and-trace training prescribed by the department and proof of completion has been validated by the department.

Note: Authority cited: Sections 26012 and 26013, Business and Professions Code. Reference: Sections 26013 and 26067, Business and Professions Code.

§ 8110. Proof of Local License, Permit, or Other Authorization.

When the applicant provides a license, permit, or other authorization from the local jurisdiction where the licensed premises will be or is located, pursuant to section 26055(e) of the Business and Professions Code, the department will notify the local jurisdiction's contact person identified pursuant to section 26055(f) of the Business and Professions Code. If the local jurisdiction does not respond to the department's notification within ten (10) calendar days, the department may issue a license to the applicant.

Note: Authority cited: Sections 26012 and 26013, Business and Professions Code. Reference: Sections 26013 and 26055, Business and Professions Code.

§ 8111. Priority Application Review.

(a) Priority review of annual license applications shall be given to applicants that can demonstrate the applicant entity was in operation under the Compassionate Use Act of 1996 before September 1, 2016.

(b) Eligibility for priority application review shall be demonstrated by any of the following, dated prior to September 1, 2016:

(1) Local license, permit, or other authorization;

(2) Collective or cooperative membership agreement;

(3) Tax or business forms submitted to the California Department of Tax and Fee Administration or Franchise Tax Board;

(4) Incorporation documents filed with the Secretary of State;

(5) Any other verifiable business record adequate to demonstrate the operation of the business prior to September 1, 2016; or

(6) Any applicant identified by the local jurisdiction pursuant to section 26054.2(b) of the Business and Professions Code.

(c) The department may request additional documentation to verify the applicant's date of commencement of operations.

(d) This section shall cease to be operative on December 31, 2019, unless otherwise provided by law.

Note: Authority cited: Sections 26012 and 26013, Business and Professions Code. Reference: Sections 26013 and 26054.2, Business and Professions Code.

§ 8112. Annual License Application Review for Completeness.

The department shall notify the applicant in writing that the application is either:

(a) Complete and accepted for further review; or

(b) Incomplete and the reasons for the incompleteness.

(1) The department shall receive the missing information or fee, payment, or penalty from the applicant no later than ninety (90) calendar days from the date of the notification from the department. Failure to provide the designated missing information or any fees, payments, or penalties that are due and payable will result in disqualification of the application from further consideration.

(2) If disqualified, the applicant may reapply and pay a new application fee.

Note: Authority cited: Sections 26012 and 26013, Business and Professions Code. Reference: Sections 26012 and 26013, Business and Professions Code.

§ 8113. Substantially Related Offenses Review.

(a) The following convictions shall be considered substantially related to the qualifications, functions, or duties of the business for which the application is made and may be a basis for denying the license:

(1) A violent felony conviction, as specified in subsection (c) of section 667.5 of the Penal Code;

(2) A serious felony conviction, as specified in subsection (c) of section 1192.7 of the Penal Code;

(3) A felony conviction involving fraud, deceit, or embezzlement;

(4) Any felony conviction involving the hiring, employment, or use of children in transporting, carrying, selling, giving away, preparing for sale, or peddling any controlled substance to a minor, or offering, furnishing, or

selling any controlled substance to a minor; and

(5) A felony conviction for drug trafficking with enhancements pursuant to sections 11370.4 or 11379.8 of the Health and Safety Code.

(b) Except as provided in subsections (a)(4) and (5) and notwithstanding chapter 2 (commencing with section 480) of division 1.5 of the Business and Professions Code, a prior conviction, where the sentence, including any term or probation, incarceration, or supervised release, is completed for possession of, possession for sale, sale, manufacture, transportation, or cultivation of a controlled substance is not considered substantially related, and shall not be the sole ground of denial for a license. Conviction for any controlled substance felony subsequent to licensure shall be grounds for revocation of a license or denial of the renewal of the license.

(c) To determine whether an applicant who has been convicted of a criminal offense that is substantially related to the qualifications, functions, or duties of the business for which the application is made should be issued a license, the department shall conduct a review of the nature of the crime, conviction, circumstances, and evidence of rehabilitation. Evidence of rehabilitation includes:

(1) The nature and severity of the criminal offense;

(2) Whether the person has a felony conviction based on possession or use of cannabis or cannabis products that would not be a felony if the person were convicted of the offense on the date of the person's application;

(3) The applicant's criminal record as a whole;

(4) Evidence of any conviction of a criminal offense committed subsequent to the criminal offense under consideration that could be considered grounds for denial, suspension, or revocation of a commercial cannabis activity license;

(5) The time that has elapsed since commission of the act or offense;

(6) The extent to which the applicant has complied with any terms of parole, probation, restitution, or any other sanctions lawfully imposed against the applicant;

(7) If applicable, evidence of dismissal under sections 1203.4, 1203.4a, and 1203.41 of the Penal Code or another state's similar law;

(8) If applicable, a certificate of rehabilitation obtained under section 4852.01 of the Penal Code or another state's similar law; and

(9) Other evidence of rehabilitation submitted by the applicant.

(d) If an applicant has been denied a license based on a substantially related conviction, the applicant may request a hearing pursuant to section 26058 of the Business and Professions Code to determine if the applicant should be issued a license.

Note: Authority cited: Sections 26012 and 26013, Business and Professions Code. Reference: Sections 26013, 26057 and 26058, Business and Professions Code.

§ 8114. Withdrawal of Application.

An applicant may withdraw an application at any time prior to the department's issuance of a license or denial of a license.

(a) Requests to withdraw an application shall be submitted to the department in writing, dated, and signed by the designated responsible party.

(b) The department will not refund application fees for a withdrawn application.

(c) An applicant may reapply and pay a new application fee at any time following the withdrawal of an application.

Note: Authority cited: Sections 26012 and 26013, Business and Professions Code. Reference: Section 26013, Business and Professions Code.

§ 8115. Notification and Grounds for Denial of License; Petition for Reconsideration.

(a) The department shall notify the applicant in writing if the application is denied with the reasons for denial.

(b) In addition to the reasons for denial in section 26057 of the Business and Professions Code, a license may be denied for the following reasons:

(1) The applicant's premises does not fully comply with standards pursuant to this chapter;

(2) The applicant denied the department access to the premises to verify compliance with this chapter;

(3) The applicant made a material misrepresentation on the application; or

(4) The licensee had a license, permit, or other authorization to engage in commercial cannabis activity denied, suspended, or revoked by a state licensing authority or local agency.

(c) Within thirty (30) calendar days upon service of the denial of an application, the applicant may file a written petition for reconsideration. Upon receipt of a timely filed petition for reconsideration, the department shall set a date for a hearing to be conducted pursuant to chapter 5 (commencing with section 11500) of part 1 of division 3 of title 2 of the Government Code.

Note: Authority cited: Sections 26012 and 26013, Business and Professions Code. Reference: Sections 26012, 26013, 26057 and 26058, Business and Professions Code.

ARTICLE 3. CULTIVATION LICENSE FEES AND REQUIREMENTS

§ 8200. Annual License Fees.

An annual license fee shall be paid to the department prior to issuance of a license or renewal license. The fee schedule is as follows:

(a) Specialty Cottage Outdoor	$1,205
(b) Specialty Cottage Indoor	$1,830
(c) Specialty Cottage Mixed-Light Tier 1	$3,035
(d) Specialty Cottage Mixed-Light Tier 2	$5,200
(e) Specialty Outdoor	$2,410
(f) Specialty Indoor	$19,540
(g) Specialty Mixed-Light Tier 1	$5,900
(h) Specialty Mixed-Light Tier 2	$10,120

(i)   Small Outdoor $4,820

(j)   Small Indoor $35,410

(k)   Small Mixed-Light Tier 1 $11,800

(l)   Small Mixed-Light Tier 2 $20,235

(m) Medium Outdoor $13,990

(n) Medium Indoor $77,905

(o) Medium Mixed-Light Tier 1 $25,970

(p) Medium Mixed-Light Tier 2 $44,517

(q) Nursery $4,685

(r) Processor $9,370

Note: Authority cited: Sections 26012 and 26013, Business and Professions Code. Reference: Sections 26012, 26013, 26050, 26051 and 26180, Business and Professions Code.

§ 8201. Cultivation License Types.

License types include:

(a) Specialty Cottage:

>   (1) "Specialty Cottage Outdoor" is an outdoor cultivation site with up to 25 mature plants.

>   (2) "Specialty Cottage Indoor" is an indoor cultivation site with 500 square feet or less of total canopy.

>   (3) "Specialty Cottage Mixed-Light Tier 1 and 2" is a mixed-light cultivation site with 2,500 square feet or less of total canopy.

(b) Specialty:

>   (1) "Specialty Outdoor" is an outdoor cultivation site with less than or equal to 5,000 square feet of total canopy, or up to 50 mature plants on noncontiguous plots.

>   (2) "Specialty Indoor" is an indoor cultivation site between 501 and 5,000 square feet of total canopy.

>   (3) "Specialty Mixed-Light Tier 1 and 2" is a mixed-light cultivation site between 2,501 and 5,000 square feet of total canopy.

(c) Small:

>   (1) "Small Outdoor" is an outdoor cultivation site between 5,001 and 10,000 square feet of total canopy.

>   (2) "Small Indoor" is an indoor cultivation site between 5,001 and 10,000 square feet of total canopy.

>   (3) "Small Mixed-Light Tier 1 and 2" is a mixed-light cultivation site between 5,001 and 10,000 square feet of total canopy.

(d) Medium:

>   (1) "Medium Outdoor" is an outdoor cultivation site between 10,001 square feet and one acre of total canopy.

(2) "Medium Indoor" is an indoor cultivation site between 10,001 and 22,000 square feet of total canopy.

(3) "Medium Mixed-Light Tier 1 and 2" is a mixed-light cultivation site between 10,001 and 22,000 square feet of total canopy.

(e) "Nursery" is a cultivation site that conducts only cultivation of clones, immature plants, seeds, and other agricultural products used specifically for the propagation of cultivation of cannabis.

(f) "Processor" is a cultivation site that conducts only trimming, drying, curing, grading, packaging, or labeling of cannabis and nonmanufactured cannabis products.

Note: Authority cited: Sections 26012 and 26013, Business and Professions Code. Reference: Sections 26012, 26013, 26050 and 26061, Business and Professions Code.

§ 8202. General License Requirements.

(a) Cultivation licenses shall be valid for twelve (12) months from the date of issuance.

(b) Every person shall obtain a separate license for each premises where the person engages in commercial cannabis cultivation.

(c) Cultivation licenses are not transferrable or assignable to any other person or property.

(d) Licensees are prohibited from transferring any commercially cultivated cannabis or nonmanufactured cannabis products from their licensed premises. All transfers of cannabis and nonmanufactured cannabis product from a licensed cultivation premises must be conducted by a distributor licensed by the bureau.

(e) The license shall be prominently displayed on the licensed premises where it can be viewed by state or local agencies.

(f) A licensee shall not sublet any portion of the licensed premises.

(g) Outdoor licensees are prohibited from using light deprivation.

Note: Authority cited: Sections 26012 and 26013, Business and Professions Code. Reference: Sections 26010, 26012, 26013, 26050 and 26053, Business and Professions Code.

§ 8203. Renewal of License.

(a) An application for renewal of a cultivation license shall be submitted to the department no earlier than sixty (60) calendar days before the expiration of the license and no later than 5:00 p.m. Pacific Time on the last business day before the expiration of the license if the renewal form is submitted to the department at its office(s), or no later than 11:59 p.m. on the last business day before the expiration of the license if the renewal form is submitted to the department through its electronic licensing system. Failure to receive a notice for license renewal does not relieve a licensee of the obligation to renew all licenses as required.

(b) In the event an application for renewal is not submitted prior to the expiration of the license, the licensee must not sell any commercial cannabis until the license is renewed.

(c) A licensee may submit a license renewal form up to thirty (30) calendar days after the license expires. Any late renewal form will be subject to a fee of fifty (50) percent of the application fee to be paid in addition to the required annual renewal fee.

(d) A licensee that does not submit a complete license renewal application to the department within thirty (30) calendar days after the expiration of the current license shall forfeit its eligibility to apply for a license renewal and, instead, shall be required to submit a new license application.

(e) The license renewal application shall be submitted to the department and contain the following:

(1) The legal name of the licensed entity;

(2) The license number and expiration date;

(3) The licensee's mailing address and premises address;

(4) The annual license fee pursuant to section 8200 of this chapter;

(5) If applicable, documentation regarding any changes that have occurred to the information originally submitted to the department pursuant to section 8102 of this chapter;

(6) If applicable, a request for a license designation change from an A-License to an M-License or an M-License to an A-License pursuant to section 8203(f) of this chapter;

(7) An attestation that all information provided to the department is accurate and current; and

(8) If applicable, a limited waiver of sovereign immunity pursuant to section 8102 of this division.

(f) License Designation Change Request.

(1) A licensee may request a license designation change from an A-License to an M-License or an M-License to an A-License during the annual license renewal timeframes outlined in section 8203 (a)-(c) above for the annual license for which the license designation change is being requested.

(2) License designation changes will be considered only if the annual licensed premises for which the change is being requested contains only one A-License or only one M-License designation pursuant to Section 8102(b) of this chapter.

(3) If the department approves a request for a license designation change, the licensee is required to order, apply, and report applicable plant and package UIDs in accordance with the applicable process and procedures developed by the department pursuant to Article 5 of this chapter.

(g) Beginning January 1, 2022, an application for renewal of a license shall include the following records for each power source indicated on the application for licensure for the previous annual licensed period:

(1) Total electricity supplied by local utility provider, name of local utility provider, and greenhouse gas emission intensity per kilowatt hour reported by the utility provider under section 398.4(c) of the Public Utilities Code for the most recent calendar year available at time of submission;

(2) Total electricity supplied by a zero net energy renewable source, as set forth in section 398.4(h)(5) of the Public Utilities Code, that is not part of a net metering or other utility benefit;

(3) Total electricity supplied from other unspecified sources, as defined in 398.2(e) of the Public Utilities Code, and other on-site sources of generation not reported to the local utility provider (e.g., generators, fuel cells) and the greenhouse gas emission intensity from these sources;

(4) Average weighted greenhouse gas emission intensity considering all electricity use in subsections (1), (2), and (3).

Note: Authority cited: Sections 26012 and 26013, Business and Professions Code. Reference: Sections 26013, 26050, 26051.5 and 26055, Business and Professions Code.

§ 8204. Notification of License Information Change.

(a) Licensees shall notify the department in writing within ten (10) calendar days of any change to any item listed in the application and any of the following events:

(1) Disciplinary proceeding initiated by any state or local government agency;

(2) Bankruptcy filing, including any proceeding for the assignment for the benefit of creditors, by the licensee or any owner listed on the application for licensure;

(3) Temporary closure longer than thirty (30) calendar days. Include in the notification the reason for temporary closure and expected duration of closure;

(4) Modifications to the cultivation plan pursuant to section 8106 of this chapter that do not require preapproval pursuant to section 8205 of this chapter; and

(5) Any change in ownership that does not affect the business entity type. New owners shall submit all information pursuant to section 8102(i) of this chapter.

(b) Any change to the business entity type that includes any change of ownership requires a new application and application fee.

(c) Licensees shall notify the department in writing of the following within forty-eight (48) hours of:

(1) Receiving a criminal conviction or civil judgment rendered against the licensee or any owner;

(2) Receiving notification of the revocation of a local license, permit, or other authorization;

(3) Receiving an administrative order for violations of labor standards against the licensee or any owner in his or her individual capacity. The written notification shall include the date of the order, the name of the agency issuing the order, and a description of the administrative penalty or judgement rendered against the licensee; and

(4) Any change in the licensee's designated track-and-trace system account manager identified pursuant to section 8109 of this chapter.

(d) For purposes of this section, "in writing" shall mean notification to the department in the form of a letter or document, email, fax, or any other written form. Notification by mail shall be addressed to the California Department of Food and Agriculture, P.O. Box 942872, Sacramento, CA 94271-2872. Mailed notifications must be postmarked within the specified timeframe provided in subsections (a) and (c) and electronic notifications must be transmitted within the specified timeframe provided in subsections (a) and (c).

Note: Authority cited: Sections 26012 and 26013, Business and Professions Code. Reference: Sections 26012 and 26013, Business and Professions Code.

§ 8205. Physical Modification of Premises.

A licensee shall not make a physical modification of the licensed premises that materially or substantially alters the licensed premises or the use of the licensed premises as specified in the premises diagram originally filed with the license application without the prior written approval of the department.

(a) The following premises modifications require approval in writing from the department prior to modification:

(1) Modification to any area described in the licensee's cultivation plan including, but not limited to, the removal, creation, or relocation of canopy, processing, packaging, composting, harvest storage, and chemical storage areas;

(2) Change in water or power source(s); and

(3) Modifications or upgrades to electrical systems at a licensed premises shall be performed by a licensed electrician. A copy of the electrician's license shall be submitted with any premises modification requests for electrical systems.

(b) A licensee shall request approval of a physical change, alteration, or modification in writing to the department, and the request shall include a new premises diagram and/or cultivation plan pursuant to section 8106 of this chapter.

(c) A licensee shall provide any additional documentation requested by the department to evaluate the licensee's request.

(d) For purposes of this section, "in writing" shall mean notification to the department in the form of a letter or document, email, fax, or any other written form. Notification by mail shall be addressed to the California Department of Food and Agriculture, P.O. Box 942872, Sacramento, CA 94271-2872.

(e) The department shall review the licensee's written request and respond in accordance with section 8112 and notify the licensee if the premises modification is approved.

Note: Authority cited: Sections 26012 and 26013, Business and Professions Code. Reference: Sections 26012, 26013 and 26055, Business and Professions Code.

§ 8206. Death or Incapacity of an Owner.

(a) In the event of the death, incapacity, receivership, assignment for the benefit of creditors of an owner, or other event rendering an owner incapable of performing the duties associated with the license, the owner's successor in interest (e.g., appointed guardian, executor, administrator, receiver, trustee, or assignee) shall notify the department within ten (10) calendar days.

(b) To continue operations or surrender the existing license, the successor in interest shall submit to the department the following:

(1) The name of the successor in interest;

(2) The name of the owner for which the successor in interest is succeeding and the license number;

(3) The phone number, mailing address, and email address of the successor in interest; and

(4) Documentation demonstrating that the owner is incapable of performing the duties associated with the license, such as a death certificate or a court order finding the owner lacks capacity, and documentation demonstrating that the individual making the request is the owner's successor in interest, such as a court order appointing guardianship, or a will or trust agreement.

(c) The department may give the successor in interest written approval to continue operations on the licensed business premises for a period of time specified by the department if:

(1) The successor in interest or another person has applied for a license from the department for the license location and that application is under review; or

(2) The successor in interest needs additional time to destroy or sell cannabis or nonmanufactured cannabis products; or

(3) At the discretion of the department.

(d) The owner's successor in interest is held subject to all terms and conditions under which a state cannabis license is held pursuant to the Act and the regulations of this chapter.

(e) The approval creates no vested right to the issuance of a state cannabis license.

Note: Authority cited: Sections 26012 and 26013, Business and Professions Code. Reference: Sections 26012 and 26013, Business and Professions Code.

§ 8207. Disaster Relief.

(a) If a licensee is unable to comply with any licensing requirement(s) due to a disaster, the licensee may notify the department of this inability to comply and request relief from the specific licensing requirement(s).

(b) The department may exercise its discretion to provide temporary relief from specific licensing requirements for licensees whose operations have been impacted by a disaster.

(c) Temporary relief from specific licensing requirements shall be issued for a reasonable amount of time as determined by the department in order to allow the licensee to recover from the disaster.

(d) The department may require that certain conditions be followed in order for a licensee to receive temporary relief from specific licensing requirements.

(e) A licensee shall not be subject to enforcement action for a violation of a licensing requirement from which the licensee has received temporary relief.

(f) For the purposes of this section, "disaster" means condition of extreme peril to the safety of persons and property within the state or a county, city and county, or city caused by such conditions such as air pollution, fire, flood, storm, tidal wave, epidemic, riot, drought, terrorism, sudden and severe energy shortage, plant or animal infestation or disease, Governor's warning of an earthquake or volcanic prediction, or an earthquake, or similar public calamity, other than conditions resulting from a labor controversy, for which the Governor has proclaimed a state of emergency in accordance with Government Code sections 8558 and 8625, or for which a local governing body has proclaimed a local emergency in accordance with Government Code sections 8558 and 8630.

(g) A licensed premises that has been vacated by a licensee due to a disaster shall not be deemed to have been surrendered, abandoned, or quit pursuant to section 8208 of this chapter.

(h) Notwithstanding subsection (a) of this section, if a licensee needs to move cannabis and nonmanufactured cannabis products stored on the premises to another location immediately to prevent loss, theft, or degradation of the cannabis and nonmanufactured cannabis products from the disaster, the licensee may move the cannabis without obtaining prior approval from the department if the following conditions are met:

(1) The cannabis and nonmanufactured cannabis products are moved to a secure location where access to the cannabis is restricted to the licensee, its employees, and contractors;

(2) The licensee notifies the department in writing that the cannabis and nonmanufactured cannabis products have been moved and that the licensee is requesting relief from complying with specific licensing requirements pursuant to subsection (a) of this section within twenty-four (24) hours of moving the cannabis;

(3) The licensee provides the department access to the location where the cannabis and nonmanufactured cannabis products have been moved to for inspection; and

(4) The licensee submits in writing to the department within ten (10) calendar days of moving the cannabis and nonmanufactured cannabis products a request for temporary relief that clearly indicates the statutory and regulatory sections from which relief is requested, the time period for which the relief is requested, and the reasons relief is needed for the specified amount of time.

Note: Authority cited: Sections 26012 and 26013, Business and Professions Code. Reference: Sections 26012 and

§ 8208. Surrender, Revocation, or Suspension of License.

(a) Any licensee may apply to surrender any license by delivering to the department written notice that the licensee surrenders that license.

(b) The surrender of a license becomes effective thirty (30) days after receipt of an application to surrender the license or within a shorter period of time that the department may determine, unless a revocation or suspension proceeding, including but not limited to, investigation or examination, is pending when the application is filed, or a proceeding to revoke or suspend or to impose conditions upon the surrender is instituted within thirty (30) days after the application is filed. If a proceeding is pending or instituted, the surrender of a license becomes effective at the time and upon the conditions that the department determines.

(c) A licensee that abandons or quits the licensed premises, or that closes the licensed premises for a period exceeding thirty (30) consecutive calendar days without the notifying the department pursuant to section 8204 of this chapter, shall be deemed to have surrendered its license at the time and upon the conditions that the department determines.

(d) The surrender of a license does not affect the licensee's civil or criminal liability for acts committed prior to the surrender of the license.

(e) The power of investigation and examination by the department is not terminated by the surrender, suspension, or revocation of any license issued by the department and the department shall have continuous authority to exercise the powers set forth in the Act and the rules and regulations promulgated thereunder.

Note: Authority cited: Sections 26012 and 26013, Business and Professions Code. Reference: Sections 26012 and 26013, Business and Professions Code.

§ 8209. Medium Cultivation License Limits.

A person shall be limited to one (1) Medium Outdoor, or one (1) Medium Indoor, or one (1) Medium Mixed-Light A-License or M-License. This section shall remain in effect until January 1, 2023.

Note: Authority cited: Sections 26012 and 26013, Business and Professions Code. Reference: Sections 26012, 26013, 26050 and 26061, Business and Professions Code.

§ 8210. Sample Collection by the Bureau.

When a licensee transfers possession, but not title, of cannabis to a licensed distributor, the licensee shall allow the bureau to collect samples for the bureau's own laboratory analysis.

Note: Authority cited: Sections 26012 and 26013, Business and Professions Code. Reference: Sections 26013 and 26110, Business and Professions Code.

§ 8211. Prohibition of Product Returns.

Licensees are prohibited from accepting returns of cannabis plants or nonmanufactured cannabis products after transferring possession of cannabis plants or nonmanufactured cannabis products to another licensee after testing is performed pursuant to section 26110 of the Business and Professions Code.

Note: Authority cited: Sections 26012 and 26013, Business and Professions Code. Reference: Sections 26013, 26060 and 26110, Business and Professions Code.

§ 8212. Packaging and Labeling of Cannabis and Nonmanufactured Cannabis Products.

(a) All cannabis and nonmanufactured cannabis products packaged and/or labeled by a licensed cultivator shall meet all of the following:

(1) All applicable requirements including implementing regulations pursuant to sections 26120 and 26121 of the Business and Professions Code;

(2) Any other requirements for cannabis and nonmanufactured cannabis product specified by the bureau and the California Department of Public Health;

(3) Packaging and labeling requirements pursuant to chapter 6 (commencing with section 12601), division 5 of the Business and Professions Code.

(4) Beginning January 1, 2020, a package for retail sale, excluding those containing immature plants and seeds, shall be child-resistant.

(b) A label may specify the county of origin only if one hundred (100) percent of the cannabis or nonmanufactured cannabis product contained in the package was produced within the designated county, as defined by finite political boundaries.

Note: Authority cited: Sections 26012 and 26013, Business and Professions Code. Reference: Sections 26013 and 26063, Business and Professions Code.

§ 8213. Requirements for Weighing Devices and Weighmasters.

(a) Weighing devices used by a licensee shall be approved, registered, tested, and sealed pursuant to chapter 5 (commencing with section 12500) of division 5 of the Business and Professions Code and its implementing regulations and registered with the county sealer consistent with chapter 2 (commencing with section 12240) of division 5 of the Business and Professions Code and its implementing regulations. Approved, registered, tested, and sealed devices shall be used whenever any one or more of the following apply:

(1) Cannabis and nonmanufactured cannabis products are bought or sold by weight or count;

(2) Cannabis and nonmanufactured cannabis products are packaged for sale by weight or count;

(3) Cannabis and nonmanufactured cannabis products are weighed or counted for entry into the track-and-trace system; or

(4) The weighing device is used for commercial purposes as defined in section 12500 of the Business and Professions Code.

(b) In any county in which a sealer is unable or not required to approve, register, test, and seal weighing devices used by a licensee, the department may perform the duties of the county sealer in the same manner, to the same extent, and with the same authority as if it had been the duly appointed sealer in such county. In those instances, the department shall charge a licensee for its services using the schedule of fees established in Business and Professions Code section 12240.

(c) For the purposes of this chapter a licensee must use wet weight or net weight. Wet weight and net weight shall be measured, recorded, and reported in U.S. customary units (e.g., ounce or pound); or International System of Units (e.g., kilograms, grams, or milligrams).

(d) For the purposes of this chapter, "count" means the numerical count of the individual cannabis plants, seeds, or nonmanufactured cannabis product units.

(e) Any licensee weighing or measuring cannabis or nonmanufactured cannabis product in accordance with subsection (a) shall be licensed as a weighmaster.

(f) A licensed weighmaster shall issue a weighmaster certificate whenever payment for the commodity or any charge for service or processing of the commodity is dependent upon the quantity determined by the weighmaster in accordance with section 12711 of the Business and Professions Code and shall be consistent with the requirements in chapter 7 (commencing with section 12700) of division 5 of the Business and Professions Code.

Note: Authority cited: Sections 12027, 26012 and 26013, Business and Professions Code. Reference: Sections 12210, 12212, 26013 and 26060, Business and Professions Code.

§ 8214. Commercial Cannabis Activity Between Licensees.

Cultivation licensees may conduct commercial cannabis activities with any other licensee, regardless of the licensee's A or M designation of its license.

Note: Authority cited: Sections 26012 and 26013, Business and Professions Code. Reference: Sections 26001, 26013 and 26053, Business and Professions Code.

§ 8215. Personnel Prohibited from Holding Licenses.

(a) A license authorized by the Act and issued by the department may not be held by, or issued to, any person holding office in, or employed by, any agency of the State of California or any of its political subdivisions when the duties of such person have to do with the enforcement of the Act or any other penal provisions of law of this State prohibiting or regulating the sale, use, possession, transportation, distribution, testing, manufacturing, or cultivation of cannabis.

(b) This section applies to, but is not limited to, any persons employed in the State of California Department of Justice as a peace officer, in any district attorney's office, in any city attorney's office, in any sheriff's office, or in any local police department.

(c) All persons listed in subsections (a) and (b) may not have any ownership interest, directly or indirectly, in any business to be operated or conducted under a cannabis license.

(d) This section does not apply to any person who holds a license in the capacity of executor, administrator, or guardian.

Note: Authority cited: Sections 26012 and 26013, Business and Professions Code. Reference: Sections 26012 and 26013, Business and Professions Code.

§ 8216. License Issuance in an Impacted Watershed.

If the State Water Resources Control Board or the Department of Fish and Wildlife notifies the department in writing that cannabis cultivation is causing significant adverse impacts on the environment in a watershed or other geographic area pursuant to section 26069, subdivision (c)(1), of the Business and Professions Code, the department shall not issue new licenses or increase the total number of plant identifiers within that watershed or area while the moratorium is in effect.

Note: Authority cited: Sections 26012 and 26013, Business and Professions Code. Reference: Sections 26013 and 26069, Business and Professions Code.

ARTICLE 4. CULTIVATION SITE REQUIREMENTS

§ 8300. Cultivation Requirements for Specialty Cottage, Specialty, Small, and Medium Licenses.

(a) Cannabis plants maintained outside of the designated canopy area(s) for specialty cottage, specialty, small, and medium licenses are prohibited from flowering. Should plants outside of the canopy area(s) begin to flower, a UID shall be applied, the plant(s) shall be moved to the designated canopy area without delay, and reported in the track-and-trace system.

(b) All plants or portions of a plant used for seed production shall be tagged with a UID pursuant to section 8403 of this chapter.

(c) Licensees propagating immature plants for distribution or seed for distribution to another licensee shall obtain a nursery license.

(d) Licensees shall process their harvested cannabis only in area(s) designated for processing in their cultivation plan provided they are compliant with packaging and labeling requirements pursuant to section 8212 of this chapter, or transfer their harvested cannabis to a licensed processor, manufacturer, or distributor via a licensed distributor.

Note: Authority cited: Sections 26012 and 26013, Business and Professions Code. Reference: Sections 26013, 26060 and 26120, Business and Professions Code.

§ 8301. Seed Production Requirements for Nursery Licensees.

Nursery licensees producing seed for distribution shall tag all mature plants with a UID pursuant to section 8403(b)(4) of this chapter. All products, except seed, derived from these plants are prohibited from entering the commercial distribution chain.

Note: Authority cited: Sections 26012 and 26013, Business and Professions Code. Reference: Sections 26013, 26060 and 26067, Business and Professions Code.

§ 8302. Research and Development Requirements for Nursery Licensees.

Nursery licensees may maintain a research and development area, as identified in their cultivation plan, for the cultivation of mature plants. All mature plants shall be tagged with a UID pursuant to section 8403 of this chapter. All products derived from these plants are prohibited from entering the commercial distribution chain.

Note: Authority cited: Sections 26012 and 26013, Business and Professions Code. Reference: Sections 26013, 26060 and 26067, Business and Professions Code.

§ 8303. Cultivation Requirements for Processor Licensees.

Processor licensees shall comply with all of the following requirements:

(a) All aggregation of product shall adhere to track-and-trace requirements pursuant to sections 8405 and 8406 of this chapter;

(b) Licensees may produce nonmanufactured cannabis products without a manufacturing license, provided packaging and labeling requirements are met pursuant to section 8212 of this chapter; and

(c) Cultivation of cannabis plants is prohibited at a licensed processor premises.

Note: Authority cited: Sections 26012 and 26013, Business and Professions Code. Reference: Sections 26013, 26060, 26067, 26069 and 26120, Business and Professions Code.

§ 8304. General Environmental Protection Measures.

All licensees shall comply with all of the following environmental protection measures:

(a) Compliance with section 13149 of the Water Code as implemented by the State Water Resources Control Board, Regional Water Quality Control Boards, or California Department of Fish and Wildlife;

(b) Compliance with any conditions requested by the California Department of Fish and Wildlife or the State Water Resources Control Board under section 26060.1(b)(1) of the Business and Professions Code;

(c) All outdoor lighting used for security purposes shall be shielded and downward facing;

(d) Immediately halt cultivation activities and implement section 7050.5 of the Health and Safety Code if human remains are discovered;

(e) Requirements for generators pursuant to section 8306 of this chapter;

(f) Compliance with pesticide laws and regulations pursuant to section 8307 of this chapter;

(g) Mixed-light license types of all tiers and sizes shall ensure that lights used for cultivation are shielded from sunset to sunrise to avoid nighttime glare.

Note: Authority cited: Sections 26012 and 26013, Business and Professions Code. Reference: Sections 26013, 26060, 26066 and 26201, Business and Professions Code.

§ 8305. Renewable Energy Requirements.

Beginning January 1, 2023, all indoor, tier 2 mixed-light license types of all sizes, and nurseries using indoor or tier 2 mixed-light techniques, shall ensure that electrical power used for commercial cannabis activity meets the average electricity greenhouse gas emissions intensity required by their local utility provider pursuant to the California Renewables Portfolio Standard Program, division 1, part 1, chapter 2.3, article 16 (commencing with section 399.11) of the Public Utilities Code. As evidence of meeting the standard, licensees shall comply with the following:

(a) If a licensee's average weighted greenhouse gas emission intensity as provided in section 8203(g)(4) is greater than the local utility provider's greenhouse gas emission intensity, the licensee shall provide evidence of carbon offsets from any of the following sources to cover the excess in carbon emissions from the previous annual licensed period:

 (1) Voluntary greenhouse gas offset credits purchased from any of the following recognized and reputable voluntary carbon registries:

  (A) American Carbon Registry;

  (B) Climate Action Reserve;

(C) Verified Carbon Standard.

(2) Offsets purchased from any other source are subject to verification and approval by the Department.

(b) New licensees, without a record of weighted greenhouse gas emissions intensity from the previous calendar year, shall report the average weighted greenhouse gas emissions intensity, as provided in section 8203(g)(4), used during their licensed period at the time of license renewal. If a licensee's average weighted greenhouse gas emissions intensity is greater than the local utility provider's greenhouse gas emissions intensity for the most recent calendar year, the licensee shall provide evidence of carbon offsets or allowances to cover the excess in carbon emissions from any of the sources provided in subsection (a).

Note: Authority cited: Sections 26012 and 26013, Business and Professions Code. Reference: Sections 26013, 26060, 26066 and 26201, Business and Professions Code.

§ 8306. Generator Requirements.

(a) For the purposes of this section, "generator" is defined as a stationary or portable compression ignition engine pursuant to title 17, division 3, chapter 1, subchapter 7.5, section 93115.4 of the California Code of Regulations.

(b) Licensees using generators rated at fifty (50) horsepower and greater shall demonstrate compliance with either, as applicable, the Airborne Toxic Control Measure for stationary engines pursuant to title 17, division 3, chapter 1, subchapter 7.5, sections 93115 through 93115.15 of the California Code of Regulations, or the Airborne Toxic Control Measure for portable engines pursuant to title 17, division 3, chapter 1, subchapter 7.5, sections 93116 through 93116.5 of the California Code of Regulations. Compliance shall be demonstrated by providing a copy of one of the following to the department upon request:

(1) For portable engines, a Portable Equipment Registration Certificate provided by the California Air Resources Board; or

(2) For portable or stationary engines, a Permit to Operate, or other proof of engine registration, obtained from the Local Air District with jurisdiction over the licensed premises.

(c) Licensees using generators rated below fifty (50) horsepower shall comply with the following by 2023:

(1) Either (A) or (B):

(A) Meet the "emergency" definition for portable engines in title 17, division 3, chapter 1, subchapter 7.5, sections 93116.2(a)(12) of the California Code of Regulations, or the "emergency use" definition for stationary engines in title 17, division 3, chapter 1, subchapter 7.5, section 93115.4(a)(30); or

(B) Operate eighty (80) hours or less in a calendar year; and

(2) Either (A) or (B):

(A) Meet Tier 3 with Level 3 diesel particulate filter requirements pursuant to title 13, division 3, chapter 14, sections 2700 through 2711 of the California Code of Regulations;

(B) Meet Tier 4, or current engine requirements if more stringent, pursuant to title 40, chapter I, subchapter U, part 1039, subpart B, section 1039.101 of the Code of Federal Regulations.

(d) All generators shall be equipped with non-resettable hour-meters. If a generator does not come equipped with a non-resettable hour-meter an after-market non-resettable hour-meter shall be installed.

Note: Authority cited: Sections 26012 and 26013, Business and Professions Code. Reference: Sections 26013, 26060, 26066 and 26201, Business and Professions Code.

§ 8307. Pesticide Use Requirements.

(a) Licensees shall comply with all pesticide laws and regulations enforced by the Department of Pesticide Regulation.

(b) For all pesticides that are exempt from registration requirements, licensees shall comply with all pesticide laws and regulations enforced by the Department of Pesticide regulation and with the following pesticide application and storage protocols:

(1) Comply with all pesticide label directions;

(2) Store chemicals in a secure building or shed to prevent access by wildlife;

(3) Contain any chemical leaks and immediately clean up any spills;

(4) Apply the minimum amount of product necessary to control the target pest;

(5) Prevent offsite drift;

(6) Do not apply pesticides when pollinators are present;

(7) Do not allow drift to flowering plants attractive to pollinators;

(8) Do not spray directly to surface water or allow pesticide product to drift to surface water. Spray only when wind is blowing away from surface water bodies;

(9) Do not apply pesticides when they may reach surface water or groundwater; and

(10) Only use properly labeled pesticides. If no label is available consult the Department of Pesticide Regulation.

Note: Authority cited: Sections 26012 and 26013, Business and Professions Code. Reference: Sections 26013, 26060, 26066 and 26201, Business and Professions Code.

§ 8308. Cannabis Waste Management.

(a) For the purposes of this section, "cannabis waste" is organic waste, as defined in section 42649.8(c) of the Public Resources Code.

(b) A licensee shall manage all hazardous waste, as defined in section 40141 of the Public Resources Code, in compliance with all applicable hazardous waste statutes and regulations.

(c) A licensee shall manage all cannabis waste in compliance with division 30, part 3, chapters 12.8, 12.9, and 13.1 of the Public Resources Code. In addition, licensees are obligated to obtain all required permits, licenses, or other clearances and comply with all orders, laws, regulations, or other requirements of other regulatory agencies, including, but not limited to, local health agencies, regional water quality control boards, air quality management districts, or air pollution control districts, local land use authorities, and fire authorities.

(d) A licensee shall dispose of cannabis waste in a secured waste receptable or in a secured area on the licensed premises designated on the licensee's premises diagram and as identified in the licensee's cultivation plan. For the purposes of this section, "secure waste receptacle" or "secured area" means physical access to the receptacle or area is restricted to only the licensee, employees of the licensee, the local agency, a waste hauler franchised or contracted by a local agency, or a private waste hauler permitted by the local agency. Public access to the designated receptacle or area shall be strictly prohibited.

(e) A licensee shall comply with the method(s) for managing cannabis waste identified on its cannabis waste management plan in accordance with section 8108.

(f) If composting cannabis waste on the licensed premises, a licensee shall do so in compliance with title 14 of the California Code of Regulations, division 7, chapter 3.1 (commencing with section 17850).

(g) If a local agency, a waste hauler franchised or contracted by a local agency, or a private waste hauler permitted by a local agency is being used to collect and process cannabis waste, a licensee shall do all the following:

(1) Obtain and retain the following information from the local agency, waste hauler franchised or contracted by the local agency, or private waste hauler permitted by the local agency that will collect and process the licensee's cannabis waste:

(A) Name of local agency providing waste hauling services, if applicable;

(B) Company name of the waste hauler franchised or contracted by a local agency or private waste hauler permitted by the local agency, if applicable;

(C) Local agency or company business address; and

(D) Name of the primary contact person at the local agency or company and contact person's phone number.

(2) Obtain and retain a copy of a receipt from the local agency, waste hauler franchised or contracted by the local agency, or private waste hauler permitted by the local agency evidencing subscription to a waste collection service; and

(3) Cannabis waste may be collected from a licensee in conjunction with a regular organic waste collection route used by the local agency, the waste hauler franchised or contracted by a local agency, or private waste hauler permitted by the local agency.

(h) If self-hauling cannabis waste to one or more of the solid waste facilities in section 8108(c) of this chapter, a licensee shall obtain and retain, for each delivery of cannabis waste by the licensee, a copy of a certified weight ticket or receipt documenting delivery prepared by a representative(s) of the solid waste facility receiving the self-hauled cannabis waste. Transportation of self-hauled cannabis waste shall only be performed by the licensee or employees of the licensee.

(i) If cannabis waste is hauled to a recycling center that meets the requirements of section 8108(c)(6), in addition to the tracking requirement set forth in section 8405 and 8406 of this chapter, a licensee shall use the track-and-trace system and documentation required pursuant to this section to ensure the cannabis waste is identified, weighed, and tracked while on the licensed premises.

(j) In addition to all other tracking requirements set forth in sections 8405 and 8406 of this chapter, a licensee shall use the track-and-trace system and documentation required pursuant to this section to ensure the cannabis waste is identified, weighed, and tracked while on the licensed premises and when disposed of in accordance with subsections (f), (g), (h), and (i) above.

(k) A licensee shall maintain accurate and comprehensive records regarding cannabis waste that account for, reconcile, and evidence all activity related to the generation or disposition of cannabis waste. All records required by this section are records subject to inspection by the department and shall be kept pursuant to section 8400 of this chapter.

Note: Authority cited: Sections 26012 and 26013, Business and Professions Code. Reference: Sections 26013 and 26060, Business and Professions Code.

ARTICLE 5. RECORDS AND REPORTING

§ 8400. Record Retention.

For the purposes of this chapter, "record" includes all records, applications, reports, or other supporting documents required by the department.

(a) Each licensee shall keep and maintain the records listed in section 8400(d) of this chapter for at least seven (7) years from the date the document was created.

(b) Licensees shall keep records, either electronically or otherwise, identified in section 8400(d) of this chapter on the premises of the location licensed. All required records shall be kept in a manner that allows the records to be examined at the licensed premises or delivered to the department, upon request.

(c) All records are subject to review by the department during standard business hours or at any other reasonable time as mutually agreed to by the department and the licensee. For the purposes of this section, standard business hours are deemed to be 8:00am - 5:00pm (Pacific Time). Prior notice by the department to review records is not required.

(d) Each licensee shall maintain all the following records on the licensed premises, including but not limited to:

(1) Department issued cultivation license(s);

(2) Cultivation plan;

(3) All records evidencing compliance with the environmental protection measures pursuant to sections 8304, 8305, 8306, and 8307 of this chapter;

(4) All supporting documentation for data or information entered into the track-and-trace system;

(5) All UIDs assigned to product in inventory and all unassigned UIDs. UIDs associated with product that has been retired from the track-and-trace system must be retained for six (6) months after the date the tags were retired;

(6) Financial records related to the licensed commercial cannabis activity, including but not limited to, bank statements, tax records, contracts, purchase orders, sales invoices, and sales receipts;

(7) Personnel records, including each employee's full name, social security number or individual tax payer identification number, date of beginning employment, and, if applicable, date of termination of employment;

(8) Records related to employee training for the track-and-trace system or other requirements of this chapter. Records shall include, but are not limited to, the date(s) training occurred, description of the training provided, and the names of the employees that received the training;

(9) Contracts with other state licensed cannabis businesses;

(10) All permits, licenses, and other authorizations to conduct the licensee's commercial cannabis activity;

(11) Records associated with composting or disposal of cannabis waste;

(12) Documentation associated with loss of access to the track-and-trace system prepared pursuant to section 8402(d) of this chapter.

(e) All required records shall be prepared and retained in accordance with the following conditions:

(1) Records shall be legible; and

(2) Records shall be stored in a secured area where the records are protected from debris, moisture, contamination, hazardous waste, fire, and theft.

Note: Authority cited: Sections 26012 and 26013, Business and Professions Code. Reference: Sections 26013, 26055, 26060, 26060.1, 26067, 26069, 26160 and 26161, Business and Professions Code.

§ 8401. Sales Invoice or Receipt Requirements.

The licensee shall prepare a sales invoice or receipt for every sale or transfer of cannabis or nonmanufactured cannabis product to another licensee. Sales invoices and receipts may be retained electronically but must be readily accessible for examination by the department, other state licensing authorities, any state or local law enforcement authority, and the California Department of Tax and Fee Administration. Each sales invoice or receipt shall include all of the following:

(a) Name, business address, and department or other licensing authority issued license number of the seller;

(b) Name, business address, and department or other licensing authority issued license number of the purchaser;

(c) Date of sale or transfer (month, day, and year). The date of any sale or transfer of cannabis and nonmanufactured cannabis products shall be the date of transfer to the licensee receiving it;

(d) Invoice or receipt number;

(e) Weight or quantity of cannabis and nonmanufactured cannabis products sold or transferred;

    (1) Weight. For the purposes of this section a licensee must use wet weight or net weight. Wet weight and net weight shall be determined following weighing device requirements pursuant to section 8213 of this chapter and measured, recorded, and reported in U.S. customary units (e.g., ounce or pound) or International System of Units (e.g., kilograms, grams, or milligrams).

    (2) Count. For the purposes of this section, "count" means the numerical count of the individual plants or units.

(f) Cost to the purchaser, including any discount applied to the total price, shall be recorded on the invoice;

(g) Description for each item, including strain or cultivar, and all the applicable information below:

    (1) Plant;

    (2) Flower;

    (3) Leaf;

    (4) Shake;

    (5) Kief; and

    (6) Pre-rolls.

(h) Signature of the seller, or designated representative of the seller, acknowledging accuracy of the cannabis and nonmanufactured cannabis products being shipped;

(i) Signature of the purchaser, or designated representative of the purchaser, acknowledging receipt or rejection of the cannabis or nonmanufactured cannabis products.

Note: Authority cited: Sections 26012 and 26013, Business and Professions Code. Reference: Sections 26013 and 26161, Business and Professions Code.

§ 8402. Track-and-Trace System.

Except as provided in section 8405(e) of this chapter, each licensee shall report in the department's track-and-trace system the disposition of immature and mature plants, nonmanufactured cannabis products on the licensed premises, any transfers associated with commercial cannabis activity between licensees, and any cannabis waste pursuant to this chapter.

(a) The licensee is responsible for the accuracy and completeness of all data and information entered into the track-and-trace system. Data entered into the track-and-trace system is assumed to be accurate and can be used to take enforcement action against the licensee if not corrected.

(b) Each licensee shall use the track-and-trace system for recording all applicable commercial cannabis activities.

(c) Pursuant to section 8109 of this chapter, each licensee shall identify an owner in the licensee's organization to be the licensee's track-and-trace system account manager. The licensee's designated track-and-trace system account manager shall be responsible for all the following:

(1) Complete track-and-trace system training provided by the department. If the designated account manager did not complete the track-and-trace system training prior to the licensee receiving his or her annual license, the designated account manager will be required to register for the track-and-trace system training provided by the department within five (5) calendar days of license issuance;

(2) Designate track-and-trace system users, as needed, and require the users to be trained in the proper and lawful use of the track-and-trace system before the users are permitted to access the track-and-trace system;

(3) Maintain an accurate and complete list of all track-and-trace system users and update the list immediately when changes occur;

(4) Within three (3) calendar days, cancel the access rights of any track-and-trace user from the licensee's track-and-trace system account if that individual is no longer authorized to use the licensee's track-and-trace system account;

(5) Correct any data that is entered into the track-and-trace system in error within three (3) calendar days of discovery of the error; and

(6) Notify the department immediately for any loss of access that exceeds three (3) calendar days.

(d) The licensee is responsible for all access and use of the licensee's track-and-trace system account.

(e) If a licensee loses access to the track-and-trace system for any reason, the licensee shall prepare and maintain comprehensive records detailing all required inventory tracking activities conducted during the loss of access.

(1) Once access to the track-and-trace system is restored, all inventory tracking activities that occurred during the loss of access shall be entered into the track-and-trace system within three (3) calendar days.

(2) A licensee shall document the date and time when access to the track-and-trace system was lost, when it was restored, and the cause for each loss of access.

(3) A licensee shall not transfer cannabis or nonmanufactured cannabis products to a distributor until such time as access to the system is restored and all information is recorded into the track-and-trace system.

Note: Authority cited: Sections 26012 and 26013, Business and Professions Code. Reference: Sections 26013, 26067, 26069 and 26160, Business and Professions Code.

§ 8403. Track-and-Trace System Unique Identifiers (UID).

(a) Within five (5) calendar days of the date the licensee's designated account manager(s) was credentialed by the department to use the track-and-trace system, the designated account manager shall request UIDs using the track-and-trace system as prescribed by the department in Article 5 of this chapter.

(1) The licensee shall only use UIDs provisioned and distributed by the department or the department's designee.

(2) The licensee shall maintain a sufficient supply of UIDs in inventory to support tagging in accordance with this section.

(3) The licensee shall use the track-and-trace system to document receipt of provisioned and distributed UIDs within three (3) calendar days of physical receipt of the UIDs by the licensee.

(4) Except as provided in section 8407 of this chapter, all cannabis shall be entered into the track-and-trace system by the licensee starting with seed, cannabis which has been propagated onsite or purchased from a licensed nursery, or seedling purchased from a licensed nursery pursuant to this chapter.

(b) The UID shall accompany the cannabis products through all phases of the growing cycle, as follows:

(1) Licensees with immature plants shall assign a UID to each established lot respectively. The lot UID shall be placed in a position so it is visible and within clear view of an individual standing next to the immature lot to which the UID was assigned, and all UIDs shall be kept free from dirt and debris. For the purposes of this subsection, each lot of immature plants shall be uniform in strain or cultivar and shall not have more than one hundred (100) immature plants at any one time. All immature plants in a lot shall be labeled with the corresponding UID number assigned to the lot and shall be contiguous to one another to facilitate identification by the department.

(2) Immature plants transferred from a licensed nursery, via a distributor, to a licensed cultivator shall meet requirements of subsection (b)(1) above. Each immature plant intended for retail sale shall have a UID affixed, or be labeled with the corresponding UID number of the lot, and be recorded in the track-and-trace system prior to transfer from the licensed nursery.

(3) The licensee shall apply a UID to all individual plants at the time any plant is moved to the designated canopy area or when an individual plant begins flowering, as defined in section 8000(l) of this chapter. The licensee may tag individual immature plants prior to movement to the designated canopy area or prior to flowering.

(4) UIDs are required for each mature plant. UIDs shall be attached to the main stem, at the base of each plant. The UID shall be attached to the plant using a tamper evident strap or zip tie and placed in a position so it is visible and within clear view of an individual standing next to the mature plant to which the UID was assigned and UIDs shall be kept free from dirt and debris. Licensees are prohibited from removing the UID from the mature plant to which it was attached and assigned until the plant is harvested, destroyed, or disposed.

(c) Each harvest batch shall be assigned a unique harvest batch name which will be associated with all UIDs for each individual plant, or portion thereof, contained in the harvest batch.

(d) UIDs are required for all cannabis and nonmanufactured cannabis products and shall be associated with the corresponding harvest batch name from which the cannabis and nonmanufactured cannabis products were derived.

(e) Upon destruction or disposal of any cannabis or nonmanufactured cannabis products, the applicable UIDs shall be retired in the track-and-trace system by the licensee within three (3) calendar days of the destruction or disposal and be performed in accordance with the licensee's approved cannabis waste management plan.

Note: Authority cited: Sections 26012 and 26013, Business and Professions Code. Reference: Sections 26013, 26067, 26069 and 26160 Business and Professions Code.

§ 8404. Track-and-Trace System User Requirements.

(a) All track-and-trace account managers or users, as identified pursuant to section 8402 of this chapter, shall enter all commercial cannabis activities in the track-and-trace system.

(b) Each track-and-trace account manager and user shall have a unique log-on, consisting of a username and password, which shall not be used by or shared with any other person.

(c) No track-and-trace account manager, user, or other licensee, employee, or agent shall intentionally misrepresent or falsify information entered into the track-and-trace system.

(d) The account manager shall monitor all notifications from the track-and-trace system and resolve all issues included in the notification in the timeframe specified in the notification. An account manager shall not dismiss a notification from the track-and-trace system until the issue(s) included in the notification has been resolved.

Note: Authority cited: Sections 26012 and 26013, Business and Professions Code. Reference: Sections 26012, 26013, 26067 and 26069, Business and Professions Code.

§ 8405. Track-and-Trace System Reporting Requirements.

(a) Except as provided in subsection (e) below, the track-and-trace account manager or users shall report in the track-and-trace system any and all transfers of cannabis or nonmanufactured cannabis products to another licensee prior to the movement of the cannabis or nonmanufactured cannabis products off the licensed premises.

(b) The track-and-trace account manager or users shall report in the track-and-trace system any and all cannabis or nonmanufactured cannabis products physically received or rejected from another licensee within twenty-four (24) hours of receipt or rejection of the products.

(c) The track-and-trace account manager or users shall report in the track-and-trace system information related to the disposition of cannabis and nonmanufactured cannabis products, as applicable, on the licensed premises. All applicable information for each event listed below shall be reported in the track-and-trace system within three (3) calendar days of the applicable event.

> (1) Creating a planting of an immature plant lot;
>
> (2) Moving immature plants to a designated canopy area, or when an individual plant begins flowering, or when applying a UID to an immature plant, in accordance with section 8403(b)(3) of this chapter;
>
> (3) Destruction or disposal of an immature or mature plant;
>
> (4) Harvest of a mature plant, or portion thereof. The following information must be reported into the track-and-trace system for each harvested plant, or portion thereof, or harvest batch:
>
> > (A) The wet weight of each harvested plant, or portion thereof, which must be obtained by the licensee immediately after harvest of the plant, or portion thereof;
> >
> > (B) The net weight of each harvest batch, obtained pursuant to section 8406(b) of this chapter;
> >
> > (C) The weight of cannabis waste associated with each harvest batch;
> >
> > (D) The unique name of the harvest batch and the initiating date of the harvest. For the purposes of this section, the initiating date of the harvest is the month, day, and year the first mature cannabis plant(s) in the harvest batch were cut, picked, or removed from the soil or other growing media. The initiating date of the harvest shall be recorded using the MM/DD/YYYY format. For example, January 1, 2018 would be recorded as 01/01/2018.

(5) Packaging.

(d) The account manager or user shall report information in the track-and-trace system for each transfer of cannabis or nonmanufactured cannabis products to, or cannabis or nonmanufactured cannabis products received from, another licensee. Required information to be entered includes, but is not limited to:

(1) Name, business address, and department or other licensing authority issued license number of the seller;

(2) Name, business address, and department or other licensing authority issued license number of the purchaser;

(3) Name and department issued license number of the distributor;

(4) Date of sale, transfer, or receipt (month, day, and year) of cannabis or nonmanufactured cannabis products;

(5) Weight or count of individual units of cannabis or nonmanufactured cannabis products sold, transferred, or received;

> (A) Weight. For the purposes of this section a licensee must use wet weight or net weight. Wet weight and net weight shall be determined following weighing device requirements pursuant to section 8213 of this chapter and measured, recorded, and reported in U.S. customary units (e.g., ounce or pound) or International System of Units (e.g., kilograms, grams, or milligrams).

> (B) Count. For the purposes of this section, "count" means the numerical count of the individual plants or units.

(6) Estimated departure and arrival time;

(7) Actual departure time;

(8) Description for each item, including strain or cultivar, and all of the applicable information below:

> (A) Plant;

> (B) Flower;

> (C) Leaf;

> (D) Shake;

> (E) Kief; and

> (F) Pre-rolls.

(9) UID(s).

(e) Temporary Licensees. A licensee operating under a temporary license, issued by the department pursuant to section 8100 of this chapter, is not required to record commercial cannabis activity in the track-and-trace system as otherwise required by this chapter. Temporary licensees shall record all commercial cannabis activity in accordance with section 8401 of this chapter.

(f) Any commercial cannabis activity conducted between a temporary licensee and an annual licensee shall be reported in the track-and-trace system by the annual licensee based upon the documentation prepared pursuant to section 8401 of this chapter.

Note: Authority cited: Sections 26012 and 26013, Business and Professions Code. Reference: Sections 26013, 26067 and 26160, Business and Professions Code.

§ 8406. Track-and-Trace System Inventory Requirements.

Licensees shall use the track-and-trace system for all inventory tracking activities at a licensed premises, including, but not limited to, all of the following:

(a) Reconciling all on-premises and in-transit cannabis or nonmanufactured cannabis product inventories at least once every thirty (30) calendar days; and

(b) Recording the net weight of all harvested cannabis once the majority of drying, trimming, and curing activities have been completed, or within sixty (60) calendar days from the initial harvest date, whichever is sooner;

(c) Licensees shall close out their physical inventory of all cannabis and nonmanufactured cannabis product and UIDs, if applicable, prior to the effective date of any of the following changes to their license:

    (1) Voluntary surrender of a temporary license or annual license;

    (2) Expiration of an annual license;

    (3) Revocation of a license.

(d) Close-out of physical inventory includes, but is not limited to, all of the following items:

    (1) Immature plants and their corresponding lot UID(s);

    (2) Mature plants and their corresponding plant UID(s);

    (3) Harvest batches and their corresponding UID(s);

    (4) Nonmanufactured cannabis products and their corresponding UID(s); and

    (5) UIDs in the licensee's possession which have not been assigned in the track-and-trace system.

(e) All transfers and sales shall be documented pursuant to sections 8401 and 8405 of this chapter.

Note: Authority cited: Sections 26012 and 26013, Business and Professions Code. Reference: Sections 26013 and 26067, Business and Professions Code.

§ 8407. Track-and-Trace System Requirements for Cannabis and Nonmanufactured Cannabis Products in Temporary Licensee Possession at the Time of Annual License Issuance.

(a) Within thirty (30) calendar days of receipt of the UIDs ordered pursuant to section 8403 of this chapter, the licensee shall enter into the track-and-trace system and assign and apply a UID to each existing immature plant lot, each individual mature plant, and all nonmanufactured cannabis products physically located on the licensed premises.

(b) After the thirty (30) day time frame referenced in subsection (a) above expires, all cannabis at the licensed premises shall be entered into the track-and-trace system starting with seed, clone propagated onsite or purchased from a licensed nursery, or seedling purchased from a licensed nursery pursuant to this chapter. This section shall remain in effect until July 1, 2019.

Note: Authority cited: Sections 26012 and 26013, Business and Professions Code. Reference: Sections 26013 and 26067, Business and Professions Code.

§ 8408. Inventory Audits.

The department may perform an audit of the physical inventory and inventory as reported in the track-and-trace system of any licensee at the department's discretion. Inventory audits of the licensee shall be conducted during standard business hours or at other reasonable times as mutually agreed to by the department and the licensee. For the purposes of this section, standard business hours are 8:00am - 5:00pm (Pacific Time). Prior notice of an inventory audit is not required.

Note: Authority cited: Sections 26012 and 26013, Business and Professions Code. Reference: Sections 26013, 26015 and 26067, Business and Professions Code.

§ 8409. Notification of Diversion, Theft, Loss, or Criminal Activity.

Licensees shall notify the department and law enforcement authorities within three (3) calendar days of discovery of any diversion, theft, loss of, or criminal activity related to licensee's cannabis or nonmanufactured cannabis products.

Note: Authority cited: Sections 26012 and 26013, Business and Professions Code. Reference: Sections 26013 and 26015, Business and Professions Code.

ARTICLE 6. INSPECTIONS, INVESTIGATIONS, AND AUDITS

§ 8500. Inspections, Investigations, and Audits Applicability.

(a) All licensees and applicants shall be subject to inspection, investigation, or audit of their licensed premises and records by the department to determine compliance with applicable laws and regulations.

(b) Inspections, investigations, and audits may be conducted by the department in coordination with the California Department of Fish and Wildlife and the State Water Resources Control Board consistent with section 12029, subdivision (c) of the Fish and Game Code.

Note: Authority cited: Sections 26012 and 26013, Business and Professions Code. Reference: Sections 26013 and 26015, Business and Professions Code.

§ 8501. Inspections, Investigations, Examinations, and Audits.

The department shall conduct inspections, investigations, examinations, and audits of licensees including, but not limited to, a review of any books, records, accounts, inventory, or onsite operations specific to the license.

(a) The department may conduct an inspection, investigation, examination, or audit for any of the following purposes:

> (1) To determine accuracy and completeness of the application prior to issuing a license;

> (2) To determine compliance with license requirements including, but not limited to, the cultivation plan;

> (3) To audit or inspect any records outlined in section 8400 of this chapter;

> (4) To respond to a complaint(s) received by the department regarding the licensee;

> (5) To inspect incoming or outgoing shipments of cannabis and nonmanufactured cannabis products; and

(6) As deemed necessary by the department.

(b) Inspections, investigations, examinations, and audits of a licensed premises shall be conducted at any time, or as otherwise agreed to by the department and the licensee or its agents, employees, or representatives. Prior notice of inspection, investigation, or examination is not required.

(c) No applicant, licensee, or any agent or employee shall interfere with, obstruct, or impede the department's inspection, investigation, or audit. This includes, but is not limited to, the following actions:

(1) Denying the department access to the licensed premises;

(2) Providing false or misleading statements;

(3) Providing false, falsified, fraudulent, or misleading documents and records; and

(4) Failing to provide records, reports, and other supporting documents.

(d) Upon completion of an inspection, investigation, examination, or audit, the department shall notify the licensee of any violation(s) and/or action(s) the department is taking.

Note: Authority cited: Sections 26012 and 26013, Business and Professions Code. Reference: Sections 26013, 26015 and 26160, Business and Professions Code.

ARTICLE 7. ENFORCEMENT

§ 8600. Enforcement Applicability.

Notwithstanding any other provision of law, the department may take an administrative action at any time within (5) years after the department discovers, or with reasonable diligence should have discovered, any violation of state law or local ordinances.

Note: Authority cited: Sections 26012 and 26013, Business and Professions Code. Reference: Sections 26013, 26031 and 26034, Business and Professions Code.

§ 8601. Administrative Actions - Operations.

The department shall use the violation classes and applicable fine amounts as follows:

(a) For the purpose of this section, violation classes are designated as "Minor," "Moderate," and "Serious."

(1) "Serious." Violations which preclude or significantly interfere with enforcement of any state law, or those that cause significant false, misleading, or deceptive business practices, potential for significant level of public or environmental harm, or for any violation that is a repeat of a Moderate violation that occurred within a two-year period and that resulted in an administrative civil penalty. All Serious violations are subject to license suspension or revocation.

(2) "Moderate." Violations that undermine enforcement of any state law, are likely to cause public or environmental harm, or are a repeat of a Minor violation that occurred within a two-year period and resulted in an administrative civil penalty.

(3) "Minor." Violations that are not likely to have an adverse effect on public safety or environmental health.

(b) Repeat violations may result in an escalation of violation class.

(c) Table A below shall be used to establish the initial level of severity of the referenced violations of Division 10 of the Business and Professions Code and referenced regulations and the corresponding penalty range for "Serious," "Moderate," and "Minor" violation classes. For violations of other state law, including state labor laws and related regulations, the department shall utilize the definitions of violation classes in subsection (a).

TABLE A:		Violation Type		
		Minor	Moderate	Serious
Authority	Description of Violation	Fine Range	Fine Range	Fine Range
		$100 – $500	$501 – $1,000	$1,001 – $5,000
BPC 26053(a)	Licensee engaged in commercial cannabis activity with an unlicensed person.	-	-	X
BPC 26055(b)	Licensee continued to operate after revocation of state license.	-	-	X
BPC 26060.1(a)	Licensee used a water source that was not identified or permitted on his or her application.	-	-	X
BPC 26050.1(a) 3 CCR 8100(b)	After January 1, 2018, licensee engaged in commercial cannabis activity prior to obtaining a temporary license.	-	-	X
BPC 26060 3 CCR 8106(a)(1)(B)	Licensee shared area(s) outside the canopy where only immature plants shall be maintained, as designated on the licensee's premises diagram, with another cultivation license held by the licensee.	X	-	-
BPC 26060 3 CCR 8106(a)(1)(D)	Licensee shared processing area(s), as designated on the licensee's premises diagram, with another cultivation license held by the licensee.	-	X	-
BPC 26060 3 CCR 8106(a)(1)(E)	Licensee shared packaging area(s), as designated on the licensee's premises diagram, with another cultivation license held by the licensee.	-	X	-

BPC 26060 3 CCR 8106(a)(1)(I)	Licensee shared area(s) for physically segregating cannabis or nonmanufactured cannabis products subject to administrative hold pursuant to section 8604 of this chapter, as designated on the licensee's premises diagram, with another cultivation license held by the licensee.	-	X	-
BPC 26031 3 CCR 8108	Failure to dispose of cannabis waste as identified in the licensee's approved waste management plan.	-	X	-
BPC 26031 3 CCR 8108	Failure to deposit cannabis waste at a manned, fully permitted solid waste landfill or transformation facility; manned, fully permitted composting facility or manned composting operation; manned, fully permitted in-vessel digestion facility; manned, fully permitted in-vessel digestion operation; or manned, fully permitted chip and grind operation or facility.	-	X	-
BPC 26031 3 CCR 8201	Licensee total canopy size on licensed premises exceeded the total allowable canopy size for the license type.	-	-	X
BPC 26031 3 CCR 8202(b)	Failure to obtain a separate license for each premises where the person engaged in commercial cannabis cultivation.	-	-	X
BPC 26031 3 CCR 8202(c)	Licensee transferred or assigned his or her cultivation license to another person or property.	-	-	X
BPC 26031 3 CCR 8202(d)	Licensee transferred cannabis and nonmanufactured cannabis products from his or her licensed premises to another licensee without using a licensed distributor.	-	-	X
BPC 26031 3 CCR 8202(e)	Failure to prominently display license on licensed premises where it can be viewed by state and local agencies.	X	-	-
BPC 26031 3 CCR 8202(f)	Licensee sublet a portion of the licensed premises.	X	-	-
BPC 26031 3 CCR 8202(g)	Licensee used light deprivation at a licensed outdoor cultivation site.	-	X	-

BPC 26031 3 CCR 8204(a)	Failure to notify the department in writing within ten (10) calendar days of any changes to any item listed in the application or any of the events pursuant to section 8204(a) (1)-(5) of this chapter.	X	-	-
BPC 26031 3 CCR 8204(b)	Failure to submit a new application for a change in business entity type that includes any change of ownership.	-	X	-
BPC 26031 3 CCR 8204(c)(1)	Failure to notify the department in writing of a penalty or judgment of a criminal conviction or civil judgment rendered against the licensee or any owner within forty-eight (48) hours of receiving a penalty or judgement of a criminal penalty or civil judgement.	X	-	-
BPC 26031 3 CCR 8204(c)(2)	Failure to notify the department in writing of a revocation of a local license, permit, or other authorization within forty-eight (48) hours of the revocation.	X	-	-
BPC 26031 3 CCR 8204(c)(3)	Failure to notify the department in writing within 48 hours of receiving an administrative order for violations of labor standards against the licensee or any owner in his or her individual capacity.	X	-	-
BPC 26031 3 CCR 8204(c)(4)	Failure to notify the department in writing within 48 hours of a change in the licensee's designated track-and-trace system account manager.	-	X	-
BPC 26031 3 CCR 8205 (first paragraph)	Licensee made physical modifications to the licensed premises that materially or substantially altered the licensed premises or use of the licensed premises from the premises diagram originally filed with the license application without receiving prior written approval from the department.	-	X	-
BPC 26031 3 CCR 8205(b)	Failure to file a request for approval of a premises modification with the department associated with a physical modification of the licensed premises.	X	-	-
BPC 26031 3 CCR 8205(c)	Failure to provide additional documentation requested by the department to evaluate the request for approval of a premises modification.	X	-	-

BPC 26031 3 CCR 8206(a)	Failure of an owner's successor in interest as specified in section 8206(a) to notify the department within ten (10) calendar days of the death, incapacity, receivership, assignment for the benefit of creditors of an owner, or other event rendering a licensee incapable of performing the duties associated with the license.	-	X	-
BPC 26031 3 CCR 8207(h)(1)	Failure to move cannabis and nonmanufactured cannabis products to a secure location where access to the cannabis is restricted to the licensee, its employees, and contractors.	X	-	-
BPC 26031 3 CCR 8207(h)(2)	Failure to notify the department, in writing, within twenty-four (24) hours of moving cannabis and nonmanufactured cannabis products and requesting relief pursuant to section 8207 of this chapter.	X	-	-
BPC 26031 3 CCR 8207(h)(3)	Failure to provide the department access to the location where cannabis and nonmanufactured cannabis products were moved pursuant to section 8207 of this chapter.	X	-	-
BPC 26031 3 CCR 8207(h)(4)	Failure to submit, in writing, a request for temporary relief that clearly indicates the statutory and regulatory sections from which relief is being requested, the time period for which the relief is requested, and the reason relief is needed, within ten (10) calendar days of moving cannabis and nonmanufactured cannabis products pursuant to section 8207 of this chapter.	X	-	-
BPC 26031 3 CCR 8210	Failure to allow the bureau to collect samples for the bureau's own laboratory analysis from cannabis transferred to a licensed distributor.	-	X	-
BPC 26031 3 CCR 8211	Licensee accepted returns of cannabis plants or nonmanufactured products transferred to another licensee after testing performed pursuant to section 26110 of the Business and Professions Code.	X	-	-
BPC 26031 3 CCR 8212	Failure to comply with packaging requirements.	X	-	-

BPC 26031 3 CCR 8212	Failure to comply with labeling requirements.	X	-	-
BPC 26031 3 CCR 8213(a)	Failure to use weighing devices approved, tested, and sealed pursuant to chapter 5 (commencing with section 12500) of division 5 of the Business and Professions Code, and registered with the county sealer pursuant to chapter 2 (commencing with section 12240) of division 5 of the Business and Professions Code.	X	-	-
BPC 26031 3 CCR 8213(e)	Failure to become licensed as a weighmaster for determining any weight or measurement of cannabis and nonmanufactured cannabis products in accordance with 8213(e) of this chapter.	X	-	-
BPC 26031 3 CCR 8213(e)	Failure to issue weighmaster certificate pursuant to chapter 7 (commencing with section 12700) of division 5 of the Business and Profession Code.	X	-	-
BPC 26031 3 CCR 8300(a)	Failure to prohibit cannabis plants maintained outside the designated canopy area from flowering.	-	-	X
BPC 26031 3 CCR 8300(a)	Failure to move flowering cannabis plants located outside the designated canopy area(s) to the designated canopy area(s) without delay and report the movement and UID tagging in the track-and-trace system.	-	-	X
BPC 26031 3 CCR 8300(b)	Failure to properly apply UIDs to cannabis plants used for seed production pursuant to section 8403 of this chapter.	X	-	-
BPC 26031 3 CCR 8300(c)	Licensee propagating immature plants for distribution or seed for distribution without a nursey license.	-	X	-
BPC 26031 3 CCR 8300(d)	Licensee processed cannabis on the licensed premises in an area(s) not designated for processing as identified on his or her approved cultivation plan.	-	X	-
BPC 26031 3 CCR 8300(d)	Processing cannabis on licensee's premises without compliance to packaging or labeling requirements pursuant to section 8212 of this chapter.	-	X	-

BPC 26031 3 CCR 8301	Failure to properly apply UIDs to mature cannabis plants used for seed production pursuant to section 8403 of this chapter.	-	-	X
BPC 26031 3 CCR 8301	Licensee allowed cannabis products to enter the commercial distribution chain other than seed.	-	-	X
BPC 26031 3 CCR 8302	Licensee conducted research and development in areas that were not identified in his or her approved cultivation plan.	-	-	X
BPC 26031 3 CCR 8302	Failure to properly tag with a UID mature plants maintained in the area on the licensed premises designated for research and development.	-	X	-
BPC 26031 3 CCR 8302	Licensee allowed cannabis and nonmanufactured cannabis products from the research and development area to enter the commercial distribution chain.	-	-	X
BPC 26031 3 CCR 8303(a)	Failure to adhere to track-and-trace requirements for aggregation of cannabis products pursuant to sections 8405 and 8406 of this chapter.	-	X	-
BPC 26031 3 CCR 8303(b)	Failure to adhere to product packaging and labeling requirements, pursuant to section 8212 of this chapter, for nonmanufactured cannabis products.	X	-	-
BPC 26031 3 CCR 8303(c)	Processor licensee cultivated cannabis plants on his or her licensed premises.	-	-	X
BPC 26031 3 CCR 8304(a)-(g)	Failure to comply with specified general environmental protection measures.	-	-	X
BPC 26031 3 CCR 8305(a) & (b)	Failure to comply with specified renewable energy requirements.	-	-	X
BPC 26031 3 CCR 8306(a)-(d)	Failure to comply with specified generator requirements.	-	-	X
BPC 26031 3 CCR 8307(a) & (b)	Failure to comply with specified pesticide use requirements.	-	-	X

BPC 26031 3 CCR 8308(d)	Failure to dispose of cannabis waste in a secure waste receptacle or in a secured area on the licensed premises.	-	X	-
BPC 26031 3 CCR 8308(g)(1)(A-D)	Failure to obtain and retain required information from the local agency, waste hauler franchised or contracted by the local agency, or private waste hauler permitted by the local agency that collects and processes the licensee's cannabis waste.	X	-	-
BPC 26031 3 CCR 8308(g)(2)	Failure to obtain and retain a copy of a receipt from the local agency, waste hauler franchised or contracted by the local agency, or private waste hauler permitted by the local agency evidencing subscription to a waste collection service.	X	-	-
BPC 26031 3 CCR 8308(h)	Failure to obtain and retain, for each delivery of cannabis waste by the licensee, a copy of a certified weight ticket, or receipt documenting delivery, prepared by a representative(s) of a solid waste facility receiving self-hauled cannabis waste.	X	-	-
BPC 26031 3 CCR 8308(j)	Failure to use track-and-trace system and documentation required pursuant to sections 8405 and 8406 of this chapter to ensure the cannabis waste materials are identified, weighed, and tracked while on the licensed premises and when disposed of pursuant to subsections (f), (g), (h), and (i) of section 8308.	-	X	-
BPC 26031 3 CCR 8401	Failure to prepare a sales invoice or receipt for every sale or transport of cannabis or nonmanufactured cannabis product to another licensee.	-	X	-
BPC 26031 3 CCR 8402(a)	Failure to accurately and completely enter data and information into the track-and-trace system.	X	-	-
BPC 26031 3 CCR 8402(c)	Failure to identify an owner in the licensee's organization to be the licensee's track-and-trace system account manager.	-	X	-
BPC 26031 3 CCR 8402(c)(1)	Failure of the licensee's designated track-and-trace system account manager to complete track-and-trace system training as required by the department.	-	X	-

BPC 26031 3 CCR 8402(c)(2)	Failure to properly train all track-and-trace system users before the users were permitted to access the track-and-trace system.	-	X	-
BPC 26031 3 CCR 8402(c)(3)	Failure to maintain an accurate and complete list of all track-and-trace system users and to update the list immediately when changes occurred.	-	X	-
BPC 26031 3 CCR 8402(c)(4)	Failure to cancel a track-and-trace system user account within three (3) calendar days when that individual is no longer a representative of the licensee.	-	X	-
BPC 26031 3 CCR 8402(c)(5)	Failure to correct data entered into the track-and-trace system in error within three (3) calendar days of discovery of the error.	-	X	-
BPC 26031 3 CCR 8402(c)(6)	Failure to notify the department immediately for any loss of access that exceeds three (3) calendar days.	-	X	-
BPC 26031 3 CCR 8402(e)	Failure to prepare and maintain comprehensive records detailing all tracking inventory activities which occurred during a loss of access to the track-and-trace system for any reason.	-	X	-
BPC 26031 3 CCR 8402(e)(1)	Failure to enter all inventory tracking activities that occurred during a loss of access to the track-and-trace system within three (3) calendar days of the loss of access.	-	X	-
BPC 26031 3 CCR 8402(e)(2)	Failure to document the date and time when licensee lost access to the track-and-trace system, the cause of the loss, and when access was restored.	-	X	-
BPC 26031 3 CCR 8402(e)(3)	Licensee transferred cannabis or nonmanufactured products to a distributor without having access to the track-and-trace system.	-	X	-
BPC 26031 3 CCR 8403(a)	Failure of the licensee's designated account manager to request UIDs as prescribed by the department pursuant to Article 5 of this chapter.	-	X	-

BPC 26031 3 CCR 8403(a)(1)	Failure to use only UIDs provisioned and distributed by the department or the department's designee.	-	X	-
BPC 26031 3 CCR 8403(a)(2)	Failure to maintain a sufficient supply of UIDs to support tagging requirements.	-	X	-
BPC 26031 3 CCR 8403(a)(3)	Failure to use track-and-trace system to document receipt of provisioned and distributed UIDs within three (3) calendar days of physical receipt of the UIDs by the licensee.	-	X	-
BPC 26031 3 CCR 8403(b)(1)	Failure to properly assign a UID to each lot of immature plants.	-	X	-
BPC 26031 3 CCR 8403(b)(1)	Licensee had more than one hundred (100) immature plants in a lot.	-	X	-
BPC 26031 3 CCR 8403(b)(1)	Failure to keep immature plants contiguous to one another to facilitate identification of the immature lot by the department.	-	X	-
BPC 26031 3 CCR 8403(b)(1)	Failure to label each plant in an immature lot with a label containing the UID number assigned to the immature lot by the licensee.	-	X	-
BPC 26031 3 CCR 8403(b)(2)	Licensee failed to properly apply UID to immature plants transported from a licensed nursery, via a licensed distributor, to a licensed cultivation site.	-	X	-
BPC 26031 3 CCR 8403(b)(2)	Licensee failed to properly apply UID to immature plants intended for retail sale.	-	X	-
BPC 26031 3 CCR 8403(b)(3)	Failure to apply UID to all individual plants at the time the plants were moved to the designated canopy area identified in the licensee's approved cultivation plan or when individual plants began flowering, as defined in section 8000(l) of this chapter.	-	X	-
BPC 26031 3 CCR 8403(b)(3)	Licensee applied UID to an individual plant that was not associated with the UID for the lot of immature plants from which it was derived.	-	X	-

BPC 26031 3 CCR 8403(b)(4)	Licensee failed to properly place and maintain the required UID on each mature plant.	-	X	-
BPC 26031 3 CCR 8403(b)(4)	Licensee removed UID from the mature plant to which it was attached and assigned prior to the plant being harvested, destroyed, or disposed.	-	X	-
BPC 26031 3 CCR 8403(c)	Failure to assign a unique harvest batch name that is associated with all UIDs for each individual plant, or portion thereof, contained in the harvest batch.	-	-	X
BPC 26031 3 CCR 8403(d)	Failure to assign a UID to cannabis and nonmanufactured cannabis products corresponding to the unique harvest batch name from which the cannabis and nonmanufactured cannabis products were derived.	-	-	X
BPC 26031 3 CCR 8403(e)	Failure to retire UIDs in the track-and-trace system associated with the destruction or disposal of cannabis or nonmanufactured cannabis products within three (3) calendar days of the destruction or disposal.	-	-	X
BPC 26031 3 CCR 8404(b)	Failure to obtain a unique track-and-trace system user log-on for each user entering information into the track-and-trace system.	X	-	-
BPC 26031 3 CCR 8404(b)	Licensee, designated account manager, or track-and-trace system user used or shared his or her unique log-on with another person.	X	-	-
BPC 26031 3 CCR 8404(c)	Licensee, account manager, user, employee, or agent misrepresented or falsified data and information entered into the track-and-trace system.	-	-	X
BPC 26031 3 CCR 8404(d)	Failure to monitor notifications and/or resolve issues included in the notification in the time frame specified in the notification.	X	-	-

BPC 26031 3 CCR 8405(a)	Failure to report through the track-and-trace system any and all transfers of cannabis or nonmanufactured cannabis products to another licensee prior to movement of the cannabis or nonmanufactured cannabis products off the licensed premises.	-	-	X
BPC 26031 3 CCR 8405(b)	Failure to report through the track-and-trace system any and all receipt or rejection of cannabis or nonmanufactured cannabis products received or rejected by the licensee on his or her licensed premises from another licensee within twenty-four (24) hours of receipt or rejection of the products.	-	-	X
BPC 26031 3 CCR 8405(c)(1)-(5)	Failure to report in the track-and-trace system information related to the disposition of cannabis and nonmanufactured cannabis products on the licensed premises within three (3) calendar days of the change in disposition.	-	X	-
BPC 26031 3 CCR 8405(d)(1)-(9)	Licensee failed to record all required information for each transfer of cannabis or nonmanufactured cannabis products to, or cannabis or nonmanufactured cannabis products received from, other licensed premises.	-	X	-
BPC 26031 3 CCR 8405(f)	Annual licensee failed to report all commercial cannabis activity the annual licensee conducted with temporary licensees in the track-and-trace system pursuant to section 8401 of this chapter.	-	X	-
BPC 26031 3 CCR 8406(a)	Failure to reconcile all on-premises and in-transit cannabis or nonmanufactured cannabis product inventories at least once every thirty (30) calendar days.	-	X	-
BPC 26031 3 CCR 8406(b)	Failure to record the net weight of all harvested cannabis once all drying and curing activities have been completed, or within sixty (60) calendar days from the initial harvest date, whichever is sooner.	-	X	-
BPC 26031 3 CCR 8406(c) & (d)	Failure to close out physical inventory of all cannabis, nonmanufactured cannabis products, and UIDs in the track-and-trace system.	-	X	-

BPC 26031 3 CCR 8406(e)	Failure to record all transfers and sales pursuant to section 8401 and 8405 of this chapter.	-	X	-
BPC 26031 3 CCR 8407(a)	Within 30 calendar days of receipt of UIDs ordered pursuant to section 8403 licensee failed to assign and apply UIDs to each existing immature lot, individual mature plant, and all nonmanufactured cannabis products physically located on the licensed premises on the date of license issuance. (This section shall remain in effect until July 1, 2019.)	-	X	-
BPC 26031 3 CCR 8407(b)	Within 30 calendar days of receipt of UIDs ordered pursuant to section 8403 licensee failed to enter in the track-and-trace system the information associated with each existing immature lot, individual mature plant, and nonmanufactured cannabis products physically located on the licensed premises. (This section shall remain in effect until July 1, 2019.)	-	X	-
BPC 26031 3 CCR 8409	Failure to notify the department and law enforcement authorities within three (3) calendar days of discovery of any diversion, theft, loss of, or criminal activity related to licensee's cannabis or nonmanufactured cannabis products.	-	-	X
BPC 26031 3 CCR 8501(c)(1)	Applicant, licensee, its agent, or employees denied the department access to the licensed premises.	-	-	X
BPC 26031 CCR 8501(c)(2)	Licensee provided false or misleading statements.	-	-	X
BPC 26031 3 CCR 8501(c)(3)	Licensee provided false, falsified, fraudulent, or misleading documents and records.	-	-	X
BPC 26031 3 CCR 8501(c)(4)	Failure to provide records, reports, and other supporting documents.	-	-	X
BPC 26031 3 CCR 8604(d)(3)	Failure to physically segregate all designated cannabis or nonmanufactured cannabis products subject to hold within twenty-four (24) hours of receipt of the notice of administrative hold.	-	-	X

BPC 26031 3 CCR 8604(d)(4)	Licensee sold, donated, transferred, transported, or destroyed cannabis or nonmanufactured cannabis products subject to hold.	-	-	X
BPC 26031 3 CCR 8604(d)(5)	Failure to put all cannabis and nonmanufactured cannabis products on hold into separate batches.	-	-	X
BPC 26031 3 CCR 8604(d)(6)	Failure to identify in the track-and-trace system cannabis or nonmanufactured cannabis products subject to an administrative hold which were voluntarily surrendered by the licensee.	-	-	X

Note: Authority cited: Sections 26012, 26013, and 26031, Business and Professions Code. Reference: Sections 26013 and 26031, Business and Professions Code.

§ 8602. Administrative Actions - Recordkeeping.

Pursuant to section 26160(f) of the Business and Professions Code, if a licensee, or an agent or employee of the licensee, fails to maintain or provide required records, the licensee shall be subject to a citation and a fine, which may be issued as a Notice of Violation, of up to thirty thousand dollars ($30,000) per individual violation. The department shall use the violation classes and applicable fine amounts as follows:

(a) For the purpose of this section, violation classes are designated as "Minor," "Moderate," and "Serious."

(1) "Serious." A Moderate class violation in which a licensee, or its agent or employees, willfully or knowingly refuses, impedes, obstructs, or interferes with an examination of records of the licensee, or willfully or knowingly prepares records that are falsified, misleading, deceptive, or omits any material information, or for any violation that is a repeat of a Moderate violation that occurred within a two-year period and that resulted in an administrative civil penalty. All Serious violations are also subject to license suspension or revocation.

(2) "Moderate." Violations that are likely to undermine an examination of records of the licensee, or are a repeat of a Minor violation that occurred within a two-year period and resulted in an administrative civil penalty.

(3) "Minor." Violations that are not likely to undermine an inspection of records of the licensee, or are an initial violation.

(b) For the purposes of this section willful means a purpose or willingness to commit the act or omission referred to and does not require any intent to violate the law, injure another, or to acquire any advantage.

(c) Repeat violations may result in an escalation of violation class.

(d) Table B below shall be used to establish the initial level of severity of violations of Section 26160 of Division 10 of the Business and Professions Code, and the referenced regulations and the corresponding penalty range for "Serious," "Moderate," and "Minor" violation classes.

TABLE B:		Violation Type		
		Minor	Moderate	Serious
Authority	Description of Violation	Fine Range	Fine Range	Fine Range
		$100 – $1,000	$1,001 - $10,000	$10,001 - $30,000
BPC 26160 3 CCR 8308(k)	Failure to maintain accurate and comprehensive records regarding cannabis waste material that account for, reconcile, and evidence all activity related to the generation or disposition of cannabis waste.	X	-	-
BPC 26160 3 CCR 8400(a)	Failure to keep and maintain records listed in 8400(d) for at least seven (7) years from the date the document was created.	-	X	-
BPC 26160 3 CCR 8400(b)	Failure to provide or deliver required records, upon request.	-	X	-
BPC 26160 3 CCR 8400(c)	Failure to provide the department with ability to review all records subject to review by the department during standard business hours or at any other reasonable time as mutually agreed to by the department and the licensee.	-	X	-
BPC 26160 3 CCR 8400(d)(1)	Failure to maintain on the licensed premises the department issued cultivation license.	X	-	-
BPC 26160 3 CCR 8400(d)(2)	Failure to maintain on the licensed premises the licensee's cultivation plan.	X	-	-
BPC 26160 3 CCR 8400(d)(3)	Failure to maintain on the licensed premises all records evidencing compliance with environmental protection measures pursuant to sections 8304, 8305, 8306 and 8307.	X	-	-
BPC 26160 3 CCR 8400(d)(4)	Failure to maintain on the licensed premises all supporting documentation for data or information entered into the track-and-trace system.	-	X	-
BPC 26160 3 CCR 8400(d)(5)	Failure to maintain on the licensed premises all UIDs assigned to product in inventory and all unassigned UIDs.	-	X	-

BPC 26160 3 CCR 8400(d)(5)	Failure to retain UIDs for six (6) months after the date the tags were retired.	X	-	-
BPC 26160 3 CCR 8400(d)(6)	Failure to maintain on the licensed premises all financial records related to the licensed commercial cannabis activity, including but not limited to, bank statements, tax records, contracts, purchase orders, sales invoices, and sales receipts.	X	-	-
BPC 26160 3 CCR 8400(d)(7)	Failure to maintain on the licensed premises personnel records, including each employee's full name, social security number or individual tax payer identification number, date of employment, and, if applicable, date of termination of employment.	X	-	-
BPC 26160 3 CCR 8400(d)(8)	Failure to maintain on the licensed premises records related to employee training for the track-and-trace system or other requirements of this chapter. Records shall include, but are not limited to, the date(s) training occurred, description of the training provided, and the names of the employees that received the training.	X	-	-
BPC 26160 3 CCR 8400(d)(9)	Failure to maintain on the licensed premises contracts with other state licensed cannabis businesses.	X	-	-
BPC 26160 3 CCR 8400(d)(10)	Failure to maintain on the licensed premises all permits, licenses, and other authorizations to conduct the licensee's commercial cannabis activity.	X	-	-
BPC 26160 3 CCR 8400(d)(11)	Failure to maintain on the licensed premises records associated with composting or disposal of cannabis waste.	X	-	-
BPC 26160 3 CCR 8400(d)(12)	Failure to maintain on the licensed premises documentation associated with loss of access to the track-and-trace system prepared pursuant to section 8402(d) of this chapter.	X	-	-

Note: Authority cited: Sections 26012, 26013 and 26031, Business and Professions Code. Reference: Sections 26013 and 26031, Business and Professions Code.

§ 8603. Notice of Violation.

(a) The department may issue a Notice of Violation to a licensee that is in violation of applicable statutes and regulations. A Notice of Violation shall be served upon the licensee and the legal owner of the property. The Notice of Violation shall contain all of the following:

(1) A brief statement of the violation(s) alleged;

(2) The proposed penalty;

(3) A statement of whether the violation is correctable and a time frame in which the violation shall be corrected; and

(4) Notice of an administrative hold of property, if applicable.

(b) The right to a hearing will be deemed waived if respondent fails to respond in writing within thirty (30) calendar days from the date the Notice of Violation was received by the respondent.

Note: Authority cited: Sections 26012, 26013 and 26031, Business and Professions Code. Reference: Sections 26013 and 26031, Business and Professions Code.

§ 8604. Emergency Decisions.

(a) Pursuant to Government Code sections 11460.10 through 11460.80, the department may issue an emergency decision and order for temporary, interim relief to prevent or avoid an immediate danger to the public health, safety, or welfare. Such circumstances include but are not limited to the following:

(1) To prevent the sale, transfer, or transport of illegal cannabis, nonmanufactured cannabis product, or cannabis products in the possession of the licensee.

(2) The Department has information that conditions at the licensee's premises exist that present an immediate risk to worker or public health and safety.

(3) To prevent illegal diversion of cannabis, nonmanufactured cannabis product, or cannabis product or other criminal activity at the licensee's premises.

(4) To prevent the destruction of evidence related to illegal activity or violations of the Act.

(5) To prevent immediate threats to the environment.

(6) To prevent the offer, sale or transfer of any cannabis, nonmanufactured cannabis product, or cannabis product to anyone by means of any written or oral communication that is false or misleading.

(b) Temporary, interim relief, may include one or more of the following:

(1) An order for the temporary suspension of a license.

(2) An order for the administrative hold of cannabis, nonmanufactured cannabis product, or cannabis product.

(c) The emergency decision and order issued by the department shall include a brief explanation of the factual and legal basis and reasons for the emergency decision to justify the determination of an immediate danger and the department's emergency decision to take the specific action. The emergency decision and order shall be effective when issued or as otherwise provided by the decision and order.

(d) If the department determines it is in the public interest to issue an order for the administrative hold of cannabis, nonmanufactured cannabis product, or cannabis product:

(1) The order shall provide a description of the cannabis, nonmanufactured cannabis product, or cannabis product to be subject to the administrative hold.

(2) Following the issuance of an order for administrative hold, the department shall identify the cannabis, nonmanufactured cannabis product, or cannabis product subject to the administrative hold in the track-and-trace system.

(3) Within twenty-four (24) hours of receipt of the order for administrative hold, the licensee shall physically segregate, safeguard and preserve all designated cannabis, nonmanufactured cannabis product, or cannabis product subject to the hold in the area designated on the licensee's premises diagram.

(4) While the administrative hold is in effect, the licensee is restricted from selling, donating, transferring, transporting, gifting, giving away, or destroying the cannabis, nonmanufactured cannabis, or cannabis product that is subject to the hold.

(5) Nothing herein shall prevent a licensee from continued possession, cultivation, or harvesting of the cannabis subject to the administrative hold. While the administrative hold is in effect, all cannabis or nonmanufactured cannabis product subject to the hold shall be put into separate batches.

(6) Nothing herein shall prevent a licensee from voluntarily surrendering cannabis, nonmanufactured cannabis product, or cannabis product that are subject to an administrative hold. The licensee shall identify the cannabis, nonmanufactured cannabis product, or cannabis product being voluntarily surrendered in the track-and-trace system. Voluntary surrender does not waive the right to a hearing and any associated rights.

(e) If the department determines it is in the public interest to issue an order for the temporary suspension of a license:

(1) The emergency decision and order shall specify that the licensee shall immediately cease conducting all commercial cannabis activity under its license, unless otherwise specified in the decision and order.

(2) A licensee may continue to possess, cultivate, or harvest cannabis at the licensed premises during the temporary suspension of its license only as prescribed by the department in the emergency decision and order, in which case the cannabis or nonmanufactured cannabis product shall be put into separate batches.

(f) The emergency decision and order for temporary, interim relief shall be issued in accordance with the following procedure:

(1) The department shall give notice of the emergency decision and order and an opportunity to be heard to the licensee prior to the issuance, or effective date, of the emergency decision and order, if practicable.

(2) Notice and hearing under this section may be oral or written and may be provided by telephone, personal service, mail, facsimile transmission, electronic mail, or other electronic means, as the circumstances permit.

(3) Notice may be given to the licensee, any person meeting the definition of owner of the licensee, an agent for service of process, or other personnel at the premises.

(4) Upon receipt of the notice, the licensee may request a hearing within three (3) business days by submitting a written request pursuant to Section 8605 of this chapter. The hearing shall commence within five (5) business days of receipt of the written request for hearing.

(5) The hearing may be conducted in the same manner as an informal hearing under sections 8605 through 8607 of this chapter, however, the timeframes provided in Sections 8605 through 8607 shall not apply to a hearing under this section. Discovery or cross-examination of witnesses is not required under this section.

(6) Following the hearing, the emergency decision and order shall be affirmed, modified, or set aside as determined appropriate by the department within five (5) business days of the hearing.

(g) Within ten (10) days of the issuance or effective date of the emergency decision and order for temporary, interim relief, the department shall commence an adjudicative proceeding in accordance with Chapter 5 (commencing with Section 11500) of Part 1 of Division 3 of Title 2 of the Government Code to resolve the underlying issues giving rise to the temporary, interim relief, notwithstanding the pendency of proceedings for judicial review of the emergency decision and order as provided in subsection (i).

(h) After formal proceedings pursuant to subsection (g) of this section are held, a licensee aggrieved by a final decision of the department may appeal the decision to the Cannabis Control Appeals Panel pursuant to Section 26043 of the Act.

(i) Notwithstanding administrative proceedings pursuant to subsection (g), the licensee may obtain judicial review of the emergency decision and order under Section 1094.5 of the Code of Civil Procedure in the manner provided in Section 11460.80 of the Government Code without exhaustion of administrative remedies.

Note: Authority cited: Sections 26012, 26013 and 26031, Business and Professions Code; Sections 11460.10, 11460.20, 11460.30, 11460.40, 11460.50, 11460.60, 11460.70 and 11460.80, Government Code. Reference: Sections 26013 and 26031, Business and Professions Code; Sections 11460.10, 11460.20, 11460.30, 11460.40, 11460.50, 11460.60, 11460.70 and 11460.80, Government Code.

§ 8605. Informal Administrative Hearings.

(a) The respondent may appeal a Notice of Violation by submitting a written request for an informal hearing to the Department of Food and Agriculture, Legal Office of Hearings and Appeals, 1220 "N" Street, Suite 315, Sacramento, California 95814 or via email to CDFA.LegalOffice@cdfa.ca.gov. The request shall be received within thirty (30) calendar days from the date the Notice of Violation was received by the respondent. The request shall include the following:

(1) The respondent's name, mailing address, and daytime phone number;

(2) The license number issued by the department;

(3) Copy of the Notice of Violation; and

(4) A clear and concise statement for the basis of the appeal or counts within the Notice of Violation.

(b) If the respondent fails to submit a timely request for hearing pursuant to subdivision (a) above, the Notice of Violation is not appealable and the department may proceed upon the violations noticed without a hearing.

Note: Authority cited: Sections 26012, 26013 and 26031, Business and Professions Code. Reference: Sections 26013 and 26031, Business and Professions Code.

§ 8606. Informal Hearing Schedule and Notification.

(a) The department shall schedule an informal hearing within forty-five (45) calendar days from receipt of the request for an informal hearing.

(b) The department shall provide notice of the informal hearing to the respondent containing the following information:

(1) Date, location, and time of the informal hearing;

(2) A statement to the respondent that the respondent may, but need not, be represented by counsel at any or all stages of the proceedings;

(3) Summary of the violations;

(4) Any other information or documentation necessary for the hearing;

(5) A copy of California Code of Regulations, title 3, section 8607.

Note: Authority cited: Sections 26012, 26013 and 26031, Business and Professions Code. Reference: Sections 26013 and 26031, Business and Professions Code.

§ 8607. Conduct of Informal Hearings.

Informal hearings shall be conducted as follows:

(a) The standard of proof to be applied by the hearing officer shall be a preponderance of the evidence;

(b) Hearings may be conducted by phone at the request of the respondent. The request for a hearing to be conducted by phone must be submitted with the licensee's request for an informal hearing;

(c) The decision of the hearing officer shall be in writing and shall include a statement of the factual legal basis of the decision;

(d) The written decision shall be issued within thirty (30) calendar days after the conclusion of the hearing;

(e) The decision shall be served on the respondent either by personal service, mail, email, or via facsimile based upon the method the appeal was received; and

(f) The respondent may appeal the department's decision to the Cannabis Control Appeals Panel in accordance with Business and Professions Code section 26043.

Note: Authority cited: Sections 26012, 26013 and 26031, Business and Professions Code. Reference: Sections 26013 and 26031, Business and Professions Code.

§ 8608. Licensing Actions.

(a) The department may take any action listed in subdivision (b) below against a license for any violation of this chapter.

(b) If the licensee holds multiple cultivation licenses, the department may take any one of, or combination of, the following actions on any of the licensee's cultivation licenses:

(1) Revocation of the license;

(2) Suspension of the license for a specified period of time;

(3) Issuance of a probationary license with terms and conditions determined by the department; and

(4) Order an administrative hold of cannabis or nonmanufactured cannabis products.

Note: Authority cited: Sections 26012, 26013 and 26031, Business and Professions Code. Reference: Sections 26013 and 26031, Business and Professions Code.

§ 8609. Formal Administrative Hearings.

(a) Hearings concerning the following proceedings shall be held pursuant to chapter 5 (commencing with section

11500) of part 1 of division 3 of title 2 of the Government Code:

(1) Denial of an application for a license;

(2) Denial of a license renewal;

(3) Revocation of a license; and

(4) Suspension of a license for a period of time exceeding thirty (30) calendar days.

Note: Authority cited: Sections 26012, 26013 and 26031, Business and Professions Code. Reference: Sections 26013 and 26031, Business and Professions Code.

Title 16. Professional and Vocational Regulations

DIVISION 42. BUREAU OF CANNABIS CONTROL

Chapter 1. All Bureau Licensees

ARTICLE 1. DIVISION DEFINITIONS

§ 5000. Definitions.

For the purposes of this division, the definitions in this section shall govern the construction of this division unless otherwise indicated.

(a) "Act" means the Medicinal and Adult-Use Cannabis Regulation and Safety Act.

(b) "Branded merchandise" means clothing, hats, pencils, pens, keychains, mugs, water bottles, beverage glasses, notepads, lanyards, cannabis accessories, or other types of merchandise approved by the Bureau with the name or logo of a commercial cannabis business licensed pursuant to the Act. Branded merchandise does not include items containing cannabis or any items that are considered food as defined by Health and Safety Code section 109935.

(c) "Bureau" means the Bureau of Cannabis Control, previously named the Bureau of Marijuana Control, Bureau of Medical Cannabis Regulation, and Bureau of Medical Marijuana Regulation.

(d) "Business day" is a day Monday through Friday from 8:00 a.m. to 5.00 p.m. Pacific Time, excluding state holidays, during which the Bureau is closed for business.

(e) "Cannabis accessories" has the same meaning as in Health and Safety Code section 11018.2.

(f) "Cannabis goods" means cannabis, including dried flower, and products containing cannabis.

(g) "Cannabis waste" means waste that contains cannabis and that has been made unusable and unrecognizable in the manner prescribed in section 5054 of this division.

(h) "Canopy" means the designated area(s) at a licensed premises that will contain mature plants at any point in time.

(i) "Delivery employee" means an individual employed by a licensed retailer or licensed microbusiness authorized to engage in retail sales who delivers cannabis goods from the licensed retailer or licensed microbusiness premises to a customer at a physical address.

(j) "Free cannabis goods" means any amount of cannabis goods provided to any person without cost or payment or exchange of any other thing of value.

(k) "Immature cannabis plant" or "immature plant" means a plant that is nonflowering and is shorter and narrower than 18 inches. For purposes of this division, this definition is applicable to retail activities.

(l) "Kief" means the resinous trichomes of cannabis that have been separated from the cannabis plant.

(m) "Limited-access area" means an area in which cannabis goods are stored or held and is only accessible to a licensee and its employees and authorized individuals.

(n) "Lot number" or "batch number" means a distinctive group of numbers, letters, or symbols or any combination of these that is unique to a group of cannabis goods.

(o) "Medicinal cannabis patient" includes both a qualified patient as defined in Health and Safety Code section 11362.7 and a person in possession of a valid identification card issued under Health and Safety Code section 11362.71.

(p) "Package" and "Packaging" means any container or wrapper that may be used for enclosing or containing any cannabis goods for final retail sale. "Package" and "packaging" does not include a shipping container or outer wrapping used solely for the transport of cannabis goods in bulk quantity to a licensee.

(q) "Pre-roll" means any combination of the following rolled in paper: flower, shake, leaf, or kief that is obtained from accumulation in containers or sifted from loose, dry cannabis flower or leaf with a mesh screen or sieve.

(r) "Promotional materials" means any form, letter, circular, pamphlet, publication, or other written material directed to a customer or prospective customer to induce retail sales. Promotional material does not include permitted signs, displays, decorations, cannabis accessories, or cannabis goods furnished by a licensed cultivator, licensed manufacturer, licensed distributor, licensed microbusiness, or licensed cannabis event organizer to a retail licensee for advertising purposes. Promotional materials shall have no intrinsic or secondary value.

(s) "Publicly owned land" means any building or real property that is owned, leased, or occupied by a city, county, state, federal, or other government entity.

(t) "Residential area" is an area that is within 600 feet of any single-family or multifamily residence, other than commercial hotels, motels, and similar establishments for temporary lodging.

(u) "Retail area" means a building, room, or other area that is open to the public, upon the licensed retailer or licensed microbusiness premises authorized to engage in retail sales in which cannabis goods are sold or displayed.

(v) "Sublet" means to lease or rent all or part of a leased or rented property.

(w) "Tamper-evident" means that the cannabis goods packaging is sealed in a manner that prevents the packaging from being opened without obvious destruction of the seal.

(x) "Transport" means the physical movement of cannabis goods from one licensed premises to another licensed premises.

(y) "Vehicle alarm system" is a device or series of devices installed to discourage theft of the vehicle or its contents and is intended to summon general attention or to summon law enforcement as a result of an indication of an attempted breach of the vehicle.

(z) "Wholesale cost" has the same meaning as in regulation adopted by the California Department of Tax and Fee Administration for cannabis taxes.

Note: Authority cited: Section 26013, Business and Professions Code. Reference: Section 26013, Business and Professions Code.

ARTICLE 2. APPLICATIONS

§ 5001. Temporary Licenses.

(a) A temporary license is a conditional license that authorizes the licensee to engage in commercial cannabis activity as would be permitted under the privileges of a non-temporary license of the same type. A temporary licensee shall follow all applicable rules and regulations as would be required if the licensee held a non-temporary license of the same type.

(b) A temporary license does not obligate the Bureau to issue a non-temporary license nor does the temporary license create a vested right in the holder to either an extension of the temporary license or to the granting of a subsequent non-temporary license.

(c) A temporary license issued under this section shall be valid for 120 days from the effective date. No temporary license shall be effective prior to January 1, 2018.

(d) A temporary license may be extended by the Bureau for additional 90-day periods if a complete application for an annual license has been submitted to the Bureau pursuant to section 5002 of this division prior to the initial expiration date of the temporary license.

(e) The Bureau shall not issue any temporary licenses or extensions after December 31, 2018. Any temporary license issued or extended with an expiration date after December 31, 2018, will be valid until it expires, but shall not be extended beyond the expiration date.

Note: Authority cited: Section 26013, Business and Professions Code. Reference: Section 26012, Business and Professions Code.

§ 5002. Annual License Application Requirements.

(a) Applications may be completed and submitted online at www.bcc.ca.gov or completed in hard copy and submitted by delivering a printed copy to the Bureau's office(s).

(b) Applicants who submit their applications online shall first register for a user account. To register for a user account, the applicant shall do all of the following:

> (1) Create a user name, password, and security question and answer;
>
> (2) Provide an email address; and
>
> (3) Provide the owner's first and last name, primary phone number, social security number or individual taxpayer identification number, date of birth, and mailing address.

(c) An application must be completed by an owner as defined by section 5003 of this division. An application must be submitted to the Bureau for each location and each license type. An application for an annual cannabis license includes the following:

> (1) The name of the applicant. For applicants who are individuals, the applicant shall provide both the first and last name of the individual. For applicants who are business entities, the applicant shall provide the legal business name of the applicant.
>
> (2) If applicable, the business trade name ("DBA") of the applicant.
>
> (3) The commercial cannabis license that the applicant is applying for, and whether the applicant is requesting that the license be designated as medicinal, adult-use, or both. Testing laboratory applicants do not have to

designate medicinal or adult-use, as testing laboratory licenses allow the holder to test both medicinal and adult-use cannabis.

(4) Payment of an application fee pursuant to section 5014 of this division.

(5) Whether the owner is serving or has previously served in the military. Disclosure of military service is voluntary. An applicant who has served as an active duty member of the Armed Forces of the United States and was honorably discharged and who can provide evidence of such honorable discharge shall have his or her application expedited pursuant to Business and Professions Code section 115.4.

(6) A list of the license types and the license numbers issued from the Bureau and all other state cannabis licensing authorities that the applicant holds, including the date the license was issued and the licensing authority that issued the license.

(7) Whether the applicant has been denied a license or has had a license suspended or revoked by the Bureau or any other state cannabis licensing authority. The applicant shall provide the type of license applied for, the name of the licensing authority that denied the application, and the date of denial.

(8) The physical address of the premises. If the Bureau is unable to confirm that the address provided is valid, then the applicant shall provide a document that confirms the physical address of the premises. Such a document may include a utility bill, printed information from the county assessor, deed, or title.

(9) The mailing address for the applicant, if different from the premises address.

(10) The telephone number for the premises.

(11) The website address and email address of the applicant's business.

(12) The business' federal employer identification number.

(13) Contact information for the applicant's designated primary contact person including the name, title, phone number, and email address of the individual.

(14) A description of the business organizational structure of the applicant, such as partnership or corporation.

(15) All business-formation documents, which may include, but are not limited to, articles of incorporation, bylaws, operating agreements, partnership agreements, and fictitious business name statements. The applicant shall also provide all documents filed with the California Secretary of State, which may include, but are not limited to, articles of incorporation, certificates of stock, articles of organization, certificates of limited partnership, and statements of partnership authority. If the commercial cannabis business is held in trust, the applicant shall provide a copy of the certificate of trust establishing trustee authority.

(16) A list of every fictitious business name the applicant is operating under including the address where the business is located.

(17) A commercial cannabis business that is a foreign corporation or foreign limited liability company shall include in its application a certificate of qualification, certificate of registration, or certificate of status issued by the California Secretary of State.

(18) The applicant shall supply the following financial information:

(A) A list of funds belonging to the applicant held in savings, checking, or other accounts maintained by a financial institution. The applicant shall provide, for each account, the financial institution's name, the financial institution's address, account type, account number, and the amount of money in the account.

(B) A list of loans made to the applicant. For each loan, the applicant shall provide the amount of the loan, the date of the loan, term(s) of the loan, security provided for the loan, and the name, address, and phone number of the lender.

(C) A list of investments made into the applicant's commercial cannabis business. For each investment, the applicant shall provide the amount of the investment, the date of the investment, term(s) of the investment, and the name, address, and phone number of the investor.

(D) A list of all gifts of any kind given to the applicant for its use in conducting commercial cannabis activity. For each gift, the applicant shall provide the value of the gift or description of the gift, and the name, address, and phone number of the provider of the gift.

(19) A complete list of every individual who has a financial interest in the commercial cannabis business as defined in section 5004 of this division, who is not an owner as defined in section 5003 of this division.

(20) A complete list of every owner of the applicant as defined in section 5003 of this division. Each individual named on this list shall submit the following information:

(A) The full name of the owner.

(B) The owner's title within the applicant entity.

(C) The owner's date of birth and place of birth.

(D) The owner's social security number or individual taxpayer identification number.

(E) The owner's mailing address.

(F) The owner's telephone number. This may include a number for the owner's home, business, or mobile telephone.

(G) The owner's email address.

(H) The owner's current employer.

(I) The percentage of the ownership interest held in the applicant entity by the owner.

(J) Whether the owner has an ownership or a financial interest as defined in sections 5003 and 5004, respectively, of this division in any other commercial cannabis business licensed under the Act.

(K) A copy of the owner's government-issued identification. Acceptable forms of identification are a document issued by a federal, state, county, or municipal government that includes the name, date of birth, height, gender, and picture of the person, such as a driver license.

(L) A detailed description of the owner's convictions. A conviction within the meaning of this section means a plea or verdict of guilty or a conviction following a plea of nolo contendere. Convictions dismissed under Penal Code section 1203.4 or equivalent non-California law must be disclosed. Convictions dismissed under Health and Safety Code section 11361.8 or equivalent non-California law must be disclosed. Juvenile adjudications and traffic infractions under $300 that did not involve alcohol, dangerous drugs, or controlled substances do not need to be included. For each conviction, the owner shall provide the following:

(i) The date of conviction.

(ii) Dates of incarceration, if applicable.

(iii) Dates of probation, if applicable.

(iv) Dates of parole, if applicable.

(v) A detailed description of the offense for which the owner was convicted.

(vi) A statement of rehabilitation for each conviction. The statement of rehabilitation is to be written by the owner and may contain evidence that the owner would like the Bureau to consider that demonstrates the owner's fitness for licensure. Supporting evidence may be attached to the statement of rehabilitation and may include, but is not limited to, a certificate of rehabilitation under Penal Code section 4852.01, and dated letters of reference from employers, instructors, or professional counselors that contain valid contact information for the individual providing the reference.

(M) If applicable, a detailed description of any administrative orders or civil judgments for violations of labor standards, any suspension of a commercial cannabis license, revocation of a commercial cannabis license, or sanctions for unlicensed commercial cannabis activity by a licensing authority, local agency, or state agency against the applicant or a business entity in which the applicant was an owner or officer within the three years immediately preceding the date of the application.

(N) Attestation to the following statement: Under penalty of perjury, I hereby declare that the information contained within and submitted with the application is complete, true, and accurate. I understand that a misrepresentation of fact is cause for rejection of this application, denial of the license, or revocation of a license issued.

(21) Evidence that the applicant has the legal right to occupy and use the proposed location that complies with section 5007 of this division.

(22) Evidence that the proposed premises is in compliance with Business and Professions Code section 26054(b) and section 5026 of this division.

(23) For an applicant with 20 or more employees, the applicant shall attest that the applicant has entered into a labor peace agreement and will abide by the terms of the agreement. The applicant shall submit a copy of the page of the labor peace agreement that contains the signatures of the union representative and the applicant. For applicants who have not yet entered into a labor peace agreement, the applicant shall provide a notarized statement indicating that the applicant will enter into and abide by the terms of a labor peace agreement as soon as reasonably practicable after licensure.

(24) The applicant shall provide a valid seller's permit number issued by the California Department of Tax and Fee Administration, if applicable. If the applicant has not yet received a seller's permit, the applicant shall attest that the applicant is currently applying for a seller's permit.

(25) A diagram of the premises as required by section 5006 of this division.

(26) Proof of a bond as required by section 5008 of this division.

(27) For testing laboratory applications, the certificate(s) of accreditation as required by section 5702 of this division, or the information required for an interim license as required by section 5703 of this division.

(28) When an applicant provides a license, permit, or other authorization from the local jurisdiction where the licensed premises will be or is located, the Bureau will notify the applicable local jurisdiction to confirm the validity of the authorization. If the local jurisdiction does not respond within 10 calendar days, the Bureau shall consider the authorization valid.

(29) All license applications shall include a detailed description of the applicant's operating procedures. Applicants shall use and submit to the Bureau the following forms, which are incorporated by reference:

(A) Transportation Procedures, Form BCC-LIC-015 (New 10/18)

(B) Inventory Procedures, Form BCC-LIC-016 (New 7/18)

(C) Non-Laboratory Quality Control Procedures, Form BCC-LIC-017 (New 10/18)

(D) Security Procedures, Form BCC-LIC-018 (New 10/18)

(E) Delivery Procedures, Form BCC-LIC-020 (New 10/18)

(30) For applicants applying for a microbusiness license, the application shall include a detailed description of the applicant's operating procedures required by this section for each cannabis activity the applicant intends to engage in.

(31) For applicants applying for a testing laboratory license, in addition to the operating procedures required under subsection (c)(29) of this section, the standard application shall include the operating procedures required by Chapter 6 of this division.

(32) The limited waiver of sovereign immunity required by section 5009 of this division, if applicable.

(33) Evidence of exemption from, or compliance with, the California Environmental Quality Act as required by sections 5010-5010.3 of this division.

(34) The applicant's State Employer Identification Number (SEIN) issued by the California Employment Development Department.

(35) For an applicant with more than one employee, the applicant shall attest that the applicant employs, or will employ within one year of receiving a license, one supervisor and one employee who have successfully completed a Cal-OSHA 30-hour general industry outreach course offered by a training provider that is authorized by an OSHA Training Institute Education Center to provide the course.

Note: Authority cited: Sections 115.4 and 26013, Business and Professions Code. Reference: Sections 115.4, 144, 26012, 26050, 26051.5 and 26055, Business and Professions Code.

§ 5003. Designation of Owner.

(a) All applicants for a commercial cannabis license shall have at a minimum one individual who meets the definition of "owner" under Business and Professions Code section 26001(al) and who will submit the information required of owners under section 5002 of this division.

(b) "Owner" means any of the following:

(1) A person with an aggregate ownership interest of 20 percent or more in the person applying for a license or a licensee, unless the interest is solely a security, lien, or encumbrance.

(2) The chief executive officer of a nonprofit or other entity.

(3) A member of the board of directors of a nonprofit.

(4) The trustee(s) and all persons who have control of the trust and/or the commercial cannabis business that is held in trust.

(5) An individual entitled to a share of at least 20 percent of the profits of the commercial cannabis business.

(6) An individual who will be participating in the direction, control, or management of the person applying for a license. Such an individual includes any of the following:

(A) A general partner of a commercial cannabis business that is organized as a partnership.

(B) A non-member manager or managing member of a commercial cannabis business that is organized as a limited liability company.

(C) An officer or director of a commercial cannabis business that is organized as a corporation.

(c) When an entity is an owner in a commercial cannabis business, all entities and individuals with a financial interest in the entity shall be disclosed to the Bureau and may be considered owners of the commercial cannabis business. For example, this includes all entities in a multi-layer business structure, as well as the chief executive officer, members of the board of directors, partners, trustees and all persons who have control of a trust, and managing members or non-member managers of the entity. Each entity disclosed as having a financial interest must disclose the identities of persons holding financial interests until only individuals remain.

Note: Authority cited: Section 26013, Business and Professions Code. Reference: Sections 26001 and 26012, Business and Professions Code.

§ 5004. Financial Interest in a Commercial Cannabis Business.

(a) A financial interest means an agreement to receive a portion of the profits of a commercial cannabis business, an investment into a commercial cannabis business, a loan provided to a commercial cannabis business, or any other equity interest in a commercial cannabis business except as provided in subsection (d). For the purpose of this division, an agreement to receive a portion of the profits includes, but is not limited to, the following individuals:

(1) An employee who has entered into a profit share plan with the commercial cannabis business.

(2) A landlord who has entered into a lease agreement with the commercial cannabis business for a share of the profits.

(3) A consultant who is providing services to the commercial cannabis business for a share of the profits.

(4) A person acting as an agent, such as an accountant or attorney, for the commercial cannabis business for a share of the profits.

(5) A broker who is engaging in activities for the commercial cannabis business for a share of the profits.

(6) A salesperson who earns a commission.

(b) The license application shall include the name, birthdate, and government-issued identification type and number for all individuals who have a financial interest in a commercial cannabis business but are not owners as defined in section 5003(b) of this division.These individuals shall not be required to submit the information required of owners under section 5002(c)(20) of this division.

(c) When an entity has a financial interest in a commercial cannabis business, then all individuals who are owners of that entity shall be considered financial interest holders of the commercial cannabis business. For example, this includes all entities in a multi-layer business structure, as well as the chief executive officer, members of the board of directors, partners, trustees and all persons who have control of a trust, and managing members or non-member managers of the entity. Each entity disclosed as having a financial interest must disclose the identities of persons holding financial interests until only individuals remain.

(d) Notwithstanding subsection (b), the following persons are not required to be listed on an application for licensure under section 5002(c)(19) of this division:

(1) A bank or financial institution whose interest constitutes a loan;

(2) Persons whose only financial interest in the commercial cannabis business is through an interest in a diversified mutual fund, blind trust, or similar instrument;

(3) Persons whose only financial interest is a security interest, lien, or encumbrance on property that will be used by the commercial cannabis business; and

(4) Persons who hold a share of stock that is less than 5 percent of the total shares in a publicly traded company.

Note: Authority cited: Section 26013, Business and Professions Code. Reference: Sections 26012 and 26051.5, Business and Professions Code.

§ 5005. Personnel Prohibited from Holding Licenses.

(a) A license authorized by the Act and issued by the Bureau may not be held by, or issued to, any person holding office in, or employed by, any agency of the State of California or any of its political subdivisions when the duties of such person have to do with the enforcement of the Act or any other penal provisions of law of this State prohibiting or regulating the sale, use, possession, transportation, distribution, testing, manufacturing, or cultivation of cannabis goods.

(b) This section applies to, but is not limited to, any person employed in the State of California Department of Justice as a peace officer, in any district attorney's office, in any city attorney's office, in any sheriff's office, or in any local police department.

(c) No person listed in subsection (a) or (b) of this section may have any ownership interest, directly or indirectly, in any business to be operated or conducted under a cannabis license.

(d) This section does not apply to any person who holds a license in the capacity of executor, administrator, or guardian.

Note: Authority cited: Section 26013, Business and Professions Code. Reference: Section 26012, Business and Professions Code.

§ 5006. Premises Diagram.

(a) An applicant shall submit to the Bureau, with the application, a complete and detailed diagram of the proposed premises. The diagram shall be used by the Bureau to determine whether the premises meets the requirements under this division and the Act. The Bureau shall deny an application if the premises does not qualify for licensure pursuant to Business and Professions Code section 26057.

(b) The diagram shall show the boundaries of the property and the proposed premises to be licensed, showing all boundaries, dimensions, entrances and exits, interior partitions, walls, rooms, windows, and doorways, and shall include a brief statement or description of the principal activity to be conducted therein.

(c) The diagram shall show and identify commercial cannabis activities that will take place in each area of the premises, and identify limited-access areas. Commercial cannabis activities that shall be identified on the diagram include the following, if applicable to the business operations: storage, batch sampling, loading or unloading of shipments, packaging and labeling, customer sales, loading for deliveries, extraction, infusion, cultivation, and processing.

(d) The diagram shall show where all cameras are located and assign a number to each camera for identification purposes unless the premises is exempt from the video surveillance requirement pursuant to section 5315 of this division.

(e) The diagram shall be to scale.

(f) The diagram shall not contain any highlighting and the markings on the diagram shall be in black-and-white print.

(g) If the proposed premises consists of only a portion of a property, the diagram must be labeled indicating which part of the property is the proposed premises and what the remaining property is used for.

(h) If the proposed premises consists of only a portion of a property that will contain two or more licensed premises, the diagram shall clearly show the designated entrances and walls under the exclusive control of the applicant for the premises, as well as the designated entrances and walls for each additional premises. The diagram shall also show all proposed common or shared areas of the property. Such areas may include lobbies, bathrooms, hallways, and breakrooms.

(i) If the proposed premises will be a microbusiness that includes cultivation activities, in addition to the requirements of this section, the premises diagram shall also include all the required information for a premises diagram under section 5501(d) of this division.

(j) If a proposed premises is located on only a portion of a property that also includes a residence, the diagram shall clearly show the designated buildings for the premises and the residence.

Note: Authority cited: Section 26013, Business and Professions Code. Reference: Sections 26012 and 26051.5, Business and Professions Code.

§ 5007. Landowner Approval.

(a) If the applicant is not the landowner of the real property upon which the premises is located, the applicant shall provide to the Bureau a document from the landowner or the landowner's agent that states that the applicant has the right to occupy the property and acknowledges that the applicant may use the property for the commercial cannabis activity for which the applicant is applying for licensure. An applicant shall also provide a copy of the rental agreement, as applicable.

(b) If the applicant is the landowner of the real property upon which the premises is located, the applicant shall provide to the Bureau a copy of the title or deed to the property.

(c) If the landowner is a trust, the landowner approval shall come from the person who holds equitable title in the real property.

Note: Authority cited: Section 26013, Business and Professions Code. Reference: Section 26051.5, Business and Professions Code.

§ 5007.1. Electronic Signature.

The Bureau will accept an electronic signature that complies with Civil Code section 1633.2(h) on any documents required to be submitted to the Bureau and that are submitted electronically, except documents that are required to be notarized.

Note: Authority cited: Section 26013, Business and Professions Code. Reference: Section 26013, Business and Professions Code.

§ 5007.2. Use of Legal Business Name.

Applicants and licensees shall use their legal business name on all documents related to commercial cannabis activity.

Note: Authority cited: Section 26013, Business and Professions Code. Reference: Section 26013, Business and Professions Code.

§ 5008. Bond.

An applicant shall provide proof of having obtained a surety bond of at least $5,000 payable to the State of California to ensure payment of the cost incurred for the destruction of cannabis goods necessitated by a violation of the Act or the regulations adopted thereunder. All bonds required under this regulation must be issued by a corporate surety licensed to transact surety business in the State of California and shall be issued on the Commercial Cannabis Licensee Bond form under Title 11, California Code of Regulations, Article 56, section 118.1. A bond shall be required for each license.

Note: Authority cited: Section 26013, Business and Professions Code. Reference: Section 26051.5, Business and Professions Code.

§ 5009. Limited Waiver of Sovereign Immunity.

(a) Any applicant or licensee that may fall within the scope of sovereign immunity that may be asserted by a federally recognized tribe or other sovereign entity must waive any sovereign immunity defense that the applicant or licensee may have, may be asserted on its behalf, or may otherwise be asserted in any state administrative or judicial enforcement actions against the applicant or licensee, regardless of the form of relief sought, whether monetary or otherwise, under the state laws and regulations governing commercial cannabis activity. The applicant or licensee must submit a written waiver of sovereign immunity to the Bureau with any license application or renewal, which is valid for the period of the license. The written waiver shall include that the applicant or licensee has the lawful authority to enter into the waiver required by this section, the applicant or licensee hereby waives sovereign immunity, and the applicant or licensee agrees to do all of the following:

(1) Provide documentation to the Bureau that establishes that the applicant or licensee has the lawful authority to enter into the waiver required by this section;

(2) Conduct all commercial cannabis activity in full compliance with the state laws and regulations governing commercial cannabis activity, including submission to all enforcement provisions thereof;

(3) Allow access as required by state statute or regulation by persons or entities charged with duties under the state laws and regulations governing commercial cannabis activity to any licensed premises or property at which the applicant conducts any commercial cannabis activity, including licensed premises or property where records of commercial cannabis activity are maintained by or for the applicant or licensee;

(4) Provide any and all records, reports, and other documents as may be required under the state laws and regulations governing commercial cannabis activity;

(5) Conduct commercial cannabis activity with other state commercial cannabis licensees only, unless otherwise specified by state law;

(6) Meet all of the requirements for licensure under the state laws and regulations governing the conduct of commercial cannabis activity, and provide truthful and accurate documentation and other information of the applicant's qualifications and suitability for licensure as may be requested; and

(7) Submit to the personal and subject matter jurisdiction of the California courts to address any matter related to the waiver or the commercial cannabis application, license, or activity, and that all such matters and proceedings shall be governed, construed and enforced in accordance with California substantive and procedural law, including but not limited to the Medicinal and Adult-Use Regulation and Safety Act and the Administrative Procedure Act.

(b) The Bureau shall not approve an application for a state license if approval of the license would violate the provisions of any local ordinance or regulation adopted in accordance with Business and Professions Code section 26200 that is issued by the county or, if within a city, the city, within which the licensed premises is to be located.

(c) Any applicant or licensee must immediately notify the Bureau of any changes that may materially affect the applicant or licensee's compliance with subsection (a) of this section.

(d) Any failure by an applicant or licensee to comply with the requirements of subsections (b) or (c) of this section shall be a basis for denial of an application or renewal or discipline of a licensee.

Note: Authority cited: Section 26013, Business and Professions Code. Reference: Sections 26012, 26050 and 26051.5, Business and Professions Code.

§ 5010. Compliance with the California Environmental Quality Act (CEQA).

(a) For purposes of complying with the California Environmental Quality Act (CEQA):

(1) "Project" means the commercial cannabis activity or activities for which an annual license application is submitted to the Bureau and which requires the Bureau to engage in discretionary review.

(2) "CEQA Guidelines" means the Guidelines for Implementation of the California Environmental Quality Act codified at Title 14, California Code of Regulations, section 15000 et seq.

(3) "Environmental document" has the same meaning as section 15361 of the CEQA Guidelines. Environmental documents are prepared by the applicant or the local jurisdiction that analyzes the commercial cannabis activity or activities and which assess whether the project has the potential to generate significant adverse environmental impacts.

(b) An applicant may provide evidence of compliance with CEQA by submitting a copy of an environmental document previously certified or adopted by the local jurisdiction that evaluated the project.

(c) If a previously certified or adopted environmental document is not available or does not exist, and if the Bureau does not determine that the project is exempt from CEQA as provided in section 5010.2 of this division, the applicant shall provide information to enable the Bureau to determine what type of environmental document should be prepared by submitting the CEQA Project-Specific Information Form, BCC-LIC-025 (New 10/18), incorporated herein by reference. Such information shall include at least the following:

(1) The project location and surrounding land use, which shall:

(A) Describe the project location, including street address, city, county, Assessor's Parcel Number, major cross streets, general plan designation, zoning designation, and any other physical description that clearly indicates the project site location.

(B) Describe the surrounding land uses and zoning designations within a one-half mile radius of the project and list all abutting land uses.

(C) Include a vicinity map and aerial image to show the project location.

(D) Include photographs, not larger than 8 1/2 by 11 inches, of existing visual conditions as observed from publicly accessible vantage point(s).

(2) A project description, which shall:

(A) Describe the activities included in the project application and identify any other commercial cannabis activity or activities occurring at the proposed premises.

(B) Quantify the project size (total floor area of the project), in square feet, and the lot size on which the project is located, in square feet.

(C) List and describe any other related public agency permits and approvals, including any entitlements, required for this project, including those required by a planning commission, local air district, or regional water board.

(D) Identify whether the applicant is licensed by, or has applied for licensure from, the California Department of Food and Agriculture or the State Department of Public Health to engage in commercial cannabis activity at the proposed premises.

(E) Estimate the number of anticipated employees onsite, occupancy during operating hours, and frequency of deliveries or shipments originating from and/or arriving to the project site, and describe the anticipated transportation activity at the project site including the effects of the project related to public transit, bicycle, or pedestrian facilities.

(F) Identify the location, type, and quantity of hazardous materials, as defined by Health and Safety Code section 25260, that are stored, used, or disposed of at the project site and a copy of the Hazardous Material Business Plan (HMBP) prepared for the proposed premises, if any.

(G) Discuss whether the project will increase the quantity and type of solid waste, as defined by Public Resources Code section 40191, or hazardous waste, as defined by Health and Safety Code section 25117, that is generated or stored onsite.

(H) Describe the project's anticipated operational energy needs, identify the source of energy supplied for the project and the anticipated amount of energy per day, and explain whether the project will require an increase in energy demand and the need for additional energy resources.

(3) The Bureau shall consider, for purposes of evaluating compliance with CEQA, both the individual and cumulative impacts of all commercial cannabis activities occurring at the proposed premises.

Note: Authority cited: Section 26013, Business and Professions Code. Reference: Section 26055, Business and Professions Code.

§ 5010.1. Review of Previously Prepared Environmental Documents Pursuant to CEQA.

(a) When the project has been evaluated in a previously certified or adopted environmental document, the Bureau will evaluate the project as a responsible agency as provided in section 15096 of the CEQA Guidelines.

(b) The Bureau may require subsequent environmental review if one or more of the events outlined in Public Resources Code section 21166 or section 15162 of the CEQA Guidelines occurs.

Note: Authority cited: Section 26013, Business and Professions Code. Reference: Section 26055, Business and Professions Code; and Section 21166, Public Resources Code.

§ 5010.2. CEQA Exempt Projects.

(a) An applicant may submit documentation to the Bureau demonstrating that the project is exempt from further environmental review pursuant to CEQA, because the project falls within a class of projects determined not to have significant effect on the environment, by submitting the CEQA Exemption Petition, BCC-LIC-026 (New 10/18), incorporated herein by reference.

(b) Documentation submitted to the Bureau in support of a determination that the project is exempt from further environmental review under CEQA shall, at minimum, include the following information:

(1) Project location and surrounding land use, as required in section 5010 of this division;

(2) Project description, as required in section 5010 of this division; and

(3) A written justification to support a determination that the project is categorically exempt. The written justification shall list the category and class the exemption falls under and shall explain how the project fits the specified exemption. The justification shall also demonstrate that none of the exceptions to categorical exemptions described in section 15300.2 of the CEQA Guidelines apply to the project.

(c) Upon review, if the Bureau determines that the project is exempt from further CEQA review, and approves an application for annual licensure, the Bureau will file a Notice of Exemption with the State Clearinghouse within 5 business days after approval of the project as required by section 15062(c) of the CEQA Guidelines.

Note: Authority cited: Section 26013, Business and Professions Code. Reference: Section 26055, Business and Professions Code.

§ 5010.3. Preparation of CEQA Environmental Documents for Applicant.

If the Bureau determines that a project does not qualify for an exemption, or that the circumstances described in Public Resources Code section 21166 and section 15162 of the CEQA Guidelines require subsequent environmental review, the Bureau may charge the applicant for the costs of preparation for any supplemental environmental document as well as the Bureau's costs for procedures to comply with CEQA, unless the Bureau specifies otherwise.

Note: Authority cited: Section 26013, Business and Professions Code. Reference: Section 26055, Business and Professions Code.

§ 5011. Additional Information.

The Bureau may request additional information and documents from the applicant. The Bureau will provide the applicant a deadline for submittal of additional information. The Bureau will consider the complexity of the information requested and the ease with which the information can be obtained and transmitted to the Bureau by the applicant in determining the deadline.

Note: Authority cited: Section 26013, Business and Professions Code. Reference: Sections 26031, 26050 and 26051.5, Business and Professions Code.

§ 5012. Incomplete Applications.

(a) If the Bureau determines that the application is incomplete, the Bureau may provide notice to the applicant in accordance with Business and Professions Code section 124.

(b) If the Bureau issues a notice pursuant to Business and Professions Code section 124, an applicant has one year from the date of the notice in subsection (a) of this section to correct all deficiencies. If the applicant fails to correct the deficiencies within the one-year period and has not responded to the Bureau's attempts to contact the applicant, the application shall be considered abandoned under Business and Professions Code section 142.

(c) An applicant may reapply at any time following an abandoned application.

(d) The Bureau will not refund application fees for an incomplete or abandoned application.

Note: Authority cited: Section 26013, Business and Professions Code. Reference: Sections 124, 142, 26050 and

26051.5, Business and Professions Code.

§ 5013. Withdrawal of Application.

(a) An applicant may withdraw an application at any time prior to the Bureau's issuance of a license or denial of a license.

(b) Requests to withdraw an application must be submitted to the Bureau in writing, dated, and signed by the applicant.

(c) In accordance with Business and Professions Code section 118, withdrawal of an application shall not, unless the Bureau has consented in writing to such withdrawal, deprive the Bureau of its authority to institute or continue a proceeding against the applicant for the denial of the license upon any ground provided by law or to enter an order denying the license upon any such ground.

(d) The Bureau will not refund application fees for a withdrawn application.

(e) An applicant may reapply at any time following the withdrawal of an application and will be required to submit a new application and fee.

Note: Authority cited: Section 26013, Business and Professions Code. Reference: Sections 118 and 26050, Business and Professions Code.

ARTICLE 3. LICENSING

§ 5014. Fees.

(a) The application fee for an annual license under section 5002 of this division, a cannabis event organizer license under section 5600 of this division, a temporary cannabis event license under section 5601 of this division for each event, and physical modification of the premises under section 5027 of this division shall be paid by an applicant or licensee as provided by this division. Applicants and licensees shall pay the appropriate fee as outlined in this section.

APPLICATION FEE SCHEDULE

License Type	Fee Per Application
All Annual Licenses	$ 1,000
Cannabis Event Organizer License	$ 1,000
Temporary Cannabis Event License	$ 1,000
Physical Modification of Premises	$ 500

(b) The annual licensing fee for each license shall be paid by an applicant or licensee after the Bureau has approved the application. The Bureau shall not issue the license until the annual licensing fee has been paid.

(c) To determine the appropriate license fee due, the applicant or licensee shall first estimate the gross revenue for the 12-month license period of the license. Based on the license type sought, the applicant or licensee shall identify the appropriate tier category in which their expected gross revenue belongs, as identified in the Annual License Fee Schedule chart found in this section. The license fee associated with the licensing tier category the applicant or licensee has identified using their expected gross revenue shall be the license fee due for the application or renewal.

ANNUAL LICENSE FEE SCHEDULE

License Type	Gross Revenue ($ Max. Per License)	Fee Per License
Testing Laboratory Type 8	Less than or equal to $160,000	$3,000
	More than $160,000 and less or equal to $320,000	$6,000
	More than $320,000 and less or equal to $480,000	$8,000
	More than $480,000 and less or equal to $800,000	$13,000
	More than $800,000 and less or equal to $1.2 million	$20,000
	More than $1.2 million and less or equal to $2.0 million	$32,000
	More than $2.0 million and less or equal to $2.8 million	$48,000
	More than $2.8 million and less or equal to $4.4 million	$72,000
	More than $4.4 million	$112,000
Distributor Type 11 Type 13 (unless only engaging in transport only self-distribution)	Less than or equal to $1.0 million	$1,500
	More than $1.0 million and less or equal to $2.5 million	$6,000
	More than $2.5 million and less or equal to $5.0 million	$11,250
	More than $5.0 million and less or equal to $10.0 million	$22,500
	More than $10.0 million and less or equal to $20.0 million	$45,000
	More than $20.0 million and less or equal to $30.0 million	$75,000
	More than $30.0 million and less or equal to $50.0 million	$120,000
	More than $50.0 million and less or equal to $70.0 million	$180,000
	More than $70.0 million	$240,000

Distributor Transport Only Self-Distribution Type 13	Less than or equal to $1,000	$200
	More than $1,000 and less or equal to $3,000	$500
	More than $3,000	$1,000
Retailer Type 9 Type 10	Less than or equal to $500,000	$2,500
	More than $500,000 and less or equal to $750,000	$5,500
	More than $750,000 and less or equal to $1.0 million	$7,500
	More than $1.0 million and less or equal to $1.5 million	$11,000
	More than $1.5 million and less or equal to $2.0 million	$14,500
	More than $2.0 million and less or equal to $3.0 million	$22,500
	More than $3.0 million and less or equal to $4.0 million	$30,500
	More than $4.0 million and less or equal to $5.0 million	$38,500
	More than $5.0 million and less or equal to $6.0 million	$46,500
	More than $6.0 million and less or equal to $7.5 million	$57,000
	More than $7.5 million	$96,000
Microbusiness Type 12	Less than or equal to $1.0 million	$5,000
	More than $1.0 and less or equal to $2.0 million	$12,000
	More than $2.0 and less or equal to $3.00 million	$20,000
	More than $3.0 and less or equal to $4.0 million	$32,000
	More than $4.0 and less or equal to $6.0 million	$45,000
	More than $6.0 and less or equal to $7.0 million	$60,000
	More than $7.0 and less or equal to $10.0 million	$80,000
	More than $10.0 and less or equal to $20.0 million	$100,000
	More than $20.0 and less or equal to $30.0 million	$120,000
	More than $30.0 and less or equal to $40.0 million	$140,000
	More than $40.0 and less or equal to $50.0 million	$160,000
	More than $50.0 and less or equal to $60.0 million	$180,000
	More than $60.0 and less than or equal to $80.0 million	$220,000

	More than $80 million	$300,000

(d) Notwithstanding the fees identified above, cannabis event organizers shall pay the appropriate fee as outlined in this section.

ANNUAL LICENSE FEE SCHEDULE FOR CANNABIS EVENT ORGANIZERS

License Type	Planned Operations (Number of Operations)	Fee Per License
Cannabis Event Organizer	0-5 events annually	$3,000
	6-10 events annually	$5,000
	11-20 events annually	$9,000
	Greater than 20 events annually	$20,000

(e) All fees are nonrefundable.

Note: Authority cited: Section 26013, Business and Professions Code. Reference: Sections 26012, 26051.5 and 26180, Business and Professions Code.

§ 5015. Payment of Fees.

(a) Any fee specified in this division shall be made to the Bureau of Cannabis Control by cash, check, money order, debit card, or credit card. Check and money order payments may be made out to the Bureau of Cannabis Control or the Department of Consumer Affairs.

(b) If the fee is paid by debit or credit card:

(1) The payment shall be made through the Bureau's online licensing system; and

(2) The applicant or licensee may be required to pay any associated processing or convenience fees to the third-party vendor processing the payment on behalf of the Bureau.

(c) Failure to pay the appropriate licensing fee is grounds for discipline. If the Bureau determines that the licensee paid an amount less than the appropriate licensing fee under section 5014 of this division, the licensee will be required to pay the balance of the appropriate fee and a penalty fee of 50 percent of the appropriate licensing fee. The Bureau in its discretion may waive the penalty fee.

Note: Authority cited: Section 26013, Business and Professions Code. Reference: Sections 26012, 26051.5 and 26180, Business and Professions Code.

§ 5016. Priority Licensing.

(a) Priority licensing is available for annual licenses only, and is not applicable to any temporary or cannabis event organizer license.

(b) To be eligible for priority licensing, an applicant must be able to demonstrate that the applicant operated in compliance with the Compassionate Use Act of 1996 and its implementing laws before September 1, 2016. Eligibility for priority licensing shall be established by one of the following methods:

(1) The applicant is included on the list provided to the Bureau by the local jurisdiction in response to the Bureau's request required by Business and Professions Code section 26054.2.

(2) If the local jurisdiction does not provide a list to the Bureau or the applicant's name does not appear on the list provided to the Bureau, the applicant shall provide to the Bureau evidence of operation in compliance with the Compassionate Use Act of 1996. Such evidence shall be in the form of a document issued or signed by the applicant's local jurisdiction that contains the following:

(A) Name of the applicant;

(B) Address of the premises to be licensed;

(C) License type(s) that the applicant is applying to the Bureau for;

(D) Name of the local jurisdiction;

(E) Name of the local jurisdiction office that is responsible for enforcing compliance with the Compassionate Use Act of 1996;

(F) Name and contact information for the person authorized by the local jurisdiction to sign on its behalf;

(G) Signature of the person authorized to sign on behalf of the local jurisdiction; and

(H) A statement to the effect of: "The above-named party is currently conducting commercial cannabis activity in this jurisdiction and has been operating in compliance with the Compassionate Use Act of 1996 since before September 1, 2016."

(c) The Bureau shall not provide priority licensing pursuant to this section after December 31, 2019.

Note: Authority cited: Section 26013, Business and Professions Code. Reference: Sections 26012 and 26054.2, Business and Professions Code.

§ 5017. Substantially Related Offenses and Criteria for Rehabilitation.

(a) For the purpose of license denial, convictions that are substantially related to the qualifications, functions, or duties of the business for which the application is made include:

(1) A violent felony conviction, as specified in Penal Code section 667.5(c).

(2) A serious felony conviction, as specified in Penal Code section 1192.7(c).

(3) A felony conviction involving fraud, deceit, or embezzlement.

(4) A felony conviction for hiring, employing, or using a minor in transporting, carrying, selling, giving away, preparing for sale, or peddling, any controlled substance to a minor; or selling, offering to sell, furnishing, offering to furnish, administering, or giving any controlled substance to a minor.

(5) A felony conviction for drug trafficking with enhancements pursuant to Health and Safety Code section 11370.4 or 11379.8.

(b) Except as provided in subsections (a)(4) and (a)(5) of this section and notwithstanding Chapter 2 (commencing with Section 480) of Division 1.5 of the Business and Professions Code, a prior conviction, where the sentence, including any term of probation, incarceration, or supervised release, is completed, for possession of, possession for sale, sale, manufacture, transportation, or cultivation of a controlled substance is not considered substantially related, and shall not be the sole ground for denial of a license. Conviction for any controlled substance felony subsequent to licensure shall be grounds for revocation of a license or denial of the renewal of a license.

(c) When evaluating whether an applicant who has been convicted of a criminal offense that is substantially related to the qualifications, functions, or duties of the business for which the application is made should be issued a license, the Bureau shall consider the following criteria of rehabilitation:

(1) The nature and severity of the act or offense;

(2) Whether the person has a felony conviction based on possession or use of cannabis or cannabis products that would not be a felony if the person was convicted of the offense on the date of the person's application;

(3) The applicant's criminal record as a whole;

(4) Evidence of any act committed subsequent to the act or offense under consideration that could be considered grounds for denial, suspension, or revocation of a commercial cannabis activity license;

(5) The time that has elapsed since commission of the act or offense;

(6) The extent to which the applicant has complied with any terms of parole, probation, restitution, or any other sanctions lawfully imposed against the applicant;

(7) If applicable, evidence of dismissal under Penal Code sections 1203.4, 1203.4a, 1203.41 or another state's similar law;

(8) If applicable, a certificate of rehabilitation obtained under Penal Code section 4852.01 or another state's similar law; and

(9) Other evidence of rehabilitation submitted by the applicant.

(d) If an applicant has been denied a license based on a conviction, the applicant may request a hearing pursuant to Business and Professions Code section 26058 to determine if the applicant should be issued a license.

Note: Authority cited: Section 26013, Business and Professions Code. Reference: Sections 482, 26012 and 26057, Business and Professions Code.

§ 5018. Additional Grounds for Denial of a License.

In addition to the reasons for denial in Business and Professions Code section 26057, a license may be denied for the following reasons:

(a) The applicant's proposed premises does not fully comply with standards set in regulation.

(b) The applicant's proposed or licensed premises is substantially different from the diagram of the proposed premises submitted by the applicant, in that the size, layout, location of common entryways, doorways, or passage ways means of public entry or exit, or identification of limited-access areas within the licensed premises is not the same.

(c) The applicant denied the Bureau access to the licensed premises.

(d) The applicant made a material misrepresentation on the application.

(e) The applicant did not correct the deficiencies within the application in accordance with sections 5002 and 5012 of this division.

(f) The applicant has been denied a license, permit, or other authorization to engage in commercial cannabis activity by a state or local licensing authority.

(g) The applicant's proposed premises is not in compliance with Division 13 (commencing with Section 21000) of the Public Resources Code.

(h) The applicant has failed to remit taxes as required under the Revenue and Taxation Code.

(i) The applicant may be denied a license for any violations of law related to the operations of the commercial cannabis business or for any violations of law related to licensure.

Note: Authority cited: Section 26013, Business and Professions Code. Reference: Sections 480, 490, 26012, 26030 and 26050, Business and Professions Code.

§ 5019. Excessive Concentration.

(a) In determining whether to grant, deny, or renew a license for a retail premises or microbusiness premises authorized to engage in retail sales, the Bureau shall consider if an excessive concentration exists in the area where the licensee will operate. For the purposes of this section "excessive concentration" applies when either of the following conditions exist:

(1) The ratio of licensees to population within the census tract or census division in which the applicant premises is located exceeds the ratio of licensees to population in the county in which the applicant premises is located, unless denial of the application would unduly limit the development of the legal market so as to perpetuate the illegal market for cannabis goods.

(2) The ratio of retail licenses or microbusiness licenses to the population within the census tract, census division, or jurisdiction exceeds that allowable by local ordinance adopted under Business and Professions Code section 26200.

(b) "Population Within the Census Tract or Census Division" as used in this section means the population as determined by the most recent United States decennial or special census. Such population determination shall not operate to prevent an applicant from establishing that an increase of resident population has occurred within the census tract or census division.

(c) "Population in the County" as used in this section shall be determined by the most recent annual population estimate for California counties published by the Demographic Research Unit, State Department of Finance.

(d) Beginning July 1, 2018, the Bureau shall calculate the ratios described in subsection (a) of this section once every six months using the most current available data. The Bureau's consideration of whether to grant, deny, or renew a license shall be based upon the most recent ratio calculated by the Bureau on the date of the Bureau's decision.

(e) The existence of an excessive concentration shall not be considered in determining whether to grant, deny, or extend a temporary license under Business and Professions Code section 26050.1.

(f) The applicant may provide reliable evidence establishing, to the satisfaction of the Bureau, that a denial of a license would unduly limit the development of the legal market so as to perpetuate the illegal market for cannabis goods.

Note: Authority cited: Section 26013, Business and Professions Code. Reference: Sections 26012 and 26051, Business and Professions Code.

applicant.

(c) Licenses are not transferrable or assignable to another person or owner. In the event of the sale or other transfer of the business or operations covered by the licensee, changes in ownership shall be made in accordance with the following:

(1) If one or more of the owners of a license change, the new owners shall submit the information required under section 5002(c)(20) for each new owner to the Bureau within 14 calendar days of the effective date of the ownership change. The business may continue to operate under the active license while the Bureau reviews the qualifications of the new owner(s) in accordance with the Act and these regulations to determine whether the change would constitute grounds for denial of the license, if at least one existing owner is not transferring his or her ownership interest and will remain as an owner under the new ownership structure. If all owners will be transferring their ownership interest, the business shall not operate under the new ownership structure until a new license application has been submitted to and approved by the Bureau, and all application and license fees for the new application have been paid.

(A) A change in ownership occurs when a new person meets the definition of owner in section 5003 of this division.

(B) A change in ownership does not occur when one or more owners leave the business by transferring their ownership interest to the other existing owner(s).

(2) In cases where one or more owners leave the business by transferring their ownership interest to the other existing owner(s), the owner or owners that are transferring their interest shall provide a signed statement to the Bureau confirming that they have transferred their interest.

(d) When there is a change in persons with financial interest(s) in the commercial cannabis business that do not meet the requirements for a new license application under this section, the licensee shall submit the information required by sections 5002(c)(19) and 5004 of this division to the Bureau within 14 calendar days of the change.

(e) When any of the following changes occur, the licensee shall notify the Bureau within 14 calendar days of the change:

(1) Any change to contact information from the information provided to the Bureau in the original application.

(2) Any change in name if the licensee is an individual, or any change in legal business name if the licensee is a business entity.

(3) Any change in business trade name (DBA) or fictitious business names.

(4) Any change to financial information including funds, loans, investments, and gifts required in the original application under section 5002(c)(18) of this division.

(5) Any change in the bond required under section 5008 of this division.

(6) Any change or lapse in insurance coverage required under section 5308 of this division.

(f) Licensees may request to add an A-designation or M-designation to their license by sending a notification to the Bureau signed by at least one owner as defined in section 5003 of this division. A licensee shall not operate under the requested designation until they have received approval from the Bureau.

(g) Microbusiness licensees may add a commercial cannabis activity to their license or remove a commercial cannabis activity from their license if doing so is consistent with the requirement set forth in section 5500(a) of this division that licensees engage in at least three (3) commercial cannabis activities. Licensees shall request the modification by completing a request to modify the licensed premises pursuant to section 5027 of this division. A licensee shall not engage in a new commercial cannabis activity until they have paid for the modification and received approval from the Bureau.

(h) Licenses may not be transferred from one premises to another. Licensees shall not operate out of a new premises until they have been issued a new license.

(i) For any business modification or notification under this section, licensees shall use and submit to the Bureau the Notification and Request Form, BCC-LIC-027 (New 10/18), which is incorporated herein by reference, unless the change can be made through the Bureau's online system.

Note: Authority cited: Section 26013, Business and Professions Code. Reference: Sections 136 and 26012, Business and Professions Code.

§ 5024. Death, Incapacity, or Insolvency of a Licensee.

(a) In the event of the death, incapacity, receivership, assignment for the benefit of creditors or other event rendering one or more owners incapable of performing the duties associated with the license, the owner or owners' successor in interest (e.g., appointed guardian, executor, administrator, receiver, trustee, or assignee) shall notify the Bureau in writing, within 14 calendar days, by submitting the Notification and Request Form, BCC-LIC-027 (New 10/18), which is incorporated herein by reference.

(b) To continue operations or cancel the existing license, the successor in interest shall submit to the Bureau the following:

(1) The name of the successor in interest.

(2) The name of the owner(s) for which the successor in interest is succeeding and the license number;

(3) The phone number, mailing address, and email address of the successor in interest; and

(4) Documentation demonstrating that the owner(s) is incapable of performing the duties associated with the license such as a death certificate or a court order, and documentation demonstrating that the person making the request is the owner or owners' successor in interest such as a court order appointing guardianship, receivership, or a will or trust agreement.

(c) The Bureau may give the successor in interest written approval to continue operations on the licensed business premises for a period of time specified by the Bureau:

(1) If the successor in interest or another person has applied for a license from the Bureau for the licensed premises and that application is under review;

(2) If the successor in interest needs additional time to destroy or sell cannabis goods; or

(3) At the discretion of the Bureau.

(d) The successor in interest is held subject to all terms and conditions under which a state cannabis license is held pursuant to the Act.

(e) The approval creates no vested right to the issuance of a state cannabis license.

Note: Authority cited: Section 26013, Business and Professions Code. Reference: Section 26012, Business and Professions Code.

§ 5024.1. Cannabis Goods After Termination of License.

In the event a license is terminated for any reason while cannabis goods remain on the premises, the following actions may be taken:

(a) The cannabis goods may be destroyed by the former licensee; or

(b) A licensed distributor or licensed microbusiness authorized to engage in distribution may be authorized by the Bureau to purchase and distribute the former licensee's entire inventory stock in accordance with the following;

(1) A licensed distributor or licensed microbusiness authorized to engage in distribution shall, within 14 calendar days of the termination of the former licensee's license, submit a written request to the Bureau, on the Notification and Request Form, BCC-LIC-027 (New 10/18), which is incorporated by reference, for authorization to purchase the cannabis goods from the former licensee; and

(2) Upon approval from the Bureau, the licensed distributor or licensed microbusiness authorized to engage in distribution shall transport the cannabis goods to their premises, arrange for laboratory testing, and perform quality assurance in accordance with Chapter 2 of this division. If the cannabis goods have already been tested in accordance with Chapter 6 of this division and have a valid certificate of analysis for regulatory compliance testing that is less than 12 months old, the cannabis goods are not required to undergo additional testing.

Note: Authority cited: Section 26013, Business and Professions Code. Reference: Sections 26011.5 and 26013, Business and Professions Code.

§ 5025. Premises.

(a) Each license shall have a designated licensed premises, with a distinct street address and suite number if applicable, for the licensee's commercial cannabis activity. Each licensed premises shall be subject to inspection by the Bureau.

(b) The Bureau may allow a licensee to conduct both adult-use and medicinal commercial cannabis activity on the same licensed premises if all of the following criteria are met:

(1) The licensee holds both an A-designation and an M-designation on the license for the identical type of commercial cannabis activity; and

(2) The licensee only conducts one type of commercial cannabis activity on the licensed premises.

(c) Licensed retailers and licensed microbusinesses authorized to engage in retail sales shall only serve customers who are within the licensed premises, or at a delivery address that meets the requirements of this division.

(1) The sale and delivery of cannabis goods shall not occur through a pass-out window or a slide-out tray to the exterior of the licensed premises.

(2) Licensed retailers or licensed microbusinesses authorized to engage in retail sales shall not operate as or with a drive-in or drive-through at which cannabis goods are sold to persons within or about a motor vehicle.

(3) No cannabis goods shall be sold and/or delivered by any means or method to any person within a motor vehicle.

(d) Alcoholic beverages as defined in Business and Professions Code section 23004 shall not be stored or consumed on a licensed premises.

(e) Any licensed premises that is adjacent to another premises engaging in manufacturing or cultivation shall be separated from those premises by walls, and any doors leading to the cultivation or manufacturing premises shall remain closed.

(g) Cannabis shall not be dispersed in the air throughout the premises or throughout a portion of the premises by an oil diffuser or any other vaporizing device that is intended to disperse the vapor throughout the premises or throughout a portion of the premises. This section shall not be interpreted to prohibit cannabis consumption on the premises of a licensed retailer or licensed microbusiness authorized to engage in retail sales that is conducted in accordance with Business and Professions Code section 26200(g).

(g) Notwithstanding subsection (c), of this section, an applicant or licensee may have a drive-in or drive-through window only if, prior to June 1, 2018:

(1) The licensee or applicant received a license or permit from the local jurisdiction for a premises including a drive-in or drive-through window which was disclosed on the local application; or

(2) The licensee or applicant has submitted an application to the local jurisdiction for a license or permit which, at the time of submission of the application, included information that a drive-in or drive-through window was already part of, or proposed to be part of, the premises, and after June 1, 2018, the local jurisdiction approves the premises with a drive-in or drive-through window.

Note: Authority cited: Section 26013, Business and Professions Code. Reference: Sections 26001, 26012 and 26053, Business and Professions Code.

§ 5026. Premises Location.

(a) A premises licensed under this division shall not be located within a 600-foot radius of a school providing instruction in kindergarten or any grades 1 through 12, day care center, or youth center that is in existence at the time the license is issued.

(b) Notwithstanding subsection (a) of this section, if a local jurisdiction has issued a license or permit to conduct commercial cannabis activity at a premises that is located within a 600-foot radius of a school providing instruction in kindergarten or any grades 1 through 12, day care center, or youth center, the Bureau may approve the premises for licensure if the following conditions are met:

(1) The applicant submits a copy of a valid license or permit from the local jurisdiction with the application for licensure; and

(2) The local jurisdiction notifies the Bureau that the applicant is in compliance with all applicable local ordinances and regulations pursuant to Business and Professions Code section 26055(g)(2)(C).

(c) A licensed premises shall not be in a location that requires persons to pass through a business that sells alcohol or tobacco or a private residence to access the licensed premises.

(d) A licensed premises shall not be in a location that requires persons to pass through the licensed premises to access a business that sells alcohol or tobacco or a private residence.

(e) A licensed premises shall not be located within a private residence.

(f) Licensees shall ensure that the Bureau has immediate access to their licensed premises. If the Bureau is denied access to a licensee's premises for any reason, the licensee shall be held responsible and subject to discipline. If the Bureau is denied access to one licensee's premises because of another licensee's refusal to grant access when the only access to one licensed premises is through another licensed premises, all licensees shall be held responsible and subject to discipline.

(g) Nothing in this section shall be interpreted to prohibit two or more licensed premises from occupying separate portions of the same parcel of land or sharing common use areas, such as a bathroom, breakroom, hallway, or building entrance.

(h) All structures included as part of the licensed premises shall be permanently affixed to the land by a method that would cause the structure to ordinarily remain affixed for an indefinite period of time. Structures that will not be considered to be permanent structures include, but are not limited to, shipping containers that are not affixed to the land, modular buildings that are not affixed to the land, structures that rest on wheels, or any structure that can be readily moved.

Note: Authority cited: Section 26013, Business and Professions Code. Reference: Sections 26012, 26051.5, 26054 and 26055, Business and Professions Code.

§ 5027. Physical Modification of Premises.

(a) A licensee shall not, without the prior written approval of the Bureau, make a physical change, alteration, or modification of the licensed premises that materially or substantially alters the licensed premises or the use of the licensed premises from the premises diagram originally filed with the license application. A licensee whose licensed premises is to be materially or substantially changed, modified, or altered is responsible for filing a request for premises modification with the Bureau.

(b) Material or substantial changes, alterations, or modifications requiring approval include, but are not limited to:

(c) The removal, creation, or relocation of a common entryway, doorway, passage, or a means of public entry or exit, when such common entryway, doorway, or passage alters or changes limited-access areas within the licensed premises;

    (1) The removal, creation, or relocation of a wall or barrier; or

    (2) Changing the activities conducted in or the use of an area identified in the last premises diagram provided to the Bureau.

(d) A licensee shall request approval of a physical change, alteration, or modification in writing, by submitting the Notification and Request Form, BCC-LIC-027 (New 10/18), which is incorporated herein by reference, and the request shall include:

    (1) A new premises diagram that conforms to requirements in section 5006 of this division; and

    (2) A fee pursuant to section 5014 of this division.

(e) A licensee shall provide additional documentation requested by the Bureau to evaluate the licensee's request to modify the licensed premises.

Note: Authority cited: Section 26013, Business and Professions Code. Reference: Sections 26012 and 26055, Business and Professions Code.

§ 5028. Subletting of Premises.

A licensee shall not sublet any area designated as the licensed premises for the licensee's commercial cannabis activity.

Note: Authority cited: Section 26013, Business and Professions Code. Reference: Sections 26012 and 26070, Business and Professions Code.

§ 5029. Transition to Regulated Commercial Cannabis Market. [Repealed]

§ 5030. Licensee's Responsibility for Acts of Employees and

Agents.

In construing and enforcing the provisions of the Act and the regulations in this division, the act, omission, or failure of an agent, officer, representative, or other person acting for or employed by a licensee, within the scope of his or her employment or office, shall in every case be deemed the act, omission, or failure of the licensee.

Note: Authority cited: Section 26013, Business and Professions Code. Reference: Sections 26031 and 26110, Business and Professions Code.

§ 5031. Age Restriction.

Employees or persons retained by a licensee to work within or on a licensed premises or to handle cannabis goods shall be at least 21 years of age.

Note: Authority cited: Section 26013, Business and Professions Code. Reference: Section 26140, Business and Professions Code.

§ 5032. Commercial Cannabis Activity.

(a) All commercial cannabis activity shall be conducted between licensees. Licensed retailers and licensed microbusinesses authorized to engage in retail sales may conduct commercial cannabis activity with customers in accordance with Chapter 3 of this division.

(b) Licensees shall not conduct commercial cannabis activities on behalf of, at the request of, or pursuant to a contract with any person who is not licensed under the Act.

(c) Licensees may conduct business with other licensees irrespective of the M-designation or A-designation on their licenses.

(d) Licensed distributors or licensed microbusinesses authorized to engage in distribution shall only transport and sell cannabis goods designated as "For Medical Use Only," pursuant to the requirements prescribed by the State Department of Public Health in regulation, to M-designated retailers or M-designated microbusinesses authorized to engage in retail sales.

(e) Products designated as "For Medical Use Only," pursuant to requirements prescribed by the State Department of Public Health in regulation, shall only be sold to medicinal customers by M-designated retailers or M-designated microbusinesses authorized to engage in retail sales.

Note: Authority cited: Section 26013, Business and Professions Code. Reference: Sections 26001, 26013 and 26053, Business and Professions Code.

§ 5033. Storage of Inventory.

(a) All inventory stored on the licensed premises shall be secured in a limited-access area.

(b) A licensee shall not store cannabis goods outdoors.

(c) Employee break rooms, changing facilities, and bathrooms shall be separated from all storage areas.

(d) Each location where cannabis goods are stored must be separately licensed.

Note: Authority cited: Section 26013, Business and Professions Code. Reference: Sections 26012 and 26070, Business and Professions Code.

§ 5034. Significant Discrepancy in Inventory.

A determination by a licensee on whether a discrepancy in inventory is significant shall be made in accordance with the following:

(a) A significant discrepancy in inventory means a difference in actual inventory compared to records pertaining to inventory of at least 3 percent of the average monthly sales of the licensee.

(b) For the purposes of this section, average monthly sales shall be calculated by taking a per month average of the total sales for the previous 6 months. If the licensee has not been in operation for at least 6 months, only the months in which the licensee was operating shall be used in determining average monthly sales.

(c) For the purposes of this section, the licensee's acquisition price shall be used to determine the value of cannabis goods in a licensee's inventory.

Note: Authority cited: Section 26013, Business and Professions Code. Reference: Section 26070, Business and Professions Code.

§ 5035. Notification of Criminal Acts, Civil Judgments, Violations of Labor Standards, and Revocation of a Local License, Permit, or Other Authorization After Licensure.

(a) A licensee shall ensure that the Bureau is notified in writing of a criminal conviction of any owner, either by mail or electronic mail, within 48 hours of the conviction. The written notification to the Bureau shall include the date of conviction, the court docket number, the name of the court in which the licensee was convicted, and the specific offense(s) for which the licensee was convicted.

(b) A licensee shall ensure that the Bureau is notified in writing of a civil penalty or judgment rendered against the licensee or any owner in their individual capacity, either by mail or electronic mail, within 48 hours of delivery of the verdict or entry of judgment, whichever is sooner. The written notification shall include the date of verdict or entry of judgment, the court docket number, the name of the court in which the matter was adjudicated, and a description of the civil penalty or judgment rendered against the licensee.

(c) A licensee shall ensure that the Bureau is notified in writing of an administrative order or civil judgment for violations of labor standards against the licensee or any owner in their individual capacity, either by mail or electronic mail, within 48 hours of delivery of the order. The written notification shall include the date of the order, the name of the agency issuing the order, and a description of the administrative penalty or judgment rendered against the licensee.

(d) A licensee shall ensure that the Bureau is notified in writing of the revocation of a local license, permit, or other authorization, either by mail or electronic mail, within 48 hours of receiving notice of the revocation. The written notification shall include the name of the local agency involved, a written explanation of the proceeding or enforcement action, and the specific violation(s) that led to revocation.

(e) For any notification required under this section, licensees shall use and submit to the Bureau the Notification and Request Form, BCC-LIC-027 (New 10/18), which is incorporated herein by reference.

Note: Authority cited: Section 26013, Business and Professions Code. Reference: Sections 26030 and 26031, Business and Professions Code.

§ 5036. Notification of Theft, Loss, and Criminal Activity.

(a) A licensee shall notify the Bureau and local law enforcement within 24 hours of discovery of any of the following situations:

(1) The licensee discovers a significant discrepancy, as defined in section 5034 of this division, in its inventory.

(2) The licensee discovers diversion, theft, loss, or any other criminal activity pertaining to the operations of the licensee.

(3) The licensee discovers diversion, theft, loss, or any other criminal activity by an agent or employee of the licensee pertaining to the operations of the licensee.

(4) The licensee discovers loss or unauthorized alteration of records related to cannabis goods, customers, or the licensee's employees or agents.

(5) The licensee discovers any other breach of security.

(b) The notification to the Bureau pursuant to subsection (a) of this section shall be submitted on the Notification and Request Form, BCC-LIC-027 (New 10/18), which is incorporated herein by reference, and shall include the date and time of occurrence of the theft, loss, or criminal activity, the name of the local law enforcement agency that was notified, and a description of the incident including, where applicable, the item(s) that were taken or lost.

Note: Authority cited: Section 26013, Business and Professions Code. Reference: Section 26070, Business and Professions Code.

§ 5037. Record Retention.

(a) Each licensee shall keep and maintain the following records related to commercial cannabis activity for at least seven years:

(1) Financial records including, but not limited to, bank statements, sales invoices, receipts, tax records, and all records required by the California Department of Tax and Fee Administration (formerly Board of Equalization) under title 18, California Code of Regulations, sections 1698 and 4901.

(2) Personnel records, including each employee's full name, social security or individual tax payer identification number, date employment begins, and date of termination of employment if applicable.

(3) Training records including, but not limited to, the content of the training provided and the names of the employees that received the training.

(4) Contracts with other licensees regarding commercial cannabis activity.

(5) Permits, licenses, and other local authorizations to conduct the licensee's commercial cannabis activity.

(6) Security records, except for surveillance recordings required pursuant to section 5044 of this division.

(7) Records relating to the composting or destruction of cannabis goods.

(8) Documentation for data or information entered into the track and trace system.

(9) All other documents prepared or executed by an owner or their employees or assignees in connection with the licensed commercial cannabis business.

(b) All required records shall be prepared and retained in accordance with the following conditions:

(1) Records shall be legible; and

(2) Records shall be stored in a secured area where the records are protected from debris, moisture, contamination, hazardous waste, fire, and theft.

(c) The Bureau may make any examination of the books and records of any licensee as it deems necessary to perform its duties under the Act.

(d) All records are subject to review by the Bureau any time the licensee is exercising the privileges of the license or at any other time as mutually agreed to by the Bureau and the licensee. Prior notice by the Bureau to review records is not necessary. The Bureau may review records outside of the licensee's standard daily business hours.

(e) Records shall be kept in a manner that allows records to be produced for the Bureau immediately upon request at the licensed premises in either hard copy or electronic form, whichever the Bureau requests.

Note: Authority cited: Section 26013, Business and Professions Code. Reference: Sections 26160 and 26161, Business and Professions Code.

§ 5038. Disaster Relief.

(a) If a licensee is unable to comply with any licensing requirements due to a disaster, the licensee may notify the Bureau of this inability to comply and request relief from the specific licensing requirement.

(b) The Bureau may exercise its discretion to provide temporary relief from specific regulatory requirements in this division and from other licensing requirements when allowed bylaw.

(c) Temporary relief from specific licensing requirements shall be issued for a reasonable amount of time in order to allow the licensee to recover from the disaster.

(d) The Bureau may require that certain conditions be followed in order for a licensee to receive temporary relief from specific licensing requirements.

(e) A licensee shall not be subject to an enforcement action for a violation of a licensing requirement in which the licensee has received temporary relief.

(f) For the purposes of this section, "disaster" means condition of extreme peril to the safety of persons and property within the state or a county, city and county, or city caused by such conditions as air pollution, fire, flood, storm, tidal wave, epidemic, riot, drought, terrorism, sudden and severe energy shortage, plant or animal infestation or disease, Governor's warning of an earthquake or volcanic prediction, or an earthquake, or similar public calamity, other than conditions resulting from a labor controversy, for which the Governor has proclaimed a state of emergency in accordance with Government Code sections 8558 and 8625, or for which a local governing body has proclaimed a local emergency in accordance with Government Code sections 8558 and 8630.

(g) A licensed premises that has been vacated by a licensee due to a disaster shall not be deemed to have been abandoned or quit under section 5022 of this division.

(h) Notwithstanding subsection (a) of this section, if a licensee needs to move cannabis goods stored on the licensed premises to another location immediately to prevent loss, theft, or degradation of the cannabis goods from the disaster, the licensee may move the cannabis goods without obtaining prior approval from the Bureau if the following conditions are met:

(1) The cannabis goods are moved to a secure location where access to the cannabis goods can be restricted to the licensee, its employees, and contractors;

(2) The licensee notifies the Bureau in writing, by submitting the Notification and Request Form, BCC-LIC-027 (New 10/18), which is incorporated herein by reference, that the cannabis goods have been moved and that the licensee is requesting relief from complying with specific licensing requirements pursuant to subsection (a) of

this section within 24 hours of moving the cannabis goods;

(3) The licensee agrees to grant the Bureau access to the location where the cannabis goods have been moved to for inspection; and

(4) The licensee submits in writing the Notification and Request Form, BCC-LIC-027 (New 10/18), incorporated herein by reference, to the Bureau within 14 calendar days of moving the cannabis goods a request for temporary relief that clearly indicates what statutory and regulatory sections relief is requested from, the time period for which the relief is requested, and the reasons relief is needed for the specified amount of time.

Note: Authority cited: Section 26013, Business and Professions Code. Reference: Section 26012, Business and Professions Code.

ARTICLE 4. POSTING AND ADVERTISING

§ 5039. License Posting Requirement.

Upon issuance of any license, the licensee shall prominently display the license on the licensed premises where it can be viewed by state and local agencies. If the licensed premises is open to the public, the license shall be displayed in an area that is within plain sight of the public.

Note: Authority cited: Section 26013, Business and Professions Code. Reference: Section 26012, Business and Professions Code.

§ 5040. Advertising Placement.

(a) Any advertising or marketing, as defined in Business and Professions Code section 26150, that is placed in broadcast, cable, radio, print, and digital communications:

(1) Shall only be displayed after a licensee has obtained reliable up-to-date audience composition data demonstrating that at least 71.6 percent of the audience viewing the advertising or marketing is reasonably expected to be 21 years of age or older;

(2) Shall not use any depictions or images of minors or anyone under 21 years of age;

(3) Shall not contain the use of objects, such as toys, inflatables, movie characters, cartoon characters, or include any other display, depiction, or image designed in any manner likely to be appealing to minors or anyone under 21 years of age; and

(4) Shall not advertise free cannabis goods or giveaways of any type of products, including non-cannabis products. This includes promotions such as:

(A) Buy one product, get one product free;

(B) Free product with any donation; and

(C) Contests, sweepstakes, or raffles.

(b) In addition to the requirements for advertising and marketing in subsection (a) of this section, all outdoor signs, including billboards, shall:

(1) Be affixed to a building or permanent structure;

(2) Comply with the provisions of the Outdoor Advertising Act, commencing with section 5200 of the Business

and Professions Code, if applicable; and

(3) Not be located within a 15-mile radius of the California border on an Interstate Highway or on a State Highway that crosses the California border.

(c) For the purposes of this section, "reliable up-to-date audience composition data" means data regarding the age and location demographics of the audience viewing a particular advertising or marketing medium. "Reliable up-to-date audience composition data" does not include data from the most recent United States decennial or special census, or the annual population estimate for California counties published by the Demographic Research Unit, State Department of Finance.

(d) Immediately upon request, a licensee shall provide to the Bureau audience composition data as required in subsection (a) of this section for advertising or marketing placed by the licensee.

(e) If the Bureau determines that audience composition data for advertising or marketing provided by a licensee does not comply with the requirements of subsection (a) of this section, or the licensee fails to provide audience composition data to the Bureau upon request, the licensee shall remove the advertising or marketing placement in question.

(f) In construing and enforcing the advertising provisions of the Act and this division, any action, omission, or failure of an advertising agent, representative, or contractor retained by the licensee shall in every case be deemed the act, omission, or failure of the licensee.

Note: Authority cited: Section 26013, Business and Professions Code. Reference: Sections 26151 and 26152, Business and Professions Code.

§ 5040.1. Marketing Cannabis Goods as Alcoholic Products.

Licensees shall not sell or transport cannabis goods that are labeled as beer, wine, liquor, spirits, or any other term that may create a misleading impression that the product is an alcoholic beverage as defined in Division 9 of the Business and Professions Code.

Note: Authority cited: Section 26013, Business and Professions Code. Reference: Sections 26054, 26151 and 26152, Business and Professions Code.

§ 5041. Age Confirmation in Advertising.

(a) Prior to any advertising or marketing from the licensee involving direct, individualized communication or dialogue, the licensee shall use age affirmation to verify that the recipient is 21 years of age or older.

(b) For the purposes of this section, direct, individualized communication or dialogue may occur through any form of communication, including in-person, telephone, physical mail, or electronic.

(c) A method of age verification is not necessary for a communication if the licensee can verify that the licensee has previously had the intended recipient undergo a method of age affirmation and the licensee is reasonably certain that the communication will only be received by the intended recipient.

(d) A licensee shall use a method of age affirmation before having a potential customer added to a mailing list, subscribe, or otherwise consent to receiving direct, individualized communication or dialogue controlled by a licensee.

Note: Authority cited: Section 26013, Business and Professions Code. Reference: Sections 26151 and 26152, Business and Professions Code.

§ 5041.1. Branded Merchandise Approval.

(a) If a licensed distributor, licensed retailer, or licensed microbusiness authorized to engage in distribution or retail sales wishes to sell branded merchandise that is not listed in section 5000, subsection (b), of this division, the licensee must receive written approval from the Bureau.

(b) To obtain approval, a licensee must submit a written request to the Bureau for approval to sell a specific item of branded merchandise and provide a photograph of the branded merchandise. Requests may be submitted by mail to the Bureau office or by email to bcc@dca.ca.gov.

(c) The licensee shall not sell the merchandise until receiving written approval from the Bureau for the specific item of branded merchandise.

Note: Authority cited: Section 26013, Business and Professions Code. Reference: Sections 26013 and 26152, Business and Professions Code.

ARTICLE 5. SECURITY MEASURES

§ 5042. Limited-Access Areas.

(a) Licensees shall ensure that only employees of the licensee and other authorized individuals access the limited-access areas of the licensed premises.

(b) For the purpose of this section, authorized individuals include outside vendors, contractors, or other individuals conducting business that requires access to the limited-access areas.

(c) An individual who enters the limited-access area and is not employed by the licensee shall be escorted by an employee of the licensee at all times while within the limited-access area.

(d) A licensee shall maintain a record of all authorized individuals who are not employees of the licensee who enter the limited-access areas. The record shall include the name of the individual, the company the individual works for, the reason the individual entered the limited-access area, the date, and the times the individual entered and exited the limited-access area. These records shall be made available to the Bureau immediately upon request.

(e) A licensee shall not receive consideration or compensation for permitting an individual to enter the limited-access areas.

(f) Entrances to all limited-access areas shall have a solid door and a lock meeting the requirements of section 5046 of this division. The door shall remain closed when not in use during regular business hours.

Note: Authority cited: Section 26013, Business and Professions Code. Reference: Sections 26070 and 26160, Business and Professions Code.

§ 5043. Licensee Employee Badge Requirement.

All agents, officers, or other persons acting for or employed by a licensee shall display a laminated or plastic-coated identification badge issued by the licensee at all times while engaging in commercial cannabis activity. The identification badge shall, at a minimum, include the licensee's "doing business as" name and license number, the employee's first name, an employee number exclusively assigned to that employee for identification purposes, and a color photograph of the employee that clearly shows the full front of the employee's face and that is at least 1 inch in width and 1.5 inches in height.

Note: Authority cited: Section 26013, Business and Professions Code. Reference: Section 26070, Business and Professions Code.

§ 5044. Video Surveillance System.

(a) Each licensed premises shall have a digital video surveillance system with a minimum camera resolution of 1280 x 720 pixels.

(b) The video surveillance system shall at all times be able to effectively and clearly record images of the area under surveillance.

(c) Each camera shall be permanently mounted and in a fixed location. Each camera shall be placed in a location that allows the camera to clearly record activity occurring within 20 feet of all points of entry and exit on the licensed premises, and allows for the clear and certain identification of any person and activities in all areas required to be filmed under subsection (d) of this section.

(d) Areas that shall be recorded on the video surveillance system include the following:

> (1) Areas where cannabis goods are weighed, packed, stored, loaded, and unloaded for transportation, prepared, or moved within the licensed premises;

> (2) Limited-access areas;

> (3) Security rooms;

> (4) Areas storing a surveillance-system storage device with at least one camera recording the access points to the secured surveillance recording area; and

> (5) Entrances and exits to the licensed premises, which shall be recorded from both indoor and outdoor vantage points.

(e) Licensed retailers and licensed microbusinesses authorized to engage in retail sales shall also record point-of-sale areas and areas where cannabis goods are displayed for sale on the video surveillance system. At each point-of-sale location, camera placement must allow for the recording of the facial features of any person purchasing or selling cannabis goods, or any person in the retail area, with sufficient clarity to determine identity.

(f) Cameras shall record continuously 24 hours per day and at a minimum of 15 frames per second (FPS).

(g) The physical media or storage device on which surveillance recordings are stored shall be secured in a manner to protect the recording from tampering or theft.

(h) Surveillance recordings shall be kept for a minimum of 90 calendar days.

(i) Surveillance recordings are subject to inspection by the Bureau, and shall be kept in a manner that allows the Bureau to view and obtain copies of the recordings at the licensed premises immediately upon request. The licensee shall also send or otherwise provide copies of the recordings to the Bureau upon request within the time specified by the Bureau.

(j) Recorded images shall clearly and accurately display the time and date. Time is to be measured in accordance with the standards issued by the United States National Institute of Standards and Technology.

(k) The video surveillance system shall be equipped with a failure notification system that provides notification to the licensee of any interruption or failure of the video surveillance system or video surveillance-system storage device.

(l) If multiple licensed premises are contained within the same building, a single video surveillance system covering the entire building may be used by all of the licensees under the following conditions:

(1) Each applicant or licensee shall disclose on their premises diagram where the surveillance recordings are stored.

(2) Each applicant or licensee shall include in their security operating procedures, submitted with the application pursuant to section 5002(c)(29)(D) of this division, an explanation of how the video surveillance system will be shared, including who is responsible for monitoring the video footage and storing any video recordings.

(3) All licensees shall have immediate access to the surveillance recordings to produce them pursuant to subsection (i) of this section.

(4) All licensees shall be held responsible and subject to discipline for any violations of the video surveillance requirements.

Note: Authority cited: Section 26013, Business and Professions Code. Reference: Section 26070, Business and Professions Code.

§ 5045. Security Personnel.

(a) A licensed retailer or licensed microbusiness authorized to engage in retail sales shall hire or contract for security personnel who are at least 21 years of age to provide on-site security services for the licensed retail premises during the hours of operation. All security personnel hired or contracted for by the licensee shall be licensed by the Bureau of Security and Investigative Services and shall comply with Chapters 11.4 and 11.5 of Division 3 of the Business and Professions Code.

(b) Notwithstanding subsection (a) of this section, a licensed non-storefront retailer or licensed microbusiness who is not engaged in storefront retail sale is not required to hire or contract for security personnel.

(c) If multiple licensed premises are contained within the same building, security personnel may be shared by all of the licensees to cover the entire building under the following conditions:

(1) Each licensee shall include in their security operating procedures, submitted with the application pursuant to section 5002(c)(29)(D) of this division, an explanation of how security personnel will be shared, including who is responsible for employing or contracting the security personnel.

(2) All licensees shall be held responsible and subject to discipline for any violations of the security personnel requirements.

Note: Authority cited: Section 26013, Business and Professions Code. Reference: Section 26070, Business and Professions Code.

§ 5046. Locks.

A licensee shall ensure that the limited-access areas described in section 5042 of this division can be securely locked using commercial-grade, nonresidential door locks. A licensee shall also use commercial-grade, nonresidential door locks on all points of entry and exit to the licensed premises.

Note: Authority cited: Section 26013, Business and Professions Code. Reference: Section 26070, Business and Professions Code.

§ 5047. Alarm System.

(a) A licensee shall maintain an alarm system as defined in Business and Professions Code section 7590.1(n) at the licensed premises.

(b) A licensee shall ensure a licensed alarm company operator or one or more of its registered alarm agents installs, maintains, monitors, and responds to the alarm system.

(c) Upon request, a licensee shall make available to the Bureau all information related to the alarm system, monitoring, and alarm activity.

(d) If multiple licensed premises are contained within the same building, a single alarm system covering the entire building may be used by all of the licensees under the following conditions:

(1) Each licensee shall include in their security operating procedures, submitted with the application pursuant to section 5002(c)(29)(D) of this division, an explanation of how the alarm system will be shared, including who is responsible for contracting with the alarm company.

(2) All licensees shall have access to and be able to provide the information under subsection (c) of this section.

(3) All licensees shall be held responsible and subject to discipline for any violations of the alarm system requirements.

Note: Authority cited: Section 26013, Business and Professions Code. Reference: Section 26070, Business and Professions Code.

ARTICLE 6. TRACK AND TRACE REQUIREMENTS

§ 5048. Track and Trace System.

(a) A licensee shall create and maintain an active and functional account within the track and trace system prior to engaging in any commercial cannabis activity, including the purchase, sale, test, packaging, transfer, transport, return, destruction, or disposal, of any cannabis goods.

(b) A licensee shall designate one individual owner as the track and trace system account manager. The account manager may authorize additional owners or employees as track and trace system users and shall ensure that each user is trained on the track and trace system prior to its access or use.

(1) The account manager shall attend and successfully complete all required track and trace system training, including any orientation and continuing education.

(2) If the account manager did not complete the required track and trace system training prior to receiving their annual license, the account manager shall sign up for and complete state mandated training, as prescribed by the Bureau, within five calendar days of license issuance.

(c) The account manager and each user shall be assigned a unique log-on, consisting of a username and password. The account manager or each user accessing the track and trace system shall only do so under his or her assigned log-on, and shall not use or access a log-on of any other individual. No account manager or user shall share or transfer his or her log-on, username, or password, to be used by any other individual for any reason.

(d) The account manager shall maintain a complete, accurate, and up-to-date list of all track and trace system users, consisting of their full names and usernames.

(e) A licensee shall monitor all compliance notifications from the track and trace system, and timely resolve the issues detailed in the compliance notification.

(1) A licensee shall keep a record, independent of the track and trace system, of all compliance notifications

received from the track and trace system, and how and when compliance was achieved.

(2) If a licensee is unable to resolve a compliance notification within three business days of receiving the notification, the licensee shall notify the Bureau immediately, by submitting the Notification and Request Form, BCC-LIC-027 (New 10/18), which is incorporated herein by reference.

(f) A licensee is accountable for all actions its owners or employees take while logged into or using the track and trace system, or otherwise while conducting track and trace activities.

Note: Authority cited: Section 26013, Business and Professions Code. Reference: Sections 26067, 26070, 26160 and 26161, Business and Professions Code.

§ 5049. Track and Trace Reporting.

(a) A licensee shall record in the track and trace system all commercial cannabis activity, including:

(1) Packaging of cannabis goods.

(2) Sale and transfer of cannabis goods.

(3) Transportation of cannabis goods to a licensee.

(4) Receipt of cannabis goods.

(5) Return of cannabis goods.

(6) Destruction and disposal of cannabis goods.

(7) Laboratory testing and results.

(8) Any other activity as required pursuant to this division, or by any other licensing authority.

(b) The following information shall be recorded for each activity entered in the track and trace system:

(1) Name and type of the cannabis goods.

(2) Unique identifier of the cannabis goods.

(3) Amount of the cannabis goods, by weight or count, and total wholesale cost of the cannabis goods, as applicable.

(4) Date and time of the activity or transaction.

(5) Name and license number of other licensees involved in the activity or transaction.

(6) If the cannabis goods are being transported:

(A) The licensee shall transport pursuant to a shipping manifest generated through the track and trace system, that includes items (1) through (5) of this subsection, as well as:

(i) The name, license number, and licensed premises address of the originating licensee.

(ii) The name, license number, and licensed premises address of the licensee transporting the cannabis goods.

(iii) The name, license number, and licensed premises address of the destination licensee receiving the cannabis goods into inventory or storage.

(iv) The date and time of departure from the licensed premises and approximate date and time of departure from each subsequent licensed premises, if any.

(v) Arrival date and estimated time of arrival at each licensed premises.

(vi) Driver license number of the personnel transporting the cannabis goods, and the make, model, and license plate number of the vehicle used for transport.

(B) Upon pick-up or receipt of cannabis goods for transport, storage, or inventory, a licensee shall ensure that the cannabis goods received are as described in the shipping manifest, and shall record acceptance or receipt, and acknowledgment of the cannabis goods in the track and trace system.

(C) If there are any discrepancies between the type or quantity of cannabis goods specified in the shipping manifest and the type or quantity received by the licensee, the licensee shall record and document the discrepancy in the track and trace system and in any relevant business record.

(7) If cannabis goods are being destroyed or disposed of, the licensee shall record in the track and trace system the following additional information:

(A) The name of the employee performing the destruction or disposal.

(B) The reason for destruction and disposal.

(C) The entity disposing of the cannabis waste.

(8) Description for any adjustments made in the track and trace system, including, but not limited to:

(A) Spoilage or fouling of the cannabis goods.

(B) Any event resulting in damage, exposure, or compromise of the cannabis goods.

(9) Any other information as required pursuant to this division, or by any other applicable licensing authorities.

(c) Unless otherwise specified, all transactions must be entered into the track and trace system within 24 hours of occurrence.

(d) Licensees shall only enter and record complete and accurate information into the track and trace system, and shall correct any known errors entered into the track and trace system immediately upon discovery.

Note: Authority cited: Section 26013, Business and Professions Code. Reference: Sections 26067, 26070, 26160 and 26161, Business and Professions Code.

§ 5050. Loss of Connectivity.

(a) If at any point a licensee loses connectivity to the track and trace system for any reason, the licensee shall prepare and maintain comprehensive records detailing all commercial cannabis activities that were conducted during the loss of connectivity.

(b) The licensee shall notify the Bureau immediately for any loss of connectivity, and shall not transport, receive, or deliver any cannabis goods until such time as connectivity is restored. Licensees shall submit such notices on the Notification and Request Form, BCC-LIC-027 (New 10/18), which is incorporated by reference.

(c) Once connectivity has been restored, the licensee shall:

(1) Within three calendar days, enter all commercial cannabis activity that occurred during the loss of connectivity into the track and trace system.

(2) Document the cause for loss of connectivity, and the date and time for when connectivity to the track and

trace system was lost and when it was restored.

Note: Authority cited: Section 26013, Business and Professions Code. Reference: Sections 26067, 26070 and 26160, Business and Professions Code.

§ 5051. Track and Trace System Reconciliation.

(a) In addition to other inventory reconciliation requirements under this division, a licensee shall reconcile the physical inventory of cannabis goods at the licensed premises with the records in the track and trace database at least once every 30 calendar days.

(b) If a licensee finds a discrepancy between its physical inventory and the track and trace system database, the licensee shall conduct an audit, and notify the Bureau of any reportable activity pursuant to section 5036 of this division.

Note: Authority cited: Section 26013, Business and Professions Code. Reference: Sections 26067, 26070 and 26160, Business and Professions Code.

§ 5052. Temporary Licenses; Licensees in Operation at Time of Licensure.

(a) A licensee operating under a temporary license issued pursuant to section 5001 of this division is not required to record commercial cannabis activity in the track and trace system as otherwise required by this article.

(b) Temporary licensees shall track and record all commercial cannabis activities and information required pursuant to this division and any other provision of law, at a minimum, on paper receipts, invoices, or manifests.

(c) Any commercial cannabis activity conducted between annual license holders shall be recorded in the track and trace system.

(d) Any licensee in operation at the time the annual license is issued shall enter all inventory into the track and trace system no later than 30 calendar days after the track and trace system account manager attends the training required pursuant to section 5048 of this division.

Note: Authority cited: Section 26013, Business and Professions Code. Reference: Sections 26050.1, 26067, 26070, 26160 and 26161, Business and Professions Code.

ARTICLE 7. RETURNS AND DESTRUCTION

§ 5052.1. Acceptance of Shipments.

(a) Licensees shall accept or reject, in whole, shipments of cannabis goods.

(b) Notwithstanding subsection (a) of this section, partial shipments of cannabis goods shall be rejected in the following circumstances:

(1) If a licensee receives a shipment containing cannabis goods that differ from those listed on the sales invoice or receipt, the licensee shall reject the portion of the shipment that is not accurately reflected on the sales invoice or receipt.

(2) If a licensee receives a shipment containing any cannabis goods that were damaged during transportation,

the licensee shall reject that portion of the shipment that was damaged.

(3) If a licensee receives a shipment containing cannabis goods that is non-compliant with labeling requirements or exceeds its provided expiration date, the licensee shall reject the portion of the shipment that is non-compliant with labeling requirements or expired.

(c) The licensee rejecting a shipment of cannabis goods, whether in whole or in part, shall record in the track and trace system, as required by Chapter 1, Article 6 of this division, and indicate on any relevant manifest, invoice, or sales receipt, the specific reason for rejection.

Note: Authority cited: Section 26013, Business and Professions Code. Reference: Sections 26013, 26067, 26070 and 26161, Business and Professions Code.

§ 5053. Returns Between Licensees.

(a) If a licensee discovers that a manufactured cannabis good that was purchased from another licensee is defective, the purchasing licensee may return the manufactured cannabis good to the selling licensee only in exchange for a non-defective version of the same type of manufactured cannabis good or in exchange for a manufactured cannabis good of equal value.

(b) Except as provided in subsection (a) of this section, a licensee shall not return cannabis goods purchased from another licensee.

Note: Authority cited: Section 26013, Business and Professions Code. Reference: Sections 26013 and 26070, Business and Professions Code.

§ 5054. Destruction of Cannabis Goods Prior to Disposal.

(a) Licensees shall not dispose of cannabis goods, unless disposed of as cannabis waste, defined under section 5000(g) of this division.

(b) Cannabis waste shall be stored, managed, and disposed of in accordance with all applicable waste management laws, including, but not limited to, Division 30 of the Public Resources Code.

(c) Cannabis goods intended for disposal shall remain on the licensed premises until rendered into cannabis waste. The licensee shall ensure that:

(1) Access to the cannabis goods is restricted to the licensee, its employees or agents; and

(2) Storage of the cannabis goods allocated for disposal is separate and distinct from other cannabis goods.

(d) To be rendered as cannabis waste for proper disposal, including disposal as defined under Public Resources Code section 40192, cannabis goods shall first be destroyed on the licensed premises. This includes, at a minimum, removing or separating the cannabis goods from any packaging or container and rendering it unrecognizable and unusable. Nothing in this subsection shall be construed to require vape cartridges to be emptied of cannabis oil prior to disposal, provided that the vape cartridge itself is unusable at the time of disposal.

(e) Cannabis waste on the licensed premises shall be secured in a receptacle or area that is restricted to the licensee, its employees, or an authorized waste hauler.

(f) A licensee shall report all cannabis waste activities, up to and including disposal, into the track and trace system, as required under Chapter 1, Article 6 of this division.

Note: Authority cited: Section 26013, Business and Professions Code. Reference: Sections 26013 and 26070, Business and Professions Code.

§ 5055. Cannabis Waste Management. [Repealed]

Chapter 2. Distributors

§ 5300. Distribution Activities.

A licensed distributor shall distribute only cannabis goods, cannabis accessories, and licensees' branded merchandise or promotional materials.

Note: Authority cited: Section 26013, Business and Professions Code. Reference: Section 26070, Business and Professions Code.

§ 5301. Storage Services.

(a) A licensed distributor may provide storage services, including storage-only services that are unrelated to the quality assurance and laboratory testing processes, to a licensed cultivator, licensed manufacturer, licensed microbusiness, licensed retailer, or another licensed distributor.

(b) A licensed distributor may provide storage services to other licensees for cannabis goods packaged as they will be sold at retail, cannabis accessories, and licensees' branded merchandise or promotional materials only.

(c) A licensed distributor shall ensure that each batch of cannabis goods that are stored for another licensee are stored in accordance with section 5302 of this division.

(d) Notwithstanding subsection (b) of this section, a licensed distributor shall not store live plants, except for seeds, on the licensed premises.

Note: Authority cited: Section 26013, Business and Professions Code. Reference: Sections 26070 and 26110, Business and Professions Code.

§ 5302. Storage of Batches for Testing.

(a) A licensed distributor shall ensure that all cannabis goods batches are stored separately and distinctly from other cannabis goods batches on the licensed distributor's premises.

(b) A licensed distributor shall ensure a label with the following information is physically attached to each container of each batch:

    (1) The name, license number, and licensed premises address of the licensed manufacturer or licensed cultivator who provided the batch;

    (2) The date of entry into the licensed distributor's storage area;

    (3) The unique identifiers and batch number associated with the batch;

    (4) A description of the cannabis goods with enough detail to easily identify the batch;

    (5) The weight of or quantity of units in the batch; and

(6) The best-by, sell-by, or expiration date of the batch, if any.

Note: Authority cited: Section 26013, Business and Professions Code. Reference: Sections 26110 and 26120, Business and Professions Code.

§ 5303. Packaging, Labeling, and Rolling.

(a) A licensed distributor may package, re-package, label, and re-label cannabis, including pre-rolls, for retail sale. All packages of cannabis, including pre-rolls, shall comply with the following:

(1) Until January 1, 2020, all packages shall meet the following requirements:

(A) The package shall protect the cannabis, including pre-rolls, from contamination and shall not expose the cannabis or pre-rolls to any harmful substance.

(B) The package shall be tamper-evident.

(C) If the package of cannabis or pre-rolls contains more than one serving, then the packaging shall be resealable.

(D) The package shall not imitate any package used for goods that are typically marketed to children.

(2) Beginning January 1, 2020, all packages shall meet the requirements of subsection (a)(1) of this section and shall also meet the following requirements:

(A) The package shall be child-resistant until the package is first opened. For purposes of this division, the following packages are considered child-resistant:

(i) Any package that has been certified as child-resistant under the requirements of the Poison Prevention Packaging Act of 1970 Regulations (16 C.F.R. §1700.15(b)(1)) (Rev. July 1995), which is hereby incorporated by reference.

(ii) Plastic packaging that is at least 4 mils thick and heat-sealed without an easy-open tab, dimple, corner, or flap.

(B) The package shall be labeled with the statement "This package is not child-resistant after opening."

(3) Notwithstanding subsections (a)(1)-(a)(2) of this section, immature plants and seeds shall not be required to be packaged in child-resistant, tamper-evident, and resealable packaging.

(b) A licensed distributor shall not process cannabis, but may roll pre-rolls that consist exclusively of any combination of flower, shake, leaf, or kief. Pre-rolls shall be rolled prior to regulatory compliance testing.

(c) Licensed distributors may label and re-label a package containing manufactured cannabis goods with the amount of cannabinoids and terpenoids based on regulatory compliance testing results.

Note: Authority cited: Section 26013, Business and Professions Code. Reference: Sections 26013 and 26120, Business and Professions Code.

§ 5303.1. Net Weight of Dried Flower.

For purposes of this division, the net weight on any package of dried flower shall not be considered inaccurate if the actual weight is within plus or minus 3% of the labeled weight.

Note: Authority cited: Section 26013, Business and Professions Code. Reference: Sections 26013, 26120 and 26152,

Business and Professions Code.

§ 5304. Testing Arrangements.

After taking physical possession of a cannabis goods batch, the licensed distributor shall contact a licensed testing laboratory and arrange for a laboratory employee to come to the licensed distributor's licensed premises to select a representative sample for laboratory testing.

Note: Authority cited: Section 26013, Business and Professions Code. Reference: Sections 26104 and 26110, Business and Professions Code.

§ 5305. Testing Sample.

(a) The licensed distributor shall ensure that the batch size from which the sample is taken meets the requirements of this division.

(b) A licensed distributor or an employee of the licensed distributor shall be physically present to observe the laboratory employee obtain the sample of cannabis goods for testing and shall ensure that the increments are taken from throughout the batch.

(c) The sampling shall be video recorded with the batch number stated verbally or in writing on the video at the beginning of the video and a visible time and date indication on the video recording footage. The video recordings shall be maintained for 90 calendar days by the licensed distributor.

(d) After the sample has been selected, both the licensed distributor and the laboratory employee shall sign and date the chain of custody form pursuant to section 5706 of this division, attesting to the sample selection having occurred.

(e) A licensed distributor shall not assist the laboratory employee nor touch the cannabis goods or the sampling equipment while the laboratory employee is obtaining the sample.

Note: Authority cited: Section 26013, Business and Professions Code. Reference: Sections 26104 and 26110, Business and Professions Code.

§ 5305.1. Re-sampling.

Once a sample has been obtained from a batch for regulatory compliance testing, a licensed distributor may not arrange for or allow another licensed testing laboratory to sample or re-sample the same batch for regulatory compliance testing, unless all of the requirements of section 5705 subsection (g) of this division are met.

Note: Authority cited: Section 26013, Business and Professions Code. Reference: Sections 26100, 26104 and 26110, Business and Professions Code.

§ 5306. Laboratory Testing Results.

(a) A sample batch "passes" a laboratory test when the sample meets specifications in Chapter 6 of this division.

(b) When a batch from a manufactured or harvest batch passes, the cannabis goods may be transported to one or more licensed retailers, licensed distributors, or licensed microbusinesses. A printed copy of the certificate of analysis for regulatory compliance testing shall accompany the batch and be provided to the licensee receiving the cannabis goods.

(c) A batch "fails" a laboratory test when the sample does not meet specifications in Chapter 6 of this division.

(d) If a failed batch may be remediated pursuant to section 5727 of this division, a licensed distributor may transport or arrange for the transportation of the batch to a licensed manufacturer for remediation in accordance with the following:

(1) The licensed distributor shall ensure that a corrective action plan is submitted by a licensed manufacturer to the State Department of Public Health, or by a licensed microbusiness authorized to engage in manufacturing to the Bureau, within 30 calendar days of issuance of the certificate of analysis for regulatory compliance testing by the licensed testing laboratory.

(2) The licensed distributor shall ensure that the licensed manufacturer or licensed microbusiness authorized to engage in manufacturing begins remediating the cannabis goods within 30 calendar days of receiving approval from the State Department of Public Health or the Bureau to remediate the cannabis goods.

(3) If the licensed distributor is unable to arrange for a licensed manufacturer or licensed microbusiness authorized to engage in manufacturing to remediate the cannabis goods within 30 calendar days of issuance of the certificate of analysis for regulatory compliance testing by the licensed testing laboratory, the licensed distributor shall destroy the cannabis goods immediately.

(e) A licensed distributor shall destroy a batch that failed laboratory testing and cannot be remediated pursuant to section 5727 of this division within 30 calendar days of issuance of the certificate of analysis for regulatory compliance testing by the licensed testing laboratory.

Note: Authority cited: Section 26013, Business and Professions Code. Reference: Sections 26070, 26100, 26104 and 26110, Business and Professions Code.

§ 5307. Quality Assurance Review.

When a licensed distributor receives a certificate of analysis for regulatory compliance testing from the licensed testing laboratory or upon transfer from another licensed distributor stating that the batch meets specifications required by law, the licensed distributor shall ensure the following before transporting the cannabis goods, packaged as they will be sold at retail, to one or more licensed retailers or licensed microbusinesses authorized to engage in retail sales:

(a) The certificate of analysis for regulatory compliance testing that the licensed distributor received from the licensed testing laboratory or another licensed distributor is the certificate of analysis that corresponds to the batch;

(b) The date on the certificate of analysis for the regulatory compliance testing is less than 12 months old;

(c) The label on the cannabis goods is consistent with the certificate of analysis for regulatory compliance testing regarding cannabinoid content and contaminants required to be listed by law as follows:

(1) If the cannabis goods are labeled with the content for cannabinoids, terpenoids, Total THC, and/or Total CBD prior to receiving the certificate of analysis for regulatory compliance testing, the licensed distributor shall ensure that the labeled amounts are accurate in accordance with section 5307.1 of this division.

(2) If the cannabis goods are not labeled with the content for cannabinoids, terpenoids, Total THC, and/or Total CBD prior to receiving the certificate of analysis for regulatory compliance testing, the licensed distributor shall label the cannabis goods with the amounts listed on the certificate of analysis pursuant to section 5303 of this division;

(d) The packaging and labeling of the cannabis goods complies with Business and Professions Code Section 26120 and all applicable regulations within this division as well as California Code of Regulations, Title 3, Division 8 and Title 17, Division 1, Chapter 13, except cannabis goods are not required to be labeled or otherwise identified as medicinal products prior to retail sale unless the cannabis goods must be labeled as such pursuant to the requirements prescribed by the State Department of Public Health in regulation;

(e) The cannabis goods have not exceeded their expiration or sell-by date if one is provided;

(f) The weight or count of the cannabis batch comports with that in the track and trace system. A licensed distributor shall use scales as required by the Business and Professions Code; and

(g) All events prior to receipt of the certificate of analysis for regulatory compliance testing have been entered into the track and trace system.

Note: Authority cited: Section 26013, Business and Professions Code. Reference: Sections 26070, 26110 and 26120, Business and Professions Code.

§ 5307.1. Quality-Assurance Review for Labeling Cannabinoids and Terpenoids.

(a) For purposes of this division, any one cannabinoid, Total THC, and/or Total CBD claimed to be present on a label shall not be considered inaccurate if the difference in percentage on the certificate of analysis is plus or minus 10.0%.

(b) For purposes of this division, the terpenoid testing results on the label of any one terpenoid claimed to be present shall not be considered inaccurate if the difference in percentage on the certificate of analysis is plus or minus 10.0%.

(c) For purposes of this section, the difference in percent shall be calculated using the following equation:

Difference in percent = (laboratory measurement - label claim) / (label claim) X 100%

(d) For purposes of this section, Total THC and Total CBD shall have the same meaning as defined in Chapter 6 of this division.

Note: Authority cited: Section 26013, Business and Professions Code. Reference: Sections 26100 and 26110, Business and Professions Code.

§ 5307.2. Licensed Distributor to Licensed Distributor Transfers.

Cannabis goods, packaged as they will be sold at retail, that have undergone and passed regulatory compliance testing and have an accompanying certificate of analysis may be transferred to one or more licensed distributors. However, cannabis goods that have not been transported to retail within 12 months of the date on the certificate of analysis must be destroyed or retested by the licensed distributor in possession of the cannabis goods.

Note: Authority cited: Section 26013, Business and Professions Code. Reference: Sections 26070 and 26110, Business and Professions Code.

§ 5308. Insurance Requirements.

(a) An applicant for a distributor license shall provide the Bureau with a certificate of insurance that shows the types of insurance coverage and minimum amounts that have been secured as required by this section, and documentation establishing compliance with subsection (d) of this section.

(b) A distributor licensee shall at all times carry and maintain commercial general liability insurance in the aggregate in an amount no less than $2,000,000 and in an amount no less than $1,000,000 for each loss.

(c) A distributor licensee shall maintain the insurance required in subsection (b) of this section from an insurance company that is:

(1) A non-admitted insurer that meets the requirements of Insurance Code section 1765.1 or 1765.2, and the insurance is placed pursuant to Insurance Code section 1763 and through a surplus line broker licensed under Insurance Code section 1765;

(2) An insurer qualified to do business in California by the Secretary of State and authorized by the Insurance Commissioner to write the liability and property classes of insurance as defined by Insurance Code sections 102, 103, 107, 114, 108, and 120; or

(3) A registered risk retention group compliant with the California Risk Retention Act of 1991. (See California Insurance Code sections 125-140.)

(d) Admitted insurers and risk retention groups must show proof of capitalization in the amount of at least $10,000,000.

(e) A distributor licensee shall notify the Bureau in writing, by submitting the Notification and Request Form, BCC-LIC-027 (New 10/18), which is incorporated herein by reference, within 14 calendar days of a lapse in insurance in accordance with section 5023.

Note: Authority cited: Section 26013, Business and Professions Code. Reference: Sections 26051.5 and 26070, Business and Professions Code.

§ 5309. Inventory Accounting.

(a) A licensed distributor shall be able to account for all inventory and provide that information to the Bureau upon request.

(b) To account for inventory, a licensed distributor shall ensure all batches of cannabis goods are stored in accordance with section 5302 of this division and shall be able to provide the Bureau with the status of the batch as follows:

(1) The batch is being held in; storage for another licensee;

(2) The batch is awaiting sampling for regulatory compliance testing;

(3) The batch has been sampled and is awaiting testing results;

(4) The batch has passed testing;

(5) The batch has failed testing and is awaiting approval for remediation;

(6) The batch has failed testing and is awaiting destruction; and

(7) The batch is being stored or held for any other lawful purpose under the Act or this division.

Note: Authority cited: Section 26013, Business and Professions Code. Reference: Sections 26070 and 26160, Business and Professions Code.

§ 5310. Records.

In addition to the records required by section 5037 of this division, a licensed distributor shall maintain the following records:

(a) Records relating to branding, packaging and labeling;

(b) Inventory logs and records;

(c) Transportation bills of lading and shipping manifests for completed transports and for cannabis goods in transit;

(d) Vehicle and trailer ownership records;

(e) Quality-assurance records;

(f) Records relating to destruction and disposal of cannabis goods;

(g) Laboratory-testing records;

(h) Warehouse receipts; and

(i) Records relating to tax payments collected and paid under Revenue and Taxation Code sections 34011 and 34012.

Note: Authority cited: Section 26013, Business and Professions Code. Reference: Section 26160, Business and Professions Code.

§ 5311. Requirements for the Transportation of Cannabis Goods.

The following requirements apply when transporting cannabis goods between licensees or licensed premises:

(a) Transportation shall only be conducted by persons holding a distributor license under the Act, or employees of those persons. All vehicles and trailers used for transportation shall be owned or leased, in accordance with the Vehicle Code, by the licensee.

(b) Prior to transporting any cannabis goods, the licensed distributor shall have a completed sales invoice or receipt that meets the requirements of Business and Professions Code section 26161. The licensed distributor shall only transport cannabis goods listed on the sales invoice or receipt. The sales invoice or receipt may not be altered or changed once transport begins.

(c) All vehicles transporting cannabis goods for hire shall be required to have a motor carrier permit pursuant to Chapter 2 (commencing with Section 34620) of Division 14.85 of the Vehicle Code.

(d) Transportation by means of aircraft, watercraft, drone, rail, human powered vehicle, or unmanned vehicle is prohibited.

(e) Cannabis goods shall only be transported inside of a vehicle or trailer and shall not be visible or identifiable from outside of the vehicle or trailer.

(f) Cannabis goods shall be locked in a fully enclosed box, container, or cage that is secured to the inside of the vehicle or trailer. No portion of the enclosed box, container, or cage shall be comprised of any part of the body of the vehicle or trailer. For the purposes of this section, the inside of the vehicle includes the trunk.

(g) While left unattended, vehicles and trailers shall be locked and secured.

(h) A licensed distributor shall not leave a vehicle or trailer containing cannabis goods unattended in a residential area or parked overnight in a residential area.

(i) At a minimum, a licensed distributor shall have a vehicle alarm system on all transport vehicles and trailers. Motion detectors, pressure switches, duress, panic, and hold-up alarms may also be used.

(j) Packages or containers holding cannabis goods shall not be tampered with, or opened, during transport.

(k) A licensed distributor transporting cannabis goods shall only travel between licensees shipping or receiving cannabis goods and its own licensed premises when engaged in the transportation of cannabis goods. The licensed distributor may transport multiple shipments of cannabis goods at once in accordance with applicable laws. A licensed distributor shall not deviate from the travel requirements described in this section, except for necessary rest, fuel, or vehicle repair stops.

(l) Under no circumstances may non-cannabis goods, except for cannabis accessories and licensees' branded merchandise or promotional materials, be transported with cannabis goods.

(m) Vehicles and trailers transporting cannabis goods are subject to inspection by the Bureau at any licensed premises or during transport at any time.

(n) Notwithstanding subsections (d)-(f) of this section, if it is not operationally feasible to transport cannabis goods inside of a vehicle or trailer because the licensed premises that the cannabis goods will be transported from and the licensed premises that will be receiving the cannabis goods are located within the same building or on the same parcel of land, the cannabis goods may be transported by foot, hand truck, fork lift, or other similar means. A shipping manifest that complies with this division is required when transporting cannabis goods pursuant to this subsection.

(o) Notwithstanding subsection (d) of this section, transportation of cannabis goods may be conducted via waterway to licensees located on Catalina Island. The provisions of this section and other sections regarding vehicle requirements also apply to vessels used to transport cannabis goods via waterway pursuant to this section.

Note: Authority cited: Section 26013, Business and Professions Code. Reference: Section 26070, Business and Professions Code.

§ 5312. Required Transport Vehicle Information.

(a) In addition to the information required in section 5314 of this division, any licensed distributor who will be or is transporting cannabis goods shall provide the following information to the Bureau:

> (1) Proof that the licensed distributor is the registered owner under the Vehicle Code for each vehicle and trailer used to transport cannabis goods;

> (2) The year, make, model, license plate number, and numerical Vehicle Identification Number (VIN) for each vehicle and trailer used to transport cannabis goods; and

> (3) Proof of insurance for each vehicle and trailer used to transport cannabis goods.

(b) The licensed distributor shall provide the Bureau with the information required by this section in writing for any new vehicle or trailer that will be used to transport cannabis goods prior to using the vehicle or trailer to transport cannabis goods.

(c) The licensed distributor shall provide the Bureau with any changes to the information required by this section in writing within 30 calendar days, submitted on the Notification and Request Form, BCC-LIC-027 (New 10/18), which is incorporated herein by reference.

Note: Authority cited: Section 26013, Business and Professions Code. Reference: Section 26070, Business and Professions Code.

§ 5313. Transport Personnel Requirements.

(a) No person under the age of 21 years old shall be in a commercial vehicle or trailer transporting cannabis goods; and

(b) Only a licensee, an employee of the licensed distributor, or security personnel who meets the requirements of section 5045 of this division shall be in a vehicle while transporting cannabis goods.

Note: Authority cited: Section 26013, Business and Professions Code. Reference: Section 26070, Business and Professions Code.

§ 5314. Shipping Manifest.

(a) Prior to transporting cannabis goods, a licensed distributor shall generate a shipping manifest through the track and trace system for the following activities:

(1) Testing and sampling;

(2) Sale of cannabis goods to a licensee;

(3) Destruction or disposal of cannabis goods; and

(4) Any other activity, as required pursuant to this division, or by any other licensing authority.

(b) The licensed distributor shall transmit the shipping manifest to the Bureau and the licensee that will receive the cannabis goods prior to transporting the cannabis goods.

(c) The licensed distributor shall ensure and verify that the cannabis goods being taken into possession for transport at the originating licensed premises are as described and accurately reflected in the shipping manifest. For purposes of this section, the licensed distributor may verify that the cannabis goods are accurately reflected in the shipping manifest by confirming that the number of boxes of cannabis goods, type of cannabis goods, weight and/or units of cannabis goods matches the label on the boxes containing the cannabis goods.

(1) The licensed distributor shall not take into possession or transport:

(A) Any cannabis goods that are not on the shipping manifest; or

(B) Any cannabis goods that are less than or greater than the amount reflected on the shipping manifest.

(2) The licensed distributor is responsible for any discrepancies between the shipping manifest and the cannabis goods in its possession during transport, and subject to any enforcement or disciplinary action related to such discrepancy.

(3) A licensed distributor shall not void or change a shipping manifest after departing from the originating licensed premises.

(d) A shipping manifest shall accompany every transport of cannabis goods.

(e) Notwithstanding subsection (a) of this section, if a transporting licensed distributor has not obtained access to the track and trace system, the licensed distributor shall complete the shipping manifest outside of the track and trace system and transmit it to the Bureau and the licensee receiving the shipment by electronic mail.

(f) If the transporting licensed distributor has access to the track and trace system and the licensee receiving the shipment has not obtained access to the track and trace system, the licensed distributor shall complete the shipping manifest in the track and trace system and transmit it to the Bureau. However, the licensed distributor shall send a copy to the licensee receiving the shipment by electronic mail.

Note: Authority cited: Section 26013, Business and Professions Code. Reference: Sections 26067 and 26070, Business and Professions Code.

§ 5315. Distributor Transport Only License.

(a) A licensed distributor transport only licensee may transport cannabis goods between licensees; however, they shall not transport any cannabis goods except for immature cannabis plants and seeds to a licensed retailer or licensed microbusiness authorized to engage in retail sales.

(b) A complete application for a distributor transport only license shall include all the information required in an application for a distributor license.

(c) The licensing fee for a distributor transport only license will be based in part upon whether the licensee intends to transport only cannabis goods that the licensee has cultivated or manufactured (self-distribution), or whether the licensee intends to transport cannabis goods cultivated or manufactured by other licensees.

(d) A distributor transport only licensee shall comply with all of the requirements for a holder of a distributor license, except for those related to quality assurance and testing.

(e) A distributor transport only licensee shall not hold title to any cannabis goods unless the licensee also holds a state-issued cultivation, manufacturing, retailer, or microbusiness license.

(f) Holding a distributor transport only license shall not authorize a licensee to:

> (1) Engage in the delivery of cannabis goods as defined in Business and Professions Code section 26001(p);

> (2) Engage in the wholesale, destruction, packaging, labeling, or storing of cannabis goods; or

> (3) Arrange for the testing of cannabis goods by a testing laboratory.

(g) Notwithstanding subsection (e) of this section, a distributor transport only licensee who is licensed to engage in self-distribution and whose licensed premises will be on the same property as their licensed cultivation or licensed manufacturing premises shall not be required to comply with the security provisions contained in Chapter 1, Article 5 of this division.

Note: Authority cited: Section 26013, Business and Professions Code. Reference: Sections 26012 and 26070, Business and Professions Code.

Chapter 3. Retailers

§ 5400. Access to Retailer Premises.

(a) Access to the licensed premises of a retailer with only an A-designation shall be limited to individuals who are at least 21 years of age.

(b) Access to the licensed premises of a retailer with only an M-designation shall be limited to individuals who are at least 18 years of age and have a valid physician's recommendation for medicinal cannabis, and individuals who are at least 21 years of age.

(c) Access to the licensed premises of a retailer with both an A-designation and an M-designation may include persons identified in subsections (a) and (b) of this section.

Note: Authority cited: Section 26013, Business and Professions Code. Reference: Sections 26070 and 26140, Business and Professions Code.

§ 5401. Limited-Access Areas. [Repealed]

§ 5402. Customer Access to the Retail Area.

(a) Individuals shall be granted access to the retail area to purchase cannabis goods only after the retailer or an employee of the retailer has confirmed the individual's age and identity pursuant to section 5404 of this division.

(b) The licensed retailer or at least one employee shall be physically present in the retail area at all times when individuals who are not employees of the licensed retailer are in the retail area.

(c) All sales of cannabis goods must take place within the retail area of the retailer's licensed premises, except for cannabis goods sold through delivery, or a drive-in or drive-through window as authorized by section 5025(g) of this division.

Note: Authority cited: Section 26013, Business and Professions Code. Reference: Sections 26070 and 26140, Business and Professions Code.

§ 5403. Hours of Operation.

A licensed retailer shall sell and deliver cannabis goods only between the hours of 6:00 a.m. Pacific Time and 10:00 p.m. Pacific Time.

Note: Authority cited: Section 26013, Business and Professions Code. Reference: Section 26070, Business and Professions Code.

§ 5403.1. Requirements While Not Open for Business.

At any time the licensed premises is not open for retail sales, a licensed retailer shall ensure that:

(a) The licensed premises is securely locked with commercial-grade, nonresidential door locks as required in section 5046 of this division;

(b) The licensed premises is equipped with an active alarm system pursuant to section 5047 of this division, which shall be activated when the licensed retailer or its employees are not on the licensed premises; and

(c) Only employees of the licensee and other authorized individuals are allowed access to the licensed premises. For the purposes of this section, authorized individuals include individuals employed by the licensee as well as any outside vendors, contractors, or other individuals conducting business that requires access to the licensed premises.

Note: Authority cited: Section 26013, Business and Professions Code. Reference: Section 26070, Business and Professions Code.

§ 5404. Retail Customers.

(a) A licensed retailer shall only sell adult-use cannabis goods to individuals who are at least 21 years of age after confirming the customer's age and identity by inspecting a valid form of identification provided by the customer as required by subsection (c) of this section.

(b) A licensed retailer shall only sell medicinal cannabis goods to individuals who are at least 18 years of age and possesses a valid physician's recommendation after confirming the customer's age, identity, and physician's recommendation as required by subsection (c) of this section.

(c) Acceptable forms of identification include the following:

(1) A document issued by a federal, state, county, or municipal government, or a political subdivision or agency thereof, including, but not limited to, a valid motor vehicle operator's license, that contains the name, date of birth, height, gender, and photo of the person;

(2) A valid identification card issued to a member of the Armed Forces that includes the person's name, date of birth, and photo; or

(3) A valid passport issued by the United States or by a foreign government.

Note: Authority cited: Section 26013, Business and Professions Code. Reference: Section 26140, Business and Professions Code.

§ 5405. Cannabis Goods Display.

(a) Cannabis goods for inspection and sale shall only be displayed in the retail area.

(b) Cannabis goods may be removed from their packaging and placed in containers to allow for customer inspection. The containers shall not be readily accessible to customers without assistance of retailer personnel. A container must be provided to the customer by the licensed retailer or its employees, who shall remain with the customer at all times that the container is being inspected by the customer.

(c) Cannabis goods removed from their packaging for display shall not be sold, shall not be consumed, and shall be destroyed pursuant to section 5054 of this division when the cannabis goods are no longer used for display.

Note: Authority cited: Section 26013, Business and Professions Code. Reference: Section 26070, Business and Professions Code.

§ 5406. Cannabis Goods for Sale.

A licensed retailer shall not make any cannabis goods available for sale or delivery to a customer unless:

(a) The cannabis goods were received by the retail licensee from a licensed distributor or licensed microbusiness authorized to engage in distribution;

(b) The licensed retailer has verified that the cannabis goods have not exceeded their best-by, sell-by, or expiration date if one is provided;

(c) In the case of manufactured cannabis products, the product complies with all requirements of Business and Professions Code section 26130 and California Code of Regulations, Title 3, Division 8 and Title 17, Division 1, Chapter 13;

(d) The cannabis goods have undergone laboratory testing as required by the Act and Chapter 6 of this division;

(e) The batch number is labeled on the package of cannabis goods and matches the batch number on the corresponding certificate of analysis for regulatory compliance testing;

(f) The packaging and labeling of the cannabis goods complies with Business and Professions Code Section 26120 and all applicable regulations within this division as well as California Code of Regulations, Title 3, Division 8 and Title 17, Division 1, Chapter 13; and

(g) The cannabis goods comply with all applicable requirements found in the Act and applicable regulations.

Note: Authority cited: Section 26013, Business and Professions Code. Reference: Sections 26070 and 26120, Business and Professions Code.

§ 5407. Sale of Non-Cannabis Goods.

In addition to cannabis goods, a licensed retailer may sell only cannabis accessories and licensee's branded merchandise. Licensed retailers may provide customers with promotional materials.

Note: Authority cited: Section 26013, Business and Professions Code. Reference: Sections 26070, 26151 and 26152, Business and Professions Code.

§ 5408. Sale of Live Plants and Seeds.

(a) A licensed retailer shall only sell live, immature cannabis plants and cannabis seeds if all of the following requirements are met:

(1) The plant is not flowering;

(2) The plant or seed originated from a nursery that holds a valid license from the Department of Food and Agriculture or a licensed microbusiness authorized to engage in cultivation; and

(3) A label is affixed to the plant or package containing any seeds which states "This product has not been tested pursuant to the Medicinal and Adult-Use Cannabis Regulation and Safety Act."

(b) A licensed retailer may not sell any other live plants.

(c) A licensed retailer shall not apply nor use any pesticide, nor cause any pesticide to be applied nor used, on live plants.

Note: Authority cited: Section 26013, Business and Professions Code. Reference: Sections 26070 and 26100, Business and Professions Code.

§ 5409. Daily Limits.

(a) A licensed retailer shall not sell more than the following amounts to a single adult-use cannabis customer in a single day:

(1) 28.5 grams of non-concentrated cannabis.

(2) 8 grams of cannabis concentrate as defined in Business and Professions Code section 26001, including cannabis concentrate contained in cannabis products.

(3) 6 immature cannabis plants.

(b) A licensed retailer shall not sell more than the following amounts to a single medicinal cannabis patient, or to a patient's primary caregiver purchasing medicinal cannabis on behalf of the patient, in a single day:

(1) 8 ounces of medicinal cannabis in the form of dried mature flowers or the plant conversion as provided in Health and Safety Code section 11362.77.

(2) 12 immature cannabis plants.

(c) Notwithstanding subsection (b) of this section, if a medicinal cannabis patient's valid physician's recommendation contains a different amount than the limits listed in this section, the medicinal cannabis patient may purchase an amount of medicinal cannabis consistent with the patient's needs as recommended by a physician and documented in the physician's recommendation.

(d) The limits provided in subsection (a) and subsection (b) of this section shall not be combined to allow a customer to purchase cannabis goods in excess of any of the limits provided in this section.

(e) For the purposes of this section, a licensed retailer shall be responsible for determining that the amount of cannabis concentrates found in manufactured cannabis products sold to customers comply with the requirements of this section.

Note: Authority cited: Section 26013, Business and Professions Code. Reference: Section 26012, Business and Professions Code; and Sections 11362.1 and 11362.77, Health and Safety Code.

§ 5410. Customer Return of Cannabis Goods.

(a) For the purposes of this section, "customer return" means a customer's return of cannabis goods that were purchased from a licensed retailer, back to the licensed retailer the cannabis goods were purchased from.

(b) A licensed retailer may accept customer returns of cannabis goods that were previously sold to a customer.

(c) A licensed retailer shall not resell cannabis goods that have been returned.

(d) A licensed retailer shall treat any cannabis goods abandoned on the licensed retailer premises as a customer return.

(e) Defective manufactured cannabis products returned by customers to a licensed retailer may be destroyed pursuant to section 5054 of this division, or returned to the licensed distributor from whom the cannabis goods were obtained in accordance with section 5053 of this division.

Note: Authority cited: Section 26013, Business and Professions Code. Reference: Sections 26011.5, 26012 and 26070, Business and Professions Code.

§ 5411. Free Cannabis Goods.

(a) A licensed retailer shall not provide free cannabis goods to any person. A licensed retailer shall not allow individuals who are not employed by the licensed retailer to provide free cannabis goods to any person on the licensed premises.

(b) Notwithstanding subsection (a) of this section, in order to provide access to medicinal cannabis patients who have difficulty accessing medicinal cannabis goods, a licensee who holds an M-Retailer license, an M-Retailer Non-storefront license, or an M Microbusiness license that is authorized for retail sales may provide free medicinal cannabis goods if the following criteria are met:

> (1) Free cannabis goods are provided only to a medicinal cannabis patient or primary caregiver for the patient in possession of an identification card issued under Section 11362.71 of the Health and Safety Code.

> (2) The cannabis goods comply with all applicable laboratory testing requirements under this division.

> (3) Prior to being provided to the patient or primary caregiver, the cannabis goods have been properly recorded in the track and trace system as belonging to the licensed retailer.

> (4) The cannabis goods shall not leave the licensed premises unless placed in a resealable child-resistant opaque package as required for purchased cannabis goods under Business and Professions Code section 26070.1.

> (5) The cannabis goods shall be applied toward the daily purchase limit for a medicinal cannabis customer pursuant to section 5409 of this division.

> (6) The event shall be properly recorded in the licensed retailer's inventory records and the track and trace system.

(c) In addition to the provision of free cannabis goods in subsection (b) of this section, a licensee may donate cannabis goods and the use of equipment in compliance with any compassionate use, equity, or other similar program administered by a local jurisdiction. The licensee shall ensure that all cannabis goods provided pursuant to this subsection comply with subsections (b)(2) and (b)(6) of this section.

Note: Authority cited: Section 26013, Business and Professions Code. Reference: Sections 26013, 26153 and 26160, Business and Professions Code.

§ 5412. Prohibition on Packaging and Labeling by a Retailer.

(a) A licensed retailer shall not accept, possess, or sell cannabis goods that are not packaged as they will be sold at final sale, in compliance with this division.

(b) A licensed retailer shall not package or label cannabis goods.

(c) Notwithstanding subsection (b) of this section, a licensed retailer may place a barcode or similar sticker on the packaging of cannabis goods to be used in inventory tracking. A barcode or similar sticker placed on the packaging of a cannabis goods shall not obscure any labels required by the Act or this division.

Note: Authority cited: Section 26013, Business and Professions Code. Reference: Section 26120, Business and Professions Code.

§ 5413. Cannabis Goods Packaging and Exit Packaging.

(a) All cannabis goods sold by a licensed retailer shall be in compliance with the packaging requirements.

(b) Beginning January 1, 2020, a package containing cannabis goods shall be resealable, tamper-evident, and child resistant.

(c) All cannabis goods purchased by a customer shall not leave the licensed retailer's premises unless the goods are placed in an opaque exit package.

(d) Notwithstanding subsections (a)-(c) of this section, immature plants and seeds sold by a licensed retailer are not required to be placed in resealable, tamper-evident, child resistant packaging.

Note: Authority cited: Section 26013, Business and Professions Code. Reference: Sections 26070.1 and 26120, Business and Professions Code.

§ 5414. Non-Storefront Retailer.

(a) A non-storefront retailer licensee shall be authorized to conduct retail sales exclusively by delivery as defined in Business and Professions Code section 26001 (p).

(b) A complete application for a non-storefront retailer license shall include all the information required in an application for a retailer license.

(c) A non-storefront retailer licensee shall comply with all the requirements applicable to retailer licensees, except for those provisions related to public access to the licensed premises and the retail area.

(d) The licensed premises of a non-storefront retailer licensee shall be closed to the public.

Note: Authority cited: Section 26013, Business and Professions Code. Reference: Sections 26012 and 26070, Business and Professions Code.

§ 5415. Delivery Employees.

(a) All deliveries of cannabis goods shall be performed by a delivery employee who is directly employed by a licensed retailer.

(b) Each delivery employee of a licensed retailer shall be at least 21 years of age.

(c) All deliveries of cannabis goods shall be made in person. A delivery of cannabis goods shall not be made through the use of an unmanned vehicle.

(d) The process of delivery begins when the delivery employee leaves the retailer's licensed premises with the cannabis goods for delivery. The process of delivering ends when the delivery employee returns to the retailer's licensed premises after delivering the cannabis goods, or attempting to deliver cannabis goods, to the customer(s). During the process of delivery, the licensed retailer's delivery employee may not engage in any activities except for cannabis goods delivery and necessary rest, fuel, or vehicle repair stops.

(e) A delivery employee of a licensed retailer shall, during deliveries, carry a copy of the retailer's current license, the employee's government-issued identification, and an identification badge provided by the employer pursuant to section 5043 of this division.

(f) Prior to providing cannabis goods to a delivery customer, a delivery employee shall confirm the identity and age of the delivery customer as required by section 5404 of this division and ensure that all cannabis goods sold comply with requirements of section 5413 of this division.

(g) A licensed retailer shall maintain an accurate list of the retailer's delivery employees and shall provide the list to the Bureau upon request.

Note: Authority cited: Section 26013, Business and Professions Code. Reference: Sections 26070 and 26090, Business and Professions Code.

§ 5415.1. Deliveries Facilitated by Technology Platforms.

(a) A licensed retailer or licensed microbusiness shall not sell or otherwise transfer any cannabis goods to a customer through the use of an unlicensed third party, intermediary business, broker, or any other business or entity.

(b) Notwithstanding subsection (a) of this section, a licensed retailer or licensed microbusiness may contract with a service that provides a technology platform to facilitate the sale and delivery of cannabis goods, in accordance with all of the following:

    (1) The licensed retailer or licensed microbusiness does not allow for delivery of cannabis goods by the technology platform service provider.

    (2) The licensed retailer or licensed microbusiness does not share in the profits of the sale of cannabis goods with the technology platform service provider, or otherwise provide for a percentage or portion of the cannabis goods sales to the technology platform service provider.

    (3) The licensed retailer or licensed microbusiness shall not advertise or market cannabis goods in conjunction with the technology platform service provider, outside of the technology platform, and shall ensure that the technology platform service provider does not use the licensed retailer's or licensed microbusiness's license number or legal business name on any advertisement or marketing that primarily promotes the services of the technology platform.

    (4) The licensed retailer or licensed microbusiness shall ensure the following information is provided to customers:

(A) Any cannabis goods advertised or offered for sale on or through the technology platform shall disclose, at a minimum, the licensed retailer's or licensed microbusiness's legal business name and license number.

(B) Customers placing an order for cannabis goods through the technology platform shall be able to easily identify the licensed retailer or licensed microbusiness that each cannabis good is being ordered or purchased from. This information shall be available to the customer prior to the customer placing an order or purchasing the cannabis goods.

(5) All required sales invoices and receipts, including any receipts provided to the customer, shall disclose, at a minimum, the licensed retailer's or licensed microbusiness's legal business name and license number.

(6) All other delivery, marketing, and advertising requirements under this division are complied with.

Note: Authority cited: Section 26013, Business and Professions Code. Reference: Sections 26001, 26070, 26090, 26151 and 26152, Business and Professions Code.

§ 5416. Delivery to a Physical Address.

(a) A delivery employee may only deliver cannabis goods to a physical address in California.

(b) A delivery employee shall not leave the State of California while possessing cannabis goods.

(c) A delivery employee shall not deliver cannabis goods to an address located on publicly owned land or any address on land or in a building leased by a public agency. This prohibition applies to land held in trust by the United States for a tribe or an individual tribal member unless the delivery is authorized by and consistent with applicable tribal law.

(d) A delivery employee may deliver to any jurisdiction within the State of California provided that such delivery is conducted in compliance with all delivery provisions of this division.

(e) A delivery employee shall not deliver cannabis goods to a school providing instruction in kindergarten or any grades 1 through 12, day care center, or youth center.

Note: Authority cited: Section 26013, Business and Professions Code. Reference: Sections 26070 and 26090, Business and Professions Code.

§ 5417. Delivery Vehicle Requirements.

(a) A licensed retailer's delivery employee, carrying cannabis goods for delivery, shall only travel in an enclosed motor vehicle. Any vehicle used in the delivery of cannabis goods shall be operated by a delivery employee of the licensee. A vehicle used in the delivery of cannabis goods shall not have any marking or other indications on the exterior of the vehicle that may indicate that the delivery employee is carrying cannabis goods for delivery. Only the licensee or an employee of the retailer licensee for whom delivery is being performed shall be in the delivery vehicle.

(b) While carrying cannabis goods for delivery, a licensed retailer's delivery employee shall ensure the cannabis goods are not visible to the public. Cannabis goods shall be locked in a fully enclosed box, container, or cage that is secured on the inside of the vehicle. No portion of the enclosed box, container, or cage shall be comprised of any part of the body of the vehicle or trailer. For purposes of this section, the inside of the vehicle includes the trunk.

(c) A licensed retailer's delivery employee shall not leave cannabis goods in an unattended motor vehicle unless the motor vehicle is locked and equipped with an active vehicle alarm system. Any cannabis goods left in an unattended vehicle must be stored in a container as required in subsection (b) of this section.

(d) A vehicle used for the delivery of cannabis goods shall be outfitted with a dedicated Global Positioning System (GPS) device for identifying the geographic location of the delivery vehicle and recording a history of all locations traveled to by the delivery employee while engaged in delivery. A dedicated GPS device must be owned by the licensee and used for delivery only. The device shall be either permanently or temporarily affixed to the delivery vehicle and shall remain active and inside of the delivery vehicle at all times during delivery. At all times, the licensed retailer shall be able to identify the geographic location of all delivery vehicles that are making deliveries for the licensed retailer and document the history of all locations traveled to by a delivery employee while engaged in delivery. A licensed retailer shall provide this information to the Bureau upon request. The history of all locations traveled to by a delivery employee while engaging in delivery shall be maintained by the licensee for a minimum of 90 days.

(e) Upon request, a licensed retailer shall provide the Bureau with information regarding any motor vehicle used for the delivery of cannabis goods, including the vehicle's make, model, color, Vehicle Identification Number, license plate number and Department of Motor Vehicles registration information.

(f) Any motor vehicle used by a licensed retailer to deliver cannabis goods is subject to inspection by the Bureau. Vehicles used to deliver cannabis goods may be stopped and inspected by the Bureau at any licensed premises or during delivery.

Note: Authority cited: Section 26013, Business and Professions Code. Reference: Sections 26070 and 26090, Business and Professions Code.

§ 5418. Cannabis Goods Carried During Delivery.

(a) A licensed retailer's delivery employee shall not carry cannabis goods in the delivery vehicle with a value in excess of $5,000 at any time. The value of cannabis goods carried in the delivery vehicle for which a delivery order was not received and processed by the licensed retailer prior to the delivery employee departing from the licensed premises may not exceed $3,000.

(b) For the purposes of this section, the value of cannabis goods shall be determined using the current retail price of all cannabis goods carried by, or within the delivery vehicle of, the licensed retailer's delivery employee.

(c) A delivery employee may only carry cannabis goods in the delivery vehicle and may only perform deliveries for one licensed retailer at a time. A delivery employee must depart and return to the same licensed premises before taking possession of any cannabis goods from another licensee to perform deliveries.

(d) A licensed retailer's delivery employee shall not leave the licensed premises with cannabis goods without at least one delivery order that has already been received and processed by the licensed retailer.

(e) Before leaving the licensed premises, the licensed retailer's delivery driver must have a delivery inventory ledger of all cannabis goods provided to the licensed retailer's delivery driver. For each cannabis good, the delivery inventory ledger shall include the type of good, the brand, the retail value, the track and trace identifier, and the weight, volume or other accurate measure of the cannabis good. All cannabis goods prepared for an order that was received and processed by the licensed retailer prior to the delivery driver's departure from the licensed premises must be clearly identified on the inventory ledger. After each customer delivery, the delivery inventory ledger must be updated to reflect the current inventory in possession of the licensed retailer's delivery driver. Delivery inventory ledgers may be maintained electronically.

(f) The licensed retailer's delivery driver shall maintain a log that includes all stops from the time the licensed retailer's delivery driver leaves the licensed premises to the time that the licensed retailer's delivery driver returns to the licensed premises, and the reason for each stop. The log shall be turned in to the licensed retailer when the licensed retailer's delivery driver returns to the licensed premises. The licensed retailer must maintain the log as a commercial cannabis activity record as required by this division. The log may be maintained electronically.

(g) Prior to arrival at any delivery location, the licensed retailer must have received a delivery request from the customer and provided the delivery request receipt to the licensed retailer's delivery driver electronically or in hard copy. The delivery request receipt provided to the licensed retailer's delivery driver shall contain all of the information required in section 5420 of this division, except for the date and time the delivery was made, and the signature of the customer.

(h) Immediately upon request by the Bureau or any law enforcement officer, the licensed retailer's delivery driver shall provide:

(1) All delivery inventory ledgers from the time the licensed retailer's delivery driver left the licensed premises up to the time of the request;

(2) All delivery request receipts for cannabis goods carried by the driver, in the delivery vehicle, or any deliveries that have already been made to customers; and

(3) The log of all stops from the time the licensed retailer's delivery driver left the licensed premises up to the time of the request.

(i) If a licensed retailer's delivery driver does not have any delivery requests to be performed for a 30-minute period, the licensed retailer's delivery driver shall not make any additional deliveries and shall return to the licensed premises. Required meal breaks shall not count toward the 30-minute period.

(j) Upon returning to the licensed premises, all undelivered cannabis goods shall be returned to inventory and all necessary inventory and track-and-trace records shall be updated as appropriate that same day.

Note: Authority cited: Section 26013, Business and Professions Code. Reference: Sections 26070, 26090 and 26160, Business and Professions Code.

§ 5419. Cannabis Consumption During Delivery.

A licensed retailer's delivery employees shall not consume cannabis goods while delivering cannabis goods to customers.

Note: Authority cited: Section 26013, Business and Professions Code. Reference: Sections 26070 and 26090, Business and Professions Code.

§ 5420. Delivery Request Receipt.

A licensed retailer shall prepare a hard copy or electronic delivery request receipt for each delivery of cannabis goods.

(a) The delivery request receipt shall contain the following:

(1) The name and address of the licensed retailer;

(2) The first name and employee number of the licensed retailer's delivery employee who delivered the order;

(3) The first name and employee number of the licensed retailer's employee who prepared the order for delivery;

(4) The first name of the customer and a licensed retailer-assigned customer number for the person who requested the delivery;

(5) The date and time the delivery request was made;

(6) The delivery address;

(7) A detailed description of all cannabis goods requested for delivery. The description shall include the weight, volume, or any other accurate measure of the amount of all cannabis goods requested;

(8) The total amount paid for the delivery, including any taxes or fees, the cost of the cannabis goods, and any other charges related to the delivery; and

(9) Upon delivery, the date and time the delivery was made, and the handwritten or electronic signature of the customer who received the delivery.

(b) At the time of the delivery, the delivery employee of the retailer shall provide the customer who placed the order with a hard or electronic copy of the delivery request receipt. The delivery employee shall retain a hard or electronic copy of the signed delivery request receipt for the licensed retailer's records.

(c) For the purposes of this section, an employee number is a distinct number assigned by a licensed retailer to an employee that would allow the licensed retailer to identify the employee in documents or records using the employee number rather than the employee's full name. A licensed retailer shall be able to identify the employee associated with each employee number upon request from the Bureau.

(d) For the purposes of this section, a customer number is a distinct number assigned by a licensed retailer to a customer that would allow the licensed retailer to identify the customer in documents or records using the customer number rather than the customer's full name. A licensed retailer shall be able to identify the customer associated with each customer number upon request from the Bureau.

Note: Authority cited: Section 26013, Business and Professions Code. Reference: Sections 26070, 26090 and 26160, Business and Professions Code.

§ 5421. Delivery Route.

While making deliveries of cannabis goods, a licensed retailer's delivery employee shall only travel from the retailer's licensed premises to the delivery address; from one delivery address to another delivery address; or from a delivery address back to the retailer's licensed premises. A delivery employee of a licensed retailer shall not deviate from the delivery path described in this section, except for necessary rest, fuel, or vehicle repair stops, or because road conditions make continued use of the route unsafe, impossible, or impracticable.

Note: Authority cited: Section 26013, Business and Professions Code. Reference: Sections 26070 and 26090, Business and Professions Code.

§ 5422. Receiving Shipments of Inventory.

(a) A licensed retailer shall receive a shipment of cannabis goods only from a licensed distributor or licensed microbusiness authorized to engage in distribution.

(b) A licensed retailer shall accept shipments of cannabis goods only between the hours of 6:00 a.m. Pacific Time and 10:00 p.m. Pacific Time.

(c) During business hours, shipments of cannabis goods shall not enter the licensed premises through an entrance or exit that is available for use by the public.

(d) A licensed retailer whose licensed premises only has one entryway may be exempt from the requirements of subsection (c) of this section if the licensed retailer obtains authorization from the local jurisdiction explicitly authorizing this activity. The licensed retailer shall be required to provide this authorization to the Bureau upon request. For this section to apply, the licensed premises must physically have only one entryway and cannot have any other entryways.

Note: Authority cited: Section 26013, Business and Professions Code. Reference: Sections 26012 and 26070, Business and Professions Code.

§ 5423. Inventory Documentation.

A licensed retailer shall maintain an accurate record of its inventory. A licensed retailer shall provide the Bureau with the record of inventory immediately upon request. A licensed retailer shall keep a record of the following information for all cannabis goods the licensed retailer has in its inventory:

(a) A description of each item such that the cannabis goods can easily be identified;

(b) An accurate measurement of the quantity of the item;

(c) The date and time the cannabis goods were received by the licensed retailer;

(d) The sell-by or expiration date provided on the package of cannabis goods, if any;

(e) The name and license number of the licensed distributor or licensed microbusiness that transported the cannabis goods to the licensed retailer; and

(f) The price the licensed retailer paid for the cannabis goods, including taxes, delivery costs, and any other costs.

Note: Authority cited: Section 26013, Business and Professions Code. Reference: Section 26160, Business and Professions Code.

§ 5424. Inventory Reconciliation.

(a) A licensed retailer shall be able to account for all of its inventory.

(b) In conducting an inventory reconciliation, a licensed retailer shall verify that the licensed retailer's physical inventory is consistent with the licensed retailer's records pertaining to inventory.

(c) The result of inventory reconciliation shall be retained in the licensed retailer's records and shall be made available to the Bureau upon request.

(d) If a licensed retailer identifies any evidence of theft, diversion, or loss, the licensed retailer shall notify the Bureau and law enforcement pursuant to section 5036 of this division.

(e) If a significant discrepancy as defined in section 5034 of this division is discovered between a licensed retailer's physical inventory and the licensed retailer's inventory records, the licensed retailer shall notify the Bureau and law enforcement pursuant to section 5036 of this division.

Note: Authority cited: Section 26013, Business and Professions Code. Reference: Section 26160, Business and Professions Code.

§ 5425. Record of Sales. [Repealed]

§ 5426. Records.

All licensed retailer-specific records in this chapter shall be maintained in accordance with section 5037 of this division.

Note: Authority cited: Section 26013, Business and Professions Code. Reference: Section 26160, Business and Professions Code.

§ 5427. Retailer Premises to Retailer Premises Transfer.

(a) A licensee who holds multiple retail licenses may arrange for the transfer of cannabis goods from one licensed retail premises to another licensed retail premises if both retail licenses are held under the same ownership.

(b) Cannabis goods transferred to a licensed retail premises under subsection (a) of this section may be sold by the licensed retailer receiving the cannabis goods only if the cannabis goods comply with all requirements found in the Act and this division.

(c) The transportation of cannabis goods under this section must comply with all requirements found within the Act and this division.

(d) Any movement of cannabis goods under this section shall be properly entered into the state track and trace system.

Note: Authority cited: Section 26013, Business and Professions Code. Reference: Section 26070, Business and Professions Code.

Chapter 4. Microbusiness

§ 5500. Microbusiness.

(a) In order to hold a microbusiness license, a licensee must engage in at least three (3) of the following commercial cannabis activities: cultivation, manufacturing, distribution, and retail sale. License types created by the California Department of Food and Agriculture or the State Department of Public Health in regulation shall not be considered qualifying commercial cannabis activities for purposes of obtaining a microbusiness license, except for the Type N manufacturing license.

(b) An applicant for a microbusiness license shall indicate on the application for licensure which commercial cannabis activities the applicant intends to engage in.

(c) An application for a microbusiness license shall include:

(1) For an application indicating that the applicant intends to engage in cultivation under the microbusiness license, all the required information under sections 5002, 5501, 5502 and 5503 of this division.

(2) For an application indicating that the applicant intends to engage in manufacturing under the microbusiness license, all the required information under sections 5002, and 5506 of this division.

(3) For an application indicating that the applicant intends to engage in distribution under the microbusiness license, all the required information for an application seeking a distributor license.

(4) For an application indicating that the applicant intends to engage in distribution, transport-only under the microbusiness license, all the required information for an application seeking a distributor, transport-only license.

(5) For an application indicating that the applicant intends to engage in retail sale under the microbusiness license, all the required information for an application seeking a retailer license.

(6) For an application indicating that the applicant intends to engage in non-storefront retail sale under the

microbusiness license, all the required information for an application seeking a non-storefront retailer license.

(d) All cultivation, manufacturing, distribution, and retail activities performed by a licensee under a microbusiness license shall occur on the same licensed premises.

(e) A holder of a microbusiness license shall comply with the following:

(1) A holder of a microbusiness license engaged in cultivation shall comply with all the rules and requirements applicable to the cultivation license type suitable for the cultivation activities of the licensee.

(2) A holder of a microbusiness license engaged in manufacturing shall comply with all the rules and requirements applicable to a Manufacturer 1 license in Division 1 of Title 17 of the California Code of Regulations.

(3) A holder of a microbusiness license engaged in distribution shall comply with all the rules and requirements applicable to a distributor license in this division.

(4) A holder of a microbusiness license engaged in retail sale shall comply with all the rules and requirements applicable to a retailer license, or a non-storefront retailer license if retail sales are conducted by delivery only, in this division.

(f) A holder of a microbusiness license may only engage in the commercial cannabis activity requested in the license application and approved by the Bureau at the time the license is issued. If the holder of a microbusiness license wants to engage in an additional commercial cannabis activity after the license is issued, the licensee shall submit a request for a modification of the licensed premises pursuant to section 5027 of this division.

(g) A holder of a microbusiness license shall comply with all the security rules and requirements applicable to the corresponding license type suitable for the activities of the licensee.

(h) Areas of the licensed premises for manufacturing and cultivation shall be separated from the distribution and retail areas by a wall and all doors between the areas shall remain closed when not in use.

(i) A suspension or revocation of a microbusiness licensee shall affect all commercial cannabis activities allowed pursuant to that license.

Note: Authority cited: Section 26013, Business and Professions Code. Reference: Sections 26012, 26050, 26051.5 and 26070, Business and Professions Code.

§ 5501. Microbusiness Applications Including Cultivation Activities.

In addition to the information required in section 5002 of this division, an application for a microbusiness license to engage in cultivation shall include the following:

(a) Evidence of enrollment with the applicable Regional Water Quality Control Board or State Water Resources Control Board for water quality protection programs or written verification from the appropriate Board that enrollment is not necessary.

(b) Evidence that the applicant has conducted a hazardous materials record search of the EnviroStor database for the proposed premises. If hazardous sites were encountered, the applicant shall provide documentation of protocols implemented to protect employee health and safety.

(c) For indoor and mixed-light cultivation, identification of all power sources for cultivation activities, including, but not limited to: illumination, heating, cooling, and ventilation.

(d) A premises diagram pursuant to section 5006 of this division that shall also include:

(1) All roads and water crossings on the property.

(2) If the applicant is proposing to use a diversion from a waterbody, groundwater well, or rain catchment system as a water source for cultivation, the following locations on the property diagram with locations also provided as coordinates in either latitude and longitude or the California Coordinate System:

(A) Sources of water used, including the location of waterbody diversion(s), pump location(s), and distribution system; and

(B) Location, type, and capacity of each storage unit to be used for cultivation.

(e) A proposed cultivation plan pursuant to section 5502 of this division.

(f) Identification of all water sources used for cultivation activities and the applicable supplemental information for each source as required by section 5503 of this division:

(1) A retail water supplier;

(2) A groundwater well;

(3) A rainwater catchment system; or

(4) A diversion from a surface waterbody or an underground stream flowing in a known and definite channel.

(g) A copy of any final lake or streambed alteration agreement issued by the California Department of Fish and Wildlife, pursuant to Fish and Game Code sections 1602 and 1617, or written verification from the California Department of Fish and Wildlife that a lake and streambed alteration agreement is not required.

(h) An attestation that the applicant entity is an "agricultural employer" as defined by the Alatorre-Zenovich-Dunlap-Berman Agricultural Labor Relations Act of 1975; Division 2, Part 3.5 (commencing with Section 1140) of the Labor Code.

(i) An attestation that the local fire department has been notified of the cultivation site if the applicant entity is an indoor license type.

(j) An acknowledgement that the applicant understands that the information provided in the application that is relevant to the cultivation operation may be shared with the Department of Food and Agriculture for purposes of evaluating the applicant's qualifications for licensure. If the Department of Food and Agriculture corresponds directly with the applicant on matters related to the application, the applicant shall agree to cooperate. The applicant shall further agree that the Department of Food and Agriculture may conduct inspections on the areas of the premises related to their respective oversight authority.

(k) If applicable, a detailed description of any fines or penalties for cultivation or production of a controlled substance on public or private land pursuant to Fish and Game Code section 12025 or 12025.1 against the applicant or a business entity in which the applicant was an owner or officer within 3 years preceding the date of application.

Note: Authority cited: Section 26013, Business and Professions Code. Reference: Sections 26012, 26050, 26051.5 and 26070, Business and Professions Code.

§ 5502. Cultivation Plan Requirements.

A cultivation plan shall include all of the following:

(a) A detailed premises diagram showing all cultivation activity areas, boundaries, and dimensions in feet. The total area of the following cultivation activity areas shall be less than 10,000 square feet as provided in Business and

Professions Code section 26070.

    (1) Canopy area(s) (which shall contain mature plants, at any point in time), including aggregate square footage if the canopy areas are noncontiguous.

    (2) Area(s) outside of the canopy where only immature plants shall be maintained, if applicable.

    (3) Designated pesticide and other agricultural chemical storage area(s).

    (4) Designated processing area(s) if the licensee will process on site.

    (5) Designated packaging area(s) if the licensee will package products on site.

    (6) Designated composting area(s) if the licensee will compost plant or cannabis waste on site.

    (7) Designated secured area(s) for cannabis waste if different than subsection (a)(6) of this section.

    (8) Designated area(s) for harvested cannabis storage.

    (9) Designated research and development area(s) which may contain mature plants for nursery only.

    (10) Designated seed production area(s) which may contain mature plants for nursery only.

(b) For purposes of subsection(a)(1) in this section, canopy shall be calculated in square feet and measured using clearly identifiable boundaries of all areas(s) that will contain mature plants at any point in time, including all of the space(s) within the boundaries. Canopy may be noncontiguous, but each unique area included in the total canopy calculation shall be separated by an identifiable boundary which include, but are not limited to: interior walls, shelves, greenhouse walls, hoop house walls, garden benches, hedgerows, fencing, garden beds, or garden plots. If mature plants are being cultivated using a shelving system, the surface area of each level shall be included in the total canopy calculation. Immature plants for cultivation activities of a microbusiness shall have the same definition as defined by the California Department of Food and Agriculture in regulation.

(c) For indoor and mixed-light cultivation, a lighting diagram with the following information shall be included:

    (1) Location of all lights in the canopy area(s); and

    (2) Maximum wattage, or wattage equivalent, of each light.

(d) A pest management plan which shall include, but not be limited to, the following:

    (1) Product name and active ingredient(s) of all pesticides to be applied to cannabis during any stage of plant growth; and

    (2) Integrated pest management protocols including chemical, biological, and cultural methods the applicant anticipates using to control or prevent the introduction of pests on the cultivation site.

Note: Authority cited: Section 26013, Business and Professions Code. Reference: Sections 26050, 26051.5 and 26070, Business and Professions Code.

§ 5503. Supplemental Water Source Information.

The following information shall be provided for each water source identified by the applicant:

(a) Retail water supply sources:

    (1) If the water source is a retail water supplier, as defined in Water Code section 13575, identify the retail water supplier.

(2) If the water source is a small retail water supplier, such as a delivery service, and is subject to Business and Professions Code section 26060.1(a)(1)(B):

(A) If the retail water supplier contract is for delivery or pickup of water from a surface water body or an underground stream flowing in a known and definite channel, provide all of the following:

(i) The name of the retail water supplier under the contract;

(ii) The geographic location coordinates in either latitude and longitude or the California Coordinate System of any point of diversion used by the retail water supplier to divert water delivered to the applicant under the contract;

(iii) The authorized place of use of any water right used by the retail water supplier to divert water delivered to the applicant under the contract; and

(iv) The maximum amount of water delivered to the applicant for cannabis cultivation in any year.

(B) If the retail water supplier contract is for delivery or pickup of water from a groundwater well, provide all of the following:

(i) The name of the retail water supplier;

(ii) The geographic location coordinates for any groundwater well used to supply water delivered to the applicant, in either latitude and longitude or the California Coordinate System;

(iii) The maximum amount of water delivered to the applicant for cannabis cultivation in any year; and

(iv) A copy of the well log filed with the Department of Water Resources pursuant to Water Code section 13751 for each percolating groundwater well used to divert water delivered to the applicant. If no well log is available, the applicant shall provide evidence from the Department of Water Resources indicating that the Department of Water Resources does not have a record of the well log. When no well log is available, the State Water Resources Control Board may request additional information about the well.

(b) If the water source is a groundwater well:

(1) The groundwater well's geographic location coordinates in either latitude and longitude or the California Coordinate System; and

(2) A copy of the well log filed with the Department of Water Resources pursuant to Water Code section 13751. If no well log is available, the applicant shall provide evidence from the Department of Water Resources indicating that the Department of Water Resources does not have a record of the well log. If no well log is available, the State Water Resources Control Board may request additional information about the well.

(c) If the water source is a rainwater catchment system:

(1) The total square footage of the catchment footprint area(s);

(2) The total storage capacity, in gallons, of the catchment system(s); and

(3) A detailed description of the type, nature, and location of each catchment surface. Examples of catchment surfaces include a rooftop and greenhouse.

(d) If the water source is a diversion from a waterbody, provide any applicable statement, application, permit, license, or small irrigation use registration identification number(s), and either:

(1) A copy of any applicable registrations, permits, or licenses or proof of a pending application, issued under

Part 2 (commencing with Section 1200) of Division 2 of the Water Code as evidence of approval of a water diversion by the State Water Resources Control Board;

(2) A copy of any statements of diversion and use filed with the State Water Resources Control Board before October 31, 2017, detailing the water diversion and use; or

(3) A copy of documentation submitted to the State Water Resources Control Board before October 31, 2017, demonstrating that the diversion is authorized under a riparian right and that no diversion occurred in any calendar year between January 1, 2010, and January 1, 2017.

(4) If the applicant has claimed an exception from the requirement to file a statement of diversion and use pursuant to Water Code section 5101, the applicant shall provide a copy of the documentation submitted to the State Water Resources Control Board before January 1, 2019, demonstrating that the diversion is subject to Water Code section 5101, subdivision (a), (c), (d), or (e).

Note: Authority cited: Section 26013, Business and Professions Code. Reference: Sections 26050, 26051.5 and 26070, Business and Professions Code; and Section 13149, Water Code.

§ 5504. License Issuance in an Impacted Watershed.

If the State Water Resources Control Board or the Department of Fish and Wildlife finds, based on substantial evidence, that a licensed microbusiness' cannabis cultivation is causing significant adverse impacts on the environment in a watershed or other geographic area, the Bureau shall not issue new microbusiness licenses that include cultivation activities or increase the total number of plant identifiers within that watershed or area.

Note: Authority cited: Section 26013, Business and Professions Code. Reference: Sections 26011.5, 26055 and 26070, Business and Professions Code.

§ 5505. Cultivation Records for Licensees Engaging in Cultivation Activities.

In addition to the records required by section 5037 of this division, a licensed microbusiness engaging in cultivation activities shall maintain the following records:

(a) Cultivation plan(s);

(b) All records evidencing compliance with the environmental protection measures required in sections 5501, 5502, 5503 and 5504 of this division; and

(c) All unique identifiers (UID) assigned to product in inventory and all unassigned UIDs. UIDs associated with product that has been retired from the track and trace system must be retained for six (6) months after the date the tags were retired.

Note: Authority cited: Section 26013, Business and Professions Code. Reference: Sections 26069, 26160 and 26161, Business and Professions Code.

§ 5506. Microbusiness Applications Including Manufacturing Activities.

In addition to the information required in section 5002 of this division, an application for a microbusiness license that engages or will engage in manufacturing shall include the following:

(a) The type of activity conducted at the premises (extraction, infusion, packaging, and/or labeling).

(b) The types of products that will be manufactured, packaged, or labeled.

(c) The name, title, and phone number of the on-site individual who manages the operation of the premises.

(d) The name, title, and phone number of an alternate contact person for the premises.

(e) The number of employees at the premises.

(f) The following information:

> (1) A description of inventory control procedures sufficient to demonstrate how the applicant will comply with the requirements of section 40282 of Title 17 of the California Code of Regulations, or a copy of the standard operating procedure addressing inventory control;

> (2) A copy of the product quality plan that meets the requirements of section 40253 of Title 17 of the California Code of Regulations; and

> (3) A description of security procedures sufficient to demonstrate how the applicant will comply with the requirements of section 40200 of Title 17 of the California Code of Regulations, or a copy of the standard operating procedure addressing security procedures.

Note: Authority cited: Section 26013, Business and Professions Code. Reference: Sections 26012, 26050, 26051.5, 26055 and 26070, Business and Professions Code.

§ 5506.1. Microbusiness Failed Manufactured Cannabis Product Batches.

A microbusiness licensee that engages or will engage in manufacturing shall handle failed manufactured cannabis product batches in accordance with the following:

(a) A finished manufactured cannabis product batch that fails any laboratory testing requirement established by the Bureau pursuant to Business and Professions Code section 26100 shall be destroyed unless a corrective action plan for remediation or reprocessing is approved by the Bureau pursuant to subsection (d) of this section.

(b) Remediation or reprocessing of a failed manufactured cannabis product batch or the use of a harvest batch that has failed any laboratory test shall comply with the requirements and procedures established by the Bureau in section 5727 of this division.

(c) Edible cannabis products that fail laboratory testing requirements shall not be remediated or reprocessed and shall be destroyed. If any edible cannabis product that has failed laboratory testing is remediated, reprocessed, or otherwise mixed with another batch of cannabis product, such action shall render the final cannabis product adulterated, as defined in Business and Professions Code section 26131, regardless of the defect level of the final cannabis product.

(d) A manufactured cannabis product batch or a harvest batch that fails laboratory testing or quality assurance review shall not be remediated or reprocessed unless the Bureau has approved a corrective action plan submitted by the microbusiness licensee. The corrective action plan shall include, at minimum, a description of how the product or harvest batch will be remediated so that the product or harvest batch, or any product produced therefrom, will meet all laboratory testing and quality assurance requirements. Corrective action plans will be reviewed by the Bureau on a case-by-case basis.

(e) All remediation of harvest or manufactured cannabis product batches shall be documented in the microbusiness' manufacturing records. Remediated products, harvest batches, or products produced therefrom shall be tested and undergo quality assurance review in accordance with the requirements established by the Bureau in Chapter 2 of this division.

(f) Notwithstanding subsection (c) of this section, if the edible cannabis products are orally-dissolving products, as defined in section 5700 of this division, and fail laboratory testing because the per-package limit of THC for adult-use products has been exceeded, the orally-dissolving products may be remediated by repackaging the orally-dissolving products as medicinal products in accordance with the following:

(1) A corrective action plan pursuant to subsection (d) of this section shall be submitted to and approved by the Bureau;

(2) The orally-dissolving edible cannabis products batch is returned to the licensed microbusiness that packaged the products;

(3) The orally-dissolving edible cannabis products are not altered in any way; and

(4) The orally-dissolving edible cannabis product is labeled to accurately state the contents.

Note: Authority cited: Section 26013, Business and Professions Code. Reference: Sections 26012, 26050 and 26070, Business and Professions Code.

§ 5507. Microbusiness Records for Licensees Engaging in Manufacturing Activities.

In addition to the records required by section 5037 of this division, a licensed microbusiness engaging in manufacturing activities shall maintain all records required to be maintained by manufacturers under Chapter 13, Division 1 of Title 17 of the California Code of Regulations.

Note: Authority cited: Section 26013, Business and Professions Code. Reference: Section 26160, Business and Professions Code.

Chapter 5. Cannabis Events

§ 5600. Cannabis Event Organizer License.

(a) To obtain a temporary cannabis event license, the event organizer must first apply for and obtain a cannabis event organizer license.

(b) A cannabis event organizer licensed under this section shall comply with chapter 1 of this division except for sections 5001-5002, 5006-5008, 5010-5010.3, 5016, 5019, 5025-5028, 5032-5034, 5038, 5042, 5044, and 5046-5054.

(c) A cannabis event organizer licensee is not authorized or licensed to cultivate, distribute, manufacture, or retail cannabis or cannabis products without first obtaining the appropriate licenses or authorizations to engage in such commercial cannabis activities.

(d) A cannabis event organizer licensee shall comply with the record retention provisions of section 5037 of this division. Records shall be kept by the cannabis event organizer licensee in a manner that allows the records to be produced for the Bureau in either hard copy or electronic form, whichever the Bureau requests. Failure to produce records upon the Bureau's request may result in disciplinary action against the cannabis event organizer license and/or denial of a temporary cannabis event license.

(e) Cannabis event organizer applications may be completed online at www.bcc.ca.gov or by delivering a printed copy to the Bureau's office(s).

(f) Applicants who submit their applications online shall first register for a user account as provided by section 5002(b) of this division.

(g) An application must be completed by an owner as defined by section 5003 of this division. An application for a cannabis event organizer license includes the following:

(1) The name of the applicant. For applicants who are individuals, the applicant shall provide both the first and last name of the individual. For applicants who are business entities, the applicant shall provide the legal business name of the applicant.

(2) If applicable, the business trade name ("DBA") of the applicant.

(3) Payment of an application fee pursuant to section 5014 of this division.

(4) Whether the owner is serving or has previously served in the military. Disclosure of military service is voluntary. An applicant who has served as an active duty member of the Armed Forces of the United States and was honorably discharged and who can provide evidence of such honorable discharge shall have his or her application expedited pursuant to Business and Professions Code section 115.4.

(5) A list of the license types and the license numbers issued from the Bureau and all other state cannabis licensing authorities that the applicant holds, including the date the license was issued and the licensing authority that issued the license.

(6) Whether the applicant has been denied a license or has had a license suspended or revoked by the Bureau or any other state cannabis licensing authority. The applicant shall provide the type of license applied for, the name of the licensing authority that denied the application, and the date of denial.

(7) The mailing address for the applicant.

(8) The telephone number for the applicant.

(9) The website address of the applicant's business, if applicable.

(10) The email address for the applicant's business.

(11) Contact information for the applicant's designated primary contact person including the name, title, phone number, and email address of the individual.

(12) The federal employer identification number for the applicant's business.

(13) A description of the business organizational structure of the applicant, such as partnership or corporation.

(14) All business-formation documents, which may include, but are not limited to, articles of incorporation, bylaws, operating agreements, partnership agreements, and fictitious business name statements. The applicant shall also provide all documents filed with the California Secretary of State, which may include, but are not limited to, articles of incorporation, certificates of stock, articles of organization, certificates of limited partnership, and statements of partnership authority. If the commercial cannabis business is held in trust, the applicant shall provide a copy of the certificate of trust establishing trustee authority.

(15) A list of every fictitious business name the applicant is operating under including the address where the business is located.

(16) A commercial cannabis business that is a foreign corporation shall include in its application the certificate of qualification, certificate of registration, or certificate of status issued by the California Secretary of State.

(17) The applicant shall supply the following financial information:

(A) A list of funds belonging to the applicant's cannabis event organizing business held in savings, checking, or other accounts maintained by a financial institution. The applicant shall provide, for each account, the financial institution's name, the financial institution's address, account type, account number, and the amount of money in the account.

(B) A list of loans made to the applicant for its use in cannabis event organizing activities. For each loan, the applicant shall provide the amount of the loan, the date of the loan, term(s) of the loan, security provided for the loan, and the name, address, and phone number of the lender.

(C) A list of investments made into the applicant's cannabis event organizing activities. For each investment, the applicant shall provide the amount of the investment, the date of the investment, term(s) of the investment, and the name, address, and phone number of the investor.

(D) A list of all gifts of any kind given to the applicant for its use in cannabis event organizing activities. For each gift, the applicant shall provide the value of the gift or description of the gift, and the name, address, and phone number of the provider of the gift.

(18) A complete list of every individual that has a financial interest in the cannabis event organizing business as defined in section 5004 of this division, who is not an owner as defined in section 5003 of this division.

(19) A complete list of every owner of the applicant as defined in section 5003 of this division. Each individual named on this list shall submit the following information:

(A) The full name of the owner.

(B) The owner's title within the applicant entity.

(C) The owner's date of birth and place of birth.

(D) The owner's social security number or individual taxpayer identification number.

(E) The owner's mailing address.

(F) The owner's telephone number. This may include a number for the owner's home, business, or mobile telephone.

(G) The owner's email address.

(H) The owner's current employer.

(I) The percentage of the ownership interest held in the applicant entity by the owner.

(J) Whether the owner has an ownership or a financial interest as defined in sections 5003 and 5004, respectively, of this division in any other commercial cannabis business licensed under the Act.

(K) A copy of the owner's government-issued identification. Acceptable forms of identification are a document issued by a federal, state, county, or municipal government that includes the name, date of birth, height, gender, and picture of the person, such as a driver license.

(L) A detailed description of the owner's convictions. A conviction within the meaning of this section means a plea or verdict of guilty or a conviction following a plea of nolo contendere. Convictions dismissed under Penal Code section 1203.4 or equivalent non-California law must be disclosed. Convictions dismissed under Health and Safety Code section 11361.8 or equivalent non-California law must be disclosed. Juvenile adjudications and traffic infractions under $300 that did not involve alcohol, dangerous drugs, or controlled substances do not need to be included. For each conviction, the owner shall provide the following:

(i) The date of conviction.

(ii) Dates of incarceration, if applicable.

(iii) Dates of probation, if applicable.

(iv) Dates of parole, if applicable.

(v) A detailed description of the offense for which the owner was convicted.

(vi) A statement of rehabilitation for each conviction. The statement of rehabilitation is to be written by the owner and may contain evidence that the owner would like the Bureau to consider that demonstrates the owner's fitness for licensure. Supporting evidence may be attached to the statement of rehabilitation and may include, but is not limited to, a certificate of rehabilitation under Penal Code section 4852.01, and dated letters of reference from employers, instructors, or professional counselors that contain valid contact information for the individual providing the reference.

(M) If applicable, a detailed description of any administrative orders or civil judgments for violations of labor standards, any suspension of a commercial cannabis license, revocation of a commercial cannabis license, or sanctions for unlicensed commercial cannabis activity by a licensing authority, local agency, or state agency against the applicant or a business entity in which the applicant was an owner or officer within the three years immediately preceding the date of the application.

(N) Attestation to the following statement: Under penalty of perjury, I hereby declare that the information contained within and submitted with the application is complete, true, and accurate. I understand that a misrepresentation of fact is cause for rejection of this application, denial of the license, or revocation of a license issued.

(20) For an applicant with 20 or more employees, the applicant shall attest that the applicant has entered into a labor peace agreement and will abide by the terms of the agreement. The applicant shall submit a copy of the page of the labor peace agreement that contains signatures of the union representative and the applicant. For applicants who have not yet entered into a labor peace agreement, the applicant shall provide a notarized statement indicating the applicant will enter into and abide by the terms of a labor peace agreement as soon as reasonably practicable after licensure.

(21) The limited waiver of sovereign immunity required by section 5009 of this division, if applicable.

(22) The applicant's State Employer Identification Number (SEIN) issued by the California Employment Development Department.

(23) For an applicant with more than one employee, the applicant shall attest that the applicant employs, or will employ within one year of receiving a license, one supervisor and one employee who have successfully completed a Cal-OSHA 30-hour general industry outreach course offered by a training provider that is authorized by an OSHA Training Institute Education Center to provide the course.

Note: Authority cited: Sections 115.4 and 26013, Business and Professions Code. Reference: Sections 115.4, 144, 26012 and 26200, Business and Professions Code.

§ 5601. Temporary Cannabis Event License.

(a) A temporary cannabis event license authorizes a licensed cannabis event organizer to hold a temporary cannabis event where the onsite sale and consumption of cannabis goods is authorized at the location indicated on the license during the dates indicated on the license.

(b) A temporary cannabis event license shall only be issued to a person who holds a cannabis event organizer license issued by the Bureau.

(c) Violations of the requirements applicable to temporary cannabis events may result in disciplinary action against the cannabis event organizer license or any other licenses held by a licensee participating in the temporary cannabis event and responsible for a violation under this division or the Act.

(d) A temporary cannabis event license shall only be issued for a single day or up to 4 consecutive days. No temporary cannabis event license will be issued for more than 4 days.

(e) An application for a temporary cannabis event license shall be submitted to the Bureau no less than 60 calendar days before the first day of the temporary cannabis event.

(f) A temporary cannabis event may only be held at a county fair event, district agricultural association event, or at another venue expressly approved by a local jurisdiction for the purpose of holding a temporary cannabis event.

(g) A temporary cannabis event license shall not be issued for a premises that is licensed for the sale of alcohol or tobacco.

(h) An application for a temporary cannabis event license shall include the following:

(1) The name of the applicant. For applicants who are individuals, the applicant shall provide both the first and last name of the individual. For applicants who are business entities, the applicant shall provide the legal business name of the applicant.

(2) The license number for each state cannabis license held by the applicant.

(3) The address of the location where the temporary cannabis event will be held.

(4) The name of the temporary cannabis event.

(5) A diagram of the physical layout of the temporary cannabis event. The diagram shall clearly indicate where the temporary cannabis event will be taking place on the location grounds, all entrances and exits that will be used by participants during the event, all cannabis consumption areas, and all retail areas where cannabis goods will be sold. The hours during which cannabis goods will be sold shall be noted on the diagram. The diagram shall also clearly indicate the area where cannabis waste will be stored, all areas where cannabis goods will be stored, and the specific location of each cannabis licensee who will be participating in the event. Each cannabis licensee participating in the event shall be identified with an assigned temporary cannabis event location number. The diagram shall not contain highlighting and the markings on the diagram shall be in black-and-white print.

(6) The dates and hours of operation for which the temporary cannabis event license is being sought. A temporary event license is required for any date in which the applicant engages in onsite cannabis sales or allows onsite cannabis consumption.

(7) Contact information for the applicant's designated primary contact person regarding the temporary event license, including the name, title, address, phone number, and email address of the individual.

(8) Contact information for a designated contact person(s) who shall be onsite at the event and reachable by telephone at all times that the event is occurring.

(9) Written approval from the local jurisdiction authorizing the applicant to engage in onsite cannabis sales to, and onsite consumption by, persons 21 years of age or older at the temporary cannabis event at the proposed location.

(10) A list of all licensees and employees that will be providing onsite sales of cannabis goods at the temporary cannabis event.

(11) Attestation to the following statement: Under penalty of perjury, I hereby declare that the information contained within and submitted with the application is complete, true, and accurate. I understand that a

misrepresentation of fact is cause for rejection of this application, denial of the license, or revocation of a license issued.

(i) If the list of licensees and employees participating in the temporary cannabis event changes after the application is submitted or after the license is issued, the applicant shall submit with the Notification and Request Form, BCC-LIC-027 (New 10/18), incorporated herein by reference, an updated list and an updated diagram, as required in subsection (f)(5) of this section, to the Bureau no less than 72 hours before the event. Licensees not on the list submitted to the Bureau shall not participate in the temporary cannabis event.

(j) The licensed cannabis event organizer shall hire or contract for security personnel to provide security services at the licensed temporary cannabis event. All security personnel hired or contracted for by the licensee shall be at least 21 years of age, licensed by the Bureau of Security and Investigative Services, and comply with Chapters 11.4 and 11.5 of Division 3 of the Business and Professions Code. Security personnel shall be present on the licensed premises at all times cannabis goods are available for sale and/or cannabis consumption is allowed on the licensed premises.

(k) A licensed cannabis event organizer shall maintain a clearly legible sign, not less than 7" x 11" in size reading, "No Persons Under 21 Allowed" at or near each public entrance to any area where the sale or consumption of cannabis goods is allowed. The lettering of the sign shall be no less than 1 inch in height.

(l) All cannabis waste generated at a temporary cannabis event shall be collected and disposed of in accordance with the requirements of section 5054 of this division. The licensed cannabis event organizer may contract or arrange for the collection and disposal of cannabis waste generated during the temporary cannabis event.

(m) A licensed cannabis event organizer and all other licensees participating in a temporary cannabis event are required to comply with section 5037 of this division and all other applicable requirements in the Act and this division pertaining to recordkeeping.

(n) The Bureau may require the event organizer and all participants to cease operations without delay if, in the opinion of the Bureau or local law enforcement, it is necessary to protect the immediate public health and safety of the people of the state. Upon notification from the Bureau that the event is to cease operations, the event organizer shall immediately stop the event and all participants shall be removed from the premises within the time frame provided by the Bureau.

(o) Upon notification from the Bureau, the event organizer shall immediately expel from the event any person selling cannabis goods without a license from the Bureau that authorizes the participant to sell cannabis goods. The event organizer or their representative shall remain with the person being expelled from the premises at all times until he or she vacates the premises. If the person does not vacate the premises, the Bureau may inform the event organizer that the event must cease operations. Upon notification from the Bureau that the event is to cease operations, the event organizer shall immediately stop the event and all participants shall be removed from the premises within the time frame provided by the Bureau.

Note: Authority cited: Section 26013, Business and Professions Code. Reference: Sections 26012 and 26200, Business and Professions Code.

§ 5602. Temporary Cannabis Event Sales.

(a) Only persons age 21 or older may purchase and consume cannabis goods at a temporary cannabis event. Prior to selling cannabis goods to a customer, the licensee making the sale shall confirm, using valid identification as specified in section 5404 of this division, the age and identity of the customer.

(b) All sales of cannabis goods at a temporary cannabis event must occur in a retail area as designated in the premises diagram pursuant to section 5601(h)(5) of this division.

(c) Each sale at a temporary cannabis event shall be performed by a licensed retailer, a licensed non-storefront retailer, or licensed microbusiness that is authorized to engage in retail sales. The cannabis event organizer may also sell cannabis goods at the temporary cannabis event if the organizer separately holds a license authorizing the retail sale of cannabis goods.

(1) Licensed retailers or licensed microbusinesses shall only conduct sales activities within their specifically assigned area, identified in the diagram of the physical layout of the temporary cannabis event.

(2) Mobile sales activities via wagon, cart, or similar means are prohibited at the temporary cannabis event site.

(d) Licensed retailers or licensed microbusinesses must prominently display their temporary cannabis event location number and state license within plain sight of the public.

(e) All sales at a temporary cannabis event shall occur on the dates stated on the license and shall occur at the location stated on the license. All onsite sales of cannabis goods must comply with the hours of operation requirements of section 5403 of this division.

(f) Sale of alcohol or tobacco shall not be allowed on the licensed temporary cannabis event premises.

(g) The cannabis goods sold onsite at a temporary cannabis event shall be transported by a licensed distributor or licensed microbusiness in compliance with the Act and this division. All shipments of cannabis and non-cannabis goods intended for sale at a temporary cannabis event must be checked by the temporary cannabis event organizer staff to prevent prohibited items, such as alcohol and tobacco, from entering the licensed premises.

(h) Except small amounts of cannabis goods used for display, all cannabis goods for sale at a temporary cannabis event shall be stored in a secure, locked container that is not accessible to the public. Cannabis goods being stored by a licensee at a temporary cannabis event shall not be left unattended. Licensees may share the secure, locked container; however, each licensee using the container shall be held responsible for any violations of this section and subject to disciplinary action.

(i) All cannabis goods made available for sale at a cannabis event shall comply with all requirements for the retail sale of cannabis goods within the Act and section 5406 of this division.

(j) All cannabis goods made available for sale at a temporary cannabis event shall comply with all track and trace requirements within the Act and this division.

(k) All cannabis goods used for display at a temporary cannabis event shall comply with the requirements of section 5405 of this division.

(l) All cannabis goods sold at a temporary cannabis event shall comply with section 5413 of this division.

(m) All customer returns of cannabis goods at a temporary cannabis event shall comply with section 5410 of this division.

(n) The daily sales limits under section 5409 of this division apply to all sales made at a temporary cannabis event.

(o) A licensed retailer shall only provide free cannabis goods to a person at a temporary cannabis event if the licensed retailer complies with all requirements of section 5411 of this division.

(p) The licensed cannabis event organizer shall be responsible for ensuring that all rules and requirements for the onsite sale of cannabis goods are followed.

(q) Any compensation paid from a licensed retailer to a licensed cannabis event organizer for participation in a temporary cannabis event shall not be determined based on, or be contingent on, the sale of cannabis goods.

Note: Authority cited: Section 26013, Business and Professions Code. Reference: Sections 26070 and 26200, Business and Professions Code.

§ 5603. Temporary Cannabis Event Consumption.

(a) Access to the area where cannabis consumption is allowed shall be restricted to persons 21 years of age or older.

(b) The event organizer licensee shall ensure that cannabis consumption is not visible from any public place or non-age-restricted area.

(c) Consumption of alcohol or tobacco shall not be allowed on the licensed premises.

(d) All requirements for onsite cannabis consumption imposed by the relevant local jurisdiction shall be followed and smoking of cannabis goods shall be prohibited in any areas where smoking is prohibited by law.

(e) The licensed cannabis event organizer, who holds the temporary cannabis event license, shall be responsible for ensuring that all rules and requirements for the onsite consumption of cannabis goods are followed.

(f) A licensed cannabis event organizer and all other licensees participating in a temporary cannabis event are required to follow all applicable requirements in this division pertaining to record keeping and waste management.

Note: Authority cited: Section 26013, Business and Professions Code. Reference: Section 26200, Business and Professions Code.

§ 5604. Informational or Educational Cannabis Events.

(a) Informational or educational cannabis events where no sales of cannabis goods or consumption of cannabis goods is occurring are not required to be licensed by the Bureau.

(b) A person may display cannabis goods for informational or educational purposes consistent with Health and Safety Code sections 11362.1 and 11362.77.

Note: Authority cited: Section 26013, Business and Professions Code. Reference: Section 26013, Business and Professions Code; and Sections 11362.1 and 11362.77, Health and Safety Code.

Chapter 6. Testing Laboratories

ARTICLE 1. CHAPTER DEFINITIONS

§ 5700. Definitions.

In addition to the definitions in section 5000 of this division, the following definitions apply to this chapter.

(a) "Acceptance criteria" means the specified limits placed on the characteristics of an item or method that are used to determine data quality.

(b) "Accreditation body" means an impartial non-profit organization that operates in conformance with the International Organization for Standardization (ISO) / International Electrotechnical Commission (IEC) standard 17011 and is a signatory to the International Laboratory Accreditation Cooperation (ILAC) Mutual Recognition Arrangement (MRA) for Testing.

(c) "Accredited college or university" means a college or university accredited by a regional or national accrediting agency that is an accreditor recognized by the Secretary of the US Department of Education.

(d) "Action level" means the threshold value that provides the criterion for determining whether a sample passes or fails an analytical test.

(e) "Analyte" means a chemical, compound, element, bacteria, yeast, fungus, or toxin to be identified or measured.

(f) "Analytical batch" means a set of no more than 20 samples that is prepared together for the same analysis and are prepared with laboratory quality control (LQC) samples.

(g) "Analytical method" means a technique used qualitatively or quantitatively to determine the composition of a sample or a microbial contamination of a sample.

(h) "Analytical sequence" means a group of samples that are analyzed sequentially using the same instrument calibration curve.

(i) "Cannabinoid" means a class of diverse chemical compounds derived from a cannabis plant.

(j) "Cannabis concentrate" means cannabis that has undergone a process to concentrate one or more active cannabinoids, thereby increasing the product's potency. For purposes of this chapter, "cannabis concentrate" includes, but is not limited to, the separated resinous trichomes of cannabis, tinctures, capsules, suppositories, extracts, vape cartridges, inhaled products (such as dab, shatter, and wax), and tablets as defined by the State Department of Public Health in regulation.

(k) "CAS number" means the unique numerical identifier assigned to every chemical substance by Chemical Abstracts Service, a division of the American Chemical Society.

(l) "CBD" means cannabidiol, CAS number 13956-29-1.

(m) "CBDA" means cannabidiolic acid, CAS number 1244-58-2.

(n) "CBG" means cannabigerol, CAS number 25654-31-3.

(o) "CBN" means cannabinol, CAS number 521-35-7.

(p) "Certificate of accreditation" means a document issued by an accreditation body that attests to the laboratory's competence to carry out specific testing analysis.

(q) "Certificate of analysis" (COA) means the report prepared by the laboratory about the analytical testing performed and results obtained by the laboratory.

(r) "Certified reference material" means a reference material prepared by a certifying body or a party independent of the laboratory with ISO/IEC 17034 accreditation.

(s) "Chain of Custody" (COC) means the chronological documentation that records the sequence of custody, control, transfer, analysis, and disposal of a sample.

(t) "Coefficient of Determination" (commonly denoted as "r2") means a statistical measure that determines how well the regression approximates the actual data points in the calibration curve, with a regression of 1 being a perfect fit.

(u) "Continuing calibration verification" (CCV) means a type of quality control sample that includes each of the target method analytes that is a mid-range calibration standard which checks the continued validity of the initial calibration of the instrument.

(v) "Corrective action" means an action taken by the laboratory to resolve, and prevent from recurrence, a problem with the technical operations of the laboratory.

(w) "Exclusivity" means the specificity of the test method for validating microbial testing methods. It evaluates the ability of the method to distinguish the target organisms from similar but genetically distinct non-target organisms.

(x) "Foreign material" means any filthy, putrid, or decomposed substance including hair, insects, excreta, or related adulterant that may be hazardous or cause illness or injury to the consumer.

(y) "Frequency" means the number of items occurring in each category. Frequency may be determined by analytical method or laboratory specific requirements for accuracy, precision of the analysis, or statistical calculation.

(z) "Good laboratory practice" (GLP) means a system of management controls for laboratories to ensure the uniformity, consistency, reliability, reproducibility, quality, and integrity of analyses performed by the testing laboratory.

(aa) "Inclusivity" means, related to microbiological method validation, the sensitivity of the test method. It evaluates the ability of the test method to detect a wide range of target organisms by a defined relatedness.

(bb) "Inhalable" means consumable in gaseous or vapor form through the lungs.

(cc) "Initial Calibration Verification" (ICV) means a solution of each of the target method analytes of known concentration that is obtained from a source external to the laboratory and different from the source of calibration standards.

(dd) "ISO/IEC" means the joint technical committee of the International Organization for Standardization (ISO) and the International Electrotechnical Commission (IEC).

(ee) "ISO/IEC 17025" means the general requirements specified by the ISO/IEC for the competence of testing and calibration laboratories.

(ff) "ISO/IEC 17034" means the general requirements established by the ISO/IEC for the competence of reference material producers.

(gg) "ISO/IEC 17043" means the general requirements established by the ISO/IEC for proficiency testing.

(hh) "Laboratory" means "testing laboratory" as defined at Business and Professions Code section 26001 (at).

(ii) "Laboratory Control Sample" (LCS) means a blank matrix to which known concentrations of each of the target method analytes are added. The spiked concentration must be at a mid-range concentration of the calibration curve for the target analytes. The LCS is analyzed in the same manner as the representative sample.

(jj) "Laboratory replicate sample" means a sub-sample taken of the representative sample used for laboratory quality control purposes to demonstrate reproducibility. It is prepared and analyzed in the identical manner as the representative sample. The results from replicate analyses are used to evaluate analytical precision.

(kk) "Laboratory employee" means any person directly employed by the laboratory for wages, salary, barter, or trade by the laboratory and who is not employed by any other licensee under the Act except for another testing laboratory. "Laboratory employee" does not mean an independent contractor, third party entity, or any other entity acting on behalf of the laboratory.

(ll) "Laboratory quality assurance" means the set of operating principles that enable laboratories to produce defensible data of known accuracy and precision and includes employee training, equipment preventative maintenance procedures, calibration procedures, and quality control testing, among other things.

(mm) "Limit of detection" (LOD) means the lowest quantity of a substance or analyte that can be distinguished from the absence of that substance within a stated confidence limit.

(nn) "Limit of quantitation" (LOQ) means the minimum concentration of an analyte in a specific matrix that can be reliably quantified while also meeting predefined goals for bias and imprecision.

(oo) "Linear regression" means the determination, in analytical chemistry, of the best linear equation for calibration data to generate a calibration curve. The concentrate of an analyte in a sample can then be determined by comparing a measurement of the unknown to the calibration curve. A linear regression uses the following equation:

$y = mx + b$; where m = slope, b = intercept

(pp) "Matrix" means the substances that are present in a sample except for the analyte(s) of interest.

(qq) "Matrix spike sample" means a sample prepared by adding a known quantity of each of the target analyte to a sample matrix or to a matrix that is as closely representative of the matrix being analyzed as possible. The spiked concentration must be at a mid-range concentration of the calibration curve for the target analytes.

(rr) "Method blank" means an analyte free matrix to which all reagents are added in the same volumes or proportions as used in the sample preparation and is processed in exactly the same manner as the samples.

(ss) "Moisture content" means the percentage of water in a sample, by weight.

(tt) "Non-target organism" means an organism that the test method or analytical procedure is not testing for and can be used in evaluating the specificity of a test method.

(uu) "Orally-consumed product containing alcohol" means a liquid solution that contains more than 0.5% alcohol by volume as an ingredient, is not otherwise an alcoholic beverage as defined in Business and Professions Code section 23004, is packaged in a container no larger than two (2) fluid ounces and includes a capped calibrated dropper capable of accurately measuring servings.

(vv) "Orally-dissolving product" means an edible cannabis product that is intended to dissolve and release cannabinoids directly into the mouth, which allows them to enter the bloodstream through the tissue, such as sublingual lozenges or mouth strips. Orally dissolving products are not intended to be eaten or swallowed to enter the digestive system.

(ww) "Percent recovery" means the percentage of a measured concentration relative to the added (spiked) concentration in a reference material or matrix spike sample. A laboratory shall calculate the percent recovery by dividing the sample result by the expected result then multiplying the quotient by 100.

(xx) "Practical experience" means experience performing scientific analytical tests in a laboratory setting using equipment, instruments, kits, and materials routinely found in a laboratory. "Practical experience" includes experience in any type of laboratory setting and is not limited to cannabis-specific laboratories.

(yy) "Pre-roll" has the same meaning as in section 5000(q) of this division and also includes, for purposes of this chapter, pre-rolls infused with cannabis concentrate.

(zz) "Proficiency test" means an evaluation of a laboratory's performance against pre-established criteria by means of interlaboratory comparisons of test measurements.

(aaa) "Proficiency test sample" means a sample that is prepared by a party independent of the testing laboratory with the ISO/IEC 17043 accreditation, where the concentration and identity of an analyte is known to the independent party, but is unknown to the testing laboratory and testing laboratory employees.

(bbb) "Quadratic regression" means the determination, in analytical chemistry, of the best parabola equation for calibration data to generate a calibration curve. The concentrate of an analyte in a sample can then be determined by comparing a measurement of the unknown to the calibration curve. A quadratic regression uses the following equation:

$y = ax^2 + bx + c$; where a, b, and c are numerical coefficients

(ccc) "Quality control" means the set of measures implemented within an analytical procedure to ensure that the measurement system is operating in a state of statistical control for which errors have been reduced to acceptable levels.

(ddd) "Quality control sample" means a sample that is produced and used by a laboratory for the purpose of assuring the quality of the data and results. Quality control samples include blank samples, matrix spike samples, laboratory control samples, replicate samples, and reference material samples.

(eee) "Reagent" means a compound or mixture added to a system to cause a chemical reaction or test if a reaction occurs. A reagent may be used to tell whether a specific chemical substance is present by causing a reaction to occur with the chemical substance.

(fff) "Reference material" means material containing a known concentration of an analyte of interest that is in solution or in a homogeneous matrix.

(ggg) "Reference method" means the method by which the performance of an alternate method is measured or evaluated.

(hhh) "Relative percent difference" (RPD) means the comparative statistic that is used to calculate precision or random error. RPD is calculated using the following equation:

RPD = (representative sample measurement - replicate sample measurement) / ([representative sample measurement + replicate sample measurement] / 2) X 100%

(iii) "Relative standard deviation" (RSD) means the standard deviation expressed as a percentage of the means recovery. RSD is calculated using the following equation:

RSD = (s / x) X 100%; where s = standard deviation and x = mean

(jjj) "Representative" means a small quantity of the batch whose characteristics represent, as accurately as possible, the entire batch, thus allowing the results to be generalized.

(kkk) "Representative sample" means a sample that is comprised of several sample increments of cannabis goods that are collected from a batch for testing.

(lll) "Requester" means the person who submits a request to the laboratory for testing of cannabis goods from an entity licensed under the Act.

(mmm) "Reserve sample" means any portion of a representative sample that was not used in the testing process.

(nnn) "Sample" means a representative part of, or a single item from, a batch which is comprised of several sample increments.

(ooo) "Sample increment" means a portion of a batch that, together with other increments, makes up the sample.

(ppp)"Sampler" means the laboratory employee responsible for obtaining samples of cannabis goods from a licensed distributor or licensed microbusiness authorized to engage in distribution.

(qqq)"Sanitize" means to sterilize, disinfect, or make hygienic.

(rrr) "Scope of accreditation" means the tests or types of tests performed, materials or products tested, and the methods used for testing cannabis or cannabis products for which the accreditation has been granted.

(sss) "Standard operating procedure" (SOP) means a written document that provides detailed instructions for the performance of all aspects of an analysis, operation, or action.

(ttt) "Target organism" means an organism that is being tested for in an analytical procedure or test method.

(uuu) "THC" and "delta-9 THC" means tetrahydrocannabinol, CAS number 1972-08-3.

(vvv) "THCA" means tetrahydrocannabinolic acid, CAS number 23978-85-0.

(www) "Topical cannabis goods" means cannabis products intended to be applied to the skin and not intended to be ingested or inhaled. Liquid solutions that contain more than 0.5% alcohol by volume as an ingredient and are not otherwise an alcoholic beverage as defined in Business and Professions Code section 23004 shall only be considered topical cannabis goods if they are packaged in a container no larger than two (2) fluid ounces.

(xxx) "Total CBD" means the sum of CBD and CBDA. Total CBD is calculated using the following equation:

Total CBD concentration (mg/g) = (CBDA concentration (mg/g) X 0.877) + CBD concentration (mg/g)

(yyy) "Total THC" means the sum of THC and THCA. Total THC is calculated using the following equation:

Total THC concentration (mg/g) = (THCA concentration (mg/g) X 0.877) + THC concentration (mg/g)

(zzz) "Validation" means the confirmation by examination and objective evidence that the requirements for a specific intended use or analytical method are fulfilled.

(aaaa) "Water activity" means the measure of the quantity of water in a product that is available and therefore capable of supporting bacteria, yeasts, and fungi and which is reported in units Aw.

Note: Authority cited: Section 26013, Business and Professions Code. Reference: Sections 26013 and 26100, Business and Professions Code.

ARTICLE 2. LABORATORY LICENSE

§ 5701. General Laboratory License Requirements.

(a) A licensed laboratory shall maintain ISO/IEC 17025 accreditation for the testing of the following:

(1) Cannabinoids;

(2) Heavy metals;

(3) Microbial impurities;

(4) Mycotoxins;

(5) Residual pesticides;

(6) Residual solvents and processing chemicals; and

(7) If tested, terpenoids.

(b) Each testing laboratory licensed premises shall have ISO/IEC 17025 accreditation.

(c) A licensed laboratory shall retain, and make available to the Bureau upon request, all records associated with the licensee's ISO/IEC 17025 certificate of accreditation.

Note: Authority cited: Section 26013, Business and Professions Code. Reference: Sections 26012 and 26100, Business and Professions Code.

§ 5702. Laboratory License Application.

In addition to the information required in section 5002 of this division, an application for a testing laboratory license includes the following:

(a) A valid certificate of accreditation, issued by an accreditation body, that attests to the laboratory's competence to perform testing, including all the required analytes for the following test methods:

(1) Cannabinoids;

(2) Heavy metals;

(3) Microbial impurities;

(4) Mycotoxins;

(5) Residual pesticides;

(6) Residual solvents and processing chemicals; and

(7) If tested, terpenoids.

(b) Standard operating procedures for the following testing methods:

(1) Cannabinoids;

(2) Foreign material;

(3) Heavy metals;

(4) Microbial impurities;

(5) Moisture content and water activity;

(6) Mycotoxins;

(7) Residual pesticides;

(8) Residual solvents and processing chemicals; and

(9) If tested, terpenoids.

(c) Method validation reports for the following testing methods:

(1) Cannabinoids;

(2) Heavy metals;

(3) Microbial impurities;

(4) Water activity;

(5) Mycotoxins;

(6) Residual pesticides;

(7) Residual solvents and processing chemicals; and

(8) If tested, terpenoids.

(d) Standard operating procedures for the sampling of cannabis goods.

Note: Authority cited: Section 26013, Business and Professions Code. Reference: Sections 26012, 26050, 26055, 26102 and 26104, Business and Professions Code.

§ 5703. Interim Testing Laboratory License.

(a) An applicant may apply for an interim license prior to receiving ISO/IEC 17025 accreditation provided that the applicant meets all other licensure requirements for a testing laboratory and submits to the Bureau an application in compliance with section 5002 of this division and an attestation that the applicant has or intends to seek ISO/IEC 17025 accreditation for all testing methods required by this division.

(b) An interim testing laboratory license shall be valid for 12 months. The annual license fee for an interim license shall be determined pursuant to the requirements in section 5014 of this division for determining the annual license fee for a testing laboratory license.

(c) To timely renew an interim license, a completed license renewal form and the annual renewal license fee pursuant to section 5014 of this division shall be received by the Bureau from the licensee no earlier than 60 calendar days before the expiration of the license and no later than 5:00 p.m. Pacific Time on the last business day before the expiration of the license if the renewal form is submitted to the Bureau at its office(s), or no later than 11:59 p.m. on the last business day before the expiration of the license if the renewal form is submitted to the Bureau through its electronic licensing system. Failure to receive a notice for license renewal does not relieve a licensee of the obligation to renew an interim license as required.

(d) In the event the license is not renewed prior to the expiration date, the licensee must not test any commercial cannabis goods until the license is renewed.

(e) A licensee may submit a license renewal form up to 30 calendar days after the license expires. Any late renewal form will be subject to a late fee equal to 50 percent of the applicable licensing fees required by subsection (c) of this section.

(f) The license renewal application shall contain the following:

(1) The name of the licensee. For licensees who are individuals, the applicant shall provide both the first and last name of the individual. For licensees who are business entities, the licensee shall provide the legal business name of the applicant;

(2) The license number and expiration date;

(3) The licensee's address of record and licensed premises address; and

(4) An attestation that all information provided to the Bureau in the original application under section 5002 of this division or subsequent notification under section 5023 of this division is accurate and current.

(g) The Bureau may renew an interim license for an initial renewal period of 12 months.

(h) After one renewal, the Bureau may renew the interim license for additional 12-month periods if the licensee has submitted an application for the ISO/IEC 17025 accreditation. In addition to the information required for a renewal form pursuant to subsection (f) of this section, any renewal request pursuant to this section shall also include an attestation that the licensee's application for each ISO/IEC 17025 is pending with the accrediting body, the name of the accrediting body, and the date the application was submitted to the accrediting body.

(i) The licensee shall notify the Bureau if the application for each ISO/IEC 17025 accreditation is granted or denied within 1 business day of receiving the decision from the accrediting body. The Licensee shall submit to the Bureau the information required, on the Notification and Request Form, BCC-LIC-027 (New 10/18), which is incorporated herein by reference. If the accrediting body grants or denies the licensee's application for any ISO/IEC 17025 accreditation before the expiration of the interim license, the Bureau may terminate the interim license at that time.

(j) The Bureau may revoke an interim license at any time.

Note: Authority cited: Section 26013, Business and Professions Code. Reference: Sections 26012, 26031, 26050 and 26102, Business and Professions Code.

ARTICLE 3. SAMPLING CANNABIS AND CANNABIS PRODUCTS

§ 5704. Sampling Standard Operating Procedures.

(a) The laboratory shall develop and implement a sampling standard operating procedure (SOP) that describes the laboratory's method for obtaining representative samples of cannabis goods. The laboratory shall use and submit to the Bureau Sampling - Standard Operating Procedures, Form BCC-LIC-021 (New 7/18), which is incorporated herein by reference.

(b) The laboratory shall retain a copy of the sampling SOP on the licensed laboratory premises and ensure that the sampling SOP is accessible to the sampler during sampling.

Note: Authority cited: Section 26013, Business and Professions Code. Reference: Sections 26100, 26102, 26104 and 26110, Business and Professions Code.

§ 5705. General Sampling Requirements.

(a) The laboratory that obtains a representative sample from a licensed distributor or licensed microbusiness shall perform all the required testing at one licensed laboratory premises.

(b) The laboratory may obtain and analyze samples only from batches in final form as required by Business and Professions Code section 26100.

(c) The laboratory sampler shall collect a representative sample from each batch following the procedures specified in the laboratory's sampling standard operating procedure(s).

(d) The laboratory shall ensure that the sample is transported and subsequently stored at the licensed laboratory premises in a manner that prevents degradation, contamination, commingling, and tampering. If the cannabis good specifies on the label how the cannabis good shall be stored, the laboratory shall store the sample as indicated on the label.

(e) The laboratory shall complete a chain of custody form for each sample that the laboratory collects and analyzes.

(f) Once a representative sample has been obtained for regulatory compliance testing, the licensed testing laboratory that obtained the sample must complete the regulatory compliance testing.

(g) If a licensed laboratory is unable to competently complete the regulatory compliance testing after sampling and before a COA is issued, the licensed distributor or microbusiness authorized to engage in distribution who arranged for the testing of the batch(s) may request approval from the Bureau to have the impacted batch(s) re-sampled and tested by another licensed laboratory.

(1) The request shall be made in writing via email to bcc.labs@dca.ca.gov and shall include all of the following:

(A) The name and license number of the distributor;

(B) The batch numbers;

(C) The type and quantity of cannabis goods;

(D) The name and license number of the laboratory that took the initial sample and is not able to competently complete the regulatory compliance testing;

(E) The name and license number of the laboratory proposed to re-sample and complete the regulatory compliance testing for the batch(s); and

(F) The reason why the laboratory that initially took the sample cannot competently complete the regulatory compliance testing.

(2) The Bureau will review the request and determine if the laboratory that initially took the sample is unable to competently complete the regulatory compliance testing. If the Bureau determines that the laboratory is

unable to competently complete the regulatory compliance testing, the Bureau, in its discretion, may approve the request in whole or part and set conditions for the re-sampling and testing.

(3) No re-sampling of any batch shall occur prior to the licensed distributor or licensed microbusiness authorized to engaged in distribution receiving written approval from the Bureau.

Note: Authority cited: Section 26013, Business and Professions Code. Reference: Sections 26100, 26104 and 26110, Business and Professions Code.

§ 5706. Chain of Custody (COC).

(a) The laboratory shall develop and implement a COC protocol to ensure accurate documentation is recorded for the transport, handling, storage, and destruction of samples.

(b) The COC protocol shall require the use of a COC form. The sampler shall use a COC to record the following information for each sampled batch:

(1) Laboratory's name, licensed premises address, and license number;

(2) Date and time sampling started and ended;

(3) Licensed distributor or licensed microbusiness' name, licensed premises address, and license number;

(4) Licensed cultivator's, licensed manufacturer's, or licensed microbusiness' name, licensed premises address, and license number;

(5) Batch number of the batch from which the representative sample was obtained and assigned unique sample identifier;

(6) Sample matrix;

(7) Total batch size, by weight, or unit count;

(8) Total weight, or unit count of the representative sample;

(9) Sampling conditions or problems encountered during the sampling process, if any;

(10) Printed name and signature of the licensed distributor or licensed microbusiness' authorized to engage in distribution employee; and

(11) Printed name and signature of the sampler.

(c) Each time a sample changes custody between licensees, is transported, or is destroyed, the date, time, and the names and signatures of persons involved in these activities shall be recorded on the COC form.

(d) Once the custody of the sample changes between licensees, the COC form for that change of custody may not be altered.

Note: Authority cited: Section 26013, Business and Professions Code. Reference: Sections 26100, 26102, 26104 and 26110, Business and Professions Code.

§ 5707. Harvest Batch Sampling.

(a) The sampler shall obtain a representative sample from each prepacked or unpacked harvest batch. The representative sample must weigh 0.35% of the total harvest batch weight.

(b) A sampler may collect a representative sample greater than 0.35% of the total harvest batch weight of a prepacked or unpacked harvest batch if necessary to perform the required testing or to ensure that the samples obtained are representative.

(c) The prepacked or unpacked harvest batch from which a sample is obtained shall weigh no more than 50.0 pounds. Laboratory analyses of a sample collected from a harvest batch weighing more than 50.0 pounds shall be deemed invalid and the harvest batch from which the sample was obtained shall not be released for retail sale.

(d) When the sampler obtains a representative sample from an unpacked harvest batch, the sampler shall do all the following:

(1) Collect the number of sample increments relative to the unpacked harvest batch size as listed in the following table;

(2) Obtain sample increments from random and varying locations of the unpacked harvest batch, both vertically and horizontally. To the extent practicable, the sample increments obtained from an unpacked harvest batch shall be of equal weight; and

(3) To the extent practicable, collect an equal number of sample increments from each container if the unpacked harvest batch is stored in multiple containers.

Unpacked Harvest Batch Size (pounds)	Number of Increments (per sample)
≤ 10.0	8
10.1 – 20.0	16
20.1 – 30.0	23
30.1 – 40.0	29
40.1 – 50.0	34

Note: Authority cited: Section 26013, Business and Professions Code. Reference: Sections 26100, 26104 and 26110, Business and Professions Code.

§ 5708. Cannabis Product Batch and Pre-Roll Sampling.

(a) The sampler shall obtain a representative sample from each cannabis product batch or pre-roll batch.

(b) The sampler may collect a greater number of sample increments if necessary to perform the required testing or to ensure that the samples obtained are representative.

(c) The cannabis product batch or pre-roll batch from which a representative sample is obtained shall contain no more than 150,000 units. Laboratory analyses of a sample collected from a cannabis product batch containing more than 150,000 units shall be deemed invalid and the cannabis product batch or pre-roll batch from which the representative sample was obtained shall not be released for retail sale.

(d) The sampler shall obtain a representative sample of a cannabis product or pre-roll batch by collecting, at minimum, the number of sample increments relative to the batch size as listed in the following table. Each sample increment consists of 1 packaged unit.

Cannabis Product or Pre-roll Batch Size (units)	Number of Sample Increments (per sample)
≤ 50	2
51 – 150	3
151 – 500	5
501 – 1,200	8
1,201 – 3,200	13
3,201 – 10,000	20
10,001 – 35,000	32
35,001 – 150,000	50

Note: Authority cited: Section 26013, Business and Professions Code. Reference: Sections 26100, 26104 and 26110, Business and Professions Code.

§ 5709. Laboratory Transportation of Cannabis Goods Samples.

(a) The following requirements apply when a licensed testing laboratory transports cannabis goods samples:

(1) While transporting cannabis goods samples, a licensed testing laboratory employee shall ensure the cannabis goods are not visible to the public. Cannabis goods shall be locked in a fully enclosed box, container, or cage that is secured to the inside of the vehicle or trailer. No portion of the enclosed box, container, or cage shall be comprised of any part of the body of the vehicle or trailer. For the purposes of this section, the inside of the vehicle includes the trunk.

(2) While left unattended, vehicles and trailers shall be locked and secured.

(3) The laboratory shall not leave a vehicle or trailer containing cannabis goods samples unattended in a residential area or parked overnight in a residential area.

(4) The laboratory shall ensure that any vehicle or trailer transporting cannabis goods samples has an alarm system.

(5) The laboratory shall ensure that packages or containers holding cannabis goods samples are neither tampered with, nor opened during transport.

(6) The laboratory transporting cannabis goods samples shall only travel between licensees for whom the laboratory is conducting regulatory compliance testing or quality assurance testing. A laboratory shall not deviate from the travel requirements described in this section, except for necessary rest, fuel, or vehicle repair stops.

(7) The laboratory may transport multiple cannabis goods samples obtained from multiple licensees at once.

(8) Vehicles or trailers transporting cannabis goods samples are subject to inspection by the Bureau at any licensed premises or during transport at any time.

(9) No person under the age of 21 years old shall be in a vehicle or trailer transporting cannabis goods samples.

(10) Only an employee of the laboratory or security personnel who meets the requirement of section 5045 of this division shall be in a vehicle while transporting cannabis goods samples.

(b) The laboratory shall provide the following required transport vehicle information to the Bureau:

(1) Proof that the laboratory is the registered owner under the Vehicle Code for each vehicle used to transport cannabis goods samples;

(2) The year, make, model, license plate number, and numerical Vehicle Identification Number (VIN) for each vehicle or trailer used to transport cannabis goods samples; and

(3) Proof of insurance for each vehicle used to transport cannabis goods samples.

(c) The laboratory shall provide the Bureau with the information required by this section in writing for any new vehicle or trailer that will be used to transport cannabis goods samples prior to using the vehicle or trailer.

(d) The laboratory shall provide the Bureau with the information required under subsection (c) of this section and with any changes to the information required by this section in writing within 30 calendar days, submitted on the Notification and Request Form, BCC-LIC-027 (New 10/18), which is incorporated herein by reference.

Note: Authority cited: Section 26013, Business and Professions Code. Reference: Sections 26100, 26102, 26104 and 26110, Business and Professions Code.

§ 5710. Laboratory Receipt of Samples Obtained from a Distributor or Microbusiness.

(a) The laboratory may accept and analyze a sample from a licensed distributor or licensed microbusiness authorized to engage in distribution for the required testing under section 5714 of this division only if there is an accompanying COC form for the sample.

(b) The laboratory employee who receives the sample shall date, print, and sign their name on the accompanying sample COC.

(c) The laboratory shall not analyze a sample obtained from a licensed distributor or licensed microbusiness authorized to engage in distribution, and the batch from which the sample was obtained may not be released for retail sale, if any of the following occur:

(1) The sample is received at the laboratory without the requisite COC form;

(2) The tamper-evident material is broken prior to the sample being received at the laboratory; or

(3) There is evidence of sample commingling, contamination, degradation, or a related occurrence rendering the sample unusable for analytical testing when the sample is received at the laboratory.

Note: Authority cited: Section 26013, Business and Professions Code. Reference: Sections 26100, 26104 and 26110, Business and Professions Code.

ARTICLE 4. STANDARD OPERATING PROCEDURES

§ 5711. Laboratory Analyses Standard Operating Procedures.

(a) The laboratory shall develop, implement, and maintain written standard operating procedures (SOP) for sample preparation and each required test method. The laboratory shall use and submit to the Bureau the following forms which are incorporated by reference:

(1) Sample Preparation - Standard Operating Procedures, Form BCC-LIC-022 (New 7/18), which is incorporated herein by reference; and

(2) Test Methods - Standard Operating Procedures, Form BCC-LIC-023 (New 7/18), which is incorporated herein by reference.

(b) The laboratory shall keep each SOP at the licensed laboratory premises and ensure that each SOP is accessible to laboratory employees during operating hours.

(c) The laboratory shall make each SOP available for inspection by the Bureau upon request, as well as any other SOPs associated with the licensee's ISO/IEC 17025 certificate of accreditation.

Note: Authority cited: Section 26013, Business and Professions Code. Reference: Sections 26012, 26100, 26102, 26104 and 26110, Business and Professions Code.

§ 5712. Test Methods.

(a) The laboratory shall develop, implement, and validate test methods for the analyses of samples as required under this division.

(b) To the extent practicable, the laboratory test methods shall comport with the following guidelines:

(1) US Food and Drug Administration's Bacterial Analytical Manual, 2016;

(2) AOAC International's Official Methods of Analysis for Contaminant Testing of AOAC International, 20th Edition, 2016; and

(3) United States Pharmacopeia and the National Formulary's Methods of Analysis for Contaminant Testing, 2016.

Note: Authority cited: Section 26013, Business and Professions Code. Reference: Sections 26100, 26102, 26104 and 26110, Business and Professions Code.

§ 5713. Validation of Test Methods.

(a) The laboratory may use a nonstandard, amplified, or modified test method or a method that is designed or developed by the laboratory to validate the methods for analyses of samples.

(b) The laboratory shall follow the guidelines set forth in the US Food and Drug Administration's Guidelines for the Validation of Analytical Methods for the Detection of Microbial Pathogens in Foods and Feeds, 2nd Edition, April 2015, incorporated herein by reference, to validate test methods for the microbial analysis of samples. The laboratory shall include and address the criteria listed in the following table when validating test methods for microbial analyses of samples.

Criteria	Requirement
Number of target organisms; inclusivity	5
Number of non-target organisms; exclusivity	5
Number of analyte levels per matrix: Qualitative methods	3 levels: high and low inoculum levels and 1 uninoculated level
Number of analyte levels per matrix: Quantitative methods	4 levels: low, medium and high inoculum levels and 1 uninoculated level
Replicates per food at each level tested	2 or more replicates per level

(c) The laboratory shall follow the guidelines set forth in the US Food and Drug Administration's Guidelines for the Validation of Chemical Methods for the FDA FVM Program, 2nd Edition, April 2015, incorporated herein by reference, to validate test methods for chemical analysis of samples.

(1) The laboratory shall include and address the following criteria to validate test methods for chemical analyses of samples:

(A) Accuracy;

(B) Precision;

(C) Linearity and range;

(i) The Coefficient of Determination (r2) for all calibration curves shall be greater than or equal to 0.99.

(ii) Linear regression or quadratic regression shall only be used for calibration curves. Curves shall not be weighted at all or only weighted at 1/X.

(iii) LOQ for analytes tested shall be within the range of the calibration curve.

(D) Calibration standard;

(i) For calibration curves, there shall be a minimum of five calibration standards, not including zero; and

(ii) Each calibration curve must include an Initial Calibration Verification (ICV). The percent recovery must be between 70% to 130%.

(E) Sensitivity and selectivity;

(F) Limit of detection and limit of quantitation;

(G) Recovery;

(H) Reproducibility; and

(I) Robustness.

(2) The laboratory shall use certified reference materials to validate the following chemical analyses. The test method used for analysis is valid if the percent recovery of the certified reference material is between 80% to 120% for all required analytes.

(A) Cannabinoids, if available;

(B) Heavy metals;

(C) Microbial impurities;

(D) Mycotoxins;

(E) Residual pesticides;

(F) Residual solvents and processing chemicals; and

(G) Terpenoids, if available.

(d) The laboratory shall generate a validation report for each test method. Each validation report shall include the following information:

(1) Instrument calibration data, if any;

(2) Raw data, including instrument raw data, for each test method, if any;

(3) Cannabis reference materials or certified reference material results;

(4) Data and calculations pertaining to LOD and LOQ determinations, if any;

(5) LQC report, as described in this chapter, for the validation of each method; and

(6) Worksheets, forms, pictures, or copies of laboratory notebook pages and any other documentation necessary to meet the requirements described in subsections (b) and (c) of this section.

(7) The supervisory or management laboratory employee shall review, approve, sign, and date the validation report for each test method.

(8) Upon new test methods or altered test methods being used in the laboratory, the new validation report shall be submitted to the Bureau within 5 business days, accompanied by the Notification and Request Form, BCC-LIC-027 (New 10/18), which is incorporated herein by reference.

Note: Authority cited: Section 26013, Business and Professions Code. Reference: Sections 26012, 26100, 26104 and 26110, Business and Professions Code.

ARTICLE 5. LABORATORY TESTING AND REPORTING

§ 5714. Required Testing.

(a) All sample increments collected must be homogenized prior to sample analyses, notwithstanding foreign material testing.

(b) The laboratory shall test each representative sample for the following:

(1) Cannabinoids;

(2) Foreign material;

(3) Heavy metals;

(4) Microbial impurities;

(5) Mycotoxins;

(6) Moisture content and water activity;

(7) Residual pesticides;

(8) Residual solvents and processing chemicals; and

(9) If applicable, terpenoids.

(c) The laboratory shall report the results of each analysis performed by the laboratory on the certificate of analysis.

(d) The laboratory that obtained the representative sample shall complete all required testing for each representative sample for regulatory compliance testing.

Note: Authority cited: Section 26013, Business and Professions Code. Reference: Sections 26100, 26104 and 26110, Business and Professions Code.

§ 5715. Phase-In of Required Laboratory Testing.

(a) Cannabis goods shall not be sold or transferred to a licensed retailer or licensed microbusiness, or released for retail sale, unless a representative sample of the cannabis goods has undergone and passed all testing as required by this section.

(b) All cannabis harvested on or after January 1, 2018, and all cannabis products manufactured on or after January 1, 2018, shall be tested for the following analytes, if applicable:

(1) Cannabinoids as required in section 5724 of this division;

(2) Moisture content as required in section 5717 of this division;

(3) Category II Residual Solvents and Processing Chemicals as required in section 5718 of this division;

(4) Category I Residual Pesticides as required in section 5719 of this division; and

(5) Microbial Impurities as required in section 5720 of this division.

(c) In addition to the requirements of subsection (b) of this section, all cannabis harvested on or after July 1, 2018, and all cannabis products manufactured on or after July 1, 2018, shall be tested for the following analytes, if applicable:

(1) Category I Residual Solvents and Processing Chemicals as required in section 5718 of this division;

(2) Category II Residual Pesticides as required in section 5719 of this division; and

(3) Foreign Material as required in section 5722 of this division.

(d) In addition to the requirements in subsections (b) and (c) of this section, all cannabis harvested on or after December 31, 2018, and all cannabis products manufactured on or after December 31, 2018, shall be tested for the following analytes, if applicable:

(1) Terpenoids as required in section 5725 of this division;

(2) Mycotoxins as required in section 5721 of this division;

(3) Heavy Metals as required in section 5723 of this division; and

(4) Water Activity as required in section 5717 of this division.

(e) Licensees may have a sample of cannabis goods tested for analytes that are not yet required to be tested. However, if the sample fails any additional test(s) not required pursuant to this section on the date of testing, the batch from which the sample was collected fails testing and shall not be released for retail sale.

Note: Authority cited: Section 26013, Business and Professions Code. Reference: Sections 26100, 26104 and 26110, Business and Professions Code.

§ 5716. Homogeneity Testing of Edible Cannabis Products. [Repealed]

§ 5717. Moisture Content and Water Activity Testing.

(a) The laboratory shall analyze at minimum 0.5 grams of the representative sample of dried flower to determine the level of water activity and the percentage of moisture content.

(1) The dried flower sample, including pre-rolls, shall be deemed to have passed water activity testing if the

water activity does not exceed 0.65 Aw. The laboratory shall report the result of the water activity test on the certificate of analysis (COA) and indicate "pass" or "fail" on the COA.

(2)The laboratory shall report the result of the moisture content test on the COA as a percentage.

(b) The laboratory shall analyze at least 0.5 grams of the representative sample of solid edible cannabis products to determine the level of water activity. A solid edible cannabis product shall be deemed to have passed water activity testing if the water activity does not exceed 0.85 Aw. The laboratory shall report the result of the water activity test on the COA and indicate "pass" or "fail" on the COA.

(c) If the sample fails water activity testing, the batch from which the sample was collected fails water activity testing and shall not be released for retail sale.

Note: Authority cited: Section 26013, Business and Professions Code. Reference: Sections 26100, 26104 and 26110, Business and Professions Code.

§ 5718. Residual Solvents and Processing Chemicals Testing.

(a) The laboratory shall analyze at minimum 0.25 grams of the representative sample of cannabis product or pre-rolls to determine whether residual solvents or processing chemicals are present.

(b) The laboratory shall report the result of the residual solvents and processing chemicals testing in unit micrograms per gram (µg/g) on the COA and indicate "pass" or "fail" on the COA.

(c) The sample shall be deemed to have passed the residual solvents and processing chemicals testing if the presence of any residual solvent or processing chemical listed in the following tables in Category I and Category II does not exceed the indicated action levels.

(1) Notwithstanding subsection (c), the limit for ethanol does not apply to cannabis goods that are intended to be orally-consumed products containing alcohol as defined in section 5700 of this division.

(2) Notwithstanding subsection (c), the limit for ethanol or isopropyl alcohol does not apply to cannabis goods that are intended to be topical cannabis goods as defined in section 5700 of this division.

Category I Residual Solvent or Processing Chemical	CAS No.	Cannabis Product or Pre-Roll Action Level (µg/g)
1,2-Dichloroethane	107-06-2	1.0
Benzene	71-43-2	1.0
Chloroform	67-66-3	1.0
Ethylene oxide	75-21-8	1.0
Methylene chloride	75-09-2	1.0
Trichloroethylene	79-01-6	1.0

Category II Residual Solvent or Processing Chemical	CAS No.	Cannabis Product or Pre-roll Action Level (µg/g)
Acetone	67-64-1	5000
Acetonitrile	75-05-8	410
Butane	106-97-8	5000
Ethanol	64-17-5	5000

Ethyl acetate	141-78-6	5000
Ethyl ether	60-29-7	5000
Heptane	142-82-5	5000
Hexane	110-54-3	290
Isopropyl alcohol	67-63-0	5000
Methanol	67-56-1	3000
Pentane	109-66-0	5000
Propane	74-98-6	5000
Toluene	108-88-3	890
Total xylenes (ortho-, meta-, para-)	1330-20-7	2170

(d) If the sample fails residual solvents and processing chemicals testing, the batch from which the sample was collected fails residual solvents and processing chemicals testing and shall not be released for retail sale.

Note: Authority cited: Section 26013, Business and Professions Code. Reference: Sections 26100, 26104 and 26110, Business and Professions Code.

§ 5719. Residual Pesticides Testing.

(a) The laboratory shall analyze at minimum 0.5 grams of the representative sample of cannabis goods to determine whether residual pesticides are present.

(b) The laboratory shall report whether any Category I Residual Pesticides are detected above the limit of detection (LOD) and shall report the result of the Category II Residual Pesticides testing in unit micrograms per gram (µg/g) on the COA. The laboratory shall indicate "pass" or "fail" on the COA.

(c) The laboratory shall establish a limit of quantitation (LOQ) of 0.10 µg/g or lower for all Category I Residual Pesticides.

(d) The sample shall be deemed to have passed the residual pesticides testing if both of the following conditions are met:

(1) The presence of any residual pesticide listed in the following tables in Category I are not detected, and

(2) The presence of any residual pesticide listed in the following tables in Category II does not exceed the indicated action levels.

Category I Residual Pesticide	CAS No.
Aldicarb	116-06-3
Carbofuran	1563-66-2
Chlordane	57-74-9
Chlorfenapyr	122453-73-0
Chlorpyrifos	2921-88-2
Coumaphos	56-72-4
Daminozide	1596-84-5
DDVP (Dichlorvos)	62-73-7
Dimethoate	60-51-5

Ethoprop(hos)	13194-48-4
Etofenprox	80844-07-1
Fenoxycarb	72490-01-8
Fipronil	120068-37-3
Imazalil	35554-44-0
Methiocarb	2032-65-7
Methyl parathion	298-00-0
Mevinphos	7786-34-7
Paclobutrazol	76738-62-0
Propoxur	114-26-1
Spiroxamine	118134-30-8
Thiacloprid	111988-49-9

Category II Residual Pesticide	CAS No.	Action Level (µg/g)	
		Inhalable Cannabis Goods	Other Cannabis Goods
Abamectin	71751-41-2	0.1	0.3
Acephate	30560-19-1	0.1	5
Acequinocyl	57960-19-7	0.1	4
Acetamiprid	135410-20-7	0.1	5
Azoxystrobin	131860-33-8	0.1	40
Bifenazate	149877-41-8	0.1	5
Bifenthrin	82657-04-3	3	0.5
Boscalid	188425-85-6	0.1	10
Captan	133-06-2	0.7	5
Carbaryl	63-25-2	0.5	0.5
Chlorantraniliprole	500008-45-7	10	40
Clofentezine	74115-24-5	0.1	0.5
Cyfluthrin	68359-37-5	2	1
Cypermethrin	52315-07-8	1	1
Diazinon	333-41-5	0.1	0.2
Dimethomorph	110488-70-5	2	20
Etoxazole	153233-91-1	0.1	1.5
Fenhexamid	126833-17-8	0.1	10
Fenpyroximate	111812-58-9	0.1	2
Flonicamid	158062-67-0	0.1	2
Fludioxonil	131341-86-1	0.1	30
Hexythiazox	78587-05-0	0.1	2
Imidacloprid	138261-41-3	5	3
Kresoxim-methyl	143390-89-0	0.1	1

Category II Residual Pesticide	CAS No.	Action Level (µg/g)	
		Inhalable Cannabis Goods	Other Cannabis Goods
Malathion	121-75-5	0.5	5
Metalaxyl	57837-19-1	2	15
Methomyl	16752-77-5	1	0.1
Myclobutanil	88671-89-0	0.1	9
Naled	300-76-5	0.1	0.5
Oxamyl	23135-22-0	0.5	0.2
Pentachloronitrobenzene	82-68-8	0.1	0.2
Permethrin	52645-53-1	0.5	20
Phosmet	732-11-6	0.1	0.2
Piperonylbutoxide	51-03-6	3	8
Prallethrin	23031-36-9	0.1	0.4
Propiconazole	60207-90-1	0.1	20
Pyrethrins	8003-34-7	0.5	1
Pyridaben	96489-71-3	0.1	3
Spinetoram	187166-15-0, 187166-40-1	0.1	3
Spinosad	131929-60-7, 131929-63-0	0.1	3
Spiromesifen	283594-90-1	0.1	12
Spirotetramat	203313-25-1	0.1	13
Tebuconazole	107534-96-3	0.1	2
Thiamethoxam	153719-23-4	5	4.5
Trifloxystrobin	141517-21-7	0.1	30

(e) If the sample fails residual pesticides testing, the batch from which the sample was collected fails residual pesticides testing and shall not be released for retail sale.

Note: Authority cited: Section 26013, Business and Professions Code. Reference: Sections 26100, 26104 and 26110, Business and Professions Code.

§ 5720. Microbial Impurities Testing.

(a) The laboratory shall analyze at minimum 1.0 grams of the representative sample of cannabis goods to determine whether microbial impurities are present.

(b) The laboratory shall report the result of the microbial impurities testing by indicating "pass" or "fail" on the COA.

(c) The sample of inhalable cannabis goods shall be deemed to have passed the microbial impurities testing if all of the following conditions are met:

(1) Shiga toxin-producing Escherichia coli is not detected in 1 gram;

(2) Salmonella spp. is not detected in 1 gram; and

(3) Pathogenic Aspergillus species A. fumigatus, A. flavus, A. niger, and A. terreus are not detected in 1 gram.

(d) The sample of non-inhalable cannabis goods shall be deemed to have passed the microbial impurities testing if both the following conditions are met:

(1) Shiga toxin-producing Escherichia coli is not detected in 1 gram, and

(2) Salmonella spp. is not detected in 1 gram.

(e) If the sample fails microbial impurities testing, the batch from which the sample was collected fails microbial impurities testing and shall not be released for retail sale.

Note: Authority cited: Section 26013, Business and Professions Code. Reference: Sections 26100, 26104 and 26110, Business and Professions Code.

§ 5721. Mycotoxin Testing.

(a) The laboratory shall analyze at minimum 0.5 grams of the representative sample of cannabis goods to determine whether mycotoxins are present.

(b) The laboratory shall report the result of the mycotoxins testing in unit micrograms per kilograms (µg/kg) on the COA and indicate "pass" or "fail" on the COA.

(c) The sample shall be deemed to have passed mycotoxin testing if both the following conditions are met:

(1) Total of aflatoxin B1, B2, G1, and G2 does not exceed 20 µg/kg of substance, and

(2) Ochratoxin A does not exceed 20 µg/kg of substance.

(d) If the sample fails mycotoxin testing, the batch from which the sample was collected fails mycotoxin testing and shall not be released for retail sale.

Note: Authority cited: Section 26013, Business and Professions Code. Reference: Sections 26100, 26104 and 26110, Business and Professions Code.

§ 5722. Foreign Material Testing.

(a) The laboratory shall analyze the representative sample of cannabis goods to determine whether foreign material is present.

(b) The laboratory shall report the result of the foreign material test by indicating "pass" or "fail" on the COA.

(c) The laboratory shall perform foreign material testing on the total representative sample prior to sample homogenization.

(d) When the laboratory performs foreign material testing, at minimum, the laboratory shall do all of the following:

(1) Examine both the exterior and interior of the dried flower sample, and

(2) Examine the exterior of the cannabis product sample.

(e) The sample shall be deemed to have passed the foreign material testing if the presence of foreign material does not exceed:

(1) 1/4 of the total sample area covered by sand, soil, cinders, or dirt;

(2) 1/4 of the total sample area covered by mold;

(3) 1 insect fragment, 1 hair, or 1 count mammalian excreta per 3.0 grams; or

(4) 1/4 of the total sample area covered by an imbedded foreign material.

(f) If the sample fails foreign material testing, the batch from which the sample was collected fails foreign material testing and shall not be released for retail sale.

Note: Authority cited: Section 26013, Business and Professions Code. Reference: Sections 26100, 26104 and 26110, Business and Professions Code.

§ 5723. Heavy Metals Testing.

(a) The laboratory shall analyze at minimum 0.5 grams of the representative sample of cannabis goods to determine whether heavy metals are present.

(b) The laboratory shall report the result of the heavy metals test in unit micrograms per gram (µg/g) on the COA and indicate "pass" or "fail" on the COA.

(c) The sample shall be deemed to have passed the heavy metals testing if the presence of heavy metals does not exceed the action levels listed in the following table.

Heavy Metal	Action Level (µg/g)	
	Inhalable Cannabis Goods	Other Cannabis Goods
Cadmium	0.2	0.5
Lead	0.5	0.5
Arsenic	0.2	1.5
Mercury	0.1	3.0

(d) If the sample fails heavy metals testing, the batch from which the sample was collected fails heavy metals testing and shall not be released for retail sale.

Note: Authority cited: Section 26013, Business and Professions Code. Reference: Sections 26100, 26104 and 26110, Business and Professions Code.

§ 5724. Cannabinoid Testing.

(a) The laboratory shall analyze at minimum 0.5 grams of the representative sample of cannabis goods to determine the cannabinoid profile such as THC; THCA; CBD; CBDA; CBG; and CBN.

(b) The laboratory shall establish a limit of quantitation (LOQ) of 1.0 mg/g or lower for all cannabinoids analyzed and reported.

(c) The laboratory shall report the result of the cannabinoid testing on the COA, including, at minimum:

(1) A percentage for THC, THCA, CBD, and CBDA;

(A) When the laboratory reports the result of the cannabinoid testing for harvest batch representative samples on the COA in dry-weight percent, they shall use the following equation:

Dry-weight percent cannabinoid = wet-weight percent cannabinoid / (1 - percent moisture / 100)

(2) A percentage for Total THC and Total CBD, if applicable;

(3) Milligrams per gram (mg/g) if by dry-weight or milliliters per milliliter (mg/mL) if by volume for THC, THCA, CBD, and CBDA.

(4) Milligrams per gram (mg/g) if by dry-weight or milliliters per milliliter (mg/mL) if by volume for Total THC and Total CBD, if applicable;

(A) The laboratory shall calculate the total cannabinoid concentration as follows:

(i) For concentration expressed in weight:

Total cannabinoid concentration (mg/g) = (cannabinoid acid form concentration (mg/g) X 0.877) + cannabinoid concentration (mg/g)

(ii) For concentration expressed in volume:

Total cannabinoid concentration (mg/mL) = (cannabinoid acid form concentration (mg/mL) X 0.877) + cannabinoid concentration (mg/mL)

(5) Milligrams per package for THC and CBD;

(6) Milligrams per package for Total THC and Total CBD, if applicable;

(7) Milligrams per serving for THC and CBD, if any;

(8) Milligrams per serving for Total THC and Total CBD, if any and if applicable; and

(9) The laboratory shall report the results of all other cannabinoids analyzed on the COA both as a percentage and in either milligrams per gram (mg/g) if by weight or milligrams per milliliter (mg/mL) if by volume.

(d) The sample shall be deemed to have passed the cannabinoid testing if the following conditions are met:

(1) For all edible cannabis products, the milligrams per serving for THC does not exceed 10 milligrams per serving.

(2) For edible cannabis products that are not orally-dissolving products labeled "FOR MEDICAL USE ONLY," the milligrams per package for THC does not exceed 100 milligrams per package.

(3) For edible cannabis products that are orally-dissolving products labeled "FOR MEDICAL USE ONLY," the milligrams per package for THC does not exceed 500 milligrams per package.

(4) For cannabis concentrates and topical cannabis goods not labeled "FOR MEDICAL USE ONLY," the milligrams per package for THC does not exceed 1000 milligrams per package.

(5) For cannabis concentrates and topical cannabis goods labeled "FOR MEDICAL USE ONLY," the milligrams per package for THC does not exceed 2000 milligrams per package.

(e) The laboratory shall report the test results and indicate an overall "pass" or "fail" for the cannabinoid testing on the COA.

(f) Any cannabinoids found to be less than the LOQ shall be reported on the COA as "<1 mg/g" if by dry-weight or "<1 mg/mL" if by volume.

(g) If the sample fails cannabinoid testing, the batch from which the sample was collected fails cannabinoid testing and shall not be released for retail sale.

Note: Authority cited: Section 26013, Business and Professions Code. Reference: Sections 26100, 26104 and 26110,

Business and Professions Code.

§ 5725. Terpenoid Testing.

(a) If requested, the laboratory shall analyze at minimum 0.5 grams of the representative sample of cannabis goods to determine the terpenoid profile of the sample.

(b) The laboratory shall report the result of the terpenoid testing on the COA both as a percentage and in either milligrams per gram (mg/g) if by weight or milligrams per milliliter (mg/mL) if by volume.

Note: Authority cited: Section 26013, Business and Professions Code. Reference: Sections 26100, 26104 and 26110, Business and Professions Code.

§ 5726. Certificate of Analysis (COA).

(a) The laboratory shall generate a COA for each representative sample that the laboratory analyzes.

(b) The laboratory shall ensure that the COA contains the results of all required analyses performed for the representative sample.

(c) The laboratory shall, within 1 business day of completing all analyses of a sample, both upload the COA into the track and trace system and simultaneously provide a copy of the COA to the Bureau via email at bcc.labs@dca.ca.gov.

(d) The laboratory shall not release to any person any cumulative or individual test results prior to completing all analyses and providing the COA to the Bureau.

(e) The COA shall contain, at minimum, the following information:

(1) The term "Regulatory Compliance Testing" in font no smaller than 14-point, which shall appear in the upper-right corner of each page of the COA. No text or images shall appear above the term "Regulatory Compliance Testing" on any page of the COA.

(2) Laboratory's name, licensed premises address, and license number;

(3) Licensed distributor's or licensed microbusiness authorized to engage in distribution's name, licensed premises address, and license number;

(4) Licensed cultivator's, licensed manufacturer's, or licensed microbusiness' name, licensed premises address, and license number;

(5) Batch number of the batch from which the sample was obtained. For cannabis goods that are already packaged at the time of sampling, the labeled batch number on the packaged cannabis goods shall match the batch number on the COA;

(6) Sample identifying information, including matrix type and unique sample identifiers;

(7) Sample history, including the date collected, the date received by the laboratory, and the date(s) of sample analyses and corresponding testing results;

(8) A picture of the sample of cannabis goods. If the sample is pre-packaged, the picture must include an unobstructed image of the packaging;

(9) For dried flower samples, the total weight of the batch, in grams or pounds, and the total weight of the representative sample in grams;

(10) For cannabis product or pre-rolls samples, the total unit count of both the representative sample and the total batch size;

(11) Measured density of the cannabis goods;

(12) The analytical methods, analytical instrumentation used, and corresponding Limits of Detection (LOD) and Limits of Quantitation (LOQ);

(13) An attestation on the COA from the laboratory supervisory or management employee that all LQC samples required by section 5730 of this division were performed and met the acceptance criteria; and

(14) Analytes detected during the analyses of the sample that are unknown, unidentified, or injurious to human health if consumed, if any.

(f) The laboratory shall report test results for each representative sample on the COA as follows:

(1) Indicate an overall "pass" or "fail" for the entire batch;

(2) When reporting qualitative results for each analyte, the laboratory shall indicate "pass" or "fail";

(3) When reporting quantitative results for each analyte, the laboratory shall use the appropriate units of measurement as required under this chapter;

(4) When reporting results for each test method, the laboratory shall indicate "pass" or "fail";

(5) When reporting results for any analytes that were detected below the analytical method LOQ, indicate "<LOQ", notwithstanding cannabinoid results;

(6) When reporting results for any analytes that were not detected or detected below the LOD, indicate "ND"; and

(7) Indicate "NT" for any test that the laboratory did not perform.

(g) The laboratory supervisory or management employee shall validate the accuracy of the information contained on the COA and sign and date the COA.

Note: Authority cited: Section 26013, Business and Professions Code. Reference: Sections 26100, 26104 and 26110, Business and Professions Code.

ARTICLE 6. POST TESTING PROCEDURES

§ 5727. Remediation and Retesting.

(a) A cannabis goods batch that has been additionally processed after failed testing must be retested and successfully pass all the analyses required under this chapter.

(b) The licensed distributor or licensed microbusiness authorized to engage in distribution shall arrange for remediation of a failed cannabis goods batch. If the batch cannot be remediated, the batch shall be destroyed by the licensed distributor or licensed microbusiness authorized to engage in distribution.

(c) If a failed batch is not remediated or reprocessed in any way it cannot be retested. Any subsequent COAs produced without remediation or reprocessing of the failed batch will not supersede the initial regulatory compliance testing COA.

(d) A cannabis goods batch may only be remediated twice. If the batch fails after the second remediation attempt and the second retesting, the entire batch shall be destroyed.

(e) Within one business day of completing the required analyses of a representative sample obtained from a remediated cannabis goods batch, the laboratory shall upload the COA information into the track and trace system, or if the licensee does not yet have access to the track and trace system, it shall be emailed to the Bureau.

(f) Nothing in this section shall be interpreted to prevent a cannabis goods batch from being retested when the COA is 12 or more months old.

Note: Authority cited: Section 26013, Business and Professions Code. Reference: Sections 26100, 26104 and 26110, Business and Professions Code.

§ 5728. Post Testing Sample Retention.

(a) The laboratory shall retain the reserve sample, consisting of any portion of a sample that was not used in the testing process. The reserve sample shall be kept, at minimum, for 45 business days after the analyses, after which time it may be destroyed and denatured to the point the material is rendered unrecognizable and unusable.

(b) The laboratory shall securely store the reserve sample in a manner that prohibits sample degradation, contamination, and tampering.

(c) The laboratory shall provide the reserve sample to the Bureau upon request.

Note: Authority cited: Section 26013, Business and Professions Code. Reference: Sections 26100, 26104 and 26110, Business and Professions Code.

ARTICLE 7. LABORATORY QUALITY ASSURANCE AND QUALITY CONTROL

§ 5729. Laboratory Quality Assurance (LQA) Program.

(a) The laboratory shall develop and implement a LQA program to assure the reliability and validity of the analytical data produced by the laboratory. The LQA program shall, at minimum, include a written LQA manual that addresses the following:

> (1) Quality control procedures;
>
> (2) Laboratory organization and employee training and responsibilities, including good laboratory practice (GLP);
>
> (3) LQA objectives for measurement data;
>
> (4) Traceability of data and analytical results;
>
> (5) Instrument maintenance, calibration procedures, and frequency;
>
> (6) Performance and system audits;
>
> (7) Corrective action procedures;
>
> (8) Steps to change processes when necessary;
>
> (9) Record retention and document control;
>
> (10) Test procedure standardization; and
>
> (11) Method validation.

(b) The supervisory or management laboratory employee shall annually review, amend if necessary, and approve the LQA program and manual both when they are created and when there is a change in methods, laboratory equipment, or the supervisory or management laboratory employee.

Note: Authority cited: Section 26013, Business and Professions Code. Reference: Sections 26100, 26104 and 26110, Business and Professions Code.

§ 5730. Laboratory Quality Control (LQC) Samples.

The laboratory shall use LQC samples and adhere to good laboratory practice (GLP) in the performance of each analysis according to the following specifications.

(a) The laboratory shall analyze LQC samples in the same manner as the laboratory analyzes cannabis goods samples.

(b) The laboratory shall use at least one negative control, one positive control, and one laboratory replicate sample in each analytical batch for each target organism during microbial testing. If one of the controls produces unexpected results, the samples shall be re-prepped and reanalyzed with a new set of controls.

(c) If the result of the microbial analyses is outside the specified acceptance criteria in the following table, the laboratory shall determine the cause and take steps to remedy the problem until the result is within the specified acceptance criteria.

Laboratory Quality Control Sample	Acceptance Criteria	Corrective Action
Positive control	Produces expected result, positive result	Re-prep and reanalyze the entire analytical batch, once. If problem persists, locate and remedy the source of unexpected result, then re-prep samples and reanalyze with a new set of controls.
Negative control	Produces expected result, negative result	Re-prep and reanalyze the entire analytical batch, once. If problem persists, locate and remedy the source of unexpected result, then re-prep samples and reanalyze with a new set of controls.
Laboratory replicate sample	Sample results must concur	Reanalyze sample and associated replicate sample once. If problem persists, re-prep samples and reanalyze.

(d) The laboratory shall prepare and analyze at least one of each of the following LQC samples for each analytical batch:

(1) Method blank;

(2) Laboratory control sample (LCS); and

(3) Laboratory replicate sample or matrix spike sample.

(e) The laboratory shall analyze, at minimum, a continuing calibration verification (CCV) sample at the beginning of each analytical sequence and every 10 samples thereafter.

(f) If the result of the chemical analyses is outside the specified acceptance criteria in the following table, the laboratory shall determine the cause and take steps to remedy the problem until the result is within the specified acceptance criteria.

Laboratory Quality Control Sample	Acceptance Criteria	Corrective Action
Method blank sample	Not to exceed LOQ	Reanalyze entire analytical batch once. If method blank is still greater than the LOQ for any analyte, locate the source of contamination then re-prep samples and reanalyze.
LCS	Percent recovery 70% to 130%	Reanalyze the entire analytical batch, once. If problem persists, re-prep samples and reanalyze or re-run the initial calibration curve.
Laboratory replicate sample	RPD ≤30%	Reanalyze sample and associated replicate sample once. If problem persists, re-prep samples and reanalyze.
Matrix spike sample	Percent recovery between 70% to 130%	Reanalyze sample and associated matrix spike sample once. If problem persists, re-prep samples and reanalyze.
CCV	Percent recovery between 70% to 130%	Reanalyze all samples that followed the last CCV that met the acceptance criteria. If CCV still fails, re-run the initial calibration curve and all samples in the analytical sequence.

(g) If any analyte is detected above any action level, as described in this chapter, the sample shall be re-prepped and reanalyzed in replicate within another analytical batch.

> (1) For quantitative analyses, the re-prepped sample and its associated replicate must meet the acceptance criteria of RPD ≤ 30%.

> (2) For qualitative analyses, the re-prepped sample and its associated replicate results must concur.

(h) If any LQC sample produces a result outside of the acceptance criteria, the laboratory cannot report the result and the entire batch cannot be released for retail sale. The laboratory shall determine the cause and take steps to remedy the problem until the result is within the specified acceptance criteria.

(i) If the laboratory determines that the result is a false-positive or a false-negative, the Bureau may ask for the laboratory to re-sample or re-test.

(j) The laboratory shall compile and generate one LQC sample report for each analytical batch that includes LQC acceptance criteria, measurements, analysis date, and matrix.

Note: Authority cited: Section 26013, Business and Professions Code. Reference: Sections 26100, 26104 and 26110, Business and Professions Code.

§ 5731. Limits of Detection (LOD) and Limits of Quantitation (LOQ) for Quantitative Analyses.

(a) The laboratory shall calculate the LOD for chemical method analyses according to any of the following methods:

> (1) Signal-to-noise ratio of between 3:1 and 2:1;

> (2) Standard deviation of the response and the slope of calibration curve using a minimum of 7 spiked blank samples calculated as follows:

LOD = (3.3 X standard deviation of the response) / slope of the calibration curve; or

(3) A method published by the United States Food and Drug Administration (USFDA) or the United States Environmental Protection Agency (USEPA).

(b) The laboratory shall calculate the LOQ for chemical method analyses according to any of the following methods:

(1) Signal-to-noise ratio of 10:1, at minimum;

(2) Standard deviation of the response and the slope using a minimum of 7 spiked blank samples calculated as follows:

LOQ = (10 X standard deviation of the response) / slope of the calibration curve; or

(3) A method published by the USFDA or the USEPA.

Note: Authority cited: Section 26013, Business and Professions Code. Reference: Sections 26100, 26104 and 26110, Business and Professions Code.

§ 5732. Data Package.

(a) The laboratory shall compile and generate one data package for each representative sample that the laboratory analyzes.

(b) The laboratory shall create a data package and use the Data Package Cover Page and Checklist Form, BCC-LIC-024, which is incorporated herein by reference. The materials data package and form BCC-LIC-024 shall be provided to the Bureau immediately upon request.

Note: Authority cited: Section 26013, Business and Professions Code. Reference: Sections 26100, 26104, 26110 and 26160, Business and Professions Code.

§ 5733. Required Proficiency Testing.

(a) The laboratory shall participate in a proficiency testing program provided by an organization that operates in conformance with the requirements of ISO/IEC 17043, at least once every six months.

(b) The laboratory shall annually, successfully participate in a proficiency testing program for each of the following test methods:

(1) Cannabinoids;

(2) Heavy metals;

(3) Microbial impurities;

(4) Mycotoxins;

(5) Residual pesticides;

(6) Residual solvents and processing chemicals; and

(7) If tested, terpenoids.

(c) The laboratory shall report all analytes available by the proficiency testing program provider and for which the licensee is required to test as required under this chapter.

(d) The laboratory shall participate in the proficiency testing program by following the laboratory's existing SOPs for testing cannabis goods.

(e) The laboratory shall rotate the proficiency testing program among the laboratory employees who perform the test methods.

(f) Laboratory employees who participate in a proficiency testing program shall sign the corresponding analytical reports or attestation statements to certify that the proficiency testing program was conducted in the same manner as the laboratory tests of cannabis goods.

(g) A supervisory or management laboratory employee shall review and verify the accuracy of results reported for all proficiency testing program samples analyzed.

(h) The laboratory shall request the proficiency testing program provider to send results concurrently to the Bureau, if available, or the laboratory shall provide the proficiency testing program results to the Bureau within 3 business days after the laboratory receives notification of their test results from the proficiency testing program provider. Any results shall be reported by submitting the Notification and Request Form, BCC-LIC-027 (New 10/18), which is incorporated herein by reference.

Note: Authority cited: Section 26013, Business and Professions Code. Reference: Sections 26100 and 26110, Business and Professions Code.

§ 5734. Satisfactory and Unsatisfactory Proficiency Test Performance.

(a) The laboratory shall be deemed to have successfully participated in a proficiency testing program for an analyte tested in a specific method if the test results demonstrate a "satisfactory" or otherwise proficient performance determination by the proficiency testing program provider.

(b) The laboratory may not report test results for analytes that are deemed by the proficiency testing program provider as "unacceptable," "questionable," "unsatisfactory", or otherwise deficient.

(c) The laboratory may resume reporting test results for analytes that were deemed "unacceptable," "questionable," "unsatisfactory", or otherwise deficient, only if both of the following conditions are met:

(1) The laboratory satisfactorily remedies the cause of the failure for each analyte; and

(2) The laboratory submits, to the Bureau, a written corrective action report demonstrating how the laboratory has fixed the cause of the failure.

Note: Authority cited: Section 26013, Business and Professions Code. Reference: Sections 26100 and 26110, Business and Professions Code.

§ 5735. Laboratory Audits.

(a) The laboratory shall conduct an internal audit at least once per year or in accordance with the ISO/IEC 17025 accrediting body's requirement, whichever is more frequent.

(b) The internal audit must include all of the components required by the ISO/IEC 17025 internal-audit standards.

(c) Within 3 business days of completing the internal audit, the laboratory shall submit the results of the internal audit to the Bureau.

(d) Within 3 business days of receiving the accrediting body on-site audit findings, the laboratory shall submit the results to the Bureau.

(e) The laboratory shall submit any audit results to the Bureau, accompanied by the Notification and Request Form, BCC-LIC-027 (New 10/18), which is incorporated herein by reference.

Note: Authority cited: Section 26013, Business and Professions Code. Reference: Sections 26100 and 26104, Business and Professions Code.

ARTICLE 8. LABORATORY EMPLOYEE QUALIFICATIONS

§ 5736. General Laboratory Employee Qualifications.

(a) The laboratory may only employ persons who are at least 21 years of age.

(b) The laboratory shall develop and implement an employee training program to ensure competency of laboratory employees for their assigned functions.

(c) The laboratory shall ensure and document that each laboratory employee meets the employee qualifications.

Note: Authority cited: Section 26013, Business and Professions Code. Reference: Sections 26102 and 26104, Business and Professions Code.

§ 5737. Supervisor or Management Responsibilities and Qualifications.

(a) The laboratory shall employ a supervisor or management employee who must be responsible for:

(1) Overseeing and directing the scientific methods of the laboratory;

(2) Ensuring that the laboratory achieves and maintains a laboratory quality assurance program as required by section 5729 of this division; and

(3) Providing ongoing and appropriate training to laboratory employees.

(b) To be considered qualified, the supervisor or management employee must have at minimum:

(1) A doctoral degree in biological, chemical, agricultural, environmental, or related sciences from an accredited college or university;

(2) A master's degree in biological, chemical, agricultural, environmental, or related sciences from an accredited college or university, plus at least 2 years of full-time practical experience;

(3) A bachelor's degree in biological, chemical, agricultural, environmental, or related sciences from an accredited college or university, plus at least 4 years of full-time practical experience; or

(4) A bachelor's degree in any field from an accredited college or university, plus at least 8 years of full-time practical experience, 4 years of which must have been in a supervisory or management position.

Note: Authority cited: Section 26013, Business and Professions Code. Reference: Sections 26102 and 26104, Business and Professions Code.

§ 5738. Analyst and Sampler Qualifications.

(a) The laboratory shall employ an analyst who, at minimum, must have either:

(1) Earned a master's degree or a bachelor's degree in biological, chemical, agricultural, environmental, or related sciences from an accredited college or university; or

(2) Completed 2 years of college or university education that included coursework in biological, chemical, agricultural, environmental, or related sciences from an accredited college or university, plus at least 3 years of full-time practical experience.

(b) The laboratory shall employ a sampler who, at minimum, must have either:

(1) Completed 2 years college or university education; or

(2) Earned a High School Diploma or passed a General Educational Development or High School Equivalency exam, plus at least 1 year of full-time practical experience.

Note: Authority cited: Section 26013, Business and Professions Code. Reference: Sections 26102 and 26104, Business and Professions Code.

ARTICLE 9. RECORD RETENTION

§ 5739. Records.

All laboratory records described in this chapter shall be maintained in accordance with section 5037 of this division.

Note: Authority cited: Section 26013, Business and Professions Code. Reference: Section 26160, Business and Professions Code.

Chapter 7. Enforcement

§ 5800. Right of Access.

(a) The Bureau, and its authorized representatives, shall have full and immediate access to inspect and:

(1) Enter onto any premises licensed by the Bureau.

(2) Test any vehicle or equipment possessed by, in control of, or used by a licensee or their agents and employees for the purpose of conducting commercial cannabis activity.

(3) Test any cannabis goods or cannabis-related materials or products possessed by, in control of, or used by a licensee or their agents and employees for the purpose of conducting commercial cannabis activity.

(4) Copy any materials, books, or records of any licensee or their agents and employees.

(b) Failure to cooperate with and participate in any Bureau investigation pending against the licensee may result in a licensing violation subject to discipline. This subsection shall not be construed to deprive a licensee of any privilege guaranteed by the Fifth Amendment to the Constitution of the United States, or any other constitutional or statutory privileges. This subsection shall not be construed to require a licensee to cooperate with a request that would require the licensee to waive any constitutional or statutory privilege or to comply with a request for information or other matters within an unreasonable period of time in light of the time constraints of the licensee's business. Any constitutional or statutory privilege exercised by the licensee shall not be used against the licensee in a regulatory or disciplinary proceeding against the licensee.

(c) The Bureau, and its authorized representatives, shall have the rights of full and immediate access under subsection (a) of this section, during any inspection, investigation, review, or audit, or as otherwise allowed by law.

(d) Prior notice of an inspection, investigation, review, or audit is not required.

(e) Any inspection, investigation, review, or audit of a licensed premises shall be conducted anytime the licensee is exercising privileges under the license, or as otherwise agreed to by the Bureau and the licensee or its agents, employees, or representatives.

(f) If the licensed premises is not accessible because access is only available by going through another licensed premises and the licensee occupying the other licensed premises denies the Bureau access, the licensees shall both be held responsible and subject to discipline.

Note: Authority cited: Section 26013, Business and Professions Code. Reference: Sections 26012, 26015 and 26160, Business and Professions Code; and Section 11181, Government Code.

§ 5801. Notice to Comply.

(a) The Bureau may issue a notice to comply to a licensee for violation(s) of the Act or regulations discovered during an investigation or observed during an inspection.

(b) The notice to comply shall be in writing and describe the nature and facts of each violation, including a reference to the statute or regulation violated, and may indicate the manner in which the licensee must correct the violation(s) to achieve compliance.

(c) The Bureau will serve the notice to comply prior to leaving the licensed premises after the inspection on any licensee, employee, agent, or person delegated by any of those listed, to facilitate the inspection or accept such notice, or will mail the notice to comply within 15 calendar days of the discovery of violation or the last date of inspection.

(d) The notice to comply shall inform the licensee that the licensee may, within 20 calendar days from the date of personal service or mailing of the notice to comply, sign and return the notice to comply declaring under penalty of perjury that each violation was corrected and describing how compliance was achieved.

(e) Failure to correct the violation(s) in the notice to comply may result in a disciplinary action.

Note: Authority cited: Section 26013, Business and Professions Code; Reference: Sections 26012 and 26018, Business and Professions Code.

§ 5802. Citations; Orders of Abatement; Administrative Fines.

(a) The Bureau may issue citations containing orders of abatement and fines against a licensee, or an unlicensed person, for any acts or omissions which are in violation of any provision of the Act or any regulation adopted pursuant thereto, or for any violation of state law or regulations applicable to cannabis licensees, including, but not limited to, state labor law.

(b) The Bureau may issue a citation under this section to a licensee for a violation of a term or condition contained in a decision placing that licensee on probation.

(c) Each citation may contain either order(s) of abatement, monetary fine(s), or both, and shall:

(1) Be in writing and describe with particularity the nature of the violation, including a reference to the law or regulation determined to have been violated;

(2) Fix a reasonable time for abatement of the violation if the citation contains an order of abatement, or assess an administrative fine of up to $5,000 if the citation contains a fine;

(3) Be served personally or by certified mail; and

(4) Inform the licensee or person that they may request an informal conference, or contest the citation, or both, pursuant to section 5803 of this division.

(d) Failure to pay a fine within 30 calendar days of the date of assessment, unless the citation is being contested, may result in further action being taken by the Bureau including, but not limited to, suspension or revocation of a license. If a citation is not appealed and the fine is not paid, the full amount of the assessed fine shall be added to the fee for renewal of the license. A license shall not be renewed without the payment of the renewal fee and fine.

(e) The amount of any fine assessed by the Bureau under this section shall take into consideration the factors listed in Business and Professions Code section 125.9(b)(3).

(f) Nothing in this section shall be deemed to prevent the Bureau from filing an accusation to suspend or revoke a license where grounds for such suspension or revocation exist.

Note: Authority cited: Sections 125.9 and 26013, Business and Professions Code. Reference: Sections 125.9, 148, 149 and 26012, Business and Professions Code.

§ 5803. Contesting Citations.

(a) A cited licensee or person may, within 30 calendar days of service of the citation, contest the citation by submitting to the Bureau a written request for a hearing, conducted in accordance with Chapter 5 (commencing with Section 11500) of Part 1 of Division 3 of the Government Code. If a hearing is not requested, it is waived and payment of a fine will not constitute an admission of the violation charged.

(b) In addition to requesting a hearing provided for in subsection (a) of this section, the cited licensee or person may, within 15 calendar days after service of the citation, submit a written request for an informal conference with the Bureau regarding the acts or omissions charged in the citation.

(c) The Bureau shall, within 15 calendar days from receipt of the written request, hold an informal conference with the licensee or person cited, and/or his or her legal counsel or authorized representative.

(d) At the conclusion of the informal conference, the Bureau may affirm, modify, or dismiss the citation, including any fines levied or orders of abatement issued. A written decision stating the reasons for the decision shall be mailed to the cited licensee or person and his or her legal counsel, if any, within 15 calendar days from the date of the informal conference. This decision shall be deemed to be a final order with regard to the citation issued, including the levied fine and the order of abatement, if any.

(e) If the citation is dismissed, any request for a hearing shall be deemed withdrawn. If the citation is affirmed or modified, the cited licensee or person may, in his or her discretion, withdraw the request for a hearing or proceed with the administrative hearing process.

(f) If the citation, including any fine levied or order of abatement, is modified, the citation originally issued shall be considered withdrawn and new citation issued. If a hearing is requested for the subsequent citation, it shall be requested within 30 calendar days in accordance with Business and Professions Code section 125.9(b)(4).

Note: Authority cited: Section 26013, Business and Professions Code. Reference: Sections 125.9, 26012 and 26016, Business and Professions Code.

§ 5804. Citation Compliance.

(a) The time to abate or correct a violation as provided for in an order of abatement may be extended for good cause. If a cited licensee or person who has been issued an order of abatement is unable to complete the correction within the time set forth in the citation because of conditions beyond his or her control after the exercise of reasonable diligence, the licensee or person cited may request an extension of time from the Bureau in which to complete the correction. Such a request shall be in writing and shall be made within the time set forth for abatement.

(b) When a citation is not contested, or if it is appealed and the person cited does not prevail, failure to abate the violation within the time allowed or pay a fine that was imposed shall constitute a violation and a failure to comply with the citation or order of abatement.

(c) Failure to timely comply with an order of abatement or pay a fine that was imposed may result in further action being taken by the Bureau, including, but not limited to, suspension or revocation of a license, or further administrative or civil proceedings.

Note: Authority cited: Section 26013, Business and Professions Code. Reference: Sections 125.9 and 26012, Business and Professions Code.

§ 5805. Minor Decoys.

(a) Peace officers may use a person under 21 years of age to attempt to purchase cannabis goods, for the purposes of enforcing the Act, and to apprehend licensees, employees, or agents of licensees who sell cannabis goods to minors. For purposes of this section, a "minor" is a person under 21 years of age.

(b) The following minimum standards shall apply to the use of a minor decoy:

(1) At the time of the operation, the decoy shall be less than 20 years of age.

(2) A decoy shall either carry his or her own identification showing the decoy's correct date of birth, or carry no identification. A decoy who carries identification shall present it upon request to any seller of cannabis goods.

(3) A decoy shall answer truthfully any questions about his or her age.

(4) Following any completed sale, but not later than the time a citation, if any, is issued, the peace officer directing the decoy shall make a reasonable attempt to enter the licensed premises or respond to the location where the licensee is located and have the minor decoy who purchased cannabis goods identify the alleged seller of the cannabis goods.

Note: Authority cited: Sections 26013 and 26140, Business and Professions Code. Reference: Section 26140, Business and Professions Code.

§ 5806. Attire and Conduct.

No license shall allow the following:

(a) Employment or use of any person in the sale or service of cannabis goods in or upon the licensed premises while such person is unclothed or in such attire, costume, or clothing as to expose to view any portion of the male or female breast below the top of the areola or of any portion of the pubic hair, anus, cleft of the buttocks, vulva, or genitals.

(b) Employment or use of the services of any host or other person to mingle with the patrons while such hostess or other person is unclothed or in such attire, costume, or clothing as described in subsection (a) of this section.

(c) Encouraging or permitting any person on the licensed premises to touch, caress, or fondle the breasts, buttocks, anus, or genitals of any other person.

(d) Permitting any employee or person to wear or use any device or covering, exposed to view, which simulates the breast, genitals, anus, pubic hair, or any portion thereof.

Note: Authority cited: Section 26013, Business and Professions Code. Reference: 26011.5, Business and Professions Code.

§ 5807. Entertainers and Conduct.

(a) Live entertainment is permitted on a licensed premises, except that no licensee shall permit any person to perform acts of or acts that simulate:

> (1) Sexual intercourse, masturbation, sodomy, bestiality, oral copulation, flagellation, or any sexual acts that are prohibited by law.

> (2) Touching, caressing, or fondling of the breast, buttocks, anus, or genitals.

> (3) Displaying of the buttocks, breasts, pubic hair, anus, vulva, or genitals.

(b) No licensee shall permit any person to use artificial devices or inanimate objects to depict any of the prohibited activities described in this section.

(c) No licensee shall permit any person to remain in or upon the licensed premises who exposes to public view any portion of his or her breast, buttocks, genitals, or anus.

Note: Authority cited: Section 26013, Business and Professions Code. Reference: 26011.5, Business and Professions Code.

§ 5808. Additional Grounds for Discipline.

The following include, but are not limited to, additional grounds that constitute a basis for disciplinary action:

(a) Failure to pay a fine imposed by the Bureau or agreed to by the licensee.

(b) Failure to take reasonable steps to correct objectionable conditions on the licensed premises, including the immediately adjacent area that is owned, leased, or rented by the licensee, that constitute a nuisance, within a reasonable time after receipt of notice to make those corrections, under Penal Code section 373a.

(c) Failure to take reasonable steps to correct objectionable conditions that occur during operating hours on any public sidewalk abutting a licensed premises and constitute a nuisance, within a reasonable time after receipt of notice to correct those conditions from the Bureau. This subsection shall apply to a licensee only upon written notice to the licensee from the Bureau. The Bureau shall issue this written notice upon its own determination, or upon a request from the local law enforcement agency in whose jurisdiction the licensed premises is located, that is supported by substantial evidence that persistent objectionable conditions are occurring on the public sidewalk abutting the licensed premises. For purposes of this subsection:

> (1) "Any public sidewalk abutting a licensed premises" means the publicly owned, pedestrian-traveled way, not more than 20 feet from the licensed premises, that is located between a licensed premises, including any immediately adjacent area that is owned, leased, or rented by the licensee, and a public street

> (2) "Objectionable conditions that constitute a nuisance" means disturbance of the peace, public intoxication, drinking alcoholic beverages in public, smoking or ingesting cannabis or cannabis products in public, harassment of passersby, gambling, prostitution, loitering, public urination, lewd conduct, drug trafficking, or excessive loud noise.

(3) "Reasonable steps" means all of the following:

(A) Calling the local law enforcement agency. Timely calls to the local law enforcement agency that are placed by the licensee, or his or her agents or employees, shall not be construed by the Bureau as evidence of objectionable conditions that constitute a nuisance.

(B) Requesting those persons engaging in activities causing objectionable conditions to cease those activities, unless the licensee, or his or her agents or employees, feel that their personal safety would be threatened in making that request.

(C) Making good faith efforts to remove items that facilitate loitering, such as furniture, except those structures approved or permitted by the local jurisdiction. The licensee shall not be liable for the removal of those items that facilitate loitering.

(4) When determining what constitutes "reasonable steps," the Bureau shall consider site configuration constraints related to the unique circumstances of the nature of the business.

(d) Notwithstanding that the licensee corrects the objectionable conditions that constitute a nuisance, the licensee has a continuing obligation to meet the requirements of subsections (a) and (b) of this section, and failure to do so shall constitute grounds for disciplinary action.

(e) If a licensee has knowingly permitted the illegal sale, or negotiations for the sales, of controlled substances or dangerous drugs upon his or her licensed premises. Successive sales, or negotiations for sales, over any continuous period of time shall be deemed evidence of permission. As used in this section, "controlled substances" shall have the same meaning as is given that term in Article 1 (commencing with Section 11000) of Chapter 1 of Division 10 of the Health and Safety Code, and "dangerous drugs" shall have the same meaning as is given that term in Article 2 (commencing with Section 4015) of Chapter 9 of Division 2 of the Business and Professions Code.

(f) If the licensee has employed or permitted any persons to solicit or encourage others, directly or indirectly, to buy such persons cannabis goods in the licensed premises under any commission, percentage, salary, or other profit-sharing plan, scheme, or conspiracy.

Note: Authority cited: Section 26013, Business and Professions Code. Reference: Sections 26011.5, 26012, 26030 and 26031, Business and Professions Code.

§ 5809. Disciplinary Actions.

(a) When an accusation recommending disciplinary action against a licensee has been filed pursuant to Business and Professions Code section 26031, the accusation shall be served on the licensee in accordance with Government Code section 11505.

(b) A hearing shall be conducted in accordance with the provisions of Chapter 5 (commencing with Section 11500) of Part 1 of Division 3 of Title 2 of the Government Code to determine if cause exists to take action against the licensee. At such a hearing, the Bureau shall have all the powers granted therein and by the Business and Professions Code.

(c) If a hearing on an accusation against a licensee results in a finding that the licensee has committed any of the acts or omissions constituting grounds for disciplinary action, the Bureau may order the license revoked, suspended outright for a specified period of time, suspended on probationary restriction for a specified period of time on such terms and conditions of probation as in its judgment are supported by its findings, impose a fine, or any combination thereof. The Bureau may also issue such other lawful orders it considers to be appropriate on the basis of its findings.

(d) An accusation may be terminated by written stipulation at any time prior to the conclusion of the hearing on the accusation. If a licensee submits a proposed stipulation to the Bureau for its consideration and the Bureau subsequently declines to accept the proposed stipulation, the Bureau shall not thereafter be disqualified from hearing evidence on the accusation and taking action thereon as authorized in this section.

Note: Authority cited: Section 26013, Business and Professions Code. Reference: Sections 26012, 26031 and 26034, Business and Professions Code.

§ 5810. Interim Suspension.

(a) Pursuant to Business and Professions Code section 494, the Bureau may petition for an interim order to suspend any license or impose licensing restrictions upon any licensee, if:

(1) The licensee has engaged in acts or omissions constituting a violation of the Business and Professions Code or this division, or been convicted of a crime substantially related to the licensed activity, and

(2) Permitting the licensee to continue to engage in the licensed activity would endanger the public health, safety, or welfare.

(b) An interim order for suspension or restrictions may be issued with notice, as follows:

(1) The Bureau shall provide the licensee with at least 15 days' notice of the hearing on the petition for an interim order.

(2) The notice shall include documents submitted in support of the petition.

(c) An interim order for suspension or restrictions may issue without notice to the licensee, as follows:

(1) If it appears from the Bureau's petition and supporting documents that serious injury would result to the public before the matter could be heard on notice.

(2) The Bureau shall provide the licensee with a hearing on the petition within 20 days after issuance of the initial interim order.

(3) Notice of the hearing shall be provided within two days after issuance of the initial interim order.

(d) The Bureau shall file an accusation, pursuant to Chapter 5 (commencing with Section 11500) of Part 1 of Division 3 of Title 2 of the Government Code, within 15 calendar days of the issuance of the interim order.

Note: Authority cited: Section 26013, Business and Professions Code; Reference: Sections 494, 26011.5, 26012 and 26031, Business and Professions Code.

§ 5811. Posting of Notice of Suspension.

(a) A licensee whose license has been suspended shall conspicuously and continuously display a notice on the exterior of the licensee's premises for the duration of the suspension.

(b) The notice shall be two feet in length and 14 inches in width. The notice shall read:

NOTICE OF SUSPENSION

The Bureau of Cannabis Control License(s) Issued For This Premises Has Been Suspended For Violation of State Law

(c) Advertising or posting signs to the effect that the licensed premises has been closed or that business has been suspended for any reason other than the reason provided in the decision suspending the license, shall be deemed a violation of this section.

(d) Failure to display the notice as required in this section or removal of the notice prior to the expiration of the suspension shall be a violation of this section and may result in additional disciplinary action.

(e) A licensee shall notify the Bureau, by submitting the Notification and Request Form, BCC-LIC-027 (New 10/18), incorporated herein by reference, within 24 hours of discovering that the notice under subsection (b) of this section has been removed or damaged to an extent that makes the notice illegible.

Note: Authority cited: Section 26013, Business and Professions Code. Reference: Sections 26011.5 and 26012, Business and Professions Code.

§ 5812. Posting of Notice of Revocation.

(a) A person whose license has been revoked shall conspicuously display a notice on the exterior of the premises indicating that the license has been revoked. The notice shall remain continuously on the premises for at least 15 calendar days.

(b) The notice shall be two feet in length and 14 inches in width. The notice shall read:

NOTICE OF REVOCATION

The Bureau of Cannabis Control License(s) Issued For This Premises Has Been Revoked For Violation of State Law

(c) Advertising or posting signs to the effect that the premises has been closed or that business has been suspended for any reason other than the reason provided in the decision revoking the license shall be deemed a violation of this section.

(d) If the Bureau revokes a license at a licensed premises that has one or more licenses at the location that will remain active after the revocation, the revocation notice shall remain posted for a period of at least 15 calendar days.

(e) Failure to display the notice for the time required in this section shall be a violation of this section and may result in additional disciplinary action.

(f) A licensee shall notify the Bureau, by submitting the Notification and Request Form, BCC-LIC-027 (New 10/18), incorporated herein by reference, within 24 hours of discovering that the notice under subsection (b) of this section has been removed or damaged to an extent that makes the notice illegible.

Note: Authority cited: Section 26013, Business and Professions Code. Reference: Sections 26011.5 and 26012, Business and Professions Code.

§ 5813. Enforcement Costs.

(a) In any order in resolution of a disciplinary proceeding for suspension or revocation of a license, the Bureau may request the administrative law judge to direct a licensee found to have committed a violation or violations of the Act, or any regulation adopted pursuant to the Act, to pay a sum not to exceed the reasonable costs of the investigation and enforcement of the case.

(b) A certified copy of the actual costs, or a good faith estimate of costs where actual costs are not available, signed by the Bureau's designated representative shall be prima facie evidence of reasonable costs of investigation and prosecution of the case. The costs shall include the amount of investigative and enforcement costs up to the date of the hearing, including, but not limited to, charges imposed by the Attorney General.

(c) The administrative law judge shall make a proposed finding of the amount of reasonable costs of investigation and prosecution of the case when requested pursuant to subsection (a). The Bureau may reduce or eliminate the cost award, or remand to the administrative law judge where the proposed decision fails to make a finding on costs requested pursuant to subsection (a).

(d) Where an order for recovery of costs is made and timely payment is not made as directed in the decision, the Bureau may enforce the order for repayment in any appropriate court. This right of enforcement shall be in addition to any other rights the Bureau may have as to any licensee to pay costs.

(e) In any action for recovery of costs, proof of the decision shall be conclusive proof of the validity of the order of payment and the terms for payment.

(f) Except as provided in subsection (g) of this section, the Bureau shall not renew or reinstate any license of any licensee who has failed to pay all of the costs ordered under this division.

(g) Notwithstanding subsection (f) of this section, the Bureau may, in its discretion, conditionally renew or reinstate for a maximum of one year the license of any licensee who demonstrates financial hardship and who enters into a formal agreement with the Bureau for reimbursement within that one-year period for the unpaid costs.

(h) Nothing in this section shall preclude the Bureau from including the recovery of the costs of investigation and enforcement of a case in any stipulated settlement.

Note: Authority cited: Section 26013, Business and Professions Code; Reference: Sections 125.3, 26012 and 26031, Business and Professions Code

§ 5814. Disciplinary Guidelines.

In reaching a decision on a disciplinary action under the Act and the Administrative Procedure Act (Govt. Code section 11400 et seq.), the Bureau shall consider the disciplinary guidelines entitled "Bureau of Cannabis Control Disciplinary Guidelines October 2018," which are hereby incorporated by reference. Deviation from these guidelines and orders, including the standard terms of probation, is appropriate where the Bureau in its sole discretion determines that the facts of the particular case warrant such a deviation, e.g., the presence of mitigating factors, the age of the case, or evidentiary problems.

Note: Authority cited: Section 26013, Business and Professions Code; Reference: Sections 26012 and 26031, Business and Professions Code.

§ 5815. Emergency Decision and Order.

(a) The Bureau may issue an emergency decision and order for temporary, interim relief to prevent or avoid immediate danger to the public health, safety, or welfare. Such circumstances include, but are not limited to, the following:

(1) The Bureau has information that cannabis goods at a licensee's premises have a reasonable probability of causing serious adverse health consequences or death.

(2) To prevent the sale, transfer, or transport of contaminated or illegal cannabis goods in possession of the licensee.

(3) The Bureau observes or has information that conditions at the licensee's premises exist that present an immediate risk to worker or public health and safety.

(4) To prevent illegal diversion of cannabis goods, or other criminal activity at the licensee's premises.

(5) To prevent the destruction of evidence related to illegal activity or violations of the Act.

(6) To prevent misrepresentation to the public, such as selling untested cannabis goods, providing inaccurate information about the cannabis goods, or cannabis goods that have been obtained from an unlicensed person.

(b) Temporary, interim relief may include a suspension or administrative hold by one or more of the following:

(1) The temporary suspension of a license.

(2) An order to segregate or isolate specific cannabis goods.

(3) An order prohibiting the movement of cannabis goods to or from the premises.

(4) An order prohibiting the sale of specific cannabis goods.

(5) An order prohibiting the destruction of specific cannabis goods.

(c) The emergency decision and order issued by the Bureau shall include a brief explanation of the factual and legal basis of the emergency decision that justify the Bureau's determination that emergency action is necessary, and the specific actions ordered. The emergency decision and order shall be effective when issued or as otherwise provided by the decision and order.

(d) To issue an administrative hold that prohibits activity related to specified cannabis goods, the Bureau shall comply with the following:

(1) The notice of the administrative hold shall include a description of the cannabis goods subject to the administrative hold.

(2) Following notice, the Bureau shall identify the cannabis goods subject to the administrative hold in the track and trace system.

(e) A licensee subject to an administrative hold shall comply with the following:

(1) Within 24 hours of receipt of the notice of administrative hold, physically segregate all designated cannabis goods in a limited-access area of the licensed premises. The licensee shall ensure that all cannabis goods subject to the administrative hold are safeguarded and preserved in a manner that prevents tampering, degradation, or contamination.

(2) While the administrative hold is in effect, the licensee shall not sell, donate, transfer, transport, gift, or destroy the cannabis goods subject to the hold.

(3) A microbusiness licensee subject to an administrative hold may continue to cultivate any cannabis subject to an administrative hold. If the cannabis subject to the hold must be harvested, the licensee shall place the harvested cannabis into separate batches.

(4) A licensee may voluntarily surrender cannabis goods that are subject to an administrative hold. The licensee shall identify the cannabis goods being voluntarily surrendered in the track and trace system. Voluntary surrender shall not be construed to waive the right to a hearing or any associated rights.

(f) To issue a temporary suspension, the Bureau shall specify in the order that the licensee shall immediately cease conducting all commercial cannabis activities under its license, unless otherwise specified in the order.

(g) A microbusiness licensee subject to a temporary suspension may continue to cultivate cannabis at the licensed premises only as prescribed by the Bureau in the order. If the order permits the cannabis to be harvested, the licensee shall place the harvested cannabis into separate batches.

(h) The emergency decision and order for temporary, interim relief shall be issued in accordance with the following procedures:

(1) The Bureau shall give notice of the emergency decision and order and an opportunity to be heard to the licensee prior to the issuance, or effective date, of the emergency decision and order, if practicable.

(2) Notice and hearing under this section may be oral or written and may be provided by telephone, personal service, mail, facsimile transmission, electronic mail, or other electronic means, as the circumstances permit.

(3) Notice may be given to the licensee, any person meeting the definition of owner for the license, or to the manager or other personnel at the licensed premises.

(4) Upon receipt of the notice, the licensee may request a hearing within three (3) business days by submitting a written request for hearing to the Bureau through electronic mail, facsimile transmission, or other written means. The hearing shall commence within five (5) business days of receipt of the written request for hearing, unless a later time is agreed upon by the Bureau and the licensee.

(5) The hearing may be conducted in the same manner as an informal conference under section 5803 of this division; however, the timeframes provided in section 5803 shall not apply to a hearing under this section. Pre-hearing discovery or cross-examination of witnesses is not required under this section.

(6) The emergency decision and order shall be affirmed, modified, or set aside as determined appropriate by the Bureau within five (5) business days of the hearing.

(i) Within ten (10) calendar days of the issuance or effective date of the emergency decision and order for temporary, interim relief, the Bureau shall commence adjudicative proceedings in accordance with Chapter 5 (commencing with Section 11500) of Part 1 of Division 3 of Title 2 of the Government Code to resolve the underlying issues giving rise to the temporary, interim relief, notwithstanding the pendency of proceedings for judicial review of the emergency decision as provided in subsection (k).

(j) After formal proceedings pursuant to subsection (i) of this section are held, a licensee aggrieved by a final decision of the Bureau may appeal the decision to the Cannabis Control Appeals Panel pursuant to Section 26043 of the Act.

(k) Notwithstanding administrative proceedings commenced pursuant to subsection (i), the licensee may obtain judicial review of the emergency decision and order pursuant to section 1094.5 of the Code of Civil Procedure in the manner provided in Section 11460.80 of the Government Code without exhaustion of administrative remedies.

(l) The Bureau's authority provided by this section may be used in addition to any civil, criminal, or other administrative remedies available to the Bureau.

Note: Authority cited: Section 26013, Business and Professions Code. Reference: Section 26012, Business and Professions Code; and Sections 11460.10, 11460.20, 11460.30, 11460.40, 11460.50, 11460.60, 11460.70 and 11460.80, Government Code.

Chapter 8. Other Provisions

ARTICLE 1. RESEARCH FUNDING

§ 5900. Eligibility.

(a) Only public universities in California shall be eligible to be selected to receive funds disbursed pursuant to Revenue and Taxation Code section 34019(b).

(b) Subject to available funding, the amounts to be disbursed to the university or universities will not exceed the sum of ten million dollars ($10,000,000) for each fiscal year, ending with the 2028-2029 fiscal year.

Note: Authority cited: Section 26013, Business and Professions Code. Reference: Section 34019, Revenue and Taxation Code.

§ 5901. Request for Proposals.

A Request for Proposal (RFP) is the document issued by the Bureau, which notifies all eligible fund recipients of the following, at a minimum:

(a) The funding available for research related to the Act or regulations adopted pursuant thereto;

(b) Disbursement of funds to eligible applicants through a review and selection process, including the criteria that will be used for review and selection;

(c) The specified timeframes for the proposal review and selection process, including the deadline for submission of proposals;

(d) Proposal requirements, including necessary documentation;

(e) Any priorities or restrictions imposed upon the use of the funds;

(f) The governing statutes and regulations; and

(g) The name, address, and telephone number of a contact person within the Bureau, who can provide further information regarding the process for submission of proposals.

Note: Authority cited: Section 26013, Business and Professions Code. Reference: Section 34019, Revenue and Taxation Code.

§ 5902. Selection Process and Criteria.

(a) The selection process shall involve eligible proposals timely received by the Bureau, in response to an applicable RFP, or similar notice.

(b) The Bureau will consider only one proposal per applicant for a given research project. Applicants may submit more than one proposal if the proposals are for separate and distinct research projects or activities.

(c) The Bureau will make a selection for funding, based on criteria including, but not limited to:

(1) The extent to which the proposed project is designed to achieve objectives as specified in Revenue and Taxation Code section 34019(b).

(2) The extent to which the proposed project is designed to achieve measurable outcomes, and the clarity of the measures for success, including, for research-based objectives, the scientific and technical merit of the proposed project as evaluated by relevant experts.

(3) The extent to which the proposed project is feasible, demonstrated by:

(A) A timeline for project completion, including readiness; and

(B) Budget detail.

(4) Qualifications of the staff who will be assigned or working on the proposed project.

(5) Any other criteria to determine the proposed project's efficacy in evaluating the implementation and effect of the Act.

(d) Applicants selected for funding will be notified in writing, along with the amount of the proposed funding.

(e) The Bureau's selection decision is final and not subject to appeal.

Note: Authority cited: Section 26013, Business and Professions Code. Reference: Section 34019, Revenue and Taxation Code.

§ 5903. Release of Funds.

(a) The Bureau shall not cause funds to be disbursed until the Applicant has executed a Grant Agreement, and any other required documents.

(b) Selected recipients shall receive a single disbursement of funds for the duration of the research project.

(c) Funds released to the recipient that will be used for the purchase of any equipment related to the research project shall, at a minimum, meet the following conditions:

(1) Prior to the purchase of any equipment, the recipient shall obtain written approval from the Bureau.

(2) Receipts or other documentation for the purchase of any equipment shall be provided to the Bureau immediately upon purchase and request, and retained pursuant to section 5904 of this division.

(d) Any funds that are not used prior to the completion of the research project shall be forfeited.

Note: Authority cited: Section 26013, Business and Professions Code. Reference: Section 34019, Revenue and Taxation Code.

§ 5904. Reports to the Bureau.

The recipient of funds shall provide regular performance reports to the Bureau.

(a) Unless otherwise specified in the Grant Agreement, performance reports shall be provided to the Bureau in the following manner:

(1) At monthly intervals for research projects with an estimated completion time not exceeding one year.

(2) At quarterly intervals for research projects with an estimated completion time exceeding one year.

(b) Performance reports shall include, at a minimum:

(1) A detailed, estimated time schedule of completion for the research project;

(2) Description of any measurable outcomes, results achieved, or other completed objectives of the research project;

(3) Description of remaining work to be completed;

(4) Summary of the expenditures of the funds, and whether the research project is meeting the proposed budget, and if not, the reasons for any discrepancies and what actions will be taken to ensure the research project will be completed; and

(5) Any changes to the information provided in the proposal, including, but not limited to, change in staff.

Note: Authority cited: Section 26013, Business and Professions Code. Reference: Section 34019, Revenue and Taxation Code.

§ 5905. Research Records.

Recipients shall retain all research and financial data necessary to substantiate the purposes for which the funds were spent for the duration of the funding, and for a period of seven years after completion of the research project. Recipients shall provide such documentation to the Bureau upon request.

Note: Authority cited: Section 26013, Business and Professions Code. Reference: Section 26160, Business and Professions Code; and Section 34019, Revenue and Taxation Code.

Title 17. Public Health

DIVISION 1. STATE DEPARTMENT OF HEALTH SERVICES

Chapter 13. Manufactured Cannabis Safety

SUBCHAPTER 1. GENERAL PROVISIONS AND DEFINITIONS

ARTICLE 1. DEFINITIONS

§ 40100. Definitions.

In addition to the definitions in Business and Professions Code section 26001, the following definitions shall govern the construction of this chapter:

(a) "A-license" means a license issued for commercial cannabis activities involving cannabis and cannabis products that are intended for individuals 21 years of age and older and who do not possess a physician's recommendations.

(b) "Act" means the Medicinal and Adult-Use Cannabis Regulation and Safety Act, codified at Business and Professions Code section 26000, et seq.

(c) "Adult-use Market" means the products intended for sale at a retailer or microbusiness to individuals 21 years of age and older and who do not possess a physician's recommendation.

(d) "Adulterated" or "adulteration" has the meaning stated in section 26131 of the Act.

(e) "Allergen" means a major food allergen including any of the following: (1) Milk, eggs, fish (e.g., bass, flounder, or cod), crustacean shellfish (e.g., crab, lobster, or shrimp), tree nuts (e.g., almonds, pecans, or walnuts), wheat, peanuts, and soybeans. (2) A food ingredient that contains protein derived from a food specified in (1). "Allergen" does not include the following: Any highly refined oil derived from a food specified in (1) and any ingredient derived from such highly refined oil.

(f) "Applicant" means the owner that is applying on behalf of the commercial cannabis business for a license to manufacture cannabis products.

(g) "Batch" or "production batch" means either:

> (1) An amount of cannabis concentrate or extract produced in one production cycle using the same extraction methods and standard operating procedures; or

> (2) An amount of a type of cannabis product produced in one production cycle using the same formulation and standard operating procedures.

(h) "Bureau" means the Bureau of Cannabis Control in the Department of Consumer Affairs.

(i) "Cannabis concentrate" means cannabis that has undergone a process to concentrate one or more active cannabinoids, thereby increasing the product's potency. For purposes of this chapter, "cannabis concentrate" includes, but is not limited to, the separated resinous trichomes of cannabis, tinctures, capsules, suppositories, extracts, vape cartridges, inhaled products (e.g., dab, shatter, and wax), and tablets as defined in subsection (rr).

(j) "Cannabis product" as used in this chapter means cannabis that has undergone a process whereby the plant material has been transformed into a concentrate, including, but not limited to, concentrated cannabis, or an edible or topical product containing cannabis or concentrated cannabis and other ingredients.

(k) "Cannabis product quality," "quality cannabis product," or "quality" means that the cannabis product consistently meets the established specifications for identity, cannabinoid concentration (as specified in Section 5724 of Title 16 of the California Code of Regulations), homogeneity, composition, and testing standards established by the Bureau in Sections 5718 to 5723, inclusive, of Title 16 of the California Code of Regulations, and has been manufactured, packaged, labeled, and held under conditions to prevent adulteration and misbranding.

(l) "Cannabis waste" means waste that contains cannabis or cannabis products but is not otherwise a hazardous waste as defined in Public Resources Code section 40141.

(m) "CBD" means the compound cannabidiol.

(n) "Commercial-grade, non-residential door lock" means a lock manufactured for commercial use.

(o) "Department" means the State Department of Public Health.

(p) "Distribution" means the procurement, sale, and transport of cannabis and cannabis products between licensees.

(q) "Edible cannabis product" means a cannabis product intended to be used orally, in whole or in part, for human consumption. For purposes of this chapter, "edible cannabis product" includes cannabis products that dissolve or disintegrate in the mouth, but does not include any product otherwise defined as "cannabis concentrate."

(r) "Extraction" means a process by which cannabinoids are separated from cannabis plant material through chemical or physical means.

(s) "Finished product" means a cannabis product in its final form to be sold at a retail premises.

(t) "Harvest batch" means a specifically identified quantity of dried flower or trim, leaves, and other cannabis plant matter that is uniform in strain, harvested at the same time, and, if applicable, cultivated using the same pesticides and other agricultural chemicals, and harvested at the same time.

(u) "Informational panel" means any part of the cannabis product label that is not the primary panel and that contains required labeling information.

(v) "Infusion" means a process by which cannabis, cannabinoids, or cannabis concentrates are directly incorporated into a product formulation to produce a cannabis product.

(w) "Infused pre-roll" means a pre roll into which cannabis concentrate (other than kief) or other ingredients have been incorporated.

(x) "Ingredient" means any substance that is used in the manufacture of a cannabis product and that is intended to be present in the product's final form.

(y) "Kief" means the resinous trichomes of cannabis that have been separated from the cannabis plant.

(z) "Labeling" means any label or other written, printed, or graphic matter upon a cannabis product, upon its container or wrapper, or that accompanies any cannabis product.

(aa) "Limited-access area" means an area in which cannabis or cannabis products are stored or held and is only accessible to a licensee and authorized personnel.

(bb) "M-license" means a license issued for commercial cannabis activity involving medicinal cannabis.

(cc) "Manufacturer licensee" or "licensee" means the holder of a manufacturer license issued pursuant to the Act.

(dd) "Manufacture" means to compound, blend, extract, infuse, or otherwise make or prepare a cannabis product.

(1) The term "manufacture" includes the following processes:

    (A) Extraction;

    (B) Infusion;

    (C) Packaging or repackaging of cannabis products; and

    (D) Labeling or relabeling the packages of cannabis products.

(2) The term "manufacture" does not include the following:

    (A) The repacking of cannabis products from a bulk shipping container by a distributor or retailer where the product's original packaging and labeling is not otherwise altered;

    (B) The preparation of pre-rolls by a licensed distributor in accordance with the requirements of the Bureau specified in Section 5303 of Division 42 of Title 16 of the California Code of Regulations;

    (C) The collection of the resinous trichomes that are dislodged or sifted from the cannabis plant incident to cultivation activities by a licensed cultivator in accordance with the requirements of the California Department of Food and Agriculture specified in Article 4 of Chapter 1 of Division 8 of Title 3 of the California Code of Regulations;

    (D) The processing of non-manufactured cannabis products, as defined in Section 8000 of Title 3 of the California Code of Regulations, by a licensed cultivator in accordance with the requirements of the California Department of Food and Agriculture specified in Article 4 of Chapter 1 of Division 8 of Title 3 of the California Code of Regulations; or

    (E) The addition of cannabinoid content on the label of a package of cannabis or cannabis product by a distributor in accordance with Section 40409.

(ee) "Manufacturing" or "manufacturing operation" means all aspects of the extraction process, infusion process, and packaging and labeling processes, including processing, preparing, holding, and storing of cannabis products. Manufacturing also includes any processing, preparing, holding, or storing of components and ingredients.

(ff) "MCLS" means the Manufacturing Cannabis Licensing System, which is the online license application system available on the Department's website (www.cdph.ca.gov).

(gg) "Nonvolatile solvent" means any solvent used in the extraction process that is not a volatile solvent. For purposes of this chapter, "nonvolatile solvents" include carbon dioxide and ethanol.

(hh) "Orally-consumed concentrate" means a cannabis concentrate that is intended to be consumed by mouth and is not otherwise an edible cannabis product. "Orally-consumed concentrate" includes tinctures, capsules, and tablets that meet the definition of subsection (rr).

(ii) "Package" or "packaging" means any container or wrapper that may be used for enclosing or containing any cannabis products. The term "package" does not include any shipping container or outer wrapping used solely for the transportation of cannabis products in bulk quantity to another licensee or licensed premises.

(jj) "Personnel" means any worker engaged in the performance or supervision of operations at a manufacturing premises and includes full-time employees, part-time employees, temporary employees, contractors, and volunteers. For purposes of training requirements, "personnel" also includes owner-operators.

(kk) "Person" includes any individual, firm, partnership, joint venture, association, corporation, limited liability company, estate, trust, business trust, receiver, syndicate, or any other group or combination acting as a unit, and the plural as well as the singular.

(ll) "Pre-roll" means any combination of the following rolled in paper: flower, shake, leaf, or kief.

(mm) "Premises" means the designated structure(s) and land specified in the application that is owned, leased, or otherwise held under the control of the applicant or licensee where the commercial cannabis activity (as defined in section 26001(k) of the Act) will be or is conducted. The premises shall be a contiguous area and shall only be occupied by one licensee.

(nn) "Primary panel" means the part of a cannabis product label that is most likely to be displayed, presented, shown, or examined under customary conditions of display for retail sale.

(oo) "Product Identity" or "identity of the product" means the generic, common, or usual name of the product by which it is most commonly known.

(pp) "Quarantine" means the storage or identification of a product to prevent distribution or transfer of the product.

(qq) "Serving" means the designated amount of cannabis product established by the manufacturer to constitute a single unit.

(rr) "Tablet" means a solid preparation containing a single serving of THC or other cannabinoid that is intended to be swallowed whole, and that is not formulated to be chewable, dispersible, effervescent, orally disintegrating, used as a suspension, or consumed in a manner other than swallowed whole, and that does not contain any added natural or artificial flavor or sweetener.

(ss) "THC" means the compound tetrahydrocannabinol. For purposes of this chapter, "THC" refers specifically to delta 9-tetrahydrocannabinol.

(tt) "Topical cannabis product" means a cannabis product intended to be applied to the skin rather than ingested or inhaled.

(uu) "Track-and-trace system" means the program for reporting the movement of cannabis and cannabis products through the distribution chain established by the Department of Food and Agriculture in accordance with section 26067 of the Act.

(vv) "UID" means the unique identifier for use in the track-and-trace system established by the Department of Food and Agriculture in accordance with section 26069 of the Act.

(ww) "Universal symbol" means the symbol developed by the Department pursuant to section 26130(c)(7) of the Act to indicate a product contains cannabinoids.

(xx) "Volatile solvent" means any solvent that is or produces a flammable gas or vapor that, when present in the air in sufficient quantities, will create explosive or ignitable mixtures. Examples of volatile solvents include, but are not limited to, butane, hexane, and propane.

Note: Authority cited: Sections 26012, 26013 and 26130, Business and Professions Code. Reference: Sections 26001, 26120 and 26130, Business and Professions Code; and Section 11018.1, Health and Safety Code.

§ 40101. Applicability.

(a) Unless otherwise specified, the requirements of this chapter apply to all licensed manufacturers and to the manufacture of cannabis products for both the medicinal-use market and the adult-use market.

(b) The requirements for the production, packaging, and labeling of cannabis products in subchapters 3, 4, and 5 shall apply to licensed microbusinesses conducting manufacturing operations.

Note: Authority cited: Sections 26012, 26013 and 26130, Business and Professions Code. Reference: Sections 26050 and 26106, Business and Professions Code.

§ 40102. Owners and Financial Interest Holders.

(a) An owner shall mean any of the following:

(1) Any person that has an aggregate ownership interest, other than a security interest, lien, or encumbrance, in a commercial cannabis business of 20 percent or more;

(A) If the owner identified in subsection (a)(1) is an entity, then the chief executive officer and members of the board of directors of the entity shall be considered owners.

(2) The chief executive officer of a commercial cannabis business;

(3) If a non-profit entity, each member of the board of directors;

(4) Any individual that will be participating in the direction, control, or management of the licensed commercial cannabis business. An owner who is an individual participating in the direction, control, or management of the commercial cannabis business includes any of the following:

(A) Each general partner of a commercial cannabis business that is organized as a partnership;

(B) Each non-member manager or managing member of a limited liability company for a commercial cannabis business that is organized as a limited liability company;

(C) Each officer or director of a commercial cannabis business that is organized as a corporation.

(5) The trustee(s) and all persons that have control of the trust and/or the commercial cannabis business that is held in trust.

(b) Financial interest holders, for purposes of section 26051.5(d) of the Act, are persons that hold an ownership interest of less than 20 percent in a commercial cannabis business, and are not otherwise specified as owners pursuant to subsection (a). Financial interest holders shall be disclosed on the application for licensure. A financial interest means an agreement to receive a portion of the profits of a commercial cannabis business, an investment into a commercial cannabis business, a loan provided to a commercial cannabis business, or any other equity interest in a commercial cannabis business.

(c) The following persons are not considered to be owners or financial interest holders:

(1) A bank or financial institution whose interest constitutes a loan;

(2) Persons whose only ownership interest in the commercial cannabis business is through an interest in a diversified mutual fund, blind trust, or similar instrument;

(3) Persons whose only financial interest is a security interest, lien, or encumbrance on the property that will be used by the commercial cannabis business; and

(4) Persons who hold a share of stock that is less than 5 percent of the total shares in a publicly traded company.

Note: Authority cited: Sections 26012 and 26013, Business and Professions Code. Reference: Sections 26001 and 26051.5, Business and Professions Code.

§ 40105. Premises Diagram.

(a) The premises diagram required pursuant to section 26051.5(c) of the Act shall meet the following requirements:

(1) The diagram shall be specific enough to enable ready determination of the bounds of the property and the

proposed premises to be licensed;

(2) The diagram shall be to scale;

(3) If the proposed premises consists of only a portion of a property, the diagram shall be labeled to indicate which part of the property is the proposed premises and identify what the remaining property is used for.

(b) The premises diagram shall include:

(1) All boundaries, dimensions, entrances and exits, interior partitions, walls, rooms, windows, and doorways.

(2) The areas in which all commercial cannabis activities will be conducted. Commercial cannabis activities that shall be identified on the diagram include the following, as applicable to the business operations: infusion activities, extraction activities, packaging activities, labeling activities, and transportation activities such as loading and unloading of cannabis and cannabis products.

(3) The limited-access areas, areas used for video surveillance monitoring and surveillance system storage devices, and all security camera locations.

(4) Cannabis waste disposal areas.

(c) If the proposed premises consists of only a portion of a property that will contain two or more licensed premises, the diagram shall clearly show any entrances and walls under the exclusive control of the applicant or licensee. The diagram shall also show all proposed common or shared areas of the property, including entryways, lobbies, bathrooms, hallways, and breakrooms.

(d) The diagram shall be used by the Department to determine whether the premises meets the requirements of the Act and this chapter.

Note: Authority cited: Section 26013, Business and Professions Code. Reference: Section 26051.5, Business and Professions Code.

ARTICLE 2. GENERAL PROVISIONS

§ 40115. License Required.

(a) Every person who manufactures cannabis products shall obtain and maintain a valid manufacturer license from the Department for each separate premises at which manufacturing operations will be conducted.

(b) No person shall manufacture cannabis products without a valid license from the Department.

(c) Licenses shall not be transferrable.

Note: Authority cited: Sections 26012, 26013 and 26130, Business and Professions Code. Reference: Section 26053, Business and Professions Code.

§ 40116. Personnel Prohibited from Holding Licenses.

(a) A license authorized by the Act and issued by the Department may not be held by, or issued to, any person holding office in, or employed by, any agency of the State of California or any of its political subdivisions when the duties of such person have to do with the enforcement of the Act or the penal provisions of law of this State prohibiting or regulating the sale, use, possession, transportation, distribution, testing, manufacturing, or cultivation of cannabis or cannabis products.

(b) This section applies to, but is not limited to, any person employed in the State of California Department of Justice as a peace officer, in any district attorney's office, in any city or county attorney's office, in any sheriff's office, or in any local police department.

(c) All persons listed in subsection (a) or (b) may not have any ownership interest, directly or indirectly, in any business to be operated or conducted under a cannabis license.

(d) This section does not apply to any person who holds a license in the capacity of executor, administrator, or guardian.

Note: Authority cited: Sections 26012 and 26013, Business and Professions Code. Reference: Section 26012, Business and Professions Code.

§ 40118. Manufacturing License Types.

The following license types are available from the Department:

(a) "Type 7," for extractions using volatile solvents as defined by Section 40100(xx). A Type 7 licensee may also:

(1) Conduct extractions using nonvolatile solvents or mechanical methods on the licensed premises, provided that the extraction process is noted on the application and the relevant information pursuant to Section 40131 is provided to the Department;

(2) Conduct infusion operations on the licensed premises, provided the infusion operations and product types are noted on the application and the relevant information pursuant to Section 40131 is provided to the Department;

(3) Conduct packaging and labeling of cannabis products on the licensed premises; and

(4) Register and operate the licensed premises as a shared-use facility in accordance with Article 6 (commencing with Section 40190) of Subchapter 2.

(b) "Type 6," for extractions using mechanical methods or nonvolatile solvents as defined by Section 40100(gg). A Type 6 licensee may also:

(1) Conduct infusion operations on the licensed premises, provided the infusion operations and product types are noted on the application and the relevant information pursuant to Section 40131 is provided to the Department;

(2) Conduct packaging and labeling of cannabis products on the licensed premises; and

(3) Register and operate the licensed premises as a shared-use facility in accordance with Article 6 (commencing with Section 40190) of Subchapter 2.

(c) "Type N," for manufacturers that produce cannabis products other than extracts or concentrates that are produced through extraction. A Type N licensee may also:

(1) Conduct packaging and labeling of cannabis products on the licensed premises; and

(2) Register and operate the licensed premises as a shared-use facility in accordance with Article 6 (commencing with Section 40190) of Subchapter 2.

(d) "Type P," for manufacturers that only package or repackage cannabis products or label or relabel cannabis product containers or wrappers.

(e) "Type S," for manufacturers that conduct commercial cannabis manufacturing activities in accordance with Article 6 (commencing with Section 40190) of Subchapter 2 at a registered shared-use facility.

Note: Authority cited: Sections 26012, 26013 and 26130, Business and Professions Code. Reference: Sections 26012, 26050 and 26130, Business and Professions Code.

§ 40120. Additional Activities.

In addition to the activities specified in Section 40118, a licensee may also roll and package pre-rolls and package dried cannabis flower.

Note: Authority cited: Sections 26012, 26013 and 26130, Business and Professions Code. Reference: Sections 26012 and 26130, Business and Professions Code.

SUBCHAPTER 2. MANUFACTURING LICENSES

ARTICLE 1. APPLICATIONS FOR LICENSURE

§ 40126. Temporary Licenses.

(a) A temporary license shall be valid for 120 days from the effective date. No temporary license shall be issued on or after January 1, 2019.

(c) Any temporary license issued or extended that has an expiration date after December 31, 2018, will be valid until it expires, but shall not be extended beyond the expiration date.

(e) Refusal by the Department to issue or extend a temporary license shall not entitle the applicant to a hearing or appeal of the decision.

(f) A temporary license does not obligate the Department to issue an annual license to the temporary license holder, nor does the temporary license create a vested right in the holder to either an extension of the temporary license or to the granting of a subsequent annual license.

Note: Authority cited: Sections 26012, 26013 and 26130, Business and Professions Code. Reference: Section 26012, Business and Professions Code.

§ 40127. Temporary Shared-Use Facility Registration; Temporary Licenses: Type S.

(a) To register a manufacturing premises as a shared-use facility as defined in Section 40190, an applicant shall submit to the Department the following:

(1) Form CDPH-9037 (03/18), which is hereby incorporated by reference;

(2) A copy of the valid license, permit, or other authorization issued by the local jurisdiction that enables the applicant to operate as a shared-use facility. Upon receipt of the registration application, the Department shall contact the applicable local jurisdiction to confirm the validity of the authorization. If the local jurisdiction does not respond within 10 calendar days, the Department shall consider the authorization valid.

(b) To request a temporary Type S license, an applicant shall submit to the Department the following:

(1) Form CDPH-9038 (03/18), which is hereby incorporated by reference;

(2) A copy of the valid license, permit, or other authorization issued by the local jurisdiction that enables the

applicant to conduct commercial cannabis activity. Upon receipt of the license application, the Department shall contact the applicable local jurisdiction to confirm the validity of the authorization. If the local jurisdiction does not respond within 10 calendar days, the Department shall consider the authorization valid;

(3) The license number and address of the shared-use facility at which the applicant will conduct manufacturing operations; and

(4) The days and hours in which the applicant will conduct manufacturing operations.

(c) Temporary licenses and registrations issued pursuant to this section shall be subject to the terms and conditions of subsections (b), (c), (d), (e), and (f) of Section 40126.

Note: Authority cited: Sections 26012, 26013 and 26130, Business and Professions Code. Reference: Section 26050.1, Business and Professions Code.

§ 40128. Annual License Application Requirements.

(a) To apply for a manufacturer license from the Department, the applicant shall submit the following on behalf of the commercial cannabis business:

(1) A completed application form as prescribed by the Department, or through MCLS, which includes all of the following information:

(A) Business information as specified in Section 40129;

(B) Owner information as specified in Section 40130; and

(C) Manufacturing premises and operations information as specified in Section 40131;

(2) For new applications, the nonrefundable application fee as specified in Section 40150(a). The annual license fee shall be paid upon approval of the application, as prescribed in Section 40155. For license renewal applications, the nonrefundable annual license fee as specified in Section 40150(b) shall be submitted with the license renewal application. The application fee described in Section 40150(a) is not required for license renewal applications;

(3) Evidence of compliance with or exemption from the California Environmental Quality Act (CEQA) as specified in Section 40132; and

(4) The limited waiver of sovereign immunity as specified in Section 40133, if applicable.

(b) The application shall be signed by the applicant under penalty of perjury that the information provided in and submitted with the application is complete, true, and accurate, and shall include the following attestations:

(1) The applicant is authorized to act on behalf of the commercial cannabis business;

(2) The applicant entity, when it has 20 or more employees, has entered, or will enter as soon as reasonably practicable, into a labor peace agreement and will abide by the terms of the agreement as required by section 26051.5 (a)(5)(A) of the Act. The applicant shall provide the Department a copy of the page of the labor peace agreement that contains the signatures of the union representative and the applicant;

(3) The commercial cannabis business is operating in compliance with all local ordinances;

(4) The proposed premises is not within a 600-foot radius of the perimeter of a school providing instruction in kindergarten or any grades 1 through 12, or a day care center, or youth center, or that the premises complies with the local ordinance specifying a different radius, as specified in section 26054(b) of the Act; and

(5) For an applicant entity with more than one employee, the applicant employs, or will employ within one

year of receiving a license, one supervisor and one employee who have successfully completed a Cal/OSHA 30-hour general industry outreach course offered by a training provider that is authorized by an OSHA Training Institute Education Center to provide the course.

(c) The Department may request additional information and documents from the applicant as necessary to determine whether the applicant or the commercial cannabis business meets the requirements and qualifications for licensure.

Note: Authority cited: Sections 26012, 26013 and 26130, Business and Professions Code. Reference: Sections 26050, 26051.5 and 26054, Business and Professions Code.

§ 40129. Annual License Application Requirements - Business Information.

(a) The applicant shall submit the following information for the commercial cannabis business:

(1) The legal business name;

(2) The federal tax identification number. If the commercial cannabis business is a sole proprietorship, the applicant shall submit the social security number or individual taxpayer identification number of the sole proprietor;

(3) The registered name(s) under which the business will operate (Fictitious Business Name, Trade Name, "Doing Business As"), if applicable;

(4) The business's mailing address which will serve as the address of record;

(5) The name, title, phone number and email address of the primary contact person for the commercial cannabis business;

(6) The seller's permit number issued by the California Department of Tax and Fee Administration or notification issued by the California Department of Tax and Fee Administration that the business is not required to have a seller's permit. If the applicant has not yet received a seller's permit, the applicant shall attest that the applicant is currently applying for a seller's permit;

(7) The business structure of the commercial cannabis business as filed with the California Secretary of State (e.g., limited liability company, partnership, corporation) or operation as a sole proprietor. A commercial cannabis business that is a foreign corporation or foreign limited liability company under the California Corporations Code shall include with its application the certificate of status issued by the California Secretary of State;

(8) A list of all owners, as defined in Section 40102;

(9) A list of all financial interest holders, as defined in Section 40102, which shall include:

(A) For financial interest holders that are individuals, the first and last name of the individual, and the type and number of the individual's government-issued identification (e.g. driver's license); or

(B) For financial interest holders that are entities, the legal business name and federal taxpayer identification number of the entity.

(10) Proof of having obtained a surety bond in the amount of $5,000, payable to the State of California as obligee, to ensure payment of the cost incurred for the destruction of cannabis or cannabis products necessitated by a violation of the Act or the regulations adopted thereunder. The bond shall be issued by a corporate surety licensed to transact surety business in the State of California;

(11) The license type applied for and whether the application is for medicinal cannabis product manufacturing, adult-use cannabis product manufacturing, or both;

(12) The business formation documents, which may include, but are not limited to, articles of incorporation, bylaws, operating agreements, partnership agreements, and fictitious business name statements. If the commercial cannabis business is held in trust, the applicant shall provide a copy of the certificate of trust establishing trustee authority;

(13) All documents filed with the California Secretary of State, which may include, but are not limited to, articles of incorporation, articles of organization, certificates of limited partnership, and statements of partnership authority.

(b) Pursuant to section 26055(e) of the Act, an applicant may voluntarily submit a copy of a license, permit, or other authorization to conduct commercial cannabis manufacturing activities issued by the local jurisdiction. When an applicant submits a local authorization, upon receipt of the application, the Department shall contact the applicable local jurisdiction to confirm the validity of the authorization. If the local jurisdiction does not respond within 10 calendar days, the Department shall consider the authorization valid.

Note: Authority cited: Sections 26012, 26013 and 26130, Business and Professions Code. Reference: Sections 26050 and 26051.5, Business and Professions Code.

§ 40130. Annual License Application Requirements - Owners.

(a) Each owner shall submit all of the following information:

(1) Name;

(2) Title or position held;

(3) Social security number or individual taxpayer identification number;

(4) Date of birth;

(5) Mailing address;

(6) Contact phone number and email address;

(7) A copy of Department of Justice form BCIA 8016, provided to the applicant by the Department of Public Health and signed by the live scan operator;

(8) Disclosure of all of the following, including any actions against the owner as an individual and against a business entity in which the owner was an officer or an owner. The information provided shall include dates and a description of the circumstances:

(A) Any criminal conviction from any jurisdiction. Adjudications by a juvenile court and infractions do not need to be disclosed. Convictions dismissed under Penal Code section 1203.4 or equivalent non-California law must be disclosed;

(B) Any civil proceeding or administrative penalty or license sanction that is substantially related to the qualifications of a manufacturer as identified in Section 40162;

(C) Any fines, penalties, or other sanctions for cultivation or production of a controlled substance on public or private lands pursuant to Fish and Game Code section 12025 or 12025.1;

(D) Any sanctions by a licensing authority, city, or county for unauthorized commercial cannabis activity within 3 years preceding the date of the application;

(E) Any suspension or revocation of a cannabis license by a licensing authority or local jurisdiction within 3 years preceding the date of the application; and

(F) Any administrative orders or civil judgements for violations of labor standards within the 3 years immediately preceding the date of the application.

(9) Disclosure of any ownership interest or financial interest in any other cannabis business licensed under the Act.

(b) The owner shall sign under penalty of perjury that the information provided in and submitted with the application is complete, true, and accurate.

(c) An owner disclosing a criminal conviction or other penalty or sanction pursuant to subdivision (a), paragraphs (8) (A) and (B), shall submit any evidence of rehabilitation with the application for consideration by the Department. A statement of rehabilitation shall be written by the owner and contain all the evidence that the owner would like the Department to consider that demonstrates the owner's fitness for licensure. Supporting evidence may be attached to the statement of rehabilitation and may include, but is not limited to, evidence specified in Section 40165, and dated letters of reference from employers, instructors, or counselors that contain valid contact information for the individual providing the reference.

Note: Authority cited: Sections 26012, 26013 and 26130, Business and Professions Code. Reference: Sections 26012, 26013, 26050, 26055 and 26130, Business and Professions Code.

§ 40131. Annual License Application Requirements - Manufacturing Premises and Operations Information.

The applicant shall submit all of the following information regarding the manufacturing premises and operation:

(a) The physical address of the manufacturing premises;

(b) Whether medicinal-use cannabis products, adult-use cannabis products, or both, are manufactured at the premises;

(c) The type(s) of activity conducted at the premises (extraction, infusion, packaging, or labeling);

(d) The types of products that will be manufactured, packaged, or labeled at the premises, including a product list;

(e) The name, title, email address, and phone number of the on-site individual who manages the operation of the premises;

(f) The name, title, email address, and phone number of an alternate contact person for the premises if applicable;

(g) The number of employees at the premises;

(h) The anticipated gross annual revenue from products manufactured at the premises as specified in Section 40152;

(i) A premises diagram as specified in Section 40105;

(j) The following information:

(1) A description of inventory control procedures sufficient to demonstrate how the applicant will comply with the requirements of Section 40282, or a copy of the standard operating procedure addressing inventory control;

(2) A description of quality control procedures sufficient to demonstrate how the applicant will comply with all of the applicable requirements specified in Sections 40235-40258 or a copy of the standard operating procedure addressing quality control;

(3) A description of the transportation process describing how cannabis or cannabis products will be transported into and out of the premises, or a copy of the standard operating procedure addressing transportation;

(4) A description of security procedures sufficient to demonstrate how the applicant will comply with the requirements of Section 40200, or a copy of the standard operating procedure addressing security procedures;

(5) A description of the cannabis waste management procedures sufficient to demonstrate how the applicant will comply with the requirements of Section 40290, or a copy of the standard operating procedure addressing cannabis waste management.

(k) A written statement signed by the owner of the property, or the owner's agent, identifying the physical location of the property and acknowledging and consenting to the manufacture of cannabis products on the property. The name, address and contact phone number for the owner or owner's agent shall be included;

(l) A copy of the signed closed-loop system certification and a document evidencing approval of the extraction operation by the local fire code official required pursuant to Section 40223 or 40225, if applicable;

(m) Any manufacturer submitting operating procedures and protocols to the Department pursuant to the Act and this chapter may claim such information as a trade secret or confidential by clearly identifying such information as "confidential" on the document at the time of submission. Any claim of confidentiality by a manufacturer must be based on the manufacturer's good faith belief that the information marked as confidential constitutes a trade secret as defined in Civil Code section 3426.1(d), or is otherwise exempt from public disclosure under the California Public Records Act in Government Code section 6250 et seq.

Note: Authority cited: Sections 26012, 26013 and 26130, Business and Professions Code. Reference: Sections 26050, 26050.1, 26055 and 26130, Business and Professions Code.

§ 40132. Annual License Application Requirements - Compliance with CEQA.

(a) An applicant for a new license shall provide evidence of exemption from or compliance with the California Environmental Quality Act (CEQA), Division 13 (commencing with section 21000) of the Public Resources Code.

(b) The evidence provided pursuant to subsection (a) shall be one of the following:

(1) If the premises is located in a local jurisdiction that has adopted an ordinance, rule, or regulation pursuant to Business and Professions Code section 26055(h), a copy of the local license, permit, or other authorization shall be sufficient to demonstrate compliance.

(2) If the applicant does not provide a copy of the local license, permit, or other authorization pursuant to subsection (b)(1), or if the premises is located in a local jurisdiction that has not adopted an ordinance, rule, or regulation pursuant to Business and Professions Code section 26055(h), a copy of the Notice of Exemption or Notice of Determination and a copy of the CEQA document from the local jurisdiction, or a reference to where it can be found electronically to demonstrate compliance.

(3) Any other permit or local authorization issued by the local jurisdiction in compliance with CEQA may be submitted to demonstrate compliance.

(c) If an applicant does not have the evidence specified in subsection (b), or if the local jurisdiction did not prepare a CEQA document, the applicant shall be responsible for the preparation of an environmental document in compliance with CEQA that can be approved or certified by the Department, if applicable.

Note: Authority cited: Sections 26012, 26013 and 26130, Business and Professions Code. Reference: Section 26055,

§ 40133. Limited Waiver of Sovereign Immunity.

(a) Any applicant or licensee that may fall within the scope of sovereign immunity that may be asserted by a federally recognized tribe or other sovereign entity must waive any sovereign immunity defense that the applicant or licensee may have, may be asserted on its behalf, or may otherwise be asserted in any state administrative or judicial enforcement actions against the applicant or licensee, regardless of the form of relief sought, whether monetary or otherwise, under the state laws and regulations governing commercial cannabis activity. The applicant or licensee must submit a written waiver of sovereign immunity to the Department with any license application or renewal, which is valid for the period of the license. The written waiver shall include that the applicant or licensee has the lawful authority to enter into the waiver required by this section, the applicant or licensee hereby waives sovereign immunity, and the applicant or licensee agrees to do all of the following:

(1) Provide documentation to the Department that establishes that the applicant or licensee has the lawful authority to enter into the waiver required by this section;

(2) Conduct all commercial cannabis activity in full compliance with the state laws and regulations governing commercial cannabis activity, including submission to all enforcement provisions thereof;

(3) Allow access as required by state statute or regulation by persons or entities charged with duties under the state laws and regulations governing commercial cannabis activity to any premises or property at which the applicant conducts any commercial cannabis activity, including premises or property where records of commercial cannabis activity are maintained by or for the applicant or licensee;

(4) Provide any and all records, reports, and other documents as may be required under the state laws and regulations governing commercial cannabis activity;

(5) Conduct commercial cannabis activity with other state commercial cannabis licensees only, unless otherwise specified by state law;

(6) Meet all of the requirements for licensure under the state laws and regulations governing the conduct of commercial cannabis activity, and provide truthful and accurate documentation and other information of the applicant's qualifications and suitability for licensure as may be requested;

(7) Submit to the personal and subject matter jurisdiction of the California courts to address any matter related to the waiver or the commercial cannabis application, license, or activity, and that all such matters and proceedings shall be governed, construed, and enforced in accordance with California substantive and procedural law, including but not limited to the Medicinal and Adult-Use Cannabis Regulation and Safety Act and the Administrative Procedure Act.

(b) The Department shall not approve an application for a state license if approval of the license would violate the provisions of any local ordinance or regulation adopted in accordance with section 26200 of the Act that is issued by the county or, if within a city, the city, within which the licensed premises is to be located.

(c) Any applicant or licensee must immediately notify the Department of any changes that may materially affect the applicant and licensee's compliance with subsection (a).

(d) Any failure by an applicant or licensee to comply with the requirements of subsections (a) or (c) shall be a basis for denial of an application or renewal or discipline of a licensee.

Note: Authority cited: Sections 26012, 26013 and 26130, Business and Professions Code. Reference: Sections 26011.5, 26012, 26050 and 26051.5, Business and Professions Code.

§ 40135. Incomplete and Abandoned Applications.

(a) Incomplete applications will not be processed. Applications will only be considered complete if all of the information requested under Sections 40128 to 40131 is included. The Department shall issue a written notice to the applicant, by mail or through MCLS, informing them of any information missing from the application.

(b) If the applicant fails to submit the required information within 180 days from the date of notice, the application shall be deemed abandoned. Application fees for abandoned applications shall not be refunded.

(c) An applicant may reapply at any time following an abandoned application. However, a new application and application fee are required.

Note: Authority cited: Sections 26012, 26013 and 26130, Business and Professions Code. Reference: Sections 26012 and 26050, Business and Professions Code.

§ 40137. Application Withdrawal.

(a) An applicant may withdraw an application for annual licensure at any time prior to the issuance or denial of the license. Requests to withdraw an application shall be submitted in writing to the Department or through MCLS.

(b) An applicant may reapply for annual licensure at any time subsequent to the withdrawal of an application. However, a new application and application fee are required.

(c) Withdrawal of an application shall not deprive the Department of its authority to institute or continue a proceeding against the applicant for the denial of the license upon any ground provided by law or to enter an order denying the license upon any such ground.

(d) The application fee paid for a new application and the annual license fee paid for a renewal application shall not be refunded if an application is withdrawn.

Note: Authority cited: Sections 26012, 26013 and 26130, Business and Professions Code. Reference: Sections 26012 and 26050, Business and Professions Code.

ARTICLE 3. FEES

§ 40150. Application and License Fees.

(a) Manufacturer application fees for new applications shall be as follows:

(1) For a Type 7, Type 6, Type N, or Type P license application, the nonrefundable application fee is $1,000 for each new application submitted;

(2) For a Type S license application, a nonrefundable application fee of $500 for each new application submitted.

(b) The annual license fee shall be as follows:

(1) For a licensed premises with gross annual revenue of up to $100,000 (Tier I), the fee shall be $2,000;

(2) For a licensed premises with gross annual revenue of $100,001 to $500,000 (Tier II), the fee shall be $7,500;

(3) For a licensed premises with gross annual revenue of $500,001 to $1,500,000 (Tier III), the fee shall be $15,000;

(4) For a licensed premises with gross annual revenue of $1,500,001 to $3,000,000 (Tier IV), the fee shall be $25,000;

(5) For a licensed premises with gross annual revenue of $3,000,001 to $5,000,000 (Tier V), the fee shall be $35,000;

(6) For a licensed premises with gross annual revenue of $5,000,001 to $10,000,000 (Tier VI), the fee shall be $50,000;

(7) For a licensed premises with an annual gross revenue of over $10,000,000 (Tier VII), the fee shall be $75,000.

(c) All fees are nonrefundable.

Note: Authority cited: Sections 26012, 26013 and 26130, Business and Professions Code. Reference: Sections 26012 and 26180, Business and Professions Code.

§ 40152. Gross Annual Revenue Calculation.

(a) The applicant shall calculate the gross annual revenue for the licensed premises based on the annual gross sales of cannabis products and, if applicable, the annual revenue received from manufacturing, packaging, labeling or otherwise handling cannabis or cannabis products for other licensees, in the twelve months preceding the date of application.

(b) For a new license applicant, the gross annual revenue shall be based on the gross sales and revenue expected during the first 12 months following licensure.

(c) For a manufacturer licensee that is also licensed as a distributor or retailer, and that sells or transfers cannabis products manufactured on the licensed premises in a non-arm's length transaction, the annual gross sales or revenue for such transactions shall be based on the product's fair market value if it were to be sold in an arm's length transaction at wholesale.

(d) For purposes of this section, an "arm's length transaction" means a sale entered into in good faith and for valuable consideration that reflects the fair market value in the open market between two informed and willing parties, neither under any compulsion to participate in the transaction.

Note: Authority cited: Sections 26012, 26013 and 26130, Business and Professions Code. Reference: Sections 26012 and 26180, Business and Professions Code.

ARTICLE 4. APPROVAL OR DENIAL OF APPLICATION FOR LICENSURE

§ 40155. New License Approval.

(a) The Department shall notify the applicant upon approval of a new license application by email or through MCLS.

(b) The applicant shall pay the applicable license fee specified in Section 40150(b) within 30 calendar days of notification. The license fee for the first year of licensure shall be based on the estimated gross annual revenue as calculated pursuant to Section 40152 and submitted in the license application.

(c) No license shall be issued before the license fee is paid to the Department in full.

Note: Authority cited: Sections 26012, 26013 and 26130, Business and Professions Code. Reference: Sections 26012 and 26130, Business and Professions Code.

§ 40156. Priority License Issuance.

(a) Priority issuance of licenses shall be given to applicants that can demonstrate that the commercial cannabis business was in operation under the Compassionate Use Act of 1996, Health and Safety Code sections 11362.5 et seq., as of September 1, 2016.

(b) Eligibility for priority in application processing shall be demonstrated by any of the following, dated prior to September 1, 2016:

(1) Local license or permit or other written authorization;

(2) Collective or Cooperative Membership Agreement;

(3) Tax or business forms submitted to the Board of Equalization or Franchise Tax Board;

(4) Incorporation documents; or

(5) Any other business record that demonstrates the operation of the business prior to September 1, 2016.

(c) Any applicant identified by the local jurisdiction pursuant to section 26054.2(b) of the Act shall be considered eligible for priority issuance.

(d) The Department may request additional documentation to verify the applicant's date of commencement of operations.

(e) This section shall expire on December 31, 2019, unless otherwise provided by law.

Note: Authority cited: Sections 26012, 26013 and 26130, Business and Professions Code. Reference: Sections 26012, 26054.2 and 26130, Business and Professions Code.

§ 40159. Denial of License.

(a) The Department may deny an application for a new or renewal license for any reason specified in section 26057 (b) of the Act. Further, the Department may deny a new or renewal license application for any of the following additional reasons:

(1) The applicant, an owner, or licensee made a material misrepresentation in the application for the license;

(2) An owner of the commercial cannabis business has been convicted of a crime or has committed a violation of law substantially related to the qualifications, functions, or duties of a manufacturer as identified in Section 40162;

(3) The applicant, an owner, or licensee has been denied a license to engage in commercial cannabis activity by a state licensing authority;

(4) The applicant, an owner, or licensee has denied the Department access to the premises; or

(5) The licensee has engaged in conduct that is grounds for disciplinary action specified in section 26030 of the Act.

(b) The Department shall deny an application for a new or renewal license if the proposed manufacturing operation or premises would violate the applicable local ordinance.

(c) A conviction within the meaning of this section means a plea or verdict of guilty or a conviction following a plea of nolo contendere.

(d) Prior to denial of a license based upon paragraph (2) of subsection (a) of this Section, the Department shall consider any evidence of rehabilitation as provided in Section 40165.

Note: Authority cited: Sections 26012, 26013 and 26130, Business and Professions Code. Reference: Sections 26030 and 26057, Business and Professions Code.

§ 40162. Substantially Related Acts.

For the purpose of denial of a license, a conviction or violation from any jurisdiction that is substantially related to the qualifications, functions, and duties of the business for which the application is made include:

(a) A violent felony conviction, as specified in subdivision (c) of Section 667.5 of the Penal Code;

(b) A serious felony conviction, as specified in subdivision (c) of Section 1192.7 of the Penal Code;

(c) A felony conviction involving fraud, deceit, or embezzlement;

(d) A felony conviction for hiring, employing, or using a minor in transporting, carrying, selling, giving away, preparing for sale, or peddling, any controlled substance to a minor; or selling, offering to sell, furnishing, offering to furnish, administering or giving any controlled substance to a minor;

(e) A felony conviction for drug trafficking with enhancements pursuant to Health and Safety Code sections 11370.4 or 11379.8;

(f) A violation of section 110620, 110625, 110630, 110760, 110765, 110770, 110775, 111295, 111300, 111305, 111440, 111445, 111450, or 111455 of the Health and Safety Code (Sherman Food, Drug, and Cosmetic Law) that resulted in suspension or revocation of a license, administrative penalty, civil proceeding or criminal conviction;

(g) A violation of Chapter 4 (sections 111950 through 112130) of Part 6 of Division 104 of the Health and Safety Code that resulted in suspension or revocation of a license, administrative penalty, civil proceeding or criminal conviction;

(h) A conviction under section 382 or 383 of the Penal Code; and

(i) A violation of law identified in subsections (f) or (g) committed by a business entity in which an owner was an officer or had an ownership interest is considered a violation that is substantially related to the owner's qualifications for licensure.

Note: Authority cited: Sections 26012, 26013 and 26130, Business and Professions Code. Reference: Sections 26011.5 and 26057, Business and Professions Code.

§ 40165. Criteria for Evidence of Rehabilitation.

When evaluating whether a license should be issued or denied when an owner has been convicted of a criminal offense or committed a violation of law that is substantially related to the qualifications, functions, or duties of the business for which the application is made, the Department shall consider the following criteria in its evaluation of evidence of rehabilitation:

(a) The nature and severity of the act or offense, including the actual or potential harm to the public;

(b) The owner's criminal record as a whole;

(c) Evidence of any act committed subsequent to the act or offense under consideration that could be considered grounds for denial, suspension, or revocation of a manufacturing license;

(d) The time elapsed since commission of the act or offense listed in Section 40162, or in section 26057(b)(4) of the Act;

(e) The extent to which the owner has complied with any terms of parole, probation, restitution, or any other sanctions lawfully imposed against the owner or licensee;

(f) If applicable, evidence of dismissal under Penal Code section 1203.4, 1203.4a, 1203.41, or a similar law in another state;

(g) If applicable, a certificate of rehabilitation obtained under Penal Code section 4852.01 or a similar law in another state; and

(h) Other evidence of rehabilitation submitted by the owner.

Note: Authority cited: Sections 26012, 26013 and 26130, Business and Professions Code. Reference: Sections 26011.5, 26055 and 26057, Business and Professions Code.

§ 40167. Appeal of License Denial.

(a) Upon denial of an application for a license, the Department shall notify the applicant in writing of the reasons for the denial and the right to a hearing to contest the denial.

(b) The applicant may request a hearing by filing a written petition for a license with the Department within 30 calendar days of service of the notice of denial. The written request for hearing must be postmarked within the 30-day period. If a request is not filed within the 30-day period, the applicant's right to a hearing is waived.

(c) Upon receipt of a timely filed petition, the Department shall set the petition for hearing. The hearing shall be conducted in accordance with Chapter 5 (commencing with Section 11500) of Part 1 of Division 3 of Title 2 of the Government Code.

Note: Authority cited: Sections 26012, 26013 and 26130, Business and Professions Code. Reference: Section 26058, Business and Professions Code.

§ 40169. Notification of Criminal Acts, Civil Judgments, and Revocation of a Local License, Permit, or Other Authorization after Licensure. [Repealed]

ARTICLE 5. LICENSING

§ 40175. License Constraints.

(a) A manufacturer licensee shall not manufacture, prepare, package or label any products other than cannabis products at the licensed premises. For purposes of this section, the term "cannabis products" also includes packaged cannabis, pre-rolls, and products that do not contain cannabis, but are otherwise identical to the cannabis-containing product, and are intended for use as samples.

(b) No licensee shall employ or retain an individual under 21 years of age.

(c) A manufacturer licensee shall only use cannabinoid concentrates and extracts that are manufactured or processed from cannabis obtained from a licensed cannabis cultivator.

(d) A manufacturer licensee shall not manufacture, prepare, package, or label cannabis products in a location that is operating as a retail food establishment or as a processed food registrant.

(e) A manufacturer licensee shall not manufacture, prepare, package, or label cannabis products in a location that is licensed by the Department of Alcoholic Beverage Control pursuant to Division 9 (commencing with section 23000) of the Business and Professions Code.

Note: Authority cited: Sections 26012, 26013 and 26130, Business and Professions Code. Reference: Sections 26050 and 26140, Business and Professions Code.

§ 40177. Change in Licensed Operations.

(a) At any time during the license period, a licensee may request to change the manufacturing activities conducted at the licensed premises. The following changes require pre-approval from the Department:

(1) The addition of any extraction method subject to the requirements of Section 40225;

(2) The addition of any other extraction method that necessitates a substantial or material alteration of the premises;

(3) The addition of infusion operations if no infusion activity is listed in the current license application on file with the Department;

(4) A substantial or material alteration of the licensed premises from the current premises diagram on file with the Department.

(b) For purposes of this section, a "substantial or material alteration" includes: the removal, creation, or relocation of an entryway, doorway, wall, or interior partition; a change in the type of activity conducted in, or the use of, an area identified in the premises diagram; or remodeling of the premises or portion of the premises in which manufacturing activities are conducted.

(c) To request approval for a change listed in subsection (a), the licensee shall submit the following:

(1) Any changes to the information and documents required under Section 40131 by email or through MCLS; and

(2) A non-refundable $700 change request processing fee for review of all documents.

(d) The request shall be evaluated on a case-by-case basis by the Department, and upon approval of the request by the Department, the licensee may begin conducting the additional manufacturing operation or make the requested change to the premises. The existing license shall be amended to reflect the change in operations, if applicable, but the date of expiration shall not change.

(e) Licensees that choose to cease operation of any activity identified in the current license application on file with the Department shall notify the Department within 10 days of cessation of the activity. License fees shall not be pro-rated or refunded upon cessation of any activity.

(f) A licensee shall notify the Department through MCLS of any changes to the product list on file with the Department and provide a new product list within 10 business days of making any change.

Note: Authority cited: Sections 26012, 26013 and 26130, Business and Professions Code. Reference: Sections 26050 and 26055, Business and Professions Code.

§ 40178. Add or Remove Owner(s) and Financial Interest Holders.

(a) The licensee shall notify the Department of the addition or removal of an owner through MCLS within 10 calendar days of the change.

(b) Any new owner shall submit the information required under Section 40130 to the Department through MCLS or on a form prescribed by the Department. The Department shall review the qualifications of the new owner in accordance with the Act and these regulations to determine whether the change would constitute grounds for denial of the license. The Department may approve the addition of the owner, deny the addition of the owner, or condition the license as appropriate, to be determined on a case-by-case basis.

(c) An owner shall notify the Department through MCLS of any change in their owner information submitted pursuant to Section 40130 within 10 calendar days of the change.

(d) A licensee shall notify the Department through MCLS of any change in the list of financial interest holders, as specified in to Section 40129(a)(9) within 10 calendar days of the change.

Note: Authority cited: Sections 26012, 26013 and 26130, Business and Professions Code. Reference: Sections 26050 and 26057, Business and Professions Code.

§ 40179. Death, Incapacity, or Insolvency of a Licensee.

(a) In the event of the death, incapacity, receivership, assignment for the benefit of creditors or other event rendering one or more owners' incapable of performing the duties associated with the license, the owner or owners' successor in interest (e.g., appointed guardian, executor, administrator, receiver, trustee, or assignee) shall notify the Department in writing within 10 business days.

(b) To continue operations or cancel the existing license, the successor in interest shall submit to the Department the following:

   (1) The name of the successor in interest;

   (2) The name of the owner(s) for which the successor in interest is succeeding and the license number;

   (3) The phone number, mailing address, and email address of the successor in interest; and

   (4) Documentation demonstrating that the owner(s) is incapable of performing the duties associated with the license such as a death certificate or a court order, and documentation demonstrating that the person making the request is the owner or owners' successor in interest such as a court order appointing guardianship, receivership, or a will or trust agreement.

(c) The Department may give the successor in interest written approval to continue operations on the licensed manufacturing premises for a period of time specified by the Department:

   (1) If the successor in interest or another person has applied for a license from the Department for the licensed premises and that application is under review;

   (2) If the successor in interest needs additional time to destroy or sell cannabis or cannabis products; or

   (3) At the discretion of the Department.

(d) The successor in interest is held subject to all terms and conditions under which a state cannabis license is held pursuant to the Act.

(e) The approval pursuant to subsection (c) creates no vested right to the issuance of a state cannabis license.

Note: Authority cited: Sections 26012, 26013 and 26130, Business and Professions Code. Reference: Section 26012, Business and Professions Code.

§ 40180. License Renewal.

(a) To apply for a license renewal, the licensee shall submit any changes to their current license application information (as required by Section 40128) on a form prescribed by the Department or through MCLS; submit a document demonstrating the gross annual revenue for the licensed premises calculated pursuant to Section 40152, such as a copy of the licensee's state tax return filed with the California Department of Tax and Fee Administration; sign the license renewal application under penalty of perjury; and submit the annual license fee as specified in Section 40150(b).

(b) To timely renew a license, a completed license renewal application and annual license fee pursuant to Section 40150(b) shall be received by the Department from the licensee no earlier than 60 calendar days before the expiration of the license and no later than 5:00 p.m. Pacific Time on the last business day before the expiration of the license if the renewal form is submitted to the Department at its office(s), or no later than 11:59 p.m. on the last business day before the expiration of the license if the renewal form is submitted through MCLS. Failure to receive a notice for license renewal does not relieve a licensee of the obligation to renew all licenses as required.

(c) In the event the license renewal application is not submitted by the deadline established in subsection (b), the licensee shall not conduct commercial cannabis activity until the license is renewed.

(d) A licensee may submit an application for license renewal up to 30 calendar days after the license expires. A late license renewal application shall be subject to a late fee of $500. A licensee that does not submit a complete license renewal application, including the late fee, to the Department within 30 calendar days after the expiration of the license shall forfeit their eligibility to apply for a license renewal and, instead, shall be required to submit a new license application.

(e) Any changes to owner and financial interest holder information shall be made in accordance with Section 40178.

(f) The Department shall notify the licensee upon approval of the license renewal application through email or MCLS. The Department shall notify a licensee of the denial of an application in accordance with Section 40167.

Note: Authority cited: Sections 26012, 26013 and 26130, Business and Professions Code. Reference: Sections 26050, 26051.5 and 26180, Business and Professions Code.

§ 40182. Disaster Relief.

(a) If a licensee is unable to comply with any licensing requirement due to a disaster, the licensee may notify the Department of this inability to comply and request relief from the specific licensing requirement.

(b) The Department may exercise its discretion to provide temporary relief from specific regulatory requirements in this chapter and from other licensing requirements when allowed by law.

(c) Temporary relief from specific licensing requirements shall be issued for a reasonable amount of time in order to allow the licensee to recover from the disaster.

(d) The Department may require that certain conditions be followed in order for a licensee to receive temporary relief from specific licensing requirements.

(e) A licensee shall not be subject to an enforcement action for a violation of a licensing requirement in which the licensee has received temporary relief.

(f) For purposes of this section, "disaster" means condition of extreme peril to the safety of persons and property within the state or a county, city and county, or city caused by such conditions such as air pollution, fire, flood, storm, tidal wave, epidemic, riot, drought, terrorism, sudden and severe energy shortage, plant or animal infestation or disease, Governor's warning of an earthquake or volcanic prediction, or an earthquake, or similar public calamity, other than conditions resulting from a labor controversy, for which the Governor has proclaimed a state of emergency in accordance with Government Code sections 8558 and 8625, or for which a local governing body has proclaimed a local emergency in accordance with Government Code sections 8558 and 8630.

(g) Notwithstanding subsection (a) of this section, if a licensee needs to move cannabis or cannabis products stored on the premises to another location immediately to prevent loss, theft, or degradation of the cannabis or cannabis products from the disaster, the licensee may move the cannabis or cannabis products without obtaining prior approval from the Department if the following conditions are met:

(1) The cannabis or cannabis products are moved to a secure location where access to the cannabis or cannabis products can be restricted to the licensees, its employees, and its contractors;

(2) The licensee notifies the Department in writing that the cannabis or cannabis products have been moved and that the licensee is requesting relief from complying with the specific licensing requirements pursuant to subsection (a) of this section within 24 hours of moving the cannabis or cannabis products;

(3) The licensee agrees to grant the Department access to the location where the cannabis or cannabis products have been moved;

(4) The licensee submits in writing to the Department within 10 days of moving the cannabis or cannabis products a request for temporary relief that clearly indicates what regulatory sections relief is requested from, the time period for which the relief is requested, and the reasons relief is needed for the specified amount of time.

Note: Authority cited: Sections 26012, 26013 and 26130, Business and Professions Code. Reference: Section 26012, Business and Professions Code.

§ 40184. Notification of Criminal Acts, Civil Judgments, and Revocation of a Local License, Permit, or Other Authorization after Licensure.

(a) A licensee shall notify the Department in writing of a criminal conviction of any owner, either by mail or electronic mail, within 48 hours of the conviction. The written notification to the Department shall include the date of conviction, the court case number, the name of the court in which the owner was convicted, and the specific offense(s) for which the owner was convicted.

(b) A licensee shall notify the Department in writing of a civil penalty or judgment rendered against the licensee or any owner in their individual capacity, either by mail or electronic mail, within 48 hours of delivery of the verdict or entry of judgment, whichever is sooner. The written notification to the Department shall include the date of verdict or entry of judgment, the court case number, the name of the court in which the matter was adjudicated, and a description of the civil penalty or judgement rendered against the licensee or owner.

(c) A licensee shall notify the Department in writing of the revocation of a local license, permit, or other authorization, either by mail or electronic mail, within 48 hours of receiving notice of the revocation. The written notification shall include the name of the local agency involved, a written explanation of the proceeding or enforcement action, and the specific violation(s) that led to revocation.

(d) A licensee shall notify the Department in writing of an administrative order for violations of labor standards against the licensee or any owner in their individual capacity, either by mail or electronic mail, within 48 hours of delivery of the order. The written notification shall include the date of the order, the name of the agency issuing the order, and a description of the administrative penalty or judgment against the licensee.

Note: Authority cited: Sections 26012, 26013 and 26130, Business and Professions Code. Reference: Section 26031, Business and Professions Code.

ARTICLE 6. SHARED-USE FACILITIES

§ 40190. Definitions.

For purposes of this Article, the following definitions shall apply:

(a) "Common-use area" means any area of the manufacturer's registered shared-use facility, including equipment that is available for use by more than one licensee, provided that the use of a common-use area is limited to one licensee at a time.

(b) "Designated area" means the area of the manufacturer's registered shared-use facility that is designated by the primary licensee for the sole and exclusive use of a Type S licensee, including storage of the Type S licensee's cannabis, cannabis concentrates, and cannabis products.

(c) "Primary licensee" means the Type 7, Type 6, or Type N licensee that has registered and been approved to operate its licensed premises as a shared-use facility.

(d) "Shared-use facility" means a manufacturing premises operated by a Type 7, Type 6, or Type N licensee in which Type S licensees are authorized to conduct manufacturing operations.

(e) "Use agreement" means a written agreement between a primary licensee and a Type S applicant or licensee that specifies the designated area of the Type S licensee, the days and hours in which the Type S licensee is assigned to use the common-use area, any allocation of responsibility for compliance pursuant to Section 40196, and an acknowledgement that the Type S licensee has sole and exclusive use of the common-use area during the Type S licensee's assigned time period.

Note: Authority cited: Sections 26012, 26013 and 26130, Business and Professions Code. Reference: Sections 26001, 26050, 26051.5 and 26130, Business and Professions Code.

§ 40191. Type S License.

(a) Applications for a Type S license shall:

> (1) Be submitted in accordance with Section 40128;

> (2) Include the license number and address of the registered shared-use facility at which the applicant will conduct manufacturing operations;

> (3) Include a copy of the use agreement signed by both the Type S applicant and the primary licensee; and

> (4) On the premises diagram submitted pursuant to Section 40131(i), indicate the designated area to be used by the Type S applicant and detail where the applicant will store its cannabis, cannabis concentrates, and cannabis products.

(b) A Type S license shall only be available to applicants with a gross annual revenue of less than $1,000,000 as calculated pursuant to Section 40152.

(c) A Type S licensee may conduct the following operational activities:

> (1) Infusions, as defined in Section 40100(v);

> (2) Packaging and labeling of cannabis products; and

> (3) Extractions with butter or food-grade oils, provided that the resulting extract or concentrate shall be used solely in the manufacture of the Type S licensee's infused product, and shall not be sold to any other licensee.

Note: Authority cited: Sections 26012, 26013 and 26130, Business and Professions Code. Reference: Sections 26050, 26051.5 and 26130, Business and Professions Code.

§ 40192. Registration to Operate a Shared-Use Facility.

(a) No licensee shall operate as a shared-use facility without prior approval by the Department.

(b) To register as a shared-use facility, a Type 7, Type 6, or Type N licensee shall submit the following to the Department through MCLS:

    (1) A copy of the license, permit, or other authorization issued by the local jurisdiction that enables the licensee to operate as a shared-use facility. The Department shall contact the applicable local jurisdiction to confirm the validity of the authorization upon receipt of the application for registration. If the local jurisdiction does not respond within 10 calendar days, the Department shall consider the authorization valid.

    (2) A registration form prescribed by the Department, which includes the following information:

        (A) The proposed occupancy schedule that specifies the days and hours the common-use area will be available for use by Type S licensees and when the common-use area will be used by the primary licensee. The occupancy schedule shall allow for maintenance and sanitizing between uses by individual licensees.

        (B) A diagram indicating:

            (i) Each designated area for Type S licensee(s).

            (ii) The common-use area, including identification of any shared equipment.

(c) The Department shall notify the Type 7, Type 6, or Type N licensee upon approval of the registration to operate as a shared-use facility. Notification shall be made through MCLS.

(d) At least one business day prior to a Type S licensee commencing manufacturing operations at a registered shared-use facility, the primary licensee shall provide written notification to the Department. The notification to the Department shall include the Type S licensee's business name, contact person, contact phone number, and license number. The primary licensee shall also provide an updated occupancy schedule that includes the Type S licensee and an updated diagram that specifies the Type S licensee's designated area. Notification shall be provided by email or through MCLS.

(e) A primary licensee that wishes to discontinue operation as a shared-use facility may cancel its registration by providing written notice to the Department and each Type S licensee authorized to use the shared-use facility at least 30 calendar days prior to the effective date of the cancellation.

Note: Authority cited: Sections 26012, 26013 and 26130, Business and Professions Code. Reference: Sections 26051.5, 26055 and 26130, Business and Professions Code.

§ 40194. Shared-Use Facility Conditions for Operation.

(a) A primary licensee shall operate the shared-use facility in accordance with the conditions of operation specified in this section.

(b) Each Type S licensee shall be assigned a "designated area" that, at minimum:

    (1) Is for exclusive use by the Type S licensee;

    (2) Provides an area for storage that is secure, fixed in place, locked with a commercial-grade lock, and accessible only to the Type S licensee for storage of that Type S licensee's cannabis, cannabis concentrates, and cannabis products.

(c) Any part of the premises used for manufacturing activities that is a common-use area shall be occupied by only one licensee at a time by restricting the time period that each licensee may use the common-use area. During the assigned time period, one licensee shall have sole and exclusive occupancy of the common-use area.

(d) The use of the shared-use facility shall be restricted to the primary licensee and the Type S licensees authorized by the Department to use the shared-use facility.

(e) Any cannabis product or other materials remaining after a Type S licensee ceases operation and discontinues use of its designated area shall be considered cannabis waste and disposed of by the primary licensee consistent with the requirements of the Act and regulations.

(f) The shared-use facility shall meet all applicable requirements of the Act and regulations.

(g) The occupancy schedule shall be prominently posted near the entrance to the shared-use facility.

(h) The primary licensee may conduct manufacturing activities as permitted under its Type 7, Type 6, or Type N license and may use the common-use area during its scheduled time period.

Note: Authority cited: Sections 26012, 26013 and 26130, Business and Professions Code. Reference: Sections 26011.5 and 26130, Business and Professions Code.

§ 40196. Shared-Use Facility Compliance Requirements.

(a) As part of the use agreement, the primary licensee and Type S licensee(s) may allocate responsibility for providing and maintaining commonly used equipment and services, including, but not limited to security systems, fire monitoring and protection services, and waste disposal service. However, such agreement is not binding on the Department and the Department may take enforcement action against either the primary licensee or Type S licensee(s), regardless of the allocation of responsibility in the use agreement.

(b) A primary licensee or a Type S licensee is liable for any violation found at the shared-use facility during that licensee's scheduled occupancy or within that licensee's designated area. However, a violation of any provision of the Act or regulations may be deemed a violation for which each Type S licensee and the primary licensee are responsible. In the event of a recall or embargo of a cannabis product produced at a shared-use facility, the Department, in its sole discretion, may include any or all cannabis products produced at the shared-use facility.

(c) The occupancy schedule and designated area for a Type S licensee shall not be altered without prior notification to the Department. Prior to making any changes to the occupancy schedule or the designated area, written notification shall be submitted to the Department that includes the intended changes. Notification shall be submitted by email or through MCLS.

Note: Authority cited: Sections 26012, 26013 and 26130, Business and Professions Code. Reference: Sections 26011.5, 26055 and 26130, Business and Professions Code.

SUBCHAPTER 3. REQUIREMENTS OF OPERATION

ARTICLE 1. SAFETY AND SECURITY

§ 40200. Security Plan.

Every licensee shall develop and implement a written security plan. At a minimum, the security plan shall include a description of the security measures to:

(a) Prevent access to the manufacturing premises by unauthorized persons and protect the physical safety of employees. This includes, but is not limited to:

(1) Establishing physical barriers to secure perimeter access and all points of entry into a manufacturing premises (such as locking primary entrances with commercial-grade, non-residential door locks, or providing fencing around the grounds and driveway, and securing any secondary entrances including windows, roofs, or ventilation systems);

(2) Installing a security alarm system to notify and record incident(s) where physical barriers have been breached;

(3) Establishing an identification and sign-in/sign-out procedure for authorized personnel, suppliers, and visitors;

(4) Maintaining the premises such that visibility and security monitoring of the premises is possible; and

(5) Establishing procedures for the investigation of suspicious activities.

(b) Prevent against theft or loss of cannabis and cannabis products. This includes but is not limited to:

(1) Establishing an inventory system to track cannabis and cannabis products and the personnel responsible for processing it throughout the manufacturing process;

(2) Limiting access of personnel within the premises to those areas necessary to complete job duties, and to those time-frames specifically scheduled for completion of job duties, including access by outside vendors, suppliers, contractors or other individuals conducting business with the licensee that requires access to the premises;

(3) Supervising tasks or processes with high potential for diversion, including the loading and unloading of cannabis transportation vehicles; and

(4) Providing areas in which personnel may store and access personal items that are separate from the manufacturing areas.

(c) Secure and back up electronic records in a manner that prevents unauthorized access and that ensures the integrity of the records is maintained.

Note: Authority cited: Sections 26012, 26013 and 26130, Business and Professions Code. Reference: Sections 26011.5 and 26051.5, Business and Professions Code.

§ 40205. Video Surveillance.

(a) At a minimum, licensed premises shall have a digital video surveillance system with a minimum camera resolution of 1280 x 720 pixels. The video surveillance system shall be able to effectively and clearly record images of the area under surveillance.

(b) To the extent reasonably possible, all video surveillance cameras shall be installed in a manner that prevents intentional obstruction, tampering with, or disabling.

(c) Areas that shall be recorded on the video surveillance system include the following:

(1) Areas where cannabis or cannabis products are weighed, packed, stored, quarantined, loaded and unloaded for transportation, prepared, or moved within the premises;

(2) Limited-access areas;

(3) Security rooms;

(4) Areas containing surveillance-system storage devices, which shall contain at least one camera to record the access points to such an area; and

(5) The interior and exterior of all entrances and exits to the premises.

(d) The surveillance system shall record continuously 24 hours per day and at a minimum speed of 15 frames per second.

(e) Any on-site surveillance system storage devices shall be located in secure rooms or areas of the premises in an access-controlled environment.

(f) The licensee shall ensure that all surveillance recordings are kept for a minimum of 90 days.

(g) All video surveillance recordings shall be available on the licensed premises and are subject to inspection by the Department and shall also be copied and sent, or otherwise provided, to the Department upon request.

(h) The video recordings shall display the current date and time of recorded events. Time is to be measured in accordance with the U.S. National Institute of Standards and Technology standards. The displayed date and time shall not significantly obstruct the view of recorded images.

(i) If multiple licensed premises are contained within the same building, a single video surveillance system covering the entire building may be used by all of the licensees under the following conditions:

(1) Each applicant or licensee shall disclose on their premises diagram where the surveillance recordings are stored;

(2) Each applicant or licensee shall include in their security operating procedures an explanation of how the video surveillance system will be shared, including who is responsible for monitoring the video footage and storing any video recordings;

(3) All licensees shall have immediate access to the surveillance recordings to produce them pursuant to the requirements of this section;

(4) All licensees shall be held responsible and subject to discipline for any violations of the video surveillance requirements.

Note: Authority cited: Sections 26012, 26013 and 26130, Business and Professions Code. Reference: Sections 26011.5 and 26070, Business and Professions Code.

§ 40207. Notification of Theft, Loss, or Diversion.

If a licensee finds evidence of theft or diversion of cannabis or cannabis products, the licensee shall report the theft or diversion to the Department and local law enforcement within 24 hours of the discovery. The notice to the Department shall be in writing and shall include the date and time of the incident: a description of the incident, including items that were taken or missing; and the name of the local law enforcement agency that was notified of the incident.

Note: Authority cited: Sections 26012, 26013 and 26130, Business and Professions Code. Reference: Sections 26011.5 and 26070, Business and Professions Code.

ARTICLE 2. EXTRACTIONS

§ 40220. Permissible Extractions.

(a) Except as provided in subsection (b), cannabis extraction shall only be conducted using the following methods:

(1) Mechanical extraction;

(2) Chemical extraction using a nonvolatile solvent such as a nonhydrocarbon-based or other solvent such as water, vegetable glycerin, vegetable oils, animal fats, or glycerin. Nonhydrocarbon-based solvents shall be food grade;

(3) Chemical extraction using a professional closed loop CO_2 gas extraction system. CO_2 gas used for extraction shall be food grade;

(4) Chemical extraction using a volatile solvent, as defined in Section 40100(xx), using a professional closed loop extraction system; or

(5) Any other method authorized by the Department pursuant to subsection (b).

(b) To request authorization from the Department to conduct cannabis extraction using a method other than those specified in paragraphs (1) through (4) of subsection (a), the applicant or licensee shall submit a detailed description of the extraction method, including any documentation that validates the method and any safety procedures to be utilized to mitigate any risk to public or worker health and safety.

Note: Authority cited: Sections 26012, 26013 and 26130, Business and Professions Code. Reference: Sections 26011.5 and 26130, Business and Professions Code.

§ 40222. Volatile Solvent Extractions.

Chemical extractions using volatile solvents shall be subject to the following requirements:

(a) Hydrocarbon-based solvents shall be at least 99 percent purity;

(b) All extractions shall be performed in a closed loop extraction system as described in Section 40225; and

(c) No volatile solvent extraction operations shall occur in an area zoned as residential.

Note: Authority cited: Sections 26012, 26013 and 26130, Business and Professions Code. Reference: Sections 26011.5, 26105 and 26130, Business and Professions Code.

§ 40223. Ethanol Extractions.

(a) Ethanol used for extractions or for post-extraction processing shall be food-grade.

(b) Ethanol extraction operations shall be approved by the local fire code official and shall be operated in accordance with applicable Division of Occupational Safety and Health (Cal/OSHA) regulations and any other state and local requirements.

Note: Authority cited: Sections 26012, 26013 and 26130, Business and Professions Code. Reference: Sections 26011.5 and 26130, Business and Professions Code.

§ 40225. Closed-Loop Extraction System Requirements.

(a) Chemical extractions using CO_2; a volatile solvent; or chlorofluorocarbon, hydrocarbon, or other fluorinated gas shall be conducted in a professional closed loop extraction system designed to recover the solvents. The system shall be commercially manufactured and bear a permanently affixed and visible serial number. The system shall be certified by a California-licensed engineer that the system was commercially manufactured, safe for use with the intended solvent, and built to codes of recognized and generally accepted good engineering practices, such as:

(1) The American Society of Mechanical Engineers (ASME);

(2) American National Standards Institute (ANSI);

(3) Underwriters Laboratories (UL); or

(4) The American Society for Testing and Materials (ASTM).

(b) Professional closed loop systems, other equipment used, the extraction operation, and facilities must be approved for use by the local fire code official and comply with any required fire, safety, and building code requirements related to the processing, handling, and storage of the applicable solvent or gas.

(c) The certification document required pursuant to subsection (a) shall contain the signature and stamp of a California-licensed professional engineer and the serial number of the extraction unit being certified.

(d) The licensee shall establish and implement written procedures to document that the closed loop extraction system is maintained in accordance with the equipment manufacturer specifications and to ensure routine verification that the system is operating in accordance with specifications and continues to comply with fire, safety, and building code requirements.

(e) A licensee shall develop standard operating procedures, good manufacturing practices, and a training plan prior to producing extracts. Any personnel using solvents or gases in a closed loop system to create extracts must be trained on how to use the system, have direct access to applicable safety data sheets, and handle and store solvents and gases safely.

(f) The extraction operation shall be operated in an environment with proper ventilation, controlling all sources of ignition where a flammable atmosphere is or may be present, and shall be operated in accordance with applicable Division of Occupational Safety and Health (Cal/OSHA) regulations and any other state and local requirements.

(g) No closed loop extraction system operation shall occur in an area zoned as residential.

Note: Authority cited: Sections 26012, 26013 and 26130, Business and Professions Code. Reference: Sections 26011.5, 26105 and 26130, Business and Professions Code.

ARTICLE 3. GOOD MANUFACTURING PRACTICES

§ 40230. Manufacturing Practices Definitions.

In addition to the definitions in section 26001 of the Act and Section 40100 of these regulations, the following definitions shall govern the construction of this article:

(a) "Allergen cross-contact" means the unintentional incorporation of a food allergen into a cannabis product.

(b) "Component" means any substance or item intended for use in the manufacture of a cannabis product, including those substances or items that are not intended to appear in the final form of the product. "Component" includes cannabis, cannabis products used as ingredients, raw materials, other ingredients, and processing aids.

(c) "Contact surface" means any surface that contacts cannabis products and cannabis product components and those surfaces from which drainage, or other transfer, onto the cannabis product or cannabis product components, occurs during the normal course of operations. Examples of contact surfaces include containers, utensils, tables, and equipment.

(d) "Easily cleanable" means a characteristic of a surface that allows effective removal of soil, food residue, or other organic or inorganic materials by normal cleaning methods.

(e) "Environmental pathogen" means a pathogen capable of surviving and persisting within the manufacturing environment such that cannabis products may be contaminated and may result in illness if consumed or used without treatment to significantly minimize the environmental pathogen. Examples of environmental pathogens include Listeria monocytogenes and Salmonella spp. but do not include the spores of pathogenic spore-forming bacteria.

(f) "Hazard" means any biological, chemical, radiological, or physical agent that has the potential to cause illness or injury.

(g) "Holding" means storage of cannabis or cannabis products and includes activities performed incidental to storage of a cannabis product and activities performed as a practical necessity for the distribution of that cannabis product.

(h) "Microorganisms" means yeasts, molds, bacteria, viruses, protozoa, and microscopic parasites and includes species that are pathogens. The term "undesirable microorganisms" includes those microorganisms that are pathogens, that subject a cannabis product to decomposition, that indicate that a cannabis product is contaminated with filth, or that otherwise may cause a cannabis product to be adulterated.

(i) "Monitor" means to conduct a planned sequence of observations or measurements to assess whether preventive measures are operating as intended.

(j) "Pathogen" means a microorganism that can cause illness or injury.

(k) "Pest" means an undesired insect, rodent, nematode (small worm), fungus, bird, vertebrate, invertebrate, weed, virus, bacteria, or other microorganism (except microorganisms on or in humans or animals) injurious to health or the environment.

(l) "Potable" means water that meets the requirements of Health and Safety Code section 113869.

(m) "Preventive measures" means those risk-based, reasonably appropriate procedures, practices, and processes that a person knowledgeable about the safe manufacturing, processing, packing, or holding of food would employ to significantly minimize or prevent the hazards identified pursuant to a product quality plan as specified in Section 40253.

(n) "Processing aid" means any substance that is added to a cannabis product during manufacture but is removed in some manner from the cannabis product before it is packaged in its finished form. This includes substances that are converted into constituents normally present in the product, and do not significantly increase the amount of the constituent naturally found in the product. This also includes substances that are added to a product for their technical or functional effect in the processing but are present in the finished product at insignificant levels and do not have any technical or functional effect in that product.

(o) "Qualified individual" means a person who has the education, training, or experience (or a combination thereof) necessary to manufacture quality cannabis products as appropriate to the individual's assigned duties. A qualified individual may be, but is not required to be, an employee of the licensee.

(p) "Quality control" means a planned and systematic operation or procedure for ensuring the quality of a cannabis product.

(q) "Quality control operation" means a planned and systematic procedure for taking all actions necessary to prevent cannabis product(s) from being adulterated or misbranded.

(r) "Quality control personnel" means any person, persons, or group, designated by the licensee to be responsible for quality control operations.

(s) "Raw material" means any unprocessed material in its raw or natural state that is intended to become part of the components of a cannabis product.

(t) "Sanitize" means to treat cleaned surfaces by a process that is effective in destroying vegetative cells of pathogens, and in substantially reducing numbers of other undesirable microorganisms, but without adversely affecting the product or its safety for the consumer.

(u) "Smooth" means any of the following:

(1) A contact surface that is free of pits, pinholes, cracks, crevices, inclusions, rough edges, and other surface imperfections detectable by visual or tactile inspection.

(2) A floor, wall, or ceiling having an even or level surface with no roughness or projections that render it difficult to clean.

(v) "Utensil" means an implement, tool, or container used in the storage, preparation, manufacture, or processing of cannabis and cannabis products. In addition to kitchenware, examples of utensils include, but are not limited to, gloves, screens, sieves, implements to create pre-rolls, buckets, and scissors.

(w) "Validate" means obtaining and evaluating scientific and technical evidence that a control measure, combination of control measures, or quality control procedures as a whole, when properly implemented, is capable of ensuring the quality of a cannabis product or effectively controlling an identified hazard.

(x) "Verification" means the application of methods, procedures, tests, or other evaluations, in addition to monitoring, to determine whether a control measure or combination of control measures is or has been operating as intended and to establish the validity of the quality control procedures.

(y) "Yield" means the quantity of a particular cannabis product expected to be produced at a given step of manufacture or packaging, as identified in the master manufacturing protocol. The expected yield is based upon the quantity of components or packaging to be used, in the absence of any loss or error in actual production. "Actual yield" means the quantity of a particular cannabis product that is actually produced at a given step of manufacture or packaging that is recorded in the batch production record.

Note: Authority cited: Sections 26012, 26013 and 26130, Business and Professions Code. Reference: Sections 26001 and 26130, Business and Professions Code.

§ 40232. Requirements for Personnel. [Repealed]

§ 40234. Grounds. [Repealed]

§ 40235. Quality Control Program.

(a) Each licensee is responsible for implementing a quality control program to ensure that cannabis products are not adulterated or misbranded. The quality control program shall include quality control operations for all of the following:

(1) The grounds, building, and manufacturing premises, as specified in Section 40240;

(2) Equipment and utensils, as specified in Section 40243;

(3) Personnel, as specified in Section 40246;

(4) Cannabis product components, as specified in Section 40248; and

(5) Manufacturing processes and procedures, as specified in Section 40250.

(b) Quality control shall be under the supervision of one or more qualified individuals assigned responsibility for this function.

(c) For purposes of this article, for those requirements that are contained in the Health and Safety Code, use of the term "food" shall include cannabis, cannabis products, components, and contact surfaces.

Note: Authority cited: Sections 26012, 26013 and 26130, Business and Professions Code. Reference: Sections 26011.5 and 26131, Business and Professions Code.

§ 40236. Premises Construction and Design. [Repealed]

§ 40238. Sanitary Operations. [Repealed]

§ 40240. Grounds, Building, and Manufacturing Premises.

(a) Exterior facility and grounds. The licensee shall ensure the facility exterior and grounds under the licensee's control meet the following minimum standards:

(1) Grounds shall be equipped with draining areas in order to prevent pooled or standing water;

(2) Weeds, grass, and vegetation shall be cut within the immediate vicinity of the cannabis manufacturing premises, litter and waste shall be removed, and equipment shall be stored in order to minimize the potential for the grounds to constitute an attractant, breeding place, or harborage for pests;

(3) Roads, yards, and parking lots shall be maintained so that these areas do not constitute a source of contamination in areas where cannabis products are handled or transported;

(4) Openings into the building (such as windows, exhaust fans, ventilation ducts, or plumbing vent pipes) shall be screened, sealed, or otherwise protected to minimize potential for pests to enter the building;

(5) Waste treatment and disposal systems shall be provided and maintained so as to prevent contamination in areas where cannabis products may be exposed to such a system's waste or waste by-products.

(6) The licensee shall implement precautions within the premises such as inspection or extermination if the premises is bordered by grounds outside the licensee's control that are not maintained in the manner described in paragraphs (1) through (5) of this subsection, in order to eliminate any pests, dirt, and filth that pose a source of cannabis product contamination. Any use of insecticide, rodenticide, or other pesticide within the premises shall meet the requirements of Health and Safety Code section 114254.

(b) Interior facility. The licensee shall ensure construction, design, and maintenance of the interior of the manufacturing premises as follows:

(1) Walls, ceilings, and floors. Walls, ceilings, and floors shall be constructed of material that is smooth, nonporous, easily cleanable, corrosion-resistant, and suitable to the activity that will be conducted. Fixtures, ducts, and pipes shall not pose a source of drip or condensate that may contaminate cannabis products, contact surfaces or packaging material.

(2) Lighting. Interior facility lighting shall meet the requirements of subdivisions (a)(1) and (3), (b)(3) and (4), and (c) of section 114252 of the Health and Safety Code. Interior facility lighting shall also meet the requirements for shatter-resistant lighting in section 114252.1 of the Health and Safety Code. The requirements of Health and Safety Code section 114252.1, subdivision (a), shall also apply to all areas where glass breakage may result in the contamination of exposed cannabis, components or cannabis products at any step of preparation.

(3) Plumbing system and fixtures.

(A) Water supply. Running water shall be supplied as required by Health and Safety Code section 114192 in all areas where required for the processing of cannabis products; in all areas used for the cleaning of equipment, utensils, and packaging materials; and for employee sanitary facilities. Any water that contacts cannabis, components, cannabis products, contact surfaces, or packaging materials shall be potable.

(B) Plumbing. Plumbing systems shall meet the requirements of Health and Safety Code section 114190.

(C) Sewage disposal. The sewage system shall be maintained and kept in good repair so that it does not pose a potential source of contamination to cannabis products, contact surfaces, or packaging materials.

(D) Toilet facilities. Each manufacturing premises shall provide employees with access to toilet facilities that meet the requirements of Health and Safety Code section 114250. Toilet facilities shall be kept clean and shall not pose a potential source of contamination of cannabis, components, cannabis products, contact surfaces, or packaging materials.

(E) Hand-washing facilities. Each manufacturing premises shall provide hand-washing facilities that meet the requirements of Health and Safety Code section 113953, subdivision (a) through (d).

(F) Waste disposal. The premises shall provide waste disposal in accordance with Health and Safety Code sections 114244(a), 114244(c), and 114245.1. Cannabis waste shall be disposed of in accordance with Section 40290 of these regulations.

(4) Ventilation. Ventilation systems shall meet the requirements of Health and Safety Code sections 114149 and 114149.3.

(5) Cleaning and maintenance. The premises, including any fixtures, and other physical facilities therein, shall be maintained in a clean and sanitary condition and kept in good repair so as to prevent cannabis products from becoming adulterated, and shall meet the requirements of Health and Safety Code section 114257.1.

(A) The premises shall have a janitorial facility that meets the requirements of Health and Safety Code section 114279(a).

(B) Cleaning equipment and supplies shall be stored in a manner that meets the requirements of Health and Safety Code section 114281.

(C) Poisonous or toxic materials such as cleaning compounds, sanitizing agents, and pesticide chemicals that are necessary for premises and equipment maintenance and operation shall be handled and stored in a manner that meets the requirements of Health and Safety Code sections 114254.1, 114254.2 and 114254.3.

Note: Authority cited: Sections 26012, 26013 and 26130, Business and Professions Code. Reference: Sections 26011.5 and 26131, Business and Professions Code.

§ 40242. Equipment and Utensils. [Repealed]

§ 40243. Equipment and Utensils.

Licensees shall utilize equipment and utensils that meet the following minimum requirements:

(a) Design. Equipment and utensils shall meet the requirements of Health and Safety Code sections 114130.1, 114130.2, 114130.3, and 114130.4 and shall be used in accordance with their operating instructions to avoid the adulteration of cannabis products with lubricants, fuel, metal fragments, contaminated water, or any other contaminants.

(b) Installation. Equipment shall be installed so as to allow the cleaning and maintenance of the equipment and of adjacent spaces. Equipment that is not easily moveable shall meet the requirements of Health and Safety Code section 114169.

(c) Cleaning, sanitizing, and maintenance. The quality control program for cleaning, sanitizing, and maintenance of equipment and utensils shall include the following elements, at minimum:

(1) A detailed, written procedure for cleaning, sanitizing, and maintaining (including calibrating) equipment and utensils;

(2) A schedule for cleaning, sanitizing, and maintaining equipment and utensils;

(3) A procedure, including a log, for documentation of the date and time of maintenance, cleaning, and sanitizing of equipment and utensils; and

(4) A detailed, written procedure for storing cleaned and sanitized equipment and utensils in a manner to protect the equipment and utensils from contamination.

Note: Authority cited: Sections 26012, 26013 and 26130, Business and Professions Code. Reference: Sections 26011.5 and 26131, Business and Professions Code.

§ 40246. Personnel.

Licensees shall implement written procedures for personnel that include, at minimum:

(a) Disease control. Any individual who by medical examination or supervisory observation is shown to have, or appears to have, an illness specified in Health and Safety Code section 113949.2(a), or an open lesion (such as boils, sores, cut, rash, or infected wounds) unless covered in accordance with the requirements of Health and Safety Code section 113949.2(b), shall be excluded from any manufacturing operations until their health condition is corrected. Personnel shall be instructed to report such health conditions to their supervisors.

(b) Cleanliness. All individuals working in direct contact with cannabis products, contact surfaces, and packaging materials shall maintain personal cleanliness in order to protect against allergen cross-contact and contamination of cannabis products while on duty. The methods for maintaining personal cleanliness include:

(1) Wearing clean outer clothing to protect against allergen cross-contact and contamination of cannabis products, contact surfaces, and packaging materials;

(2) Washing hands thoroughly in a hand-washing facility that meets the requirements of Section 40240 before starting work, after each absence from the work station, and at any time when the hands may have become soiled or contaminated;

(3) Removing all unsecured jewelry and other objects that might fall into cannabis products, equipment, or containers. Hand jewelry that cannot be sanitized shall be removed during periods in which cannabis products are manipulated by hand. If such hand jewelry cannot be removed, it shall be covered by material which can be maintained in an intact, clean, and sanitary condition and which effectively protects against the contamination by these objects of the cannabis products, contact surfaces, or packaging materials;

(4) Maintaining any gloves, if they are used in cannabis product handling, in an intact, clean, and sanitary condition;

(5) Wearing hair nets, caps, beard covers, or other hair restraints that are designed and worn to prevent hair contact with cannabis, cannabis products, contact surfaces, or packaging materials;

(6) Storing clothing and personal belongings in areas separate from those where cannabis products are exposed or where equipment or utensils are washed;

(7) Confining the following activities to areas separate from those where cannabis products may be exposed or where equipment or utensils are washed: eating food, chewing gum, drinking beverages, and using tobacco;

(c) Nothing in this section prohibits a licensee from establishing any other precautions to protect against allergen cross-contact and against contamination of cannabis products, contact surfaces, or packaging materials by microorganisms or foreign substances (including perspiration, hair, cosmetics, tobacco, chemicals, and medicines applied to the skin).

Note: Authority cited: Sections 26012, 26013 and 26130, Business and Professions Code. Reference: Sections 26011.5 and 26131, Business and Professions Code.

§ 40248. Cannabis Product Components.

(a) In order to prevent adulteration of cannabis products, licensees shall establish and implement written policies and procedures to ensure and maintain the quality of product components.

(b) Components are subject to the following minimum requirements:

(1) Raw materials and other components shall be inspected upon intake to ensure that they are clean and suitable for processing into cannabis products, and shall be stored under conditions that protect against allergen cross-contact and contamination, and in such a way as to minimize deterioration.

(2) Raw materials shall be washed or cleaned as necessary to remove soil and other visible contaminants. Water used for washing, rinsing, or conveying cannabis product ingredients shall be potable.

(3) Raw materials and other components shall not contain levels of microorganisms that render the cannabis product injurious to human health, or shall be pasteurized or otherwise treated during manufacturing so that they no longer contain levels of microorganisms that would cause the cannabis product to be adulterated.

(4) Raw materials and other components susceptible to contamination with aflatoxin or other natural toxins, pests, or extraneous material shall not exceed generally acceptable limits set by the U.S. Food and Drug Administration in the Defect Levels Handbook (Rev. February 2005), which is hereby incorporated by reference, before these raw materials or other ingredients are incorporated into finished cannabis products.

(5) Raw materials and other components shall be held in containers designed and constructed so as to protect against allergen cross-contact or contamination, and shall be held at such temperature and relative humidity and in such a manner as to prevent the cannabis products from becoming adulterated.

(6) Frozen raw materials and other components shall be kept frozen. If thawing is required prior to use, it shall be done in a manner that prevents the raw materials and other ingredients from becoming adulterated.

(7) Raw materials and other components that are food allergens shall be identified and held in a manner that prevents cross-contact with other raw materials or ingredients.

(c) Holding and storage of raw materials and other components shall meet the requirements of section 114047, subdivisions (a) and (b), section 114049, and section 114051 of the Health and Safety Code.

Note: Authority cited: Sections 26012, 26013 and 26130, Business and Professions Code. Reference: Sections 26011.5 and 26131, Business and Professions Code.

§ 40250. Manufacturing Processes and Procedures.

(a) The licensee shall implement and maintain manufacturing processes and procedures that ensure cannabis product quality. Manufacturing processes and procedures shall be identified through a product quality plan, as described in Section 40253.

(b) The licensee shall maintain written master manufacturing protocols, as described in Section 40255, for each unique formulation of cannabis product manufactured to ensure only intended components are included and that the cannabis product is packaged and labeled in accordance with product specifications and these regulations.

(c) The licensee shall maintain written batch production records, as described in Section 40258, to document the production process and, if needed, to verify that the established processes and procedures, including the preventive measures and master manufacturing protocol, were implemented correctly.

(d) All manufacturing records are subject to inspection by the Department, its inspectors and agents.

Note: Authority cited: Sections 26012, 26013 and 26130, Business and Professions Code. Reference: Sections 26011.5 and 26131, Business and Professions Code.

§ 40252. Quality of Raw Materials and Ingredients. [Repealed]

§ 40253. Product Quality Plan.

(a) Licensees shall create and implement a written product quality plan for each type of product manufactured at the premises. The product quality plan shall address the hazards associated with the premises or the manufacturing process that, if not properly mitigated, may cause the product to be adulterated or misbranded, or may cause the product to fail laboratory testing or quality assurance review.

(b) To create the product quality plan, licensees shall conduct a comprehensive assessment of the overall manufacturing process, identifying each step from component intake through transfer of product from the premises, to determine the potential risks associated with each step, the preventive measures to mitigate the potential risks identified, the methods to evaluate and monitor the effectiveness of the preventive measures, and action to take if a preventive measure was unsuccessful.

(c) The product quality plan shall evaluate the following potential risks to cannabis product quality:

(1) Biological hazards, including microbiological hazards;

(2) Chemical hazards, including radiological hazards, pesticide contamination, solvent or other residue, natural toxins, decomposition, or allergens;

(3) Physical hazards, such as stone, glass, metal fragments, hair, or insects;

(4) Process failures that may lead to product contamination, allergen cross-contact, packaging errors, labeling errors, or other errors affecting cannabis product quality.

(d) The product quality plan shall identify the preventive measure that will be implemented to mitigate each potential risk identified pursuant to subsection (c). Examples of preventive measures include, but are not limited to:

(1) Cleaning and sanitizing of equipment and utensils to mitigate against risk of microbiological hazards;

(2) Conducting in-house testing of raw cannabis to mitigate against the risk of pesticide contamination;

(3) Establishing an allergen control program to ensure that allergen cross-contact does not occur between product types;

(4) Implementing procedures to ensure homogeneity of cannabinoids into a cannabis product to mitigate against the risk of a non-homogeneous product.

(e) The product quality plan shall identify methods to evaluate and monitor the effectiveness of the preventive measures in mitigating the potential risks identified in subsection (c). Methods for evaluation and monitoring of preventive measures include, but are not limited to, the following:

(1) Review of test results conducted to determine contamination such as pesticide residue;

(2) Maintaining and reviewing cleaning, sanitizing, or maintenance logs to verify such actions have been taken;

(3) Conducting environmental testing to determine if equipment or utensils are contaminated with pathogens;

(4) Monitoring the temperature of raw materials that need to be held below 41 degrees Fahrenheit to prevent microbial contamination.

(f) The product quality plan shall identify actions to be taken if the evaluation and monitoring of the preventive measure indicates that the risk was not properly mitigated. The corrective action shall be specific to the type of product under evaluation and the specific risk to be mitigated. Examples of corrective actions that may be taken include, but are not limited to:

(1) Destruction of product components or finished product;

(2) Further processing of cannabis extract to remove impurities;

(3) Reworking the unfinished product to further homogenize the cannabinoids.

(g) The licensee shall maintain the product quality plans and documentation of preventive measures, monitoring results, and corrective actions and make the records available to the Department upon the Department's request, including during the Department's onsite inspection of the premises. Nothing in this chapter requires the disclosure of product quality plans other than to the Department and its inspectors and agents. The licensee may consider the product quality plan subject to trade secret protection.

Note: Authority cited: Sections 26012, 26013 and 26130, Business and Professions Code. Reference: Sections 26011.5 and 26131, Business and Professions Code.

§ 40254. Manufacturing Operations. [Repealed]

§ 40255. Master Manufacturing Protocol.

(a) The licensee shall establish and follow a written master manufacturing protocol for each unique formulation of cannabis product manufactured, and for each batch size, in order to mitigate against the potential for adulteration through incorporation of incorrect amounts of cannabinoids, unintended ingredients, or hazards identified in the product quality plan; against the potential for misbranding through incorporation of ingredients not identified on the label or the mislabeling of product; and to ensure uniformity in finished batches and across all batches produced.

(b) The master manufacturing protocol shall include:

(1) The name and intended cannabinoid(s) concentration of the cannabis product to be manufactured;

(2) A complete list of components to be used;

(3) The weight or measure of each component to be used. The master manufacturing protocol for any given product may include the ability to adjust the weight or measure of cannabinoid-containing ingredients in order to account for the variability of cannabinoid content in harvest batches;

(4) The identity and weight or measure of each ingredient that will be declared on the ingredients list of the cannabis product;

(5) The expected yield of the finished product, based upon the quantity of components or packaging to be used in the absence of any loss or error in actual production, and the maximum and minimum percentages of expected yield beyond which a deviation investigation of a batch is necessary and material review is conducted and a decision on the disposition of the product is made;

(6) A description of packaging and a representative label, or a cross-reference to the physical location of the actual or representative label;

(7) Written instructions for each point, step, or stage in the manufacturing process; and

(8) Written instructions for any action to mitigate an identified risk established in the product quality plan.

(c) Nothing in this chapter requires disclosure of the master manufacturing protocol to any person other than the individuals conducting activities that utilize the protocol or to the Department and its inspectors and agents. The licensee may consider the master manufacturing protocol subject to trade secret protection.

Note: Authority cited: Sections 26012, 26013 and 26130, Business and Professions Code. Reference: Sections 26011.5 and 26131, Business and Professions Code.

§ 40256. Hazard Analysis. [Repealed]

§ 40258. Batch Production Record.

(a) The licensee shall prepare a written batch production record every time a batch of a cannabis product is manufactured. The batch production record shall accurately follow the appropriate master manufacturing protocol, and each step of the protocol shall be performed in the production of the batch.

(b) The batch production record shall document complete information relating to the production and control of each batch, including all of the following details:

(1) The UID and the batch or lot number of the finished batch of cannabis product and the UIDs of all cannabis or cannabis products used in the batch.

(2) The equipment and processing lines used in producing the batch;

(3) The date and time of the maintenance, cleaning, and sanitizing of the equipment and processing lines used in producing the batch, or a cross-reference to records, such as individual equipment logs, where this information is retained;

(4) The identification number assigned to each component, packaging, and label used, and, if applicable, to a cannabis product received from another licensee for packaging or labeling as a cannabis product;

(5) The identity and weight or measure of each component used;

(6) A statement of the actual yield and a statement of the percentage of expected yield at appropriate phases of processing;

(7) The actual results obtained during any monitoring operation;

(8) The results of any testing or examination performed during the batch production, or a cross-reference to such results; and

(9) Documentation, at the time of performance, of the manufacture of the batch, including:

(A) The date on which each step of the master manufacturing protocol was performed; and

(B) The initials of the persons performing each step, including:

(i) The initials of the person responsible for weighing or measuring each component used in the batch;

(ii) The initials of the person responsible for verifying the weight or measure of each component used in the batch;

(iii) The initials of the person responsible for adding the component to the batch; and

(iv) The initials of the person responsible for verifying the addition of components to the batch.

(10) Documentation, at the time of performance, of packaging and labeling operations, including:

(A) An actual or representative label, or a cross-reference to the physical location of the actual or representative label specified in the master manufacturing record;

(B) The expected number of packaging and labels to be used, the actual quantity of the packaging and labels used, and, when label reconciliation is required, reconciliation of any discrepancies between issuance and use of labels; and

(C) The results of any tests or examinations conducted on packaged and labeled cannabis products (including repackaged or relabeled cannabis products), or a cross-reference to the physical location of such results.

(11) Documentation, at the time of performance, that quality control personnel:

(A) Reviewed the batch production record;

(B) Reviewed all required monitoring operation(s);

(C) Reviewed the results of all tests and examinations, including tests and examinations conducted on components, finished batches of cannabis product, and packaged and labeled cannabis products;

(D) Either approved and released, or rejected, the batch for distribution; and

(E) Either approved and released, or rejected, the finished cannabis product, including any repackaged or relabeled cannabis product.

(12) Documentation, at the time of performance, of any required material review and disposition decision; and

(13) The Certificate of Analysis issued for the batch by the licensed testing laboratory, which shall be added to the record after regulatory compliance testing has been completed.

(c) The batch production record shall:

(1) Contain the actual values and observations obtained during monitoring and, as appropriate, during verification activities;

(2) Be accurate, indelible, and legible;

(3) Be created concurrently with performance of the activity documented; and

(4) Be as detailed as necessary to provide a history of work performed; including:

(A) Information to identify any associated manufacturing premises (e.g., the name, license number, and the location of the premises);

(B) The date and the time of the activity documented;

(C) The signature or initials of the person performing the activity; and

(D) The identity of the product, the UID, and the batch or lot number.

Note: Authority cited: Sections 26012, 26013 and 26130, Business and Professions Code. Reference: Sections 26011.5 and 26131, Business and Professions Code.

§ 40260. Equipment and Machinery Qualification. [Repealed]

§ 40262. Master Manufacturing Protocol. [Renumbered]

§ 40264. Batch Production Record. [Renumbered]

§ 40266. Product Complaints. [Repealed]

§ 40268. Recalls. [Repealed]

ARTICLE 5. SPECIAL PROCESSING REQUIREMENTS

§ 40270. Juice Processing.

(a) Requirements of this section shall apply to manufacturers of cannabis juice, and cannabis-infused juice or beverages.

(b) Manufacturers of cannabis juice or cannabis-infused juice or beverages shall prepare and implement a written juice hazard analysis and critical control plan in accordance with the requirements of 21 CFR, Part 120, subpart A, section 120.8, and subpart B, section 120.24, (Rev. January 2001), which is hereby incorporated by reference.

Note: Authority cited: Sections 26012, 26013 and 26130, Business and Professions Code. Reference: Sections 26011.5 and 26131, Business and Professions Code.

§ 40272. Dried Meat Processing.

Manufacturing of cannabis-infused dried meat products shall be conducted in accordance with the United States Department of Agriculture Compliance Guideline for Meat and Poultry Jerky Produced by Small and Very Small Establishments: 2014 Compliance Guideline (Rev. 2014), which is hereby incorporated by reference. Meat for processing into dried meat products shall be acquired from a commercially-available source.

Note: Authority cited: Sections 26012, 26013 and 26130, Business and Professions Code. Reference: Sections 26011.5 and 26131, Business and Professions Code.

ARTICLE 6. OTHER RESPONSIBILITIES

§ 40275. Standard Operating Procedures.

(a) A licensee shall establish and maintain written standard operating procedures that are easily accessible to onsite personnel. The standard operating procedures shall, at minimum, include the following:

    (1) Policies or procedures developed in accordance with the security plan required by Section 40200;

    (2) Emergency response procedures, including safety data sheets for any chemicals on-site;

    (3) Policies and procedures developed in accordance with Section 40225;

    (4) Policies and procedures developed in accordance with Article 3 of this subchapter (Good Manufacturing Practices);

    (5) Procedures for complying with the track-and-trace requirements established in Article 2 of subchapter 6;

    (6) Inventory control procedures in compliance with Section 40282; and

    (7) Cannabis waste management procedures in compliance with Section 40290.

(b) Procedures shall be written in English but may be made available in other languages, as necessary for the licensee's personnel.

Note: Authority cited: Sections 26012, 26013 and 26130, Business and Professions Code. Reference: Sections 26011.5, 26130 and 26160, Business and Professions Code.

§ 40277. Weights and Measures.

(a) Weighing devices used by a licensee shall be approved, tested, and sealed in accordance with the requirements in Chapter 5 (commencing with section 12500) of Division 5 of the Business and Professions Code, and registered with the county sealer consistent with Chapter 2 (commencing with section 12240) of Division 5 of the Business and Professions Code. Approved and registered devices shall be used whenever:

    (1) Cannabis or cannabis product is bought or sold by weight or count;

    (2) Cannabis or cannabis product is packaged for sale by weight or count;

    (3) Cannabis or cannabis product is weighed or counted for entry into the track-and-trace system; and

    (4) The weighing device is used for commercial purposes as defined in section 12500 of the Business and Professions Code.

(b) For the purposes of this chapter, "count" means the numerical count of the individual cannabis product units.

(c) Whenever the licensee is determining the weight, measure, or count of cannabis and cannabis products for the purposes specified in subsection (a), the weight, measure, or count shall be determined by a licensed weighmaster as required by Chapter 7 (commencing with section 12700) of Division 5 of the Business and Professions Code. The weighmaster certificate required under section 12711 of the Business and Professions Code shall not be required when cannabis or cannabis products are weighed for entry into the track-and-trace system.

Note: Authority cited: Sections 26012, 26013 and 26130, Business and Professions Code. Reference: Sections 26011.5 and 26060, Business and Professions Code.

§ 40280. Training Program.

(a) The licensee shall implement a training program to ensure that all personnel present at the premises are provided information and training that, at minimum, covers the following topics:

(1) Within 30 days of the start of employment:

    (A) Health and safety hazards;

    (B) Hazards presented by all solvents or chemicals used at the licensed premises as described in the safety data sheet for each solvent or chemical;

    (C) Emergency response procedures;

    (D) Security procedures;

    (E) Record keeping requirements; and

    (F) Training requirements.

(2) Manufacturing and production personnel, prior to independently engaging in any cannabis manufacturing process:

    (A) An overview of the cannabis manufacturing process and standard operating procedure(s);

    (B) Quality control procedures;

    (C) The product quality plans developed in accordance with Section 40253;

    (D) Proper and safe usage of equipment or machinery;

    (E) Safe work practices applicable to an employee's job tasks, including appropriate use of any necessary safety or sanitary equipment;

    (F) Cleaning and maintenance requirements;

    (G) Emergency operations, including shutdown; and

    (H) Any additional information reasonably related to an employee's job duties.

(3) Additionally, a licensee that produces edible cannabis products shall ensure that all personnel who prepare, handle, or package edible products successfully complete a California food handler certificate course from an entity accredited by the American National Standards Institute (ANSI) within 90 days of commencing employment at the premises and again every three years during employment. The licensee shall obtain documentation evidencing the fulfillment of this requirement;

(4) The licensee shall ensure that all personnel receive annual refresher training to cover, at minimum, the topics listed in this subsection. This annual refresher training must be completed within 12 months of the previous training completion date.

(b) The licensee shall maintain a record of training which contains at minimum:

    (1) A list of all personnel at the premises, including at minimum, name and job duties of each individual;

    (2) Documentation of training topics and dates of training completion, including refresher training, for all personnel;

    (3) The signature of each individual personnel and the licensee verifying receipt and understanding of each training or refresher training completed by the individual; and

    (4) Any official documentation attesting to the successful completion of required training by personnel.

(c) The licensee may assign responsibility for the training of individual personnel to supervisory personnel. Assigned supervisory personnel must have the education, training, or experience (or a combination thereof) necessary to ensure the production of quality cannabis products by all personnel. The assigned training personnel shall sign and date a document on an annual basis attesting that he or she has received and understands all information that will be provided to individual personnel in the training program. This documentation shall be maintained as part of the record requirements.

(d) For licensees in operation pursuant to Section 40126, applicable personnel shall receive required training no later than 90 days after the effective date of the annual license.

Note: Authority cited: Sections 26012, 26013 and 26130, Business and Professions Code. Reference: Sections 26011.5, 26130 and 26160, Business and Professions Code.

§ 40282. Inventory Control - Cannabis and Cannabis Products.

(a) A licensee shall establish and implement a written inventory control plan capable of tracking the location and disposition of all cannabis and cannabis products at the licensed premises.

(b) A licensee shall reconcile the on-hand inventory of cannabis and cannabis products at the licensed premises with the records in the track-and-trace database least once every thirty (30) calendar days.

(c) If a licensee finds a discrepancy between the on-hand inventory and the track-and-trace database, the licensee shall conduct an audit.

(d) If the inventory reconciliation conducted pursuant to subsection (b) or the audit conducted pursuant to subsection (c) reveals a discrepancy that is more than five percent of the documented inventory, the licensee shall notify the Department within 24 hours of the discovery.

Note: Authority cited: Sections 26012, 26013 and 26130, Business and Professions Code. Reference: Sections 26011.5 and 26130, Business and Professions Code.

§ 40290. Waste Management.

(a) A licensee shall have a written cannabis waste management plan and shall dispose of all waste, including cannabis waste, in accordance with the Public Resources Code and any other applicable state and local laws, including laws regulating "organic waste" as defined in Public Resources Code section 42649.8(c). It is the responsibility of the licensee to properly evaluate waste to determine if it should be designated and handled as a hazardous waste, as defined in section 40141 of the Public Resources Code.

(b) A licensee shall dispose of any cannabis waste in a secured waste receptacle or secured area on the licensed premises. For the purposes of this section, "secured waste receptacle" or "secured area" means that physical access to the receptacle or area is restricted to the licensee, employees of the licensee, the local agency, waste hauler franchised or contracted by the local agency, or private waste hauler permitted by the local agency only. Public access to the designated receptacle or area shall be prohibited.

(c) No cannabis product shall be disposed of in its packaging, and all cannabis waste shall be unrecognizable and unusable as cannabis or a cannabis product at the time of disposal. Nothing in this subsection shall be construed to require waste vape cartridges to be emptied of cannabis oil prior to disposal, provided that the vape cartridge is itself unrecognizable and unusable at the time of disposal.

(d) Cannabis waste shall be entered into the track-and-trace system as required under Section 40512.

(e) Cannabis waste may be collected from a licensee in conjunction with a regular organic waste collection route used by the local agency, a waste hauler franchised or contracted by the local agency, or a private waste hauler permitted by the local agency. If a local agency, a waste hauler franchised or contracted by the local agency, or a private waste hauler permitted by the local agency is being used to collect and process cannabis waste, a licensee shall do all of the following:

(1) Maintain and make available to the Department upon request the business name, address, contact person, and contact phone number of the entity hauling the waste; and

(2) Obtain documentation from the entity hauling the waste that evidences subscription to a waste collection service.

(f) If a licensee is self-hauling cannabis waste as allowed by the local jurisdiction, the licensee shall be subject to all of the following requirements:

(1) Self-hauled cannabis waste shall only be transported by the licensee or its employees;

(2) Self-hauled cannabis waste shall only be transported to one or more of the following:

(A) A manned fully permitted solid waste landfill or transformation facility;

(B) A manned fully permitted composting facility or manned composting operation;

(C) A manned fully permitted in-vessel digestion facility or manned in-vessel digestion operation; or

(D) A manned fully permitted transfer/processing facility or manned transfer/processing operation.

(3) The licensee or its employee who transports the waste shall obtain for each delivery of cannabis waste a copy of a certified weight ticket or receipt from the solid waste facility.

Note: Authority cited: Sections 26012, 26013 and 26130, Business and Professions Code. Reference: Sections 26011.5, 26013 and 26130, Business and Professions Code.

§ 40292. Consent to Sample Collection.

A manufacturer licensee that transfers possession but not title of cannabis products to a licensed distributor shall allow the Bureau, upon the Bureau's request, to collect samples for purposes of conducting oversight of licensed testing laboratories.

Note: Authority cited: Sections 26012, 26013 and 26130, Business and Professions Code. Reference: Sections 26011.5, 26013 and 26130, Business and Professions Code.

§ 40295. Product Complaints.

(a) The licensee shall establish and implement written procedures to ensure that:

(1) A qualified individual shall review and investigate all product complaints to determine whether such complaints involve a possible failure of a cannabis product to meet any of its specifications;

(2) Quality control personnel shall review and approve decisions determining whether to investigate a product complaint and shall review and approve the findings and follow up action(s) of any investigation performed;

(3) Pursuant to subsections (a) and (b) in this section, any review or investigative activities by qualified individuals and quality control personnel shall extend to all relevant batches and records.

(4) Quality control personnel shall maintain written records for every product complaint and subsequent investigation, if any. The records shall include:

(A) The name and description of the cannabis product;

(B) The batch number or UID of the cannabis product if available;

(C) The date the complaint was received and the name, address, and telephone number of the complainant, if available;

(D) The nature of the complaint including, if known, how the product was used;

(E) The reply to the complainant, if any;

(F) The findings of the investigation or follow-up action taken when an investigation is performed; and

(G) The basis for any determination not to conduct an investigation.

(b) For purposes of this section, "product complaint" means any written, electronic, or oral communication that contains any allegation expressing concern, for any reason, with the quality of a cannabis product that could be related to the manufacturing practices. Examples of product complaints may include but are not limited to: foul odor, off taste, illness or injury, disintegration time, color variation, foreign material in a cannabis product container, improper packaging, mislabeling, cannabis products that contain an incorrect concentration of cannabinoids, or cannabis products that contain an unidentified ingredient, or any form of contaminant.

Note: Authority cited: Sections 26012, 26013 and 26130, Business and Professions Code. Reference: Sections 26011.5 and 26131, Business and Professions Code.

§ 40297. Recalls.

(a) Licensees shall establish and implement written procedures for recalling cannabis products manufactured by the licensee that are determined to be misbranded or adulterated. These procedures shall include:

(1) Factors which necessitate a recall;

(2) Personnel responsible for implementing the recall procedures; and

(3) Notification protocols, including:

(A) A mechanism to notify all customers that have, or could have, obtained the product, including communication and outreach via media, as necessary and appropriate;

(B) A mechanism to notify any licensees that supplied or received the recalled product;

(C) Instructions to the general public and other licensees for the return or destruction of the recalled product.

(4) Procedures for the collection and destruction of any recalled product. Such procedures shall meet the following requirements:

(A) All recalled products that are intended to be destroyed shall be quarantined for a minimum of 72 hours. The licensee shall affix to the recalled products any bills of lading, shipping manifests, or other similar documents with product information and weight. The product held in quarantine shall be subject to auditing by the Department.

(B) Following the quarantine period, the licensee shall render the recalled cannabis product unusable and unrecognizable and dispose of it in accordance with Section 40290, and do so on video surveillance in accordance with Section 40205.

(b) In addition to the tracking requirements set forth in Section 40512, a licensee shall use the track-and-trace database and on-site documentation to ensure that recalled cannabis products intended for destruction are identified, weighed, and tracked while on the licensed premises and when disposed of in accordance with this section.

For recalled cannabis products, the licensee shall enter the following details into the track-and-trace database: the weight and count of the product, reason for destruction, and the date the quarantine period will begin.

(c) The licensee shall notify the Department of any recall within 24 hours of initiating the recall.

Note: Authority cited: Sections 26012, 26013 and 26130, Business and Professions Code. Reference: Sections 26011.5 and 26131, Business and Professions Code.

SUBCHAPTER 4. PRODUCTS

ARTICLE 1. CANNABIS PRODUCT STANDARDS

§ 40299. Applicability. [Repealed]

§ 40300. Prohibited Products.

The following types of products shall not be sold as cannabis products:

(a) Alcoholic beverages, as defined in section 23004 of the Business and Professions Code. This prohibition does not apply to tinctures that meet the requirements of Section 40308;

(b) Any product containing any non-cannabinoid additive that would increase potency, toxicity, or addictive potential, or that would create an unsafe combination with other psychoactive substances. Prohibited additives include, but are not limited to, nicotine and caffeine. This prohibition shall not apply to products containing naturally-occurring caffeine, such as coffee, tea, or chocolate;

(c) Any cannabis product that must be held at or below 41 degrees Fahrenheit to keep it safe for human consumption, including, but not limited to, cream or custard-filled pies; pies or pastries which consist in whole or in part of milk or milk products, or eggs; and meat-filled pies or pastries. This prohibition shall not apply to juices or beverages that need to be held below 41 degrees Fahrenheit if the juice or beverage was processed in accordance with Section 40270, or to infused butter manufactured as permitted by subsection (g);

(d) Any thermally-processed low-acid cannabis product packed in a hermetically sealed container that, if it did not contain cannabis, would be subject to the manufacturing requirements of Title 21, Code of Federal Regulations, Part 113;

(e) Any acidified cannabis product that, if it did not contain cannabis, would be subject to the manufacturing requirements of Title 21, Code of Federal Regulations, Part 114;

(f) Any juice that is not shelf-stable or that is not processed in accordance with Section 40270;

(g) Dairy products of any kind, as prohibited by section 26001(t) of the Act, except that butter purchased from a licensed milk products plant or retail location that is subsequently infused or mixed with cannabis may be sold as a cannabis product;

(h) Meat products other than dried meat products prepared in accordance with Section 40272;

(i) Seafood products of any kind;

(j) Any product that is manufactured by application of cannabinoid concentrate or extract to commercially available candy or snack food items without further processing of the product. Commercially available candy or snack food items may be used as ingredients in a cannabis product, provided that they are used in a way that renders them unrecognizable as the commercially available items and the label, including the ingredient list, does not note that the final cannabis product contains the commercially available item;

(k) Any cannabis product that the Department determines, on a case-by-case basis, is attractive to children, as specified in Section 40410;

(l) Any cannabis product that the Department determines, on a case-by-case basis, is easily confused with commercially available foods that do not contain cannabis;

(m) Any cannabis product in the shape of, or imprinted with the shape, either realistic or caricature, of a human being, animal, insect, or fruit.

Note: Authority cited: Sections 26012, 26013 and 26130, Business and Professions Code. Reference: Sections 26011.5 and 26130, Business and Professions Code; and Section 37104, Food and Agricultural Code.

§ 40305. Requirements for Edible Cannabis Products.

(a) Except for cannabis, cannabis concentrate, or terpenes, no product ingredient or component shall be used in the manufacture of an edible cannabis product unless that ingredient or component is permitted by the United States Food and Drug Administration for use in food or food manufacturing, as specified in Substances Added to Food in the United States, available at https://www.fda.gov/Food/ IngredientsPackagingLabeling/FoodAdditivesIngredients/ucm115326.htm or is Generally Recognized as Safe (GRAS) under sections 201(s) and 409 of the Federal Food, Drug, and Cosmetic Act (codified in 21 U.S.C. 321(s) and 348).

(b) Edible cannabis products that consist of more than a single serving shall be either:

(1) Scored or delineated to indicate one serving, if the edible cannabis product is in solid form. For purposes of this section, "delineated" includes directly marking the product to indicate one serving or providing a means by which a consumer can accurately identify one serving; or

(2) If the edible cannabis product is not in solid form, packaged in a manner such that a single serving is readily identifiable or easily measurable.

(c) An edible cannabis product consisting of multiple servings shall be homogenized so that each serving contains the same concentration of THC.

Note: Authority cited: Sections 26012, 26013 and 26130, Business and Professions Code. Reference: Sections 26011.5 and 26130, Business and Professions Code.

§ 40306. Requirements for Topical Cannabis Products, Concentrates, and Other Cannabis Products.

(a) Except for cannabis, cannabis concentrate, or terpenes, topical cannabis products shall only contain ingredients permitted for cosmetic manufacturing in accordance with Title 21, Code of Federal Regulations, Part 700, subpart B (section 700.11 et seq.) (Rev. March 2016), which is hereby incorporated by reference.

Note: Authority cited: Sections 26012, 26013 and 26130, Business and Professions Code. Reference: Section 26011.5, Business and Professions Code.

§ 40308. Orally-Consumed Products Containing Alcohol.

Any orally-consumed product that contains more than 0.5% alcohol by volume as an ingredient, and is not otherwise an alcoholic beverage as defined in Business and Professions Code section 23004, shall be packaged in a container no larger than two (2) fluid ounces and shall include a calibrated dropper or other similar device capable of accurately measuring servings.

Note: Authority cited: Sections 26012, 26013 and 26130, Business and Professions Code. Reference: Section 26011.5, Business and Professions Code.

§ 40310. Failed Product Batches. [Repealed]

ARTICLE 2. CANNABINOID CONCENTRATION LIMITS

§ 40315. THC Concentration Limits.

(a) An edible cannabis product shall not contain more than:

  (1) 10 milligrams THC per serving; and

  (2) 100 milligrams THC per package.

(b) Notwithstanding subsection (a), a package containing an edible product that is an orally-dissolving product, such as sublingual lozenges or mouth strips, may contain up to 500 milligrams THC per package, if:

  (1) The cannabis product consists of discrete servings of no more than 10 milligrams THC per piece;

  (2) The cannabis product is labeled "FOR MEDICAL USE ONLY;" and

  (3) The cannabis product is only available for sale to a medicinal-use customer.

(c) A topical cannabis product or a cannabis concentrate shall not contain more than 1,000 milligrams THC per package.

(d) Notwithstanding subsection (c), a topical cannabis product or a cannabis concentrate may contain more than 1,000 milligrams THC per package, but not more than 2,000 milligrams THC per package, if the product is labeled "FOR MEDICAL USE ONLY" and is only available for sale to a medicinal-use customer.

Note: Authority cited: Sections 26012, 26013 and 26130, Business and Professions Code. Reference: Sections 26011.5, 26120 and 26130, Business and Professions Code.

ARTICLE 3. FAILED PRODUCT BATCHES

§ 40330. Failed Product Batches.

(a) A finished cannabis product batch that fails any regulatory compliance laboratory testing requirement established by the Bureau pursuant to section 26100 of the Act shall be destroyed unless:

  (1) The cannabis product batch may be remediated by relabeling pursuant to subsection (d); or

  (2) A corrective action plan for remediation or reprocessing is approved by the Department pursuant to subsection (e).

(b) Remediation or reprocessing of a failed product batch or the use of a harvest batch that has failed any regulatory compliance laboratory test shall comply with the requirements and procedures established by the Bureau in Section 5727 of Title 16 of the California Code of Regulations, in addition to the requirements of this article.

(c) Except as provided in subsections (d) and (f), edible cannabis products that fail regulatory compliance laboratory testing shall not be remediated or reprocessed and shall be destroyed. If any edible cannabis product that has failed regulatory compliance laboratory testing is remediated, reprocessed, or otherwise mixed with another batch of cannabis product in violation of this section, such action shall render the final cannabis product adulterated, regardless of the defect level of the final cannabis product.

(d) A cannabis product batch that fails regulatory compliance laboratory testing for cannabinoid or terpenoid content may be remediated by relabeling the product with the correct information from the laboratory certificate of analysis, provided that the THC limits in Section 40315 are met. In addition, the following conditions apply:

(1) The manufacturer licensee shall notify the Department within 3 business days of notification by a distributor that the product failed cannabinoid content testing and is required to be relabeled.

(2) Notification shall be given to the Department by email and shall include a copy of the certificate of analysis for the batch and the name and license number of the licensee relabeling the product.

(e) Except as provided in subsection (d), a cannabis product batch or a harvest batch that fails regulatory compliance laboratory testing or quality assurance review shall not be remediated or reprocessed unless the Department has approved a corrective action plan submitted by the manufacturer licensee. The corrective action plan shall include, at minimum, a description of how the product or harvest batch will be remediated so that the product or harvest batch, or any product produced therefrom, will meet all regulatory compliance laboratory testing and quality assurance requirements. Edible cannabis products may only be remediated by relabeling or repackaging as provided in subsection (f). Corrective action plans will be reviewed by the Department on a case-by-case basis.

(f) Edible cannabis products that fail regulatory compliance laboratory testing because the per package limit of THC has been exceeded may be remediated by repackaging under the following conditions:

(1) The Department has approved a corrective action plan for repackaging the product;

(2) The product batch is returned to the manufacturer that packaged the product;

(3) The product itself is not altered in any way; and

(4) The product is labeled to accurately state the contents.

(g) All remediation of harvest or product batches shall be documented in the batch production records. Remediated products, harvest batches, or products produced therefrom, shall be tested and undergo quality assurance review in accordance with the requirements established by the Bureau in Chapter 2 of Division 42 of Title 16 of the California Code of Regulations prior to retail sale.

Note: Authority cited: Sections 26012, 26013 and 26130, Business and Professions Code. Reference: Section 26131, Business and Professions Code.

SUBCHAPTER 5. LABELING AND PACKAGING REQUIREMENTS

ARTICLE 1. GENERAL PROVISIONS

§ 40400. Applicability.

The requirements in this subchapter shall apply to finished cannabis products or dried flower and pre-rolls packaged for retail sale and shall not apply to cannabis or cannabis products that are transferred between licensees for the purpose of further processing or packaging.

Note: Authority cited: Sections 26012, 26013 and 26130, Business and Professions Code. Reference: Section 26130,

Business and Professions Code.

§ 40401. Release to Distributor as Finished Product.

(a) Prior to release of a cannabis product to a distributor, a licensee shall ensure that the product is in finished form and is labeled and packaged in its final form for sale.

(b) For purposes of this section, "final form" does not include:

(1) Labeling of cannabinoid content if the cannabinoid content is to be added to the label at the distribution premises after issuance of the Certificate of Analysis in accordance with Section 40409; or

(2) Placing the cannabis or cannabis product into child-resistant packaging as prescribed in Section 40417. This provision shall expire on December 31, 2019.

Note: Authority cited: Sections 26012, 26013 and 26130, Business and Professions Code. Reference: Sections 26011.5 and 26130, Business and Professions Code.

ARTICLE 2. LABELING REQUIREMENTS

§ 40403. General Provisions.

(a) Any information required to be listed on a label shall be written in English.

(b) A label shall be unobstructed and conspicuous so that it can be read by the consumer.

(c) All required label information shall be located on the outside container or wrapper of the finished product to be sold at a retailer. If the product container is separable from the outer-most packaging (e.g., a container placed inside of a box), the product container shall also include the following:

(1) For edible cannabis products, topical cannabis products, suppositories, or orally-consumed concentrates, all of the information specified in Sections 40405 and 40406, except for cannabinoid content.

(2) For inhaled products (e.g., dab, shatter, and wax), the universal symbol as prescribed in Section 40412.

Note: Authority cited: Sections 26012, 26013 and 26130, Business and Professions Code. Reference: Section 26120, Business and Professions Code.

§ 40404. Labeling Requirements: Pre-Rolls and Packaged Flower.

(a) The label for a package of pre-rolls or packaged flower shall include a primary panel that includes the following information in a type size no less than 6 point font and in relation to the size of the primary panel and container:

(1) Identity of the product;

(2) The net weight of cannabis in the package, listed in both metric and U.S. customary units; and

(3) Universal symbol, as prescribed in Section 40412.

(b) The label for a package of pre-rolls or packaged flower shall include an informational label that includes the following information in a type size no less than 6 point font and in relation to the size of the informational panel and container:

(1) The UID;

(2) The licensed cultivator or licensee packaging the product (either the legal business name or the registered name under which the business will operate listed on the license certificate), and its contact number or website address;

(3) The date of packaging for retail sale;

(4) The following statement in bold print: "GOVERNMENT WARNING: THIS PACKAGE CONTAINS CANNABIS, A SCHEDULE I CONTROLLED SUBSTANCE. KEEP OUT OF REACH OF CHILDREN AND ANIMALS. CANNABIS MAY ONLY BE POSSESSED OR CONSUMED BY PERSONS 21 YEARS OF AGE OR OLDER UNLESS THE PERSON IS A QUALIFIED PATIENT. CANNABIS USE WHILE PREGNANT OR BREASTFEEDING MAY BE HARMFUL. CONSUMPTION OF CANNABIS IMPAIRS YOUR ABILITY TO DRIVE AND OPERATE MACHINERY. PLEASE USE EXTREME CAUTION."

(c) Nothing in this section prohibits the inclusion of additional information on the label, provided that the label does not violate the requirements of Section 40410.

(d) The cannabinoid content for a package of pre-rolls or packaged flower shall be labeled as specified in Section 40409.

Note: Authority cited: Sections 26012, 26013 and 26130, Business and Professions Code. Reference: Section 26120, Business and Professions Code.

§ 40405. Primary Panel Labeling Requirements: Manufactured Products.

(a) The label for a manufactured cannabis product shall include a primary panel that includes the following information in a type size no less than 6 point font and in relation to the size of the primary panel and container:

(1) The identity of the product in a text size reasonably related to the most prominent printed matter on the panel;

(2) The universal symbol as prescribed in Section 40412; and

(3) The net weight or volume of the contents of the package, listed in both metric and U.S. customary units.

(b) Cannabinoid content may be included on the primary panel. Cannabinoid content for manufactured cannabis products shall be labeled as specified in Section 40409.

(c) Nothing in this section prohibits the inclusion of additional information on the primary panel, provided that the label does not violate the requirements of Section 40410.

Note: Authority cited: Sections 26012, 26013 and 26130, Business and Professions Code. Reference: Section 26120, Business and Professions Code.

§ 40406. Additional Primary Panel Labeling Requirements: Edible Products.

In addition to the requirements of Section 40405, the primary panel of an edible cannabis product shall include the words "cannabis-infused" immediately above the identity of the product in bold type and a text size larger than the text size used for the identity of the product.

Note: Authority cited: Sections 26012, 26013, 26120 and 26130, Business and Professions Code. Reference: Section 26120, Business and Professions Code.

§ 40408. Informational Panel Labeling Requirements.

(a) The label for a manufactured cannabis product shall include an informational panel that includes the following:

(1) The name of the licensed manufacturer (either the legal business name or the registered name under which the business will operate listed on the license certificate) that manufactured the cannabis product and its contact number or website address;

(2) The date of the cannabis product's manufacture and packaging;

(3) The following statement in bold print: "GOVERNMENT WARNING: THIS PRODUCT CONTAINS CANNABIS, A SCHEDULE I CONTROLLED SUBSTANCE. KEEP OUT OF REACH OF CHILDREN AND ANIMALS. CANNABIS PRODUCTS MAY ONLY BE POSSESSED OR CONSUMED BY PERSONS 21 YEARS OF AGE OR OLDER UNLESS THE PERSON IS A QUALIFIED PATIENT. THE INTOXICATING EFFECTS OF CANNABIS PRODUCTS MAY BE DELAYED UP TO TWO HOURS. CANNABIS USE WHILE PREGNANT OR BREASTFEEDING MAY BE HARMFUL. CONSUMPTION OF CANNABIS PRODUCTS IMPAIRS YOUR ABILITY TO DRIVE AND OPERATE MACHINERY. PLEASE USE EXTREME CAUTION."

(4) The statement "FOR MEDICAL USE ONLY," if:

(A) The cannabis product is intended by the manufacturer only for sale to medicinal-use customers;

(B) The product is an orally-dissolving edible product containing more than 100 milligrams THC per package, as specified in Section 40315(b); or

(C) The product is a topical cannabis product or concentrate containing more than 1,000 milligrams THC per package, as specified in Section 40315(d).

(5) A list of all product ingredients in descending order of predominance by weight or volume. If any product ingredient contains subingredients, the list shall either:

(A) Include the common name of the ingredient followed by a parenthetical listing of all ingredients in descending order by weight or volume; or

(B) List all subingredients as individual ingredients in descending order of predominance.

(C) This paragraph shall not apply to flavoring, which shall instead be compliant with the requirement of 21 C.F.R. 101.22 (Rev. Jan 2009), hereby incorporated by reference.

(6) If the cannabis product contains an ingredient, flavoring, coloring, or an incidental additive that bears or contains a major food allergen, the word "contains," followed by a list of the applicable major food allergens;

(7) The names of any artificial colorings contained in the product;

(8) If an edible cannabis product, the amount, in grams or milligrams, of sodium, sugar, carbohydrates, and total fat per serving;

(9) Instructions for use, such as the method of consumption or application, and any preparation necessary prior to use;

(10) The product expiration date, "use by" date, or "best by" date, if any;

(11) The UID and the batch or lot number; and

(12) If the cannabis product is perishable or is perishable after opening, the statement, "KEEP REFRIGERATED" or "REFRIGERATE AFTER OPENING," as applicable.

(b) The informational panel text shall be in a text size of no less than 6 point font and in relation to the size of the primary panel and container.

(c) Except for the information required by paragraph (a)(11), the requirements of subsection (a) may be fulfilled through the use of supplemental labeling, which may include, but is not limited to, a package insert, fold-out or booklet label, or a hanging tag.

(d) Cannabinoid content may be included on the informational panel. Cannabinoid content for manufactured cannabis products shall be labeled as specified in Section 40409.

(e) Nothing in this section prohibits the inclusion of additional information on the informational panel provided that the label does not violate the requirements of Section 40410.

Note: Authority cited: Sections 26012, 26013 and 26130, Business and Professions Code. Reference: Sections 26120 and 26121, Business and Professions Code.

§ 40409. Cannabinoid Content Labeling.

(a) Each package for retail sale of cannabis product, cannabis flower, or pre-rolls shall be labeled with the cannabinoid content on either the primary panel or an informational panel. Cannabinoid content may be included on the product label at the manufacturing premises prior to release to a distributor as described in subsection (b) or it may be added to the product at the distribution premises after issuance of the regulatory compliance testing Certificate of Analysis for the batch as described in subsection (c). Cannabinoid content labeling shall include the following:

(1) For an edible product or a cannabis concentrate for which the manufacturer has established serving designations, THC and CBD content, expressed in milligrams per serving and milligrams per package.

(2) For a topical cannabis product or a cannabis concentrate without serving designations, THC and CBD content, expressed in milligrams per package.

(3) Packages of pre-rolls or cannabis flower that do not include cannabinoids other than that naturally occurring in the plant material are not required to list cannabinoid content in milligrams. Instead, such packages shall be labeled with the cannabinoid content expressed as a percentage.

(4) Packages of infused pre-rolls shall be labeled with either:

(A) The cannabinoid content in milligrams; or

(B) The cannabinoid content of the dried flower expressed as a percentage and the added cannabinoid content in milligrams.

(b) A manufacturer that includes the cannabinoid content on the product label prior to release to a distributor shall label products as specified in paragraphs (1) through (4) of subsection (a), as appropriate to the product. For THC or CBD concentration that is less than two (2) milligrams per serving or per package, the THC or CBD may be labeled as "<2.0 mg per serving" or "<2.0 mg per package."

(c) A manufacturer may arrange for cannabinoid content labeling at the distribution premises after issuance of the Certificate of Analysis in accordance with the following:

(1) Each package of cannabis product in the batch shall be labeled with the cannabinoid content as specified in subsection (a) that is indicated on the Certificate of Analysis, as well as any other cannabinoid that is 5 percent or greater of the total cannabinoid content;

(2) The manufacturer shall identify a location for the cannabinoid content label on the outer packaging of the product. The location shall be sufficient in size for the required cannabinoid content to be printed in at least 6 point font;

(3) The cannabinoid content label shall be affixed to the identified location on the outer packaging of the product and shall not obscure any other label information.

(d) Nothing in this section precludes the labeling of terpenes or additional cannabinoid content on the product, provided that such information is verified by the Certificate of Analysis.

Note: Authority cited: Sections 26012, 26013 and 26130, Business and Professions Code. Reference: Section 26120, Business and Professions Code.

§ 40410. Labeling Restrictions.

Cannabis product labeling shall not contain any of the following:

(a) The name of a California county, including any similar name that is likely to mislead consumers as to the origin of the product, unless one hundred percent of the cannabis contained in the product was grown in that county.

(b) Content that is, or is designed to be, attractive to individuals under the age of 21, including but not limited to:

(1) Cartoons;

(2) Any likeness to images, characters, or phrases that are popularly used to advertise to children;

(3) Any imitation of candy packaging or labeling; or

(4) The terms "candy" or "candies" or variants in spelling such as "kandy" or "kandeez."

(c) Any information that is false or misleading.

(d) Any health-related statement that is untrue or misleading. Any health-related statement must be supported by the totality of publicly available scientific evidence (including evidence from well-designed studies conducted in a manner which is consistent with generally recognized scientific procedures and principles), and for which there is significant scientific agreement, among experts qualified by scientific training and experience to evaluate such claims.

(e) If the product is an edible cannabis product, a picture of the product contained therein.

(f) For purposes of this section, false or misleading information includes any indication that the cannabis or cannabis product is organic, unless the National Organic Program (Section 6517 of the federal Organic Foods Production Act of 1990 (7 U.S.C. Section 6501 et seq.)) authorizes organic designation and certification for cannabis and the cannabis or cannabis product meets the requirements for such designation and certification. This includes use of the word "organic" on the labeling or variants in spelling such as "organix."

(g) Any labeling in violation of Section 5040.1 of Division 42 of Title 16 of the California Code of Regulations.

Note: Authority cited: Sections 26012, 26013 and 26130, Business and Professions Code. Reference: Sections 26062.5, 26063, 26120, 26121 and 26154, Business and Professions Code.

§ 40411. Statement of Characteristic Anticipated Effects.

A cannabis product may include information on the characteristic anticipated effects of the cannabis product if the manufacturer has substantiation that the information is truthful and not misleading. Such information may be located on the informational panel of the label or as an insert included in the cannabis product package. For purposes of this section, "characteristic anticipated effect" includes any physiological effect (a temporary effect on the body related to the consumption of cannabis) that is common to or expected from the particular cannabis strain, but excludes any claim of health benefits (i.e. claims of therapeutic action as a result of the consumption of cannabis).

Note: Authority cited: Sections 26012, 26013 and 26130, Business and Professions Code. Reference: Sections 26120 and 26130, Business and Professions Code.

§ 40412. Universal Symbol.

(a) The primary panel of a cannabis product shall be marked, stamped, or otherwise imprinted with the universal symbol.

(b) The symbol shall replicate the following in form:

CA

(c) The symbol shall be black in color. For packaging that is dark in color, the symbol may be made conspicuous by printing the symbol on, or outlining the symbol with, a contrasting color.

(d) The symbol shall be no smaller in size than one half (.5) inch by one half (.5) inch and shall be printed legibly and conspicuously.

(e) The symbol shall not be altered or cropped in any way other than to adjust the sizing for placement on the primary panel.

Note: Authority cited: Sections 26012, 26013 and 26130, Business and Professions Code. Reference: Sections 26120, 26121 and 26130, Business and Professions Code.

ARTICLE 3. PACKAGING

§ 40415. Packaging.

A package used to contain cannabis or a cannabis product shall comply with the following requirements:

(a) The package shall protect the product from contamination and shall not expose the product to any toxic or harmful substance.

(b) The package shall be tamper-evident, which means that the product packaging is sealed so that the contents cannot be opened without obvious destruction of the seal.

(c) If the product has multiple uses, the package shall be resealable.

(d) The package shall not imitate any package used for products typically marketed to children.

(e) If the product is an edible product, the package shall be opaque. Amber bottles shall be considered opaque for purposes of this section.

(f) Notwithstanding subsection (e), opaque bottles used to contain a cannabis beverage product may utilize a single, vertical, clear strip of no wider than 0.25 inches for the purpose of determining serving amounts.

(g) The package shall be child-resistant, as described in Section 40417.

Note: Authority cited: Sections 26012, 26013 and 26130, Business and Professions Code. Reference: Sections 26120 and 26121, Business and Professions Code.

§ 40417. Child-Resistant Packaging Requirements.

(a) Beginning January 1, 2020, a package containing cannabis or cannabis products transferred to a distributor for retail sale shall be child-resistant, as follows:

(1) An edible product, an orally-consumed concentrate, or a suppository shall be child-resistant for the life of the product. A package that contains more than a single serving is not required to be child-resistant if each individual serving is packaged in child-resistant packaging.

(2) Cannabis or a cannabis product intended to be inhaled or a cannabis product that is applied topically may utilize packaging that is child-resistant only until first opened, if the package is labeled with the statement "This package is not child-resistant after opening."

(b) The following packages are considered child-resistant for purposes of this Article:

(1) Any package that has been certified as child-resistant under the requirements of the Poison Prevention Packaging Act of 1970 Regulations (16 C.F.R. §1700.15(b)(1)) (Rev. July 1995), which is hereby incorporated by reference.

(2) A bottle sealed with a pry-off metal crown cork style bottle cap, provided that the bottle contains only a single serving.

(3) Plastic packaging that is at least 4 mils thick and heat-sealed without an easy-open tab, dimple, corner, or flap, provided that the package contains a cannabis product described in subsection (a)(2) or is a cannabis product that is only a single serving.

(c) Until the date specified in subsection (a), the child-resistant package requirement specified in section 26120 of the Act may be met through the use of a child-resistant exit package at retail sale.

Note: Authority cited: Sections 26012, 26013 and 26130, Business and Professions Code. Reference: Sections 26011.5, 26120 and 26121, Business and Professions Code.

SUBCHAPTER 6. COMPLIANCE

ARTICLE 1. RECORDS

§ 40500. Record Keeping Requirements.

(a) The licensee shall maintain the following documents on the premises at all times and shall make the documents available to the Department upon request:

(1) The valid state license issued by the Department, which shall be prominently displayed;

(2) Any other valid license issued by a state cannabis licensing agency;

(3) The valid license, permit, or other approval issued by the local jurisdiction;

(4) The premises diagram, as specified in Section 40105;

(5) The current standard operating procedures as defined in Section 40275;

(6) Shipping manifests;

(7) Personnel records, including evidence of personnel qualifications and training procedures and records, as specified in Section 40280;

(8) Contracts with other licensees regarding commercial cannabis activity;

(9) Financial records related to the commercial cannabis activity including, but not limited to, bank statements, and tax records;

(10) Sales invoices and receipts as described in section 26161 of the Act and Section 40505 of these regulations; and

(11) Any other record or documentation required to be kept pursuant to this Chapter or the Act.

(b) The records shall be maintained for a period of seven (7) years. Outdated standard operating procedures shall be maintained such that onsite employees cannot mistakenly access outdated information.

(c) All documentation shall be maintained in English. However, nothing in this subsection prohibits the maintenance of documents in languages in addition to English as needed by the licensee.

Note: Authority cited: Sections 26012, 26013 and 26130, Business and Professions Code. Reference: Sections 26011.5 and 26160, Business and Professions Code.

§ 40505. Sales Invoices and Receipts.

(a) The licensee shall prepare a sales invoice or sales receipt for every sale, transport, or transfer of cannabis products to another licensee. Sales invoices and receipts may be maintained electronically, but shall be readily accessible for examination by the Department and its inspectors and agents.

(b) Each sales invoice or receipt shall include the following information:

(1) Name, address, and license number of the seller;

(2) Name, address, and license number of the purchaser;

(3) Date of sale, transport, or transfer;

(4) Invoice or receipt number;

(5) Kind, quantity, size, and capacity of packages of cannabis or cannabis product sold, transported, or transferred; and

(6) Cost to the purchaser for the cannabis or cannabis product, including any discount or trade allowance applied to the price, which shall be recorded on the invoice.

(c) For purposes of this section, "discount or trade allowance" means any price reduction or allowance of any kind, whether stated or unstated, and includes, without limitation, any price reduction applied to a licensee's price list. The discounts may be for prompt payment, payment in cash, bulk purchases, related-party transaction, or "preferred-customer" status.

(d) Invoices and receipts for the sale, transport, or transfer of cannabis or cannabis products shall not be comingled with invoices covering other commodities.

Note: Authority cited: Sections 26012, 26013 and 26130, Business and Professions Code. Reference: Section 26161,

Business and Professions Code.

ARTICLE 2. TRACK-AND-TRACE SYSTEM

§ 40510. Track-and-Trace System General Requirements.

(a) Each applicant or licensee shall identify an owner of the commercial cannabis business to be the track-and-trace system account manager. The account manager shall register for track-and-trace system training provided by the Department of Food and Agriculture or its designee within ten (10) calendar days of receiving notice from the Department of Public Health that their application for licensure has been received.

(b) Applicants approved for an annual license shall not have access to the track-and-trace system until the account manager has completed the track-and-trace system training prescribed by the Department of Food and Agriculture or its designee and proof of completion has been validated by Department of Food and Agriculture or its designee.

(c) The licensee's track-and-trace system account manager shall be responsible for all the following:

(1) Complete track-and-trace system training provided by the Department of Food and Agriculture or its designee. If the account manager did not complete the track-and-trace system training prior to the licensee receiving their annual license, the account manager will be required to register for the track-and-trace system training provided by the Department of Food and Agriculture or its designee within five (5) calendar days of license issuance;

(2) Designate track-and-trace system users, as needed, and require the designated users to be trained in the proper and lawful use of the track-and-trace system before the users are permitted to access the track-and-trace system;

(3) Maintain an accurate and complete list of all track-and-trace system designated users and update the list immediately when changes occur;

(4) Cancel any track-and-trace designated users from the licensee's track-and-trace system account if that individual is no longer authorized to represent the licensee;

(5) Correct any data that is entered into the track-and-trace system in error within three (3) calendar days of discovery of the error;

(6) Obtain UID tags from the Department of Food and Agriculture, or its designee, and ensure that a sufficient supply of UIDs is available at all times;

(7) Ensure that all inventory is tagged and entered in the track-and-trace system as required by Section 40512 and 40517;

(8) Monitor all notifications from the track-and-trace system and resolve all issues identified in the notification. The notification shall not be dismissed by an account manager until the issue(s) identified in the notification has been resolved; and

(9) Notify the Department of any loss of access to the track-and-trace system that exceeds 72 hours.

(d) The applicant or licensee is responsible for notifying the Department in writing of any change to the designated track-and-trace system account manager within 48 hours.

(e) The licensee is responsible for all actions its owners or employees take while logged into the track-and-trace system, or are otherwise performing track-and-trace activities.

(f) No person shall intentionally misrepresent or falsify information entered into the track-and-trace system. The track-and-trace system shall be the system of record. The licensee is responsible for the accuracy and completeness of all data and information entered into the track-and-trace system. Information entered into the track-and-trace system shall be assumed to be accurate and may be used to take enforcement action against the licensee if incorrect information is not corrected.

Note: Authority cited: Sections 26012, 26013 and 26130, Business and Professions Code. Reference: Sections 26067 and 26160, Business and Professions Code.

§ 40512. Track-and-Trace System Reporting Requirements.

(a) A system account manager or designated user shall record all of the following activities in the track-and-trace system within 24 hours of the activity:

(1) Receipt of cannabis material;

(2) The transfer to or receipt of cannabis products for further manufacturing from another licensed manufacturer; and

(3) All changes in the disposition of cannabis or cannabis products. A change in disposition includes, but is not limited to:

(A) Processing of the cannabis or further processing of the cannabis product; and

(B) Packaging and labeling of the cannabis or cannabis products or repackaging or relabeling of the cannabis or cannabis products.

(4) Use of cannabis or cannabis product for internal quality control testing or product research and development.

(5) Transfer of cannabis products to a distributor.

(b) The following information shall be recorded for each activity entered into the track-and-trace system:

(1) The licensed entity from which the cannabis material or cannabis product is received, including that entity's license number, and the licensed entity to which the cannabis product is transferred, including that entity's license number;

(2) The name and license number of the distributor that transported the cannabis material or cannabis product;

(3) The type of cannabis material or cannabis product received, processed, manufactured, packaged, or transferred;

(4) The weight or count of the cannabis material or cannabis product received, processed, manufactured, packaged, or transferred;

(5) The date and time of receipt, processing, manufacturing, packaging, or transfer;

(6) The UID assigned to the cannabis material or cannabis product;

(7) Any other information required by other relevant licensing authorities.

Note: Authority cited: Sections 26012, 26013 and 26130, Business and Professions Code. Reference: Sections 26067 and 26160, Business and Professions Code.

§ 40513. Track-and-Trace System - Loss of Access.

(a) If a licensee loses access to the track-and-trace system for any reason, the licensee shall prepare and maintain comprehensive records detailing all required inventory tracking activities conducted during the loss of access.

(b) Upon restoration of access to the track-and-trace system, all inventory tracking activities that occurred during the loss of access shall be entered into the track-and-trace system within three (3) business days.

(c) A licensee shall document the date and time when access to the track-and-trace system was lost, when it was restored, and the cause for each loss of access.

(d) A licensee shall not transfer cannabis products to another licensee or receive cannabis or cannabis products from another licensee until such time as access to the track-and-trace system is restored and all information is recorded into the track-and-trace system.

Note: Authority cited: Sections 26012, 26013 and 26130, Business and Professions Code. Reference: Sections 26067 and 26160, Business and Professions Code.

§ 40515. Track-and-Trace System - Temporary Licenses.

(a) A licensee operating under a temporary license issued pursuant to Section 40126 is not required to record commercial cannabis activity in the track-and-trace system as otherwise required by this article. Temporary licensees shall track all commercial cannabis activities on a paper sales receipt or invoice that includes the following information:

(1) Name, address, and license number of the seller;

(2) Name, address, and license number of the purchaser;

(3) Date of sale or transfer and invoice number;

(4) Description or type of cannabis or cannabis product;

(5) Weight or count of the cannabis or cannabis product sold or transferred;

(6) Cost to the purchaser of the cannabis or cannabis product.

(b) After issuance of an annual license, the licensee may continue to conduct commercial cannabis activities with temporary licensees in accordance with subsection (a). Any commercial cannabis activity conducted between annual license holders shall be recorded in the track-and-trace system.

(c) The provisions of this section shall expire on July 1, 2019.

Note: Authority cited: Sections 26012, 26013 and 26130, Business and Professions Code. Reference: Sections 26067, 26160 and 26161 Business and Professions Code.

§ 40517. Track-and-Trace System - UID Tag Order.

(a) A licensee shall order UID tags within five (5) calendar days of receiving access to the track-and-trace system. The receipt of the UID tags by the licensee shall be recorded in the track-and-trace system within three (3) calendar days of receipt.

(b) Any licensee in operation at the time access to the track-and-trace system is granted shall input all inventory into the track-and-trace system no later than 30 calendar days after receipt of the UID tags. After UID tags have been received, all commercial cannabis activity shall be recorded in the track-and-trace system by the licensee as required by this Article.

Note: Authority cited: Sections 26012, 26013, and 26130, Business and Professions Code. Reference: Sections 26067, 26160 and 26161, Business and Professions Code.

ARTICLE 3. ADVERTISING AND MARKETING

§ 40525. Advertising and Marketing.

(a) A licensee shall ensure that all advertising and marketing of its cannabis products meet the requirements of Chapter 15 (commencing with section 26150) of the Act. Any health-related statement shall also meet the requirements of Section 40410.

(b) A licensee shall accurately and legibly include its name and license number on all advertising and marketing for its products.

(c) A licensee shall maintain records and documentation to establish that its advertising and marketing meet the requirements of Chapter 15 (commencing with section 26150) of the Act. The records shall be maintained in accordance with section 26160 of the Act and Section 40500 of this chapter.

(d) A licensee shall remove or discontinue advertising or marketing if the Department determines the advertising or marketing violates the provisions of the Act or these regulations or if the licensee fails to provide records to the Department upon request that establishes the advertising and marketing meets the requirements of the Act and regulations.

Note: Authority cited: Sections 26012, 26013 and 26130, Business and Professions Code. Reference: Section 26150, Business and Professions Code.

ARTICLE 4. INSPECTIONS

§ 40550. Inspections.

(a) The Department and its inspectors or agents may conduct an on-site inspection prior to issuing a new or renewal license.

(b) The Department and its inspectors or agents shall have access at reasonable times to the manufacturing premises, any area in which the licensee is conducting manufacturing activities, storage areas, records, production processes, labeling and packaging processes, and conveyances used in the manufacture, storage or transportation of cannabis products so that it may determine compliance with the provisions of the Act and these regulations.

(c) The Department may inspect any record or document that has a bearing on whether the labeling, advertising or marketing of a cannabis product complies with the requirements of Chapter 15 (commencing with section 26150) of the Act.

(d) To the extent necessary for the enforcement of the Act and this chapter, the Department may secure any sample or specimen of any cannabis product or ingredient used therein by the manufacturing operation. The Department's inspector or agent shall leave a receipt for the licensee describing any sample obtained prior to leaving the premises.

(e) The Department may analyze or examine any sample obtained. If an analysis is made of a sample, a copy of the results of the analysis shall be furnished to the licensee by the Department.

(f) The Department may conduct investigations concerning the adulteration, misbranding, false or misleading advertising or marketing, or unlicensed production of any cannabis product, and may enter and inspect any place where any cannabis product is suspected of being manufactured or held in violation of the Act or these regulations.

(g) The Department may collect evidence related to any alleged violation of the Act or the regulations for the purpose of preserving such evidence during the course of investigation and any subsequent enforcement proceedings.

(h) The Department may copy any materials, books, or records of any licensee or their agents pertaining to the commercial cannabis business.

Note: Authority cited: Sections 26012, 26013 and 26130, Business and Professions Code. Reference: Sections 26011.5, 26130, 26132, 26133, 26134, 26135 and 26160, Business and Professions Code.

§ 40551. Notice to Comply.

(a) The Department may issue a notice to comply to a licensee for violation(s) of the Act or regulations observed during an inspection.

(b) The notice to comply shall be in writing and describe the nature and facts of each violation, including a reference to the statute or regulation violated.

(c) The Department may serve the notice to comply prior to leaving the licensed premises on an owner, manager or other individual on the premises designated by the licensee to accept the notice, or may mail the notice to comply to the licensee within 15 business days of the last date of inspection.

(d) The Department shall specify a reasonable timeframe in the notice to comply for the licensee to correct the violation(s). Within the specified timeframe, the licensee shall notify the Department of the corrective action(s) taken for each violation and describe how compliance was achieved. The Department may require the licensee to provide a corrective action plan for review and approval by the Department on a case by case basis.

(e) Failure to correct the violation(s) in the notice to comply may result in a disciplinary action or additional enforcement action by the Department.

Note: Authority cited: Sections 26012 and 26013, Business and Professions Code. Reference: Sections 26011.5 and 26018; Business and Professions Code.

ARTICLE 5. SUSPENSIONS AND REVOCATIONS OF A LICENSE

§ 40570. Emergency Decision and Order.

(a) The Department may issue an emergency decision and order for temporary, interim relief to prevent or avoid immediate danger to the public health, safety, or welfare. Such circumstances include, but are not limited to, the following:

(1) The Department determines that a cannabis product manufactured, processed, packed, or held at the licensee's premises has a reasonable probability of causing serious adverse health consequences or death;

(2) The Department determines that insanitary or other conditions at the licensee's premises exist that could lead to the adulteration of finished cannabis products, and has a reasonable probability of affecting the safety of finished cannabis products;

(3) The Department observes or has information that conditions at the licensee's premises exist that present an immediate risk to worker or public health and safety;

(4) To prevent illegal diversion of cannabis or cannabis products, or other criminal activity at the licensee's premises; or

(5) To prevent the destruction of evidence related to illegal activity or violations of the Act.

(b) Temporary, interim relief may include one or more of the following:

(1) The temporary suspension of a license;

(2) An order to segregate or isolate specified cannabis products;

(3) An order prohibiting the movement of cannabis products from the premises or the receipt of cannabis or cannabis products at the premises;

(4) An order to cease some or all manufacturing operations at the premises;

(5) An order prohibiting the sale of specified cannabis products; or

(6) An order for the recall of cannabis products.

(c) The emergency decision and order issued by the Department shall include a brief explanation of the factual and legal basis for the emergency decision that justify the Department's determination that emergency action is necessary and the specific actions ordered. The emergency decision and order shall be effective when issued or as otherwise provided by the decision and order.

(d) The emergency decision and order for temporary, interim relief shall be issued in accordance with the following procedures:

(1) The Department shall give notice of the emergency decision and order and an opportunity to be heard to the licensee prior to the issuance, or effective date, of the emergency decision and order, if practicable;

(2) Notice and hearing under this section may be oral or written and may be provided by telephone, personal service, mail, facsimile transmission, electronic mail, or other electronic means, as the circumstances permit;

(3) Notice may be given to the licensee, any person meeting the definition of owner for the licensee, or to the manager or other personnel at the licensee's premises;

(4) Upon receipt of the notice, the licensee may request a hearing within three (3) business days by submitting a written request for hearing to the Department through electronic mail, facsimile transmission, or other written means. The hearing shall commence within five (5) business days of the Department's receipt of the written request for hearing, unless a later time is agreed upon by the Department and the licensee;

(5) The hearing shall be in the nature of an informal conference before the Department's Director or his or her designee, and shall permit the licensee and Department personnel to offer written or oral evidence and comments on the issues. The hearing does not require the opportunity for pre-hearing discovery or cross-examination of witnesses; and

(6) Following the hearing, the emergency decision and order shall be affirmed, modified, or set aside as determined appropriate by the Department within five (5) business days of the hearing.

(e) Within ten (10) days of the issuance or effective date of the emergency decision and order for temporary, interim relief, the Department shall commence adjudicative proceedings in accordance with Chapter 5 (commencing with Section 11500) of Part 1 of Division 3 of Title 2 of the Government Code to resolve the underlying issues giving rise to the temporary, interim relief, notwithstanding the pendency of proceedings for judicial review of the emergency decision as provided in subsection (g).

(f) After formal proceedings pursuant to subsection (e) of this section are held, a licensee aggrieved by a final decision of the Department may appeal the decision to the Cannabis Control Appeals Panel pursuant to section 26043 of the Act.

(g) Notwithstanding administrative proceedings commenced pursuant to subsection (e), the licensee may obtain judicial review of the emergency decision and order pursuant to section 1094.5 of the Code of Civil Procedure in the manner provided in section 11460.80 of the Government Code without exhaustion of administrative remedies.

(h) The Department's authority in this section is in addition to, and does not preclude the exercise of, the Department's authority governing the recall of cannabis products in section 26132 of the Act and its authority to embargo cannabis products in section 26133 of the Act. The authority provided by this section may be used in addition to any civil, criminal, or other administrative remedies available to the Department.

Note: Authority cited: Sections 26012 and 26013, Business and Professions Code. Reference: Sections 26011.5 and 26013, Business and Professions Code; and Sections 11460.10, 11460.20, 11460.30, 11460.40, 11460.50, 11460.60, 11460.70 and 11460.80, Government Code.

SUBCHAPTER 7. TRANSITIONAL PERIOD [REPEALED]

§ 40600. License Designations. [Repealed]

§ 40601. Packaging and Labeling. [Repealed]

Index

A

ADVERTISING

Advertising and Marketing Regulations (17 CCR § 40525), 522

Cannabis Goods Display (16 CCR § 5405), 392

Contracts (B&P §§ 26230 to 26230.3), 135

Physician Recommendations (B&P § 2525.5), 60

Posting and Advertising (16 CCR §§ 5039 to 5041.1), 371-373

Restrictions (B&P §§ 26150 to 26156), 111-113

ALCOHOLIC BEVERAGES

Cannabis Events (16 CCR §§ 5602, 5603), 414-416

Marketing Cannabis Goods as Alcoholic Products (16 CCR § 5040.1), 372

Motor Vehicles (Veh §§ 23152, 23220 to 23222), 258-259

Orally-Consumed Products Containing Alcohol (17 CCR § 40308), 508

Premises Location (16 CCR § 5026), 365

Restrictions on Sales of Alcohol by Retailer of Cannabis (B&P §§ 26054, 26070.2), 84, 98

Restrictions on Sales of Cannabis by Retailer of Alcoholic Beverages (B&P § 25621.5), 65

ANNUAL REPORTS

Cannabis Cooperative Associations (B&P § 26228.3), 133

Report to the Legislature by Each Licensing Authority (B&P §§ 26190 to 26191), 116-118

Public Report by Advisory Committee (B&P § 26014), 72

APPEALS

General Appeals Provisions (B&P §§ 26040 to 26047), 76-79

Cannabis Control Appeals Panel Annual Salary (Gov §§ 11553, 11553.5), 162-163

Criminal Defendant Medical Cannabis Use Appeal (H&S § 11362.795), 203

Manufacturing License Denial (17 CCR § 40167), 479

Notice of Violation Appeal (3 CCR § 8605), 337

AUDITS

Cultivation License Audits (3 CCR §§ 8408, 8500, 8501), 318

Licensing Authority Performance Audit (B&P §§ 26190 to 26191), 116-118

Tax Fund Audit (Rev&Tax § 34020), 256

Testing Laboratory Audits (16 CCR § 5735), 446

B

BUREAU OF CANNABIS CONTROL

Administration (B&P §§ 26010 to 26018), 69-73

Advertising (16 CCR §§ 5040 to 5041.1), 371-373

Advisory Committee (B&P § 26014), 72

Applications (16 CCR §§ 5001 to 5013), 341-353

Cannabis Events (16 CCR §§ 5600 to 5604), 409-416

Definition (B&P § 26010), 69

Destruction (16 CCR §§ 5052.1, 5054), 379-380

Distributors (16 CCR §§ 5300 to 5315), 381-389

Duties (B&P § 26010.5), 69

Enforcement (16 CCR §§ 5800 to 5815), 448-456

Events (16 CCR §§ 5600 to 5604), 409-416

Jurisdiction (B&P § 26010.5), 69

Laboratories (16 CCR §§ 5700 to 5739), 416-448

Licensing (16 CCR §§ 5014 to 5038), 353-370

Local Equity Program Assistance (B&P § 26246), 138

Microbusiness (16 CCR §§ 5500 to 5507), 402-409

Posting Requirement (16 CCR § 5039), 371

Powers (B&P § 26010.5), 69

Purpose (B&P § 26010.5), 69

Regulations (16 CCR §§ 5000 to 5905), 339-460

Research Funding (16 CCR §§ 5900 to 5905), 458-460

Responsibilities (B&P § 26010.5), 69

Retailers (16 CCR §§ 5400 to 5427), 390-402

Returns (16 CCR §§ 5052.1, 5053), 379-380

Security Measures (16 CCR §§ 5042 to 5047), 373-375

Testing Laboratories (16 CCR §§ 5700 to 5739), 416-448

Track and Trace (16 CCR §§ 5048 to 5042), 376-379

BUSINESS AND PROFESSIONS CODE

Alcoholic Beverages (B&P § 25621.5), 65

Cannabis Business (B&P §§ 26000 to 26250), 65-139

Farm Names, Trade Names (B&P §§ 14460 to 14465), 64-65

C

CANNABIS COOPERATIVE ASSOCIATIONS

Articles of Incorporation (B&P §§ 26224 to 26224.2), 125

Bylaws (B&P §§ 26225 to 26225.95), 126-128

Definitions (B&P §§ 26220 to 26220.3), 122

Directors and Management (B&P §§ 26226 to 26226.9), 128-130

Financial Provisions (B&P §§ 26228 to 26228.3), 132-133

General Provisions (B&P §§ 26222 to 26222.6), 122-123

Management and Directors (B&P §§ 26226 to 26226.9), 128-130

Marketing Contracts (B&P §§ 26230 to 26230.3), 135

Members (B&P §§ 26229 to 26229.8), 133-134

Powers (B&P §§ 26227 to 26227.9), 130-132

Purposes (B&P § 26223), 124

Reorganization of Corporations (B&P §§ 26231 to 26231.2), 136

CANNABIS EVENT LICENSES

Educational Cannabis Events (16 CCR § 5604), 416

Event Organizer License (16 CCR § 5600), 409

Informational Cannabis Events (16 CCR § 5604), 416

Local Control (B&P § 26200), 118

Temporary Cannabis Event License (16 CCR §§ 5601 to 5603), 412-416

CALIFORNIA CANNABIS EQUITY ACT

Definitions (B&P § 26240), 136

Provisions (B&P §§ 26242 to 26250), 137-139

CHILDREN AND MINORS

Advertising Restrictions (B&P § 26151), 111

Child-Resistant Packaging Requirements (17 CCR § 40417), 517

Parental and Custodial Rights to Minor Children Protection for Medical Cannabis Patients (H&S § 11362.84), 205

Product Specifications- Not to Appeal to Children (B&P § 26130), 106

Protection of Minors (B&P § 26140), 110

Restrictions Related to Cannabis and Minors (H&S § 11361), 184

CIVIL CODE

Contracts for Commercial Cannabis Activity Enforceability (Civ § 1550.5), 140

History of California Cannabis Legislation (Civ § 1550.5), 140

Medical Records Confidential (Civ § 56.06), 139

COMPASSIONATE USE ACT OF 1996 - Proposition 215 (H&S § 11362.5), 193

CONCENTRATED CANNABIS
Definition (H&S § 11006.5), 169
Licenses - SEE MANUFACTURING LICENSES
Penalty for Unlawful Possession of Concentrated Cannabis (H&S § 11357), 177
Personal Lawful Possession of Concentrated Cannabis (H&S § 11362.1), 190
Penalty for Unlawfully Manufacturing Concentrated Cannabis by Means of Chemical Extraction (H&S § 11379.6), 212

CONTRACTS
Cannabis Cooperative Associations Marketing Contracts (B&P §§ 26230 to 26230.3), 135
Cannabis Cooperative Associations Powers to Contract (B&P §§ 26227.7, 26227.9), 131, 132
Commercial Cannabis Activity (Civ § 1550.5), 140
Enforceability of Contracts for Commercial Cannabis Activity (Civ § 1550.5), 140
Fair Trade and Competition (B&P § 26052), 83
Marketing Contracts for Cannabis Cooperative Associations (B&P §§ 26230 to 26230.3), 135
Powers to Contract of Cannabis Cooperative Associations (B&P §§ 26227.7, 26227.9), 131, 132
Records Retention (16 CCR § 5037), 369

CONTROLLED SUBSTANCES
Cannabis Possession (H&S § 11357), 177
Cannabis Possession for Sale (H&S § 11359), 183
Cannabis Cultivation (H&S § 11358), 182
Concentrated Cannabis Possession (H&S § 11357), 177
Definition (H&S § 11007), 169
Destruction of a Suspected Controlled Substance (H&S §§ 11479, 11479.2), 216-217
Forfeiture for Violations of the Controlled Substances Act (H&S § 11470), 212
Gift of Cannabis - Unlawful (H&S § 11360), 184
Importation of Cannabis - Unlawful (H&S § 11360), 184
Lawful Cannabis (H&S § 11362.1), 190
Lawful Cannabis Restrictions (H&S § 11362.3), 191
Maintaining a Place for Selling, Giving Away, or Using Any Controlled Substance (H&S § 11366), 211
Manufacturing of a Controlled Substance (H&S § 11379.6), 212
Nuisance (H&S § 11570), 220
Personal Cultivation of Cannabis Restrictions (H&S § 11362.2), 190
Registration of Controlled Substance Offenders (H&S § 11590), 220
Renting, Leasing, or Making Available for Unlawfully Manufacturing, Storing, or Distributing Any Controlled Substance (H&S § 11366.5), 211
Sale of Cannabis- Unlawful (H&S § 11360), 184
Schedule 1 Classification (H&S § 11054), 172
Synthetic Cannabinoid Compound (H&S § 11357.5), 178
Synthetic Cannabinoid Derivative (H&S § 11357.5), 178
Transportation of Cannabis - Unlawful (H&S § 11360), 184

CONVICTIONS

Criminal Defendant Medical Cannabis Use (H&S § 11362.795), 203

Cultivation License Denial for Conviction (3 CCR § 8113), 294

Destruction of Arrest and Conviction Records (H&S § 11361.5), 185

Employers and Cannabis Convictions (Lab § 432.8), 224

License Applications and Convictions (16 CCR § 5017), 357

License Denial for Conviction (B&P §§ 26057 to 26059), 87-88

Manufacturing License Denial for Conviction (17 CCR §§ 40159 to 40167), 477-479

Notification of Conviction Requirement (3 CCR § 8204), 300

CULTIVATION

Applications (3 CCR §§ 8100 to 8115), 281-296

Audits (3 CCR §§ 8500, 8501), 318

Cannabis Cultivation Program (3 CCR §§ 8000 to 8609), 279-338

Definitions (3 CCR § 8000), 279

Diversion or Use of Water for Cannabis Cultivation (Wat §§ 1847, 13149), 266, 268

Enforcement (3 CCR §§ 8600 to 8609), 319-338

Environmental Impact of Cannabis Cultivation (F&G § 12029), 145

Establishment of Cannabis Cultivation Program (B&P § 26069), 95

Fees for Annual License (3 CCR § 8200), 296

Fees for Annual License Application (3 CCR § 8101), 282

Fish and Game General Agreement Related to Cannabis Cultivation (F&G § 1617), 143

Inspections (3 CCR §§ 8500, 8501), 318

Investigations (3 CCR §§ 8500, 8501), 318

Licensed Cultivation Sites (B&P §§ 26060 to 26066), 88-93

License Types (3 CCR § 8201), 297

Microbusiness (16 CCR §§ 5500 to 5507), 402-409

Penalty for Unlawful Cultivation of Cannabis (H&S § 11358), 182

Personal Cultivation of Cannabis Restrictions (H&S § 11362.2), 190

Records and Reporting (3 CCR §§ 8400 to 8409), 311-318

Requirements as Licensee (3 CCR §§ 8202 to 8216), 298-305

Taxes (Rev&Tax §§ 34012 to 34012.5), 246-247

Track and Trace (B&P §§ 26067 to 26069.9, 3 CCR §§ 8402 to 8407), 93-96, 313-317

Unlawful Cultivation of Cannabis (H&S § 11358), 182

Use of Water for Cannabis Cultivation (Wat §§ 1847, 13149), 266, 268

D

DEFINITIONS

Advertising and Marketing Definitions (B&P § 26150), 111

Agricultural Employees Related Definitions (Lab § 1140.4), 224

Best Available Technologies Definition (Wat § 5100), 266

Best Professional Practices Definition (Wat § 5100), 266

Bureau of Cannabis Control Definitions (16 CCR § 5000), 339

Cannabis Definition (H&S § 11018), 171

Cannabis Accessories Definition (H&S § 11018.2), 171

Cannabis Business Definitions (B&P § 26001), 66

Cannabis Cooperative Associations Definitions (B&P §§ 26220 to 26220.3), 122

Cannabis Cultivation Program Definitions (3 CCR § 8000), 279

Cannabis Products Definition (H&S § 11018.1), 171

Cannabis Tax Definitions (Rev&Tax § 34010), 244

Concentrated Cannabis Definition (H&S § 11006.5), 169

Controlled Substance Definition (H&S § 11007), 169

Drug Paraphernalia Definition (H&S §§ 11014.5, 11364.5), 170, 209

Excessive Concentration of Licensees Definition (B&P § 26051), 80

Farm Product Definition (Fd&Ag § 55403), 147

Processor Definition (Fd&Ag § 55407), 147

Producer Definition (Fd&Ag § 55408),148

Hemp Division Definitions (Fd&Ag § 81000), 154

Industrial Hemp Definition (H&S § 11018.5), 172

Manufactured Cannabis Definitions (17 CCR § 40100), 461

Manufacturing Practices Definitions (17 CCR § 40230), 490

Marketing Definitions (B&P § 26150), 111

Medical Cannabis Related Definitions (H&S § 11362.7), 194

Microbusiness Definition (B&P § 26001.1), 69

Neighbor Definition (Fd&Ag § 52452), 146

Person Definition (Wat § 5100), 266

Shared-Use Facilities Definitions (17 CCR § 40190), 484

Testing Laboratories Definitions (16 CCR § 5700), 416

The California Cannabis Equity Act Definitions (B&P § 26240), 136

Water Diversion Definition (Wat § 5100), 266

Water Recycling Act of 1991 Definitions (Wat § 13575), 276

DELIVERY

Cannabis Consumption During Delivery (16 CCR § 5419), 399

Cannabis Delivery (B&P § 26090), 100

Cannabis Goods Carried During Delivery (16 CCR § 5418), 398

Employees of Cannabis Delivery (16 CCR § 5415), 396

Jurisdictions to Which Deliveries Can Be Made (16 CCR § 5416), 397

Non-Storefront Retailer (16 CCR § 5414), 395

Physical Address Deliveries (16 CCR § 5416), 397

Receipt Request for Delivery (16 CCR § 5420), 399

Route for Delivery (16 CCR § 5421), 400

Technology Platforms (16 CCR § 5415.1), 396

Vehicle Requirements for Delivery (16 CCR § 5417), 397

DISTRIBUTOR LICENSES

Distribution Activities (16 CCR § 5300), 381

General Laws Related to Distributors (B&P §§ 26070 to 26070.5), 96-99

General Regulations Related to Distributors (16 CCR §§ 5300 to 5315), 381-389

Inspection Responsibility of Distributor (B&P § 26110), 103

Insurance Requirements (16 CCR § 5308), 385

Inventory Accounting (16 CCR § 5309), 386

Laboratory Laws Related to Distributors Generally (B&P §§ 26070 to 26070.5), 96-99

License Classifications (B&P § 26050), 79

Licensed Distributor to Licensed Distributor Transfers (16 CCR § 5307.2), 385

Local Control (B&P § 26200), 118

Net Weight of Dried Flower (16 CCR § 5303.1), 382

Packaging, Labeling, and Rolling (16 CCR § 5303), 382

Quality Assurance (B&P § 26110), 103

Quality Assurance Review (16 CCR § 5307), 384

Quality-Assurance Review for Labeling Cannabinoids and Terpenoids (16 CCR § 5307.1), 385

Records (16 CCR § 5310), 386

Regulations Related to Distributors Generally (16 CCR §§ 5300 to 5315), 381-389

Re-Sampling (16 CCR § 5305.1), 383

Responsibilities of Distributors (B&P § 26110), 103

Security and Safety Standards for Distributors (B&P § 26070), 96

Shipping Manifest (16 CCR § 5314), 389

Storage of Batches for Testing (16 CCR § 5302), 381

Storage Services (16 CCR § 5301), 381

Tax Collected by Distributor from Cultivator (Rev&Tax § 34012.5), 247

Testing Arrangements (16 CCR § 5304), 383

Testing Prior to Sale (B&P § 26110), 103

Testing Results (16 CCR § 5306), 383

Testing Sample (16 CCR § 5305), 383

Transfers from Licensed Distributor to Licensed Distributor (16 CCR § 5307.2), 385

Transport and Distribution (B&P § 26080), 100

Transportation of Cannabis Goods (16 CCR § 5311), 387

Transport Only License (16 CCR § 5315), 389

Transport Personnel Requirements (16 CCR § 5313), 388

Transport Vehicle Required Information (16 CCR § 5312), 388

DRIVING

Delivery (B&P § 26090), 100

Distribution and Transport (B&P § 26080), 100

Impaired Driving- Cannabis and Alcohol (Veh §§ 2429.7, 23152, 23220, 23221, 23222, and 40000.15), 257-260

Laboratory Transportation of Cannabis Samples (16 CCR § 5709), 427

Possession of Cannabis While Driving- Unlawful (Veh § 23222), 259

Security and Safety Transportation Requirements for Retailer, Distributor, and Microbusiness (B&P § 26070), 96

Transportation of Cannabis Goods Requirements (16 CCR §§ 5311 to 5313), 387-388

Transport of Cannabis Between Licensees (B&P § 26161), 113

Unlawful Transportation of Cannabis (H&S § 11360), 184

E

EDIBLE CANNABIS PRODUCTS

General Provisions (B&P § 26130), 106

Labeling Requirements for Edible Cannabis Products (17 CCR § 40406), 512

Milk Products (Fd&Ag § 37104), 146

Requirements for Edible Cannabis Product (17 CCR § 40305), 508

ENFORCEMENT

General Laws (B&P §§ 26030 to 26038), 73-76

General Regulation (16 CCR §§ 5800 to 5815), 448-456

Local Enforcement Authority (B&P §§ 26200 to 26202), 118-120

Minors and Cannabis (B&P § 26140), 110

Watershed Enforcement Program (Fish&G § 12029), 145

EVENT LICENSES

Educational Cannabis Events (16 CCR § 5604), 416

Event Organizer License (16 CCR § 5600), 409

Informational Cannabis Events (16 CCR § 5604), 416

Local Control (B&P § 26200), 118

Locations of Cannabis Events (B&P § 26200), 118

Temporary Cannabis Event License (16 CCR §§ 5601 to 5603), 412-416

EVIDENCE CODE

Crime/Fraud Exception to the Lawyer-Client Privilege (Evid § 956), 141

F

FEES

Cultivation Fees for Annual License (3 CCR § 8200), 296

Cultivation Fees for Annual License Application (3 CCR § 8101), 282

Hemp Cultivation or Seed Breeding Fee (Fd&Ag § 81005), 158

License Fees (B&P §§ 26180 to 26191), 116-118

Medical Cannabis ID Card (H&S §§ 11362.715 and 11362.755), 197, 200

Water Appropriation Fees (Wat §§ 1525, 1535), 261

FISH AND GAME CODE

Cannabis Cultivation Specifics General Agreement (Fish&G § 1617), 143

Environmental Impact of Cannabis Cultivation (Fish&G § 12029), 145

Water Diversion or Obstruction Notification Requirements (Fish&G § 1602), 141

FOOD AND AGRICULTURAL CODE

Cannabis Seed Labeling Requirements (Fd&Ag § 52452), 146

"Cooperative" in Business Name Restrictions (Fd&Ag § 54036), 147

Farm Product Definition (Fd&Ag § 55403), 147

Industrial Hemp (Fd&Ag §§ 81000 to 81011), 154-161

Milk Product Exception for Medical Cannabis (Fd&Ag § 37104), 146

Neighbor Definition (Fd&Ag § 52452), 146

Processor Definition (Fd&Ag § 55407), 147

Producer Definition (Fd&Ag § 55408), 148

Producer's Lien (Fd&Ag §§ 55631 to 55653), 148-153

FUNDING

California Cannabis Tax Fund (Rev&Tax §§ 34018 to 34021.5), 250-256

Cannabis Control Fund (B&P §§ 26180, 26210 to 26211), 116, 120-121

Cannabis Program Fund (B&P §§ 26210 to 26211), 120-121

Cannabis Research Funding (16 CCR §§ 5900 to 5905), 458-460

Medical Cannabis Regulation and Safety Act Fund (B&P § 205.1), 57

G

GOVERNMENT CODE

Cannabis Control Appeals Panel Chairperson Annual Salary (Gov § 11553), 162

Cannabis Control Appeals Panel Member Annual Salary (Gov § 11553), 162

Destruction of Court Records (Gov § 68152), 163

"Eligible Agency" Definition (Gov § 9147.7), 161

Sunset Review Committee (Gov § 9147.7), 161

H

HEALTH AND SAFETY CODE

Arrest and Conviction Records Destruction (H&S §§ 11361.5, 11361.7), 185-187

Butane Restrictions (H&S § 11107.2), 176

California Marijuana Research Program (H&S § 11362.9), 205

"Cannabis Accessories" Definition (H&S § 11018.2), 171

Cannabis and Hallucinogenic Drugs Research Advisory Panel (H&S § 11480), 218

Cannabis and Plants Allowed for Qualified Patients (H&S § 11362.77), 202

Cannabis Cultivation (H&S § 11358), 182

"Cannabis" Definition (H&S § 11018),171

Cannabis Possession (H&S § 11357), 177

"Cannabis Products" Definition (H&S § 11018.1), 171

Community Service Provisions for Cannabis Offense (H&S § 11362.4), 192

Compassionate Use Act of 1996- Proposition 215 (H&S § 11362.5), 193

"Concentrated Cannabis" Definition (H&S § 11006.5), 169

Concentrated Cannabis Possession (H&S § 11357), 177

"Controlled Substance" Definition (H&S § 11007), 169

Conviction and Arrest Records Destruction (H&S §§ 11361.5, 11361.7), 185-187

Counseling Provisions for Cannabis (H&S §§ 11361.1, 11362.4), 185,192

Criminal Defendant Medical Cannabis Use (H&S § 11362.795), 203

Criminal Liability Exceptions (H&S § 11362.765), 201

Cultivation of Cannabis (H&S § 11358), 182

Destruction of Arrest and Conviction Records (H&S §§ 11361.5, 11361.7), 185-187

Destruction of a Suspected Controlled Substance (H&S §§ 11479, 11479.2), 216-217

Dismissal or Reduction of Charges (H&S §§ 11361.8, 11361.9), 187-189

Drug Education Provisions for Cannabis (H&S §§ 11361.1, 11362.4), 185, 192

"Drug" Meaning (H&S § 109925), 223

"Drug Paraphernalia" Definition (H&S § 11014.5), 170

Employment Accommodation of Medical Cannabis Not Required (H&S § 11362.785), 202

Environmental Impacts of Cannabis Cultivation (H&S § 11362.769), 202

"Felony Offense" Meaning (H&S § 11362), 189

Forfeiture for Violations of the Controlled Substances Act (H&S § 11470), 212

Gift of Cannabis- Unlawful (H&S § 11360), 184

Hazardous Waste (H&S §§ 25189.5 to 25189.7), 221-222

Importation of Cannabis- Unlawful (H&S § 11360), 184

"Industrial Hemp" Definition (H&S § 11018.5), 172

Industrial Hemp Regulation (H&S § 11018.5), 172

Lawful Cannabis (H&S §§ 11362.1, 11362.45), 190, 192

Lawful Cannabis Manufacturing Restrictions (H&S §§ 11362.3, 11362.4), 191-192

Lawful Cannabis Possession and Use Restrictions (H&S §§ 11362.3, 11362.4), 191-192

Local Control Over Collectives and Cooperatives (H&S § 11362.83), 205

Location Restrictions of Medical Cannabis Business in Relation to a School (H&S § 11362.768), 201

Maintaining a Place for the Purpose of Selling, Giving Away, or Using Any Controlled Substance (H&S § 11366), 211

Manufacturing of a Controlled Substance (H&S § 11379.6), 212

Medical Cannabis Definitions (H&S § 11362.7), 194

Medical Cannabis ID Card Program (H&S §§ 11362.71 to § 11362.76, 11362.78), 195-200, 202

Medical Marijuana Provisions for Organ Transplants (H&S § 7151.36), 169

Minors and Cannabis Restrictions (H&S § 11361), 184

Offense "Punishable as a Felony" Meaning (H&S § 11362), 189

Organ Transplant Medical Marijuana Provisions (H&S § 7151.36), 169

Parental and Custodial Rights to Minor Children Protection for Medical Cannabis Patients (H&S § 11362.84), 205

Penal Institution Accommodation of Medical Cannabis Not Required (H&S § 11362.785), 202

Personal Cultivation of Cannabis Restrictions (H&S §§ 11362.2, 11362.4), 190, 192

Petition for Reduction or Dismissal of Charges (H&S § 11361.8), 187

Possession of Cannabis (H&S § 11357), 177

Possession of Cannabis for Sale (H&S § 11359), 183

Possession of Concentrated Cannabis (H&S § 11357), 177

Professional License Protection for Medical Cannabis Patient (H&S § 11362.8), 204

Professional License Protection for Primary Caregivers (H&S § 11362.8), 204

Proposition 215- Compassionate Use Act of 1996 (H&S § 11362.5), 193

Public Consumption of Cannabis Restrictions (H&S § 11362.79), 203

Reduction or Dismissal of Charges (H&S §§ 11361.8, 11361.9), 187-189

Renting, Leasing, or Making Available for Unlawfully Manufacturing, Storing, or Distributing Any Controlled Substance (H&S § 11366.5), 211

Registration of Controlled Substance Offenders (H&S § 11590), 220

Research Advisory Panel - Cannabis and Hallucinogenic Drugs (H&S § 11480), 218

Sale of Cannabis- Unlawful (H&S § 11360), 184

Schedule 1 Classification (H&S § 11054), 172

Seizure of Items for Violations of the Controlled Substances Act (H&S §§ 11472 to 11477, 11485), 215-216, 219

Synthetic Cannabinoid Compound (H&S § 11357.5), 178

Synthetic Cannabinoid Derivative (H&S § 11357.5), 178

Transportation of Cannabis- Unlawful (H&S § 11360), 184

HEMP
Attorney General Reports on Industrial Hemp (Fd&Ag § 81008), 160

Cultivation of Industrial Hemp Registration (Fd&Ag § 81003), 156

Definitions Related to Hemp Division (Fd&Ag § 81000), 154

Economic Impact Report on Industrial Hemp (Fd&Ag § 81009), 160

Fees for Industrial Hemp Cultivation or Seed Breeding (Fd&Ag § 81005), 158

Hemp Research Sites (Fd&Ag § 81011), 161

Imports of Industrial Hemp (Fd&Ag § 81006), 158

Industrial Hemp Agricultural Pilot Program (Fd&Ag § 81007), 160

"Industrial Hemp Definition (H&S § 11018.5), 172

Laboratory Testing of Industrial Hemp (Fd&Ag § 81006), 158

Limitations on Industrial Hemp Growth (Fd&Ag § 81006), 158

Operation of Hemp Division (Fd&Ag § 81010), 161

Prohibitions on Industrial Hemp Growth (Fd&Ag § 81006), 158

Research Sites (Fd&Ag § 81011), 161

Seed Breeder of Industrial Hemp Registration (Fd&Ag § 81004), 157

Seed Cultivars (Fd&Ag § 81002), 155

Seed Provisions (Fd&Ag § 81002), 155

I

INSURANCE

Distributor Licensee Insurance Requirements (16 CCR § 5308), 385

Distributors Transport Vehicle Required Information (16 CCR § 5312), 388

Medical Cannabis and Health Insurance- No Reimbursement Requirement (H&S § 11362.785), 202

L

LABELING

Bureau of Cannabis Control Packaging, Labeling, and Rolling (16 CCR § 5303), 382

Cannabinoids and Terpenoids Labeling Quality-Assurance Review (16 CCR § 5307.1), 385

Cannabis and Nonmanufactured Cannabis Products Packaging and Labeling (3 CCR § 8212), 304

Cannabis Seed Labeling Requirements (Fd&Ag § 52452), 146

Department of Public Health Labeling Standards (B&P §§ 26106, 26120, 26121), 103-105

Edible Cannabis Products Labeling Requirements (17 CCR § 40406), 512

Manufactured Cannabis Labeling and Packaging Requirements (17 CCR §§ 40400 to 40417), 510-517

Manufacturers Labeling Standards (B&P §§ 26106, 26120, 26121), 103-105

Microbusinesses Labeling Standards (B&P §§ 26106, 26120, 26121), 103-105

Nonmanufactured Cannabis Products Packaging and Labeling (3 CCR § 8212), 304

Quality-Assurance Review for Labeling Cannabinoids and Terpenoids (16 CCR § 5307.1), 385

Retailer Packaging and Labeling Prohibition (16 CCR § 5412), 395

LABORATORIES

Cannabinoid Testing (16 CCR § 5724), 438

Cannabis or Cannabis Product Testing Requirements (B&P § 26100), 100

Certificate of Analysis- COA (16 CCR § 5726), 440

Chain of Custody Protocol (B&P § 26100, 16 CCR § 5706), 100, 425

Chemical Profile (B&P § 26100), 100

Contaminants (B&P § 26100), 100

Definitions (16 CCR § 5700), 416

Destruction of Noncompliant Harvested Batches (B&P § 26104), 102

Distributors Testing Responsibilities (16 CCR §§ 5302 to 5307.1), 381-385

Employee Qualifications for Laboratory (16 CCR §§ 5736 to 5738), 447

Foreign Material Testing (16 CCR § 5722), 437

General Laboratory License Requirements (16 CCR § 5701), 421

Heavy Metals Testing (16 CCR § 5723), 438

Hemp Laboratory Testing (Fd&Ag § 81006), 158

Industrial Hemp Laboratory Testing (Fd&Ag § 81006), 158

Interim Testing Laboratory License (16 CCR § 5703), 422

Laboratory Employee Qualifications (16 CCR §§ 5736 to 5738), 447

Laboratory License Application (16 CCR § 5702), 421

Laboratory Quality Assurance and Quality Control (16 CCR §§ 5729 to 5735), 442-446

License Requirements Generally (16 CCR § 5701), 421

Medical Cannabis Patients (B&P § 26104), 102

Microbial Impurities Testing (16 CCR § 5720), 436

Moisture Content and Water Activity Testing (16 CCR § 5717), 432

Multiple Licenses (B&P § 26053), 84

Mycotoxin Testing (16 CCR § 5721), 437

Noncompliant Harvested Batches (B&P § 26104), 102

Pesticides Testing (16 CCR § 5719), 434

Phase-in of Required Laboratory Testing (16 CCR § 5715), 431

Post Testing Procedures (16 CCR §§ 5727 to 5728), 441-442

Processing Chemicals Testing (16 CCR § 5718), 433

Quality Assurance and Quality Control of Laboratories (16 CCR §§ 5729 to 5735), 442-446

Record Retention (16 CCR § 5739), 448

Required Testing (16 CCR §§ 5714 to 5715), 431

Residual Levels of Volatile Organic Compounds (B&P § 26100), 100

Residual Pesticides Testing (16 CCR § 5719), 436

Residual Solvents and Processing Chemicals Testing (16 CCR § 5718), 433

Sampling Cannabis and Cannabis Products (16 CCR §§ 5704 to 5710), 423-428

Standard Operating Procedures (16 CCR §§ 5711 to 5713), 428-429

Terpenoid Testing (16 CCR § 5725), 440

Testing Laboratories Licensee Prohibited from Licensure for Any Other Activity (B&P § 26053), 84

Testing License Requirements (B&P § 26102, 16 CCR §§ 5701 to 5702), 102, 421

Testing Methods (B&P § 26100), 100

Testing Restricted to Licensed Businesses, Qualified Patients, and Primary Caregivers (B&P § 26104), 102

Water Activity and Moisture Content Testing (16 CCR § 5717), 432

LABOR CODE

Agricultural Employees Definitions (Lab § 1140.4), 224

Agricultural Employees Rights (Lab § 1140.2), 224

Alatorre-Zenovich-Dunlap-Berman Agricultural Labor Relations Act of 1975 (Lab § 1140), 224

Cannabis Convictions Subject to the Limitations on Employers (Lab § 432.8), 224

Definitions Related to Agricultural Employees (Lab § 1140.4), 224

Employers and Cannabis Convictions (Lab § 432.8), 224

Medical Cannabis Advisory Committee (Lab § 147.5), 223

Nonmedical Cannabis Businesses Advisory Committee (Lab § 147.6), 223

Rights of Agricultural Employees (Lab § 1140.2), 224

LOCAL CONTROL

Cooperative Agreement Between State and Local Agencies (B&P § 26069.1), 96

Delivery - Local Control Limitations (B&P § 26090), 100

Distribution and Transport Limits on Local Control (B&P § 26080), 100

Limits on Local Control - Delivery (B&P § 26090), 100

Limits on Local Control - Distribution and Transport (B&P § 26080), 100

Local Control Generally (B&P §§ 26200 to 26202), 118-120

Local Equity Program Assistance (B&P § 26246), 138

M

MANUFACTURING LICENSES

Advertising and Marketing (17 CCR § 40525), 522

Alcohol- Products Containing Alcohol (17 CCR § 40308), 508

Annual License Applications (17 CCR §§ 40128 to 40137), 469-475

Application Fees (17 CCR § 40150), 475

Applications for Manufacturing Licenses (17 CCR §§ 40126 to 40167), 468-479

Batch Production Record (17 CCR § 40258), 499

Building, Grounds, and Manufacturing Premises (17 CCR § 40240), 493

Cannabinoid Concentration Limits (17 CCR § 40315), 509

Cannabinoid Content Labeling (17 CCR § 40409), 514

Cannabis Product Components (17 CCR § 40248), 496

Child-Resistant Packaging Requirements (17 CCR § 40417), 517

Closed-Loop Extraction System Requirements (17 CCR § 40225), 489

Complaints Concerning Product (17 CCR § 40295), 505

Concentrates and Other Cannabis Products (17 CCR § 40306), 508

Concentration Limits (17 CCR § 40315), 509

Consent to Sample Collection (17 CCR § 40292), 505

Cultivation Tax Collected by Distributor or Manufacturer (Rev&Tax§ 34012.5), 247

Definitions (17 CCR §§ 40100, 40190, 40230), 461,484, 490

Denial of License (17 CCR §§ 40159 to 40167), 477-479

Dried Meat Processing (17 CCR § 40272), 501

Edible Cannabis Products Requirements and Restrictions (B&P § 26130, 17 CCR § 40305), 106, 508

Emergency Decision and Order (17 CCR § 40570), 523

Equipment and Utensils (17 CCR § 40243), 494

Ethanol Extractions (17 CCR § 40223), 489

Extractions (17 CCR §§ 40220 to 40225), 488-489

Failed Product Batches (17 CCR § 40330), 509

Fees (17 CCR §§ 40150 to 40152), 475-476

Financial Interest Holders and Owners (17 CCR § 40102), 465

Good Manufacturing Practices (17 CCR §§ 40230 to 40258), 490-499

Gross Annual Revenue Calculation (17 CCR § 40152), 476

Grounds, Building, and Manufacturing Premises (17 CCR § 40240), 493

Informational Panel Labeling Requirements (17 CCR § 40408), 513

Inspections (17 CCR §§ 40550 to 40551), 522-523

Inventory Control - Cannabis and Cannabis Products (17 CCR § 40282), 504

Juice Processing (17 CCR § 40270), 501

Labeling and Packaging Requirements for Manufactured Cannabis (17 CCR §§ 40400 to 40417), 510-517

Labeling Requirements: Pre-Rolls and Packaged Flower (17 CCR § 40404), 511

Labeling Restrictions (17 CCR § 40410), 515

Labeling Standards for Manufacturers (B&P §§ 26106, 26120, 26121), 103-105

Lawful Cannabis Manufacturing Restrictions (H&S §§ 11362.3, 11362.4), 191-192

License Categories (B&P § 26130), 106

License Denial (17 CCR § 40167), 479

License Fees (17 CCR § 40150), 475

Licenses Regulated by The State Department of Public Health (B&P § 26130), 106

Licenses Required for Manufacturing (17 CCR § 40115), 466

License Types (17 CCR § 40118), 467

Licensing (17 CCR §§ 40175 to 40184), 479-483

Manufactured Cannabis Definitions (17 CCR § 40100), 461

Manufacturers and Cannabis Products (B&P § 26130), 106

Manufacturing of a Controlled Substance (H&S § 11379.6), 212

Manufacturing License Categories (B&P § 26130), 106

Manufacturing License Denial (17 CCR § 40167), 479

Manufacturing Licenses Regulated by The State Department of Public Health (B&P § 26130), 106

Manufacturing License Types (17 CCR § 40118), 467

Manufacturing Practices Definitions (17 CCR § 40230), 490

Manufacturing Processes and Procedures (17 CCR § 40250), 496

Marketing and Advertising (17 CCR § 40525), 522

Master Manufacturing Protocol (17 CCR § 40255), 498

Microbusiness Applications Including Manufacturing Activities (16 CCR § 5506), 407

Microbusiness Failed Manufactured Cannabis Product Batches (16 CCR § 5506.1), 408

Microbusiness Records for Licensees Engaging in Manufacturing Activities (16 CCR § 5507), 409

New License Approval (17 CCR § 40155), 476

Orally-Consumed Products Containing Alcohol (17 CCR § 40308), 508

Other Cannabis Products (17 CCR § 40306), 508

Owners and Financial Interest Holders (17 CCR § 40102), 465

Packaged Flower and Pre-Rolls Labeling Requirements (17 CCR § 40404), 511

Packaging (17 CCR § 40415), 516

Packaging and Labeling Requirements (17 CCR §§ 40400 to 40417), 510-517

Penalties for Unlawful Manufacturing of a Controlled Substance (H&S § 11379.6), 212

Personnel (17 CCR § 40246), 495

Personnel Prohibited from Holding Licenses (17 CCR § 40116), 466

Premises (17 CCR § 40240), 493

Premises Diagram Requirements (17 CCR § 40105), 465

Pre-Rolls and Packaged Flower Labeling Requirements (17 CCR § 40404), 511

Primary Panel Labeling Requirements: Edible Products (17 CCR § 40406), 512

Primary Panel Labeling Requirements: Manufactured Products (17 CCR § 40405), 512

Priority License Issuance (17 CCR § 40156), 477

Processes and Procedures (17 CCR § 40250), 496

Product Complaints (17 CCR § 40295), 505

Product Standards (17 CCR §§ 40300 to 40308), 507-508

Product Quality Plan (17 CCR § 40253), 497

Prohibited Products (17 CCR § 40300), 507

Quality Control Program (17 CCR § 40235), 492

Recalls (17 CCR § 40297), 506

Record Keeping Requirements (17 CCR § 40500), 517

Renting, Leasing, or Making Available for Unlawfully Manufacturing Any Controlled Substance (H&S § 11366.5), 211

Safety Standards (B&P § 26105), 103

Sales Invoices and Receipts (17 CCR § 40505), 518

Sample Collection (17 CCR § 40292), 505

Security (17 CCR §§ 40200 to 40207), 486-488

Shared-Use Facilities (17 CCR §§ 40190 to 40196), 484-486

Standard Operating Procedures (17 CCR § 40275), 501

Statement of Characteristic Anticipated Effects (17 CCR § 40411), 515

Suspensions and Revocations of a License (17 CCR § 40570), 523

Tax Collected by Distributor or Manufacturer (Rev&Tax § 34012.5), 247

Temporary Licenses (17 CCR §§ 40126, 40127), 468

Temporary Manufacturing Licenses (17 CCR § 40126), 468

Temporary Shared-Use Facility Registration (17 CCR § 40127), 468

Temporary Type S License (17 CCR § 40127), 468

Topical Cannabis Products, Concentrates, and Other Cannabis Products (17 CCR § 40306), 508

Track-and-Trace System (17 CCR §§ 40510 to 40517), 519-521

Training Program (17 CCR § 40280), 502

Type S License (17 CCR § 40191), 484

Universal Symbol (17 CCR § 40412), 516

Utensils and Equipment (17 CCR § 40243), 494

Volatile Solvent Extractions (17 CCR § 40222), 489

Volatile Solvents (B&P § 26130), 106

Waste Management (17 CCR § 40290), 504

Weights and Measures (17 CCR § 40277), 502

MARKETING
Advertising and Marketing Regulations (17 CCR § 40525), 522

Cannabis Goods Display (16 CCR § 5405), 392

Contracts (B&P §§ 26230 to 26230.3), 135

Physician Recommendations (B&P § 2525.5), 60

Posting and Advertising (16 CCR §§ 5039 to 5041.1), 371-373

Restrictions (B&P §§ 26150 to 26156), 111-113

MEDICAL CANNABIS
Cannabis and Number of Plants Allowed for Each Qualified Patient (H&S § 11362.77), 202

Compassionate Use Act of 1996 - Proposition 215 (H&S § 11362.5), 193

Confidentiality of Medical Records (Civ § 56.06), 139

Counterfeiting Medical Cannabis ID Card (H&S § 11362.81), 204

Criminal Defendant Medical Cannabis Use (H&S § 11362.795), 203

Criminal Liability Exceptions (H&S § 11362.765), 201

Definitions Related to Medical Cannabis (H&S § 11362.7), 194

Employer Accommodation of Medical Cannabis Use- No Requirement (H&S § 11362.785), 202

Exemption of Licensing Requirement for Personal Medical Use (B&P § 26033), 74

Health Insurance Provider Liability- No Requirement (H&S § 11362.785), 202

Law Enforcement's Required Consideration of Medical Cannabis ID Card (H&S § 11362.78), 202

Medical Cannabis Milk Product Exception (Fd&Ag § 37104), 146

Medical Records Confidential (Civ § 56.06), 139

Milk Product Exception for Cannabis Product (Fd&Ag § 37104), 146

Organ Transplants Medical Marijuana Provisions (H&S § 7151.36), 169

Parental and Custodial Rights to Minor Children Protection for Medical Cannabis Patients (H&S § 11362.84), 205

Penal Institution Accommodation of Medical Cannabis Use- No Requirement (H&S § 11362.785), 202

Personal Medical Use Exemption of Licensing Requirement (B&P § 26033), 74

Physician's Recommendation (H&S § 11362.712), 196

Physician's Recommendation Requirements (B&P §§ 2525 to 2525.5), 59-60

Plants Allowed for Each Qualified Patient (H&S § 11362.77), 202

Professional License Protection (H&S § 11362.8), 204

Proposition 215 - Compassionate Use Act of 1996 (H&S § 11362.5), 193

Public Consumption Restrictions (H&S § 11362.79), 203

Quantity of Cannabis and Number of Plants Purportedly Allowed for Each Qualified Patient (H&S § 11362.77), 202

Recommending Medical Cannabis Requirements (B&P § 2241.5), 58

Restrictions on Location of Medical Cannabis Business in Relation to a School (H&S § 11362.768), 201

State Medical Cannabis ID Card Program (H&S §§ 11362.71 to 11362.76), 195-200

MICROBUSINESS LICENSE

Applications Including Cultivation Activities (16 CCR § 5501), 403

Applications Including Manufacturing Activities (16 CCR § 5506), 407

Cultivation Plan Requirements (16 CCR § 5502), 404

Cultivation Records for Licensees Engaging in Cultivation Activities (16 CCR § 5505), 407

Definition of Microbusiness (B&P § 26001.1), 69

Deliveries (B&P § 26090), 100

Failed Manufactured Cannabis Product Batches (16 CCR § 5506.1), 408

Impacted Watershed (16 CCR § 5504), 407

Labeling Standards for Microbusinesses (B&P §§ 26106, 26120, 26121), 103-105

Laboratory Receipt of Samples Obtained from a Distributor or Microbusiness (16 CCR § 5710), 428

Local Control (B&P § 26200), 118

Records for Licensees Engaging in Manufacturing Activities (16 CCR § 5507), 409

Regulations (16 CCR §§ 5500 to 5507), 402-409

Security and Safety Transportation Requirements for Retailer, Distributor, and Microbusiness (B&P § 26070), 96

Supplemental Water Source Information (16 CCR § 5503), 405

MINORS

Advertising Restrictions (B&P § 26151), 111

Child-Resistant Packaging Requirements (17 CCR § 40417), 517

Parental and Custodial Rights to Minor Children Protection for Medical Cannabis Patients (H&S § 11362.84), 205

Product Specifications - Not to Appeal to Children (B&P § 26130), 106

Protection of Minors (B&P § 26140), 110

Restrictions Related to Cannabis and Minors (H&S § 11361), 184

MOTOR VEHICLES

Delivery (B&P § 26090), 100

Distribution and Transport (B&P § 26080), 100

Impaired Driving - Cannabis and Alcohol (Veh §§ 2429.7, 23152, 23220, 23221, 23222, and 40000.15), 257-260

Laboratory Transportation of Cannabis Samples (16 CCR § 5709), 427

Possession of Cannabis While Driving - Unlawful (Veh § 23222), 259

Security and Safety Transportation Requirements for Retailer, Distributor, and Microbusiness (B&P § 26070), 96

Transportation of Cannabis Goods Requirements (16 CCR §§ 5311 to 5313), 387-388

Transport of Cannabis Between Licensees (B&P § 26161), 113

Unlawful Transportation of Cannabis (H&S § 11360), 184

N

NURSERY LICENSE

Licensing- SEE CULTIVATION LICENSE

Research and Development Requirements for Nursery Licensees (3 CCR § 8302), 306

Seed Production Requirements for Nursery Licensees (3 CCR § 8301), 306

O

ORGANIC CANNABIS

Certified Organic Designation (B&P § 26062), 92

Organic Certification Program (B&P § 26062), 92

Restriction on Organic Designation and Certification (B&P § 26062 .5), 92

P

PACKAGING

Bureau of Cannabis Control Packaging, Labeling, and Rolling (16 CCR § 5303), 382

Cannabinoids and Terpenoids Labeling Quality-Assurance Review (16 CCR § 5307.1), 385

Cannabis and Nonmanufactured Cannabis Products Packaging and Labeling (3 CCR § 8212), 304

Cannabis Seed Labeling Requirements (Fd&Ag § 52452), 146

Department of Public Health Labeling Standards (B&P §§ 26106, 26120, 26121), 103-105

Edible Cannabis Products Labeling Requirements (17 CCR § 40406), 512

Manufactured Cannabis Labeling and Packaging Requirements (17 CCR §§ 40400 to 40417), 510-517

Manufacturers Labeling Standards (B&P §§ 26106, 26120, 26121), 103-105

Microbusinesses Labeling Standards (B&P §§ 26106, 26120, 26121), 103-105

Nonmanufactured Cannabis Products Packaging and Labeling (3 CCR § 8212), 304

Quality-Assurance Review for Labeling Cannabinoids and Terpenoids (16 CCR § 5307.1), 385

Retailer Packaging and Labeling Prohibition (16 CCR § 5412), 395

PENAL CODE

Conspiracy to Commit a Crime (Pen § 182), 225

Department of Food and Agriculture Employees Power of Arrest and Power to Serve Warrants (Pen § 830.11), 234

Drug Treatment Program Eligibility and Procedure (Pen § 1000), 235

Enhancement for Being Armed with a Firearm in the Commission of a Felony or Attempted Felony (Pen § 12022), 242

Enhancement for Repeat Felony Convictions (Pen § 667), 231

Hazardous Substance Spill (Pen § 374.8), 230

Power of Arrest of Department of Food and Agriculture Employees (Pen § 830.11), 234

Power to Serve Warrants of Department of Food and Agriculture Employees (Pen § 830.11), 234

Sentencing Guidelines (Pen § 1170), 236

Sex Offender Registration Act (Pen § 290), 226

PRODUCER'S LIEN

Definitions (Fd&Ag §§ 55403, 55407, 55408), 147-148

Generally (Fd&Ag §§ 55631 to 55653), 148-153

PROPOSITION 215 - Compassionate Use Act of 1996 (H&S § 11362.5), 193

R

RESEARCH

California Marijuana Research Program (H&S § 11362.9), 205

Cannabis and Hallucinogenic Drugs Research Advisory Panel (H&S § 11480), 218

Cannabis Provided for Research Purposes (H&S § 11478), 216

Center for Medicinal Cannabis Research (B&P § 2525.1), 59

Funding for Cannabis Research (16 CCR §§ 5900 to 5905), 458-460

Hemp Research Sites (Fd&Ag § 81011), 161

Nursery License Research and Development Requirements (3 CCR § 8302), 306

RETAILER LICENSES

Access to Retailer Premises (16 CCR § 5400), 390

Access to the Retail Area for Customer (16 CCR § 5402), 390

Alcohol Restrictions (B&P §§ 25621.5, 26054, 26070.2), 65, 84, 98

Cannabis Consumption During Delivery (16 CCR § 5419), 399

Cannabis Goods Carried During Delivery (16 CCR § 5418), 398

Cannabis Goods Display (16 CCR § 5405), 392

Cannabis Goods for Sale (16 CCR § 5406), 392

Cannabis Goods Packaging and Exit Packaging (16 CCR § 5413), 395

Customers (16 CCR § 5404), 391

Customer Return of Cannabis Goods (16 CCR § 5410), 394

Daily Limits (16 CCR § 5409), 393

Deliveries by Licensed Retailer (B&P § 26090), 100

Deliveries Facilitated by Technology Platforms (16 CCR § 5415.1), 396

Delivery (16 CCR §§ 5415 to 5421), 396-400

Delivery - Cannabis Goods Carried (16 CCR § 5418), 398

Delivery - Consumption of Cannabis Goods (16 CCR § 5419), 399

Delivery Employees (16 CCR § 5415), 396

Delivery Request Receipt (16 CCR § 5420), 399

Delivery Route (16 CCR § 5421), 400

Delivery to a Physical Address (16 CCR § 5416), 397

Delivery Vehicle Requirements (16 CCR § 5417), 397

Display of Cannabis Goods (16 CCR § 5405), 392

Exit Packaging (16 CCR § 5413), 395

Free Cannabis Goods (16 CCR § 5411), 394

Hours of Operation (16 CCR § 5403), 391

Inventory (16 CCR §§ 5422 to 5424), 400-401

Inventory Documentation (16 CCR § 5423), 401

Inventory - Receiving Shipment (16 CCR § 5422), 400

Inventory Reconciliation (16 CCR § 5424), 401

Labeling and Packaging by a Retailer Prohibition (16 CCR § 5412), 395

Live Plants for Sale and Seeds (16 CCR § 5408), 393

Local Control (B&P § 26200), 118

Non-Cannabis Goods for Sale (16 CCR § 5407), 392

Non-Storefront Retailer (16 CCR § 5414), 395

Packaging (16 CCR §§ 5412, 5413), 395

Packaging and Labeling Prohibition (16 CCR § 5412), 395

Prohibition on Packaging and Labeling by a Retailer (16 CCR § 5412), 395

Records (16 CCR § 5426), 401

Regulations for Retailers (16 CCR §§ 5400 to 5427), 390-402

Requirements While Not Open for Business (16 CCR § 5403.1), 391

Restrictions on Sales of Alcohol by Retailer of Cannabis (B&P §§ 26054, 26070.2), 84, 98

Restrictions on Sales of Cannabis by Retailer of Alcoholic Beverages (B&P § 25621.5), 65

Retailer Premises to Retailer Premises Transfer (16 CCR § 5427), 402

Return of Cannabis Goods by Customer (16 CCR § 5410), 394

Sale of Cannabis Goods (16 CCR § 5406), 392

Sale of Live Plants and Seeds (16 CCR § 5408), 393

Sale of Non-Cannabis Goods (16 CCR § 5407), 392

Security and Safety Transportation Requirements (B&P § 26070), 96

Seeds and Live Plants for Sale (16 CCR § 5408), 393

Transfer Retailer Premises to Retailer Premises (16 CCR § 5427), 402

REVENUE AND TAXATION CODE

Adjustments to the Tax Rate (Rev&Tax § 34017), 250

Audit of the Cannabis Tax Fund (Rev&Tax § 34020), 256

Cannabis Excise Tax Specifics (Rev&Tax § 34011), 245

Cannabis Cultivation Tax Collected by Distributor or Manufacturer (Rev&Tax § 34012.5), 247

Cannabis Cultivation Tax Specifics (Rev&Tax § 34012), 246

Cannabis Tax Administration (Rev&Tax § 34013), 248

Cannabis Tax Fund Audit (Rev&Tax § 34020), 256

Cannabis Tax Funds Disbursement (Rev&Tax § 34019), 251

California Cannabis Tax Fund (Rev&Tax § 34018), 250

Definitions (Rev&Tax § 34010), 244

Disbursement of Cannabis Tax Funds (Rev&Tax § 34019), 251

Due Dates for Taxes (Rev&Tax § 34015), 249

Electronic Funds Transfer Requirement - Cannabis Business Exception Until 1/1/2022 (Rev&Tax § 6479.3), 243

Failure to Make a Timely Return or Payment - Penalty Relief (Rev&Tax § 55044), 256

Filing Tax Report Requirement (Rev&Tax § 34015), 249

Inspections by Board Employee or Peace Officer (Rev&Tax § 34016), 249

Local Cannabis Tax Specifics (Rev&Tax §§ 34021, 34021.5), 256

Penalty Relief for Failure to Make a Timely Return or Payment (Rev&Tax § 55044), 256

Punishment for Failure to Tax Cannabis (Rev&Tax § 34016), 249

Punishment for False or Fraudulent Report (Rev&Tax § 34016), 249

Punishment for Refusal of Inspection (Rev&Tax § 34016), 249

Security to Cover Liability for Taxes (Rev&Tax § 34014), 248

Tax Due Dates (Rev&Tax § 34015), 249

Tax Report Filing Requirement (Rev&Tax § 34015), 249

Tax Rate Adjustments (Rev&Tax § 34017), 250

S

SHARED-USE FACILITIES LICENSE

Definitions (17 CCR § 40190), 484

Registration to Operate a Shared-Use Facility (17 CCR § 40192), 485

Shared-Use Facility Compliance Requirements (17 CCR § 40196), 486

Shared-Use Facility Conditions for Operation (17 CCR § 40194), 485

Temporary Shared-Use Facility Registration (17 CCR § 40127), 468

Temporary Type S License (17 CCR § 40127), 468

Type S License (17 CCR § 40191), 484

SYNTHETIC CANNABINOID

Synthetic Cannabinoid Compound (H&S § 11357.5), 178

Synthetic Cannabinoid Derivative (H&S § 11357.5), 178

T

TAX

Adjustments to the Tax Rate (Rev&Tax § 34017), 250

Audit of the Cannabis Tax Fund (Rev&Tax § 34020), 256

Cannabis Excise Tax Specifics (Rev&Tax § 34011), 245

Cannabis Cultivation Tax Collected by Distributor or Manufacturer (Rev&Tax § 34012.5), 247

Cannabis Cultivation Tax Specifics (Rev&Tax § 34012), 246

Cannabis Tax Administration (Rev&Tax § 34013), 248

Cannabis Tax Fund Audit (Rev&Tax § 34020), 256

Cannabis Tax Funds Disbursement (Rev&Tax § 34019), 251

California Cannabis Tax Fund (Rev&Tax § 34018), 250

Cultivation Tax Due - Track and Trace (B&P § 26068), 94

Deadline for Safe and Viable Way to Collect Cash Payments for Cannabis Taxes and Fees (B&P § 26180.5), 116

Deadline to Establish Offices to Collect Cash Fees and Taxes in Northern California (B&P § 26210.5), 121

Definitions (Rev&Tax § 34010), 244

Disbursement of Cannabis Tax Funds (Rev&Tax § 34019), 251

Due Dates for Taxes (Rev&Tax § 34015), 249

Electronic Funds Transfer Requirement - Cannabis Business Exception Until 1/1/2022 (Rev&Tax § 6479.3), 243

Failure to Make a Timely Return or Payment - Penalty Relief (Rev&Tax § 55044), 256

Filing Tax Report Requirement (Rev&Tax § 34015), 249

Inspections by Board Employee or Peace Officer (Rev&Tax § 34016), 249

Local Cannabis Tax Specifics (Rev&Tax §§ 34021, 34021.5), 256

Penalty Relief for Failure to Make a Timely Return or Payment (Rev&Tax § 55044), 256

Punishment for Failure to Tax Cannabis (Rev&Tax § 34016), 249

Punishment for False or Fraudulent Report (Rev&Tax § 34016), 249

Punishment for Refusal of Inspection (Rev&Tax § 34016), 249

Security to Cover Liability for Taxes (Rev&Tax § 34014), 248

Tax Due Dates (Rev&Tax § 34015), 249

Tax Report Filing Requirement (Rev&Tax § 34015), 249

Tax Rate Adjustments (Rev&Tax § 34017), 250

Track and Trace of Cultivation Tax Due (B&P § 26068), 94

TEMPORARY CANNABIS EVENT LICENSES

Consumption at Temporary Cannabis Event (16 CCR § 5603), 416

Educational Cannabis Events (16 CCR § 5604), 416

Event Organizer License (16 CCR § 5600), 409

Informational Cannabis Events (16 CCR § 5604), 416

License for Temporary Cannabis Event (16 CCR § 5601), 412

Local Control (B&P § 26200), 118

Locations of Temporary Cannabis Events (B&P § 26200), 118

Sales at Temporary Cannabis Event (16 CCR § 5602), 414

TESTING LABORATORIES

Cannabinoid Testing (16 CCR § 5724), 438

Cannabis or Cannabis Product Testing Requirements (B&P § 26100), 100

Certificate of Analysis - COA (16 CCR § 5726), 440

Chain of Custody Protocol (B&P § 26100, 16 CCR § 5706), 100, 425

Chemical Profile (B&P § 26100), 100

Contaminants (B&P § 26100), 100

Definitions (16 CCR § 5700), 416

Destruction of Noncompliant Harvested Batches (B&P § 26104), 102

Distributors Testing Responsibilities (16 CCR §§ 5302 to 5307.1), 381-385

Employee Qualifications for Laboratory (16 CCR §§ 5736 to 5738), 447

Foreign Material Testing (16 CCR § 5722), 437

General Laboratory License Requirements (16 CCR § 5701), 421

Heavy Metals Testing (16 CCR § 5723), 438

Hemp Laboratory Testing (Fd&Ag § 81006), 158

Industrial Hemp Laboratory Testing (Fd&Ag § 81006), 158

Interim Testing Laboratory License (16 CCR § 5703), 422

Laboratory Employee Qualifications (16 CCR §§ 5736 to 5738), 447

Laboratory License Application (16 CCR § 5702), 421

Laboratory Quality Assurance and Quality Control (16 CCR §§ 5729 to 5735), 442-446

License Requirements Generally (16 CCR § 5701), 421

Medical Cannabis Patients (B&P § 26104), 102

Microbial Impurities Testing (16 CCR § 5720), 436

Moisture Content and Water Activity Testing (16 CCR § 5717), 432

Multiple Licenses (B&P § 26053), 84

Mycotoxin Testing (16 CCR § 5721), 437

Noncompliant Harvested Batches (B&P § 26104), 102

Pesticides Testing (16 CCR § 5719), 434

Phase-in of Required Laboratory Testing (16 CCR § 5715), 431

Post Testing Procedures (16 CCR §§ 5727 to 5728), 441-442

Processing Chemicals Testing (16 CCR § 5718), 433

Quality Assurance and Quality Control of Laboratories (16 CCR §§ 5729 to 5735), 442-446

Record Retention (16 CCR § 5739), 448

Required Testing (16 CCR §§ 5714 to 5715), 431

Residual Levels of Volatile Organic Compounds (B&P § 26100), 100

Residual Pesticides Testing (16 CCR § 5719), 434

Residual Solvents and Processing Chemicals Testing (16 CCR § 5718), 433

Sampling Cannabis and Cannabis Products (16 CCR §§ 5704 to 5710), 423-428

Standard Operating Procedures (16 CCR §§ 5711 to 5713), 428-429

Terpenoid Testing (16 CCR § 5725), 440

Testing Laboratories Licensee Prohibited from Licensure for Any Other Activity (B&P § 26053), 84

Testing License Requirements (B&P § 26102, 16 CCR §§ 5701 to 5702), 102, 421

Testing Methods (B&P § 26100), 100

Testing Restricted to Licensed Businesses, Qualified Patients, and Primary Caregivers (B&P § 26104), 102

Water Activity and Moisture Content Testing (16 CCR § 5717), 432

TRACK AND TRACE SYSTEM

Bureau of Cannabis Control Regulations (16 CCR §§ 5048 to 5052), 376-379

Business and Professions Code Sections (B&P §§ 26067 to 26069.9), 93-96

Cultivation Regulations (3 CCR §§ 8109, 8401 to 8409), 293, 313-318

Food and Agriculture Regulations (3 CCR §§ 8109, 8401 to 8409), 293, 313-318

Laws- Business and Professions Code Sections (B&P §§ 26067 to 26069.9), 93-96

     Cooperative Agreement Between State and Local Agencies (B&P § 26069.1), 96

     Cultivation Tax Due - Track and Trace (B&P § 26068), 94

     Definitions (B&P § 26069.9), 96

     Electronic Database Creation (B&P § 26067), 93

     Electronic Seed to Sale Software Tracking System (B&P § 26068), 94

     Establishment of Track and Trace Program (B&P § 26067), 93

     Information Technology Systems (B&P § 26068), 94

     Third Party Applications (B&P § 26068), 94

     Unique Identifier Program Implementation (B&P § 26069), 95

Manufactured Cannabis Safety, Regulations (17 CCR §§ 40510 to 40517), 519-521

Professional and Vocational Regulations (16 CCR §§ 5048 to 5052), 376-379

Public Health Regulations (17 CCR §§ 40510 to 40517), 519-521

Regulations- Bureau of Cannabis Control (16 CCR §§ 5048 to 5052), 376-379

     General Requirements (16 CCR § 5048), 376

     Loss of Connectivity (16 CCR § 5050), 378

     Reconciliation (16 CCR § 5051), 379

     Reporting (16 CCR § 5049), 377

     Temporary Licenses (16 CCR § 5052), 379

Regulations- Cannabis Cultivation (3 CCR §§ 8109, 8401 to 8409), 293, 313-318

     Applicant Track-and-Trace Training Requirement (3 CCR § 8109), 293

     General Requirements (3 CCR § 8402), 313

     Inventory Audits (3 CCR § 8408), 318

     Inventory Requirements (3 CCR § 8406), 317

     Notification of Diversion, Theft, Loss, or Criminal Activity (3 CCR § 8409), 318

Record Retention (3 CCR § 8400), 311

Reporting Requirements (3 CCR § 8405), 315

Sales Invoice or Receipt Requirements (3 CCR § 8401), 312

Temporary Licensee to Annual License Process (3 CCR § 8407), 317

Unique Identifiers - UID (3 CCR § 8403), 313

User Requirements (3 CCR § 8404), 315

Regulations- Manufactured Cannabis (17 CCR §§ 40510 to 40517), 519-521

General Requirements (17 CCR § 40510), 519

Loss of Access (17 CCR § 40513), 520

Reporting Requirements (17 CCR § 40512), 520

Temporary Licenses (17 CCR § 40515), 521

UID Tag Order (17 CCR § 40517), 521

State Department of Health Services Regulations (17 CCR §§ 40510 to 40517), 519-521

V

TYPE S LICENSE

Definitions (17 CCR § 40190), 484

Registration to Operate a Shared-Use Facility (17 CCR § 40192), 485

Shared-Use Facility Compliance Requirements (17 CCR § 40196), 486

Shared-Use Facility Conditions for Operation (17 CCR § 40194), 485

Temporary Shared-Use Facility Registration (17 CCR § 40127), 468

Temporary Type S License (17 CCR § 40127), 468

Type S License (17 CCR § 40191), 484

VEHICLE CODE

Highway Definition (Veh § 23221), 259

Impaired Driving Task Force (Veh § 2429.7), 257

Influence of Alcohol or Drugs While Driving (Veh § 23152), 258

Ingesting or Smoking Marijuana While Driving (Veh §§ 23220, 23221), 259

Lands Definition (Veh § 23220), 259

Misdemeanor Vehicle Codes (Veh § 40000.15), 260

Open Container of Cannabis While Driving (Veh § 23222), 259

Passenger in Motor Vehicle Smoking or Ingesting Marijuana (Veh §§ 23220, 23221), 259

Possession of Open Alcoholic Beverages or Cannabis While Driving (Veh § 23222), 259

Smoking or Ingesting Marijuana While Driving (Veh §§ 23220, 23221), 259

W

WATER

Diversion or Use of Water for Cannabis Cultivation (Wat §§ 1847, 13149), 266, 268

Impacted Watershed (16 CCR § 5504), 407

Moisture Content and Water Activity Testing (16 CCR § 5717), 432

Supplemental Water Source Information (16 CCR § 5503), 405

Use of Water for Cannabis Cultivation (Wat §§ 1847, 13149), 266, 268

Water Appropriation Fees (Wat §§ 1525, 1535), 261-263

Water Diversion Definition (Wat § 5100), 266

Water Diversion or Obstruction Notification Requirements (Fish&G § 1602), 141

Water Recycling Act of 1991 Definitions (Wat § 13575), 276

Watershed Enforcement Program (Fish&G § 12029), 145

WATER CODE

"Best Available Technologies" Definition (Wat § 5100), 266

"Best Professional Practices" Definition (Wat § 5100), 266

"Board" = State Water Resources Control Board (Wat § 25), 260

Cannabis Cultivation Impacts on Water Quality, and on Fish and Wildlife (Wat § 13276), 274

Cease and Desist Order - Failure to Comply (Wat § 1845), 265

Cease and Desist Order for Violation (Wat § 1831), 263

Civil Liability for Trespass Water Diversion (Wat § 1052), 261

Criminal Penalties (Wat § 13387), 274

Definitions (Wat §§ 5100, 13575), 266, 276

Discharge of Waste (Wat §§ 13260, 13264, 13272), 269, 272-273

"Diversion" Definition (Wat § 5100), 266

Diversion or Use of Water for Cannabis Cultivation (Wat §§ 1847, 13149), 266, 268

Failure to Comply with Cease and Desist Order (Wat § 1845), 265

Injunctive Relief and Civil Liability for Trespass Water Diversion (Wat § 1052), 261

Liability for Term, Condition, Regulation, or Order Violation (Wat § 1846), 265

Monitoring, Recording, and Reporting Requirements for Water Diversion (Wat § 1840), 264

"Person" Definition (Wat § 5100), 266

Recording Requirements for Water Diversion (Wat § 1840), 264

Reporting Requirements for Water Diversion (Wat § 1840), 264

Statement of Diversion and Use (Wat §§ 5101 to 5103), 267

Trespass Water Diversion Injunctive Relief and Civil Liability (Wat § 1052), 261

Use of Water for Cannabis Cultivation (Wat §§ 1847, 13149), 266, 268

Violations (Wat § 13387), 274

Violations Qualified for a Cease and Desist Order (Wat § 1831), 263

Water Appropriation Fees (Wat §§ 1525, 1535), 261-263

Water Diversion Monitoring, Recording, and Reporting Requirements (Wat § 1840), 264

Water Recycling Act of 1991 Definitions (Wat § 13575), 276

www.ingramcontent.com/pod-product-compliance
Lightning Source LLC
Chambersburg PA
CBHW081438190326
41458CB00020B/6231